THE FAMILY

THE FAMILY
An Introduction

SECOND EDITION

J. Ross Eshleman
Wayne State University

Allyn and Bacon, Inc.
Boston · London · Sydney · Toronto

PHOTO CREDITS

Jeff Albertson: Chapters 3, 5, 11.
Bobbi Carrey: Chapters 4, 9, 14, 17, 19, 20.
Owen Franken/Stock, Boston: Chapter 16.
Steve Hansen/Stock, Boston: Chapter 2.
Talbot Lovering: Chapters 7, 8.
Peter Menzel/Stock, Boston: Chapters 9, 12.
George W. Perkins, III: Chapter 18.
Peter Vandermark/Stock, Boston: Chapter 13.
Joe Weiler: Chapters 1, 10, 15.

Cover photo by Jean-Claude LeJeune/Stock, Boston.

Library of Congress Cataloging in Publication Data

Eshleman, J   Ross.
   The family.

   Includes bibliographies and index.
   1. Family. 2. Marriage. I. Title.
HQ728.E83   1978   301.42   77–16632
ISBN 0–205–05949–X

Third printing . . . December, 1979

Contents

Preface

What should an introductory family textbook try to do? First, I believe it should provide a thorough and objective coverage of the basic concepts and ideas in marriage and the family. These ideas should be presented clearly and intelligibly. The coverage should include specific factual data as well as abstract principles, empirically supported findings as well as hypotheses for testing. Since many students will find this introduction to the family to be their terminal course as well, the text should arouse a curiosity toward, and include tools for, an ongoing process of observation, understanding, and analysis of marital and family relationships and organizations.

Second, and equally important, I believe an introductory family textbook should capture the interest of the student. This should not be done at the expense of accuracy but should convey realistically the processes and organization of marital and family behavior in an understandable, readable, and interesting way. From this, the student should be able to relate personal and familial values and behaviors to differing life-styles and patterns both within his own society and in relation to others. In other words, the student should be made to see more clearly his or her place in the United States or world picture.

I have tried with this book to write a text that was both interesting and highly readable, to be relatively comprehensive in the coverage of topics, to emphasize the American family and supplement it heavily with historical and cross-cultural referents, and to be accurate, yet contemporary—including alternate marital and family life-styles, yet keeping them in a realistic perspective relative to the more common traditional family forms. I have tried to document extensively in presenting the family as a scholarly discipline and have tried to encourage further thought and reading by concluding each chapter with questions for discussion and an annotated bibliography for further reading. I have tried to make extensive use of the latest census material and I have inserted (note the screened material) illustrative selections and case materials to supplement the basic text.

Each of these attempts was an outgrowth of several major objectives: 1) to present an objective description and analysis of contemporary American families within a world perspective, 2) to examine without condemnation or praise alternate family and marital life-styles, 3) to apply general theoretical schemes and frames of reference to family issues, 4) to present basic concepts and descriptive materials clearly and intelligibly, 5) to suggest questions and supplemental sources to stimulate discussion and reading beyond the textual materials, and 6) to cultivate in the student an increased awareness of his or her particular niche in the family and general social order. Whether these objectives have been fulfilled is for the reader to judge.

The Family: An Introduction, Second Edition, follows basically a sociological and social-psychological approach. Part I deals with understanding the family irrespective of time or place. It summarizes basic issues in the American family, examines approaches to the study of the family, establishes five basic frames of reference or theories central to understanding groups and systems, defines and illustrates basic concepts of the field, and looks at the family in a process of change. Part II looks at structural and subcultural variations in family life-styles: in marriage and number of spouses, in extended relationships, in couple relationships, in the kibbutz, among the Filipino, Muslim, and tribal groups in the Philippines, among the Amish and black families in the United States, and, finally, by social class. Part III brings structure and process to the creation of a marital and family status by examining the who, why, and how of mate selection in contemporary American society. Part IV singles out sexual norms and relationships as a major and significant social fact of the premarital, marital, and family system. Part V deals with the family life cycle: marriage, parenthood, child rearing or socialization, middle and later years, and the nature of crisis, disorganization, and reorganization of the American family. Part VI involves a speculative projection into the future of the family.

As a result of feedback from faculty and students who used the first edition, various changes and additions appear in this second edition. There is a much greater emphasis on sex roles and interaction patterns. New chapters appear on variations on marital and family life-styles, family systems in other cultures (kibbutz, Christian Filipinos, Muslim, Kalinga, and Mangyan), and parent-child interaction and socialization. The exchange and conflict frames of references have been added to the interactional, structural-functional, and developmental. Inserts based on interviews with four persons (Louise, Alex, Ann, and Mac) have been included throughout the text to provide personal experiences and opinions that relate to the basic topic under discussion. As in the first edition, extensive use is made of recent census data and research findings.

It is my hope that you will find the ideas stimulating and clearly explained. Where you find errors, where you disagree with particular points, when you can supply supplemental material or observations, please inform me. I hope the book will be readable and interesting, will present an accurate portrayal of the family system, will be flexible in its use, will stimulate thought and discussion, and, perhaps most important, will change behavior by expanding our awareness of, and sensitivity to, self and others. From the perspective of my particular value orientation, if this textbook does these things, the writing of it will have been worthwhile.

It is difficult to know where to begin or end in expressing a deeply felt sense of gratitude and appreciation to many people. Surely, the most sacrifices were made by my wife Janet, daughter Jill, and son Sidney, who gave up many hours of family activities to allow Dad to write. Secondly, I would want any acknowledgement to include my Ph.D. advisor, Dr. A. R. Mangus, and my department chairman for the nine years I was at Western Michigan University, Dr. Leonard Kercher. Both of these men, now retired, affected my life, interest in the family, and professional achievement far more than they will ever know.

To single out others would require a lengthy list. But several should be mentioned. Mr. Robert A. Clarke has served as a significant friend, counselor, and business associate over the past decade. Dr. Chester L. Hunt kindled within me an interest in the Philippines which led to two Fulbright experiences in that country. Dr. Leila Bradfield and I spent many hours together discussing how to get students involved and interested in the family. Drs. Greer Litton-Fox, Constantina Safilios-Rothschild and Juanne Clarke have served, in their writing, in reviews of my writing, and in personal interactions, to alert me to sex-role issues. Doris Seifert, who typed sections of the manuscript, Fred Wessells as department academic services officer, several hundred students who exchanged ideas, five or six professionals in the field who reviewed a draft of the manuscript, dozens of friends and colleagues who provided encouragement and support in areas other than writing but which made writing easier, all should be acknowledged.

Finally, two individuals at Allyn and Bacon influenced the final product in a direct fashion far more than most. Shirley Davis provided the needed editorial expertise and Gary Folven, the senior sociology editor, provided the continual contacts and a valued friendship.

J. ROSS ESHLEMAN

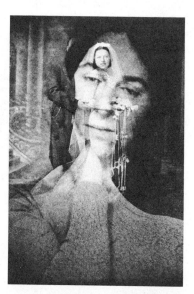

Part I

Understanding Marriage and the Family

1

An Introduction to the Family:
Issues and Characteristics

1

While there is a basic unity in the culture of the United States, there is also diversity. Most of our citizens speak the English language, wear clothes, travel in automobiles, drink Coca Cola, sleep in beds, marry, engage in sexual relations, enjoy recreational pursuits, attend school, and believe in "freedom." But while most people engage in these same things, their diversity of opinion and behavior is, at times, astounding. This diversity is accorded not only to individual differences, but to region, rural-urban residence, ethnic affiliation, religious identification, race, socioeconomic position, educational level, age, sex, and many other factors.

We are truly living in a pluralistic society that is highly differentiated. It is possible to state, although difficult to support empirically, that never in history has a society been composed of a greater multiplicity of attitudes, values, behaviors, or life-styles. Both the quality and quantity of most characteristics of our society exist in a multiple number of forms. From its very beginning, society in the U.S. has been highly pluralistic—yet even today there is hardly an adequate vocabulary for discussing this pluralism.

These social and cultural differences are reflected in family structures and behavior. The life-styles of Afro-Americans are not identical to those of the European Americans. The rural Amish family patterns contrast sharply with the urban Jewish family patterns. Divorce rates are higher in the West than in the Northeast. Upper-class families maintain greater control over the mate selection of their children than do lower-class families. The percentage of mothers who have preschool children but are employed is much lower than for mothers with older children. Catholics have a larger median family size than do Protestants. Farm families have a lower average income per person than do nonfarm families. Children of first-generation immigrants are more likely to be bilingual than later generations. First-born children are likely to be more conservative in their value orientation than are later-born children. Young couples show a higher degree of companionship in their marriage relationship than do couples in their middle years.

Most differences, including those mentioned, create little conflict or controversy. Most are not even obvious to the majority of persons who never undertake a systematic study of the family. Do parents, teachers, or business-men get disturbed over higher divorce rates in the West, employment rates of mothers, or the failure of Amish-Americans to use electricity or drive auto-mobiles? Generally not. However, social controversy does arise when Amish buggies present a highway danger to fast moving automobiles, when children of working mothers are not provided with adequate care, and when property settlements and child placements cannot be agreed upon by divorced couples. This introductory chapter alerts us to selected major issues brought about by social change and to selected characteristics of families in the United States. The following chapter discusses approaches used to examine issues such as these.

IDEAL-TYPE CONSTRUCTS

Many concepts, illustrations and ideas used in this text are treated in "ideal-type" terms. Ideal types are *not* what are implied in the common usage of the word: that which is ideal, good, best, valuable, perfect, or de-sirable. Rather, ideal types are hypothetical constructs based on "pure" characteristics.

Ideal types always represent the end, the extreme, or the pole of a continuum. Created hypothetically, they provide contrasting points with which to compare any social phenomenon. Patriarchal-matriarchal, nuclear-extended, primary-secondary, individualism-familism, or rural-urban are examples of ideal types. The "pure' characteristics of rural might include geo-graphical and social isolation, homogeneity, agricultural employment, sparse population, and a subsistence economy. Characteristics of urban are likely to include social heterogeneity, industrial employment, density of population, and impersonality. Any community in the world could be placed along this ideal-type continuum, but none is likely to include all characteristics to their maximum degree. These terms accentuate, even exaggerate, reality rather than describe it accurately. On a rural-urban construct, Chicago would fall toward the urban end of the continuum. However, New York may be more characteristic of urban than Chicago, and Tokyo more than either. Few would argue against the residents of Rough Creek, Arizona, or Mud Lick, Kentucky, being classified as rural, but compared to the Tasaday tribe found on the island of Mindanao in the Philippines, both are quite urban.

The concept "ideal type" was systematically developed by the German sociologist Max Weber.[1] He was careful to point out that, first, value conno-

---

1. Max Weber, *The Methodology of the Social Sciences*, trans. and ed. Edward H. Shils and Henry A. Finch (New York: Free Press, 1949).

tations should be avoided. The prefix "ideal" denotes a constructed model, not evaluation or approval. It makes no suggestion as to what ought to be or what norm of conduct is approved or disapproved. Second, an ideal type or ideal construct is not an average or modal characteristic. An average denotes a central tendency, whereas an ideal type is a representation derived from the extreme instances. Third, as mentioned, the ideal type is not reality. It is an abstraction, a logical construct, and by its very nature is not found in reality in its "pure" form.

Functions of Ideal-type Constructs

An ideal-type construct performs several basic functions: It provides a limiting case with which concrete phenomena may be contrasted, it provides for the analysis and measurement of social reality, and it facilitates classification and comparison. In short, the ideal type provides a means to clarify what any phenomenon would be if it always and ever would conform to its own definition. Thus, ideal types enable social scientists to make valid and precise comparisons between societies, institutions, or families separated in time and place. It enables us in a sociology of the family to have a methodological tool that provides assistance in examining the upper or lower classes, black or white families, or arranged or free choices in mate selection. At this point, it is used to examine selected issues in the American Family.

ISSUES IN THE AMERICAN FAMILY

There is little dispute that the family in United States society is changing. Change per se is not necessarily disruptive, nor does it always present a conflict of interest between groups or persons. However, not all changes occur at an equal rate, as is well-supported by the cultural-lag idea of William Ogburn (see Chapter 4), nor do all segments of a society adjust equally to the changes taking place. Thus it would be possible to deal with nearly any issue in the family by noting what patterns existed at some point in the past and then comparing them with present patterns. Similarly, it would be possible to establish a series of ideal-type constructs (extended family-conjugal family, patriarchal family-matriarchal family, arranged marriages-free choice of mate, homogamy-heterogamy), place any aspect of a given family system at different points of time on the continuum, and observe the changes or trends that seem to be taking place.

The selected issues in the family that will be discussed follow this procedure. Using polar extremes as ideal types, changes are shown that have occurred in the family primarily within this century. Thus a comparison is made between traditional and emerging family forms. A comparison is made between the ideal norms (traditional patterns) and the real norms (emerging patterns).

Issues (that is, unresolved conflicts) exist because both the traditional and the emerging sets of norms exist simultaneously. In other words, certain groups and individuals resist the emerging norms and cling vehemently to the more traditional patterns, whereas other individuals and groups find the traditional patterns unacceptable and adhere to the new set of norms and values. The result is that major issues (conflicts) occur primarily because of social change. If no change occurs and everyone accepts the traditional patterns of behavior, no issue or conflict results; or, if everyone adopts the emerging set of norms, no conflict exists.

Several ideal-type constructs are developed to illustrate the conflicts that result when an emerging set of marital and family values coexist with the traditional social values inherited from the past. It is in a pluralistic society that both the traditional and a multiple number of emerging family

The New and the Old in Contemporary Japan

Contemporary Japan remains a complex blend of the new and the old. While rapidly absorbing the most advanced scientific and technological knowledge, Japan simultaneously retains a multitude of ancient folk faiths and beliefs. In daily life, for example, the average Japanese still refers to the koyomi (zodiac almanac) in making many important decisions, even among the well educated groups. Certain days designated as tai-an, a day of "great peace," when success is said to attend all attempts made in this auspicious day, are chosen for weddings. Tomobiki (friend-pulling) days are avoided for funerals for fear the deceased may "pull" along a close friend or relative to his death. In Japan today, funeral parlors and crematoriums almost without exception remain closed on these tomobiki days for lack of business.

One folk superstition . . . based on the zodiac almanac [is] that females born in the Year of Hinoe-Uma (Elder Fire-Horse) possess unde-sirable characteristics and should be avoided as marriage partners. A female born in this year, which occurs every sixty years, is believed to be fiery and impulsive, anger quickly, and destroy her husband if she marries. This myth became a strong superstition in 1682 when it was combined with the tale of Yaoya-Oshichi, a young maiden born in the Year of Hinoe-Uma, who because of her love for a young priest started a fire which spread and almost destroyed the entire city of Edo, present day Tokyo. She was executed for arson. Kabuki plays and odori dances based on this episode have helped to perpetuate the belief down through the centuries. In more modern times, a startling news story in the mid-1930s concerned a deranged woman who had murdered her lover, cut off his penis, and carried it about in her bosom, with the added detail that she was born in the Year of Hinoe-Uma. Such incidents have reinforced the superstition.

Source: Kanae Kaku and Y. Scott Matsumoto, "Influence of a Folk Superstition on Fertility of Japanese in California and Hawaii, 1966," *American Journal of Public Health* 65 (February 1975), p. 170. Reprinted by permission.

patterns exist simultaneously. This results in conflict, confusion, and an un-settled state in the family system.

The issues that follow are not listed in any order of importance with the exception of the first.[2] It is the author's belief that all other issues relate to or basically stem from the meaning given to marriage and the family itself.

The Meaning of Marriage and the Family

The most basic issue presented centers around the meaning and the purpose of marriage and the family. It questions the sources of authority in marital and family decisions. It questions whether marriage is itself necessary.

The most traditional social norm, which represents one polar extreme of our ideal-type construct, views marriage as a *sacred* phenomenon. That is to say, the family and marriage are divine and holy institutions. They are created and maintained by God, Yahweh, or some supreme being greater than man. The phrase "marriages are made in heaven" is in many ways consistent with this perspective. This traditional social norm was perhaps most widely prevalent prior to the turn of the century. In its extreme form, marriage is not only sacred, but it is in itself a sacrament. The Catholic Church today views marriage as one of the seven sacraments. This implies that man and his personal wishes or wants are of secondary importance to that which is God created and God given. Basic to this idea is the source of authority on all family and religious matters as stemming from God or his connecting links (prophets, popes, cardinals, bishops, or priests) in the hierarchy of man-God positions.

A second traditional norm, one in widespread existence at the turn of the century and the first several decades thereafter, views the meaning of mar-riage and the family as centering primarily around *social* obligations. The social meaning of marriage, like the sacred meaning, represents traditional norms. But rather than the source of authority being God, authority becomes centered in man as represented by the kin group, community, church as a social institution, and society in general. Primary values within this meaning of marriage are to maintain social respectability, conform to kin and com-munity wishes, and maintain a "proper image" within society. Thus within this meaning of marriage, what other people think is very important. Divorce, premarital pregnancy, black-white intermarriage, and so forth, are not un-desirable per se but because "society" (friends, community, kin group, and others), in word and in action, disapproves.

The most recent meaning of marriage suggests that families and the

2. With considerable modification, these issues and ideas follow the lead of Cavan as pre-sented in Ruth S. Cavan, *The American Family*, 4th ed. (New York: Thomas Y. Crowell, 1969), pp. 21–40.

marital relationship exist for the *individual*. Thus, the concern is not with God or with society but with "me." If I choose to marry outside of my race, religion, ethnic group, social class, and educational level, that is "my business." After all, I am not marrying my family, my church, my community, or American society. If I am happy in my marriage, then it is a successful one. If I am unhappy, neither God nor society can dictate my behavior nor can force the endurance of an unsuccessful marriage. Within this meaning, the source of authority is the person alone: each individual is responsible for his or her own success or failure without regard to the community structure or the social conditions in which he or she operates. This myth, frequently perpetuated by our educational system, makes "anything possible if the individual wants it badly enough." On an ideal-type construct, this view represents the polar extreme that is directly opposite to the sacred meaning of marriage.

Thus, there are at least three basic meanings of marriage, all of which exist today. To some persons and groups, marriage is sacred or sacramental; with others, marriage is a social contract and success is viewed in terms of conformity to societal demands; to a third group, marriage is a highly personal, highly individualistic concern. The lack of uniformity in the source of authority on the meaning of marriage is basic to most issues and conflicts that exist in the marital and family system today in our society.

Family Organization

Closely related to the basic meaning of marriage is the "proper" form of marital and family organization. Traditionally, in the United States and in much of the world, the extended-family form was most common and most highly desired. Power resided in the elders, and they in turn were responsible for caring for other members of the kin group. The traditional form of family organization in our society, although monogamous, included social obligations to family members beyond the immediate nuclear-family unit.

With the passage of time and assisted by urbanization and industrialization, the extended family, although remaining important, appeared to decline in importance. Although it was expected that children would assist in providing for the needs of their aging parents, their primary responsibility centered around their own children; the nuclear family has increased in importance in our society.

The emerging form of family organization centers around pluralism. That is, the type of family organization that is preferred will vary both over time and from one individual to another. Some individuals may prefer to eliminate the marriage contract and simply live together. Others may desire some form of communal family where, at least economically, labor and goods are shared equally among all members. Others may desire to include sexual communism within their preferred form of family organization. A limited number of persons may desire a group marriage of three or four persons where all individuals recognize each other as spouse. Certain members may choose not to marry at all. Some of these who choose not to marry may choose to be parents. The point is that the emerging forms of family organization will not be uniform among families nor necessarily within the same family over time. The preferred form is that which permits the individual to, in the words of Herbert Otto, develop personal potential.[3] Thus polygyny, polyandry, homosexual marriages, nonlegal voluntary associations, progressive monogamy, trial marriages, group marriages, communal families, single-parent families, or no marriage at all have a place within the emerging forms of family organization.

A basic issue exists today over the "proper" form of family organization. Those who view marriage as sacred, those who view marriage as a monogamous lifelong relationship, and those who insist on two-parent permanent relationships will find difficulty in accepting and adjusting to the emerging forms of family organization that are increasingly becoming public. It is not that these forms are totally new or have not existed in the past; rather, it is that these forms are occurring with an increasing frequency, are being given an increasing amount of publicity, and are resulting in meaningful and realistic alternatives in the form of marital and family organization of thousands of persons in the United States today. A multiple number of acceptable forms of marriage and family life are part of the pluralistic scene of our society. These alternate marital-family styles are examined more fully in Chapter 5.

Family Functions

Many critics of the American family have included in their argument for the "breakdown" of the family the loss of functions which has taken place. Throughout written history, the family has been the major social institution. With changes that have occurred, particularly within the functions that a family has performed, the increasing specialization and complexity of modern society has led to a dehumanizing and fragmentizing process.

This issue is by no means a recent one. In the 1930s, Ogburn argued that the dilemma of the modern family was due to its loss of function.[4] It was his notion that prior to modern times the power and prestige of the family was due to the seven functions it performed.

1. Foremost was the economic function. The family was a self-sufficient unit in which the members of the family consumed primarily that which they

---

3. Herbert A. Otto, *The Family in Search of a Future* (New York: Appleton-Century-Crofts, 1970), pp. 111–118.
4. William F. Ogburn, "The Changing Family," *The Family* (1938), pp. 139–143.

produced. Thus banks, stores, and factories were not needed.

2. The family served the basic function of giving prestige and status to its members. The family name was important, and a member of the family was less an individual and more a member of the family.

3. The family performed the basic function of education, not only of the infant and child, but also of youth for their vocational education, physical education, domestic science, and so on.

4. The family provided the function of protecting its members. Not only did the father provide physical protection for his family, but children provided social and economic protection against economic and psychological needs in old age.

5. The family exercised a religious function, as was evidenced by grace at meals, family prayers, and the reading together of passages in the Bible.

6. The recreation function was performed at the homestead of some family or within the family rather than at recreation centers outside the home, provided by the school, community, or industry.

7. The final function was that of providing affection between mates and the procreation of children.

Many people in our society today are committed to the idea that these traditional functions of the family should be maintained. That is, families should be relatively sufficient, familism should have priority over individualism, education should be centered in the home, children should care for their aging parents, prayer and religious rituals should be a basic part of the daily life of the family, recreation should be engaged in by the family as a unit, and affection should be received relatively exclusively within the family unit.

The emerging norms suggest that many of these traditional family functions are being performed by other agencies. The economic function has gone to the factory, store, and office. The prestige and status function is increasingly centering around a family member rather than the family name. Teachers have become substitute parents and are basically responsible for the education of the child. Police, reform schools, social security, medicare and medicaid, unemployment compensation, and other types of social legislation provided by the state have replaced the traditional protective function. The professional priest, rabbi, or clergyman has assumed the responsibility for fulfilling the religious function. Little league baseball, industrial bowling teams, TV watching, or women's tennis groups have replaced the family as a source of recreation. And, although many would argue that the family still remains the center of the affectional life and is the only recognized place for producing children, one does not have to engage in an intensive investigation to discover the extent to which these two are sought and found outside the boundaries of the family and its members.

Not all writers agree that only losses have taken place in family functions. Talcott Parsons, for example, has emphasized that the shift in functions has produced gains as well.[5] He indicated that when functions are "lost" by one unit, that unit may thereby be freer to concentrate upon other functions. It is not merely a matter of "loss," therefore, but also a matter of what one is "freed for." Certain groups have come to specialize more now than in the past upon certain of the functions that mass-society critics fear have been lost. The family and the peer group, for example, have gained in importance as sources of emotional support. Within these primary group boundaries, its members may increasingly find a therapeutic milieu for personal and physical health problems. Also, families may be increasingly responsible for the development of family members' competence in the use of community and nonfamily resources. Existence in complex, highly specialized societies requires a knowledge of the range of options, an ability to make sound choices, and a flexibility toward new technologies and ideologies. Thus a major "new" family function is one of socialization for competence in a changing complex society and world. A further discussion of the concept and use of "function" as well as family functions is presented in Chapter 5.

Social Mobility

The issue of social mobility centers around the extent to which it is possible—or desirable—to move from one status to another. The issue includes the American Dream of going from the log cabin to the White House, from rags to riches, or from being a nobody to a Supreme Court judge.

The polar extremes of an ideal-type construct would include an open class society, where anyone could move up or down in the social structure strictly on the basis of personal effort and ability, versus a closed class society, where everyone remains in the position born with no change in position possible through individual achievement or any other means. The classic representation of the closed system is that of the caste system of ancient India, where position was based on ancestry and sustained by strict rules of same-caste marriage (endogamy), by religious beliefs, and by rigidly enforced legal and normative expectations.

No society has an absolutely open or a completely closed class system. In our own society family position exerts a major influence on one's chances for getting an education, for exposure to literature, travel, and the arts, for inheritance, for marriage choices, and the like. On the other hand, factors such as educational achievement, marriage possibilities, or business successes do provide opportunities for upward social mobility.

Traditionally, factors such as the extended family system, the predomi-

---

5. Hyman Rodman, "Talcott Parsons' View of the Changing American Family," *Merrill-Palmer Quarterly of Behavior and Development* 11 (July 1965), pp. 209–227.

nantly rural farming economy, the authority held by the elders, and religious and ethnic ties appeared to make personal upward mobility extremely difficult. Likewise today, the lack of opportunity and resources of the poor makes planning for the future and social climbing exceedingly difficult if not impossible. Yet the dream of upward social mobility, of "doing better than my parents," of economic success, and of obtaining a new and superior life-style remains widespread. A further discussion of this issue and of the meaning and consequence of social class position is presented in Chapter 9.

Mate Selection

The issue of mate selection centers around two questions: who chooses and who is chosen? The polar extremes of an ideal-type construct would include arranged marriages with no voice given to the mates involved versus absolutely free mate choice where decisions are made solely by the mates involved. Around the world and traditionally in the United States the most prevalent position falls toward the former (arranged) rather than the latter (free choice).

In our society the traditional norms suggest that parents in particular, if not doing the choosing, should give their approval to the mate chosen. It is not uncommon today to find men in the fifty and older age group who formally and directly requested the girl's parents' permission for her hand in marriage. Although mates were not chosen by the parents, as in much of the Eastern world, they were chosen with a clear consciousness of the extent to which the spouse would meet the approval of the parents. And to marry without the future spouse having been known, not only by the parents, but within the kin group and community would be unthinkable. Thus who did the choosing? The emerging norm, in the polar extreme is to have "absolute free choice" of a mate with a total absence of approval by parents, friends or others.

Closely related to who chooses is a question of who is chosen. Traditionally, in-group (endogamous) selection was extremely important. The ideal spouse was a person from one's own ethnic, social class, religious, racial, or neighborhood group. Outsiders were viewed with much suspicion, and marriage to an outsider was a sure sign of future marital problems. That the traditional norm still exists today is very obvious when one looks at the type of material taught in marriage-preparation classes within our educational system, the position taken by most religious groups, or the advice of parents or columnists. This writer knows of no Catholic priests or Catholic parents who encourage their members or children to find themselves a Protestant or Jewish spouse. But statements such as "individuals who share the same religious belief have five times as good a chance of staying married" or "almost one out of three marriages flop" (see insert) are not supported by empirical evidence. Both are in need of interpretation and will be clarified later since they

Dear Ann Landers: I know you are op-posed to interfaith marriages because I heard you say so when you spoke to our high school a few years ago. Now I am going with a young man whose religion is different from mine. I wish I could remember what you said—the reasons I mean. Please go over them again. Thank you.

                                        Undecided Girl

Dear Girl: The records show that indi- *viduals who share the same religious beliefs have five times as good a chance of staying married as those who do not. Since marriage is becoming increasingly risky (almost one out of three flop), it makes sense to start out on as solid a footing as possible. Marriage at its best, with everything going for you, is a tremen-dous challenge. Why begin with built-in trou-ble? Who needs it?*

Source: *Detroit Free Press*, February 28, 1967. Copyright by Publishers-Hall Syndicate. Reprinted by permission.

are incidental to this particular point. Here the point is that the traditional norm clearly suggests that persons should marry others like themselves and that parents, kin groups, and the community should have a hand in the selection of the marriage partner.

The emerging norm suggests that mate selection is increasingly com-ing under the control of youths themselves and that out-group selection (exogamous marriages) is increasingly common. In an informal discussion with a group of high school teachers, the comment was made that religion is no longer a crucial factor in the dating and marriage of persons from high school. You might find it interesting to inquire of your married friends whether the husband asked the wife's parents for permission to marry or, perhaps today, a more realistic question is whether either set of parents knew about their premarital cohabitation instead of, or prior to, their marriage. Consistent with the individualistic meaning of marriage is the idea that since it is "my spouse," I should choose any person with whom I am "in love" or with whom I choose to live. That the mate comes from a different com-munity, social class, religion, or race is not the concern of relatives or church groups. These issues focusing on mate selection are discussed in detail in Chapters 10 and 11.

Love

The issue of love as related to marriage centers around questions such as whether it is even necessary, to what degree of intensity, and to what extent of exclusiveness? On an ideal-type continuum, the polar extremes would be represented by 1) love as not even a factor for consideration in mar-riage versus love as the sole and prime factor for marriage, 2) zero percent or no feelings of love versus 100 percent feelings of love (whatever that is), and 3) love with one other person only versus many loves.

The reader can quickly note the linkage between this issue and both the previous one of mate selection and the next one of sexual relationships. Traditionally in North America and today in much of the world, kin, economic, and status considerations are still the key determinants for marriage. After marriage, not before, love is expected to develop. In contrast is the emerging idea that marriage without love is unthinkable. After all, does not "love make the world go round" and cannot "love conquer all?"

Closely related to whether or not love is necessary is the problem of the intensity of love feelings. Clearly feelings are subjective and the question is how intense must these subjective feelings be before they are "real"? Thus reference is made to "puppy love" or "infatuation" as feelings that are superficial and not the type upon which lasting relationships are built. Other descriptions such as romantic love, conjugal love, spiritual love (agape) or sexual love (eros) have been used to clarify different types of love or love conditions. In any case, attempts at understanding what love is, measuring how genuine or "real" it is, and analyzing its intensity have been basic problems for centuries and still engender debate and conflict today.

Finally, the issue of love—particularly as it relates to marriage—centers on the exclusiveness or nonexclusiveness of love relationships. Can two people be loved at once? Does love with one's spouse eliminate the possibility of loving someone else's spouse? The traditional view of love demands a love devoted exclusively to one person—in sickness and in health, for richer, for poorer, and so forth. This traditional relationship is all-absorbing and all-encompassing. All one's needs for affection and intimacy are found in this relationship. Forbidden are open, primary, intimate relationships with anyone other than one's spouse.

An emerging view, and one gaining widespread acceptance, is that one's spouse and/or lover neither can nor need meet all of one's intimacy needs.[6] That is, individuals who are personally growing, developing, and changing find differing needs fulfilled by different individuals. Thus, the fulfillment of various intimacy needs can be met outside of marriage without diminishing the love for one's spouse. If one is to grow and develop, it becomes difficult to imagine one other person fulfilling all intimacy needs of that individual. This type of relationship allows both self and other the right to new experiences and growth possibilities, both sexual and nonsexual. The result is a more enriched relationship with one's spouse, with a drastic reduction in feelings of possessiveness, rigidity of role expectations, or feelings of confinement.

As with the other issues, the traditional and the emerging views of love are in conflict. One cannot be both exclusive in love relationships and

---

6. An excellent treatment of this idea can be found in Carolynne Kieffer, "New Depths in Intimacy," in Roger W. Libby and Robert N. Whitehurst, *Marriage and Alternatives: Exploring Intimate Relationships* (Glenview, Ill.: Scott, Foresman, 1977). pp. 267–293.

at the same time open to other relationships. This issue of love, particularly its development and control, is discussed in Chapter 11.

Sexual Relationships

The central question surrounding the issue of sexual relationships is whether sexual relations (coitus) should be limited to marriage. Are there conditions or circumstances under which premarital, extramarital, or post-marital intercourse is legitimate? In addition, are there rational arguments for a double standard, differentiating the sexual norms for men and women?

The traditional sacred norm is quite clear. Prior to the turn of the century, extramarital, postmarital, and even sexual relations within marriage for purposes of pleasure were considered taboo. Officially, the mores allowed little deviation from this norm. Unofficially, a double standard existed whereby sexual deviation by men, although not sanctioned, was understand-able. On the other hand, women were socialized to believe that the husband

---

INTRODUCTION TO LOUISE, ALEX, ANN AND MAC

Permit me to introduce you to Louise, Alex, Ann and Mac, who are quoted in selected inserts throughout the text. With the exception of Ann, I had never met these persons prior to their arrival for an interview. Each was referred to me by another faculty member. My request was that I have a maximum of four in-dividuals; two males and two females. I preferred that at least one be single, one be black, one be from a foreign country, and one be a grandparent. There was no screening process or selection based on unique or unusual life-styles.

Each individual was told about the purpose of the interview and about the intent to insert quotations throughout the text. All gave their permission, volun-teered their time, and spoke openly about their lives, thoughts, and beliefs. As far as possible, the interview inserts are direct quotations as taken from tapes of the interviews.

Louise: *Female, age fifty-four, grandmother, widow of two years following twenty-seven years of marriage, mother of five children (one a foster child), Polish ethnic identity, currently a nurse in pediatrics.*

Alex: *Male, age twenty-two, foreign student from Turkey, white, single, resident of U.S. for four years, from an upper class family.*

Ann: *Female, age twenty-eight, black, married (but currently separated), mother of two boys, stepmother of two girls, working as receptionist.*

Mac: *Male, age twenty-nine, white single but cohabitating with divorcee with two boys, ex-factory worker, ex-marine, currently supported by veteran's benefits and "mate."*

was the one to whom sex was important, that sex should remain solely within the marital relationship, and that a good wife "submits" because she "owes this duty" to her husband.

Various changes took place when the social meaning of marriage began to emerge. As with the sacred meaning, sexual relationships outside of marriage were basically taboo except among unmarried couples who were marriage oriented or were "in love." This second traditional view of sex primarily limited intercourse to marriage, but it increasingly separated sex from reproduction and allowed it to become a source of pleasure for both sexes. Anything occurring within the marital relationship was perfectly normal and satisfactory as long as it was agreeable and unharmful to the couple involved. Although a double standard remains in effect, this latter view is likely the predominant position today.

The trend has been away from these traditional norms to an emerging sexual norm that questions the double standard and the necessity of limiting sexual relationships to marriage. If sex is fun (which an increasing number of men and women are agreeing that it is), why should it be limited to a spouse, someone whom you intend to marry, or even someone with whom you are in love? If maturity and adulthood imply independence and the capacity to make one's own decisions, then two individuals, whether married or single, male or female, should have the choice as to when, where, and with whom sexual relationships will take place. The publicity given to "swinging," "premarital cohabitation," and same-sex liaisons suggests one type of documentation of the emergence of this sexual norm. As women seek equality with men, as increasingly it is possible to separate sex from parenthood, and as primary informal means of control lessen, sexual independence and permissiveness are likely to result.

The implications of this issue are far-reaching. It has affected and will continue to affect the family, the educational system, other social institutions, and legislative processes, as well as personal behavior. The conflict is again obvious. One cannot adhere to both polar extremes of sexual relationships within marriage primarily for reproductive purposes as well as follow a philosophy of "sex as fun" in or out of marriage. These issues involving sexual relationships are discussed in a social context (Chapter 12), in a premarital context (Chapter 13), and in a marital context (Chapter 14).

Louise: *Sex must be oriented towards procreation. I think that's the way it was created. That's the way it was meant. In order to cut it off from procreation you have to interrupt some part of the sex act, and I viewed it as an element of the unnatural.*

Ann: *I don't mind telling people I enjoy it. There was a time I didn't. But now I don't mind saying to my husband or my mate—hey, let's go to bed.*

Women's Sex Role Attitudes Are Changing

Sex role attitudes of women are changing, but not because of the women's movement. So report Karen Oppenheim Mason, John L. Czajka and Sara Arber who used five sample surveys to analyze changes during the 1964–1974 decade.

Their results suggest considerable movement has taken place in the past decade toward more egalitarian role definitions with such change occurring equally among higher and lower status women. These changes were as great for the items that refer to the family as for those referring to the work place. Sizable increases occurred in the percentages of women who endorsed husbands sharing housework with wives, the right of women to

keep their jobs while bearing children, the right of women to be considered for top jobs on an equal footing with men, and the psychological feasibility or moral acceptability of a life without marriage and motherhood. While the figures suggest a tendency for women to shift toward a more egalitarian sex role stance, they also, however, indicate a continued predominance of support for the basic sex division of labor.

Little evidence was found that these changes were caused by the women's movement and its rise. Sex role attitude change occurred before 1970 as well as afterward and did not occur at a consistently faster pace after 1970 than before.

Source: Karen Oppenheim Mason, John L. Czajka, and Sara Arber, *American Sociological Review* 41 (August 1976) pp. 573–596.

Husband-Wife and Male-Female Roles

Husband-wife and male-female roles needs to include masculine-feminine and man-woman roles as well. The confusion and uncertainty over "proper" role definitions for the sexes became very evident to the author when a group of students were asked to define and list characteristics of masculinity. Extreme difficulty existed, first, in listing characteristics and, second, in securing agreement. Traditionally, male, husband, and father was the head of the family, its main economic support, and its representative in the community. The father was the boss, breadwinner, and the aggressive partner. The apostle Paul in his letters to the Ephesians and the Colossians made his views clearly known on husband-wife roles. To the Ephesians he said.

> Wives submit yourselves unto your husbands . . . for the husband is the head of the wife . . . therefore as the church is subject unto Christ so let the wives be to their own husbands in everything.[7]

To the Colossians, Paul was very clear on the "proper" hierarchy of power and authority within the family. To them he wrote:

---

7. Ephesians 5:22–24.

Wives submit yourselves unto your own husbands, as it is fit in the Lord. Husbands, love your wives and be not bitter against them. Children, obey your parents in all things: for this is well pleasing unto the Lord. Fathers, provoke not your children to anger, lest they be discouraged. Servants, obey in all things your masters according to the flesh, not with eye service, as men pleasers; but in singleness of heart, fear in God: and whatsoever ye do, do it heartily, as to the Lord, and not unto men.[8]

This traditional role pattern is consistent with the sacred meaning of marriage. The source of authority is not man, and the obligations are not fulfilled for men but for a supreme being.

The social definition of husband-wife roles, although in many ways consistent with the sacred definitions, places a greater focus on flexibility. Although traditionally the husband was the acknowledged head of the family, the wife increasingly contributed her opinions while attending to the specifics of child rearing and household tasks. Particularly in urban areas, an increasing number of wives found it necessary to work, although frequently as a supplement to the husband's functions. With the arrival of World War II, the demand for workers led to the employment of a large number of women. The result was an assurance that women had a permanent and needed position in business, industry, and the professions. It also meant the growth and acceptance of multiple social role definitions for women. It resulted in an increasing degree of economic independence and a more authoritative position for the female in family decision making. The expanding ethic of equalitarianism led to a rejection of a reverential attitude toward the husband and father.

The emerging definition of husband-wife roles suggests that husband and wife expectations, duties, rights, or responsibilities are not ascribed, fixed, or permanent. Increasingly, women are entering worlds that traditionally were for men only, and an increasing number of men are fulfilling the traditional roles of women. This emphasis on flexibility and lack of clear-cut role definitions should not be allowed to obscure the fact that today, as always, most of the time and effort of wives in the U.S. are devoted to their responsibilities within the home and family circle. Even most employed women drop out of the work force for a period of time after the birth of children. And most employed wives quit their jobs if their husbands are moved to another location, rather than vice versa.

With an increasing emphasis being placed on sexual role equality and personal fulfillment, it is of little surprise to find wives of successful men resentful of being a useful adjunct to their husband and his career or as being merely supportive of him and "his" children. An increasing number of husbands as well seem to be developing skills in human relations and participating in family activities such as child care, food preparation, or home

---

8. Colossians 3:18–23.

decoration, which were traditionally considered female, wife, and mother roles. And this too should, not surprisingly, result in a substantial feeling of self-approval and satisfaction among men.

A shift toward more equalitarian patterns generation by generation, less conventional allocation of roles in the family, and more consensus on family values in the younger generation is seen in a three-generational study by Reuben Hill and his colleagues.[9] A study of 100 grandparent, 100 parent, and 100 married-children families showed a shift in value orientations that are less fatalistic, moderately optimistic, and oriented toward the future. They found a shift in authority patterns to more equalitarianism with a greater division of tasks involving more sharing and less specialization. They found a greater degree of affectiveness, professional competence, and economic well-being among the younger generation. They found greater courage and risk taking accompanied by greater planning, flexibility, and communication.

This issue focusing on sex roles is discussed widely throughout the book. Chapter 5 includes discussions of sex roles as related to alternate marital-family life-styles, Chapter 6 as related to family systems outside the United States, Chapters 7 and 8 as related to Amish and black families, Chapter 9 as related to social class, Chapters 10 and 11 as related to mate selection, Chapters 12–14 as related to sexual relationships, Chapter 15 as related to marriage, Chapter 17 as related to socialization, and Chapter 18 as related to the middle and later years. This issue is of such magnitude that almost any topic in a text on the family should include a discussion of sex roles.

Family Size and Family Planning

Closely related and directly linked to the issues of sexual relationships and sex roles is the threefold issue of 1) limiting the number of children, 2) determining when and if to have them, and 3) selecting the appropriate means to accomplish these ends. Extensive publicity on zero population growth and on the population explosion has focused attention on family size. Controversies over abortion, sterilization, and the long-term effects of various contraceptives such as the pill have both contributed to and resulted from changing social norms pertaining to the number and the spacing of children as well as the means of achieving them.

The most traditional norm—one highly consistent with the sacred meaning of marriage—suggests that the primary purpose of sex is reproduction, and the only approved context for reproduction is within marriage. (One

---

9. Reuben Hill, "The American Family of the Future," *Journal of Marriage and the Family* 26 (February 1964), pp. 20–28; and Reuben Hill et al., *Family Development in Three Generations* (Cambridge, Mass.: Schenkman, 1970).

biblical admonition is that families should be fruitful and multiply.) One-child family situations were not viewed as the ideal, and a mother who only had one or two children was an issue of community concern. Neighborhood gossip might include such inquiries as "What is wrong with Bessie? Why, she has no children! And you know, Jake and Matilda have only one. Are they having marital problems?" Even more problematic was pregnancy apart from a marital relationship. Premarital pregnancies forced hasty marriages. Non-marital pregnancies and birth brought shame to the family unit.

Since, traditionally, large families were an economic asset and contributed to security in old age, children within marriage were highly valued. Few were the families that consciously and successfully controlled family size. Many mothers took pride in proclaiming that they had produced and raised fourteen healthy children. The spacing of children may have raised concern if pregnancy occurred very soon after a previous childbirth, but the concern centered more on the health of the mother than on the additional "blessing."

As the social norms changed, so did the view of large families. As population shifts removed families from farms, children became less of an economic asset. Increasingly, sex came to be viewed for pleasure as well as for reproduction. Children became a matter of choice rather than chance. And the emerging norm pertaining to family size now suggests that the maximum number of children should be two. For couples to have only one child or no children is granted social acceptability, to have four or six is to have too many, and to have ten or fourteen is disastrous.

Louise: *I am definitely antiviolence and I see abortion as a violent solution to probably a personal problem. I don't think people abort for any social reason like keeping down the population. I don't think that motivates people. It might be the thing they talk about. However, when the chips are down a woman has an abortion because she doesn't want the inconvenience of the pregnancy for whatever reason. And I don't accept any reason as valid for taking a human life. That doesn't mean I'm not sympathetic to the problem. I'm very sympathetic. The fact that we were foster parents all of our married life indicates we are concerned about the child of an unwanted pregnancy.*

Ann: *I kinda straddle the fence on abortion because I don't feel I should bring a child into the world that I cannot take care of. I also feel that to have an abortion is taking a life, taking a part of my life because it is my child. So, I'm like, taking the lesser of two evils. In my case I don't take birth control pills because I can't. I use a diaphragm, which doesn't all the time work, but I use one. Like I say, I straddle the fence, and I resent it. I have had an abortion and it's a very mind-blowing thing.*

The British Are Way Out Front

The rise and thrust of consumerism has come to the condom—on the other side of the Atlantic. (Consumerism, you know, refers to the public's demand for high quality standards of products and services.) In this country, every contraceptive device except the condom must meet Food and Drug Act standards.

Sometime ago, however, the British mounted a campaign to revise and raise condom standards. The British Standards Institution, noting that well over 100 million condoms per year are used in the UK, has laid

down these stiff and hard condom-quality measures:

Condoms must be sampled to check for holes and stretch strength.

Condoms must pass tests in hot-air ovens.

Packages must carry step-by-step instructions in how to use a condom.

Obviously, the U.S. has a Condom Gap. What this country needs is a good 5¢ condom, with a Goodhousekeeping Seal of Approval and Money-Back Guarantee If Product Fails To Perform As Advertised.

Source: *Sexology* 39 (April 1973), p. 13. Reprinted by permission.

The means of controlling the number of children has shifted as well. Again, the most traditional norm suggests that anything nonartificial or "God given" is appropriate. Since God has provided within each female a period of time each month when conception cannot occur, rhythm as a method of limiting family size is appropriate and consistent with the "will of God." The traditional sex role norm maintains that women are responsible for the prevention of pregnancy. The timing of sexual relationships around the menstrual cycle is consistent with the sacred meaning attached to marriage.

The social meaning of marriage, and perhaps the one most widely adhered to by couples in our society today, suggests that any means of fertility control that works, is nonharmful, and is agreeable to both spouses is legitimate. As a result, a majority of both Catholics and non-Catholics in the United States is using some form of "artificial" contraceptive or birth control method today, and widespread legalization of abortion has occurred in the last decade. The social norm in regard to family planning agrees with the sacred meaning in that the planning should be limited to the marital relationship, but it differs in the reliance on means that relate to the menstrual cycle.

The emerging norm pertaining to family size, family planning, and childbirth in or out of the marital context suggests that family limitation is an individual choice and the methods used (condoms, pills, diaphragm, jellies, abortion, sterilization) should not be limited by laws or measures that prevent couples from preventing pregnancy or childbirth. The emerging social norm places the responsibility for preventing conception on men as well as women, single as well as married. These issues of parenthood, family size and illegitimacy are presented in Chapter 16. Less attention is focused on methods of birth control and means of family planning.

Old Age

The traditional norms concerning the role of the aged strongly suggested that these persons should be given deference, respect, and recognition. Traditionally, it was the eldest person who had the most prestige, the widest experiences in living, and thus the greatest amount of wisdom. The aging family member had various important roles to fulfill, particularly in consulting and managerial positions in addition to those centering around the enjoyment and care of children and grandchildren.

The changing social scene has also changed the role of the aged person in the American family. The number of persons over the age of sixty-five in our population has increased steadily through the twentieth century. Most men and women of this age are no longer employed at their full-time jobs and, for many, retirement is an abrupt process; for most families it means a lowered income, and for the husband it means the destruction of his major role as a productive worker. The ascribed status of age no longer brings prestige per se. The emerging norm suggests that play must be substituted for work. This means a drastic shift in activities, in self-definitions, and in role performance. The basic issue and conflict of the aged centers around providing a meaningful way of life, which includes being able to make a contribution to life and the society in which the aged live. The role of the older person, their marital patterns, retirement, and postmarital family styles are discussed in Chapter 18.

Family Disorganization

The issue of family disorganization raises the question as to whether marriage should be a permanent or temporary arrangement. If viewed as temporary, what structural arrangements should be made to end one relationship and begin another, and what criteria should be used to determine when one relationship should end and another begin? Thus our ideal-type constructs might consist of models that include divorce-limited divorce-no divorce, total separation-partial separation-no separation, or any reason-no reason.

A sacred view of marriage suggests that marriage is for keeps. This most traditional view of marital conflict or disorganization views marriage as a lifelong permanent contract. Marriage exists until "death do us part" (unless one happens to be a Mormon who marries in the temple where the celestial marriage is for time and eternity). Marriage exists and remains legally intact irrespective of conflict in the relationship or personal unhappiness. This traditional norm was especially prevalent prior to 1920 or 1930.

Less extreme than the idea of marriage as a permanent relationship irrespective of persons or circumstances is a second traditional norm that suggests certain conditions or reasons as legitimate for ending marital and family commitments. Adultery has long been a socially acceptable reason for ending a legal marital contract. Even the Catholic Church, which takes a sacramental view of marriage relationships, accepts the ending of the marriage if it is due to conditions that existed prior to the start of that marriage. This structural form of ending a relationship (annulment) is a legally recognized type of marital dissolution.

The most common means for ending a marital relationship (other than death) is divorce. Since the legal grounds for divorce are determined by individual states, the reasons for permitting divorce vary widely. Traditionally, there was general agreement that one party had to be guilty. With time, several states made legal changes and most states interpreted the existing laws more leniently. Whereas many people believe that a major reason for the increasing divorce rates has been a change in the law, it is likely that the greater change has been in the increased tolerance toward divorce. Thus the changing social norm has been toward a greater acceptance of divorce, although a widely held social norm maintains that divorce should come only as a last resort after all other options have been considered. In any case, the 1970s witnessed a major increase in divorce rates, reaching levels unexcelled in U.S. history.

The emerging idea concerning family disorganization suggests that in many instances marriage is a trial. This norm maintains that marital success stems less from existence and permanence and more from a meaningful dynamic interaction of persons even if the partners may change. Immorality stems not from getting a divorce but from maintaining a relationship that is for all practical purposes broken. Thus divorce, rather than being a social problem, may be viewed as a solution for other types of problems. The end result is that marriages become more "vital and successful" than ever before in our history. Marriages exist out of personal desire rather than out of social or sacred obligations.

The same issues exist in regard to remarriage. Prior to the Civil War, remarriage was a right only of the innocent party. Many clergy would refuse to marry divorced persons. In certain fundamentalist denominations this is still the situation today. Within the Catholic Church as well, canon law prohibits the remarriage of divorced persons previously married in the church. In actual practice some priests do perform marriage ceremonies for divorced persons. And remarriage among the majority of divorced persons is high. Divorcees have a higher rate of marriage, age for age, than have the widowed or single persons entering their first marriage.

The basic nature of this issue of marital and family disorganization should be quite evident. Conflicts exist between those who adhere to a sacred meaning of marriage, accepting no reasons for ending a marriage, and those who grant social approval to a temporary marital relationship. The shift toward the greater acceptability of divorce may be seen in legal changes in several states, which permit divorce to whoever desires it, and the passage of "no-fault" divorce bills. Perhaps the day will come when divorce in U.S. society will be granted full social approval. Until this occurs, conflict on the basic issue of marital disorganization will remain. These issues of marital crisis, divorce, separation, and the like are further discussed in Chapter 19. Our attention is now directed toward selected characteristics of families in the United States.

CHARACTERISTICS OF FAMILIES IN THE UNITED STATES

The United States census is the primary source of national numerical data about families in this country. To provide an introduction to the American family, a summary of various characteristics as portrayed by census material is presented. More specific characteristics, statements of relationships, and research findings are presented throughout the book in the chapters appropriate to their discussion.

In 1975, the total resident population of the United States was estimated at 213.1 million.[10] This include 103.7 million males and 109.4 million females.[11]

The United States population by race (1975) included 185.2 million classified as white (86.9 percent), 24.5 classified as black (11.5 percent) and 3.5 classified as other races (1.6 percent).[12] Other races consists of Indians, Japanese, Chinese, and other nonwhites.

The United States population had a median age of 28.8, whites had a median age of 29.6, and blacks had a median age of 23.4. Nearly one-fourth of our population (23.2 percent) was under 14 years of age, one-fifth was age 14–24 (20.8 percent), one-fourth was 25–44 (25.1 percent), one-fifth was 45–64 (20.4 percent), and one in 10 persons (10.5 percent), was 65 years old and over.[13] Our changing age distribution shows a decrease since 1960 of about 6 percent in the proportion of the population under age 14, an increase of about 6 percent in the 14–24 age group, little change in the age groups 25–44 and 45–64, and a 1 percent increase in the proportion over age 65.

---

10. U.S. Bureau of the Census, *Statistical Abstract of the United States: 1976*, 97th ed., (Washington, D.C.: U.S. Government Printing Office, 1975), Table 24, p. 25.
11. Ibid.
12. Ibid.
13. Ibid., no. 28, p. 27.

Number of Families and Households

The term *family*, as used in census reporting, refers to a group of two or more persons related by blood, marriage, or adoption and residing together. Thus, if the son of the head of the household and the son's wife are in the household, they are treated as part of the head's family. On the other hand, a lodger and his wife who are not related to the head of the household, or an unrelated servant and his wife, are considered as additional families and not part of the household head's family.

In 1975, there were 55.7 million families in the United States. Of these, 47.0 million were considered to be husband-wife families. 11.5 million were other families with a male head, and 7.2 million were families with a female head.[14] The head of the family is usually the person regarded as such by the other members. In spite of the dominant position of many married females or the reality of sex role authority patterns, women are not classified as heads if their husbands are resident members of the family at the time of the survey. As stated above, married couples related to the head of a family are included in the head's family and are not classified separately.

A family is different from a *household*. A household consists of all persons who occupy a housing unit. A house, an apartment or other group of rooms, or a single room are regarded as a housing unit when they are occupied or intended for occupancy as separate living quarters. A household includes the related family members and all other unrelated persons, if any, such as lodgers, foster children, wards, or employees who share the housing unit. A person living alone in a housing unit, or a group of unrelated persons sharing a housing unit as partners, are also counted as a household. Thus, not all households contain a family. In 1975, there was 71.1 million households.[15]

The Bureau of the Census also makes reference to group quarters, primary families, secondary families and subfamilies. However, for current purposes of grasping an overview of families in the United States, these distinctions are unnecessary.

Size of Families and Households

The term "size of family" refers to the number of persons who are living together and are related to each other by blood, marriage, or adoption. The average size of all families was 3.42 in 1975. The average size of husband-wife families was 3.47, compared to 2.92 for families with a male head and

14. U.S. Bureau of the Census, *Current Population Reports*, Series P-20, no. 291, "Household and Family Characteristics: March 1975 (Washington, D.C.: U.S. Government Printing Office, 1976), Table 1, p. 7.

15. Ibid., Table 16, p. 74.

The Growing Popularity of Contraceptives: The Declining Size of Families

More and more American couples are adopting the pill, the IUD or sterilization as their birth control method. Charles F. Westoff cites the widespread use of these effective contraceptives as the main explanation for the 36 percent decline in unwanted births from 1965 to 1970 and a major factor in the drop in the nation's birthrate which is now at an all-time low (Family Planning Perspectives, July 1972).

Among all married couples within the reproduction age bracket, the pill is the most popular method, but it is closely followed by sterilization. Nearly six million married women were using the oral contraceptive in 1970—it accounted for about 34 percent of all use of birth control devices, taking a commanding lead of all other methods. The adoption of the pill by American women has been an amazing phenomenon, considering the various side effects, and is an indication of the wide market for effective contraception. Making its first public appearance in 1960, by 1965 it had been adopted by 23.9 percent of married women using contraceptives, and by 1970 this proportion had grown to 34.2 percent. Most of this increase was due to its widespread acceptance by young women. In 1970 about half of all younger women (30 and under) using contraception were relying on the pill, compared with 21 percent of women between 30 and 44. At the outset, the pill was first adopted by more educated

women, but by 1970 little of this association with level of education remained.

One of the surprising findings of the National Fertility Study of 1970 is the fact that voluntary sterilization—typically, tubal ligation for women and vasectomy for men—has become the most popular birth control method currently used by couples in which the wife is between 30 and 44 years old. One-quarter of all such couples have been surgically sterilized; the operations were almost equally divided between men and women. It is estimated that as of 1970 some 2.75 million couples of reproductive age (and, undoubtedly, many more since 1970) had resorted to sterilization, which is usually regarded as an extreme solution to the problem of fertility control.

The use of the three most effective contraceptive methods—sterilization, the pill and the IUD—has increased from 37.2 percent of all contraceptive practice in 1965 to 57.9 percent in 1970. Adding to these three methods the very effective diaphragm, the condom and a small fraction of multiple method usage, about four out of five couples using contraception in 1970 were highly protected from the risk of unintended pregnancy. And the 1970 data seem to indicate that low-income couples have almost caught up to the level of contraceptive protection experienced by higher-income couples.

Source: "Roundup of Current Research," *Society* 10 (November-December 1972), p. 8. Reprinted by permission.

3.21 for families headed by a female. The average size of white families was 3.36, compared to an average black family size of 3.90.[16]

Households had fewer persons per unit than did families in 1975. The average number of persons per household was 2.94,[17] compared to the 3.42

16. Ibid., Table 1, pp. 7–9.
17. Ibid., Table 17, p. 77.

average size of all families. The number of persons per household has de-creased considerably since the earliest census reports were taken. The average size of a household was 5.4 in 1790, 4.2 in 1900, 3.3 in 1940,[18] and, as shown, 2.94 in 1975. Thus the average household has 2.4 fewer persons today than at the end of the eighteenth century.

Marital Status

Census marital-status classification identifies four major categories: single, married, widowed, and divorced. A married couple is a husband and his wife, enumerated as members of the same household, who may or may not have children living with them.

As can be seen in Table 1–1, approximately 68 million men and 75 million women were age 18 or over in 1975. For men, 72.8 percent were mar-ried, 20.8 percent were single, 2.7 percent were widowed, and 3.7 percent were divorced. For women, 66.7 percent were married, 14.6 percent were single, 13.4 percent were widowed, and 5.3 percent were divorced. Thus, ignoring age differences, men are more likely than women to be married or single, and women are more likely than men to be widowed and divorced.

Marriage is a popular business: the overwhelming majority of both sexes marry at some time in their lives. More men (87.1 percent) are married in the 45–54 age category, and more women (84.8 percent) are married in the 35–44 age category than at any other age. Prior to those ages, an increasing number are single, and after those ages, an increasing number are widowed. Note the vast differences between widowed men and women after age 65 (41.9 percent women versus 8.8 percent men) and age 75 (69.4 percent women ver-sus 23.3 percent men). The percent distribution of men and women divorced holds fairly constant for men (about 5 percent) between age 25 and 64 and for women (about 7 percent) between age 25 and 54. Even at the maximum age category, only 7.6 percent of women and 5.0 percent of men are divorced. Thus, in spite of all the talk and concern about "easy divorce," "marital break-down," and "family decay," most of the United States population at any given time is married, and, when divorced, most remarry.

Family Income

Family income refers to the total amount reported by related persons who were members of the family at the time of enumeration. Each family member, fourteen years old and over, was asked the amount of income re-

---

18. U.S. Bureau of the Census, *Statistical Abstract of the United States: 1968* (Washington, D.C.: U.S. Government Printing Office, 1968), Table 40, p. 35.

TABLE 1–1. Marital Status of the Population, by Sex and Age: 1975

(In thousands of persons 18 years old and over, except percent. As of March)

Sex and Age	Total	Single	Married	Widowed	Divorced	PERCENT DISTRIBUTION				
						Total	Single	Married	Widowed	Divorced
Male	67,869	14,098	49,409	1,817	2,545	100.0	20.8	72.8	2.7	3.7
18–19 years	3,878	3,609	267	2	—	100.0	93.1	6.9	0.1	—
20–24 years	8,955	5,361	3,459	7	128	100.0	59.9	38.6	0.1	1.4
25–29 years	8,048	1,793	5,906	10	338	100.0	22.3	73.4	0.1	4.2
30–34 years	6,728	746	5,634	10	339	100.0	11.1	83.7	0.1	5.0
35–44 years	10,992	870	9,527	42	553	100.0	7.9	86.7	0.4	5.0
45–54 years	11,366	716	9,900	188	561	100.0	6.3	87.1	1.7	4.9
55–64 years	9,181	596	7,801	371	413	100.0	6.5	85.0	4.0	4.5
65–74 years	5,825	248	4,884	513	180	100.0	4.3	83.8	8.8	3.1
75 years and over	2,897	159	2,029	674	34	100.0	5.5	70.0	23.3	1.2
Female	75,345	11,007	50,257	10,104	3,978	100.0	14.6	66.7	13.4	5.3
18–19 years	4,078	3,169	879	4	25	100.0	77.7	21.6	0.1	0.6
20–24 years	9,406	3,792	5,261	27	326	100.0	40.3	55.9	0.3	3.5
25–29 years	8,345	1,150	6,615	41	540	100.0	13.8	79.3	0.5	6.5
30–34 years	6,971	522	5,892	62	496	100.0	7.5	84.5	0.9	7.1
35–44 years	11,615	568	9,849	323	877	100.0	4.9	84.8	2.8	7.6
45–54 years	12,220	563	9,768	1,045	845	100.0	4.6	79.9	8.6	6.9
55–64 years	10,305	529	7,142	2,087	546	100.0	5.1	69.3	20.3	5.3
65–74 years	7,599	438	3,726	3,183	253	100.0	5.8	49.0	41.9	3.3
75 years and over	4,806	277	1,125	3,334	70	100.0	5.8	23.4	69.4	1.5

— represents zero.

Source: U.S. Bureau of the Census, Statistical Abstract of the United States: 1976, 97th ed. (Washington, D.C., 1976), Table 46, p. 37.

ceived in the preceding calendar year from sources such as wages or salary, self-employment, social security, dividends, interest, rental income, public assistance or welfare payments, or other periodic income. It did not include amounts from sources such as the sale of property (stocks, bonds, a house, or a car), nor did it include borrowed money, tax refunds, gifts, or lump-sum inheritances or insurance payments. The total income of a family is the algebraic sum of the amounts received by all income recipients in the family.

Family income has increased considerably since 1960. The median family income in 1974 was $12,840 compared to $5,620 in 1960. However, rates of growth, as well as median income for families, varied widely by social category. For example, in 1974 the median income of white families was $13,356 compared to $7,808 for black families. Families with a man as head had median incomes more than twice as high as those with a woman as head ($13,788 versus $6,413). Husband-wife families with a wife in the paid labor force had a median income of $16,461 compared to $12,082 for identical families with a wife not in the labor force. Families with heads who had a college education of four years or more had a median income of $20,124 compared to $13,941 for the high school graduate and $7,073 for the head with less than an eighth-grade education. Families employed in professional occupations had a median family income of $19,441 ($23,553 for self-employed professionals), compared to $14,838 for craftsmen, foremen, and kindred workers, and $7,164 for farm laborers.[19] Many other examples could be given to illustrate the wide range of median incomes that exists for families in the United States.

Other Characteristics

A summary of various characteristics of families in the United States as of 1975 can be seen in Table 1–2. Of the 55 million families at that time, 89 percent were white, 59 percent were two- or three-person families, 46 percent had no children under 18, 75 percent had none under age 6.

Many additional factors could be mentioned. For example, although most families do not change residence in any given year, more than one in three lived in a different house in 1975 than in 1970.

Although most married women age 15–44 give birth to one or more children, nearly 19 percent are childless. Most births occur in a marital context, and about 13 percent of all births are defined as illegitimate.

Although men and women die at every age, in 1974 the average life expectancy was 68.2 for males and 75.9 for females. Although marriages take place every month of the year, nearly twice as many occur in June as in

19. All figures in this paragraph were taken from U.S. Bureau of the Census, *Current Population Reports*, Series P-60, no. 99, "Money Income and Poverty Status of Families and Persons in the United States: 1974," (Washington, D.C.: U.S. Government Printing Office, July, 1975).

> *Alex:* As far as family life in America is concerned, I think it's very different and unusual. Even though I've been here four years, there are sometimes instances it really freaks me out. For example, where the husband goes out and the wife goes out, and he works and she works, and they have different checking accounts. That really bugs me, you know. What kind of relationship is that? You're supposed to share everything. Like I know this one guy who is the vice president of some big company, and the company is owned by his father. He's the big shot and someday he's going to inherit the whole thing. And his wife works for a clothing store for something like $70 a week. Like, you know, she doesn't need it. She can get that allowance from her husband, but she won't ask for it. She goes out and works and that's her money. I don't know why on earth they do that. Could you explain to me why they do that?

TABLE 1–2. Families, by Characteristics: 1975

(Number in thousands. As of March. Based on current population survey)

Characteristic	ALL FAMILIES	
	Number	Percent
All Families	55,712	100.0
White	49,451	88.8
Negro and Other	6,262	11.2
Size of Family:		
2 persons	20,823	37.4
3 persons	12,137	21.8
4 persons	11,002	19.7
5 persons	6,313	11.3
6 persons	3,005	5.4
7 or more persons	2,432	4.4
Own Children under age 18:		
None	25,655	46.0
1	10,964	19.7
2	10,036	18.0
3	5,190	9.3
4 or more	3,866	6.9
Own Children under age 6:		
None	41,900	75.2
1	9,462	17.0
2	3,732	6.7
3 or more	618	1.1

Source: U.S. Bureau of the Census, *Statistical Abstracts of the United States 1976*, 97th ed. (Washington, D.C., 1976), Table 58, p. 43.

March. Although marriages occur in every state, in 1974 the rate in Nevada was 180.3 per 1,000 population, compared to 7.2 in Delaware, and a national rate of 10.5. Although divorces occur in every state, in 1974 the rate in Nevada was 17.5 per 1,000 population, compared to 2.5 in North Dakota and a national rate of 4.6 (up from 3.5 in 1970 and 2.2 in 1960).

Need more illustrations be given? Census data alone, apart from the countless number of completed research studies, illustrate quite clearly the pluralistic, complex, and diversified nature of U.S. families. More detailed breakdowns of characteristics such as these are presented at appropriate places in the text.

Summary

This first chapter is intended to introduce us to some characteristics and basic issues in the United States family. While all family systems adhere to similar basic general norms and values, great diversity exists in family structure and behavior within a given country such as ours. One way in which to note this diversity is to analyze variations in family organizations by age, race, class, religion, income, or other dimensions. Another is to examine selected issues of concern that relate to the family.

Ideal-type constructs were introduced as a way to provide a range of perspectives between two polar extremes. It was the tool used to examine eleven issues in the American family. Each of these issues was brought about by or was a result of social change; that is, traditional patterns coexist with emerging patterns. Were there no change or were there total change, no conflicts or issues would exist. In the view of the writer, the most important issue to which all other issues are related centers in the meaning given to marriage and the family. The most traditional social norm holds that marriage and the family is a sacred phenomenon created and maintained by factors that are beyond man. Less traditional is the norm that suggests that marriage is created and maintained by society or by kin, by community, or by social institutions. The emerging norm suggests that marriage is created and maintained by the individual and for the individual. Thus, at least three meanings, which are basically incompatible, exist simultaneously. Only when individual meanings are identical to social meanings, which are identical to sacred meanings, can there be no conflict.

Related issues include the "proper" form of marital and family organization, the functions of the family, social mobility, the choice of a mate and the authority to choose, the limiting of sexual relationships to marriage, husband-wife and male-female roles in relation to each other, the choice of the number and spacing of children and the means to fulfill that choice, the role of the aged in society, and the permanent or temporary nature of marriage. It is impossible to state that one issue is more important than another. For young single people, primary issues may focus on mate selection and sexual relationships, for married couples the primary issues may focus on children, birth control, and marital roles. For elderly persons, the primary issues may focus on the functions of the family and their place in society. The meaning given to marriage, if maintained consistently from one issue to another, will influence whether one is for divorce or against it, for abortion or opposed, for extramarital coitus or in opposition, or for accepting authority based on training.

This chapter, while highly descriptive, presents an overview of issues and characteristics of the family within the United States. The next chapter focuses on disciplinary and theoretical approaches to family study.

Key Terms and Topics

Ideal-type Constructs	4	Husband-Wife Roles	17
Meaning of Marriage	7	Family Size and Planning	19
Family Organization	8	Old Age	22
Family Functions	9	Family Disorganization	22
Social Mobility	11	Families and Households	25
Mate Selection	12	Family Size	25
Love	13	Marital Status	27
Sexual Relationships	15	Family Income	27

Discussion Questions

1. *How many "ideal types" of polar constructs can you list that describe issues in families?*
2. *Check with five married adults as to their perceptions of the most important issues in the U.S. family today. Do the same with five single students. Compare results.*
3. *Which issue (of those listed or others) do you perceive as the most significant or serious today? Why? How can the conflict or issue be resolved?*
4. *Why do marriages exist today? What is their purpose? What or who should be the ultimate authority?*
5. *If conflicts exist between traditional and emerging marital and family norms, do the adherents of either position have a right to impose their position on the other even if it appears detrimental to society? Take for example the family that wants twelve children versus those who argue for a maximum of two.*
6. *Can a person "love" more than one person simultaneously? Can intimate relationships with someone other than one's spouse enrich a relationship with the spouse?*
7. *Has there been a greater change in sexual norms for men or for women?*

Why is this so? Is this issue or conflict primarily a thing of the past or will it be an issue ten years from now?

8. *List the characteristics of "true" masculinity and femininity. Include behavioral as well as attitudinal characteristics.*

9. *Is an increase in divorce rates primarily indicative of a breakdown or a strengthening of the marital system in the United States? How about the increase in premarital or extramarital sexual relations, communal families, or interracial marriage? Why?*

10. *If a student from Ghana asked you to describe the typical family in the United States, how would you respond?*

11. *In what ways are families different in your community? Identify as many variables as you can.*

12. *To what extent is your family "typical"? How is it similar to or different from other families in our pluralistic society?*

Further Readings

Carr, Gwen B., ed. *Marriage and Family in a Decade of Change.* Reading, Mass: Addison-Wesley, 1972. A book of readings that attempts to compare the needs and values of the individual with what the present culture offers in the way of meeting them.

Cavan, Ruth Shonle. *The American Family.* 4th ed. New York: Thomas Crowell, 1969. See especially Chapter two of this textbook, which deals with issues in the American family.

Cox, Frank D. *American Marriage: A Changing Scene?* Dubuque, Iowa: William C. Brown, 1972. A collection of twenty-seven articles on change, many of which are oriented toward the morality and family of the future.

Glick, Paul C. "A Demographer Looks at American Families." *Journal of Marriage and the Family* 37 (February 1975), pp. 15–26. An examination of recent changes in marriage, fertility, divorce, living arrangements, and kin network ties.

Kammeyer, Kenneth C.W., ed. *Confronting the Issues: Sex Roles, Marriage and the Family.* Boston: Allyn and Bacon, 1975. A book of readings built around controversies relating to marriage, love, childbearing, child rearing, the woman's movement, and sexual behavior.

Korbin, Frances E. "The Primary Individual and the Family: Changes in Living Arrangements in the United States since 1940." *Journal of Marriage and the Family* 38 (May 1976), pp. 233–239. An article showing that an increasing proportion of the adult population is living alone or apart from relatives and that the family is declining as a locus of primary relationships.

Kubat, Daniel, and **David Thornton.** *A Statistical Profile of Canadian Society.* Toronto: McGraw-Hill Ryerson, 1974. For those interested in Canadian families, marriages, divorce, and fertility, the reader will particularly want to note pages 34–44 and 84–109.

Ross, Heather L., and **Isabel V. Sawhill.** *Time of Transition: The Growth of Families Headed by Women.* Washington, D.C.: Urban Institute, 1975. An extensive analysis of families with a single female parent, showing its unprecedented growth, its potential effects, and the role public policy has played.

Streib, Gordon F., ed. *The Changing Family: Adaptation and Diversity.* Reading, Mass.: Addison-Wesley, 1973. An examination of selected issues in the family as related to variations in family structure.

Wells, J. Gipson, ed. *Current Issues in Marriage and The Family.* New York: Macmillan, 1975. An examination of eight issues of central importance to the American Family system.

2   *Disciplinary and Theoretical*
Approaches to Family Study

2

Chapter 1 was devoted to a general introduction to the family, particularly in the United States. It provided some descriptive material on families, then examined eleven major issues in the American family by use of ideal-type constructs. This general overview was intended to set the general stage and introduce various issues, topics, and themes that follow throughout the text. There are many disciplines, approaches, and frames of reference used to study these family-related issues. These are examined in this chapter with an emphasis given to the basic approaches and orientations followed throughout this text.

DISCIPLINES INVOLVED IN FAMILY STUDY

The area of marriage and the family touches upon a wide range of topics, lends itself to many types of research, and uses in various ways the results of the research. The orientation used in dealing with families will, in large part, determine the areas to investigate, the questions to ask about those areas, the research and theoretical approaches to apply, and the results that are derived. Since no single discipline is asking all the questions, obviously none has all the answers. Note in Table 2–1, for example, the wide range of disciplines that are concerned with families or family-related topics and the examples of illustrative studies within each discipline.

Interdisciplinary Approaches and Concerns

No one discipline or occupation has a corner on the marriage and family market. The subject itself is highly interdisciplinary and, as a result, "is beset to an extreme degree by problems endemic to all interdisciplinary work:

TABLE 2–1.   Behavioral Sciences and Disciplines Involved in Family Study

Disciplines	Illustrative Studies

Anthropology
   Cultural anthropology
   Social anthropology
   Ethnology
	Cultural and subcultural family forms and functions
	Cross-cultural comparative family patterns
	Ethnic, racial, and social status family differences
	Families in primitive, developing, and industrial societies

Counseling
   Counseling theory
   Clinical practice
   Evaluation
	Dynamics of interpersonal relationships in marriage and
	   family
	Methods and results of individual, marriage, and family
	   counseling

Demography	Census and vital statistics on many facets of family life Cross-sectional, longitudinal, and record-linkage surveys Differential birth rates Family planning and population control
Economics	Consumer behavior, marketing, and motivation research Insurance, pensions, and welfare needs of families Standards of living, wage scales, socioeconomic status

Education
   Early childhood
   Early elementary
   Secondary
   College
   Parent
   Professional
	Child-rearing methods
	Developmental patterns
	Educational methods and evaluation
	Family life education
	Motivation and learning
	Preparation for marriage
	Sex education

History	Origins of family patterns Predictions of the future of families Social influences on the family Social trends and adaptations

Home economics
   Family relationships
   Home economics edu-
     cation
   Home management
   Nutrition
	Evaluation of family practices
	Family food habits and nutrition
	Home management practices
	Relationships between family members

Human development
   Child development
   Adolescent develop-
     ment
   Middle age and aging
	Child growth and development
	Developmental norms and differences
	Nature of cognitive learning
	Cross-cultural variations
	Personality development
	Social roles of aging

TABLE 2–1.   (*Continued*)

Disciplines	*Illustrative Studies*
Law	Adoption and child protection Child care and welfare Marriage and family law Divorce and marital dissolution Sexual controls and behavior Parental rights and responsibilities
Psychoanalysis	Abnormal and normal behavior Clinical diagnosis and therapy Foundations of personality Stages of development Treatment of mental illness

Psychology
  Clinical
  Developmental
  Social
	Aspirations and self-concepts
	Drives, needs, and hungers
	Dynamics of interpersonal interaction
	Learning theory
	Mental health
	Therapeutic intervention

Public health	Epidemiology and immunization Family health and preventive medicine Maternal and infant health Pediatric health education Venereal disease
Religion	Church policies on marriage and family Families of various religions Interfaith marriage Love, sex, marriage, divorce, and family in religious contexts

Social work
  Family casework
  Group work
  Social welfare
	Appraising family need
	Devising constructive programs for family assistance
	Measuring family functioning

Sociology	Courtship and mate selection Family formation and functioning Effects of social change on families Family crises and dissolution Prediction of family success Social class influence on families

From *Family Development,* by Evelyn M. Duvall. Reprinted by permission of the publisher, J. B. Lippincott Company. Copyright 1971 (Fourth Edition).

communication gaps, time lags, incommensurate concepts and definitions."[1] No one discipline can give a comprehensive and/or adequate picture of the family. Yet, the problem of interdisciplinary isolation is strikingly persistent. Anthropologists who focus on families and family structures often overlook emotional dynamics of family life. Psychologists, focusing on child development and personal adjustment, often overlook cultural variation and social organizational aspects. Sociologists, focusing on the social order, often overlook historical and personal developmental factors.

Since the late 1960s, major changes have taken place in the extent to which one discipline has challenged and/or incorporated ideas and theoretical frameworks of another discipline. Arlene Skolnick[2] claims that old social science theories are in a state of decline and that the family seems to be in a process of being rediscovered. Variation in family systems is emerging as distinct cultural phenomena rather than focusing on the abstraction and universalism of "the family." The idea of the natural state of the family being one of harmony is being replaced by notions of conflict and violence as equally natural. Treatment of individual persons has expanded to a focus on interaction and the whole family group. It is her contention that we know both more and less about the family than we thought we did a decade ago. In her words:

> We know that there is no uniform type of family, no Family that is everywhere and at all times the same. We know that there is great variation in family size, in extent of kinship, in residence patterns, in the organization of domestic functions, in the cognitive meanings of family, and in affective styles. We know that these features may vary not only from one culture to another, but also from one family to another in the same culture. We also know that we cannot extrapolate from family ideals and norms to behavior, or vice versa, but rather that behavior, norm, and symbol represent dimensions of family life that need to be analyzed separately. Finally, we know that there has been more physical and emotional conflict in families than anyone had acknowledged, and that somehow most families have coped with these strains and children have grown up amidst them without society's "falling apart."[3]

The Orientation of Specific Disciplines

Interdisciplinary new approaches may lead toward closing some of the gaps that separated disciplines and may bring forth new concepts and thus new meanings; yet each discipline will continue to focus attention in specific directions. The anthropologist will focus on family patterns in a cross-cultural and national context. The counsellor, usually in an applied context, will attempt to assist individuals, couples, or groups in resolving conflicts or modi-

1. Arlene Skolnick, "The Family Revisited: Themes in Recent Social Science Research," *Journal of Interdisciplinary History* 4 (Spring 1975), p. 703.
2. Ibid., pp. 703–719.
3. Ibid., p. 718.

fying attitude or behavioral problems. The educator will attempt to convey ideas and elicit thought on child development, preparing for marriage, sexual concerns, or parental functioning. The historian will examine family patterns, events, and change in the past and over time. The politician will formulate policy and enact laws to deal with child care, marriage age, parental duties and responsibilities, or divorce. The social worker will direct knowledge and skills toward assisting families and family members in coping with problems of income, health, or behavior.

Neither the disciplines described nor the illustrative studies in the table present an exhaustive listing of approaches to family study. The humanities have long been interested in the family.[4] Poets have been writing about love, marriage, and family matters for centuries. Theologists, philosophers, artists, musicians, and linguists have not been immune from dealing with areas pertinent to the family. Biology, genetics, anatomy, and other biological sciences are interested in many facets that affect families. In fact, it may well be the biosocial science area that will provide the next major revolution, replacing the industrial one and having an impact on families far greater than anything experienced or known at this time.

The point is that a student could take a large number of family courses and encounter different ideas, approaches, and interests. Some courses would include theories and findings from other disciplines, others would have no interdisciplinary focus. The question becomes less "Which is better or correct?" than "Which fulfills the objectives or purposes desired?" The student interested in the portrayal of mothers in the mass media may not find much satisfaction in a course on child growth and development. Neither may the student interested in sex education care much about insurance plans or marketing behavior of nineteenth century English households.

Textbooks, like disciplines or courses, approach the family with a particular focus and orientation. That this text gives minimal attention to human anatomy, childhood diseases, and family nutrition is not meant to indicate a lack of importance of these areas. Rather, the orientation and frame of reference of this text basically follows that of the social sciences and more specifically that of sociology.

A SOCIAL SCIENCE
APPROACH TO THE FAMILY

As with the other areas mentioned, and perhaps to a greater extent, the social sciences too have a primary interest in the family. Generally, the social sciences include sociology, anthropology, psychology, economics, and politi-

---

4. An excellent illustration of fiction writings related to marriage and the family can be found in Rose M. Somerville, *Intimate Relationships: Marriage, Family and Lifestyles through Literature* (Englewood Cliffs, N.J.: Prentice-Hall, 1975).

of the behavior of human beings

cal science. Sometimes history, geography, and linguistics are added to this list. Each examines the same subject matter—the behavior of human beings— employs the same body of general explanatory principles, and shares similar aims and methods. Science is determined by its aims and methods, not by its results.

Regardless of the topic that is studied, be it the family or the economy, the social scientist is obligated to view facts as they are without an insertion of personal value preferences. It is this key factor of objectivity that distinguishes a social science approach from other approaches to human behavior. Underlying the scientific perspective of objectivity are three basic assumptions:

1. Various phenomena within the universe are characterized by certain regularities or uniformities.
2. These regularities or uniformities operate independently of the characteristics of the observer.
3. These regularities or uniformities can be discovered, at least in theory, through objective observation.[5]

In brief, science is predicated upon the assumption that there is a "real world," that something exists "out there"—something that is divorced from the individuals themselves and is empirically knowable.

These, then, are the aims and goals of a social science approach to the family: to establish more-or-less general relationships, to require that they be based on empirical observation, and to view findings as tentative and open to multiple interpretations. Within the social science framework, let us examine the sociological approach to the family.

Sociology of the Family

Sociology per se is devoted to the study of how society is organized, its social structure, and its social processes. The primary units of investigation include human groups, social systems, and institutions.

As stated by Inkeles:

> If you were to insist that the basic problems to which Sociology addresses itself be described in a single phrase, we would reply: It seeks to explain the nature of social order and social disorder. Sociology shares with all other essential scientific perspectives the assumption that there is order in nature, and that it can be discovered, described, and understood. . . . When we speak of "order" we mean that events occur in a more-or-less regular sequence or pattern so that we can make an empirically verifiable statement about the relation of one event

5. James W. Vander Zanden, *Sociology: A Systematic Approach*, 3rd ed. (New York: Ronald Press, 1975), p. 7.

to another at given points in time under specified conditions. Sociology deals with several such forms of order, varying greatly in scale but each having substantially the same character.[6]

In light of the above statement, a sociology of the family seeks to explain the nature of the social order and disorder of the family. The attempt is to discover, describe, and explain the order of family systems and family groups. A sociology of the family is interested in the organization of the family: its structures, functions, and changes. It is interested in how the family as a social system is sustained and modified. It is interested in how family relationships are formed and changed, how the components within the family are interrelated, and how the family as a unit is interdependent with other groups or systems.

A sociology of the family differs from either psychological or social-psychological approaches to the family. Whereas both of the latter are primarily concerned with the behavior of individuals, sociology is interested in the social forms and structures within which this behavior takes place. Sociology has no primary interest in the individual, his personality, or his behavior but, rather, with the nature of the groups to which the individual belongs and the society in which he lives. Robert Bierstedt states that this separation is difficult and easy to oversimplify, but the reader will not be far wrong if he observes that psychology studies the individual, social psychology the individual in his social groups, and sociology the groups themselves and the larger social structures within which both individual and group processes occur.[7]

A sociology of the family will not focus on the motivation, drives, or perceptions of individuals. Technically speaking, a major segment of this book is a social psychology of marriage and the family. The sections that deal with interpersonal relationships (mate-selection processes, sexual behavior, parental interaction) focus on explaining how the structure and function of the family group influence the behavior of the members within that group and, reciprocally, how the behavior of each member modifies or shapes the family organization and its functioning.

A sociology of the family, operating within the social science framework, does not have as its major intent the direct application or utilization of the knowledge gained by the "pure," "concrete," or "basic" disciplines. On a pure-applied ideal-type continuum, and operating within an ideal-type construct (see Chapter 1), persons involved in the acquisition of knowledge do not devote their time and attention to the application of the knowledge. Thus the "basic" psychologist does not counsel family members, the sociologist does not work in adoption agencies, nor does the economist assist a family member in obtaining a job. The extent to which the two polar types should

6. Alex Inkeles, *What is Sociology?* (Englewood Cliffs, N.J.: Prentice-Hall, 1964), p. 25.
7. Robert Bierstedt, *The Social Order*, 4th ed. (New York: McGraw-Hill, 1974), p. 10.

remain separate has become an area of heated debate. Whereas some argue that the "pure" scientist should not permit social problems and human needs to dictate or influence his research, others argue that the very persons who obtain the knowledge are in a position to influence change most effectively and make maximum use of the knowledge obtained. As one student suggested recently, "In light of the urgency of today's social problems, time no longer permits debate on this issue. Scientists must get involved in the solving of these problems."

This book will not solve family problems. Hopefully, it will increase our knowledge about existing situations, present frameworks for analysis and/or action, and suggest alternate life-styles and directives. Based on the available knowledge and various interpretations of that knowledge, based on various theoretical explanations and methodological approaches, based on the presentation of multiple structures and various alternatives, the writer hopes readers will be in a better position to make their own choices of action and their own sound value judgments.

HISTORICAL APPROACHES
TO FAMILY STUDIES

It was only after the middle of the nineteenth century that a systematic study of the family began. Prior to that time, thinking about the family had been based on emotion and superstition and was expressed by means of folklore, proverbs, and moralisms. Bert N. Adams says that the beginning of the movement toward systematic understanding rather than folklore can be traced roughly to the time of the appearance of Charles Darwin's *Origin of the Species* in 1859.[8] Adams subdivides the years from 1860–1950 into three thirty-year periods: social Darwinism (1860–1890), social reform (1890–1920), scientific study (1920–1950), plus attention to family theory (1950–Present). This division closely parallels that of Harold Christensen, who sees the development of investigations concerning marriage and the family as falling into four periods or stages: preresearch (prior to about 1850), social Darwinism (1850-1900), emerging science (1900–1950), and systematic theory building (1950–Present).[9]

The preresearch period had family guidelines that were in the form of philosophical speculations, religious pronouncements, and often contradictory generalizations (such as today's "out of sight, out of mind" and "absence makes the heart grow fonder"). Although these types of speculation continue today, and many untested assumptions regarding the family are rigidly de-

8. Bert N. Adams, *The Family: A Sociological Interpretation*, 2d ed. (Chicago: Rand McNally, 1975), pp. 4–6.
9. Harold T. Christensen, ed., *Handbook of Marriage and the Family* (Chicago: Rand McNally, 1964), pp. 5–10.

Marriage Folk Beliefs

If you awaken at 12:00 midnight and look at the mirror, you will see your future partner or sweetheart.

A person with dimples will marry someone from a place far away from his place.

It is not good for a girl or woman to sit at the head of the table because she won't get married and will eventually end up as an old maid.

A layman who goes through life without being married will not be admitted in heaven. He lacks the sacrament of matrimony and fails to comply with the commandment of God.

If a man married a woman who is one year older than him their whole married life always meets problems and difficulties.

A girl who is always fainting should get married and she will be cured.

Marriage should be held at date when the moon is getting big—half moon or full moon for abundance of children.

If a husband can cut a banana plant with just one stroke of the blade (bolo), he is the master of the house. If he cannot, he is a henpecked husband.

Source: Francisco Demetrio y Radaza, S.J., ed., *Dictionary of Philippine Folk Beliefs and Customs*, Book III. (Cagayan de Oro City: Xavier University, 1970), pp. 619–622, 624–625.

fended, various shifts have taken place in the development of the study of the family. In the middle of the nineteenth century several writers began to apply Darwin's biological evolutionary scheme to changes within the family (see also the chapter on theories of family change). Basing their arguments on Darwin's work, various writers traced the evolution of the family through certain natural stages. These were generally macroanthropological schemes that traced the origin and evolution of the family institution, based on "primitive" peoples, through a series of "progressive" stages.

Toward the end of the nineteenth century and the beginning of the twentieth, especially in the United States, social problems led to a concern for social reform. Many of these problems were closely related to the family: poverty, child labor, prostitution, illegitimacy, divorce, and the like. These problems were intensified by industrialization and urbanization, both of which disrupted kin ties.

The first half of the twentieth century emphasized large-scale comparative studies, aimed at attacking some of the social problems but emphasizing more of a value-free position and a more rigorous methodology. Various statistical techniques were developed and certain social psychologists and sociologists began to focus on individual personality adjustment, the family as a major factor in this adjustment, and the relationship between certain family problems and social problems in general.

A social-psychological orientation replaced the macroanthropological approaches of the earlier periods. Christensen states that the most pronounced characteristic of this period of family study was its emphasis upon the internal relationship of family members.[10] Charles Cooley, Robert Park, George Mead, W. I. Thomas, and others contributed to this emphasis, but it was Ernest W. Burgess who did most to both conceptualize and assist in the development of family studies. In 1926 he referred to the family as "the unity of interacting personalities," a definition that is still in wide use today. This was basically the beginning of the scientific orientation to family study, and by 1950 it was perhaps accurate to speak of the specific study of marriage and the family.

Since 1950, attempts have gone beyond mere description and quantitative research to a renewed interest in theory building. Research is increasingly turning to cross-cultural and comparative studies, not purely for descriptive purposes, but to discover relationships that are generalizable beyond a given societal context. These relationships and propositions enable the building of sound family theory.

Adams suggests that to label the period from 1950 to the present as "systematic theory building" might be a bit presumptuous, at least for the decades prior to the 1970s.[11] He prefers to describe the present period as the period of summarization of findings, of conceptual frameworks, of complaint about the lack of a comprehensive theory, and of substantial theorizing. On the other hand, particularly since 1960 with the publishing of Reuben Hill and Donald Hansen's article[12] on identifying conceptual frame works utilized in family study, with Christensen's *Handbook of Marriage and the Family*[13] (where ten chapters are devoted to theoretical orientations and methodological developments) and with the development of various less grandiose theories that deal with mate selection, sexual behavior, role differentiation, socialization, and other family-related matters, the 1960s and 1970s have truly been two decades of systematic theory building. The section that follows in this chapter examines the use and nature of theory and frames of reference.

THE NATURE OF THEORIES AND FRAMES OF REFERENCE

Like the theoreticians in most other fields, family scholars are increasingly attempting to organize their accumulated knowledge in the form of concepts, generalizations, and theories. Particularly since 1960, specialists in the family area have been conscious of the need to organize concepts, develop hypotheses and propositions, and interrelate these propositions in a meaningful fashion in order to explain a particular aspect of marital or family organi-

---

10. Ibid., p. 9.
11. Adams, op. cit., p. 6.
12. Reuben Hill and Donald A. Hansen, "The Identification of Conceptual Frameworks Utilized in Family Study," *Marriage and Family Living* 22 (November 1960), pp. 299–311.
13. Christensen, op. cit., pp. 3–400.

zation and behavior. Concepts, conceptual frameworks, frames of reference, or theories are important in that they tell scholars where to focus their attention.

Family theories are neither right nor wrong but are basically ways of looking at and rationally explaining phenomena related to the family. An understanding of the most widely used frames of reference can enable the student to study and analyze family behavior in a way that is organized and logical. Rather than behavior within the family context being idiosyncratic and inconsistent, it becomes patterned, consistent, and predictable under certain given conditions.

Concepts and Variables

Basic to all theory and to all sociological research tools are *concepts*. A family concept, as in any area, is a miniature "system of meaning"—that is, a symbol, such as a word or phrase that enables a phenomenon to be perceived in a certain way. Concepts are tools by which one can share meanings. They are unitary and thus do not explain, predict, or state relationships. They are abstractions that are used as building blocks for the development of hypotheses, propositions, and theories. *In family analysis, the segments of reality that are identified by concepts are typically qualities, attributes, or properties of social behavior.* Examples of concepts within the family area would include the nuclear family, monogamy, roles, norms, values, legitimacy, sex ratio, and so on. When these concepts take on two or more degrees or values they are referred to as *variables.* "Husband" is a concept, "years married" is a variable. The variable may be classified as independent (the presumed cause) or dependent (the presumed effect). The independent variable is antecedent, or simultaneous, to the dependent variable. Family income (a variable) may be dependent (the presumed effect) upon the number of years of education (the presumed cause).

Concepts and variables are undergoing continuous revision and refinement. Frequently, new concepts must be invented to symbolize some new idea or to identify some social property that had not previously been seen.

Do Concepts Make a Difference

I used to think I was poor. Then they told me I wasn't poor, I was NEEDY. Then they told me it was self-defeating to think of myself as needy, I was DEPRIVED. Then they told me deprived was a bad image, I was UNDERPRIVILEGED. Then they told me underprivileged was overused, I was DISADVANTAGED. I still don't have a dime, but I have a great vocabulary.

Source: Anonymous.

Thus *family* may in itself serve as an adequate term for lay people, but the professional differentiates between families of orientation, procreation, nuclear, conjugal, extended, consanguine, stem, and joint. Because the particular concept used will affect what is seen, it must be constructed in a way that will not distort "reality." An extremely difficult task for the family scholar is to label phenomena in ways that will avoid undesired connotations. Notice the obviously different connotations of labels or concepts such as nigger, colored, Negro, black, or Afro-American. Or could you imagine a family text bearing titles such as the honky, WASP, palefaced, or uncolored family in American society?

Conceptual Frameworks

When a set of concepts is interrelated to describe and classify phenomena, in this case phenomena relative to the family, the concepts are generally defined as a *conceptual framework*. A definition of a conceptual framework as utilized by most family theorists might be: a cluster of interrelated, but not as yet interdefined, concepts for viewing the phenomenon of marriage and family behavior and for describing and classifying its parts.[14] In a strict sense of the term, a conceptual framework is not a theory; it is more frequently descriptive rather than explanatory and is generally employed as a classification scheme or taxonomy.

Considerable changes have occurred in the identification of current conceptual frameworks. In 1957, seven basic frameworks or approaches were defined by Hill and others: institutional-historical, interactional-role analysis, structural-functional, situational-psychological habitat, learning theory-maturational, household economics-home management, and the family development or family life-cycle approach.[15]

In 1960, in what has become a classic article by Hill and Hansen, the chief conceptual properties and basic underlying assumptions of five frameworks were provided in taxonomic tables.[16] The frameworks delineated included these approaches: interactional, structural-functional, situational, institutional, and developmental.

These two initial works have stimulated a large number of articles throughout the world. The Christensen handbook, another classic in the field, provides four extensive chapters on the five frameworks delineated by Hill

---

14. Reuben Hill, "Contemporary Developments in Family Theory," *Journal of Marriage and the Family* 28 (February 1966), p. 11.

15. Reuben Hill, Alvin M. Katz, and Richard L. Simpson, "An Inventory of Research in Marriage and Family Behavior: A Statement of Objectives and Progress," *Marriage and Family Living* 19 (February 1957), pp. 89–92.

16. Reuben Hill and Donald A. Hansen, "The Identification of Conceptual Frameworks Utilized in Family Study," *Marriage and Family Living* 22 (November 1960), pp. 299–311.

and Hansen with the interactional and situational approaches presented in one chapter.[17] Further delineation and an expansion of conceptual frameworks is provided by Carlfred Broderick who claims that of the five frameworks, three have emerged as viable: the interactional, structural-functional, and developmental.[18] He lists family analysis, balance theory, game theory, exchange theory, and general systems theory as new conceptual frameworks.

Conceptual frameworks facilitate the research process by providing adequate definitions of concepts and providing the range of variables that might be employed in investigating a given area within marriage and the family. Ivan Nye and Felix Berardo state that the delineation of the conceptual frameworks relevant to the study of the family can contribute to research in these ways:

1. Making it explicit that a number of different frameworks exist and represent varied perspectives for viewing family behavior.
2. Providing a listing and definition of the central concepts of each framework so that these are readily available to the researcher.
3. Making explicit the implicit underlying assumptions of each framework.
4. Providing a bibliography of research done employing each frame of reference, that will afford the researcher convenient access to the relevant literature.[19]

It is doubtful that "good" research or theory building would proceed very rapidly without establishing the clarification of the basic conceptual frameworks utilized in studying the family. It is for this reason that this book delineates major conceptual frameworks that are used today in studying the family.

Propositions and Hypotheses

It is from conceptual frameworks that propositions, hypotheses, and theories can most readily be established. A *proposition* is a statement about the nature of some phenomenon. It generally involves a statement of the relationship between two or more concepts. For example, "young marriage is related to marital disorganization" would be a proposition. If this, or other propositions, would be formulated for empirical testing it would be considered a *hypothesis*. Thus a testable hypothesis would be "the younger the

---

17. Harold T. Christensen, ed., *Handbook of Marriage and the Family* (Chicago: Rand Mc-Nally, 1964, Part I), pp. 33–211.
18. Carlfred B. Broderick, "Beyond the Five Conceptual Frameworks: A Decade of Development in Family Theory," *Journal of Marriage and the Family* 33 (February 1971), pp. 139–159.
19. F. Ivan Nye and Felix M. Berardo, *Emerging Conceptual Frameworks in Family Analysis* (New York: Macmillan, 1966), p. 5.

age at marriage, the higher the rate of divorce." Hypotheses and propositions
are identical, with the exception that hypotheses carry clear implications for
testing or measuring the stated relations. Hypotheses serve as the important
branch between theory and empirical inquiry.[20] Hypotheses and propositions
are formed by combining concepts into statements that set forth some meaningful relationship.

Frequently, a proposition states that if one variable changes in some
regular fashion, predictable change will take place in the other. For example,
it is suggested and discussed in the next chapter that "as industrialization
increases, extended family ties decrease." Thus the two variables (industrialization and extended family) are stated as inversely related: as one increases
the other decreases.

An extensive inventory of propositions interrelating family variables
was presented by William Goode, Elizabeth Hopkins, and Helen McClure.[21]
In 1971 they presented an estimated 10,000 propositions that interrelated
family variables. Two years later, Wesley Burr[22] identified a series of propositions useful in understanding processes in the social institution of the family
and analyzed the nature of these propositions to determine what was asserted
and the circumstances under which they were asserted to occur. In addition,
he examined the relevant empirical data to determine the amount of proof
that existed either for or against various aspects of the theoretical ideas. This
work is another step toward systematic theory building in the area of family
study.

Theory

When it is possible to interrelate logically and systematically a series
of propositions that explain some particular process, the result is a *theory*. A
"good" theory should be testable, should be abstract, should have wide application, should be cumulative, and should give grounds for prediction. Thus
a theory is far more than mere speculation or a random collection of concepts
and variables. It is a set of logically interrelated propositions that explains
some process or set of phenomena in a testable fashion. Like propositions,
theories not only provide explanations of observed reality but also serve as
important sources of new hypotheses. One example of such an effort can be

20. William J. Goode, Elizabeth Hopkins, and Helen M. McClure, *Social Systems and Family
    Patterns: A Propositional Inventory* (Indianapolis: Bobbs-Merrill, 1971).

21. A very clear example of the clarification of concepts, the use of hypotheses (empirical
    propositions), and derived propositions in theory construction can be seen in J. Kenneth
    Davidson, Sr. and Gerald R. Leslie, "Premarital Sexual Intercourse: An Application of
    Axiomatic Theory Construction," *Journal of Marriage and the Family* 39 (February 1977),
    pp. 15–25.

22. Wesley R. Burr, *Theory Construction and the Sociology of the Family* (New York: John
    Wiley, 1973).

seen in Wesley Burr's attempt to explain variation in marital satisfaction. He identified a number of propositions about factors that influence marital satisfaction as suggested by theoretical orientations such as symbolic interaction, exchange theory, and balance theory, and integrated them into a new model.[23]

The use and application of theory, or perhaps more accurately, frames of reference, are used extensively throughout this book.[24] While no chapter exists on theory per se, the reader will note subsections that use a particular frame of reference. For example, the structural functional frame of reference is applied extensively in Part II to an analysis of family life-styles, families around the world, and social class. The symbolic interaction frame of reference is applied throughout the book to an analysis of mate selection, sexual relationships, marital interaction, and child rearing (socialization). The developmental framework is applied through Part IV in viewing marriage over the life cycle. Exchange theory is applied to mate selection and marital interaction. Conflict theory is applied to the marital system. Other theories—frames of reference—not specifically summarized in detail in this chapter are presented where appropriate to offer a specific explanation of a particular aspect of the family: an orderly replacement theory of change, a complementary-need theory of mate selection, a normative-morality theory of sexual behavior, a learning-behaviorist or psychoanalytic theory of socialization, a disengagement theory of old age, and the like. From this list alone, it becomes obvious that many sets of logically interrelated propositions exist that explain some process or set of phenomena. Those more directly pertinent and widely used in a sociology of the family are summarized in the section that follows.

FAMILY THEORIES AND FRAMES OF REFERENCE

A Structural-Functional Frame of Reference

The structural-functional frame of reference, sometimes called functional analysis, is the major and dominant theoretical orientation in sociology today. Within the family area, the scope of the approach is very broad; it provides a framework for dealing with the relationships within the family (husband, wife, sibling, and so on), as well as with the reciprocal influences on the family of other systems within the wider society, such as educational, religious, or occupational influences.

---

23. Ibid., Chapter 3, pp. 41–70.
24. While a theory and frame of reference may be identical, they are not necessarily so. A social frame of reference provides certain conceptual tools and a perspective in which to view social matters. A theory explains.

The structural-functional frame of reference has its origin in the functionalist branch of psychology, especially the gestalt position; in social anthropology, especially as seen in the works of Bronislaw Malinowski[25] and A. R. Radcliffe-Brown;[26] and in sociology, especially as seen by social-systems theorists such as Talcott Parsons.[27] The gestalt position focuses on the relation between a whole and its parts. A gestalt is an organized entity or whole in which the parts, although distinguishable, are interdependent. Numerous social anthropologists as well have stressed the impossibility of studying any particular aspect of life detached from its general setting. Malinowski identified functionalism with the study of the interrelationships between the structures of any system.

To talk about social structures is to talk about social organizations, social systems, norms, values, and the like. Cultural structures, social structures, structural interrelations, or any other "structural" terminology refers to the interdependence of parts in a definite pattern of organization. The implication is that groups, systems, or behavior are not purely random, without regularity, unpredictable, and individualistic.

The social structure of a family refers to the way in which the social units are arranged, to the interrelationship of the parts, and to the patterns of organization. These patterns differ greatly around the world but, given a particular type of organization, definite recurrent consequences take place. Thus, to have one wife or several, for newlyweds to establish a residence separate from parents, for both husband and wife to share in making the basic decisions, for inheritance to be given to the oldest child, or for there to be premarital sexual freedom is to suggest that recurrent, predictable consequences will occur within that given society and/or family system. Nuclear, polyandry, patriarchy, avunculocal, bilineal, primogeniture, exogamy, arranged marriage, or consanguine are words that define specific structural arrangements of a given family system. Most of these terms are described and illustrated in a later chapter.

The concepts "structure" and "function" can be discussed separately, although they are interrelated and one implies the other. Speaking in circular terms, social structures are units of society that carry out or result in one or more basic functions. On the other hand, functions can be defined as results or consequences of given social structures. What specifically is meant by function?

Function is generally used in one of two related ways. One is to ask, "What does it do?" That is, in describing functions of the family in America

25. Bronislaw Malinowski, "The Group and the Individual in Functional Analysis," *The American Journal of Sociology* 44 (1939), pp. 938–964; and Bronislaw Malinowski, *The Dynamics of Culture Change* (New Haven, Conn.: Yale University Press, 1945).

26. A. R. Radcliffe-Brown, *Structure and Function in Primitive Society* (Glencoe, Ill.: Free Press, 1952).

27. Talcott Parsons, *The Social System* (Glencoe: Free Press, 1951).

or any given society it is asked what the family does. Why does it exist? What functions does it perform? These functions may be performed for the individual personality, a particular social system or social institution, or the wide society.

It has been suggested that for individual members, the functions of the family are to provide the basic personality formation, the basic status ascriptions, nurturant socialization, and tension management. For the larger society, some of its functions are to replace members, to socialize the members to the norms and values of the society, and to act as an agent of social control. Talcott Parsons and Robert Bales suggest that the basic and irreducible family functions are two: 1) the primary socialization of children so that they can truly become members of the society into which they have been born, and 2) the stabilization of the adult personalities of the population of the society.[28]

The second way in which function is used and highly related to the first usage is in terms of consequences or results of activities that take place. Thus, given a certain type of structural pattern—for example, working mothers—one could ask, "What are some of the consequences (results) of the employment of mothers?" Note that the question is not "What do working mothers do?" but rather "What are some of the results or consequences of this type of behavior pattern?" Are smaller family size, higher levels of mental health, delinquent children, or marital instability consequences of mothers working? Do families in societies that permit mothers to join the labor force have a higher level of living, a "closer" parent-child relationship, or more equalitarian decision-making patterns? Are the consequences similiar irrespective of cultural context, time, or location? How does this structure interrelate with other structures? Does it lead to the maintenance or the breakdown of a particular system? Is it consistent with the value scheme of the particular subculture discussed?

The central question now centers around the consequences or results of any particular social structure and its interrelationships with other structures. To learn how any system operates, whether the system is an airplane engine, a biological organism, a human society, or a family, is to understand the objective consequences or results of any part of the structure in relationship to the other parts or the system as a whole.

To repeat, these terms, structure and function, are complementary concepts. Although they can be discussed separately, they cannot be understood independently. The structure (parts) to which a social analyst imputes functions (consequences) includes norms, values, roles, rank, power, and sanctions, as well as factors such as emotions, beliefs, and goals.

Today, a major thrust of the structural-functional approach centers

---

28. Talcott Parsons and Robert F. Bales, *Family Socialization and Interaction Process* (New York: Free Press, 1955), pp. 16–17.

around explaining the parts or components (structure) of a society and the manner in which these parts interrelate with one another, both within and outside the particular system under study. If the starting point is a given society or a particular subculture within a society, that society or subculture can be described or analyzed in terms of the parts (structures) that are interrelated and interdependent. Each component of society must be seen in relationship to the whole, since each component acts and reacts upon other components. Thus the task of functional analysis is to explain the parts, the relationship between the parts, the relationship between the parts and the whole, and the functions that are performed by, or result from, the relationship formed by the parts.

On an ideal-type continuum, the level of analysis ranges from macroanalysis to microanalysis. The distinction between these is made purely in terms of the size of the unit chosen for analysis. The macrofunctionalists are concerned with the analysis of relatively large-scale systems and institutions. The microfunctionalists are concerned with the analysis of individual families or of relatively small-scale systems (often designated as "group dynamics"). Both positions conceive of their units of analysis as important to, and interrelated with, the other parts of the larger system.[29]

A Social Conflict Frame of Reference

Conflict theory may be viewed as a special case of functional theory, as does Lewis Coser[30] or as an entirely separate theory as done by Rolf Dahrendorf.[31] Perhaps the most basic assumption of a conflict frame of reference is that conflict is natural and inevitable in all human interaction. Thus, rather than stressing equilibrium, balance, or system maintenance as in functionalism, the focus is on conflict management. Rather than viewing conflict as

---

29. Key concepts in structural-functional theory in sociology are social system, social structure, social function, dysfunctions, manifest and latent functions, functional requisites and prerequisites, equilibrium and order, status and norms.

Some of the leading advocates of this perspective include Talcott Parsons, Robert Merton, Kingsley Davis, Wilbert Moore, Robin Williams, Charles Loomis, Harry Johnson, W. Lloyd Warner, Emile Durkheim, George Homans, Marion Levy, William Goode, and Robert Winch.

From the perspective of the family, readers may wish to examine Robert F. Winch, *The Modern Family* 3d ed. (New York: Holt, Rinehart and Winston, 1971); Rose Laub Coser, *The Family: Its Structures and Functions*, 2d ed. (New York: St. Martin's, 1974); and Norman W. Bell and Eyra F. Vogel, *A Modern Introduction to the Family*, rev. ed. (New York: Free Press, 1968).

30. Lewis A. Coser, *Continuities in the Study of Social Conflict* (New York: Free Press, 1967).

31. Rolf Dahrendorf, *Essays in the Theory of Society* (Stanford: Stanford University Press, 1968); and Rolf Dahrendorf, "Out of Utopia: Toward a Reorientation of Sociological Analysis," *American Journal of Sociology* 744 (September 1958), pp. 115–127.

"bad," and disruptive of social systems and human interaction, conflict is viewed as an assumed and expected part of all systems and interactions, including family systems and marital interactions. If family-employment, husband-wife, or parent-child norms or goals are in frequent conflict (as is to be expected), the issue is not how to avoid them but how to manage, deal with, and/or resolve them. In so doing, the conflict, rather than being disruptive or negative, may strengthen relationships and make them more meaningful and rewarding than they were prior to the conflict.

The classical case for conflict theory stems from Marx,[32] who assumed that economic organization, especially the ownership of property, generates revolutionary class conflict. As the exploited and oppressed proletariats become aware of their oppression and their true "interests," they will revolt and form a revolutionary political organization aimed at overthrowing the dominant, property-holding bourgeoisie. Basic to Marx and influential in the contemporary thinking of conflict theorists are ideas such as 1) social systems systematically generate conflict, which 2) is an inevitable and pervasive feature of all social systems and 3) is manifest in the bipolar opposition of interests that 4) is brought about by the distribution of scarce resources, most notably power, which 5) results in change in social systems.[33]

Hypotheses stemming from these assumptions suggest that the more unequal the distribution of scarce resources, the greater the conflict between the dominant and subordinate; as the subordinate become aware of their collective interests, they increasingly question the legitimacy of existing patterns; the greater the questioning of inequities, the more likely they are to join in overt conflict against the dominant group; and the more overt and/or violent the conflict, the greater the change and the redistribution of these resources.

These conflicts between the oppressed and the oppressor exist not merely in the economic and occupational realm but in the family as well. Friedrich Engels[34] claimed that the basic unit in a capitalist society is the family and that it serves as the chief source of female oppression. The husband is the bourgeois and the wife the proletariat. Thus within a conflict frame of reference, as wives, females, or mothers (the oppressed) become aware of their collective interests, question the legitimacy of existing patterns, then join together against the husbands, males, and fathers (the dominant), and force change and a redistribution of resources (power, money,

32. Karl Marx, *The Communist Manifesto*, trans. Samuel Moore (Baltimore: Penguin, 1967 originally published in 1849, with Fredrich Engels); C. Wright Mills, *The Marxists* (New York: Harcourt, Brace, 1948); and Rolf Dahrendorf, *Class and Class Conflict in Industrial Society* (Stanford: Stanford University Press, 1959).

33. See Jonathan H. Turner, *The Structure of Sociological Theory* (Homewood, Ill.: Dorsey, 1974), pp. 79–83.

34. Friedrich Engels, *The Origin of the Family, Private Property and the State* (Chicago: Charles H. Kerr, 1902).

education, job opportunities, and the like). Conflict, as inevitable in society, in the family, and in interpersonal relationships, leads to change. Power, decision making, marital adjustment, economic factors, and other issues related to conflict theory are discussed further, particularly in Chapter 15.[35]

A Symbolic Interaction Frame of Reference

Symbolic interactionism has come into use as a label that indicates a particular and distinctive approach to the study of man's group life and personal behavior. As a social-psychological frame of reference, it addresses itself to two major questions, both of central concern to the family: socialization and personality. The first—socialization—focuses on how the human being obtains and internalizes the behavior patterns and ways of thinking and feeling of the society. The second—personality—focuses on the way in which these attitudes, values, and behaviors are organized.

Within social psychology, symbolic interactionism constitutes both a theoretical perspective and a methodological orientation. Its theoretical uniqueness lies in the extent to which covert activity is a crucial dimension in the understanding of behavior and society. That is, *like* Pavlovian and Skinnerian radical behaviorism,[36] symbolic interactionism includes the observable actions of individuals; *unlike* radical behaviorism, it stresses the importance of "meanings," definitions of situations, symbols, interpretations, and other internalized processes.

Interaction among socialized human beings is mediated by the use of symbols, by interpretation, or by ascertaining meanings for the actions of others. Methodologically, the "world of reality" is known by any means or set of techniques that offers a likely possibility of obtaining what is going on: direct observation, interviews, listening to the conversations of people, securing life history accounts, using letters and diaries, consulting public records, arranging for group discussions, or any allowable procedure that ascertains the subjective meanings. Basically, it involves a phenomenological approach with participant observation, the use of personal documents, and ethnometh-

35. Key concepts in conflict theory are conflict, competition, struggle, resources, scarcity, interests, change, power, and class. Some of the leading advocates of the perspective include Karl Marx, Georg Simmel, Rolf Dahrendorf, Lewis A. Coser, and Pierre van de Berghe. From the perspective of the family, readers may wish to examine Jetse Sprey, "The Family as a System in Conflict," *Journal of Marriage and the Family* 31 (November 1969), pp. 699–706; Randall Collins, "A Conflict Theory of Sexual Stratification," *Social Problems* 19 (Summer 1971), pp. 3–21; and Robert N. Whitehurst, "Conflict Theory in Family Sociology: A Missing Perspective" (Paper presented at the Canadian Sociological and Anthropological Association meeting, Edmonton, Canada, May 30, 1975).

36. Pavlovian and Skinnerian radical behaviorism, parallel to classical and operant conditioning, are described in Chapter 17 under the heading, "A Learning-Behaviorist Frame of Reference."

odological accounts as the preferred techniques. The use of the quotations from personal interviews (as found in this book in the unscreened boxes) is consistent with this particular frame of reference.

The interactionist approach makes the following assumptions:

- Marriages and families must be studied at their own level; that is, we cannot infer the behavior of humans, of human interactions, or of social systems from the study of nonhumans or infrahuman forms.
- Marriage and family and their components can only be understood in the context of the social setting and society in which they exist. The language spoken, the definitions given to situations or the appropriateness of any activity only makes sense within a social context.
- The human infant at birth is neither social nor antisocial but asocial and learns in interaction with others what is good or bad, accepted or unaccepted behavior.
- A social human being is an actor as well as a reactor; that is, can communicate symbolically and share meanings. Thus individuals do not merely respond to objective stimuli but select and interpret them. Individuals can interact each with himself, can take the roles of others, and can respond to symbolic stimuli.

These assumptions, spelled out in more detail in Chapter 17, are basic to an understanding of the significance of this framework as applied to both marital and parental interaction and to human behavior in general.

Concepts from this framework are used extensively throughout the book. For example, the concept "role" is used both within a structural-functional framework and within an interactional framework. However, its use varies significantly. An institutional or structural concept of role attaches societal expectations to statuses that we occupy. Certain statuses, such as sex, age, and race, are generally ascribed, whereas our marital, occupational, and parental statuses are likely to be achieved. Each of these statuses or status sets carry with them expected, appropriate behaviors. These expectations of what is appropriate for men or women, married or single, homosexual or heterosexual are termed roles. These are culturally defined expectations, and exist independently of any given person.

Role, as it is used within an interactionist framework, does not deny the institutional usage but, rather than dealing with a package of behavioral expectations wrapped up in a set of rules, it deals with a relationship between what we do and what others do. The expectations (roles) are developed in interaction. The emphasis here is on process. The interactionist concept of role describes the processes of cooperative behavior and of communication. It involves the idea of "role taking," which is not a set of rules associated with a position but involves actions supplied in part by relationships to others whose actions reflect roles that are inferred. Role as process involves each actor adjusting his behavior and reactions to what he thinks the other person

Love, Honor, Obey

Many American women see their roles as wives and mothers as separate and distinct from each other—and men generally take a backseat to children in a woman's priorities—according to a study by Helena Znaniecki Lopata of Roosevelt University (Human Organization, Summer 1965). She asked 299 young suburban housewives and 323 older urban matrons what they thought were the most important roles of women. Only 62 percent even mentioned the role of wife and only 33 percent gave it first place. To most women in the study, the most important people are their children, not their husbands—the role of mother was mentioned by over 80 percent and 37 percent put motherhood in first place. How do such women see their husbands? Mostly as providers—87 percent listed the provider role for husbands; 65 percent listed father; and only 46 percent listed husband. Dr. Lopata believes that there are a number of possible styles for married women in America today including:

The husband-oriented wife. She is usually dependent in all the circumstances of her life on the nature of her husband's job.

The life-cycle wife. These women have a husband-oriented "honeymoon" period, shift later to an intensive interest in motherhood, and go back to primary wifeliness later in their marriages after the children have left home. Generally, the older, urban women in the study showed more interest in the wife role than the suburban women who all had young children.

The mother and her children. For these women, the basic family unit consists of herself and her children; the husband is external to this close group. At least one-third of the women in the study followed this style.

The housewife and her home. These women are more involved with house and furnishings than with anything else. They tend to see people, including children and husbands, as infringing on this relation.

Source: "Roundup of Current Research," *Trans-Action* 2 (September-October 1965), p. 24. Reprinted by permission.

is going to do. Perhaps a simple example may clarify the difference in the use of these two bodies of thought.

Suppose we have two teen-age students, one male and one female. The fact that they occupy the statuses of student and teen-ager implies that certain expectations or roles are associated with these statuses. But for the moment let us concentrate on the students as male and female. Some of the rules or expectations traditionally associated with the status "male" in relationship to "female" are that he walk on the outside, open doors, permit her to proceed first, assist her with a chair, and pay the bill. Thus the institutional concept of role emphasizes the prescribed expectations for behavior given by the society. Whether these rules are actually followed is secondary. The roles (expectations) exist independently of a given individual's fulfillment of them. Failure to conform to the expectations appropriate to status does not eliminate the normative expectations.

In contrast to the institutionalized concept of role, the interactionist concept involves the *process* of determining appropriate behavior in inter-action with others. Now, the actor is not the occupant of a position for which there is a standardized set of rules; he is a person whose expectations for behavior are supplied in part by his relationship to another person or persons. Since the expectations of the other person can only be inferred rather than directly known there is a continuous process of testing. The clues given by the other person in part determine the expected behaviors (roles) appropriate to that situation. Getting back to our male and female, as they interact the expectations (roles) for appropriate and approved behavior may vary widely from the socially ascribed expectations. The female may quite appropriately pay the bills, open the doors, be the aggressive sexual partner, drive the auto-mobile, and the like. But these too become patterned and recurrent. This is what makes behavior predictable and interaction possible with either strangers or intimate lifelong friends.

These two conceptions of roles are not totally independent and sepa-rate, for one never escapes the norms or roles provided by a given society. At best, however, the expectations associated with a given status offer only generalized guidelines; they do not determine specific behavior patterns for every situation. Thus the norm prescribing that a teen-age male does not have intercourse with a teen-age female on a first date nevertheless may, as the couple interacts, result in coitus. The gestures, the clues, the symbols, the verbal communications, and the clarity of shared meanings may lead to intercourse as a highly appropriate role expectation for the dating partners—within the interaction concept of role. The behavior of intercourse on a first date, within the institutional concept of role, however, is inconsistent with the culturally prescribed rules for teen-agers in the United States.

Other concepts that are key to the understanding of this frame of refer-ence include the social self, significant others, reference groups, and the generalized other. These are clarified and illustrated in various chapters throughout the text, with a more extensive presentation of the symbolic in-teractionist frame of reference in Chapter 17. At this point, let us be satisfied with recognizing the family as a "unit of interacting personalities"[37] involved in a never-ending, completed, or fixed process.[38]

---

37. Ernst W. Burgess, "The Family as a Unit of Interacting Personalities," *Family* 7 (1926), pp. 3–9.

38. Key concepts in symbolic interaction theory are symbols, interaction, process, status, role, role playing, role taking, role conflict, meaning, reference group, significant other, generalized other, social self, "I," "me," socialization, actor, and identity. Some of the leading advocates of the perspective include George Herbert Mead, Charles Cooley, Wil-liam James, Herbert Blumer, Tomatsu Shibutani, Alfred Lindesmith, Anselm L. Strauss, Erving Goffman, Bernard Meltzer, Jerome Manis, Ralph Turner, Sheldon Stryker. From the perspective of the family, readers may wish to examine Ralph H. Turner, *Family Interaction* (New York: John Wiley, 1970); and Sheldon Stryker, "Symbolic Interaction Theory: A Review and Some Suggestions for Comparative Family Research," *Journal of Comparative Family Studies* 3 (Spring 1972), pp. 17–32.

A Social Exchange
Frame of Reference

Seldom does a day pass in which certain exchanges do not take place. Work, gifts, cards, affection, or ideas are given in hopes of getting something in return. Certain exchanges, such as many economic ones, are institutionalized and predetermined—clarified in precise terms prior to the exchange. Thus I know that I can exchange 25 cents for a newspaper or $30 in exchange for a membership in the National Council on Family Relations. Other exchanges, including the type found in the social exchange frame of reference, leave unspecified the exact nature of the return, although a return—an expectation of reciprocity—does exist. For example, neighbors who borrow tools or food, friends who invite you to dinner, politicians who promise lower taxes, all expect something in return. That exact something is often unspecified.

Social exchange theory seeks to explain why certain behavioral outcomes occur (marriage, sex, employment), given a set of structural conditions (age, race, gender, class) and interactional potentialities. These assumptions are made:

- Most gratifications of humans have their source in the actions of other humans (spouse, children, friends, colleagues, fellow workers).
- New associations are entered into because they are expected to be rewarding and old associations continue because they are rewarding.
- As we receive rewards or benefits from others, we're under an obligation to reciprocate by supplying benefits to them in return.
- In general, giving is more blessed than receiving, because having social credit is preferable to being socially indebted.

While it may be true that persons (saints) exist who selflessly work for others with no thought of reward, saints are rare, and even they seek social (or spiritual) approval. In brief, social exchange refers to voluntary social actions that are contingent on rewarding reactions from others. These actions cease when the actual or expected reactions are not forthcoming.

Social exchange theory has followed two differing schools of thought best represented by George Homans[39] and Peter Blau.[40] Homans, the recognized initiator of exchange theory, represents a perspective consistent with that of behavioral psychologists who believe in psychological reductionism and reinforcement theory where the focus is on actual behavior that is rewarded or punished by the behavior of other persons. Humans, like animals, react to stimuli based on need, reward, and reinforcement. It is expected that

39. George C. Homans, Social Behavior: Its Elementary Forms (New York: Harcourt, Brace and World, 1961); George C. Homans, "Social Behavior as Exchange," American Journal of Sociology 63 (May 1958), pp. 597–606.
40. Peter M. Blau, Exchange and Power in Social Life (New York: John Wiley, 1964); Peter Blau, "Justice in Social Exchange," Sociological Inquiry 34 (Spring 1964), pp. 193–206.

in exchange relationships the rewards will be proportional to the cost (a notion of distributive justice).

Blau differs considerably from Homans, and represents a perspective consistent with that of the symbolic interactionist.[41] That is, not all exchange is explained in terms of actual behavior of individuals. The exchange is more subjective and interpretative. The exchange, like interaction, is a creative process between actors and not within individuals or in external factors. While humans want rewards, the choices and decisions are limited by social influences such as friends or kin. The human mind responds subjectively to stimuli through conceptualizing, defining, valuing, reflecting, and symbolizing. As a result, the explaining of behavorial outcomes (the goal of social exchange theory) is a function of the actors who interact symbolically, have a social self, and can take roles.

Both Homans and Blau agree that what is important is that each party receives in the exchange something perceived as equivalent to that which is given (to Homans—distributive justice, to Blau—fair exchange). All social exchange involves a mutually held expectation that reciprocation will occur.[42] If resources or exchange criteria are unequal or imbalanced, one person is at a distinct disadvantage and the other has power over or controls the relationship. Specific resources (money, position, physical assets, personality) may be more applicable in one exchange over another and may have differing values in one exchange over another. Their worth can only be accurately assessed through participation in actual social markets. Therefore, socialization in exchange and bargaining skills becomes vital to maximize the use of available resources.

The family literature is filled with many examples of social exchange. As you will note in the chapters on mate selection, Kingsley Davis explains the greater frequency of black male-white female marriage than vice versa by suggesting that black males exchange a higher social status for the "higher" racial status of the white female. Willard Waller suggests in his "principle of least interest" that interest is exchanged for control of the relationship in that the person who is least interested in continuing the dating relationship is in a position to dominate. In arranged marriages, labor, gifts, or a bride price are often exchanged for the right to marry. Robert Winch talks of complementary needs involving an exchange of needs that provide maximum gratification. The higher incidence of premarital sexual behavior of engaged females has been explained by an exchange of sex on the part of the female in return for a commitment on the part of the male. Throughout

41. See Peter Singelmann, "Exchange as Symbolic Interaction: Convergence between Two Theoretical Perspectives," *American Sociological Review* 37 (August 1972), pp. 414–424; Robert B. Schafer, "Exchange and Symbolic Interaction," *Pacific Sociological Review* 17 (October 1974) pp. 417–434; and Richard M. Emerson, "Social Exchange Theory," *Annual Review of Sociology* 2 (1976), pp. 335–362.

42. Alvin W. Gouldner, "The Norm of Reciprocity," *American Sociological Review* 25 (April 1960) pp. 161–178.

the text, note the value of different types of resources and the exchange processes at work in understanding authority and power, husband-wife interaction, mate selection, kin relationships, sexual patterns, parent-child conflict, and the like.[43]

A Developmental Frame of Reference

Having its beginning in the 1930s, the family development approach to family study attempts to join together various parts of previously delineated theoretical efforts. Hill and Hansen, discussing the characteristics of the developmental-conceptual framework, have indicated that as of 1960 this approach was not a precisely unique framework but was an attempt to transcend the boundaries of several approaches through incorporation of their compatible sections into one unified theme.[44]

> From rural sociologists it borrowed the concept of stages of the family life cycle. From child psychologists and human development specialists came the concepts of developmental needs and tasks. From the sociologists engaged in work in the professions it incorporated the concept of the family as a convergence of intercontingent careers. From the structure-function and interactional approaches were borrowed the concepts of age and sex roles, plurality patterns, functional prerequisites, and the many concepts associated with the family as a system of interacting actors.[45]

The developmental approach attempts to account for the societal-institutional, interactional-associational, and individual-personality variables of family phenomena.[46] Obviously, it covers a very broad area tending to be both macro- and microanalytic in nature. The peculiar character of this

---

43. Key concepts in social exchange theory are exchange, reciprocity, negotiation, transaction, resources, cost, distributive justice, fair exchange, and power. Some of the leading advocates of this perspective include George C. Homans, Peter M. Blau, Kingsley Davis, Alvin W. Gouldner, John W. Thibaut, Harold H. Kelley, John N. Edwards and John Scanzoni. From the perspective of the family, readers may wish to examine John N. Edwards, "Familial Behavior as Social Exchange," *Journal of Marriage and the Family* 31 (August 1969) pp. 518–526; John N. Edwards and Mary Ball Brauburger, "Exchange and Parent-Youth Conflict," *Journal of Marriage and the Family* 35 (February 1973), pp. 101–107; Constantina Safilios-Rothschild, "A Macro- and Micro-Examination of Family Power and Love: An Exchange Model," *Journal of Marriage and the Family* 38 (May 1976) pp. 355–362; and Roger W. Libby and John E. Carlson, "Exchange as Concept, Conceptual Framework or Theory? The Case of Goode's Application of Exchange to the Family," *Journal of Comparative Family Studies* 12 (Autumn 1973), pp. 159–170.

44. Hill and Hansen, op. cit., pp. 299–311.

45. Ibid., p. 307.

46. Reuben Hill and Roy H. Rodgers, "The Developmental Approach," in Christensen, op. cit., p. 171.

approach lies in its attempt to account for change in the family system over time as well as account for changes in patterns of interaction over time. The major conceptual tool for this time analysis has been termed the family life cycle.

As a descriptive device, the family life cycle has been used to compare structures and functions of marital interaction in different stages of development. Over the years, the family life-cycle idea has been used in a variety of ways. In its earliest conceptualization, it was seen essentially as a control factor or as an independent variable that might explain certain kinds of family phenomena such as expenditure patterns, levels of living, and consumption patterns. As early as 1906, in England, B. S. Rowntree advanced a theory of the life cycle of families in poverty.[47] His life cycle included a period of poverty when the children are young, a period of relative prosperity when the children grow up and become earners, and a second period of poverty in old age when the grown children leave home to establish families of their own.

In the 1930s, Sorokin and others, as well as E. L. Kirkpatrick and his colleagues, discussed four-stage family life cycles. Sorokin based his life cycles upon the changing family-member constellation within the family: 1) married couples just starting their independent economic existence, 2) couples with one or more children, 3) couples with one or more adult self-supporting children, and 4) couples growing old.[48] Kirkpatrick saw the stages of the family life cycle in terms of the place of the children in the educational system in the four-stage cycle: 1) preschool family, 2) grade school family, 3) high school family, and 4) all-adult family.[49]

In the 1940s, a more elaborate set of stages of the family life cycle was developed by an economist, Howard Bigelow.[50] In plotting the changing financial patterns through the family life cycle, he elaborated on the school-placement factor in a cycle he divided into seven periods: 1) establishment, 2) child-bearing and preschool period, 3) elementary school period, 4) high school period, 5) college, 6) period of recovery, and 7) period of retirement.

By the 1960s, the family life-cycle idea had been more fully developed and used as a research tool by Paul Glick,[51] Evelyn Duvall,[52] and Roy Rod-

47. B. S. Rowntree, *Poverty: A Study of Town Life* (London: Macmillan, 1906), pp. 136–138.

48. P. Sorokin, C. C. Zimmerman, and C. J. Galpin, *A Systematic Source Book in Rural Sociology*, vol. 2 (Minneapolis: University of Minnesota Press, 1931), p. 31.

49. E. L. Kirkpatrick, et. al., *The Life Cycle of the Farm Family in Relation to its Standard of Living*, Agricultural Experiment Station Research Bulletin no. 121 (Madison, Wisc.: University of Wisconsin, 1934).

50. Howard F. Bigelow, "Money and Marriage," Chapter 17, in Howard Becker and Reuben Hill, eds., *Marriage and the Family* (Boston: D. C. Heath, 1942), pp. 382–386.

51. Paul C. Glick, *American Families* (New York: John Wiley, 1957); Paul C. Glick, "The Family Cycle," *American Sociological Review* 14 (April 1947), pp. 164–174; Paul C. Glick, "The Life Cycle of the Family," *Marriage and Family Living* 17 (February 1955), pp. 3–9.

52. Evelyn M. Duvall, *Family Development* (Philadelphia: J. B. Lippincott, 1957).

> All the world's a stage,
> And all the men and women merely players,
> They have their exits and their entrances,
> And one man in his time plays many parts,
> His acts being seven ages. At first the infant,
> Mewling and puking in the nurse's arms.
> Then the whining school-boy, with his satchel
> And shining morning face, creeping like snail
> Unwillingly to school. And then the lover,
> Sighing like furnace, with a woeful ballad
> Made to his mistress' eyebrow. Then a soldier,
> Full of strange oaths, and bearded like the pard,
> Jealous in honour, sudden, and quick in quarrel,
> Seeking the bubble reputation
> Even in the cannon's mouth. And then the justice,
> In fair round belly with good capon lin'd,
> With eyes severe and beard of formal cut,
> Full of wise saws and modern instances;
> And so he plays his part. The sixth age shifts
> Into the lean and slipper'd pantaloon,
> With spectacles on nose and pouch on side,
> His youthful hose, well sav'd, a world too wide
> For his shrunk shank; and his big manly voice
> Turning again toward childlish treble, pipes
> And whistles in his sound. Last scene of all,
> The ends this strange eventful history,
> Is second childishness and mere oblivion,
> Sans teeth, sans eyes, sans taste, sans everything.

William Shakespeare, *The Seven Ages of Man.*

gers.[53] The work of Glick provided the transition from the treatment of life-cycle stages as a demographic category (a statistical analysis of human population) to the use of life-cycle stages as periods in the family life span that are descriptively different, with implications unique to a particular stage. In his analysis of United States census material, he attempts to clarify some of the content and effects of changes in the family as it moves through various stages.

The most systematic, widespread, and long-term use of the family life-cycle idea is provided by Evelyn Duvall. She, too, has attempted to provide a clarification of the developmental-task concept.[54] "A developmental task is

---

53. Roy H. Rodgers, *Improvements in the Construction and Analysis of Family Life Cycle Categories* (Kalamazoo: Western Michigan University, 1962).

54. A history of this concept is provided in the preface to Evelyn M. Duvall, *Family Development*, op. cit., pp. v–ix.

one that arises at or about a certain period in the life of an individual, successful achievement of which leads to his happiness and to success with later tasks, while failure leads to unhappiness in the individual, disapproval by society, and difficulty with later tasks."[55] These tasks have two primary origins: 1) physical maturation and 2) cultural pressures and privileges.[56] The number of developmental tasks an individual faces are innumerable. Many of them are delineated in human development textbooks.

It is Duvall's contention that, like the individual, families too have tasks that arise at a given stage in the family life cycle. She defines a family's developmental task as "a growth responsibility that arises at a certain stage in the life of a family, successful achievement of which leads to satisfaction and success with later tasks, while failure leads to unhappiness in the family, disapproval by society, and difficulty with later developmental tasks."[57] For families to continue to grow as a unit they need to satisfy at a given stage the 1) biological requirements, 2) cultural imperatives, and 3) personal aspirations and values.

Duvall recognizes and depicts the family life cycle as consisting of eight stages:

Stage 1. Married couples (without children)

Stage 2. Childbearing families (oldest child birth–thirty months)

Stage 3. Families with preschool children (oldest child two and one half–six years)

Stage 4. Families with school children (oldest child six–thirteen years)

Stage 5. Families with teenagers (oldest child thirteen–twenty years)

Stage 6. Families as launching centers (first child gone to last child's leaving home)

Stage 7. Middle-aged parents (empty nest to retirement)

Stage 8. Aging family members (retirement to death of both spouses)[58]

These stages are determined by the age and school placement of the oldest child up to the launching stage, after which the situation facing those remaining in the original family is used. This type of scheme fails to recognize explicitly multiple-child families, overlapping stages, death of a spouse, and many other variations in families. But this scheme, as any, serves as a division for study and analysis, though in reality the family life cycle and each stage within it has no beginning and no end.

Rodgers, elaborating on the eight-stage cycle of Duvall, provides today

55. Robert J. Havighurst, *Human Development and Education* (New York: Longmans, Green, 1953), p. 2.

56. Duvall, op. cit., p. 142.

57. Ibid., pp. 149–150.

58. Ibid., pp. 116–117.

Buying Patterns and the Family Life Cycle

Market researchers, men who advise ad agencies and manufacturers about the sort of people who buy their products, have begun to use the sociological notion of the family life cycle. William D. Wells of the University of Chicago Graduate School of Business and George Gubar of Seton Hall University, in a study sponsored by the advertising agency Benton & Bowles, Inc., show how knowledge of the stage a family has reached in its life cycle can help to predict the kind of products it buys (Journal of Marketing Research, November 1966). It may be that some of the specific buying patterns Wells and Gubar refer to will, in turn, add to sociologists' knowledge about families:

Before the children come: Newly married couples spend more on coin-operated laundry machines, rent, new cars, luxury goods, and vacations.

Children under six: These families are the major buyers of TV sets and washing machines, "practical" furniture, baby food (especially for the first baby who is fed 50 percent more processed—and expensive—baby food than his later-born sibling), cough syrup,

and laundry detergents. They don't take expensive vacations, and they make do with their old car. They buy houses, but they're still a long way from owning them.

Older children at home: Now families are big buyers of corn flakes, large, economy-sized packages, new cars (the old one wore out, finally), bicycles and pianos, (and if they have daughters old enough to date) new "decorator" furniture, more shampoo.

The empty nest: By now the mortgage is paid off, and home ownership is at its peak. People start taking vacations again—percentage of couples who took a vacation trip costing at least $100 in 1962, which went down to 30 for couples with children under six, is now back up to 41. They buy air conditioners and floor waxers, whisky, manicures, commercial laundering, gifts, and pay contractors to improve the houses they now own.

Older couples living in retirement: The spending on whisky and beauty drops off sharply; vacation trips are rare (only 21 percent of such couples in 1962); spending is at a peak for nursing home care, decaffeinated coffee, and prunes.

Source: "Roundup of Current Research," *Trans-Action* 4 (May 1967), p. 4. Reprinted by permission.

the most complex breakdown of the family life cycle.[59] He uses a twenty-four-stage cycle that follows not only the predictable development of a family as the oldest child grows, but keeps the youngest child in focus. His delineation therefore calls for two preschool, three school-age, four teen-age, five young-adult, and five launching stages.

Whereas Duvall used the oldest child as the basic determinant of stage divisions, Rodgers believes that this usage does not account adequately for group initiates, thus giving a false impression of a smooth progression from one life-cycle stage to the next. He also rejected using the oldest child on the grounds that there was no way to account for families in which the death of a spouse or child occurred prior to the launching of all children, nor was there

59. Rodgers, op. cit.; Roy H. Rodgers, "Toward a Theory of Family Development," *Journal of Marriage and the Family* 26 (August 1964), pp. 262–270; and Hill and Rodgers, op. cit., pp. 181–185.

a way to handle families in which divorce, disability, or other events might interrupt the smooth progress from one stage to the next.

Rodgers also preferred to use the term *category* in preference to *stage* on the grounds that categories are analytical devices constructed by the researcher, rather than any "real" condition of families. It was Rodgers's belief that "a conceptual framework for family development investigations should lead to a better understanding of the phenomenon being described in the various life-cycle category schemes and, ultimately, should lead to some theory of family development."[60] One example of an empirical study using family life-cycle categories can be seen in Chapter 15, which includes a section on marital satisfaction over the family life cycle. Chapters 15 through 18 in general follow a family life-cycle model.[61]

Summary

This chapter noted the range of disciplines, approaches, and selected frames of reference widely used in the study of the family. The marriage and family area is highly interdisciplinary with no single discipline either asking all the questions or knowing all the answers. This book uses a social science orientation with a major concentration focused on a sociology of the family.

Only in the last 100 years has there been any systematic study of the family. In the mid-1800s, family interests focused on grand evolutionary schemes of change and philosophical speculation. By the turn of the century, social problems relating to the family led to a concern for social reform and with it some systematic data gathering. This was followed by refinements in research methodology and a concern over social theory. It was only since the middle of this century that the findings of earlier studies were summarized, conceptual frameworks were systematically presented, and theory building was of central concern.

As the foundation upon which the entire book is based, this chapter summarizes the nature of conceptual frameworks, frames of reference and theory in general, then provides an overview of five basic approaches: struc-

---

60. Ibid., p. 263. His attempt to produce and apply this theory can be seen in Roy H. Rodgers, *Family Interaction and Transaction: The Developmental Approach.* Englewood Cliffs, N.J.: Prentice-Hall, 1973.

61. Key concepts in the developmental approach are life cycle, developmental tasks, norms, roles, role sequence, role cluster, role complex, position, positional career, and sanction. Some of the leading advocates of this perspective include Reuben Hill, Roy H. Rodgers, Evelyn Duvall, and Robert J. Havighurst. From the perspective of the family, readers may wish to examine Evelyn M. Duvall, *Family Development*, 4th ed. New York: J. B. Lippincott, 1971; Roy H. Rodgers, *Family Interaction and Transaction: The Developmental Approach* (Englewood Cliffs, N.J.: Prentice-Hall, 1973); and Atlee L. Stroup, *Marriage and Family: A Developmental Approach* (New York: Appleton-Century-Crofts, 1966).

tural-functional, social conflict, symbolic interaction, social exchange, and developmental.

In this chapter and several that follow, considerable attention is given to concepts and their definitions. Although definitions of concepts are seldom the most interesting reading, they are miniature "systems of meaning" that permit the viewing of a phenomenon in a certain way and the sharing of that view with others. In addition, concepts are basic to the development of hypotheses, propositions, and theories. When concepts are interrelated to describe and classify phenomena, the result is a conceptual framework. Conceptual frameworks, generally descriptive classification schemes, provide a basis for the establishment of hypotheses and propositions: statements interrelating concepts. When propositions are logically and systematically interrelated to explain some particular process, the result is theory.

One of the most dominant "theories" or frames of reference in sociology today is the structural-functional. This frame of reference has the social system as the basic autonomous unit of which the family is a subsystem. All systems have interdependent parts (structures) that do certain things for the individual or society and have various social consequences (functions). The basic task of functional analysis is to explain the parts, the relationship between the parts and the whole, and the functions that are performed by or result from the relationship formed by the parts. Chapters 3 through 9, as well as major portions of this text, clearly fall within the structural-functional framework.

A second frame of reference receiving increasing attention is that of social conflict. Two basic factors of significance in the recognition of this perspective is in the view of conflict as natural and inevitable and as a major factor in leading to social change. It is particularly applicable to a further understanding of the marital relationship.

The symbolic-interaction frame of reference addresses itself to two major questions, both of central concern to the family: socialization and personality. The basic premises of this approach are that human beings act toward things on the basis of the meanings things have for them; these meanings are derived from interaction with others; and these meanings are modified through an interpretive process. The approach assumes that man must be studied on his own level, that the most fruitful approach to man's behavior is through an analysis of society, that the human infant at birth is asocial, and that a socialized human being is an actor as well as a reactor. In brief, the human being is unique unto himself, understood only in his social context, is neither inherently good nor bad, and responds to self-stimulating or symbolically interpreted stimuli. This frame of reference, second only to the structural-functional, is the most used throughout the text.

The social exchange framework helps us to understand why certain behavioral outcomes occur given a set of structural conditions and interactional potentialities. Two different approaches to exchange were examined. One was consistent with a behavioral frame of reference and the other more consistent with an interactional frame of reference. At various points throughout the text, the reader will note the use of this framework in dealing with mate selection, marriage, power, and other topics.

The developmental frame of reference attempts to join together various parts of other delineated theoretical efforts but has the peculiar characteristic of attempting to account for change in the family system and change in patterns of interaction over time. Thus, the central concepts include many used in the other frameworks with the additional basic concept of the family life cycle. An outgrowth of this concept has been numerous attempts to establish, describe, and analyze stages of development.

In this text, the general outline from Chapters 10 through 16 follow broad stages of the life cycle, moving from premarital processes to marital, parental, middle years, and aging.

Our attention next turns to the family as a social institution, establishing the boundaries of marital, family, and kin groups and systems and examining selected structural features of this basic institution.

Key Terms and Topics

Discussion Questions

1. *Examine the family and marriage books suggested for reading. What disciplines are represented? How do they differ in their content and approach to the family?*
2. *Since no one discipline has "all the answers" to any family problem, why is not all research of an interdisciplinary nature? What problems exist in interdisciplinary research?*
3. *Of what value is a social science approach to the family? How does it differ from any other approach?*

4. Are there any disciplines that are completely removed from family study and to which research findings about families are irrelevant?

5. Differentiate between a psychology, a social psychology, a social anthropology, and a sociology of the family.

6. Discuss the "pure" versus the "applied" orientation to the family.

7. Identify folklore that relates to mate selection, weddings, sexual behavior, childbirth, "successful" marriages, and so on. Which tales are likely to be changed by "science"?

8. The period of 1890–1920 was characterized as an era of social reform, followed by empirical studies (1920–1950), and, more recently, theory building. Is it likely these patterns are cyclical? That is, are we likely to get away from theory and return to reform, which will later be followed by a stress on science, followed by theory, etc.? Why or why not?

9. Differentiate between concepts and variables, hypotheses and propositions, conceptual frameworks and theories, descriptive and explanatory theory, and partial and grand theory.

10. Make a listing of as many family "structures" as you can. Can you think of any form of family organization that exists only as an idea and not as a concrete reality?

11. Discuss what you perceive to be the major functions of the family in the United States. How are these different from the functions of families thirty years ago? What functions do you expect the family to perform thirty years hence?

12. Do you believe that conflict is natural and inevitable in all marriages and families? Is conflict essential for change?

13. What types of assumptions, questions, and concerns are basic to a symbolic-interaction frame of reference? How is it similar to or different from other psychological or social-psychological theories? What difference does it make to assume that man must be studied on his own level, the human infant is asocial, and the like? Relate these ideas to marriage or the family.

14. Write a paragraph on "who am I." How often did you identify yourself by listing statuses you occupy? Lengthen this list of statuses and write one or two social expectations appropriate to each status. Which role expectations do you personally find displeasing? Are there conflicts between different expectations or between your personal preference and the social expectation? How do you handle them?

15. What exchanges can you identify in explaining male-female sexual behavior, husband-wife spending patterns or parent-child disciplinary behavior? What is given by each and received in return? Can you think of examples where no reciprocity is expected or given in return for a favor or gift?

16. Identify the stage of the family life cycle for yourself and for your parents. Identify the central problems, concerns, and tasks of families at these particular stages.

17. *Develop a family life-cycle model. How many stages does it have? What criteria were used to separate stages? What types of families are omitted from your particular model?*

Further Readings

Bell, Robert R., ed. *Studies in Marriage and the Family,* 2d ed. New York: Thomas Y. Crowell, 1973. This second edition includes the eight studies included in the first edition, plus four new studies dealing with the lower-class family and with sex roles. These selections represent important studies in substantive areas where no new large-scale studies in marriage and the family have emerged. They represent a wide range of methodological and theoretical approaches.

Blumer, Herbert. *Symbolic Interactionism: Perspective and Method.* Englewood Cliffs, N. J.: Prentice-Hall, 1969. A collection of articles, each written by Blumer, on the point of symbolic interactionism or on methodological matters related to it.

Broderick, Carlfred B. "Beyond the Five Conceptual Frameworks: A Decade of Development in Family Theory." *Journal of Marriage and the Family* 33 (February 1971), pp. 139–159. Presents changes in conceptual frameworks in the 1960s including the emergence of balance, game, exchange, and general systems theory, plus various substantive theories.

Burr, Wesley R. *Theory Construction and the Sociology of the Family.* New York: John Wiley, 1973. A methodological and substantive attempt at identifying, analyzing, and improving theoretical propositions useful in understanding family processes.

Christensen, Harold T., ed. *Handbook of Marriage and the Family.* Chicago: Rand McNally, 1964. Part I of the handbook deals with the major theoretical orientations of family study.

Duvall, Evelyn Millis. *Marriage and Family Development,* 5th ed. Philadelphia: J. B. Lippincott, 1977. Follows families through stages of development.

Edwards, John N. "Familial Behavior as Social Exchange." *Journal of Marriage and the Family* 31 (August 1969) pp. 518–526. Assays the relevance of a social exchange frame of reference and shows how it is utilized in familial behavior.

Gordon, Michael, ed. *The American Family in Social-Historical Perspective.* New York: St. Martin's, 1973. A collection of articles reflecting facets of a history of the family.

Lee, Gary R. *Family Structure and Interaction: A Comparative Analysis.* Philadelphia: J. B. Lippincott, 1977. An attempt to document the contributions made by comparative social research to an understanding of family structure and behavior.

Manis, Jerome G., and **Bernard N. Meltzer.** *Symbolic Interaction: A Reader in Social Psychology,* 2nd ed. Boston: Allyn and Bacon, 1972. A collection of readings bringing together previously published contributions to symbolic interaction theory.

Nye, Ivan, and **Felix Berardo.** *Conceptual Frameworks for the Study of the Family.* New York: Macmillan, 1966. A discussion of frameworks for studying the family, including the anthropological, structural-functional, institutional, interactional, situational, psychoanalytic, developmental, economic, legal, and western Christian.

Rodgers, Roy H. *Family Interaction and Transaction: The Developmental Approach.* Englewood Cliffs, N. J.: Prentice-Hall, 1973. The most complete source at this time on analyzing internal and external familial relationships using a developmental approach.

Somerville, Rose M., ed. *Intimate Relationships: Marriage, Family and Lifestyles through Literature.* Englewood Cliffs, N. J.: Prentice-Hall, 1975. A collection of more than fifty writings of fiction focusing on various stages and types of family-related relationships.

Sprey, Jetse, "The Family as a System in Conflict." *Journal of Marriage and the Family* 31 (November 1969), pp. 699–706. Examines the major premises underlying a conflict frame of reference and offers this as an alternative and fruitful theoretical approach to family study.

Stephens, William N. *The Family in Cross-Cultural Perspective.* New York: Holt, Rinehart and Winston, 1963. An anthropological approach to exploring family themes in various cultures.

Tavuchis, Nicholas and **William J. Goode.** *The Family through Literature.* New York: McGraw-Hill, 1975. Can you imagine sociologists choosing articles primarily for reading pleasure? Here it is. A look at a range of family subjects as viewed through literature.

Turner, Ralph H. *Family Interaction.* New York: John Wiley, 1970. Applies basic interaction theory to an analysis of the family.

Winch, Robert F. *The Modern Family,* 3d ed. New York: Holt, Rinehart and Winston, 1971. A sociology of the family text that follows the structural-functional approach.

3

Understanding Family Groups
and Systems

3

The second chapter noted a variety of interdisciplinary, historical, social science, and theoretical approaches to family study. Basic to any approach are selected concepts and distinctions that provide "systems of meaning" to an aspect of the world in which we live. You have already noted various ways in which "function" is used by family scholars, dual perceptions of "role"—depending upon its use in a structural or interactional frame of reference—and the different schools of thought evident in the social exchange framework. Likewise, families take on new and varied perspectives when viewed in institutional terms, when seen as a social group or social system, or when differentiated from marriages and kin, orientation and procreation, nuclear and extended, and the like. This chapter makes note of these and other conceptual distinctions in a study and understanding of the family.

THE FAMILY AS A SOCIAL INSTITUTION

Frequent reference is made to the family as the most basic of all institutions. It is most closely linked to the supporting institution of marriage. What is meant by this? The concept *institution* is one of the most important in the entire field of sociology. It refers to certain specific areas of human social life that have become broadly organized into discernible patterns. It refers to the principal organized means whereby the essential tasks of a society are organized, directed, and carried out. In short, it denotes the system of norms that organize human behavior into stable patterns of activity.

"Institution" is a noun, "institutionalize" is a verb. The noun *institution* "refers to a set of norms that cohere around a relatively distinct and socially important complex of values."[1] All societies must deal with sexual

---

1. Robin M. Williams, Jr., *American Society* (New York: Alfred A. Knopf, 1970), p. 37.

activity, the care of dependent children, the social relations established by sexual unions, and the birth of children. The institutional norms concerned with these matters constitute the familial or kinship institutions.

The verb *institutionalize* means the establishment of expected, patterned, regular, and predictable behavior; thus, noninstitutionalized behavior is spontaneous and irregular. Typically, a husband-wife fight is noninstitutionalized behavior; a professional boxing match is institutionalized. When something such as dating, premarital sexual behavior, or child rearing becomes institutionalized, this means that it becomes accepted by the society as a necessary, proper, and predictable activity. At this time, although extramarital intercourse is a very common activity in American society, it has not been institutionalized; that is, it has not become a part of our standardized, approved, and culturally safeguarded expected behavior.

Several basic social institutions can be identified in all societies: the familial and kinship, educational, economic, political, and religious institutions appear to have existed in some form in all societies throughout every period of history. Each of these five institutions performs certain functions that are basic for the existence of a given society. However, these are not the only areas that have become institutionalized. In American society, marriage, war, business, communications, medicine, law, science, and recreation have become institutionalized, standardized, and basic to our way of life.

Few institutions have received more recognition, criticism, and critiques than the family system. It has been claimed to be the solution of most problems, on one hand, and to be the basic cause of problems, on the other. It has been looked upon with hope and dismay. Scientists, clergy, newspaper columnists, parents, and even stockbrokers speak out with authority on this institution. This book is intended to examine the nature of, to describe and interpret, and, hopefully, to get the student to examine and redefine his understanding of this particular system: the family as a social institution.

FAMILIES AS GROUPS OR SYSTEMS

Family and marital groups and systems are basic to a sociology of the family and to the family as a social institution. Family systems are used in sociology much as physicists and biologists speak of solar or biological systems. In each instance a reference is made to a configuration of parts that are related interdependently. All systems, whether living or nonliving, have a characteristic organization and pattern of functioning. All major systems have subsystems that are part of the larger system.

To treat the family as a social system is to note the forms of social organization and its modes of functioning. The family system is one example of interrelated statuses that fulfill certain basic functions. It is a subsystem of the larger society that is related to and interdependent with other subsystems in the society. It fulfills selected tasks for the society that are highly patterned, recurrent, and organized. Within the family system are subsystems (marital systems, mate-selection systems, sexual systems, child-rearing systems) which are also highly patterned, recurrent, and organized in order to fulfill selected tasks. Although persons are a part of the system, it is the statuses, roles, norms, ways of ranking, means of social controls, and the values of those persons (the abstractions) that are of significance in dealing with social systems.

The basic units, therefore, of a marital or family system are not persons but the interrelated statuses (positions) and the accompanying expectations that accompany the interrelated statuses. These interrelated statuses in the family system would include parent-child, husband-wife, uncle-aunt, grandparent-grandchild, father-mother, or brother-sister, for example. The norms (folkways and mores) and roles, the expectations and values that accompany these positions, are of primary concern to the sociologist. Thus, married males occupy the status of husband. They interact with married females who occupy the status of wife. These interrelated statuses (husband and wife) comprise the marital system. This system too, like the family system or any other system, has sets of norms and expectations that prescribe appropriate and inappropriate behaviors for the specific persons involved. Thus systems are abstractions, forms of social organization comprised of interrelated statuses.

Family and marital groups, in contrast to systems, are comprised of people. These people are concrete realities, rather than abstractions, who are physically present and who interact with one another in terms of their ascribed or achieved statuses. If married, we would belong to a two-person marital group. Our family group would consist of the married partners, the children, plus any other relatives included in the extended family context. Marital or family groups can have a specific address, a specific number of members, a specific income, and specific shared rituals. Marital and family groups are temporary, disbanding when their members depart. The system of which they are a part may continue for centuries—long after the departure or death of any specific member or specific family group.

It is the task of a sociology of the family to examine the nature of marital and family groups within societies and to understand the patterns of organization, the marital and family systems that provide order within and between the groups involved.

A Classification of Family Groups

Sociologists view groups as the core of their attention. They speak of in- and out-groups, primary and secondary groups, formal and informal groups, large and small groups, minority and majority groups, open and closed groups, organized and unorganized groups, independent and dependent groups, voluntary and involuntary groups, and others. Some of these ideal-type constructs are more useful to our understanding of family groups than others. In this writer's mind, the group-classification scheme suggested by Robert Bierstedt is particularly useful.[2]

Bierstedt distinguishes four different kinds of groups: 1) the statistical, 2) the societal, 3) the social, and 4) the associational. These groups differ depending on the presence of certain characteristics or properties such as 1) a consciousness of kind, 2) social interaction, and 3) social organization. His general group characterization will be modified to clarify different types of family groupings.

Statistical Groups

Families as statistical groups would not be included by some sociologists as a group at all since no social interaction is involved. This type of group is "formed" not by the members themselves but by sociologists or statisticians. For example, in 1974 there were 55,053,000 families in the United States with an average population per family of 3.4. Thirty-seven percent of these families were two-person families, 40 percent were three- or four-person families, 19 percent were five- or six-person families, and 5 percent had seven persons or more. Fifty-six percent of these families had a member under the age of eighteen and 18 percent had a member age sixty-five or over.[3]

Persons or families within these statistical groups probably are not conscious of belonging to them, may never interact socially, and will probably never form any type of organization. This is not to imply a lack of importance to these or other statistical categories or groupings. In fact, figures such as those cited could well influence social policy or act on programs within schools, businesses, planned parenthood, or communities in general. Throughout the text you will find many examples of statistical groupings—often in the form of demographic rather than social arrangements, but nevertheless important to those who want to understand the family in our American or in other societies.

Societal Groups

Families as societal groups differ from statistical groups in that they are composed of people who have a consciousness of kind. People in a societal group are aware of the similarity or identity of the traits or characteristics

2. Robert Bierstedt, *The Social Order*, 3d ed. (New York: McGraw-Hill, 1970), pp. 276–284.
3. U.S. Bureau of the Census, *Current Population Reports*, Series P-20, no. 276, "Household and Family Characteristics: March, 1974," (Washington, D.C.: U.S. Government Printing Office, 1972). Table 1, pp. 13 and 17.

that they all possess. They recognize others like themselves and are more interested or may be pressured into associating with them. Members who comprise a societal group usually have visible signs of similarity by which the members recognize one another. Language, accent, manner of dress, skin color, age, or particular symbols (rings, pins, peace signs) enable people to recognize that they are "soul brothers," members of the "faith," or "peaceniks." The twenty-three million single males age fourteen and over seem to be highly conscious of and pay particular attention to the marital status of the nineteen million single females over age fourteen. Divorced and single-parent family members often express a sensitivity to being omitted from activities that involve primarily married couples. The slow pace of integrating neighborhoods suggests a consciousness of kind among the races.

Whatever the reason for it, people tend to live and associate with others who share certain characteristics. Interracial couples, the aged, mothers of young children, or widows, although not necessarily in social interaction with all other members of the societal group and not organized in any systematic manner, share an awareness of similarity.

Social Groups

Families as social groups are those families in which the members actually interact and associate with one another. Each member of the family is conscious of belonging to the group. This is the family group in which we live and interact. The Jones family is a social group. They might live at 6815 Orinoco Circle, have four members who share the same household, and have eighteen kin members who visit, write, and provide assistance and sharing when in need or on special occasions.

Other social groups such as classroom groups, friendship groups, passengers on the same bus, congregations, or play groups share with the family as a social group the characteristic of social interaction and an awareness of some interest in common. The type of interaction may vary from the sharing of intimate verbal and physical exchanges to polite conversation or even simple mutual awareness of one another's presence.

Associational Groups

Families as associational groups are those in which the members are formally organized, that is, an organization or association is formed. Associations are groups of people who interact socially and share a consciousness of kind but, in addition, ban together in some organized way to pursue some common interest. The Oneida Community, which existed in New York State from about 1848–1880, was a family group of this nature. Under the leadership of John Humphrey Noyes, a group marriage was created. The members believed in spiritual, economic, and sexual equality. The objective was to live a sinless and selfless life and, of course, few things are more selfish than monogamy—*my* husband or *my* wife to the sexual exclusion of others. This family was an associational group who interacted socially, shared a consciousness of similarity to one another, and formally organized to pursue the common goal of living a "perfect sinless life."

Generally, rather than families as associational groups, it is more common to find associational groups organized around interests of concern to families. The National Council on Family Relations, the Planned Parenthood Association, the YMCA, or the American Association of Marriage Counselors are groups that are formally organized for fulfilling a particular interest.

People form social groups—family or nonfamily—to accomplish things that cannot be done alone. Later, several functions of marital and family groups will be discussed, but one significant factor in the family group is its primary as opposed to secondary nature.

Primary and Secondary Groups

Because of its size and degree of intimacy, the marital and family group is generally perceived to be a "primary" group. According to the group classification just established, primary groups are always *social* groups—never statistical, societal, or associational. The concept of primary groups was introduced by Charles Horton Cooley who defined them thus:

> By primary groups I mean those characterized by intimate face to face association and cooperation. They are primary in several senses, but chiefly in that they are fundamental in forming the social nature and ideals of the individual. The result of intimate association, psychologically, is a certain fusion of individualities and a common whole, so that one's very self, for many purposes at least, is the common life and purpose of the group. Perhaps the simplest way of describing this wholeness is by saying that it is a "we"; it involves a sort of sympathy and mutual identification for which "we" is a natural expression.[4]

Primary-group relationships are facilitated by 1) face-to-face contact, 2) smallness of size, and 3) frequent and intense contact. Most families in the western world operate under these conditions. Unlike most primary groups, the family is of a special nature in that it is so essential both to individuals and to society that its formation is usually legitimized by the community through religious and legal rituals. Whereas most other primary groups can disband voluntarily if the members wish it, the dissolution of the family can only be accomplished through institutionalized means.

---

4. Charles Horton Cooley, *Social Organization* (New York: Charles Scribner's, 1929), pp. 23–24.

Much of the importance of marital and family groups centers around its function as a primary group. First, for most individuals it is this primary group that serves as the basic socializing agent for the acquisition or internalization of beliefs and attitudes. Second, the family as a primary group constitutes the chief focus for the realization of personal satisfaction. Perhaps more than any other source it is the family that provides each of us with a general sense of well-being, companionship, ego worth, security, and affection. Most of us, when away from home for the first time, experience "homesickness" or a nostalgia for the primary group from which our immediate ties have been severed. Third, the family as a primary group also serves as a basic instrument of social control. The family has an extraordinary capacity to punish deviation and reward conformity, since most of us are dependent upon other group members for meeting psychological needs and for realizing meaningful social experiences.

The polar extreme to the primary group is the secondary group. Many, if not most, of our involvements in school, work, or the community are not characterized by the intimate, informal, and personal nature of primary groups but rather are characterized by impersonal, segmental, and utilitarian contacts. Secondary groups are basically goal oriented rather than person oriented. The personal life of the bus driver, classmate in a lecture, or cigarette salesman are not of major significance in the fulfillment of the goals established for those situations.

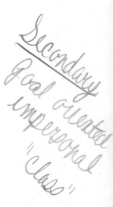

In a society dominated by secondary-group relationships, the family, time and again, provides the primary relationships that are vital to our health and happiness. With no primary-group relationships, it is doubtful that even survival itself would be possible. Suicide rates, as indicated in the insert, may be directly related to social isolation, the lack of primary relationships, and the absence of intimate family bonds.

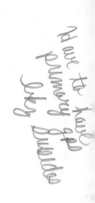

This idea has been fairly well substantiated with infants and with adults who have "no" family or close friends. One conclusion would suggest that rather than the American family being in a state of decay, losing its significant function, and being "on its way out," the family may be fulfilling a primary-group function that has seldom been more crucial and important to the stability of the person or society.

MARRIAGE, FAMILY, AND KINSHIP

Marriage, family, and kin groups are institutionalized social arrangements in all known societies. However, the nature of the arrangements differ greatly across societies, over time, and even within a given society at a specific point in time. Frequently, the legal and social norms themselves lack

---

Young Suicide

The suicide rate among the young is sky-rocketing according to the American Association of Suicidology. About 25,000 Americans, or 11 in each 100,000 kill themselves each year. The sharpest increase in suicide rates has been among people under 30. At the same time, suicides among the old have dropped almost as sharply.

"Younger people are breaking away much earlier from their support—the family," stated Jerome Motto, president of the American Association of Suicidology. The resulting isolation may in part explain the dramatic rise reported at the association's annual convention in Detroit in early April.

Other speakers cited an interest in death as a new phenomenon to be explained as another possible rationale for the young suicides. Addressing the convention, Sam Heilig, executive director of the Los Angeles Suicide Prevention Center said, "I've never known a generation as interested in death as an experience, something you can pass through."

Whatever the causes, the statistics are alarming. For example, in Los Angeles, the suicide rate for women under 20 went from 0.4 to 8 per 100,000 from 1960–70 and from 6 to 26 for women 20 to 29. Among men the suicide rate for those under 20 went from 3 to 10 per 100,000 in the decade and for those 20 to 29 from 18 to 41. And other cities report similar increases.

It was also noted that women have always had a much higher rate of attempted suicide but that more men actually succeed in killing themselves. Yet the suicide rate for women rose rapidly from 1960 to 1970—a rise attributed by some to the conflict over the woman's role in society.

At the same time, convention participants noted that suicides by the old, particularly by old white men (the typical suicides of the past) have declined. For example, in Los Angeles County, the suicide rate among those over 70 years of age dropped to 41 per 100,000 in 1970 from 60 five years before and 55 in 1960. For men 60 to 69 years of age the rate dropped to 43 per 100,000 from 52 a decade before. One authority attributed this decline to Medicare. Presumably, patients with incurable illnesses are awaiting natural deaths in hospitals rather than taking their own lives.

Source: "Roundup of Current Research," *Society* 9 (June 1972), p. 12. Reprinted by permission.

---

clarity as to what does or does not constitute a marriage, family, or kin group. For example, is it a marriage if two males live together and recognize each other as spouse, a male and a female live together but have no marriage contract or ever experience a wedding ceremony, or a man and a woman go through a marriage ceremony and then separate permanently? Can any group of persons be considered a marriage, a family, or a kin group? In an earlier work, the author wrote that:

> The difficulty of definitions becomes acute when one attempts to distinguish between marriages and nonmarriages; between families and nonfamilies; between marriages and families in America as opposed to those that exist around the world; between wives versus mistresses or concubines; between parents who provide and care for their own children as contrasted with situations where children are provided for by the community and cared for by

professional nurses; between sexual relationships in marriage between spouses versus sexual relationships prior to marriage involving the same or other individuals; between relationships that last until death versus those that last for several days or months; between those that sign legal documents versus those that simply agree to a certain type of relationship; or between those that share the same house versus those that live close to one another.[5]

The Boundaries of Marriage

Marriage has been defined in a number of ways. Harold Christensen says that marriage is an institutionalized mating arrangement between human males and females.[6] Thus marriage is viewed as a precondition of family organization. Marriage, being institutionalized, is a social institution that is strictly human and that assumes some permanence and conformity to societal norms.

Burgess and his coauthors write:

> The animal mates, but man marries. The significance of this distinction is simple and clear. Mating is biological, while marriage is social and cultural. Marriage implies a ceremony, a union with social sanctions, a recognition of obligations to the community assumed by those entering this relationship. . . . Marriage may be defined as a socially sanctioned union of one or more men with one or more women with the expectation that they will play the roles of husband and wife.[7]

In a dictionary of the social sciences, compiled under the auspices of UNESCO, marriage was denoted as a mating arrangement approved in society with special reference to the institutionalized relationships of husband and wife, also the ceremonies that established such relationships. It stated:

> In ordinary usage *marriage* included two distinct ideas: (a) that a man and a woman cohabit, generally with the intention of founding a family; (b) that some distinction can be drawn between marriage and other forms of sexual union, qualifiable as *pre-marital*, *extra-marital*, adulterous, etc. A mere casual commerce, without the intention of cohabitation, and bringing up children, would not constitute marriage under any supposition.[8]

5. J. Ross Eshleman, *Perspectives in Marriage and the Family* (Boston: Allyn and Bacon, 1969), pp. 7–8.
6. Harold T. Christensen, ed., *Handbook of Marriage and the Family* (Chicago: Rand McNally, 1964), p. 3.
7. Ernest W. Burgess, Harvey J. Locke, and Mary Margaret Thomas, *The Family*, 3d ed. (New York: American Book, 1963), p. 1.
8. Julius Gould and William L. Kolb, *A Dictionary of the Social Sciences*. Compiled under the auspices of The United Nations Educational, Scientific, and Cultural Organization (Glencoe: Free Press, 1964), p. 409.

Can Two Women Marry?

Dear Ann Landers: Can two women get married? I don't wish to go into detail as to the reason I am asking this question. You may assume it is either a gag (like to win a bet) or perhaps the women are lesbians and wish to live together as "man" and "wife." What I need to know is would a marriage between two people of the same sex be considered legal.

Please don't toss this in the circular file. I am serious.

G.C.N.Y.

Dear G.C.N.Y.: If you know a couple of women who want to get married, tell them OK, but not to each other. The word marriage means the state of being wedded to a person of the opposite sex.

In Illinois, failure to consummate a marriage in the sexual sense is grounds for annulment. Since it is understood that marriage guarantees the privileges of heterosexual relationship, two members of the same sex could not possibly be considered suitable marriage partners.

Source: **Ann Landers**, *Kalamazoo Gazette.* Copyright by Publishers-Hall Syndicate. Reprinted by permission.

William Stephens, an anthropologist, says that marriage is a) a socially legitimate sexual union, begun with b) a public announcement, undertaken with c) some idea of permanence, and assumed with a more or less explicit d) marriage contract, which spells out reciprocal obligations between spouses and between spouses and their children.[9]

Finally, Ira Reiss, who is interested in providing a universal definition of marriage, says that marriage is an institution composed of a socially accepted union of individuals in husband and wife roles, with the key function of legitimation of parenthood.[10]

There seems to be a general consensus that marriage involves several criteria that are found to exist cross-culturally and throughout time. These criteria include:

- Heterosexual, including at least one male and one female
- Legitimizing or granting approval to the sexual relationship and the bearing of children without any loss of standing in the community or society
- A public affair rather than a private personal matter
- A highly institutionalized and patterned mating arrangement
- An assuming of mutual and reciprocal rights and obligations between the spouses
- A binding relationship that assumes some permanence

9. William N. Stephens, *The Family in Cross Cultural Perspective* (New York: Holt, Rinehart, and Winston, 1963), p. 7.

10. Ira L. Reiss, *Family Systems in America.* 2d ed. (Hinsdale, Ill.: Dryden, 1976), p. 41.

The Boundaries of the Family

The family, like marriage, has been defined in various ways. Christensen says that family refers to marriage plus progeny. Family, in other words, signifies a set of statuses and roles acquired through marriage and procreation.[11] Thus the family is a product of marital interaction.

Burgess says that the following characteristics are common to the human family in all times and all places and differentiate the family from other social groups:

1. The family is composed of persons united by ties of marriage, blood, or adoption. *marriage blood*

2. The members of a family typically live together under one roof and constitute a single household; or, if they live apart, they consider the household their home. *probably live together*

3. The family is composed of persons who interact and communicate with each other in their social roles, such as husband and wife, mother and father, son and daughter, brother and sister. *interact*

4. The family maintains a common culture. It is derived mainly from the general culture, but each family has some distinctive features.[12] *common culture*

The UNESCO dictionary defines the human family as an institutionalized biosocial group made up of adults (at least two of whom, unrelated by blood and of the opposite sex, are married) and children (the offspring of the maritally related adults). The minimal functions of this group are the providing of satisfaction and control of affectional needs, including sexual

---

11. Christensen, op. cit., p. 3.
12. Burgess et. al., op. cit., p. 2.

Gay Couples Win Family Status

NEW YORK—(AP)—Eligibility for a family membership used to mean that a couple had to be married. Not any more, says the New York State Division of Human Rights.

Under the state's new human rights law, gay couples, and people living alone can now have family memberships available to them.

The Metropolitan Museum is the first membership organization to adapt the redefinition of family membership in compliance with the state's human rights law.

Family membership is now open to any two people living at the same address, even if they are not married or blood relations, the human rights division said yesterday.

Source: *The Detroit News*, September 23, 1976, p. 3-B. Reprinted by permission of The Associated Press.

relations, and the provision of a sociocultural situation for the procreation, care, and socialization of offspring.[13]

Stephens defines a family as a social arrangement based on marriage and the marriage contract, including recognition of the rights and duties of parenthood, common residence for husband, wife, and children, and reciprocal economic obligations between husband and wife.[14]

Finally, Reiss provides a definition of the family institution as a small kinship-structured group with the key function being nurturant socialization of the newborn.[15]

Thus the family, like marriage, shares various elements:

- It arises as a result of marriage.
- It includes persons who are united by marriage, blood, or adoption.
- These persons share a common residence.
- These persons assume reciprocal rights and obligations to one another.
- It provides the key function of socialization, particularly of the infant.

It could be said that all marriages are families but not all families are marriages. And certain functions, expected in the marital relationship, are taboo among certain family members (such as sexual relationships between brother and sister).

Louise: *Definitely the family is necessary. The longer I live the more committed I am to it. When I was setting up my own family I never really knew how deprived people lived. Although we never had much materially, we had a very rich spiritual heritage. We had a very rich family life. All of my friends came from the same background. I didn't know anyone that came from families where they weren't cared for. There were no broken families. My ideal was to marry and establish a very solid family. I couldn't visualize personal happiness without it. As I lived through a whole lot more years and learned a whole lot more about how other people live and have to live I'm still more committed than ever to the family. I think everything else is a substitute.*

Ann: *To me, the family is necessary. Not having a family is like being completely alone. If you ask me is it necessary to be married or to have a man in the home, no, but it's necessary for it to start out that way, to me.*

---

13. Gould and Kolb, op. cit., p. 257.
14. Stephens, op. cit., p. 8.
15. Reiss, op. cit., p. 19.

The Boundaries of Kinship

The kinship system, like marital and family systems and groups, involves special ties, bonds, and linkages among its members. However, family groups and systems are units upon which the kinship system is built. A kinship system refers to a pattern of social norms regulating those relationships that are directly based on the facts of birth and the birth cycle.[16] It is also a *set* of interpersonal social relationships involving strong interests and emotions, urgent problems of authority and order, and many reciprocal bonds of dependence and support.[17] These relationships, whether created biologically or socially, exist among people who are descended from one another (parents-children) or with common descent relations (brother-sister).

Birth is the primary biological point of reference for kinship. But kin relationships are also determined and defined by sex (male or female), birth order (older or younger children), time together (living together or casual visits), as well as seniority within the kin grouping. These characteristics combine to give each individual a different social position. As Robin William states:

> Children are not merely children; they are male or female, older or younger, with siblings or without. The sister of one's father is not in the same biological category as one's mother's sister, but both in our society are "aunt."

As defined, these relationships based on the birth cycle (kinship system) are regulated by patterns of social norms. These norms vary widely from one society to another. Thus, it is impossible to categorize all of them. On the other hand, certain norms exist universally among kin relationships. The most widely used example is that of a taboo on incest. All societies forbid sexual relations between persons in certain kinship positions. Violations of these norms arouse strong feelings among the kin group as well as in the larger society. All societies also forbid intermarriage between certain kin occupants. The circle of prohibited relatives for marriage does, however, vary widely in different societies. At one extreme were brother-sister and father-daughter marriages in ancient Egypt.[18] The other extreme may be represented by the traditional clan system of China or certain extended families in India where the prohibition extended to a very wide group of relatives including cousins to the sixth degree.[19]

The pattern of social norms tends to give differential treatment to members of the kin group. In most societies, women are accorded lower

16. Robin M. Williams, Jr., "Kinship and the Family in the United States," in *American Society* 3d ed. (New York: Alfred A. Knopf, 1970), p. 47.

17. Ibid., p. 60.

18. Russell Middleton, "Brother-Sister and Father-Daughter Marriage in Ancient Egypt." *American Sociological Review* 27 (October 1962), pp. 603–611.

19. David F. Mandlebaum, "The Family in India" in Ruth N. Anshen, ed., *The Family: Its Function and Destiny* (New York: Harper, 1949), pp. 167–187.

status than men. The eldest male or the eldest son may be accorded greater prestige, power, and responsibility than younger men. In general, status positions in the kinship network are differentiated by rights, privileges, and obligations, by inheritance, and by general social expectations.

In some societies kinship is such an integral part of all aspects of the society that it is difficult to differentiate it from other (non-kin) kinds of social institutions and relationships. Particularly in primitive and peasant societies, the political, educational, religious, economic, or property units

Main Structural Features of the American Kinship System

The American kinship system is marked by the following characteristics:

First, the incest taboo everywhere forbids a person to marry father, mother, child, grandparent, uncle, aunt, niece, or nephew. In twenty-nine states intermarriage of first cousins is forbidden; intermarriage of blood relatives is seldom otherwise limited.

Second, marriage is monogamous, and there is no prescriptive pattern for kinship marriages.

Third, no discrimination is made between paternal and maternal relatives for marriage purposes.

Fourth, although the family name descends through the male line, there is little other emphasis upon the male line of descent. The descent system tends to be bilineal or, more strictly, multilineal.

Fifth, there is an emphasis on the immediate conjugal family. In a highly developed consanguine kinship system, by contrast, the tightest unit is the descent group of siblings, a group of brothers and sisters whose spouses enter as strangers and remain always somewhat so. In America, the solidarity of spouses is stressed, to the exclusion of in-laws.

Sixth, the immediate family of father, mother, and children tends to be the effective residence, consumption, and social unit. No extended kin groupings are of more than secondary importance in these respects, except among a few relatively small population elements.

Seventh, in urban communities, which are increasingly representative of the country as a whole, the family group is typically a consuming rather than a producing unit. Kinship units as work groups and productive organizations have largely disappeared except in farming and certain types of small retail businesses.

Eighth, because the nuclear family is the unit and the kinship system is multilineal, American society places relatively little emphasis on family tradition and family continuity.

Ninth, there is comparatively free choice of mates. In fact, American mate selection is to a considerable extent an application of free competition in the institution of marriage. The choice of spouses is purely personal; the kin of the prospective mates have no right to interfere. Parents are usually asked to sanction the marriage choice, but this convention is residual. The individualistic system of mate choice is favored by the autonomous conjugal unit, the discontinuity of generations, the deemphasis of kinship, and the extensive geographic and social mobility found in American society.

Tenth, linked to the father-mother-children unit and free marriage-choice is the tendency for adult children to disperse from the parental household.

Source: Selected sentences taken from Robin M. Williams, *American Society*, 3d ed. (New York: Alfred A. Knopf, 1970), pp. 56–59.

are so interlinked and meshed with the kinship system or group that it becomes impossible to separate kin networks from non-kin networks. That is, other institutions are part of the kinship system itself.[20] In contrast are the kinship systems known in most western societies where kinship is separate and clearly distinguished from other institutions and relationships. The economic system, while not totally independent of kin networks or influences, exists separate from and is distinguishable from the kin network. This same differentiation is true for other institutionalized patterns of norms and activity.

Bert Adams[21] suggests that kin groups have tended to fulfill certain functions even when the kinship network is indistinguishable from other institutions. These include: 1) property holding and inheritance; 2) housing and the maintenance of residential proximity; 3) obligation, or helping in time of need; and 4) affection, emotional ties, or primary relationships. Regarding property holding and inheritance, readers familiar with legal and social norms in the United States will recognize a gradual shift from male lineage dominance of name and property to an increasing number of female-wife property and credit assumers who keep their own name. Regarding housing, readers will recognize the pattern of married children living in proximity or close to primary kin but not sharing the same housing unit. Some will even recognize husbands and wives, usually professional persons, who occupy separate residences. Regarding obligation and helping patterns, readers will note the shift from adult children caring for their aging parents to increasing kin independence and self-suffiency. Regarding affection and primary relationships, readers will note a movement toward nonkin networks in finding emotional gratification and persons with whom one shares most intimate thoughts. However, in spite of noting these kinds of shifts, it should become clear as one reads this text, that kin groups have not lost their importance or significance in the U.S. or elsewhere and are still basic sources of inheritance, residential sharing or proximity, obligation and affection.

Centripetal and Centrifugal Kinship and Organization

The importance of kinship is further argued by Bernard Farber[22] who sees kinship structures in modern and traditional societies as providing the dual functions of promoting special interests of members in the system of

20. To note the linkage between kinship and political organization see, for example, Jeffery M. Paige, "Kinship and Polity in Stateless Societies," *American Journal of Sociology* 80 (September 1974), pp. 301–320.

21. Bert N. Adams, "Kinship Systems and Adaptation to Modernization," *Studies in Comparative International Development* 4 (1968–1969), p. 55.

22. Bernard Farber, "Bilateral Kinship: Centripetal and Centrifugal Types of Organization," *Journal of Marriage and the Family* 37 (November 1975), pp. 871–888.

stratification and furthering the common interests that weld the population into a coherent society. These two competing functions of kinship (promoting *special* interests versus furthering *common* interests) can coexist because of the existence of two types of kinship systems: centripetal and centrifugal.

Centripetal kinship organization stresses kinship autonomy, kinship independence, vying for superiority over non-kin, giving priority to special interests, and the like. This results in societal factionalism since special interest groups each seek superiority over other kin groups for access to wealth or power. The very presence of this factionalist polity is a mechanism for stratifying a society. The general emphasis in centripetal kinship is on a long-range perspective, a stability of kin relationships, and an accumulation of relatives. Thus, one would expect in societies with factional regimes, married couples residing close to kin, little emigration from the local community, high access to relatives, the accumulation of property rights over generations, the use of the family as a means for stratifying the society, and the family as a power base to manipulate other institutions such as the government or church.

Centrifugal kinship organization stresses communalism and a subordination of special interests to common concerns. These common concerns may emerge from economic interdependence, the presence of a common enemy, the presence of a universal religion, nationalism, values of political, social, and economic equality, and so on. Thus, one might expect societies with communal norms to have a high divorce rate, loose-knit kin networks, a high degree of migration, early emancipation of children, little kinship inheritance of property, and a diffusion of power and wealth throughout the society. Individuals are not forced to a single set of kinship norms. The diversity of norms creates cross pressures and inhibits the development of society factions.

Perhaps these two types of kinship organizations can be illustrated by the difference in Jewish and Catholic norms. In general, Jewish norms tend to promote centripetality and Catholic norms tend to promote centrifugality. In early modern Europe, Jewish family law was effective in maintaining centripetal norms in Jewish communities. Bound together by strong economic ties, outside animosity, a sense of communal responsibility, and a profound feeling for tradition, each Jewish community established a legal, corporate structure by which to survive. Membership in the corporate unit was compulsory, and control by the legally constituted authority was pervasive.[23] In contrast, in order to scatter family ties "to widen the range of human sympathy and love," Catholic law imposes broad impediments to marriage among consanguineous (blood-linked) and affinal (marriage-linked) relatives. Guy Swanson[24] speculates as to whether the stress in Catholicism

---

23. Ibid.

24. Guy E. Swanson, "Descent and Polity: The Meaning of Paige's Findings," *American Journal of Sociology* 80 (September 1974), p. 326.

on female symbols (the Virgin, the Mother, the Church as the bride of Christ, the many women in the role of saints) is not an indication of relating communal polities with a collective parent who places great importance upon the common interest of all her "children."

This distinction in kinship organization may be helpful in understanding differing socialization patterns, differences in marital selection and prohibitions, stability in marriage, residence and migration patterns, property rights, kinship terminology, relation to stratification systems, the relationship between kin systems and other institutions, and the general issues discussed in Chapter 1. Centripetal forms of organization stress kin solidarity resulting in societal factionalism. Centrifugal forms of organization stress societal communalism and a subordination of special interests. Given these contrasting forms of kinship organization and the dual functions that result, the kinship system is not in a state of decay but in a state of change. People are being and will be forced to choose from competing alternatives. The trend in modern society appears to be moving from centripetal to centrifugal norms. Hence, Farber[25] opposes the views that 1) kinship structure is slowly disintegrating in American society, starting with the urban poor and spreading like a cancer throughout the society, or 2) lower-class kinship exists in a highly disorganized state, or 3) changes in domestic arrangements represent a demoralization of American society. These changes represent the dual functions of the kinship structure and a movement from one form to another.

A Typology of Family Structures

One controversy in the family literature has focused on the extent to which families, particularly in the United States, are small, isolated, independent units as opposed to large interdependent networks. The polar extremes are usually represented by a nuclear versus extended dichotomy with modified-extended and modified-nuclear as intermediate positions. The major characteristics of these types are outlined in Table 3–1.

The Nuclear and Conjugal Family

Nuclear and conjugal families refer to the family unit in its smallest form. Generally it includes the husband, wife, and their immediate children. The terms nuclear and conjugal are at times used interchangeably; however, the *conjugal* family must include a husband and wife. A *nuclear* family may or may not include the marriage partners but consists of any two or more persons related to one another by blood, marriage, or adoption, assuming they

---

25. Farber, op. cit., p. 886.

TABLE 3–1.   A Typology of Family Structures

Nuclear	Modified Nuclear	Modified Extended	Extended
Completely self-sufficient, economically no help.	Largely self-sufficient economically, recreation and friendship ties, occasional help in emergencies.	Independent economic resources in nuclear family units, but daily exchange of goods and services.	Complete economic interdependence of kin network—common ownership of economic resources, occupational cooperation, daily exchange of goods and services.
Nuclear family, friends, experts, distant models exclusive agents of socialization, emotional support, protection.	Weak kin network role in socialization, emotional support, protection.	Strong kin network psychological interdependence, but more reliance on non-kin for socialization, emotional support, protection.	Psychological interdependence—socialization, emotional support, protection—almost completely confined to kin network.
Complete nuclear family autonomy, kin network influence absent.	Nuclear family autonomy, weak kin network influence.	Nuclear family autonomy, but strong kin network influence in decision making, resolving conflicts.	Arbitrary, linear, inter-generational authority.
Minimal contact, geographic isolation, visits on holidays or for family rituals, contact primarily by letter or telephone in literate societies.	Regular but not daily contact, kin network within easy visiting distance.	Daily contact, geographic proximity.	Daily contact, geographic proximity.

Source: Betty Yorburg, "The Nuclear and the Extended Family: An Area of Conceptual Confusion," *Journal of Comparative Family Studies* 6 (Spring 1975), p. 6.

are of the same or adjoining generations. Thus a brother and sister or a single parent and child are nuclear families but would not, technically speaking, be conjugal families.

Since most persons marry, it is likely that during their lifetimes they will be members of two different but overlapping nuclear families. The nuclear family in which they are born and reared (consisting of self, brothers and sisters, and parents) is termed the *family of orientation*. This is the family where the first and most basic socialization processes occur. When an individual marries, he forms a new nuclear (and conjugal) family: a *family of procreation.* This family is composed of self, spouse, and children.

The controversy over whether the family in the U.S. and Canada is nuclear centers on questions related to geographical isolation, economic independence, and social autonomy. Are families living separately from kin? Do other relatives outside the nuclear unit provide financial assistance or aid in times of need? Are kin ties significant in relation to emotional support, visiting patterns, or social activities? And if the nuclear family is isolated, independent, and autonomous, would this not lead to high divorce, the need for more public assistance programs for the aged, single parents, or the poor, and an increase in personal instability (alcoholism, suicide, mental illness, and the like)? Whatever the actual state of the family, it has been referred to as isolated,[26] in crisis,[27] and brutal.[28] To Parsons, the isolated nuclear family is its most important feature.[29]

The Modified-Nuclear and Modified-Extended Family

Marvin Sussman[30] and others[31] suggest that the isolated nuclear family is largely fiction, that families of procreation are actually functioning within a network of other nuclear families, offering services, and maintaining close contact with them. Research by Eugene Litwak led him to suggest that both the idea of an isolated family and the idea of a network of families have some merit. Thus he wrote of a *modified-extended* family structure where nuclear families retain considerable autonomy and yet maintain a coalition with other nuclear families where they exchange goods and services.[32] The modified-extended family differs from the modified-nuclear family in Table 3–2 only in its degree of kin network exchange and support. It differs from extended families in that geographical propinquity, occupational nepotism or family integration is not required.

26. Talcott Parsons, "The Kinship System of the Contemporary United States," *American Anthropologist* 45 (1943), pp. 22–38.

27. Michael Gordon, ed., *The Nuclear Family in Crisis: The Search for an Alternative* (New York: Harper, 1972).

28. Richard Sennett, "The Brutality of Modern Families," *Trans-action* 7 (September 1970), pp. 29–37.

29. Parsons, op. cit., pp. 22–38.

30. Marvin B. Sussman, "The Isolated Nuclear Family: Fact or Fiction," *Social Problems* 6 (Spring 1959), pp. 333–340.

31. Leonard Blumberg and Robert R. Bell, "Urban Migration and Kinship Ties," *Social Problems* 6 (Spring 1959), pp. 328–333; and Ethel Shanas, "Family Help Patterns and Social Class in Three Countries," *Journal of Marriage and the Family* 29 (May 1967), pp. 257–266.

32. Eugene Litwak, "Occupational Mobility and Extended Family Cohesion," *American Sociological Review* 25 (February 1960), pp. 9–21; and "Geographic Mobility and Extended Family Cohesion," *American Sociological Review* 25 (June 1960), pp. 385–394.

when you marry a family of procreation arises

Modified nuclear are... are isolated yet interact with or nuclear families

Modified extended...

The Extended Family

Extended family refers to family structures that extend beyond the nuclear family. As stated, within the extended family may be a multiple number of nuclear family groupings. Sometimes *consanguine* families and *joint* families are used interchangeably with extended families. The consanguine family refers to the joining of nuclear families on the basis of blood relationships or on the basis of descent from the same ancestors so that several generations of offspring are included within one family unit as in an extended family. The difference is that blood ties are emphasized—those between parents and children or between brothers and sisters—over marital ties. The joint family is not used as frequently today as in times past. The term has most often been associated with the large families of India. As stated by Nimkoff:

> Traditionally, the term *joint family* has been used to identify the Hindu and its ilk, consisting of married couples and their children living together in the same household, the men related by blood. The family is joint in that there is a common treasury, common property, a common kitchen and dining room, and common tutelary deities worshiped by all.[33]

The smallest variety of extended family type is the *stem* family. Normally the stem family consists of two families in adjacent generations, based on economic blood ties. An example of this type of family would be the rural Irish where the family consists, for example, of a father and mother living in the same household with a married son, his wife, and children. This type of family is a common device for maintaining intact the family estate. In contrast to the joint family, the plural number of male members of the original family would not pool their resources. Rather, the estate would belong only to the son to whom it is given by the father. The father would continue to live in the place to contribute his labor and derive his living from it. The other sons are given a cash settlement in lieu of their share of the land, and they then leave the family place.

> Alex: *Back home we don't have nuclear families living alone; we have families where you have the grandfather and grandmother or sometimes even the in-laws beside the immediate family. You're talking about at least six to eight people in a family, that's the average family.*

Irrespective of the specific structure of the extended family, Kempler[34] argues that extended kin have both instrumental and psychological value.

---

33. M. F. Nimkoff, *Comparative Family Systems* (Boston: Houghton Mifflin, 1965), pp. 19–20.
34. Hyman L. Kempler, "Extended Kinship Ties and Some Modern Alternatives," *The Family Coordinator* 25 (April 1976), pp. 143–149.

Close emotional relationships, especially between grandparents and grand-children, can be quite important. Close kin serve to relieve parents from being the sole sources of affection and care and can often diffuse overly intense relationships between parents and children. Kin can become important ob-jects of identification and social learning. Older kin can provide experiences of historical continuity and awareness of important aspects of the life cycle. Extended kin are also important for stable transmission of an ideology and value system. Given the importance of these extended relationships, it may seem logical that as and if ties with extended kin weaken or decrease, people would increasingly suggest and experiment with new family forms that in-corporate these extended kin features. Thus he suggests that communes, family networks and affiliated families serve as possible substitutes for ex-tended kin. These variations in extended relationships are discussed in Chapter 5 as variant marital and family life-styles.

First, let us examine what happens to the extended family network as societies become more urbanized and industrialized. It has been argued that as societies move away from agrarian, rural, traditional, or folk culture to-ward a more industrialized and urbanized culture, extended family ties break down and decrease in importance. Is this the case?

Industrialization, Urbanization, and Family Structure

The issue of the interrelation of family structure, urbanism, and mod-ernization is one of the most complex and theoretical debates in recent sociological writing on the family. Some writers argue for a direct link be-tween a nuclear family form and industrialization or urbanization, while others argue that the link isn't quite so direct. Let us examine each briefly.

The Conjugal-Urban Linkage

In his book *World Revolution and Family Patterns*, William J. Goode has concluded that as the nations of the world become industrialized and urbanized, their familial systems converge on the conjugal family system. His basic argument for a "fit" between the conjugal family and modern indus-trialized societies goes something as follows:

> Wherever the economic system expands through industrialization, family patterns change. Extended kinship ties weaken, lineage patterns dissolve, and a trend toward some form of the conjugal system generally begins to appear— that is, the nuclear family becomes a more independent kinship unit. Modern commentators have reported this process in many parts of the world, some in-

terpreting it as one aspect of the "Americanization" of Europe or even of the world.[35]

It is suggested that several factors associated with industrialization tend to move the family structure toward some form of conjugal system. For example, a modern system of industry and a rise in technological development rarely if ever occur without urbanization and bureaucratization, both of which are generally associated with industrialization. Jobs in a modern system of industry are generally based on achievement rather that ascription. That is, at least ideally, an individual is given a job on the basis of ability rather than on nepotism or land ownership. This also means that, ideally, success or failure will be on the basis of performance, persons must be free to change locations and cannot be hampered by extended kin in their geographical mobility, and the family should not prevent the individual from rising in the class structure. Some consequences of these patterns associated with industrialization are likely to be: less allegiance to kin, allocation of resources to personal ends, and a greater separation between family and work activities.

These factors will differ greatly according to the class system. Goode contends that in the modern industrial system, the middle and upper strata are by definition more "successful" in the obvious sense that they own it, dominate it, occupy its highest positions, and direct its future.[36] Paradoxically, the upper strata recognize the widest extension of kin, maintain most control over the courtship and marriage choices of their young, and are most likely to give and receive help from one another. Consequently, Goode argues that the lower strata's freedom from kin is like their "freedom" to sell their labor in an open market. They are less encumbered by the weight of kin when they are able to move upward, but they also get less help from their kin. In short, Goode contends that lower-strata families are most likely to be "conjugal" and to serve the needs of the industrial system. This means that when industrialization begins, it is the lower-class family that loses least by participating in it, and that lower-class family patterns are the first to change in the society. Although there are some disharmonies, the general argument shows a fit between the needs of industrialization and a conjugal family structure.

The Conjugal-Urban Dispute

Various researchers have seriously questioned the argument just stated which links the conjugal family to industrialized societies. At least three major questions emerge:

---

35. William J. Goode, *World Revolution and Family Patterns* (Glencoe, Ill.: Free Press, 1963), p. 6.
36. Ibid., p. 12.

1. Does not evidence exist that shows a nuclear or conjugal family structure prior to industrialization and urbanization and, if so, how could industrialization, which had not yet occurred, explain the existence of the conjugal family?
2. Conversely, does not evidence exist that shows extended family structures in existence after periods of industrialization and urbanization and, if so, how does one explain this "lack of fit" between urbanization and an extended family structure.
3. Does a single familial form emerge from industrialization and urbanization, or are multiple familial forms possible?

As to the first question—what about evidence of the nuclear family in nonindustrial or agricultural societies—Peter Laslett[37] using household composition as the unit for testing, argued that the nuclear family was prevalent in England from the time of the sixteenth century.[38] Sydney Greenfield[39] and Frank Furstenberg[40] also document the presence of the nuclear family apart from or prior to industrialization and urbanization. Furstenberg, using accounts of foreign travelers who visited the United States in the early 1800s suggests that the extent to which the industrial system has affected the family has been greatly exaggerated. Not only did a nuclear family structure exist but a lack of extended family controls existed as well. Family strains commonly attributed to industralization were found to exist prior to industrialization: women's discontent arising from total domesticity, lack of discipline of children, the abrupt loss of freedom for women at marriage, strains from the voluntary choice of mates, and the like. Thus it appears accurate to conclude that many of our present day family and marital patterns, including the conjugal structure, preceded the industrial revolution and helped to shape it.

Note that this argument does not deny that urbanization and industrialization often have negative results in terms of their effect on kin ties nor the assumption that high mobility associated with industrial societies leads to social isolation, loneliness, and separation from kin networks. One study among Ozark residents and out-migrants[41] tended to support the argument that *kin ties* are weakened by migration and by urbanism. However, the argument did not hold true for *acquaintance ties*. Strong ties with acquain-

37. Peter Laslett, "The Comparative History of Household and Family," *Journal of Social History* 4 (Fall 1970), pp 75–87.
38. Caution must be extended here in reminding our readers that household residence ignores the essential qualities of extended-family relationships involving kin influence, contact, economic, and psychological interdependence.
39. Sydney M. Greenfield, "Industrialization and the Family in Sociological Theory," *American Journal of Sociology* 67 (September 1961), pp. 312–322.
40. Frank F. Furstenberg, Jr., "Industrialization and the American Family: A Look Backward," *American Sociological Review* 31 (June 1966), pp. 326–337.
41. Lewellyn Hendrix, "Kinship, Social Networks, and Integration among Ozark Residents and Out-migrants," *Journal of Marriage and the Family* 38 (February 1976) pp. 97–104.

tances, unlike kin ties, were not to any extent affected by migration and by urbanism. Thus acquaintance ties were important in promoting integration in urban, industrial society. They promoted a feeling of meaningful involvement in the community.

As to whether extended family structures can be found where industrialization and urbanization are prevalent, this question was partially answered earlier in this chapter in connection with a discussion of centripetal kinship organization and later on the modified extended family. Evidence exists to show extensive patterns of extended family help and assistance, an exchange of goods and services, and an interdependence of affectional and emotional ties. While the extended family was possibly never the dominant family form in America, it was and is, as Goode also suggests, more prevalent among the higher classes or the wealthier family networks. Thus the lack of fit between industrialization and an extended family network may be partially explained by noting social class differentials and by defining extended family networks in terms of psychological and social linkages rather than in terms of common residence patterns.

Referring to the third question, Goode's formulation that societies around the world are moving toward a conjugal family system as they industrialize has led Winch and others to question whether there is a single emerging familial form and to look for familial variation.[42] To do this, two major questions are raised: 1) Under what conditions does the nuclear family occur? and 2) Under what conditions and in which aspects does the nuclear family vary in societies where it is imbedded in the social and cultural pattern?

To explore the conditions under which a nuclear family occurs, Winch prefers to use the term "societal complexity" to Goode's term "world revolution." Winch remarks that familial complexity is a curvilinear function of societal complexity. In his words:

> Very simple and very developed societies show the pattern of the nuclear family, whereas societies of intermediate complexity show the pattern of the extended family. From intersocietal data it appears that the existence of the extended family is associated with a reliable food supply, a demand for the family as a unit of labor, little geographical mobility in subsistence activities, and the collective (familial) ownership of land.[43]

---

42. Robert F. Winch, Scott Greer, and Rae Lesser Blumberg, "Ethnicity and Extended Familism in an Upper-Middle-Class Suburb," *American Sociological Review* 32 (April 1967), pp. 265–272; Robert F. Winch and Scott Greer, "Urbanism, Ethnicity, and Extended Familism," *Journal of Marriage and the Family* 30 (February 1968); Robert F. Winch and Rae Lesser Blumberg, "Societal Complexity and Familial Organization," in Robert F. Winch and Louise Wolf Goodman, *Selected Studies in Marriage and the Family*, 3d ed. (New York: Holt, Rinehart and Winston, 1968), pp. 70–92; and Rae Lesser Blumberg and Robert F. Winch, "Societal Complexity and Familial Complexity: Evidence for the Curvilinear Hypothesis," *American Journal of Sociology* 77 (March 1972), pp. 898–920.

43. Winch and Blumberg, op. cit. p. 92.

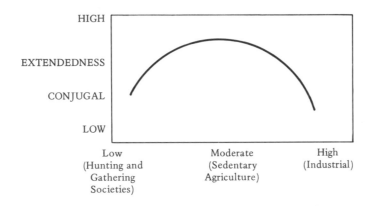

FIGURE 3–1.

The Relationship between Societal Complexity and Extendedness of Kinship Systems

To explore under what conditions and in what respects nuclear families vary, Winch and others studied an upper-middle-class suburb of Chicago and a probability sample of the state of Wisconsin. In the Chicago sample, they found that ethnicity (as indexed by religious preference) was the strongest predictor of the degree of extended familism. Compared with Protestants and Catholics, Jews had more kin in the Chicago area, interacted with more of their kin and did so more frequently, and exchanged more goods and services with their relatives. Even though there was very little variation in socio-economic status among the groups, and although Jews were less likely to be migrants than were Protestants or Catholics (non-migrants were most familistic), still Jews were more familistic than others when migratory status was held constant. Thus it was evident that in the Chicago setting there was a relationship between ethnicity and extended familism.[44]

In a somewhat parallel study in Wisconsin, ethnicity, migration, and residence (rural versus urban) all had some predictive power with respect to extended familism. In general, socioeconomic status proved to be a very weak predictor of extended familism, but one index of it—occupation of the husband—was about as strong as ethnicity.

Thus the authors note that toward the simpler end of the scale of societal complexity, it appears that spatial immobility, collectively owned property, and family labor are indicative of the higher level of subsistence. At the more complex end, it seems that certain segments of the population show much higher degrees of extended familism than others.[45]

There are many unresolved issues in this question of the relationship between type of family and industrialization. Questions such as whether the urban family is less familistic and more "isolated" than the farm family are

44. Winch, Greer, and Blumberg, op. cit., pp. 265–272.

not clearly settled.[46] Also unsettled is the question whether the prevalence of extended families is lessening with the passage of time, irrespective of industrialization and urbanization. Numerous investigators emphasize the extent to which contemporary working and middle-class families in Western society are not isolated.[47] They indicate that these families, although nuclear, engage in considerable interaction with other related nuclear families. They found that this interaction provided instrumental aid in times of illness and need.

Although no definitive answers exist as to whether the modern, urban middle-class family is relatively more or less isolated from close interaction with kin than the working-class and farm families, it does seem likely on the basis of the present research and theoretical analysis available that the urban middle-class family is somewhat more isolated.

Straus suggests two bases for hypothesizing greater isolation from close interaction with extended kin among urban families.

First is the fact that the United States has only recently become an urban nation. Thus, a substantial part of the urban population has been made up of migrants from rural areas or the children of such migrants. With geographic mobility, the kin are less readily accessible. . . . However, now that the United States is almost entirely an urban nation, generational depth in urban residence will be predominant. With the passing of the period of large rural-to-urban migration, it might be argued that there is nothing inherent in urban residence pushing family organization toward a nuclear emphasis and minimal kinship contacts.

Second, the hypothesis of a greater frequency of relatively isolated nuclear family units in the urban setting is based on the idea that a society which is predominantly organized into large-scale bureaucratic, industrial, and governmental units—and especially a society with a rapidly changing and expanding technological, economic, and social order—requires relatively high rates of social mobility and interurban geographic mobility for maximal efficiency. Under

45. Ibid., p. 84. See also Rae Lesser Blumberg and Robert F. Winch, "Societal Complexity and Familial Complexity: Evidence for the Curvilinear Hypothesis," in Robert F. Winch and Graham B. Spanier, *Selected Studies in Marriage and the Family*, 4th ed. (New York: Holt, Rinehart and Winston, 1974), pp. 94–113.

46. See, for example, P. K. Roy, "Industrialization and Fitness of Nuclear Family: A Case Study in India," *Journal of Comparative Family Studies* 5 (Spring 1974) pp. 74–86; and E. Wilbur Bock et al., "Maintenance of the Extended Family in Urban Areas of Argentina, Brazil and Chile," *Journal of Comparative Family Studies* 6 (Spring 1975) pp. 31–45.

47. Marvin B. Sussman, "The Help Pattern in the Middle Class Family," *American Sociological Review* 18 (February 1953), pp. 22–28; Eugene Litwak, op. cit., pp. 9–21 and 385–394; Michael Young and Peter Wilmott, *Family and Kinship in East London* (London: Routledge and Kegan Paul, 1957), pp. 159–166; Murray A. Straus, "Social Class and Farm-City Differences in Interaction with Kin in Relation to Societal Modernization," *Rural Sociology* 34 (December 1969), pp. 476–495; Betty Yorburg, "The Nuclear and the Extended Family: An Area of Conceptual Confusion," *Journal of Comparative Family Studies* 6 (Spring 1975), pp. 5–14; and Sandro Segre, "Family Stability, Social Classes and Values in Traditional and Industrial Societies," *Journal of Marriage and the Family* 37 (May 1975), pp. 431–436.

such conditions, individuals typically have economic opportunities that can only be maximized by mobility: a managership is open in a branch store in a distant city; a son receives a degree in chemical engineering, but there are no chemical firms in his home town. If the level of interaction with, and attachment to, the kin group is low, there is relative freedom from at least this aspect of localistic loyalty.[48]

With structural pressures such as these toward geographic and social mobility, the society will come to emphasize a relatively isolated nuclear or modified-extended family organization. This is so because it involves the least conflict with a rapidly expanding and changing economic, technological, and social order. On the other hand, because a decline in interaction with the extended kin appears to take place under the impact of rapid urbanization and industrialization, this does not necessarily mean that a decline in interaction will continue to occur in the future. Perhaps the "post-industrial" and affluent society of the latter half of the twentieth century will enable kinship ties to be maintained via long-distance telephone or air travel to a much greater extent than was practiced in the first half of the twentieth century. In addition, if social control by extended kin networks declines and if the desire for and availability of privacy increases,[49] one could predict a continued and increasing experimentation with variant marital and family styles that include nuclear, extended and non-kin networks.

Interchanges between the Family System and Other Systems

The discussion linking a particular type of family organization with the extent or degree of industrialization or urbanization of a society is one of many illustrations of the linkage and interdependence between components or structures of society. As indicated, instances exist where the kinship system is synonymous with and performs the functions of the educational, political, religious, and economic system. In other instances, such as most of the western world, a clearer differentiation in structure and function exists between these basic institutions.[50]

Most scholars assume that in all societies the family system is a functional and interdependent part of the larger totality. Thus it becomes impos-

---

48. Straus, op. cit., pp. 478–479.

49. An interesting historical analysis of family change as related to privacy can be seen in Barbara Laslett, "The Family as a Public and Private Institution: An Historical Perspective," *Journal of Marriage and the Family* 35 (August 1973), pp. 480–492.

50. Two research examples of family-societal linkages can be seen in Veronica Stolte-Heiskanen, "Family Needs and Societal Institutions: Potential Empirical Linkage Mechanisms," *Journal of Marriage and the Family* 37 (November 1975), pp. 903–916; and Michael Cernea "The Large-Scale Formal Organization and the Family Primary Group," *Journal of Marriage and the Family* 37 (November 1975), pp. 927–936.

sible for marriage and family systems to exist separately and independently of other systems. The family affects and is affected by laws and governmental policy, churches and religious thought, schools and educational experiences, and jobs and economic mechanisms. In the framework of structural-functionalism, these basic institutions exist universally because they fulfill basic prerequisites: needs or requirements essential for the existence and survival of society itself.

Any group of students could quickly come up with its own list of basic activities or things that need to be done in order for a society to exist. It would be highly unusual to have a list that does not include certain activities or needs that are currently performed basically by the family system. Most lists are likely to include the following:

- Replacement of members
- Provision of food, shelter, and clothing for all members
- Training (socialization) of new members into functioning adults
- Maintaining of order
- Reduction of conflict among members
- Motivation of members to perform tasks that need to be fulfilled
- Production, distribution, and consumption of various goods and services
- Provision of a sense of significance or "worthwhileness"

These are a few of the tasks that must be met for a society to exist. Although it is likely that they could be met apart from the family system, few deny that the family system is very basic and instrumental in the fulfilling of some of these prerequisites.

Adaptation

The best known prerequisites in sociology are those stated by Parsons: adaptation, goal attainment, integration, and pattern maintenance.[51] Adaptation refers to the necessity of the family to "adapt" or fit in with the social and physical environment in which it is located. College fraternities have an adaptive problem in the total college environment. Federal governments have the need for successful adaptation to the international environment.

Bell and Vogel term this prerequisite the economy.[52] The economy is viewed as that part of a society concerned with the creation and distribution of valued goods and services. One interchange between the nuclear family and the economy is in the contribution of labor by the family in exchange

---

51. See Talcott Parsons, *The Social System* (New York: Free Press, 1951); and Talcott Parsons and Neil Smelser, *Economy and Society* (New York: Free Press, 1956).

52. Norman W. Bell and Ezra F. Vogel, *A Modern Introduction to the Family* (New York: Free Press, 1968), p. 11.

for rewards. In industrial societies these rewards are usually money wages received for the labor contributed by a family member. In more primitive societies the reward may be goods and services or an informal verbal agreement to return assistance when needed. Families have an adaptive problem in meeting the conditions of the economy in terms of getting to work, job skills, encouragement, and so on. The economy and private industry too have an adaptive problem in meeting the needs and demands of the family: minimum wages, healthful working conditions, flexibility in handling sickness, births, funerals, and the like.

The interchanges between the family and the economy are basic (as seen in the professionalization of the housewife, unemployment, minimum incomes for families, and purchasing power for homes, automobiles, or education). The family, a substructure of the total system, takes as one of its primary functional mandates or prerequisites the task of adaptation. It acts in many ways to manipulate the economy in such a way as to facilitate or aid the goals and needs of the family.

Goal Attainment

Goal attainment refers to the basic understanding and general agreement as to what the family is all about. All social systems including the family have and need a reason to exist. Colleges exist to create and disseminate knowledge, and the persons within the academic environment (or at least many of them) concentrate their activities toward this end. General Motors and Ford exist to make automobiles and in turn provide a profit to their shareholders. Thus within any social system, a means-ends framework exists. There are personal and collective goals to be reached and means to reach these goals. This is a basic prerequisite of any system.

Bell and Vogel term this prerequisite of goal attainment the polity.[53] The polity is viewed as that part of a society that administers the activities enabling society to obtain its goals. In contemporary societies this is often seen as "government" but it is not coterminous with government. The family may act as a unit in relation to the polity—providing loyalty and compliance in return for leadership and decisions. Unlike the economy, where a family may decide to change jobs if the employment situation is unsatisfactory, the family does not have any option in relation to the polity since governing bodies are given mandates to remain in power for certain lengths of time. If the elected is not of one's choice, the burden of adjustment is on the family. In return for this compliance, the polity provides leadership, legal protection, security, and the like. In times of war, state expansion, austerity programs, or national crises, the family must be willing to forego certain

general agreement to what a family is all about

---

53. Ibid., p. 14.

Income Support Programs and the Family

In noting the interchange between the family system and other systems, one cannot ignore the role of the government. Government taxes income and gifts and in turn transfers these taxes to others in the form of security, roads, welfare, administrative costs, and the like. Many local state or national programs are of direct consequence to families. Note the following welfare type of examples:

- Aid to Families with Dependent Children (AFDC) provides cash payments to families with children whose parent(s) are absent, incapacitated, or deceased.

- Supplementary Security Income (SSI) provides cash payments to the disabled, blind, and aged.

- The Food Stamp program provides food vouchers for households that purchase food in common.

- Medicaid provides health benefits for welfare families.

- Public housing programs provide housing, rent, and purchase subsidies for the poor.

- Select public day care programs such as Head Start and social services provide day care payments or programs for poor families.

While these and other programs have been subject to major criticism, particularly among the middle and upper classes, few would deny that these programs have had a major impact (both positively and negatively) on the life-styles of large numbers of families in our society.

gratifications. In turn it is expected that the leadership will work to provide optimum conditions for the society.

> Because the family is stable, compared to many other concrete units, and because family sentiments tend to become associated with attitudes toward the polity, the family is always a unit of importance. This is most evident at the symbolic level, with leaders striving to present themselves as "solid family men (or women)," and to gather support by favoring the "family farm" or the values of strong family life. But the polity's orientation to the family is also evident in its decisions and policies, which protect the privacy of the home, refuse to compel spouses to testify against each other, distribute welfare benefits in relation to the family's condition, and act in various ways to inhibit the dissolution of marriages.[54]

The interchanges between the family and the polity are basic for the existence of either system. As with the economy, the family takes as one of its primary functional mandates or prerequisites the task of goal attainment. It elects certain types of leaders to make the types of decisions that are consistent with the objectives and goals of the family. In turn, the family is loyal to this leadership and complies with the decisions made.

---

54. Ibid., p. 16.

Integration

Integration, unlike adaptation and goal attainment, deals purely with matters within the system. It refers primarily to a condition between or among the units or parts within the system, in this instance the family. Dobriner states that:

> Essentially the integrative problem is the focusing of relationships within the system so as to achieve solidarity, cohesion, stability, order, and the comparative permanence of the relational system. Since no actor is ever completely socialized, since no social system is perfectly balanced and congruent to the internal structure of relationships, since the private ends of actors may indeed be subversive to group goals and intentions, since there is never perfect adaptation to the external environment, and since the human social condition seems inherently unstable and volatile, there is constant need to renew the integrative mechanism.[55]

The subsystem of society concerned with the integrative prerequisite is, as termed by Bell and Vogel, the community.[56] The community is not seen as a single concrete group, such as a village, but as diffuse affective relationships of varying extensiveness in reference to the family system. Daily interaction, gifts, special kindnesses, and the like, come to symbolize the solidarity of the bonds among families. The interchanges that take place between the nuclear family and the community can be seen in the extent to which the family participates in industrial, religious, or community activities. In turn, the community provides meaning (an identity) and family support, particularly in times of crisis.

Under usual circumstances the bonds of solidarity within the nuclear family are reinforced by the community. However, at other times, it may be the community that makes it difficult for the family to deal intensively with its own internal processes. Under such conditions the family may withdraw from participation in community affairs. Ordinarily, the family is exempt from participation in community activities at times of serious family problems, marriage, or death. At these times the affective relationships (community) offer social support to the family.

Cohesion, solidarity, and identity within the nuclear family may be highly related to the type of community network within which it operates. When societies are relatively stable and the group patterns operate in a relatively closed network, identity may not be a serious problem. In more mobile, highly industrialized societies, the multiple and changing group memberships may increase the difficulty in maintaining a clear stable identity.

As with the other prerequisites, integration of the family is basic to

---

55. William M. Dobriner, *Social Structures and Systems: A Sociological Overview* (Pacific Palisades, Calif.: Goodyear, 1969), p. 112.
56. Bell and Vogel, op. cit., p. 16.

its very existence. Again a considerable amount of effort is expended in maintaining solidarity, cohesion, stability, or order within the family system.

Pattern Maintenance and Tension Management

Pattern maintenance and tension management, like integration, deal primarily with the internal state of the social (family) system. But unlike integration, which deals with relationships (community), the prerequisite of pattern maintenance and tension management deals with the persons—the actors—and the expectations, ideologies, and values held. The person may suffer from role conflict, be an agnostic, or suffer from anomie, but if too far removed from the normative structure, the system will lack congruency and in the extreme will "break down."

The family is again basic in the meeting of this prerequisite. The family provides a wide range of tension display, provides an approved outlet for emotional expression, and devotes considerable time and attention to the socialization of its members to the ideologies, norms, and values of the system. Bell and Vogel refer to this prerequisite as the value system.[57] It is the value system that maintains the appropriate norms, determines what is important, and what general orientation principles should exist.

The nuclear family is the smallest social unit responsible for the preservation of the value system but is peculiarly suited for the task by virtue of the prolonged dependency of the human infant and the intensity and priority of relationships within the family. The nuclear family, then, gives to the value system conformity and an acceptance of the standards specified by the value system. The value system, determined in part by the religious and educational systems, defines what types of behavior are desirable and legitimate. Children internalize these values within a family context, and it is the family that is crucial in the preservation of these values. Conflict and differences between the value system of the society and the specific norms of importance to the family may mean the nuclear family either is considered nonconformist by the community or conforms to the basic value system. In any case, the family is basically responsible for enforcing the conformity of its members and for the managing of tension. Without the fulfillment of this prerequisite, the family system and the society would and could not exist.

In summary, the four basic prerequisites or functional imperatives— 1) adaptation, 2) goal attainment, 3) integration, and 4) pattern maintenance and tension management—are essential and universal to all social systems including the family. Concrete examples of familiar family situations and phrases to illustrate these prerequisites are as follows:

---

57. Ibid., p. 18.

1. "The neighborhood has simply gone to pieces. The only thing we can do is move."—Adaptation
2. "Well, if this family wants a new car next year we are going to have to do something about expenses this year."—Goal attainment
3. "Now I realize Johnny got in too late last night, but you spoke to him much too harshly. I think it would be a good idea if you two had a talk before things get out of hand."—Integration
4. "Tommy, nice little boys do not spit at their mothers."—Pattern maintenance
5. "Mary, I don't want you to speak to me in that tone of voice and in that manner again—particularly in front of the neighbors."—Pattern maintenance, tension management[58]

Summary

The family as a social institution refers to an organized, formal, and regular way of carrying out certain essential tasks in a society. It refers to the wide system of norms that organizes family units into stable and ongoing social systems. This chapter presents numerous ways in which marital, family, and kin groups and systems are organized to fulfill certain tasks.

The family system consists of interrelated statuses and their accompanying expectations. The family group consists of a concrete reality of persons who are physically present and who interact with one another. Four kinds of family groups—the statistical, the societal, the social, and the associational—are distinguished from one another based on the properties of a consciousness of kind, social interaction, and social organization. The family as a primary group, with face-to-face contact, smallness of size, and frequent and intense contact, is distinguished from the secondary group of more formal, impersonal contacts that characterize much of our lives. Conjugal families that always include a husband and wife are distinguished from other kin networks such as the extended, consanguine, joint, and stem families that extend beyond the two-generational family.

While it is often difficult to differentiate the kin network from other institutions in society, selected property and inheritance functions are generally attributed to it. In addition, certain kin groups function to promote special interests of its members (centripetal kinship) while other kin groups are oriented toward furthering interests of the wider community or society (centrifugal kinship).

Considerable debate has focused upon the extent to which the family in the U.S. is an isolated nuclear unit. This issue is directly related to the larger more complex theoretical issue of the interrelation of family structure, urbanism, and modernization. Three questions examined include 1) the ex-

---

58. Dobriner, op. cit., p. 126.

tent of a nuclear or conjugal family structure prior to industrialization and urbanization, 2) the extent of extended family structures after periods of industrialization and urbanization, and 3) whether or not a single familial form emerges. While the issue remains unresolved, research and theoretical arguments are presented to deal with each of these questions.

The family system is linked closely with other systems in a society. Each of these systems are thought to fulfill basic needs or requirements for the society to survive. These prerequisites have been labeled by Parsons as adaptation, goal attainment, integration, and pattern maintenance. The family is linked in with the economy, polity, the community, religion, and other systems in an exchange of support, services, and labor for wages, goods, or order, to mention only a few.

The next chapter provides a continuation in our understanding of family groups and systems by examining the issue of change.

Key Terms and Topics

Discussion Questions

1. What is meant by the family as a social institution? What does it mean for factors like homosexuality, illegitimacy, or child support to be institutionalized?

2. Differentiate family groups from family systems. Since systems are abstractional, of what relevance are they to an understanding of the family?

3. List examples of statistical groups, societal groups, social groups, and associational groups. What different functions does each serve? Which ones fulfill tasks similar to family groups?

4. Describe what would be likely to happen to a person who is removed from all primary-group relationships? Why are they so crucial?

5. In your own words, define marriage and family in a way that would be comprehensive enough to include most societies in the world. How are

the two similar or different? Is one necessary for the other? How do they differ from any other group or relationship?

6. *Thinking of your own kin group, how many persons do you know (uncles, cousins, and so on)? With how many do you interact on a regular basis? What differentiations do you make between kin on the mother's side and kin on the father's side?*

7. *Would you label your kinship network as centripetal or centrifugal? Why? Why are certain ethnic groups highly centripetal?*

8. *Debate the following issues: 1) The American family is an isolated nuclear unit. 2) As nations become urbanized and industrialized, the family systems converge on the nuclear family system.*

9. *Show how the family engages in interchanges with the economic, educational, religious, political, and community systems. What does each contribute to and receive from the other?*

10. *Are there functional imperatives or prerequisites other than adaptation, goal attainment, integration, and pattern maintenance and tension management? What might some of them be?*

Further Readings

Adams, Bert N. *The Family: A Sociological Interpretation.* 2d ed. Chicago: Rand McNally, 1975. An introductory sociology text that emphasizes current analytic frameworks and theoretical conceptions for organizing the wide body of information available on the U.S. family.

Adams, Bert N. *Kinship in an Urban Setting.* Chicago: Markham, 1968. A study of urban kinship relationships in Greensboro, N. C.

Bell, Norman W., and **Ezra F. Vogel.** *A Modern Introduction to the Family.* New York: Free Press, 1968. A functional analysis of the family system as it relates to external systems (economy, polity, community, and value systems), internal processes (adaptive, coordinative, integrative, and pattern maintaining), and personality.

Farber, Bernard. *Family and Kinship in Modern Society.* Glenview, Ill.: Scott, Foresman, 1973. A discussion of the role of the family and kinship in the destiny of western society, making use of family law pertaining to marriage and divorce, support of indigent relatives, illegitimacy, adoption, and intestacy to indicate trends. The family is viewed as a property system shifting from a "natural-family" to a "legal-family" model.

Goode, William J. *World Revolution and Family Patterns.* Glencoe, Ill.: Free Press, 1963. A description and interpretation of the main changes in family patterns that have occurred over the past half-century in the West, Arabic Islam, sub-Saharan Africa, India, China, and Japan.

Leslie, Gerald R. *The Family in Social Context.* 3d ed. New York: Oxford University

Press, 1976. An introductory textbook providing an extensive coverage of a sociological approach to the family.

Safilios-Rothschild, Constantina. "Toward a Cross-Cultural Conceptualization of Family Modernity." *Journal of Comparative Family Studies* 1 (Autumn 1970), pp. 17–25. A proposed conceptualization of modernity at different levels for societies, families, and individuals.

Stolte-Heiskanen, Veronica. "Family Needs and Societal Institutions: Potential Empirical Linkage Mechanisms." *Journal of Marriage and the Family* 37 (November 1975) pp. 903–916; and "Social Indicators for Analysis of Family Needs Related to the Life Cycle." *Journal of Marriage and the Family* 36 (August 1974) pp. 592–600. Two articles that link and show interrelationships between the family and society.

Winch, Robert F. "Some Observations on Extended Familism in the United States." In Robert F. Winch and Graham B. Spanier, eds. *Selected Studies in Marriage and the Family.* 4th ed. New York: Holt, Rinehart and Winston, 1974, pp. 147–160. An overview and testing of the arguments presented by Parsons of the isolated nuclear family and by Zimmerman of the atomistic family.

Yorburg, Betty. "The Nuclear and the Extended Family: An Area of Conceptual Confusion." *Journal of Comparative Family Studies* 6 (Spring 1975), pp. 5–14. An examination of controversies relating family organization to various types of societies.

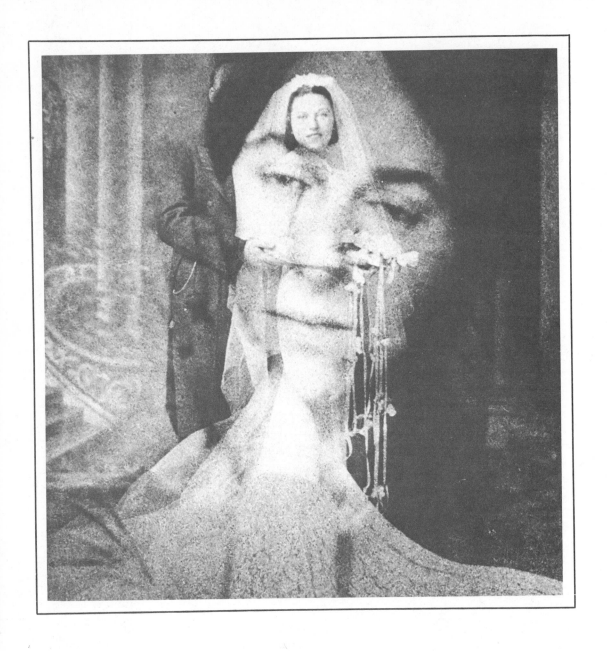

4

The Family in a Process
of Change

4

Although families have existed for thousands of years and their structures and functions have varied widely, no theory or explanation is adequate enough to explain the changes that have occurred within the institution. Nor is there agreement on the criteria to be used for a comprehensive understanding and analysis of change. Think of some of the questions that could be raised concerning this issue. What is the time period under consideration—this month, this year, this century, or longer? Should scholarly efforts be focused on description or analysis? Can family change be understood simply by dealing with the family as an internal system or does family change involve forces external to the system? Are these changes accidental or planned? Is change behavioral or attitudinal? Is our concern with material changes, such as automobiles, wedding rings, and houses, or with nonmaterial changes, such as sex roles, decision-making patterns or mate-selection values? Is the change in what actually occurred or in what was preferred (the ideal)? Is the family an agent or simply the recipient of change? Is change in a family system patterned or unpatterned, peaceful or violent, continuous or spasmodic, directional or nondirectional, rapid or slow, personal or social?

Stated simply, the word "change" denotes a difference in anything observed over some period of time, whether a fraction of a second or eons. The most untrained scholar of the family can readily point to changes that are taking place within the family system. Who has not heard of the "good old days"? Anyone over thirty can tell you that things "ain't like they used to be" (and probably never were). People proclaim with authority a rising divorce rate, a lack of obedience by children, or an increasing sexual permissiveness. Even if conscious efforts were made to do so, it would be difficult to avoid the matter of change in dealing with any family or marital issue.

The primary concern of this chapter is to describe the evolution of marriage and the family, present an idealistic-cyclical theory of change, review several ideal-type constructs of change in the American family, and present several explanations for change. Evolutionary theory covers the greatest time span and is the most global explanation of change in family systems. Second is Carle Zimmerman's idealistic-cyclical theory of family change covering a span of several thousand years. The ideal-type constructs of change cover several decades only with a particular focus on families in the United States.

THE EVOLUTION OF MARRIAGE AND THE FAMILY

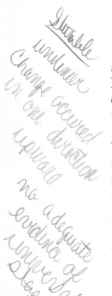

Evolutionary theory dominated sociological thought in the nineteenth and early twentieth centuries,[1] but since about 1920 interest in it appears to have waned. However, there does seem to be a recent revival of interest in an evolutionary perspective that coincides with a growing interest in comparative studies.

Some of the older evolutionary models ran into two major stumbling blocks. One was the assumption that the development of human societies or of the family system was unilinear. It was postulated that change occurred in a single direction and, generally, that direction was upward or an "improvement." The second stumbling block centered around a failure to specify and provide adequate evidence of the major "stages" of universal development and the factors that affected the transition from one stage to another. Many times, the field data and the evidence from "primitive" societies did not always fit into the evolutionary scheme.

Strongly influenced by Darwin, whose theory of natural selection provided a solid base for biological evolution, theorists sought a sociological analogy to the living organism.[2] Herbert Spencer, in particular, saw evolution as a unilinear development—a continuing process by which matter was synthesized at ever higher levels of complexity.[3] Man in society, like other living forms, followed an inevitable course from amorphous and homogeneous structures to increasingly differentiated and specialized ones.

To support his theory, Spencer traced the development of marriage and the family from an original state of promiscuity, through stages of polyandry and polygyny, to the final and, in his view, most highly developed stage of monogamy.

Spencer had unbounded faith in the natural development of society and the family. Evolution was in the natural order of things and man could not hope to alter the process by legislation. In fact, the government should adopt a policy of laissez-faire, so as not to interfere with the "natural selec-

1. A. W. Calhoun, *A Social History of the American Family* (Cleveland: Clark, 1917).
2. Charles Darwin, *Origin of Species* (New York: Appleton, 1859); and *The Descent of Man* (New York: Appleton, 1880).
3. Herbert Spencer, *The Principles of Sociology* (New York: D. Appleton, 1898).

tion" of those most fit to survive. Education, or anything that disturbed the orderly evolution of increasingly improved social forms, was considered pathological. Spencer did not oppose change or conflict. Conflict itself was part of an orderly process: what *was* at any time *ought* to be. Spencer's idea of change occurring by evolution and natural selection (sometimes called social Darwinism) was related to the elaborate analogy developed between society and a biological organism.

An anthropologist, Lewis Henry Morgan, was one of the first systematic field workers to provide a detailed outline of phases in the evolution of societies.[4] He believed that societies could be divided into three basic types—savage, barbaric, and civilized. Also influenced by Darwin, Morgan developed his evolutionary scheme to include various social institutions including the family. His "sequence of institutions" connected with the family began with promiscuity, which he termed "promiscuous intercourse." He was never certain that promiscuity ever actually existed since knowledge of it was beyond the reach of definiteness. But if promiscuity did exist, it was followed by group marriage, polygamy (commencing with polyandry and followed by polygyny), and monogamy. And since at the time of his writing monogamy was well-established in society, it was equated with the highest form of development.

Another early authority, Edward Westermarck, said that the origin of the institution of marriage most probably developed out of a primeval habit.[5] He believed that it was the habit for a man and a woman (or several women) to live together, to have sexual relations, and to rear their offspring in common: the man being the protector and supporter of his family and the woman being his helpmate and the nurse of their children. This habit was first sanctioned by custom and afterwards by law and was thus transformed into a social institution. Thus in contrast to Morgan, Westermarck was impressed by the absence of promiscuity and the presence of monogamy among primitive groups. Consistent with most other evolutionary theorists, Westermarck drew upon the animal world and primitive families to find evidence to support his theory of family change. It was his conviction that not a single authoritative statement could be made to support even a probable existence of promiscuity.

Most of these evolutionary attempts to provide a grand synthesis of family change have not been accepted. As stated by Goode, these theorists made four great assumptions that today cannot be accepted:

1. That the family and religious patterns of a society with a low level technology are closer to, say, Paleolithic man than to modern man; consequently, we can reconstruct the time stages in between by observing contemporary primitive societies.

---

4. Lewis H. Morgan, *Ancient Society* (New York: Henry Holt, 1877), pp. 325–328, 441–442.

5. Edward Westermarck, *A Short History of Marriage* (New York: Humanities Press, 1968), p. 2. (First published in 1926.)

2. That we can view a "cultural survival" like ritual wife capture as equivalent to a social "fossil," and thus reconstruct a past.
3. That observable family patterns evolved because they contributed more to the survival of the society than did the patterns which were discarded in the past.
4. That, as in biological evolution, a standard set of sequences could be found, through which all family and kinship systems would pass.[6]

The evolutionary frameworks were generally discarded after World War I in favor of precise descriptions of ongoing family systems, analyses of short-term trends, and diffusion studies, because it was agreed that the available data did not confirm the larger theory.[7] At this point, all attempts to reconstruct the earlier forms of organization of the family remain as hypotheses and lack empirical evidence.

AN IDEALISTIC-CYCLICAL THEORY OF CHANGE

Change occurs through the role of ideas

An idealistic explanation of change is based on the organization of norms and values. Rather than evolutionary or materialistic in origin, change in family organization occurs through the role of ideas. A cyclical explanation views change as occurring in giant historical swings or cycles. A combination of these explanations is provided by Zimmerman and developed in his book *Family and Civilization*.[8]

According to Zimmerman, the most outstanding fact about the family in all its manifestations is the presence or absence of power.[9] Families throughout history should be classified according to their power or ability to function and their field of action. That is, of the total power in the society, how much belongs to the family? What role does the family play in the total business of society? If individuals want to marry or break up a family, whom do they consult—the family, the church, or the state? If a rule is violated, does the family, the church, or the state dispense the punishment?

Zimmerman argues that families can be typed according to the amount of power they wield compared to the rest of the society.[10] Using the "ideal-type" or typological method, he developed three main family types: 1) the *trustee* family, which has the most power, the widest field of action, and the

---

6. William J. Goode, "The Theory and Measurement of Family Change," in Eleanor B. Sheldon and Wilbert E. Moore, *Indicators of Social Change* (New York: Russell Sage Foundation, 1968), p. 301.

7. Ibid., p. 302.

8. Carle C. Zimmerman, *Family and Civilization* (New York: Harper, 1947).

9. Ibid., p. 121.

10. Ibid., p. 125.

greatest amount of social control; 2) the *atomistic* family, which has the least power and the smallest possible field of action; and 3) the *domestic* family, in which the balance of power is distributed between the family and other agencies.

The Trustee Family

The trustee family is so named because it more or less considers itself immortal. As a result, the living members are not *the* family, but merely "trustees" of its blood, rights, property, name, and position for their life-times.[11] Family duties have priority over each individual. This type of family, as stated, has the greatest degree of power, even to the point of determining the right of life or death over its members.

Zimmerman claims that no great civilization is possible under purely trustee family conditions because the family is given responsibilities for which it is essentially unsuited and incapable of properly fulfilling. The family has to carry out the functions of government—make wars, rule commerce, incorporate strangers, inflict the death penalty, regulate matters between families, distribute justice, and perform many other acts for which it is in no way fit.[12]

Although Zimmerman describes the trustee family system as a historical phenomenon, as seen in ancient Greece, Rome, and in the families of the Dark Ages, he also sees the trustee family in the contemporary United States, particularly in the southern Appalachian-Ozark Highland regions. Family feuds, attempts by families to have their own members elected as sheriffs, judges, justices of the peace, and other public officials, and a high degree of nepotism in government and jobs are all indicative of a trustee-type family.

The Domestic Family

The domestic family arises out of modifications of the trustee family or by being revived by governmental or religious sanctions from the atomistic family. This type is the most common in the world. As stated by Zimmerman, the domestic family satisfies to some extent the natural desires for freedom from family bonds and for individualism, yet it also preserves sufficient social structure to enable the state or body politic to depend upon it as an aid in government and as a source of the extreme power needed by states in carrying out their functions.[13]

---

11. Ibid., p. 128.
12. Ibid., p. 719.
13. Ibid., p. 130.

The domestic family can be illustrated in contemporary America by looking at farm and rural families. They include in their major conceptions of the family all members of the domestic group who are living and who influence decisions about family living, family behavior, and family property. Unlike the trustee family, relatives outside the household limits may still gossip, advise, quarrel, aid, and interfere informally in the domestic institution, but fundamentally the members of the household are largely free from outside influences as long as they keep within the bounds of accepted public behavior.[14]

The domestic family can develop into the atomistic type. This change will result primarily from forces external to the family. The state seeks to gain power by taking over the functions of many of the other institutions. Political, religious, economic, and other conditions affect changes from a pro-family to an anti-family attitude in the society.

The Atomistic Family

The atomistic family is so termed because of the rise of the conception that the individual is to be freed of family bonds and the state is to become an organization of individuals.[15] Whereas the trustee family represents social power and responsibilities given to the family, the atomistic family represents social power and responsibility given to the individual. Whereas in the trustee family the family was held responsible for the individual and the individual was held accountable to the family, the atomistic family holds that the individual is responsible for himself; he alone is accountable to the state or through the state to other persons. Whereas in the trustee family the family was sacred, in the atomistic family the individual becomes sacred.

Zimmerman leaves no doubt that he believes the present period in American society to be one of widespread domination by the atomistic family. Present family relations are almost as completely individualized as it is possible to have them and still retain any familism at all.[16] The individual is free to do largely what he wishes as long as the state and public have no workable objections.

The system of atomistic familism is carried by its own momentum to its extinction, largely unchecked by anything other than the total dispersal of biological, psychological, and social resources of the society.[17] Some

14. Ibid., p. 732.
15. Ibid., p. 134.
16. Ibid., p. 760.
17. Ibid., p. 762.

familism will exist in societies that are basically atomistic; however, these will be in the minority and will consist largely of an informal, domestic type of family. These persons will possess considerable insight into the difficulties of the system but will be relatively silent or a futile minority. The "silent majority" phrase of the Nixon era must certainly have appeared prophetic to Zimmerman.

In general, when a social system reaches the latter phases of developed atomism, it reaches a point where certain forms of behavior gain great prominence. These forms of action and thought, which are identical with those during the high periods of atomism in Greece, Rome, and the modern world (a repeating of the giant cycle), include the following:

- Increased and rapid easy divorce (guilty- and innocent-party theory becoming pure fiction).
- Decreased number of children, population decay, and increased public disrespect for parents and parenthood.
- Elimination of the real meaning of the marriage ceremony.
- Popularity of pessimistic doctrines about the early heroes.
- The refusal of many people married under the older family form to maintain their traditions while other people escape these obligations.
- The spread of the anti-familism of the urbane and pseudo-intellectual classes to the very outer limits of civilization.
- Breaking down of most inhibitions against adultery.
- Revolts of youth against the parents so that parenthood becomes more and more difficult for those who did try to raise children.
- Rapid rise and spread of juvenile delinquency.
- Common acceptance of all forms of sex perversions. These would include adultery, fornication, homosexuality, bestiality, rape, incest, and others.[18]

What of the future as seen by Zimmerman? That the American family of the immediate future will move further toward atomism seems highly probable.[19] Except for the Christian church, which at present is not popular among the directive forces of Western society, no agency or group of persons seems fundamentally interested in doing anything other than facilitating this increasing atomism. Zimmerman claims that history has shown that we are seeing a reappearance of a family decay identical to that which preceded the complete nihilism of the great cultures of Greece and Rome.[20] Would you agree?

---

18. Ibid., p. 776.
19. Ibid., p. 806.
20. See sources such as J. A. Folsom, *Family & Democratic Society* (New York, 1943); Leslie Paul, *The Annihilation of Man* (New York, 1945); and Philip Wylie, *Generation of Vipers* (New York, 1942).

IDEAL-TYPE CONSTRUCTS
OF CHANGE IN THE
AMERICAN FAMILY

Most research work on change in the marital or family system is aimed at ascertaining the descriptive aspects of change. Many of these descriptions involved simply the past several decades (due to the availability of records) or concentrate on specific, concrete events (such as age at marriage, family size, or attitudes toward family planning). Other descriptions of trends or shifts in family orientation are established in broad "ideal-type" categories: institution to companionship, traditional to developmental, entrepreneurial to bureaucratic, gender role differentiation to androgyny, or orderly replacement to universal permanent availability. These five polar constructs are designed to describe major trends or changes that are taking or have taken place. Of the five, perhaps only the orderly replacement construct could be classified as a theory of family change. The other four could be classified as general descriptive typologies of change in the American family system. Each will be examined briefly.

From Institution to
Companionship

On an ideal-type construct continuum the family as an institution and the family as companionship represent two polar conceptions. The basic thesis of Ernest Burgess et al. is that the family has been in transition from an institution, with family behavior controlled by mores, public opinion, and law, to a companionship, with behavior arising from the mutual affection, equality, and consensus of its members.[21] The companionship form of the family was conceived by Burgess as an emerging form.

In its extreme conceptual formulation, the institutional family is one in which its unity is determined entirely by traditional rules and regulations, specified duties and obligations, and other social pressures impinging on family members. It is the extended patriarchal type that most closely approximates historically the ideal construct of the institutional family. At the polar extreme it involved the complete subordination of the individual family members to the authority of the husband or perhaps older male (the patriarch) combined with the strong sanctions of the law, religion, and established mores.

The companionship family at its polar extreme would focus on the unity that develops out of mutual affection and intimate association of husband and wife, parents and children. This type of family includes: 1) affection

21. Ernest W. Burgess, Harvey J. Locke, and Mary Margaret Thomes, *The Family: From Institution to Companionship*, 3d ed. (New York: American Book, 1963).

Census Bureau Shows Changing Marriage Patterns

An examination of census reports shows that ways of living today are vastly different from those of earlier generations. The behavior of U.S. residents in 1976 contrasts significantly with those of 1960 and even 1970. For example:

The median age at first marriage has increased by one year. In 1976 the median age at marriage was 23.8 for males and 21.3 for females. In 1960 these figures were 22.8 for males and 20.3 for females.

The percentage single (never married) increased considerably for those under age 35. In 1976, the percentage single of those between age 14 and 35 was 56.2 for males and 45.3 for females. In 1960 these figures were 50.7 for males and 37.6 for females.

The number of divorced persons per 1,000 married persons increased to 75 in 1976 from 35 in 1960. For those under age 45 the number increased to 80 in 1976 from 30 in 1960.

The number of two-person adult households shared by unrelated persons of the opposite sex increased by about 40 percent in the six-year period between 1970 and 1976 (from 991,000 to 1,479,000).

Female family heads increased by 34 percent between 1970 and 1976 (from 5.6 million persons to 7.5 million).

Eighty percent of the children under 18 years old in 1976 lived in families with both of their parents present, a decline from 85 percent in 1970.

Source: U.S. Bureau of the Census, *Current Population Reports*, Series P-20, No. 306, "Marital Status and Living Arrangements: March 1976" (Washington, D.C.: U.S. Government Printing Office, 1977), Tables A-G.

as a basis for its existence, 2) husband and wife with equal status and authority, 3) major decisions made by consensus, and 4) common interest and activities coexisting with division of labor and individuality of interests.[22] Most closely approximating the companionship family is the democratic family in which the members enjoy a high degree of self-expression and at the same time are united by the bonds of affection, congeniality, and common interests.

Burgess compares the historical approximations of these two types of families, indicating the differences between the larger extended patriarchal family and the smaller, more nuclear form of democratic family.

1. The patriarchal family is authoritarian and autocratic, with power vested in the head of the family and with the subordination of his wife, sons, and their wives and children, and his unmarried daughters to his authority. The democratic family is based on equality of husband and wife, with consensus in making decisions and with increasing participation by children as they grow older.
2. Marriage is arranged by the parents in the patriarchal family, with emphasis on prudence, on economic and social status, and on adjustment of the son-in-law or daughter-in-law to the family group. In the small democratic family, selection of a marriage partner is in the hands of young people, and choice is on the basis of affection and personality adjustment to each other.

22. Ibid., p. 4.

> *Alex:*   *In Turkey, our marriage events usually last three or four days: Thurs-*
> *day, Friday, Saturday, Sunday. Thursday the immediate family comes*
> *together. As the days go on, more people come into the marriage.*
> *Thursday would be the immediate family, and the next day you*
> *would have the extended family. The day after that you have the*
> *friends and the whole shot. Saturday and Sunday is the actual wed-*
> *ding day. The whole town would be there. Nowadays, the male and*
> *female can dance together and stuff like that. Everybody brings gifts.*
> *You can start out with no penny but the gifts you receive will be*
> *tremendous. After the wedding you go on a honeymoon.*
>
> *I'll tell you how it is with the Moslems, though. The Moslems are a*
> *little different. They don't go on a honeymoon. Let's say on Sunday,*
> *the last day of the marriage, they will go to an arranged room. This*
> *room is arranged by the bride and her family. In this room they will*
> *spend their first night together. There is always a suspicion whether*
> *she is a virgin. And the suspicion on the boy's side would be, like,*
> *would he achieve? And the next day you will see the mother, pulling*
> *out the bloody sheets and showing to the whole town that she was a*
> *virgin. If there are no bloody sheets, oh boy. Watch out then. That's*
> *a scandal. See in the upper class we don't have that, but the lower*
> *class they still have such, they put the bloody sheets all over the place.*
> *The mother of the boy will proudly put the bloody sheets on a string*
> *and let everybody see that. If there are no bloody sheets, watch out.*

3. Compliance with duty and the following of tradition are major expectations of the patriarchal family, while the objectives of the small democratic family are the achievement of happiness and the personal growth of the individuals.
4. The primary historic functions of the family—economic, educational, recreational, health, protective, and religious—are found in their fullest development in the patriarchal family. These historic functions have been greatly modified in the small democratic family.[23]

Changes in the American family are moving in the direction of the companionship type. The factors that once maintained stability within the family, such as control by custom and community opinion, are being replaced by factors such as the bond of affection, compatibility, and mutual interest to maintain family and marital stability.

From Traditional to Developmental

A second ideal-type construct of change in the American family, and one which closely parallels the Burgess model, is Evelyn Duvall's conception

---

23. Ibid., p. 4.

of traditional and developmental.[24] This formulation first grew out of a study of differential conceptions of parenthood.[25] In that study Duvall recorded the verbatim responses of more than 300 mothers to the question "What are five things a good mother does?" and "What are five things a good child does?" The responses were then grouped into categories that distinguished traditional mothers and children from developmental ones. Following the Duvall methods, Rachel Elder explored fathers' conceptions of parenthood and childhood.[26] Both studies were then replicated with highly similar results.[27]

The traditional father was defined as providing for the family financially, disciplining and advising the children, and setting a good example. Compared to developmental fathers, he would discipline his children for more reasons and would use fewer methods. As a strong individual, the traditional father is always right, knows what the child "should be," and does what he feels is his responsibility for the child's well-being. Parenthood is viewed as a duty that society and/or the church expect him to discharge. The developmental father fosters the growth and development of the child and other family members. He seeks to understand the child as an individual and is interested in having the child attain his own goals. Parenthood is a privilege he has chosen to assume rather than a duty demanded of him.

The traditional mother tends to be relatively steady and rigid, with specific behavioral expectancies consistent with her formal child-rearing orientations. This type of mother keeps house, washes, cooks, cleans, mends, sews, manages the household, takes care of the child physically (feeding, clothing, bathing, and guarding his safety), and trains the child to regularity with a specific schedule for activities. This conception of motherhood focuses on what a mother expects herself to do to and for her home and children. In contrast, the developmental conceptions of motherhood emphasize a mother's encouraging her children to develop and grow, sharing with the child, and focusing on the development of a happy, growing person. This does not mean that the developmental mother does not wash, cook, clean, mend, sew, or manage the household. Rather it implies that the focus of attention and the major orientation to herself, her children, and her husband is one that centers on the growth and development of persons rather than on any specific form of discipline or behavior. These conceptions are recognized as dynamic and flexible.

In light of these conceptions of mother and father, the good child (from

---

24. Evelyn Millis Duvall, *Family Development*, 4th ed. (Philadelphia: J. B. Lippincott, 1971).

25. Evelyn Millis Duvall, "Conceptions of Parenthood," *American Journal of Sociology* 52 (November 1946), pp. 193–203.

26. Rachel Ann Elder, "Traditional and Developmental Conceptions of Fatherhood," *Marriage and Family Living* 11 (Summer 1949), pp. 98–100.

27. Ruth Connor, Theodore B. Johannis, Jr., and James Walters, "Intra-Familial Conceptions of the Good Father, Good Mother, and Good Child," *Journal of Home Economics* 46 (March 1954), pp. 187–191.

the traditional perspective) is one who pleases his parents. He keeps neat and clean, obeys his parents and other adults, respects his teachers, is dependable, takes responsibility, and does what the family expects of him. The good child from the developmental perspective is one who loves and confides in his parents and is eager to learn by showing initiative, asking questions, and expressing himself. As a child he is emotionally well-adjusted, gets along with other people, and grows and develops as a person.

The traditional conceptions are more likely to be found among working-class parents, and the developmental conceptions are more frequent among middle-class parents. For both classes it is believed that change is in the direction of the person-centered developmental orientation and away from the institution-centered traditional conception.

From Entrepreneurial to Bureaucratic

A third ideal-type construct of change in the American family, and one which is highly related to the two models previously presented, is Daniel Miller and Guy Swanson's change from individuated-entrepreneurial to welfare-bureaucratic.[28] This formulation was developed in their study of child rearing from more than 1,000 Detroit-area homes in 1953.

The *individuated-entrepreneurial* (for brevity, entrepreneurial) refers to organizations having features such as small size, a simple division of labor, a relatively small capitalization, and provision for mobility and income through risk taking and competition. Miller and Swanson term social situations individuated if they isolate people from one another and from the controlling influence of shared cultural norms. It was the authors' contention that children reared in individuated and entrepreneurial homes would be encouraged to be highly rational, to exercise great self-control, to be self-reliant, and to assume an active, manipulative stance toward their environment.[29]

In their study a family was classified as entrepreneurial if any one of the following characteristics was met by the husband: He 1) was self-employed, 2) he gained at least half his income in the form of profits, fees, or commissions; 3) he worked in a small-scale organization having only two levels of supervision; 4) he was born on a farm; or 5) he was born outside the United States.[30]

The *welfare-bureaucratic* (for brevity, bureaucratic) is characterized by large organizations employing many kinds of specialists and coordinating

---

28. Daniel R. Miller and Guy E. Swanson, *The Changing American Parent* (New York: John Wiley, 1958).
29. Ibid., p. 57.
30. Ibid., pp. 68 and 71.

their activities by supervisors who follow a codified set of rules of practice. Toward the end of the nineteenth century and the beginning of the twentieth, new organizational trends appeared that were to transform the life of all Americans. Essential conditions in bringing about the change to a bureaucratic organization are classified by the authors as 1) the increase in the size of the organization of production, 2) the growth of specialization in organizations, 3) the great increase in the real incomes of the population, and 4) the enlarged power in the hands of lower-class workers.[31] It was believed that the methods of rearing children and the changes in these methods can be explained as flowing from the experiences that parents encounter in a bureaucratic society.

A family was classified as bureaucratic if 1) the husband and wife were born in towns or cities in the United States, 2) the husband in his occupational experience worked for someone else in an organization of at least moderate complexity (three or more supervisory levels); and 3) the husband received most of his income from a salary or wage.[32] The income and job security of the bureaucratic husband do not depend in as large a measure on his taking frequent risks as is the case of the entreprenurial husband.

It was predicted that, among whites, entrepreneurial middle-class mothers would be more likely than those with a bureaucratic orientation to emphasize the child's development of strong self-control. Also, it was predicted that entrepreneurial middle-class mothers would train their children to take a more accommodative and adjustive way of life.[33]

In regard to self-control, it was found that entrepreneurial mothers among the middle classes were significantly more likely than bureaucratic mothers of a similar social status to feed their babies on a schedule, to begin urinary training before the baby was eleven months old, and to use symbolic rather than direct punishments. They were also more likely to give a baby who was crying some attention—when "nothing was wrong with him"— only after he had sobbed for a while or, in some cases, to pay no attention to him at all.[34]

In regard to a more accommodative and adjustive way of life, none of twelve activity indices was in the direction predicted. Entrepreneurial middle-class mothers were more likely than bureaucratic mothers in the same social class to use harsh means to stop a child from sucking his body, to declare that their children did not touch their sex organs, to take measures to stop a child who touched his sex organs, to feel that it is desirable for a mother's sake that a child frequently be left at home with a competent woman while the mother shops, to say that children should be put on their

31. Ibid., p. 43.
32. Ibid., p. 78.
33. Ibid., p. 92.
34. Ibid., p. 97.

own as soon as possible to solve their own problems, and that, among adolescents, only males should perform activities traditionally associated with their sex, like washing the family car and shoveling sidewalks.[35] In general, their predictions have been borne out that entrepreneurial middle-class mothers would make greater use of internalization techniques and emphasize an active manipulative approach to life.

The trend toward a welfare-bureaucratic society leads to the emergence of a family type that Miller and Swanson term the *colleague family*.[36] The bureaucratic way of life has created new conditions for relations in families. Women and men are increasingly equal; they are also similar and different. The colleague family, placed on the ideal-type continuum of Burgess's institution-companionship model, would replace companionship as a polar extreme. In the companionship family, husband and wife are fairly equal partners whose vote on various subjects carry the same weight. As stated by Miller and Swanson:

> We feel that the distinctive characteristics of the bureaucratic order have led to what might be called a neotraditional family. The specialization on the job has entered the home, and the equal partners have been able to see that differences in talent, interest, and function, as long as they are complementary, do not threaten equality. Instead, they may enrich and promote the common life. For this reason we call this type of family the "colleague" family. As specialists at work may find in each other skills they lack, but skills they equally need, and as they may defer to one another's judgment on the grounds of differing competence without feeling that they have personally lost in prestige, so husband and wife may now relate in this way.[37]

As can be seen, three related ideal-type constructs are suggested by Miller and Swanson: 1) entrepreneurial-bureaucratic, 2) traditional-neotraditional, and 3) institution-companionship-colleague. The formal social controls of large-scale organizations are reshaping the American family, providing a new sense of obligation, and remolding traditional family patterns along revised lines.

From Gender Role Differentiation to Androgyny

A fourth ideal-type construct of change in the American family is that of male-female role differentiation versus androgyny. At one polar extreme is male-female or gender role differentiation with distinct and separate marital and family role expectations and behaviors based on sex. The other polar extreme is androgyny, which implies "both male and female in one" or a

35. Ibid., pp. 105–106.
36. Ibid., p. 200.
37. Ibid., p. 200.

society with no set of expectations or behaviors that differentiates males and females on the basis of sex.

The traditional expectations of appropriate gender roles are clear and unmistakable. Women are expected to have marriage, home, and children as their primary concerns. The wife takes the husband's name, shares his income, and relies on him for status and identity. Women should be sympathetic, caring, loving, compassionate, gentle, and submissive, which in turn makes them excellent wives, mothers, nurses, and teachers of young children. To be feminine, the skin must be smooth and soft and the body slim and erotic. Of course, the lady or "nice girl"[38] is chaste, gracious, good, clean, kind, virtuous, noncontroversial, and above suspicion and reproach.

In contrast, men earn livings to support their wife and children. To be masculine is to be self-reliant, strong, verbally and physically aggressive, dominant, tall, and muscular. Men are risk-takers, decision-makers, and protectors of those around them. The "ideal male" is thus hard working, responsible, achieving, and reliable. In addition, heterosexuality is greatly stressed in interests and activities, and departures from this, particularly as related to sexual desires and conduct, is strongly condemned.

This type of gender role differentiation has benefits for both sexes, but it has great costs as well.[39] For females, satisfaction may be derived from the stress on beauty, the lack of pressure to achieve, the wide range of emotional expression and intimacy, and the right to claim support. For males, satisfaction may be derived from the access to power, the ideology of male supremacy, the opportunities to develop skills and talents, the exercise of autonomy and independence, and the ability to be self-supporting. On the other hand, it is often at great cost to females that restrictions are placed on self-development, on training to cope with an increasingly complicated world, and on ability to obtain a loan, open a business, and be economically equal or superior to men. It is often at great cost to men to be pressured to achieve, to assume responsibility for family members, to be in constant competition to excel, and to be unable to shed tears and express themselves emotionally.

The traditional differentiation of male-female roles has come into serious question. While androgyny, or a society with no gender role differentiation, has not been achieved in full, pressures exist in this direction, (note insert). Nonfamilial roles available to women, an increasing egalitarian emphasis in intimate family and nonfamily relationships, changing beliefs in both work and play, and changes in patterns of socialization and education are leading to increased alternatives for males and females as to appropriate attitudes and behavior. While the labels may vary—androgyny, unisex,

---

38. Greer Litton-Fox, "Nice-Girl": The Behavioral Legacy of a Value Construct." Paper presented at the 1973 annual meeting of the National Council on Family Relations, Toronto, October 16–20, 1973.

39. For an excellent treatment of this, see Suzanne Keller, "Male and Female: A Sociological View," University Programs Modular Studies (Morristown, N. J.: General Learning Press, 1975).

desegregation, new neuter—the message is similar: men and women are increasingly pursuing their similarities, experiencing the thrill of escaping from traditional gender role stereotypes, and choosing to behave as persons rather than as male or female. Both sexes are increasingly behaving in ways that are instrumental as well as expressive, assertive as well as yielding, and masculine as well as feminine. Bem[40] argues that the androgynous individual should be able to remain sensitive to the changing constraints of the situation and engage in whatever behavior seems most effective at the moment, regardless of its stereotype as appropriate for one sex or the other.

Evidence does indicate an increasing acceptance of androgyny as a life style.[41] As discussed in other chapters, women's participation in the world of paid employment is increasing, household responsibilities by husbands and wives are increasingly shared, alternative marital styles are gaining in acceptance, variations in child-rearing patterns are becoming more common, and both sexes are increasingly thinking and behaving in ways traditionally linked to the opposite sex. Thus change is taking place from gender role differentiation to androgyny. These changes are more fully described, particularly in chapters 5, 11, 15, 17, 18, and 19.

From Orderly Replacement to Universal Permanent Availability

A fifth ideal-type model of family change, one of a more global nature, is provided by Bernard Farber.[42] His basic approach involves an attempt to explain why a particular form of family life is sustained or changed. That is, how is the persistence of the family institution from one generation to another maintained, and what factors determine whether one generation will be a duplication of the previous generation? It is his contention that the family is moving from orderly replacement to universal permanent availability. Let us briefly examine these two polar extremes.

Orderly Replacement

The concept orderly replacement suggests that each family of orientation must be organized to produce in its children's families of procreation patterns of norms and values identical to its own. This organization of family life implies that:

40. Sandra L. Bem, "Sex Role Adaptability: One Consequence of Psychological Androgyny." *Journal of Personality and Social Psychology* 31 (April 1975) pp. 634–643.

41. Jay D. Osofsky and Howard J. Osofsky, "Androgyny as a Life Style," *The Family Coordinator* 21 (October 1972), pp. 411–418.

42. Bernard Farber, *Family Organization and Interaction* (San Francisco: Chandler, 1964), Chapters 1 and 4.

New Rule Helps Women Get Credit

Washington—(AP)—A woman is entitled to her own credit identity under U.S. law, so couples with joint credit accounts will soon be invited to have their financial information recorded under both names.

A Federal Reserve Board rule that took effect Wednesday requires credit companies to record information about a married couple in the name of both the wife and the husband when requested.

The rule is designed to aid women who become divorced or widowed or who want their own accounts.

"If a married woman gets divorced or widowed and tries to open a new account, it's very, very hard to do," a Federal Reserve Board spokesman said. "She has no credit identity, so this is an attempt to rectify this situation."

Asked if the rule might cause a dispute among some couples, the spokesman said, "That's a family matter."

The new rule is a result of a 1974 law banning discrimination by marital status in the granting of credit. The Federal Reserve Board, which sets monetary policy, was instructed by Congress to write the regulation.

Under the rule, credit card companies and some big merchants will mail out letters with their bills in the next few months describing rights under the Equal Credit Opportunity Act.

"If your account with us is one that both husband and wife signed for or is an account that is being used by one of you who did not sign, then you are entitled to have us report credit information relating to the account in both your names," the letter says.

"If you choose to have credit information concerning your account with us reported in both your names, please fill in and sign the statement below and return it to us."

The letter goes on: "Federal regulations provide that signing your name below will not change or increase your or your spouse's legal liability on the account."

The form can be returned to the credit company with the signature of either spouse.

Source: *Detroit Free Press*, June 2, 1977, p. 12–A. Reprinted by permission of The Associated Press.

1. Values and norms relating to patterns and behavior in the family remain constant from one generation to the next.
2. Socialization of children is aimed at making children duplicates of their parents as these children achieve adulthood.
3. Because of its part in duplicating succeeding generations, the family and its auxiliary kinship system do not initiate change in society; the family is a force for conservatism in social arrangements.[43]

To maintain constancy from one generation to the next, the system must be closed:

- The family institution and the society have to be completely isolated from outside contacts.
- The members have to be in intimate communication with one another based on an oral tradition.

---

43. Ibid., p. 105.

- The group contacts have to be of an intimate and primary nature.
- Only one set of rules could be followed.
- The norms, rules, and values of family life have to be regarded as sacred.
- There has to be a slow turnover of family members in terms of persons entering or leaving the nuclear family.
- Close emotional ties need to exist between parents and their children or between the generations.

Given this type of closed system, the probability would be very great that there would be orderly replacement of one generation by the next to carry on the family culture.

Farber suggests that within such a closed system various controls would have to be instituted for the family system to retain its constancy.[44] First, constancy could be maintained most efficiently if an individual outside the particular nuclear family, such as the patriarch in a patrilineal society or mother's brother in a matrilineal society, were given authority and responsibility for judging and directing replacement within the family. Second, marriage would be restricted to individuals who come from families with identical norms and values of family behavior. Third, authority would be time based rather than skill based, with older generations in authority.

Universal Permanent Availability

In contrast to the orderly replacement concept, the universal permanent availability concept suggests that individuals become available for marriage with anyone at anytime. Given a bilineal type of system (in contrast to patrilineal or matrilineal), homogamous social characteristics decline in importance (exogamy occurs) and marriage becomes a personal rather than a kinship problem. Thus, love marriages rather than arranged marriages become prevalent, the rates of divorce and remarriage increase, the number of children decline, less emphasis is placed on premarital chastity and marital fidelity, emphasis is placed on competence and interpersonal relations, more married women enter the work force, and youth and glamor are emphasized.

In the words of Farber, the family operating in terms of universal permanent availability of individuals as potential mates can be expected to have the following characteristics:

- The family group takes the form of a voluntary association in which a person continues membership as long as his personal commitments to the other family members exceed his commitments elsewhere.
- If the individual is to sustain a high desirability as a potential mate, he is mo-

---

44. Ibid., p. 105.

tivated to develop and maintain certain personal skills and attributes enhancing his ability to perform activities and his appeal to members of the opposite sex.

- The socialization of children will be aimed at maximizing their market position in permanent availability. . . . The child is required to develop (a) a pleasing personality, (b) competence in interpersonal relations, (c) a pleasant appearance, (d) occupational skill regardless of sex.

- Having children is a voluntary pledge by the parents to maintain their marital relationship. . . . The presence of children diminishes flexibility in changing marriage partners.

- Without temporal or marital-status restrictions on availability, neither premarital chastity nor marital fidelity has bearing on availability as a potential mate.

- Since neither time nor prior marriage (including current marriage status) reduces the availability of the individual as a potential mate, there is no incentive to delay marriage.[45]

Since both orderly replacement and universal permanent availability are polar extremes, no society is likely to be totally closed and exclusively unilineal (as in orderly replacement), nor is any society expected to be totally open and exclusively bilineal (as in universal permanent availability). Conflict between these two polar constructs will be a continuing one because, in reality, 1) each nuclear family is to some extent a closed system isolated from other families, and 2) some restrictions do exist in regard to availability as a mate even in bilateral systems.[46] It is Farber's contention that the conflict will tend to be resolved in favor of permanent availability.

That change in American society is occurring in this direction may be evidenced by the increase in interfaith and interracial marriages, the unmarried cohabitation arrangements, group marriages, communal families, the increasing sale of wigs, cosmetics, and beauty aids to maintain youthfulness and glamour, the emphasis (particularly by women) to remain slim and never to become older than thirty-nine, the increase in "swinging" and sexual permissiveness among both married and single, and the value placed on controlling family size as well as preventing pregnancy from occurring at all. Perhaps the women's movement in general, stressing equal pay and equal status with the male sex, contributes to availability as a potential spouse. From the perspective of permanent availability, even the married woman who is not consciously looking for a spouse inadvertently may be "keeping in shape" (or "keeping up her resale values") in case the contingency arises.[47]

These five ideal-type constructs, from institution to companionship, from traditional to developmental, from entrepreneurial to bureaucratic,

45. Ibid., pp. 110–112.
46. Ibid., pp. 109–110.
47. Ibid., p. 119.

Women and Flirting Behavior

All women are a bunch of flirts. Well, almost all. According to recent research conducted by West German psychologist Susanne Rodrian, nearly all women between 16 and 50 like to flirt. "It is the solitary acceptable form in which they can seize the initiative from the man," said Dr. Rodrian.

Up to age 20, reports Dr. Rodrian, girls flirt "mainly as a form of curiosity, often unconsciously." By the time married women reach 30, flirting becomes for them "a form of revenge against their husbands." After age 40, said Dr. Rodrian, females continue to flirt because they want "to see whether they're still interesting enough to have a chance."

Source: *Sexology* 39 (September 1972), p. 55. Reprinted by permission.

from gender role differentiation to androgyny and from orderly replacement to universal permanent availability, parallel one another in their central idea of change. Each suggests that a major shift has taken place in the family system from an adherence to traditional, authoritarian, community, kin-group, and informal control to a more individualistic, equalitarian, formal type of control. How are these or other changes explained? What factors or events are most central in causing a modification in attitudes or behaviors related to marital and family life.

Sociological literature contains a wide variety of writings that stress a single "prime mover" to account for and explain variations over time in the marriage and family system. These accounts are not theories of family or social change but are unifactorial hypotheses.[48] In other words, they assert that family or social change has been shaped or caused primarily by one great factor. Although not complete in and of themselves, they do add significantly to our understanding and explaining of family change.

Let us take a brief look at some of these monocausative and unifactorial explanations of social change.

MONOCAUSATIVE EXPLANATIONS OF FAMILY CHANGE

The Geographical Factor

Some early attempts to explain family organization and behavior were in terms of geographical factors: climate, topography, resources, location, and so on. Obviously, all families are always located at a certain place, and the nature of this place will influence the activities of the family. Changes in

48. William J. Goode, *The Family* (Englewood Cliffs, N. J.: Prentice-Hall, 1964). pp. 104–105.

geographical conditions will lead to changes in the family. An earthquake in California, a flood in Louisiana, or polluted air in New York City will likely produce certain changes in attitudes and behavior of family members who reside in these areas.

The Demographic Factor

Sometimes demographic factors are used to explain change in families. Demography, the statistical study of populations, their size, distribution, and composition, is concerned with such matters as the changes over time in fertility, mortality, and migration. In addition, demographers have long been interested in fertility differentials, age distributions, regional differences, ethnic compositions, sex ratios, rural-urban differences, and mortality rates, as well as immigration and emigration.

Throughout history, any significant increase or decrease in the population has tended to modify patterns of family life. A rapid population growth poses problems such as adequate food supplies, job opportunities, schools, and housing. A major decline in population poses problems of keeping the social institutions going, of defense, of marriage, or of sufficient income. Particularly since World War II, and particularly as related to developing nations, the population explosion and the immigration to urban centers has been used to explain everything from family discord to environmental pollution. A demographic explanation of change leaves many questions unanswered but should not be ignored or overlooked.

The Economic Factor

One of the most widely used explanations of change in families has been an economic one. Basic to most families is a sufficient money supply, jobs, availability of goods and services, and the like. As noted in Chapter 2, the social conflict frame of reference as illustrated by Marx was based on economic determinism. Change would be brought about as the workers (the proletariat), who are exploited by the owners (the bourgeoisie), develop a strong feeling of solidarity and overthrow the capitalist class. The final outcome of the class struggle would be the emergence of a classless society. In regard to the family, Marx and Engels believed that change was determined by the modification of property relations.[49] Private ownership of property leads to the enslavement of women and the treatment of children as economic goods.

Whether one agrees or disagrees with Marx's interpretation, the effect of economic factors cannot be overlooked. Note what happens to divorce

---

49. Frederick Engels, *The Origin of the Family, Private Property and the State* (Chicago: C. H. Curr, 1902).

It Takes Money

What poor families need most is more money. This truism, however, is not always clear to social service agencies, who believe (or hope) they can work miracles with casework. But Irene Olson, director of the Baltimore County Department of Social Services, believes that welfare mothers whose grants are too small to pay the rent or buy enough food for the month cannot be salvaged by casework, however well intentioned (Child Welfare, February 1970).

To find out what a more adequate grant could mean to the welfare of its clients, the Baltimore County Department of Social Services began an experiment in July 1966. The agency gave its regular grant ($1,987 for a family of four, on the average) to half of a sample of 150 Aid For Dependent Children cases and gave a higher grant ($3,400 for a family of four) to the other half. It assigned half the families on the higher grants to inexperienced social workers and the other high grant families to workers with Master of Social Work degrees and at least four years of experience. The regular grant families were divided between the two groups of workers in the same way.

Each family was interviewed by an outside research firm one month after the grant began, and 131 of them were interviewed again six months afterwards. The families who seemed to be in the best shape were the 32 families with higher grants and inexperienced social workers. Almost all reported they were getting enough to eat and never had to go without food for a whole day or longer—a

reasonable measure of the adequacy of their grant and their ability to make it last out the month. They worried less than any of the others about money and felt better able to manage what they had. They spent more time improving their homes, were more likely to see a doctor regularly, and more of them said they were happy and involved with friends and relatives. The 34 cases with higher grants and experienced workers also did well: they were adequately fed, went about their daily tasks, and their morale was high.

The families on the regular grants, even those who had the help of experienced workers, could not meet these standards. Nothing an experienced worker could suggest seemed to help these clients in getting enough to eat, and many reported they had been without food for a day or longer. They worried about money and had great difficulty managing what they had. Many had withdrawn from their friends and from all participation in the community.

Most of the mothers in this study were young white women whose husbands had deserted them, leaving them with two or three young children to bring up. Almost all said they would like to work if they could, and half had tried to support themselves before they turned to welfare. They are women who try to bring up their children responsibly. It is a tragic waste of human potential, Olson concludes, to offer these women grants so niggardly they are driven to despair and withdrawal. It is a waste that no amount of skilled social work can remedy.

Source: "Roundup," *Trans-Action* 7 (September 1970), p. 8. Reprinted by permission.

rates in periods of depression or prosperity. Note differences in family size, place of residence, or spending patterns by income. As with other monocausative explanations of change, economic factors alone are hardly sufficient but need to be recognized.

The Technological Factor

Related to an economic explanation of change in families is a technological explanation. Technology consists of the application of knowledge and beliefs into action that aims to transform material things, psychological states, or social phenomena.[50] There is a technology of teaching as well as a technology of making automobiles. The technological explanation of change has been most clearly enunciated by William F. Ogburn.[51] In the 1920s he noted that material aspects of culture tend to soar ahead in their rate of change, while norms, values, and patterns of social organization (nonmaterial aspects) change much more slowly. The result of such differing rates of change he termed *cultural lag*.[52] For example, he claimed that the invention of the self-starter in automobiles had something to do with the emancipation of women. Had it not been for the self-starter, the "weaker sex" would have been unable to use the automobile on terms equal with men and thus would have had to remain in the home. Some other changes, such as the utilization of electricity, which led to the invention of labor-saving devices in the home, had a major effect in changing the role of the wife. Similarly, Ogburn suggests that the invention of the elevator, which made possible the construction of tall apartment buildings (in which it is difficult to rear children), had a depressing effect on the urban birth rate.[53]

50. Robin M. Williams, Jr., *American Society: A Sociological Interpretation* 3d ed. (New York: Alfred A. Knopf, 1970), p. 27.
51. William F. Ogburn, *Social Change* (New York: Huebach, 1923); and William F. Ogburn and Meyer F. Nimkoff, *Technology and the Changing Family* (Boston: Houghton Mifflin, 1955).
52. Ogburn, op. cit., pp. 200–237.
53. William F. Ogburn, *Machines and Tomorrow's World*, rev. ed., Public Affairs Pamphlets, no. 25, 1946, p. 6.

Pill Takers Better Workers

In a survey of 825 women, an Australian, Dr. Margaret Raphael, found that women on the Pill were out sick 4.7 days a year compared to 5.6 days missed by women not on the Pill. Also, fewer Pill-takers were off on workmen's compensation: They took an average 5.3 days compared to the non-Pill-takers, who averaged 12.1 days lost.

Of the women surveyed, 321 had been using the Pill at least six months. Almost all of them agreed that their efficiency at work was either unchanged or improved.

Dr. Raphael noted that women using oral contraceptives seemed to have fewer complaints of menstrual distress, and were less accident-prone than the nonusers.

Source: *Sexology* 39 (September 1972), p. 56. Reprinted by permission.

The Cultural-Contact Explanation:
Borrowing and Diffusion

A cultural-contact hypothesis suggests that major changes occur in a society and thus in the family within that society as a result of intersocietal contact and a diffusion of social elements from one society to another. It assumes that societies in isolation tend to be more closed and have family systems that are more stable and unchanging. Would Japanese teen-agers be wearing miniskirts while their grandmothers are wearing kimonos if contact with the Western World had not occurred? Would the worldwide distribution of Coca-Cola have come into existence without mass transportation and the advertising media? The assumption is that when people with divergent backgrounds come into contact with one another, people will borrow certain cultural elements from the other.

Today, U.S. citizens make extensive use of coffee from Brazil, silk from India, sugar from the Philippines, and silver from Africa. But in addition to material aspects, values, language, and behavior patterns are transmitted as well. The mass media brings us instantaneously into contact with persons and ideas different from our own. Diversity of life and family styles will increase as multiple patterns of behavior are diffused.

Social Movements

Most of the theories of change described thus far come about gradually and without any conscious or deliberate effort. However, a social-movement theory of change in the family system focuses upon a conscious effort of a number of people who feel dissatisfied with some aspect of their social structure for preventing them from achieving something they want. As they interact, they become aware that their feeling is not an isolated one but is shared by others who occupy similar positions. They come to common understandings that their needs can be satisfied by making certain changes in the social structure. As their ideas are publicized, if support exists, a process of public opinion formation occurs in which larger numbers of persons believe that change can be activated. At first, the movement may be very amorphous; later it may take on organization, a division of labor, rules, traditions, and a hierarchy of social values.[54]

Social movements are only likely to take place in societies that are already in the process of change and to some extent disorganized. Where social disorganization occurs, alienation and anomie, with symptoms of powerlessness, insecurity, restlessness, and suggestability, are widespread.

---

54. Arnold M. Rose and Carolyn B. Rose, *Sociology: The Study of Human Relations*, 3d ed. (New York: Alfred A. Knopf, 1969), p. 524.

Such a setting is ideal for the appearance and growth of social movements. Consistent with the individual's lack of integration into his society is the subjective evaluation that social injustice pervades. This injustice provides the issue or issues around which to establish a social movement.

Marriage and a family often deter participation in social movements. Both sexes are likely to lose the urge to "man the barricades" when presented with mortgages, diapers, and family responsibilities. The more radical the movement, the more likely the members are single or estranged from their families. The more extreme and unpopular the cause, the more strongly do family ties discourage one's participation.

In the United States, the women's movement is an organized attempt to initiate change within and outside the family system. Basically, the movement seeks equality between the sexes and seeks to eliminate the myth that men are superior to women and to eliminate practices within our society that perpetuate the myth. The National Organization for Women (NOW) is the best known and largest organization in the movement. NOW has among its major concerns the end of discrimination against women in obtaining employment and in equal pay, changing laws that discriminate against women, equalizing educational opportunities, providing child-care, facilities and the like.

At a more local level, thousands of professional, community, and education groups perceive themselves to be a part of the movement but engage in activities more specifically related to their profession or community. Some groups get together for "consciousness raising" or general discussion. These groups are generally autonomous of one another but basically agree that the institutions of our society, including the family, are male dominated, female oppressive, and in need of change.

The women's movement, like other movements, emerged from sociohistorical conditions of dissatisfaction and strain. It started out as a vague expression of a fundamental search for new directions. With the aid of writers such as Margaret Mead, Simone de Beauvoir, Betty Friedan, Jessie Bernard, and others, the formation of various radical women's groups,[55] and the assistance of the mass media (TV, newspapers, magazines) in publicizing feminist thoughts and activities, the general population was awakened to the issues. Over time, the movement became accepted as fact rather than a passing fad and today many women's activities and groups are highly institutionalized. While not solely a movement to change families, the impact of the women's movement on the social expectations, behaviors, and relationships of husbands, wives, and children is of significance.

---

55. Examples are the Redstockings, SCUM (Society for Cutting Up Men), WITCH (Women's International Terrorist Conspiracy from Hell), the Feminists, and New York Radical Women. Some would also include various left-wing political groups that subscribe to a basically Marxian analysis of society: International Socialists, Socialist Workers Party, Radical sociologists, and the like.

Louise: Some women seem to want to paint themselves as being subjugated to the men, under the rule of a man, having second-class citizenship. That is so often thrown up. I've debated with women on this issue. They have said, we don't have equal rights under the Constitution. We are second-class citizens. And yet, if I ask them to pinpoint where it says that or how that is worked through today, they really can't do it. It's like an emotional thing they want to keep throwing up. And yet, I know as I came of age, I could do anything I wanted to do. Anything I had the talent or the energy or the ambition or the money to do. And that was also true for all of my married life. I had joint ownership of all of our property. I had an account of my own when I started working. My husband said if you're earning the money, you be responsible for it too. He insisted I start my own bank account.

I just wonder how these women were socialized. Where do they come from? Are they just looking for a scapegoat to cover up their own deficiencies. If they aren't what they want to be today, are they looking for someone else to blame instead of themselves? Or are they the kind that are just never content. There are an awful lot like that around. The women's movement kind of gives them a platform for speaking out against things they could easily have corrected themselves in their lives. However, I definitely feel that women that do the same job as a man deserve the same pay. I think any woman who is qualified for a job ought to get the same as a man. I believe that a woman ought to have the same education that a man gets if that's what she wants. I have observed with my own generation and my daughter's also that their goals are different in education. My daughter, definitely, and my daughter-in-law could have any education they wanted and they have gone into more traditional women's roles. They were not restricted at all by their family structure or by society. They could just as well have gone into engineering, I'm sure, if that's what they wanted. My point is that I see the world as wide open—at least in America—to women, and I don't have too much sympathy with some of their goals. Any goal that assures equality of treatment in all situations in the business world, I favor. However, I do not favor the Equal Rights Amendment because I see that as viewing men and women as exactly the same and that is idiotic. We aren't the same.

Ann: I really don't have strong feelings about the woman's movement. I mean, oh well, maybe I do. I think she does have the right to bitch. She's treated as a second-class person. She's not treated like she's a person and unless she's with a man, she's a nobody really. If you think about it, really that's the way we've been treated. But until someone says it no one will really be aware of it. Till it was brought out, the women really weren't unhappy, were they? They didn't get unhappy till it said hey, you're a second-rate citizen. You can't get a charge account in your name if you're not married. What the hell, I make more than my husband does.

Other Change Factors

The list of factors influential in the change of family structures and functions is by no means complete. As indicated, many "theories" of family change or, perhaps more realistically, "unifactorial hypotheses" of family change, assert that change has been shaped or caused primarily by a single great factor. Many other key factors could be listed. Max Weber emphasized the importance of religion and value systems.[56] More specifically he emphasized the *ideological factor* (the role of ideas) as powerful motivating forces in changing people.

Many textbooks stress the role of *"great men."* In the Western world few charismatic leaders had as great an impact on family values and norms as did Christ and perhaps the apostle Paul. In much of Africa and Asia few charismatic leaders changed the course of family patterns as much as Muhammad. Apart from religious leaders, would the Russian family be what it is today without the reign of Stalin? Would the German family be different had it not known a Hitler? Would the American family be as it is without a Lincoln, or a Roosevelt?

Other explanations of change in families stress *military factors*. If change is considered by historians, perhaps it is explained primarily by the story of battles and skirmishes, of victories and defeats, of dynasties and wars. Obviously a high death rate among potential or current husbands as a result of war affects the sex ratio and the family system. Who is to deny the change brought about in U.S. families as a result of World War II and in Vietnamese families as a result of the military confrontation of the 1960s and 1970s? But this explanation, like other unifactorial explanations, suffers from many inadequacies.

In some instances *law* is seen as an effective means of change or prevention of change. As states and countries legalize abortion, will birth rates and sexual norms change? If states raise the legal age for marriage, will fewer people marry and divorce rates drop? It has been suggested (basically erroneously) that it is the law, in western culture that permits the innovator to function effectively.

A final theory of family change stresses *psychological and individual motivation*. It is often assumed, again basically erroneously, that change is due to the decision making of each individual apart from all other forces taking place in society. Perhaps many students reading this will strongly defend the idea that they alone make the choice as to how to treat their wives, bed mates, or sweethearts (whether the same or different persons). As any psychologist will tell you, individual motivation is usually a complex matter. As with family change, seldom can we find a single cause for the behavior of a given individual. However, it should be noted that a person who becomes too

---

56. Max Weber, *The Protestant Ethic and the Spirit of Capitalism*, trans. Talcott Parsons. London: George Allen & Unwin, 1930.

innovative in his behavior and either over- or underconforming in his relationships with others maybe confronting a psychiatrist or hospital staff in due time.

Summary

Various attempts have been made to explain family change, including grand
evolutionary theories that encompass all of time and space, less grandiose
theories that encompass specific periods and locales, and partial theories that
examine one particular societal phenomenon. Examples of each are provided
in this chapter.

In the nineteenth and twentieth centuries evolutionary theory dominated thought on family change. Generally these explanations assumed that
change was unilinear, always moving toward an "improved" system. Thus,
if promiscuity is viewed as the least-developed and lowest form of marital and
mating practice, with time families would move toward group arrangements,
then toward one woman marrying several men, to one man marrying several
women, and finally to one man marrying one woman. This final stage, monogamy, was seen as the highest and most advanced form of marital structure.
For this progression to occur, it became essential that man not interfere with
the "natural selection" of those most fit to mate and survive. As might be
expected, these grand theories, without exception, have been widely criticized
on many counts, one being the lack of empirical data to support them.

A refinement of the unilinear evolutionary explanation of family
change was provided by Zimmerman who saw change as occurring in giant
historical cycles. The change was based on the modification of man's ideas
according to the amount of power held by the family in relation to the rest of
society. Based on this power dimension, three major family types could exist:
the trustee, the domestic, or the atomistic. The trustee family has the most
power and the greatest amount of social control over its members. The
domestic family divides power among the state, the church, and the individual. The atomistic family places the social power and responsibility on the
individual who alone is accountable to the state and to others.

As was used in Chapter 1, ideal-type constructs are again used as the
tool to deal with five major trends in family orientation. Four could be classified as generally descriptive, whereas the fifth could be classified as a theory
of change in the family system. Although formulated independently, all
portray a similar theme: a shift from informal, authoritative community and
kin controls to a more formal, individualistic type of control.

The change from an institutional family system to a companionship
family system signifies a change from an extended patriarchal form of family
to a more nuclear democratic form. The change from traditional to developmental implies a change from the more rigid authoritarian parent to an
emphasis on sharing, self-expression, and personal growth and development.
The change from entrepreneurial to bureaucratic, while seemingly contra-

dictory with the other constructs presented, is basically a shift from family and kin controls to large-scale organizational controls. The change from gender role differentiation to androgyny is basically a shift from distinct and separate marital expectations and behaviors based on sex to a society that has few differentiated roles based on sex. The change from orderly replacement to universal permanent availability suggests a change from a stable, closed, constant family system from one generation to the next to a flexible, open, and variable form of family and marriage. These five general constructs indicate polar extremes that contrast the most traditional, authoritarian, stable family system with an extremely democratic or individualistic, flexible family system.

A wide range of explanations of family change focus on single dimensions as of prime importance. Some early attempts to explain modifications in family systems and groups include geographic factors such as climate topography, resources, location, and the like. Others base their explanations on demographic factors, including changes in fertility, mortality, and migration.

Perhaps the most widely used single-factor explanation of change is the economic. Economic determinism was basic to the theory of Karl Marx, who attempted to account for social change in terms of the relationship between people and the means of production. Related to the economic factor is the technological factor.

Change in family systems has also been explained by the borrowing and diffusion that result from intercultural contact. Closed systems, having little contact with others, tend to change very slowly. Open systems and societies where mass media or transportation systems permit rapid exposure to new ideas and ways of life tend to change rapidly. The one explanation of change that is conscious and deliberate centers around social movements. Social movements involve a collective effort toward effective change by persons dissatisfied with something that exists. Of interest in the family area is the women's movement, an organized attempt to modify male-female roles.

Many other explanations of change exist. Religion, great men, wars, laws, and a wide range of psychologies have been offered to explain family behavior variations, change in family groups, and change in the family institution. None appears adequate to explain change at all levels in all societies, but each makes a contribution to our understanding.

Key Terms and Concepts

Discussion Questions

1. *What are some of the pros and cons of an evolutionary idea of family change?*

2. *Why are social scientists hesitant to refer to change as progress?*

3. *Do you agree with Zimmerman's types of families? Are we an atomistic-type family today? Does this mean nihilism, disruption, and a downfall of American society?*

4. *Is it possible for a single society to have trustee, domestic, and atomistic family types all at the same time? How is it possible? What conflicts or consequences are likely to result?*

5. *What evidence exists to support the theory that the U.S. is moving from gender role differentiation to androgyny? What evidence exists to the contrary?*

6. *Do you believe that all persons (married, aged, poor, male, female) are potentially available spouses? What categories of persons are less available or less desirable?*

7. *Which monocausative explanation of change seems most plausible to explain the changes occurring in the American family today?*

8. *What effect does the theory of change which you adhere to affect your willingness to initiate or prevent change? Your satisfaction with the status quo? How does your geographical location, amount of wealth, or family status affect your response?*

9. *List several "great" persons in history. Were they persons who achieved greatness by promoting changes or by preventing changes? What, if any, effect did their lives have on the family system of their time?*

10. *Explain why the trend in the world has been toward monogamy and away from polygyny? Why are plural spouses illegal in all states in the United States? Would not polygyny be functional for certain groups (such as the aged) in our society? Which theory or theories of change best explain the process for the elimination or the addition of a polygynous family system to a society?*

11. *Would you agree that the women's movement has been more successful than the gay movement? Why or why not? How do you explain the success of certain social movements and the strong resistance to others?*

12. *Establish a model of the "ideal family system(s)" in American society. What explanations or conditions of change would be necessary to achieve that result?*

Further Readings

Appelbaum, Richard P. *Theories of Social Change.* Chicago: Markham, 1970. A brief paperback summarizing evolutionary, equilibrium, conflict, and rise and fall theories of social change.

Burgess, Ernest W., Harvey J. Locke, and **Mary Margaret Thomes.** *The Family.* 3d ed. New York: American Book, 1963. Explores the theme of the American family as in a transition from an institutional to a companionship form.

Calhoun, Arthur W. *A Social History of the American Family.* Cleveland: Arthur H. Clark, Company, Vol. I, 1917; Vol. II, 1918; and Vol. III, 1919. Volume I presents a history of the American family during the colonial period. Volume II covers the period from independence through the Civil War and Volume III covers the period between the Civil War and World War I.

Carr, Gwen B., ed. *Marriage and Family in a Decade of Change.* Reading, Mass.: Addison-Wesley, 1972. A brief book of readings with the goal of examining the needs and values of the individual and comparing these needs with what the present culture offers in the way of meeting them.

Edwards, John N., ed. *The Family and Change.* New York: Alfred A. Knopf, 1969. One of the best collections of articles that deal with this subject.

Eshleman, J. Ross. *Perspectives in Marriage and the Family.* Boston: Allyn and Bacon, 1969. Chapter 2 deals with the American family in the process of change.

Farber, Bernard. *Family Organization and Interaction.* San Francisco: Chandler, 1964. A book that concentrates on the explanation of stability and change in the family. Chapter 4 presents the orderly replacement—universal permanent availability model of change.

Ferriss, Abbott L. *Indicators of Change in the American Family.* New York: Russell Sage Foundation, 1970. A compilation from published government sources of changes in marriage rates, marital status, households, fertility, dependency, divorce, work and income, and poverty in America.

Goode, William J. "The Theory and Measurement of Family Change." In Eleanor B. Sheldon and Wilbert E. Moore, *Indicators of Social Change.* New York: Russell Sage Foundation, 1968, pp. 295–348. For the more serious student of change, an excellent source covering the types of problems in dealing with family change and the types of units to be observed.

Gordon, Michael, ed. *The American Family in Social-Historical Perspective.* New York: St. Martin's Press, 1973. A social history of the American family from the colonial era to the turn of the twentieth century. Areas covered include aspects of domestic life, childhood and youth, women's roles and relationships, sex behavior and ideology, and demographic trends.

Ogburn, William F., and **Meyer F. Nimkoff.** *Technology and the Changing Family.* Boston: Houghton Mifflin, 1955. One of a series of books by Ogburn on social change.

Zimmerman, Carle C. *Family and Civilization.* New York: Harper, 1947. Examines the role of the family in Western civilization and presents the trustee, domestic, and atomistic typology of families.

Part II

Family Life-Styles: Structural and Subcultural Variations

5

Variant Marital and
Family Life-Styles

5

Part I of this book (Chapters 1–4) was intended to provide an overview of families in the United States and around the world. Discussed were characteristics and issues of the U.S. family, theoretical and disciplinary approaches to family study, understanding the family as a social institution, clarifying key conceptual distinctions and recognizing and analyzing change. The observant reader has already noted the tremendous amount of variability in marital and family life-styles both in the U.S. and in other countries. Thus, in a sense, Part II is an extension of the variant approaches, forms and marital life-styles previously covered. However, this section will examine selected variations in the structure or organization of marriages and families and present examples of cultural and subcultural family forms that differ from the more traditional nuclear patterns.

Use of the word "variant" is meant to convey simply differences in styles of living, not improper, deviant or unethical styles. While given individuals may not approve of more than one spouse, would not choose to live among the Amish, or have negative reactions to the unmarried parent, the author is treating family forms and behavioral variations from the perspective of the social scientist. Personal preferences become secondary in an attempt to understand and analyze marital and family forms and life-styles that may be somewhat at variance with our own value systems.

As will become evident upon reading this and the other chapters in Part II, differences in family forms and life-styles could cover every imaginable topic: number of spouses, relationship with kin, patterns of rearing children, legal factors, sexual behavior, equality between the sexes, ad infinitum. Some variations from the traditional nuclear family form such as single-parent families, gay relationships, or consensual adultery are discussed in some detail later in the text. However, other topics such as retired cohabitating couples, differences in third and fourth marriages from first or second, or behaviors such as spouse beating or public exhibitionism for erotic responses are covered minimally if at all.

Apes Provide Man with Many Models for Family Structure

According to the book, Sociobiology: The New Synthesis, *the great apes, man's closest relatives, exhibit a wide variety of family structures. Author Edward Wilson says the social organization varies greatly between species of higher primates, from solitary adults and mother-offspring groups in the orangutans, to monogamous pairs and offspring in the gibbon apes, to large social groups in the baboons, gorillas, and chimpanzees. Baboons,* he states, *are organized in male-dominated harems that are zealously guarded, while gorillas live in very gentle but male-dominated societies where overt sexual behavior is very rare, and chimpanzees live in large, loosely organized groups characterized by amiable, cooperative activities and sexual promiscuity. Thus, nature provides man with many different models for family structure.*

Source: **Edward O. Wilson,** *Sociobiology: The New Synthesis* (Cambridge: Harvard University Press, 1975).

Some variant family forms are widespread and established when viewed in a world perspective. Polygyny, extended family networks, or sexual relationships with persons other than spouse, for example, can be found in most societies of the world and date prior to recorded history. Other variant family forms appear to be infrequent and rare when viewed in a world perspective: incestuous marriages, group marriage, equality between the sexes, free choice of marital partner, voluntary childless marriages, or homosexual marriages.

It has been suggested[1] that life-styles are shared tastes and preferences. Life-styles bear a relationship to and stem from subcultures, social classes, or status groups but often do not involve the degree of collective consensus or the collectively shared meanings found in subcultures or social classes. Thus, life-styles will change more readily and rapidly than social class or subcultural systems and can be studied for clues as to the direction of emerging culture. Empirically, these life-styles are revealed in economic consumption patterns, political beliefs, and moral, ethical, and aesthetic standards. Benjamin Zablocki and Rosabeth Kanter[2] suggest that the proliferation of alternative life-styles in U.S. society has been brought on by, among others, preferences for two-career families over one-career families, ethnic reidentification over assimilation, homosexual relationships over heterosexual relationships, communal living over family living, and immediate gratification over deferred gratification.

Given this background, let us turn to selected structural or organizational variations in the number of spouses. The structural-functional frame

---

1. Benjamin D. Zablocki and Rosabeth Moss Kanter, "The Differentiation of Life Styles," *Annual Review of Sociology* 2 (1976), pp. 269–298.

2. Ibid., p. 269.

of reference (see Chapter 2) leads us to assume that if the structure or form varies or differs, the functions or consequences—including life-styles—will differ as well.

VARIATIONS IN MARRIAGE AND NUMBER OF SPOUSES

Marital status (single, married, separated, widowed, divorced) and number of spouses (none, one, more than one) are two major components of, and influences on, life-style. With variations such as these come variations in marital interaction patterns, living and sleeping arrangements, exclusive or nonexclusive sexual interactions in marriage, the likelihood of and number of children, patterns of support, decision making and authority, and male-female roles, to mention a few. Obviously, never to have had a spouse is to have a nonmarital status and a distinctive life-style.

Singlehood

According to U.S. Census data,[3] in 1976, 29.8 percent of males and 23.0 percent of females fourteen years and over were single (never married). Since 1960, the percentage of those remaining single has risen sharply for persons under thirty-five years of age. The increase in the percentage that are single is particularly apparent in the age groups where most men and women have traditionally married. At ages twenty to twenty-four years, for example, there has been a 14 percent increase in the number of single women (from 28.4 in 1960 to 42.6 in 1976) and an 11 percent increase in the number of single men (from 53.1 in 1960 to 62.1 in 1976). Whether the tendency among the younger groups to refrain from marrying represents merely a postponement of first marriage or a development of a trend toward lifelong singleness is not known. However, Paul Glick[4] states that just as cohorts of young women who have postponed childbearing for an unusually long time seldom make up for the child deficit as they grow older, so also young people who are delaying marriage may never make up for the marriage deficit later on. They may try alternatives and like them.

Apparently a new style of singlehood is emerging that represents one

---

3. U.S. Bureau of the Census, *Current Population Reports*, Series P-20, no. 306, "Marital Status and Living Arrangements: March 1976" (Washington, D.C.: U.S. Government Printing Office, 1977), Table C, p. 3.

4. Paul C. Glick, "A Demographer Looks at American Families," *Journal of Marriage and the Family* 37 (February 1975), p. 18.

of choice.[5] Traditionally, the social norm implied that single people were single, not because they wanted to be or because it was a life-style that successfully fulfilled human needs, but because they, particularly females, had no one to marry. Bachelors and spinsters or old maids were men and women respectively who were past the common age of marriage and who seemed unlikely to marry. Bachelorhood, while viewed less negatively than spinsterhood, often implied selfishness, immaturity or, in some instances, not liking women. This image is in sharp contrast to the male who was "smart enough not to get trapped" and the freedom to live a carefree blissful life of wine and women without the "burden of marriage." Seldom did the "old maid" or "spinster" concept carry similar positive images. To be an old maid was to be frustrated, unattractive, and less desirable as a person.

Available data on single males and single females show a sharp contrast to the image of a "carefree liberated" male and the frustrated female. George Gilder,[6] speaking in defense of marriage, states:

> No way of life has been more glowingly celebrated in recent years than that of the "liberated" single male. Yet the truth is that men without wives in America generally seem to have a far harder time of it than married men— living lives that tend to be not only shorter, but also more destructive, both to themselves and to society. Compared to others in the population, the single man tends to be poor and neurotic. He is much less healthy and stable than the single woman. He is disposed to criminality, drugs and violence. He is irresponsible about his debts, alcoholic, accident prone and subject to venereal disease. Unless he can marry, he is often destined to a Hobbesean life—solitary, poor, nasty, brutish, and short.

The life of the single female appears, in general, to be superior to the life of the single male. Rather than finding the frustrated old maid, Gerald Gurin et al.[7] found that single women experience less discomfort than do single men, report greater happiness, show far less expected frequency of symptoms of psychological distress, and suffer fewer neurotic and antisocial tendencies. Jessie Bernard,[8] as well, argues for the superior status of the single female when compared to the single male. The single female is less likely to have a nervous breakdown, insomnia, nightmares, and dizziness, and more likely to have a higher education and higher median income, and a greater percentage occupy a professional or managerial occupation.

In an attempt to discover who stays single, Elmer Spreitzer and Lawrence Riley[9] analyzed demographic characteristics and family-of-orien-

5. See: Roger W. Libby, "Creative Singlehood as a Sexual Life-Style: Beyond Marriage as a Rite of Passage," in Roger W. Libby and Robert N. Whitehurst, *Marriage and Alternatives: Exploring Intimate Relationships* (Glenview, Ill.: Scott, Foresman, 1977), pp. 37–61.

6. George Gilder, "In Defense of Monogamy," *Commentary* 58 (November 1974), p. 31.

7. Gerald Gurin, Joseph Veroff and Sheila Feld, *Americans View Their Mental Health* (New York: Basic Books, 1960), pp. 42, 72, 190, 110, 234–35.

8. Jessie Bernard, *The Future of Marriage* (New York: World, 1972), Chapter 3 and Tables 19 and 20.

9. Elmer Spreitzer and Lawrence E. Riley, "Factors Associated with Singlehood" *Journal of Marriage and the Family* 36 (August 1974), pp. 533–542.

tation experiences as correlates of singlehood. They found that higher intelligence, education, and occupation are conducive to singlehood among females. Poor interpersonal relations with parents and siblings in the family of orientation predisposes males to singlehood.

Stein[10] analyzed singlehood as a positive alternative to marriage by conducting in-depth interviews with single persons (more than half of whom were previously married) who intentionally made the choice to stay single. Why did they so choose? Some indicated that dependency on one's mate could not satisfy the multiple demands of self-development. Some felt that marriage, rather than singlehood, paradoxically created conditions of loneliness that they did not want to experience. Other reasons included the greater extent to which single persons have freedom, enjoyment, and opportunities to meet people and develop friendships, economic independence, more and better sexual experiences, and personal development. While not void of negative social pressures and uncertainties about their own social identity, it became clear that for these respondents, singlehood provided a situation conducive to human growth and self-fulfillment. Clearly, the marital status is not essential for all to find emotional support, sex, and an active social life. For some, it is an alternative to marriage.

Monogamy

Who would expect to find monogamy included in a chapter on variant marital life-styles? To most Americans, the least variant and the "most proper" form of marriage is monogamy: one man to one woman (at a time). This form of marriage is the only one universally recognized and is the predominant form even within societies where other forms exist. Where other forms do exist, most men are too poor to have more than one wife. However, it should be noted that on a societal basis, only about 20 percent of the societies are designated as strictly monogamous, that is, the required form.[11]

10. Peter J. Stein, "Singlehood: An Alternative to Marriage," *The Family Coordinator* 24 (October 1975), p. 489–503; and Peter J. Stein, *Single* (Englewood Cliffs, N. J.: Prentice-Hall, 1976).

11. George P. Murdock, "World Ethnographic Sample," *American Anthropologist* 59 (August 1957), p. 686.

The Name of the Bride

When a woman in the United States marries, the chances are very high that she will take the surname of the husband. Is this a matter of law or social tradition? Apparently social custom and tradition prevail.

According to a comment in Parade *(No-*

vember 9, 1975), in forty-nine of our states, the bride has a right to use any name she wishes and to maintain her own identity. Only in Hawaii does a law exist that requires the wife to assume the husband's name.

In the United States, although designated as strictly monogamous, it is possible to have more than one husband or one wife. Since monogamy has never achieved perfect stability, certain married persons end their relationship and most of these remarry. Thus, the second spouse, although not existing simultaneously with the first, is sometimes referred to as fitting into a pattern of *sequential monogamy* or *serial monogamy*. Thus, in American society it is both legally and socially approved to have more than one wife or more than one husband as long as they occur sequentially and not simultaneously. To a sizable proportion of our population, the replacing of marriage partners in a sequentially monogamous fashion is a variation on the lifelong, same-spouse, monogamous pattern. In addition, most variant marital life-styles occur within the context of monogamy. Swinging, childless marriages, sexual equality, dual careers, androgynous role patterns, and the like are more likely to occur in a one-male, one-female marriage than in any other type. These variant marital life-styles are discussed elsewhere throughout this book, usually as found within a monogamous situation.

Polygamy

Distinguished from monogamy is polygamy. The suffix "-gamy" refers to marriage or a union for propagation and reproduction. Thus monogamy (single), bigamy (two), polygamy (several or many), allogamy (closely related), endogamy (within), or exogamy (outside or external) describe the nature of marriage. Polygamy refers to the marriage of several or many. Theoretically, there could exist several or many wives (polygyny), several or many husbands (polyandry), or several or many husbands and wives (group marriage), all of which are polygamous marriages, as distinguished from monogamous (one) or bigamous (two) marriages.

The frequency with which the marriage of a plural number of spouses occurs normatively, i.e., as an expected or desired type of marriage, was investigated by Murdock. In a world sample of 554 societies, polygyny was culturally favored in 415 (77 percent), whereas polyandry was culturally favored in only four (less than 1 percent):[12] Toda, Marquesas, Nayar, and Tibet. There is no known society in which group marriage is clearly the dominant, or most frequent, marriage form.[13]

Several words of caution need to be suggested concerning polygamy. First, it is necessary to maintain a clear distinction between ideology and actual occurrence. Occasionally in the United States, a group advocates the right to have as many or as few spouses as one desires. Also when multiple-spouse marriages or communes are located and/or studied, the results are exploited by the mass media and given considerable attention. Perhaps it is

---

12. Ibid., p. 686.
13. William N. Stephens, *The Family in Cross-Cultural Perspective* (New York: Holt, Rinehart and Winston, 1963), p. 33.

> *Alex:*   In southern Turkey it is still practiced that you can have one legally
> married wife and still have two or three other wives. You can go to
> the temple or the Turkish mosque and the Islamic priest will marry
> you. Women never have more than one husband though. How can
> she? She is inferior, a servant.
>
> *Mac:*   My mother believes in polyandry. She's living with one man now,
> goes out with another, and both have knowledge of each other. She's
> been married at least five times and has at least nine children not
> counting what she says has been fourteen abortions.
>
> Personally, I would like to have the . . . uh . . . marriage where the
> man can have more than one wife. With my present mate, it would
> be an experiment and I think I could accept it. I feel she is free to do
> the same thing if she wanted. But, uh . . . this is against her values to
> share.

uniqueness or rarity that attracts the attention rather than commonality in
numerical terms. Second, multiple spouses (except for group marriage) are
only possible on a large scale where an unbalanced sex ratio (the number of
males per 100 females) exists. Only if the sex ratio is either high or low will
polygamy be possible without increasing the number of single persons of one
sex. Third, polygamy where it exists, like all forms of marriage, is highly
regulated and normatively controlled. Rarely does it involve a strictly personal or psychological motive. Rather it is likely to be supported by the
attitudes and values of both sexes and linked closely to the sex ratio, economic conditions, and belief systems. Polygamy involves a normative system
that includes a wide range of obligations between the spouses, children, and
wider society. Fourth, polygamy itself has many forms and variations of
normative structure that determine who the spouse should be. Examples
would be where all the multiple husbands are brothers (fraternal polyandry),
where all the multiple wives are sisters (sororal polygyny), or a levirate and
sororate arrangement as existed in the ancient Hebrew family. The levirate
was a situation (technically sequential monogamy) in which the wife married
the brother of her deceased husband, whereas the sororate was a situation in
which the preferred mate for a husband was the sister of his deceased wife.
Each of the above represents a variant family form. Polygyny and polyandry
are examined in greater detail.

Polygyny

Polygyny is the most frequent form of polygamy. It is common in
primitive societies but less so in more advanced societies, where it is the privilege of the wealthy few. Often, having several wives is a mark of prestige,

distinction, and high status. Chiefs, the wealthy, the best hunters, and the leaders get the second or third wife. Even in Israel, throughout the Old Testament biblical period, polygyny was practiced but often restricted to men who were rich, occupied leading positions, or had some other claim to distinction. Even today in the Middle East, the "common man" has to be satisfied with only one wife.

Why more than one wife? Many circumstances and motives contribute to polygyny. The prestige and status dimension has been mentioned. Sometimes there is a need or a desire to facilitate procreation, particularly male children; however, evidence also exists to show that polygyny tends to reduce fertility for groups as a whole.[14] Other reasons for polygyny may include wife capture, the economic value of wifely services, and in some instances religious revelation. The frequently cited example of Mormon polygyny originated in a religious revelation of Joseph Smith, the founder of the Mormon religion. Interestingly, some of the very factors that led to the occurrence of polygyny were the same factors that led to its being outlawed. It was begun and maintained by a devout conviction of carrying out God's will. It was ended by a revelation from God to the president of the church forbidding the continuation of polygyny.

One way in which the Christian Church stamped Western society was in this very manner—by outlawing polygyny. Polygyny was very frequent among the pre-Christian tribes of Europe as well as in the Old Testament Hebrew accounts.

> Gideon, the Israelite judge, had many wives who bore him seventy sons (Judges 8:30). Judging from the number of sons, Jair with thirty sons (Judges 10:4), Izban with thirty sons and thirty daughters (Judges 12:9), Abdon with forty sons (Judges 12:14), all judges in Israel must have had several wives each. King David had several wives (Samuel 25:39, 43; II Samuel 3:2 FF 5:13), and King Solomon, of course, had a huge number of them (I King 9:16; Song of Solomon 6:8). Also of King Rehoboam, Solomon's son, it is stated that he had eighteen wives and sixty concubines (II Chron. 11:21). Each of Rehoboam's twenty-eight sons also had many wives (II Chron. 11:23). The frequency of marriage with two women necessitated legislation with reference to the rights of their children (Deut. 21:15).[15]

Stephens notes that often polygynous women are jealous; however, this is not a universal characteristic.[16] Jealousy among plural wives, however, does seem to be considerably more frequent than jealousy among co-husbands. Several reasons may exist for this, of which one is *not* "women are naturally jealous." Rather, the greater likelihood of jealousy among co-wives

---

14. See Alfred O. Ukaegbu, "Fertility of Women in Polygynous Unions in Rural Eastern Nigeria," *Journal of Marriage and the Family* 39 (May 1977), pp. 397–404.

15. Stephens, op. cit., pp. 51–52.

16. Ibid., p. 57.

may stem from the fact that they are more frequently chosen, whereas men are more likely to do the choosing in determining whether to be a co-spouse. Having less choice in the matter of being married may contribute to a much greater potential for jealousy. In addition, it has been suggested that multiple husbands are more likely to be brothers than are co-wives. If this is the case, it is possible that jealousy would be less among siblings than among nonsiblings. However, this factor needs additional clarification.

Viewing polygyny cross-culturally, polygynous families evidence organizational features:

> 1) In certain matters, sex particularly, co-wives have clearly defined equal rights; 2) each wife is set up in a separate establishment; and 3) the senior wife is given special powers and privileges.[17]

It has been suggested that if co-wives are sisters, they usually live in the same house; if co-wives are not sisters, they usually live in separate houses. The deduction follows: For some reason, siblings can better tolerate, suppress, and live with a situation of sexual rivalry than can nonsiblings.

What about polygyny in the United States today? The most frequently cited sources of polygyny are those of certain Mormon fundamentalists living in underground polygynous family units in Utah and neighboring states. The number of these marriages is unknown. One study of group marriages in the United States included numerous triads (one male-two females or one female-two males) but these are discussed in pages that follow.

Victor Kassel, writing in *Geriatrics*, has suggested that the United States return to a practice that at one time was considered proper in the Judeo-Christian ethic, namely, a limited polygyny: polygyny after sixty. He presented ten arguments or advantages:[18]

1. *Greater ratio of older women to older men.* The need for polygyny is obvious: There are just not enough men.
2. *The family constellation.* Besides the opportunity to remarry, polygyny offers to these women the opportunity to reestablish meaningful family groups.
3. *Diet.* Studies have demonstrated that married couples subsist on a more adequate diet than do widows and widowers.
4. *Living conditions.* By pooling funds the family can live more graciously.
5. *Illness.* Many aged persons would not need nursing-home care if responsible people at home were available to nurse the infirm person.

---

17. Ibid., p. 63. Note also Joyce Sweep and Remi Clignet, "Type of Marriage and Residential Choices in an African City." *Journal of Marriage and the Family* 36 (November 1974), pp. 780–793.
18. Victor Kassel, "Polygamy after Sixty," *Geriatrics* 21 (April 1966), pp. 214–218. Also reprinted in Herbert A. Otto, ed., *The Family in Search of a Future* (New York: Appleton-Century-Crofts, 1970), pp. 138–142.

6. *Housework.* Many aged find it impossible to keep their homes in order because of the fatigue produced by the physical labor of housework. Two or more women working together lighten the burden for one another.
7. *Sex.* Various studies have misproved the misconception that older people are not interested in sexual activity. Marriage sanctions sexual activity and the polygynous marriage enables the unmarried older woman to find a partner.
8. *Grooming.* Where you have many women competing for the attention of a a lone male, both the woman and the man will show an increased interest in better grooming.
9. *Depression and loneliness.* In the practice of geriatrics, one of the major psychiatric problems encountered is depression. Depression results from loneliness and uselessness.
10. *Health insurance.* Recent years have seen the growth of group health insurance. Membership in it offers advantages over individual policy. There is no reason why group insurance should not consider the polygynous family within its coverage and charge less expensive premiums.

Polyandry

Polyandry appears to be very unusual and quite rare. Stephens makes several generalizations about polyandry.[19] First, he notes that polyandry and group marriage tend to go together: where you find one you are likely to find the other.

Second, co-husbanding is fraternal. In the few cases in which the husbands are not brothers, they are clan-brothers, that is, they belong to the same clan and are of the same generation. This factor of being brothers may reduce the likelihood of jealousy. Among the Todas, the non-Hindu tribe in India, it is understood that when a woman marries a man she becomes the wife of his brothers at the same time. In that tribe, jealousy does not seem to present difficulty, and disputes among the brothers rarely arise.

Third, an economic inducement is often mentioned. A man tries to recruit co-husbands so that they will work for him. In other instances co-husbandry is practiced for economic security or as an answer to the land shortage. When several men marry one woman, the fragmentation of holdings, especially in land, is avoided. Thus polyandry, although rare, is one device for conserving limited economic assets.

Stephens suggests that polyandrous societies resort to infanticide to "correct" the ratio of husbands to wives; apparently polygynous societies do so rarely if at all. Where polyandry is frequent, female infanticide is frequently practiced. It is a curious anomaly that male infanticide is rarely, if ever, mentioned in the literature. Female infanticide eliminates the wife surplus among polyandrous families; however, male infanticide does not seem to be used to eliminate the husband surplus in polygynous societies.

19. Stephens, op. cit., pp. 39–49.

A recent study of polyandry among a tribal group in Brazil tended to support some of the ideas just presented.[20] Polyandry was more prevalent in the tribe in earlier years when the sex ratio was very unbalanced (149 males per 100 females), female infanticide had been known to exist, and fraternal polyandry appeared to minimize family conflict. Unlike other reports, the Brazilian tribe had no marriage ceremonies for primary or secondary husbands, and property and inheritance rights were not considerations for marriage. It is interesting to note that polyandry has proved to be functional, in Brazil and elsewhere, providing adequately for family life and family identity. While perhaps rarely found throughout the world and not acceptable for most of us, it is another variation of the marital life-style.

Group Marriage

Group marriage exists when several males are married simultaneously to several females. It exists also when each of three or more participants considers themselves to be married to at least two other members of the group. Pair-bonded or multilateral marriage are substitute terms for group marriage.[21] Except on an experimental basis it is an extremely rare occurrence and may never have existed as a viable form of marriage for any society in the world. The Oneida community of New York State has been frequently cited as an example of a group marriage experiment. It involved economic and sexual sharing based on spiritual and religious principles. The Oneida group was an experimental religious community and not representative of the society. In addition, like most group marriages on record, its time span was limited. Rarely do they endure beyond one or two generations. Experiments in group marriage practices usually occur in the transitional stages of societies undergoing drastic reorganization.

Recently, there has been widespread publicity and interest in matters such as group marriage, swinging, mate swapping, cohabitation, and the like. A best seller by a Utopian novelist, Robert Rimmer, deals with two nuclear-family units that swapped marital mates sexually and later joined their families into one unit.[22] Recently, some empirical evidence on group marriage has appeared by Larry and Joan Constantine, who have spent several years of their life studying group marriage in America.

The Constantines[23] reported on multilateral marriages including three

20. John F. Peters and Chester L. Hunt, "Polyandry among the Yanomama Shirishana," *Journal of Comparative Family Studies* 6 (Autumn 1975), pp. 197–207.

21. See James W. Ramey, "Communes, Group Marriage, and the Upper Middle Class," *Journal of Marriage and the Family* 34 (November 1972), pp. 647–655.

22. Robert H. Rimmer, *Proposition Thirty-One* (New York: New American Library, 1968).

23. Larry L. and Joan M. Constantine, *Group Marriage: A Study of Contemporary Multilateral Marriage* (New York: Macmillan, 1973); and Larry L. and Joan M. Constantine, "The Group Marriage," in Michael Gordon, *The Nuclear Family in Crisis: The Search for an Alternative* (New York: Harper, 1972), pp. 204–222.

Oneida Today: A Thriving Business

The old commune's philosophy strikes a familiar chord in this day and age.

Women were granted an equal role with men in managing its affairs. Marriage was abolished, and children were looked after in a day-care center. Every day, members met in a form of group therapy, called "mutual criticism." They referred to themselves as "Bible Communists."

But the commune's spiritual orientation didn't exclude materialistic gains. In fact, it decreed that "to prosper is good."

This all transpired more than a century ago. Today, the talk around Oneida is apt to be about import quotas, dollar devaluation and market share. For that original commune, known as the Oneida Community, has prospered and evolved into Oneida Ltd., a publicly held international concern that is listed on the New York Stock Exchange and that is the nation's largest maker of stainless-steel tableware.

The social ways of the share-the-wealth commune dissolved in the late 19th-Century amid intra-commune strife and troubles with civil authorities. At the time, Oneida was an early-day conglomerate involved in the manufacture of steel animal traps, silk, fruit preserves, carpetbags, straw hats, mop handles and tableware.

"Sin No More; Repent No More." Few descendants of the original members remain with the company, but one is Pierrepont (Peter) T. Noyes. Mr. Noyes is the president of Oneida Ltd. and the 58-year-old grandson of the commune's founder, John Humphrey Noyes. John Humphrey Noyes was an ordained minister who in 1848 led a band of 80 people from Vermont in search of a new life.

The elder Mr. Noyes had concluded that the second coming of Christ had already occurred, in 70 A.D., so the millenium had arrived and it was no longer possible to follow the paths of alternate sinning and repentence. His command was: "Sin no more; repent no more; so regulate your lives to eliminate that worst of evils—selfishness."

For his grandson, the worst of evils has been unlimited imports of flatware, particularly from Japan. In the late 1960s, the U.S. eliminated quotas on stainless-steel flatware and imports soon more than quadrupled, directly affecting Oneida's business. In the fiscal year ended Jan. 29, 1972, for instance, Oneida earned $2.2 million, or $1.56 a share, on sales of $72.6 million.

Source: Stanley H. Slom, *The Wall Street Journal*, April 4, 1973, p. 12. Reprinted with permission of *The Wall Street Journal*. © 1973 Dow Jones and Co., Inc. All rights reserved.

or more people. The respondents were very diverse: more than half were over age thirty, nearly all groups had children, and their incomes and occupations varied widely.

Why did these individuals choose to enter group marriages? Public pronouncements of reasons included a search to restore a lost sense of community, an expansion of family identification, and benefits to children. At a more private level, sex emerged as fairly central to participation, and discussions of personal growth potential were dominant. Few groups began with love relationships but rather originated at more practical or intellectual levels based on ideas of community sexual freedom, economic efficiency, or admiration of the concept of group marriage. In many instances, the initial nonemotional relationships grew to deep affection.[24]

Most of the group marriages had four persons, a few included only three, and one had six. Considerable instability appeared to characterize group marriage. After one year only 44 percent of the group marriages were intact and after three years only 17 percent were intact. The average life span of a group marriage was believed to be between six and twelve months. The interaction within the groups was typically intense and intimate, often like encounter groups but different in that the marriages are leaderless and exitless.

The Constantines reported:

> What we find is that the majority of both the men and women in group marriages particularly enjoy the element of secure sexual variety afforded by their marriage. The criterion of responsibility and interpersonal involvement appears to be preeminent over sexual involvement. Thus, while some individuals engage in sexual activities outside the group marriage, these too tend to reflect interpersonal criteria and none would properly be described as promiscuous. . . .
>
> The mechanisms by which groups resolve the issues of sexual sharing and sleeping arrangements vary but have certain elements in common. Most multilateral families aspire to natural, spontaneous sexual relations. . . . Unfortunately, immediate preference for one partner is too easily read as sexual rejection of another. . . . A group may spend a significant portion of its collective energy on this one decision, that is, who sleeps with whom.[25]

It was found that multiperson and bisexual activities were accepted as permissible but that very little had taken place. Multiple-couple sex was quite rare.

The one recurring theme reported was "coping with complexity."

> All the mechanisms of living are more complicated. Money, discipline, food, personality conflicts, all are multiplied in terms of problem potential. Fortunately, tradition, formal rules, and habits set in to reduce the continued level of complexity; unfortunately, this affect is only partial and the individual participant must be of that temperament that makes for the good of a large family or a commune.[26]

It would appear that multilateral marriages are a viable alternative to monogamy for a very small proportion of our population. The Constantines estimated that in the entire country there probably are not more than 1,000 group marriages. Where it does exist, the strong negative reactions of persons who are aware of it force anonymity and secrecy. Thus, it seems reasonable to assume that group marriages will never become very popular in spite of the various advantages they may offer.

Albert Ellis doubts that group marriage will ever gain widespread pop-

24. Ibid., p. 210.
25. Ibid., p. 214–215.
26. Ibid., pp. 217–218.

ularity. It has various difficulties and shortcomings that include, among others:

1. The difficulty in finding groups of three or more adults of both sexes who can truly live harmoniously with each other.
2. The difficulty in establishing a workable division of labor in occupational, recreational and household tasks.
3. The difficulty in finding other individuals with whom one would like to have a group-marriage arrangement and with whom each of the other members can accept and tolerate as spouse.
4. The difficulty of avoiding problems relating to sex, love and jealousy.
5. The difficulty, at the present time, of finding females who are interested in group marriage.[27]

Group marriages are likely to face reactions similar to those faced by "swingers", homosexuals, or even interracially married couples. Until the wider society comes to either accept or tolerate practices of this sort, open involvement in them will be extremely difficult.

VARIATIONS IN EXTENDED RELATIONSHIPS

The previous section sought variation in marital life-styles by an examination of the number of spouses involved. With the exception of the single or unmarried, the focus was on the organization of the nuclear or conjugal unit. Chapter 3 included a discussion of the nuclear-modified-extended family issue that raised the question of the extent of isolation of today's families. If it is true that extended kinship relationships have diminished, and if it is true that extended kinship relationships are highly functional as systems of support, continuity, and exchange, then it becomes logical that alternatives to the traditional extended family are being sought. This section examines three of these alternatives: communes, family networks, and affiliated families.

Communes

The large-scale group marriage takes the form of a commune.[28] Many communes are family type but not marriage type. That is, some may share

27. Albert Ellis, "Group Marriage: A Possible Alternative?" in Herbert A. Otto, ed., *The Family in Search of a Future* (New York: Meredith, 1970), pp. 92–94; see also Reese D. Kilgo, "Can Group Marriage Work," *Sexual Behavior* 2 (March 1972), pp. 8–14.
28. For an excellent collection of readings on communal family life in historical, cross-cultural, and contemporary perspectives see Michael Gordon, ed., *The Nuclear Family in Crisis: The Search for an Alternative* (New York: Harper, 1972).

Commune Differences

Utopian Commune	Evolutionary Commune	Religious Commune
Drop out orientation	High achievers	Highly structured
Do your own thing	Highly mobile	Authoritarian leader
Loosely organized	Straight jobs	Work ethic
Usually subsidized	Upper middle class	Usually self-sustaining
Youth oriented	Opinion leaders	Withdrawn from society
Sometimes revolutionary	Most over 30	Family oriented
Usually short-lived	Many post-children	

Source: James W. Ramey, "Emerging Patterns of Innovative Behavior in Marriage," *The Family Coordinator* 21 (October 1972), p. 449.

labor, goods, and services, while raising their children in common, yet maintain monogamous marital relationships. Many of the current youth-oriented communes operate much as a group marriage in which economic, sexual, and child-rearing functions are shared in common. However, in these members frequently come and go, and the group relationship is relatively short-lived.

Many of today's communes seek a family warmth, intimacy, and desire to become extended families, but not all communes are of this type. *The Modern Utopian*, a publication of Alternatives Foundation in San Francisco, lists in its table of contents a wide range or types of communes: new-age religious communes, old-order religious communes, ideological communes, scientific communes, hip-psychedelic communes, group marriage communes, miscellaneous communes, and historical communes.[29] As can be seen, these communes exist for a wide range of purposes. Most share a request for togetherness and share economic and child-rearing responsibilities. Some are small urban groups that live together but hold outside jobs. Others are rural farming communities that combine work and living. Some, such as the Bruderhof, are formal organizations with their own business enterprise (in this case, manufacturing community playthings). Some communes experiment sexually to change the man-woman relationship. Communes have been started by political radicals, return-to-the-land homesteaders, intellectuals, pacifists, hippies, dropouts, ex-drug addicts, behavioral psychologists, self-actualizing humanistic psychologists, Quakers, ex-monks, Hasidic Jews, and many others. Estimates of the number of communal experiments today would run into the hundreds. Most have been and will be characterized by failure.[30]

Many communes do not define themselves as families at all. Rural communes are more likely to define themselves as families than are urban communes. They are likely to involve a greater degree of commitment with

29. "Communes U.S.A.," *The Modern Utopia* 5, nos, 1, 2, 3 (1971), published by Alternatives Foundation, P.O. Drawer A, Diamond Heights Station, San Francisco, California 94131.

30. William M. Kephart, "Why They Fail: A Socio-Historical Analysis of Religious and Secular Communes," *Journal of Comparative Family Studies* 5 (Autumn 1974), pp. 130–140.

less turnover of members, are more likely to have their economic base in agriculture and are more likely to be physically isolated from the surrounding community. These factors enable the group (family) to work together, to separate members from outsiders, and to more selectively monitor visitors and new members. In contrast, many urban communes are linked in with university settings, offer financial advantages in food and housing, have many visitors and changes of members, and have their base in expediency rather than a commitment to the group, to a particular ideology, or to the particular life-style. As a result of such factors, Bennett Berger et al.[31] believe that rural communes represent a relatively more advanced stage, a purer form of the "new age" movement than do urban communes.

It has been suggested that in traditional family forms, the drive was to find a mission in life. In the newer communal family forms, the drive is to find a meaning to life.[32] This implies a search for a sense of belonging and self-actualization rather than the establishment of frontiers, making money, acquiring consumer goods, and the like. However, communal living is not without strain. Dennis Jaffe and Rosabeth Kanter[33] suggest that four factors account for strain within the commune and for couple separation from each other.

First, they write of *contextual conduciveness*. The risk of couple separation is greater in a communal living situation because many couples moved into a collective household in the first place to withdraw from a difficult relationship or to revitalize a sagging one. When in the commune, pressures exist for autonomy and individualization of couple members and for egalitarian roles. In addition, the pressure of others provides alternatives other than the spouse in having personal needs met. Couple identity is defused in that the household structure itself encourages couple members to think of themselves as individuals first and part of the couple unit second. With the accessibility of resources other than the partner, with the enlarged division of labor, with the loss of joint interest and joint decision making, and with the single status as a viable option, the communal household operates as conducive to couple separation.

Second, a *systemic strain* exists between each member's definition of the relationship and between communal versus traditional role relations. With many couples, the decision to live communally was based on different reasons. Many couples make incorrect assumptions about what their partners want or intend. Certain behaviors, such as sexual liberation, emerge as accept-

31. Bennett Berger, Bruce Hackett, and R. Mervyn Millar, "The Communal Family," *The Family Coordinator* 21 (October 1972), pp. 419–420.

32. Joy G. Schulterbrandt and Edwin J. Nichols, "Ethical and Ideological Problems for Communal Living: A Caveat," *The Family Coordinator* 21 (October 1972), pp. 432–433.

33. Dennis T. Jaffe and Rosabeth Moss Kanter, "Couple Strains in Communal Households: A Four Factor Model of the Separation Process," *The Journal of Social Issues* 32 (Winter 1976), pp. 169–191.

able for one member but not the other. Thus, much strain is a result of differing men-women perceptions and definitions as well as a result of accommodating to the communal life-style.

Third, *generalized beliefs* are a source of strain. The commune is likely to place a negative value on feelings of obligation to marriage and on private, exclusive relationships and place a positive value on individual autonomy and feminism with its emphases on sex-role equality, male participation in child care, sharing of housework and the like.

Fourth, *precipitating events* prove to be a source of stress and often serve as the final prod in separation. Whether suddenly or gradually, new occurrences force a choice. A job offer in another city or a new sexual partner may be the event that crystallizes or focuses the discontent. Extracouple sexual relationships cause the most conflict for communal couples and precede most of the breakups. Both Zablocki[34] and Kanter[35] found support for the contention that multiple sexual relationships are unconducive to the stability of either the couple or the collective unit. Communal solidarity was most often maintained by the buildup of community ties of an intimate but nonsexual nature.

The prior discussion indicates that for couples to enter a collective household represents both a risk to a couple—as structurally conducive to autonomy and perhaps separation—and an opportunity for learning and the development of more egalitarian, flexible styles of couple relationship.[36] Jaffe and Kanter[37] state that the fragility of some couple relationships in the households in their study was more than matched by the fragility of the communal groups themselves: generally they are short term, with minimal shared ideology or shared functions beyond the running of a household. Clearly, communes represent a variant life-style to certain members of our society. For communes to represent a variant marital style for couples who wish to enhance their relationship, this form appears to be one of high risk.[38]

34. Benjamin Zablocki, *The Joyful Community: An Account of the Bruderhof, a Communal Movement Now in Its Third Generation* (Baltimore: Penguin, 1971).

35. Rosabeth M. Kanter, *Commitment and Community: Communes and Utopias in Sociological Perspective* (Cambridge, Mass.: Harvard University Press, 1972).

36. Jaffe and Kanter, op. cit., p. 189.

37. Ibid., p. 189.

38. Readings other than those mentioned that may be of interest and include: Patrick W. Conover, "An Analysis of Communes and International Communities with Particular Attention to Sexual and Genderal Relations," *The Family Coordinator* 24 (October 1975), pp. 453–464; Rosabeth Moss Kanter, Dennis Jaffe, and D. Kelly Weisberg, "Coupling, Parenting and the Presence of Others: Intimate Relationships in Communal Households," *The Family Coordinator* 24 (October 1975), pp. 433–452; Rosabeth Moss Kanter, ed., *Communes: Creating and Managing the Collective Life* (New York: Harper, 1973); Rosabeth Moss Kanter, "Getting It All Together: Some Group Issues in Communes," *American Journal of Orthopsychiatry* 42 (July 1972), pp. 632–643; Richard Fairfield, *Communes, U.S.A.: A Personal Tour* (Baltimore: Penguin, 1972); Judson Jerome, *Families of Eden: Communes and the New Anarchism* (New York: Seabury, 1974); Kathleen Kinkade, *A Walden Two Experiment: The First Five Years of Twin Oaks Community* (New York:

Family Networks or Clusters

Another variation in marital and family relationships that extends beyond the primary network of the nuclear family is the family network or cluster. It can be described as a circle of families who meet together regularly and frequently, share in reciprocal fashion any of their intimate secrets, offer one another a variety of services, and do not hesitate to influence one another in terms of values and attitudes.[39]

As outlined by Frederick Stoller[40] these networks would include the following:

1. *A circle of families.* The number of families would range from two to four. Two families may not be adequate to deal with many of the problems that would arise and would not provide enough variety. A group of more than four families would be difficult to manage.

2. *Regular and frequent meetings.* Frequency of contact is required before intimacy and sharing can be attained and maintained. If meetings are infrequent, families are likely to be on their best behavior, and the issues discussed will focus on major crises rather than the mundane day-to-day features of family life.

3. *Reciprocal sharing.* All families must voluntarily be open to their own as well as to others' feelings, behaviors, and relationships. Reciprocity is essential.

4. *Exchange of services.* While an expected exchange of services would include assistance in crises, on a less dramatic level it would include the development of an interfamily consultation service in which various members of each family are called upon to aid in the negotiations that are constantly required within families from time to time.

5. *The extension of values.* Networks would become less reluctant to express whatever comes to mind. Differences in attitudes and values would be shared, and the interchange could lead to the development of new systems of values that did not exist before in any of the members' families.

To the extent that the nuclear family is an isolated unit, a network of families would provide a variety of functions. This network would give parents feedback in regard to child rearing practices, would provide opportunities to witness the interaction patterns of marriages other than their own, would eliminate much of the secrecy that is operative in marriages, would provide a

Morrow, 1973); Keith Melville, *Communes in the Counter Culture: Origins, Theories, Styles of Life* (New York: Morrow, 1972); Lewis Mumford, *The Story of Utopias* (New York: Viking, 1922); Ron E. Roberts, *The New Communes: Coming Together in America.* Englewood Cliffs, N. J.: Prentice-Hall, 1971).

39. Frederick H. Stoller, "The Intimate Network of Families as a New Structure," in Herbert A. Otto, ed., *The Family in Search of a Future* (New York: Appleton-Century-Crofts, 1970), p. 145–159; and Bruce M. Pringle, "Family Clusters as a Means of Reducing Isolation among Urbanites," *The Family Coordinator* 23 (April 1974), pp. 175–179.

40. Ibid., pp. 152–155.

source of help and assistance as needed, and would serve as a source for the interchange of ideas and attitudes.

Family networks, like communes, may present certain difficulties. It may be impossible for all families to meet regularly. Certain couples may be more open than others or may dominate the group. While development of openness and intimacy may be easy, the retention of intimacy and the sustaining of relationships may be more difficult. What about provisions for persons other than the couples: children, grandparents, other friends, and the like? While difficulties may be associated with the establishment and continuation of long-term networks, it is another variation in life-style. In certain ways, the family network resembles an extension of group therapy,[41] providing opportunities for openness, sharing, and assisting others without the added complications of sharing housing, pooling incomes, swapping mates, disturbing the neighbors, or continually living together. It involves a voluntary involvement of both open sharing and self-contained areas of living.

Affiliated Families

A third variation to the traditional extended family is that of the affiliated family. Clavan and Vatter[42] describe the family form as any combination of husband-father, wife-mother, and their children, plus one or more older persons, recognized as part of the kin network and called by a designated kin term. The older person or persons may or may not be part of the residential household, but the basic bond between the persons involved is one of voluntary commitment to responsibility for one another.

This variation in family organization and life-style appears to be best suited to older women who are retired and/or widowed and younger single or divorced women with children who desire paid employment in addition to caring for their children. It could also be suited to any nuclear family, separated geographically from their own kin but who desire the services of and interaction with older persons. The taking on of a new "affiliated" kin need not obliterate past ties. Most of us recognize and accept the adoption of children. Although biological ties are absent, parents commit themselves emotionally and socially to their adopted children. Could not the same process occur (although not necessarily in a legal sense) with single parents or nuclear family units and an older person?

An affiliated family structure has three basic attributes: propinquity, commitment of its members to responsibility for one another, and flexi-

---

41. Jonathan Clark and Hyman L. Kempler, "Therapeutic Family Camping: A Rationale," *The Family Coordinator* 22 (October 1973), pp. 437–442.
42. Sylvia Clavan and Ethel Vatter, "The Affiliated Family: A Continued Analysis," *The Family Coordinator* 21 (October 1972), p. 499.

bility.[43] Propinquity, the idea of living close to one another, has been a basic factor in discussions of extended kin relationships in the United States and in highly mobile industrialized societies. With an affiliated kin member living in the same area or neighborhood, the negative effects of geographic distance from traditional kin can be minimized. Second, a commitment of affiliated family members to one another implies caring, sharing, and the assuming of responsibility for other "family" members. This commitment is a voluntary one between both natural and "adopted" kin members. This linkage can serve to provide an opportunity for retroactive socialization of the elderly, anticipatory socialization of the young, and freedom for the middle generation to pursue occupational goals, all within a family context. Third, the flexibility of the affiliated family permits an extension of kinship beyond traditional definitions. Each relationship is developed within a particular situation—not predetermined, but adaptive to the demands of a changing and complex situation. The affiliative role is broad enough to include any age, either sex, and be either intra- or intergenerational. This offers the potential for a wide variety of family life-styles.

The affiliated family establishes a three-generation family network by substituting friends for elements of the kin group. Like the other variations of extended relationships mentioned, this one has some problematic aspects. As described by Hyman Kempler[44] the intimacy needed for the relationship benefits must be cultivated, and it requires considerable time and effort. Forming extended families may prove too stressful and unrealistic for the people involved. Commitment between the elderly and the family depends on a finely balanced mutuality of needs. This may be difficult to achieve. Nevertheless, the affiliated family may lend itself well to modern industrial life by permitting an extended form of family that is highly flexible and suitable to personal situations.

VARIATIONS IN COUPLE RELATIONSHIPS

As mentioned in the brief section on monogamy in this chapter, most variant marital life-styles occur within the context of a one-husband, one-wife situation. The triad, group, and extended network arrangements may provide increased opportunities for growth, development, and intimate interaction, but with these opportunities come an added complexity of decision making and role patterns as well.

---

43. Ibid., p. 503. See also Sylvia Clavan and Ethel Vatter, "The Affiliated Family: A Device for Integrating Old and Young," *The Gerontologist* 12 (Winter 1972), pp. 407–412.

44. Hyman L. Kempler, "Extended Kinship Ties and Some Modern Alternatives," *The Family Coordinator* 25 (April 1976), p. 147.

Sociologists have long recognized the importance of the primary group, the need for personal fulfillment in small, face-to-face intimate group interaction. But they have also recognized that as the group gets larger, so does the potential and the likelihood for the development of secondary group characteristics. At what numerical point primary groups become secondary is impossible to determine, because the key determinants do not reside purely in numbers. But clearly, as a group gets larger the number of internal relationships increases disproportionately.

Caution should be taken against viewing numbers in absolute terms. For any given person, there are degrees of intimacy and variations in numbers from one social context to another. Even in the two-person marriage, the variation in life-styles, relationships, and behaviors is vast. Let us turn our attention to three variations in couple relationships: dual-career marriages, childless marriages, and androgynous marriages.

Dual-career Marriages

While dual-employed marriages and the employment of women have been common, particularly increasing since the second world war, dual-career marriage as a common occurrence is viewed as a newer variant life-style. Career is used in place of "work" or "paid employment" to designate a level of commitment and a continuous developmental sequence that is less

---

Another Alternative: Man Adopts Girlfriend

WESTERLY, R.I.—(AP)—Elaine Ivy Tattersall has taken Joseph A. Comolli as her lawfully adopted father.

The Westerly couple decided to take a new approach to cohabitation. Instead of marriage or simply living together, the man has adopted the woman as his daughter.

Comolli, 33, adopted Miss Tattersall, 32, in Westerly's Probate Court this week. Her parents are still alive.

A spokeswoman at the town clerk's office said the adoption of Miss Tattersall was legal because "she is of age and can be adopted by whomever she chooses."

"The daughter can use the name of the

father. People will believe they are married because they use the same name. They obtain respectability in the eyes of their peers."

Said the couple's lawyer, Aram K. Berberian. "To legitimize the cohabitation, they became related."

Berberian, who claimed he used the legal tactic himself three years ago while divorcing his first wife, said the adoption of a lover can offer other benefits.

"The daughter can never force the father to pay alimony," the lawyer said.

"Each party bends over backwards to be pleasant, rather than to be obnoxious with impunity."

Source: *Detroit Free Press*, December 19, 1976, p. 2-A. Reprinted by permission of The Associated Press.

likely to be found in a job taken primarily for additional income purposes.

Several decades age, Talcott Parsons[45] dismissed marriage between professionals as a viable means of "emancipation from domesticity" for most American wives. He argued that such marriages could cast the wife into destructive occupational role competition with her mate. It follows, according to his thesis, that such employment patterns would adversely affect the professional careers of both, to say nothing about the difficulties imposed on the marriage itself.

One test of the Parsonian argument was carried out by Martin et al.[46] with sociologist husbands, their sociologist wives, and other female sociologists in the profession. They measured career patterns in terms of 1) possession of Ph.D., 2) achievement of academic rank, 3) frequency of promotion, 4) degree of employment, and 5) career half-life or longevity. They found that when compared to other females in the profession, sociologist wives were proportionately much more successful at obtaining the Ph.D., achieving higher academic ranks, gaining more promotions, avoiding demotions, and practicing longer professional careers. The only data that did not clearly indicate the professional advantage of collegial marriage for the wife was that concerning degree of employment. Here it was found that wives tended to be employed on a half-time basis more than other females and husbands. It would appear that, for sociologists at least, support does not exist for the Parsonian idea of disruptive consequences of professional marriage, particularly for the wife whose accomplishments far exceeded other female sociologists. The success of the sociologist wife might be seen as a result of professional-marital endogamy where a professional husband and wife take advantage of close marital interaction to accelerate the wife's professional success. Ironically, it is not disruptive marital consequences that occur but rather professional advantages, at least where both spouses are in the same profession. Whether similar advantages result where spouses are in different professions remains to be tested.

Perhaps the consequences are far different when the emphasis is placed on the marriage rather than the profession. The Rapoports[47] isolated five dilemmas of the dual-career marriage which in their nature set up strains. These were common to all the couples they studied. They are 1) overload, 2) environmental sanction, 3) personal identity and self-esteem, 4) social network dilemmas, and 5) dilemmas of multiple-role cycling.

45. Talcott Parsons, *Essays in Sociological Theory* (Glencoe, Ill.: Free Press, 1954), pp. 94–96.
46. Thomas W. Martin, Kenneth J. Berry, and R. Brooke Jacobsen, "The Impact of Dual-Career Marriages on Female Professional Careers: An Empirical Test of a Parsonian Hypothesis," *Journal of Marriage and the Family* 37 (November 1975), pp. 734–742.
47. Rhona and Robert N. Rapoport, *Dual-Career Families* (Harmondsworth, Middlesex, England: Penguin, 1971), pp. 286–296. See also A. C. Bebbington, "The Function of Stress in the Establishment of the Dual-Career Family," *Journal of Marriage and the Family* 35 (August 1973), pp. 530–537.

The overload factor refers to the redistribution or carrying out of tasks that are traditionally done by the wife at home: domestic supervision, child care, social arrangements, and the like. How this overload factor is handled depends on the individuals and their situations but usually involves a considerable strain in their heavy schedule, cutting heavily into free time. Domestic help intruded into family privacy and their work was not always satisfactory. Sometimes standards were deliberately lowered for the maintenance of the household. Sometimes the children were pressed into helping roles. The latter tended to be seen as a constructive socialization policy as well as an expedient in the overload situation.

Environmental sanctions refer to societal pressures with which women must endure: sex-role stereotyping, competing with men, child-rearing expectations, and so on. While the mass media and the general sentiment toward married women working is changing in the direction of disparaging the idea of highly qualified women being exclusively housewives, the other factors mentioned are other matters. Unless women at work are outstanding, their deficiencies are likely to be reacted to stereotypically and attributed to "shortcomings" of their sex. If couples have no children, they face the possible hazard of feeling unfulfillment as human beings or as being viewed as odd or unfortunate by others. If they have children, they are expected to provide conventional care, i.e., with the mother staying at home.

Personal identity and self-esteem were dilemmas experienced more or less autonomously of environmental sanctions. The individuals studied were socialized in terms of norms and values of thirty years ago and more. Boys were and are considered to be interested in machines, money, fame, power, and authority. Girls "normally" are interested in beauty, the arts, human relations, and care functions. Variance from these stereotyped interest and activities often produced guilt, ambivalence, sensitivity to criticism, self-doubt, and depression. Some husbands showed irritation or resentment at having to modify their own identities to incorporate a successful wife into their pattern. However, it should be noted that dual-career marriages appear to be as good or better at working through problems that confront them than other families. These families may engage in more purposeful decision making, more open communication, and often by a very sharp segregation between home and work roles. What this often means is that at home, the wife becomes "cook" and "my husband's wife."

Social network dilemmas involve relationships with schools, medical facilities, work organizations, friends, or kin. In general, the dual-career families tend to make their network of relationships on a couple basis rather than an individual basis, their relationships with kin tend to diminish except where there are clear responsibilities and/or compatibilities, and they tend to increase the number of people in their networks who are in service relationships with them.

The dilemmas of multiple-role cycling involve the need to dovetail the demands of marriage, husband's work, wife's work, children, and so forth as each changes with different stages of the life cycle. For example, in dual-career marriages, occupational establishment often preceded child bearing. With the arrival of children, new demands of time, money, and family tasks posed new dilemmas that needed solutions. This type or role shift, while not unique to the dual-career marriage, is another source of strain.

After reading of the dilemmas and the resultant strain produced by dual careers, one could ask: Why dual careers? Clearly, there are gains in this type of life-style. The financial gains are more important than are often acknowledged. The Rapoport study, however, found money to be less crucial than what they subsume under the general category of "self-expression."[48] These are satisfactions derived from creating something, achieving recognition, expanding energies beyond the home and children, or marital enrichment. One study comparing one- and two-career families[49] found the women in the two-career family to report fewer life pressures and worry, more communication with husbands, more happiness with their marriages, and better physical and mental health. In contrast, men in the two-career family were in poorer health and were less content with marriage, work, and life in general. It would appear that the husband of the employed wife loses part of his active support system when the wife fails to function as a servant, homemaker, and mother. Employed wives, on the other hand, expand into roles that have more positive value for them.

It would appear that participation in the dual-career pattern results in more severe identity problems for husbands than for wives. However, care must be taken about overgeneralizing. The husbands in a study by Holmstrom[50] were found to be very supportive of the wife's career, took their wives' work seriously, actively helped their wives, did not complain about the inconvenience of the dual careers, and did not feel hindered by the wife's career. On the other hand, wives in the Holmstrom study accommodated more to the husband's career than vice versa, were more likely to face anti-nepotism rules, and were viewed as ultimately responsible for the domestic realm.[51]

It is possible that the findings of the studies just cited are not as contradictory as it appears at first glance. There are strains in dual-career marriages, husbands and wives do have differential gains and losses in their

---

48. Ibid., p. 297.

49. Ronald J. Burke and Tamara Weir, "Relationship of Wives' Employment Status to Husband, Wife and Pair Satisfaction and Performance," *Journal of Marriage and the Family* 38 (May 1976), pp. 279–287.

50. Lynda Lytle Holmstrom, *The Two-Career Family* (Cambridge, Mass.: Schenkman, 1972), pp. 134–136.

51. Ibid., p. 155. Similar findings were reported by Norma A. Heckman, Rebecca Bryson, and Jeff B. Bryson, "Problems of Professional Couples: A Content Analysis," *Journal of Marriage and the Family* 39 (May 1977), pp. 323–330.

Don't Marry, Hire a Spouse

Two years ago, Edmund L. Van Deusen, a grandfather, found himself divorced and lonely after 26 years but unwilling to marry again. So he hired a "wife."

Elaine Peterson, 35, answered Van Deusen's newspaper ad asking for a woman to live with him as an informal wife for $500 a month.

The 50-year-old chemist and Miss Peterson, who said she had been living outdoors the past six years and welcomed the chance to spend the coming winter in out of the rain, are still together. And Van Deusen says he and his "hired" wife "feel very good about each other."

Miss Peterson agreed enthusiastically, "It's really sexy."

Van Deusen said in an interview last week that after his long marriage he decided to go solo "unsuppressed by togetherness and by love possessed" or by anyone possessed.

He said he found brief love affairs with intermittent periods of loneliness too much to bear, and he struck on the idea of hiring a "wife" he could shed without government interference. He put an ad in a Los Angeles underground paper.

"Scores of women, all sorts of women, replied," he said. His choice was Elaine.

During the interview he presented a bespectacled, professorial appearance, while she sat smiling in blue jeans beneath an unruly mop of curls.

"Sex without love is different," Van Deusen said. "It's very free and natural."

Before setting out on their unconventional conjugal life, Van Deusen and Ms. Peterson signed documents spelling out the duties of both parties: for Van Deusen, the compensation and all other requirements of an employer; for Ms. Peterson—who prefers the Ms. designation—the requirements of the bedroom and the kitchen, in that order.

The document also outlines Ms. Peterson's "duty hours," "days off," and "vacation" time.

Source: *Detroit News*, November 10, 1974. Reprinted by permission of The Associated Press.

marriages, and while the professional employment of women is gaining increasing respectability and acceptance, a state of sexual equality has not been achieved. Wives are still generally expected to give up their own jobs for the sake of the husbands and to see their family as their first duty.[52]

In spite of strain and sex-role inequality, it appears that much is to be gained from dual-career marriages. They are a variant and increasingly common life-style for married couples.

---

52. Benson Rosen, Thomas Jerdee, and Thomas Prestwick, "Dual-Career Marital Adjustment: Potential Effects of Discriminatory Managerial Attitudes," *Journal of Marriage and the Family* 37 (August 1975), pp. 565–572; Janet E. Harrell and Carl A. Ridley, "Substitute Child Care, Maternal Employment and the Quality of Mother-Child Interaction," *Journal of Marriage and the Family* 37 (August 1975), pp. 556–564; R. Paul Duncan and Carolyn Cummings Perrucci, "Dual Occupation Families and Migration," *American Sociological Review* 41 (April 1976), pp. 252–261; and Janet G. Hunt and Larry L. Hunt, "Dilemmas and Contradictions of Status: The Case of the Dual-career Family," *Social Problems* 24 (April 1977), pp. 407–416.

Childless Marriages

The dual-career marriage just described is highly compatible with the marriage that has no children. Much of the strain in employment for women is directly related to the social norms that view the fulfilled married woman 1) as a mother and 2) as a mother in the home. The childless marriage, while rejecting the norm that married people should have and want children, makes more acceptable the career path for the professional or employed woman outside the home.

In recent years the subject of voluntary childlessness[53] and the acceptability of childless marriages as a viable alternate marital life-style has gained increasing attention. It has been viewed by one author as the Ultimate Liberation.[54] There is little doubt that children place enormous demands on parents in terms of emotional and financial costs. Yet, most married couples, either voluntarily or involuntarily, have children.

For many years the myth existed that because of a maternal instinct, all women wanted children. This "instinct" even went one step further and assumed that once a child is born, the mother will "instinctively" want, love, and care for the child. These assumptions were given major blows as statistics, research reports, newspaper accounts, and gossip networks revealed the widespread termination of pregnancies through legal and/or illegal abortions, the commonality of mothers abusing and even killing their children, and the discovery that women who never had children—in or out of marriage—did not suffer physical or emotional damage. These and other factors tended to dispel the notion of the biological linkage between being female and a natural desire for and love of children.

Couples have children for many reasons, some planned and conscious and others not. It seems logical to believe that many people have children because they were never socialized to believe that not having them is a viable alternative to marriage and family life. Since marriage legitimizes the sexual union and the birth of children, voluntary childless marriages were not viewed as a realistic choice. Most cultures and societies impose social pressures upon couples to be "fruitful", meaning to bear children. The marriage is not complete or socially mature until children are born of the union.

With such an orientation, J. E. Veevers[55] listed voluntary childlessness

53. J. E. Veevers, "Voluntary Childlessness: A Neglected Area of Family Study," *The Family Coordinator* 22 (April 1973), pp. 199–205; J. E. Veevers, "Voluntary Childlessness and Social Policy," *The Family Coordinator* 23 (October 1974), pp. 397–406; J. E. Veevers, "Voluntary Childless Wives: An Exploratory Study," *Sociology and Social Research* 57 (1973), pp. 356–366; and J. E. Veevers, "Rural-Urban Variation in the Incidence of Childlessness," *Rural Sociology* 36 (December 1971), pp. 547–553.

54. Margaret Movius, "Voluntary Childlessness—the Ultimate Liberation," *The Family Coordinator* 25 (January 1976), pp. 57–63.

55. J. E. Veevers, "The Violation of Fertility Mores: Voluntary Childlessness as Deviant Behavior," in C. Boydell et al., eds., *Deviant Behavior and Societal Reaction* (Toronto: Holt, Rinehart, and Winston, 1972), pp. 571–592.

> Louise: *I can't understand couples marrying who say right from the very beginning they don't want any children. Why do they marry! I view it as cutting themselves off from a very important source of life and joy and entertainment and it's like boxing themselves in . . . boxing themselves into a very narrow concept of a good life. They aren't allowing themselves to experience the joys that are meant to be part of married life. And I just wonder for how long their sex is going to be all that important if there's no fruit from it. I view it as a very unnatural selfish thing.*
>
> Mac: *Well, I like children, that's for sure. But now that I'm getting more educated, and my mate has become older, and the risk of being pregnant . . . it's gonna be greater and more of a struggle for her, uh . . . physically that is, to give birth. She's working, you know, and becoming very skeptical now of having kids.*
>
> Alex: *No kids, that's not a family. Where I come from my family that I lived with was around 35, 37 people depending. . . .*

as constituting a deviant category—statistically, socially, ethically, and perhaps even psychologically. In her many writings on voluntary childlessness, she reports on the results of intensive depth interviews with childless wives living with their husbands. These wives who, according to conventional definitions, have opted for the "deviant" kind of married life, held a number of unusual beliefs about the absence of parenting and the kinds of persons who so choose. For example, almost all of the wives were married to husbands who concurred with their opinion on the nondesirability of child rearing. Together with their husbands, they evolved a deviant belief system in which motherhood was defined in negative rather than in positive terms and which, therefore, enabled them to disregard most of the social pressures toward parenthood.[56] The existence of a maternal instinct was denied, and the accusation that childlessness was abnormal was thereby dismissed. Pregnancy and childbirth were perceived to be at best unpleasant and at worst difficult and dangerous. Child care was seen as excessively burdensome and unrewarding. Motherhood was perceived as having a directly deleterious effect on a woman's life chances. Parenthood was defined as a "trap" that directly and indirectly interfered with personal happiness and the maximization of one's freedom, options, and resources.

How are these variant belief systems maintained? Veevers[57] suggests that four mechanisms are used. First, selective perception can allow one to give special attention to those perceptions that are congruent with one's be-

---

56. J. E. Veevers, "The Moral Careers of Voluntary Childless Wives: Notes on the Defense of a Variant World View," *The Family Coordinator* 24 (October 1975), p. 475.

57. Ibid., pp. 476–483.

liefs and to ignore those perceptions that suggest contradictory conclusions. Second, differential association can lead to interaction with those who share one's beliefs and separation from those whose beliefs differ.[58] This interaction will occur most often with the husband, since women may be largely unaware of others who also reject the motherhood mystique. But physical and/or psychological isolation is possible from friends who have children and take their child responsibilities very seriously. Third, social situations can be actively structured so that their outcomes support one's beliefs. For example, to "borrow" other peoples' children for the weekend seldom produces positive evaluations toward children since they are in an unfamiliar and often threatening environment that has not been "child-proofed." Fourth, one can capitalize on the ambivalence of the divergent larger culture toward one's beliefs. For example, while children are viewed within the society as desirable, unlimited reproduction is not. While children can be chosen, many mothers had little choice in that they conceived accidently or succumbed to cultural pressures. Many childless couples believe that persons who react to them with scorn are secretly jealous of the freedom they enjoy.

Veevers suggests that under some conditions, the child-free alternative may be a viable family form, conducive both to personal and to marital satisfaction and adjustment.[59] These conditions include: 1) a genuine agreement of husband and wife on the undesirability of child rearing, 2) an awareness of the advantages of a child-free life-style and an ability to utilize these advantages in the sustaining interests outside the home, and 3) an adequate defense of their variant world view as described in the previous paragraph. Veevers suggests that while this life-style will never be a viable option for a large proportion of families, it is quite possible that it might be the best life-style for more than 5 percent of all couples.[60]

Androgyny

Androgyny was discussed in the previous chapter but needs to be mentioned here as another life-style variation in couple relationships. The Osofsky's[61] view androgyny as a society with no sex-role differentiation. As a marital life-style it would imply no sex-role differentiation between husbands and wives. Within marriage, the husband may desire to be nurturant

---

58. Reference groups were found to be sources of major support in the decision to remain childless by Sharon K. Houseknecht, "Reference Group Support for Voluntary Childlessness: Evidence for Conformity," *Journal of Marriage and the Family* 39 (May 1977), pp. 285–292.

59. Ibid., pp. 483–484.

60. Ibid., p. 486.

61. Joy D. and Howard J. Osofsky, "Androgyny as a Life Style," *The Family Coordinator* 21 (October 1972), pp. 411–418.

and catering, to do the cooking, and to take care of the children. The wife may prefer to work full time or to share household responsibilities. She may wish to be assertive, competitive, and independent.

Safilios-Rothschild[62] has delineated an entire map of strategies, social actions, policies, and laws necessary to effectively eradicate sexism from all aspects of our lives and from the entire society. In relation to marital roles, she contends that the prevailing sex differentiation based on sex stereotypes restricts married women's and men's behavior in that some options cannot be even theoretically considered.[63] For example, since the main role of hus-

---

62. Constantina Safilios-Rothschild, *Women and Social Policy* (Englewood Cliffs, N. J.: Prentice-Hall, 1974).

63. Ibid., p. 111.

Words Can't Keep Up with the New Morality

At a party a few weeks ago, a man kept introducing the woman with him as "my lady," and I still don't know if she was his wife, mistress, girlfriend or cleaning woman.

There's a whole new set of problems growing out of the new morality, or whatever it is, this business of not knowing the exact nature of a couple's relationship and, worse, not knowing how to find out without sounding like a snoop. At another party, a man named Quigley introduced me to a woman named McGuffin, so I stupidly asked her, "Have you known each other long?" and she smiled, "Oh, we're married," neatly putting me in my place.

This overlapping protocol of the new morality, open marriage and women's liberation is mixing up everything. Feminists, for instance, are not about to be referred to as anybody's "lady." No man in his right mind would publicly call his girlfriend his "girlfriend," and to label a woman your "wife" is just asking for it when you get home. These days, you have to say: "I'd like you to meet my great and good female friend with whom I live in equal partnership that some call 'marriage' but which Ms. Simpkin and I prefer to think of as a continually growing and sharing
experience in which open communication is allowed to flourish."

Next time somebody says, "This is my lady," I'm not going to ask how long they've known one another. I'm going to seize the offensive and simply say, "Look here, are you two lovers or what?" He's liable to reply, "Well, we're going together but we're not committed. Just put us down as very involved."

There should be some new terms, by the way, for all these people who are "committed" or "involved": "Charley, say hello to Lois Gwertz, my new involvee," or, "I'd like to announce that Lois and I are being committed." Of course, the pair may be living together but not lovers—they may be husband and wife. Or she may say, "We're living together but we're on different floors." Or: "We're having a fling but we're not talking." Or: "We're separated but we're eating all our meals together." Or: "I'm living with two guys but I'm dating someone else." Or: "Wally and I are divorced but it's kind of a secret."

And if the woman is visibly pregnant, I just excuse myself and try to get out of there fast. There's no point in looking for trouble.

Source: Gerald Nachman, *Detroit Free Press*, August 16, 1975, p. 11-A. Reprinted by special permission of the Chicago Tribune–New York News Syndicate.

bands has been the "instrumental" breadwinning role, the option to not work could not be considered as a possibility, even for a short period of time. Since the main roles of women have been those of "housekeeper" and "mother," the option to have a continuous career has been unavailable to married women.

Up to now the option for men to be the "househusband" has never existed. Even if the desire were there, the option could not be voiced since it would represent an extreme deviance. In Sweden where this option exists with social approval, an increasing number of men are choosing to work only part-time to permit an increased amount of time at home.

Similar stereotypes exist in regard to family dynamics as well. The stereotype suggests that men must always take initiative, play the most active role, and dominate interaction. Women must follow in a passive, submissive, and supportive role. In addition, men cannot express their feelings, their worries, their anxieties, their insecurities, and their weaknesses and fears to their wives, because they would lose their "cool" and their rational, brave, tough facade.[64] Communication with wives is kept at a minimum, informative, superficial level. As to empathy, husbands are not expected to understand the feelings and desires of their wives. In contrast, wives are endowed with "feminine" intuition and are supposed to understand their husbands, even guessing their feelings and desires in order to satisfy them.[65]

Safilios-Rothschild[66] suggests a number of strategies to liberate family structure and dynamics:

1. Have marital experts (counselors, educators, social scientists, social workers, and the like) assist marital partners in expressing themselves freely according to their own needs rather than according to a stereotype role pattern.

2. Use and develop textbooks that do not perpetuate traditional sex-role stereotypes.

3. Legalize individual marital contracts mutually agreed upon by those entering a marital relationship.

4. Pass and enforce an equal rights amendment allowing women to keep their maiden name, establish another domicile, manage community property, and establish credit.

5. Obtain passage of a legal reform where all types of cohabitation, with or without marriage, with the same or the opposite sex, with two or more persons, are legally valid.

6. Modify certain zoning ordinances to permit occupants the right to determine how they will use owned or leased housing units even if it differs from the husband-wife-child nuclear family unit.

64. Ibid., p. 112.
65. Ibid., p. 113.
66. Ibid., p. 115–120.

7. Work with the mass media in presenting familial models and behaviors that
   are free of sex stereotypes.

It is believed that strategies such as these would go a long way toward liberating husbands and wives from the stereotyped and traditional dynamics of marital life.

These and other variant marital styles will not be adopted by everyone. However, the elimination of sex-role differentiation in marriage is a style highly suitable as a realistic alternate way of life.

Summary

This chapter covered a range of variant or alternate family life-styles. These were categorized as variations in: marriage and number of spouses, extended relationships, and couple relationships. While certain of these variant life-styles are common in many countries of the world, many are viewed as relatively new or emerging family forms and as realistic alternatives to the traditional models in existence in the United States.

The variations in marriage and number of spouses cover singlehood, monogamy, polygyny, polyandry, and group marriage. The choice to remain single has risen dramatically since 1960. Available data indicate some extreme differences for the male and female who choose or who involuntarily occupy this particular nonmarital life-style. Monogamy, while not a variant life-style for most Americans, is the form of marriage in which most variant styles occur.

Polygyny and polyandry, two forms of polygamy, occur in a wide range of contexts and take numerous forms. The plural spouses may be all brothers or sisters, may marry simultaneously or sequentially, and may perform various functions. While polygyny is very common, polyandry is quite rare. Group marriage, as well, occurs extremely infrequently and may never have existed as a viable form of marriage for any society in the world.

The variations in extended relationships included communes, family networks or clusters, and affiliated families. Communes in the United States are frequently utopian, evolutionary, or religious in their purpose and may or may not be marriage and family oriented. Most communes exist under a range of strains that cause them to be short-lived. Family networks or clusters involve a circle of families who meet together regularly, share reciprocally thoughts and feelings, and offer one another a variety of services. Affiliated families include the basic nuclear family unit plus an additional—often older—member who becomes part of the family unit and all share responsibility for one another. Friends are substituted for the biologically related kin group.

Variations in couple relationships take many forms. Three are described in this chapter: dual-career marriages, childless marriages, and androgynous marriages. The dual-career marriage is one in which both husband and wife are employed full time and committed to their careers or professions. These marriages face various strains but also provide many rewards.

A new form of marital life-style is one in which a choice is made to have no children. While not widespread, a number of couples are selecting a career path or a marital style that rejects "mothering" and parenthood. Finally, androgyny as a life-style is one in which the husband and wife do not stereotype or differentiate roles on the basis of sex. As a result, wives may at times desire to be aggressive, work full time, or fix appliances. Husbands may at times desire to be soft and tender, not be employed, or prefer to sweep carpets.

Many other variant life-styles exist. The next four chapters look at various major cultural and subcultural variations. Later chapters, while not always labeling them as such, are in reality variant life-styles: interracial marriage, cohabitation, homosexual marriages, swinging, and the like.

Key Terms and Topics

Singlehood	149	Family Networks	164
Monogamy	151	Affiliated Families	165
Polygamy, Polygyny, and		Dual-career Marriages	167
Polyandry	152	Childless Marriages	172
Group Marriage	157	Androgyny	174
Communes	160		

Discussion Questions

1. *What is meant by a family life-style? Why will a marital or family life-style change more rapidly than changes in a social class or a subculture?*
2. *Make a listing of variations in marital and family life-styles. Which life-styles would be acceptable to you personally? Which ones favor marital stability? Individual growth? Kin relationships?*
3. *What is the likelihood of an increasing percentage of people choosing to remain single? Why or why not? Will this be equally true for males and females?*
4. *Why is monogamy so strongly stressed in the United States as the appropriate form of marriage? What advantages or disadvantages do you see in polygyny, polyandry, or group marriage for adults in the United States?*
5. *Around the world, when polygamy is culturally approved, polygyny appears to be far more common than polyandry. How is this explained? What factors explain the exceptions?*
6. *Differentiate family networks from communes, friendship groups, or affiliated families. Under what conditions are these variant life-styles con-*

sistent with or in conflict with industrialized, highly mobile types of societies?

7. *Discuss strains likely to be found in dual-career as opposed to one-career marriages? What rewards exist in each type?*

8. *Attempt to predict the likelihood of trends in regard to open, dual-career, childless, or androgynous marriages over the next thirty years. How are trends in these variant marital styles likely to be influenced by economic conditions, wars, depressions, or new technology?*

9. *Discuss the myth of the "maternal instinct." How do you explain the widespread acceptance of it? What factors disprove its existence?*

10. *Why are childless marriages not likely to become the norm? Are there not advantages to marriage without children?*

Further Readings

Constantine, Larry L. and **Joan N.** *Group Marriage: A Study of Contemporary Multilateral Marriage.* New York: Macmillan, 1973. Based on nearly three years of research with more than thirty marriages involving three or more people, this book provides an intensive report on the psychological and sociological meaning of group marriage.

Eshleman, J. Ross. *Perspectives in Marriage and the Family.* Boston: Allyn and Bacon, 1969. A text and reader providing a current overview of a sociology of marriage and the family, emphasizing the major frames of reference that characterize the area.

Glazer-Malbin, Nona, ed. *Old Family/New Family.* New York: D. Van Nostrand, 1975. An undergraduate-level book on interpersonal relationships in social systems and on some of the variant life-styles and family forms.

Gordon, Michael, ed. *The Nuclear Family in Crisis: The Search for an Alternative.* New York: Harper, 1972. A book of readings chosen to provide insight into communal family life in historical, cross-cultural, and contemporary perspectives.

Holmstrom, Lynda Lytle. *The Two-Career Family.* Cambridge, Mass.: Schenkman, 1972. A study of twenty couples in which both spouses were professionals, the wife having an independent career of her own.

Kephart, William M. *Extraordinary Groups: The Sociology of Unconventional Life Styles.* New York: St. Martin's, 1976. A look at seven different culture groups that have appeared on the American scene: The Old-Order Amish, the Oneida Community, the Father Divine movement, the Shakers, the Mormons, the Hutterites, and the modern communes.

O'Neill, Nena, and **George O'Neill.** *Open Marriage: A New Life Style for Couples.* New York: M. Evans, 1972. An attempt to examine and to define a marriage in which the individuals involved have freedom yet a mutual commitment in a relationship that does not bind or restrict growth.

Rapoport, Rhona, and **Robert Rapoport.** *Dual-Career Families.* Harmondsworth, Middlesex, England: Penguin, 1971. A case study of five families in England in which both the husband and the wife pursue active careers and family lives.

Safilios-Rothschild, Constantina. *Women and Social Policy.* Englewood Cliffs, N. J.: Prentice-Hall, 1974. A book written to delineate the entire map of strategies, social action, policies and laws necessary to effectively eradicate sexism from all aspects of our lives and from the entire society.

Stein, Peter J. *Single.* Englewood Cliffs, N. J.: Prentice-Hall, 1976. A broad overview of singles in the U.S.: who they are, their experience in society, their sexual lives, their marital choices, their source of support, and their future.

Sussman, Marvin B., special guest editor. "Variant Marriage Styles and Family Forms." *The Family Coordinator* 21 (October 1972); and "The Second Experience: Variant Family Forms and Life Styles." *The Family Coordinator* 24 (October 1975). Two special issues of *The Family Coordinator*, both of which include approximately fifteen articles on marital and family life-styles that vary from the more traditional nuclear-extended forms.

Teselle, Sallie, ed. *The Family, Communes and Utopian Societies.* New York: Harper, 1972. A small paperback of seven papers dealing with the contemporary dialectic of reality and Utopia, of city and country, and of alternative lifestyles.

6

*Family Life-Styles of
Various Cultures*

6

The previous chapter examined a wide range of marital and family life-styles with primary but not exclusive attention devoted to variations within the United States. This chapter examines family systems outside the United States: the kibbutz of Israel and selected family systems in the Philippines. Each of these basic patterns of family organization have been in existence for decades if not centuries and are no longer viewed as experimental or trial within the dominant society. They are ways of life that its members regard as good and important. Thus, while communal households exist as a variant pattern in the United States, it is the dominant pattern among the kibbutz. While polygyny was known to exist historically, with cases existing today among the Mormons in the United States, it is a socially accepted practice among the higher status Moslems in the Philippines. Clearly a wide range of variations in marital and family life-styles exist in Israel and the Philippines; however, major attention is focused on a few selected subcultural groupings that illustrate issues of importance in the world today and are likely to be of interest to the student who is primarily exposed to the life-styles of the more dominant U.S. families.

THE KIBBUTZ OF ISRAEL

To examine the kibbutz is to look at a life-style that for seventy years and covering three generations has been concerned with issues that are pronounced today: women's liberation, the protection of the family, communal child care, and a production-oriented, profit-motivated economy.

A kibbutz (plural kibbutzim) is an agricultural collective in Israel whose main features include communal living, collective ownership of all property (and hence, the absence of "free enterprise" and the "profit motive"), and the communal rearing of children. Kibbutz culture is informed by its explicit guiding principle, "from each according to his ability, to each according to his needs."[1]

The first attempt to establish a kibbutz—or kvutza, as it was called initially—was in 1907 and lasted less than two years. The first permanent settlement was formed in 1910 by ten men and two women. By 1920, there were forty agricultural collectives with 660 members.[2] Many of those early settlers came from Poland and Russia. By the 1920s many youth joined "The Movement" which was a combination of the European youth movement and the Zionist movement. This represented a rebellion against artificial convention, against the traditional Jewish culture, and in favor of emancipation from urban mores, of regeneration of the individual, of the joy of work, of a love of nature and nation, of a sense of belonging and identification in a world of anti-Semitism. The emphasis was on changing Jewish life, not escaping it. Israel (Palestine) was where a national culture, a sense of belonging, a simple, ascetic life could be established. A belief in Zionism (a Jewish state) and socialism (collective ownership) were two motivating forces.

Melford Spiro outlines the moral postulates of kibbutz culture:

1. The value of labor as an end in itself, particularly self-physical labor as opposed to hired labor or intellectual work.
2. Property that belongs to the entire nation or kibbutz community where the individual owns nothing except small personal gifts, receives no wages, and pays for no rent, food, clothes, or medical care.
3. Social and economic equality with no class structure.
4. Individual expression in reading or speaking and individual liberty in having no one hold power over or be superior to others.
5. Group domination in that the individual, while free in personal expression, directs his energies toward the promotion of the interests of the group.[3]

One of the early founders summarized the goal of the kvutza: "to enable us to decide how to run our own lives and to create economic equality and equality between the sexes."[4] The latter has remained a problem throughout its history as will be shown later.

Today, it is estimated that there are approximately 230 existing kibbutzim. Membership of the existing kibbutzim constitutes a diminishing percentage of Israel's total population—it is now 85,000 or 2.8 percent of the total.[5] The kibbutz population has grown much slower than the nonkibbutz Israeli population, primarily because of the low birth rate and the lower im-

---

1. Melford E. Spiro, "Is the Family Universal?—The Israeli Case," in Norman W. Bell and Ezra F. Vogel, eds., *A Modern Introduction to the Family* (New York: Free Press, 1968), p. 69.
2. Yosef Criden and Saadia Gelb, *The Kibbutz Experience* (New York: Herzl, 1974), pp. 8–11.
3. Melford E. Spiro, *Kibbutz: Venture in Utopia* (Cambridge, Mass.: Harvard University Press, 1956), Chapter 2, pp. 10–37.
4. Criden and Gelb, op. cit., p. 12.
5. Michael Curtis, "Utopia and the Kibbutz," in Michael Curtis and Mordecai Chertoff, *Israel: Social Structure and Change* (New Brunswick, N.J.: Transaction, 1973), p. 107.

migrant rate. Many immigrants from the Soviet Union, Middle East countries, and certain countries in the Western World wanted to live in Israel but had a dislike for collective life and no interest in giving up the patriarchal patterns of their homeland. Michael Curtis claims that the kibbutz has always been more attractive to people from European than from Oriental backgrounds, was originally more attractive to bachelors than to family units which are not the normal form of immigrant pattern, and is no longer serving the double purpose of development and military protection.[6] Each of these factors influenced the growth of the kibbutz.

The Organization of the Kibbutz

Most of Israel's kibbutzim are organized on a national basis with three major national kibbutz federations and several minor ones. All national kibbutz federations belong to the Agricultural Center, which is part of Israel's general federation of labor. Central offices handle the purchase of clothing, shoes, fuel, fertilizer, grain, building materials, and the like from which each kibbutz can get credit and make purchases.

Every kibbutz has a certain amount of autonomy in its daily activities. The kibbutzim has no constitution or by-laws, only certain rules and regulations defining things like working hours. The governing body is the kibbutz general meeting where any member can come to express views, air grievances, or raise issues. At these meetings, all members vote on new members and discuss construction plans, travel, purchases, discipline, or whatever.

The operations are supervised by a kibbutz secretariat comprised of five officers: treasurer, general manager, secretary, purchasing agent, and work manager. They perform in accordance with the policies established at the general meeting. Many functions are, however, delegated to committees: economic, children's, youth, aged, landscaping, athletics, culture, and countless others. Each committee approves the plans within its area consistent with the goals and interest of the collective.

As indicated, a high value is placed on physical work. Everybody does as much as possible for the common welfare with no special remunerations for special jobs. Whether on general duty, kitchen work, field activity, teaching, dressmaking, or milking, all are expected to take pride in their assigned tasks and their contribution to the community.

Members of the kibbutz view themselves as comrades, each of whom are intimately related to one another. Like the Amish described in the next chapter, the kibbutz constitutes a gemeinschaft, a "folk" society, a feeling of togetherness and interdependence. Childless couples contribute as much to the support of the children, ill, aged, and others as does anyone else. The welfare of each individual is bound up with the welfare of all others.

---

6. Ibid., p. 108.

The Family in the Kibbutz

Menachem Gerson[7] notes that in comparing the kibbutz family with the modern western family, three special features are salient: 1) the kibbutz family is not a self-interested economic unit, 2) while day-care centers exist in the western world, in the kibbutz all the parents cooperate with a professional educator from the first days of the infant's life, and 3) unlike the typical employed husband-housewife relationship, in the kibbutz both spouses live and work in the same social framework.

The founder generation of the older kibbutz viewed the family with suspicion and as a remnant of the bourgeois past. As a result, family relationships were played down. Couples were to eat their meals separately, not sit together at the weekly assembly, and not demonstrate their relationship in public. Parents were supposed to convey love and acceptance to children but were not to be directly involved in the children's upbringing.

It was noted that this outlook was short-lived and not shared by all the kibbutzim. It soon became apparent that relationships between kibbutz members could not substitute for family ties. As a result, the homes were improved, the status of parents in education was enhanced, and the kibbutz family became recognized as honorable. In the fully developed kibbutzim the three-generation family is the rule. Such a family meets together regularly and particularly makes itself felt at festivals, weddings, and the like. The family is said to have become of such importance that bachelors or childless couples may find their lot harder to bear in a kibbutz than in town.[8]

In short, the family is alive and well.[9] This is not to say that family life on a kibbutz is like life outside the kibbutz or that leaders desire to undermine the communal foundations of the movement. The basic structure of the community remains intact, the method of education remains basically the same, children continue to live in children's houses (with few exceptions[10]), and—as many would view as unfortunate—women still occupy service and often "inferior" positions.

The Kibbutz Couple

In the traditional sense of a husband-wife and a parent-child unit characterized by a marriage ceremony, economic support of one another, common residence, and the like, marriage and/or family do not exist among the kib-

7. Menachem Gerson, "The Family in the Kibbutz," *Journal of Child Psychology and Psychiatry* 15 (1974), pp. 47–48.

8. Ibid., p. 49.

9. Leslie Y. Rabkin, "The Institution of the Family Is Alive and Well," *Psychology Today* (February 1976), pp. 66–73.

10. Gerson notes that about 22 kibbutzim, among 230, have private sleeping arrangements for children. Gerson, op. cit., p. 50.

butz. Single kibbutz members live in small private rooms. When a couple asks for permission to share a room, the request is a sign they wish to become a "couple." This union does not require the sanction of a marriage ceremony or of any other event. Neither does this union change the status or the responsibilities of either the male or the female. The female retains her maiden name and both continue to work as they did prior to their union. The union is not essential for sexual purposes, for few sanctions exist against sexual relationships among young people, particularly after graduation from high school. But asking for a room does establish a relatively permanent relationship with another person both physically and psychologically.

The couple relationship does differ from any other adult relationship in a number of significant features.

- It alone includes common domicile for persons of the opposite sex.
- It entails a higher rate of interaction than is to be found in any other bisexual relationship.
- It involves a higher degree of emotional intimacy than is to be found in any other relationship.
- It establishes (ideally) an exclusive sexual relationship.
- It leads to the deliberate decision to have children.[11]

The Kibbutz Household and Division of Labor

While a kibbutz couple lives in a single bedroom-living room, meals are eaten in a communal dining room. This communal living and dining was expected to relieve women of dependence on a husband for financial support, from child-rearing responsibilities, and from the cooking, cleaning, and other domestic tasks. An attempt was made to redefine marriage, work, and motherhood. As indicated, couples were discouraged from spending their leisure time together. Divorce was made painless and displays of affection were kept to a minimum.

Keller indicates that the kibbutz has made extraordinary achievements in the sphere of family life and has accomplished a large part of what its founders set out to do:

1. It broke the power of the father, or of the patriarchy, and women, children, and household.
2. It eliminated the legal, economic, and personal dependency of the wife on the husband.
3. It developed an effective method of child rearing.[12]

---

11. Spiro, in Bell and Vogel, op. cit., p. 77.
12. Suzanne Keller, "The Family on the Kibbutz: What Lessons for Us?" in Curtis and Chertoff, op. cit., p. 117–118.

However, with time—and contrary to ideology and public pronounce-ment—a fairly pervasive and clear-cut division of labor by sex has emerged in the kibbutz, both within the household and in the wider community. Women have become responsible for the operation of the household, for the welfare of young infants, and for the bodily well-being of children. The ma-jority of women are engaged in nonincome-producing activities, are under-represented in the managerial and leadership positions, are totally absent from certain committees, and are predominant in those committees dealing with health, education, and services. Men are associated with agriculture, produc-tion, and central public administration. The result is that women did become free from individual household and child-care responsibilities only to do these tasks on a community-wide basis. This issue has been and continues to be one of the main problems of concern within the community.[13]

Child Rearing in the Kibbutz

The kibbutz is extremely child centered. Children represent the future. For our purposes, an examination of the parent-child relationship is signifi-cant in that it represents a unique form of communal socialization covering several decades. It illustrates the impact of a different kind of mothering for women and to children.

Kibbutz child rearing is performed by communal agents, and whatever its difficulties, it has proved to be an effective method of raising children. Kel-ler claims this is attested to by numerous studies that show the superiority of kibbutz-reared children in a number of areas, including their idealism, au-tonomy, cooperation, capacity for leadership, courage, and loyalty to the community.[14]

The manner in which child rearing occurs follows a collective pattern from infancy to adulthood. The infant is born of a kibbutz couple who gen-erally marry just before or soon after the first child is born. This is done in ac-cordance with the laws of Israel and gives the child legal rights. Upon return from the hospital, the infant is placed in the infant house. During the first year of the infant's life his mother comes to this house to breast-feed the in-fant as long as she physically can. Young fathers participate at this period in bottle feeding and diapering. In a radical departure from child rearing in most of the world, neither an infant nor any older children live with or are directly supported by the biological father and mother. The socialization and educa-tion of kibbutz children are functions of nurses and teachers.

During the first year, the general pattern of child care emerges. Most

---

13. This issue is discussed at length in Keller, ibid., pp. 118–130.
14. Gerson, op. cit., p. 53.

of the child's time is spent with peers in the children's house. In the afternoon, two or three hours may be spent with parents in their flat or room, meeting with other families or engaging in some joint activity. On the Sabbath, only the essential chores are performed, and children of all ages spend much time with their parents. To recognize the significance of the parent-child sessions is to understand the first sentence in this section: "The kibbutz is extremely child centered." Gerson asks the reader to ask themselves: How does this compare, both quantitatively and qualitatively with the arrangements of parent-child contact in the "normal" family situation in the United States?[15]

In addition to these hourly and Sabbath visits, the child frequently sees parents while they work or by attending the weekly assembly of the kibbutz. Thus parents are extremely important in the life of the child but parents are, in a sense, junior partners. The early training is carried out by caretakers—nurses and teachers.

This training occurs, for the most part, separate from the residence of the parents. For the first year, the infant is in the nursery. The child is then moved to a toddler's house, each of which has approximately two nurses and eight children. This is where toilet training, learning to feed oneself, and learning to interact with age-mates occurs. When the children reach the ages of two or three, a nursery teacher replaces one of the nurses. By the fourth and fifth birthday, the children move into the kindergarten. This involves a different building, sometimes a new nurse and teacher, and an enlargement of the original group to approximately sixteen members. This enlarged group remains together as a unit until age twelve and the completion of sixth grade. At this point they enter high schools where for the first time they encounter male educational teachers and begin to work directly in the kibbutz economy. Their work varies from one to three hours per day, depending on age, and is done in one of the economic branches under the supervision of adults (not parents). Upon completion of high school, the students are expected to live outside the kibbutz for approximately one year. Membership in the kibbutz follows this experience.

While the children do not sleep with, do not have their physical needs cared for, are not taught social, book, or economic skills by, and are not—for the most part—disciplined or socialized by their parents, most writers stress the importance of parents in the psychological development of the child. They serve as the object of identification and provide a certain security and love not obtained from others.

This factor was used in one study to explain differences in emotional problems between adopted and biological children.[16] The attempt of the study

15. Gerson, op. cit., p. 53.
16. Michaela Lifshitz, Ronie Bau, Irith Balgur, and Channa Cohen, "The Impact of the Social Milieu upon the Nature of Adoptees' Emotional Difficulties," *Journal of Marriage and the Family* 37 (February 1975), pp. 221–228.

was to assess whether adopted children raised within the kibbutz system had emotional problems that differed from biological kibbutz children. One key difference was found to be feelings of aloneness and insecurity among the adopted children. The kibbutz adoptees were more resigned to apathy and sadness. This finding was explained by the perceived importance of the family in the kibbutz on the one hand and the educational strategies exercised within the peer group on the other. That is, the family served as the source of identity and of belonging to a small and unique unit, in contrast to the educational atmosphere, which stressed cooperation. The adopted child perceived less points of resemblance between himself and his parents, and this promoted feelings of insecurity and alienation that were not allowed open expression in the cooperative style of education and were not acted out within the family unit out of fear of destroying even those seemingly precarious ties.

This is not meant to suggest that all biological kibbutz children have no conflicts or insecurities either personally or with parents. It has been demonstrated, however, that kibbutz children in general evidence less conflict with parents than nonkibbutz children,[17] and that kibbutz girls indicated less ambivalent attitudes toward and less emotional dependence on parents.[18] Parents in the kibbutz exhibit an absence of cruelty toward children and an absence of authoritarianism. As Keller states, the success and failures of kibbutz child rearing suggests that in principle children may derive considerable benefit from an upbringing that stresses peer relations, a merging of home and community, and voluntary mothers.[19]

Changes in the Kibbutz

Few, if any, family systems or societies, be they Chinese, Amish, or the kibbutz remain static and unchanging. As was shown in Chapter 4, change is brought about by many factors and forces: demographic, economic technological, cultural-contact, social movements, ideology, and others. Many of these forces seem to exist among the kibbutz.

According to Curtis, attention has been focused on a wide range of issues:

- Growth of industrialization
- Hiring of outside labor
- Dissatisfaction of women, especially older women
- Importance of the family
- The gap and difference in perception between the generations
- Stress on education

---

17. A. I. Robin, *Growing Up in the Kibbutz*, (New York: Springer, 1965), p. 179.
18. Gerson, op. cit., p. 56–57.
19. Keller, op. cit., p. 135.

- Rise in the standard of living
- Greater prominence and status accorded to production
- Need for expertise
- Resources that must be devoted to the handicapped and the elderly
- Concern for privacy
- Reduced interest in democratic participation
- Incompatibility between individuality and equality[20]

More specifically, in regard to the family, husband-wife relationships have been affected by a greater division of labor between husband and wife, an increase in the number of children, a greater role of the family in the socialization process, the fact that many children now sleep in the family home and the existence of three generations.[21] All this, while creating a greater family solidarity, has put a heavier domestic burden on the woman. Women have not been employed in an equal number of senior positions as men and clearly have not obtained the degree of liberation originally anticipated. Likewise, children have not been freed from sex typing in their process of socialization.

In spite of change, the kibbutz may be one of the biggest and most successful utopias in the world. In the words of Curtis:

> Despite changes in ideology, population (numbers and structure) and economic needs and values, the kibbutz remains a unique institution with a remarkable record: self-sufficiency without greed or materialist spirit; cooperation without a coercive apparatus; equality without a reduction of cultural or intellectual standards; freedom without disorder; work with neither boredom nor need of incentives; self-expression without license; specialization without stratification; guidance of public opinion without repression; moral concern without dogmatism; industrialization without urbanization; rural life without idiocy.[22]

FAMILIES OF THE PHILIPPINES

The Philippines is a country of more than 42 million people and more than 7100 islands. However, the number of islands can be misleading in that eleven of the islands comprise 90 percent of the total land area. Nearly 4500 of the islands have never been named, and some of the islands even appear and disappear with the tide. Nevertheless, that it is a country of islands becomes significant in understanding the extremely wide variation in family life-styles and in the communication, travel, and interchange of its people.

---

20. Curtis, op. cit., p. 108.
21. Ibid., p. 112.
22. Ibid., p. 113.

The country, slightly larger than the British Isles, is bounded by Taiwan and Japan to the north, China, Malaysia, and Vietnam to the west, Indonesia and Australia to the south, and the United States and Mexico to the east (about 6000 miles east). The country is often divided into three major areas: Luzon, Mindanao, and the Visayas. The largest, Luzon, is in the north. Here is found the largest city, Manila, which serves as the major industrial, political, education, and population center of the country. This area also includes the mountain province tribes, including the Kalingas, described later in the chapter. The second largest area, Mindanao, is in the south. This area includes cities such as Davao, Zamboanga and Cagayan de Oro and is the location of the newly found tribe, the Tasaday, as well as the home of one and a half million Muslims, also described in this chapter. The middle group of islands, the Visayas, includes Cebu, and, here are found the Mangyans, briefly illustrated later.

Space and focus of this book do not permit a complete explanation of the history, the contrasting topography and social groupings, and the diversity of family life-styles found within this country. The author has often referred to the country as one of extreme contrasts.[23] The modern structures in the business area of Makati (a section of Manila) serve as a polar extreme to the typical barrio of the rural areas. The rice terraces carved on the side of mountains in northern Luzon serve as a polar extreme to the typical rice paddy in the lowland. The beautifully decorated borong serves as a polar extreme to the G-string dress styles of many tribal minorities. The fancy decorated, privately owned Jeepney and the horse-drawn calesas (carriages) as modes of public transportation serve as polar extremes to air conditioned buses and the 747's of Philippine Air Lines. Even the exciting cockfights with screaming adult males serve as a polar extreme to the quiet, shy Filipino child.

Recognizing many variations in family life-styles, this section on families of the Philippines will focus primarily on four groupings: the dominant Christian Filipino family, the Muslim Filipino family of Mindanao, the Kalinga mountain province family of Luzon, and the Mangyan family of the Visayas.

THE CHRISTIAN FILIPINO FAMILY

An estimated 90 percent of the population in the Philippines is Catholic, a result of more than 300 years under Spanish domination. This factor produced the unique situation of a Christian country in a non-Christian Asia.

---

23. Various statements in the chapter are based on the personal observations of the author who lived in the Philippines for one year and went back for two months on a short-term, two-month lectureship several years later.

Like most other developing Asian nations, the crude birth rate is high[24] but abortion, and until very recently, vasectomy, birth control pills, and the like were basically taboo.

The Christian Filipino family described in this section refers to the majority of the population but excludes the Muslim and non-Christian tribal groups. Primary reference is made to the family and legal system prior to the declaration of martial law by President Marcos in September of 1972; however, most family practices remain basically unchanged since that time. The elimination of a free press, the confiscation of firearms, the locking up of dissident political and social leaders, the creation of a military regime, and an attempted land reform program, may have, if anything, stabilized the family system along more traditional lines. Yet, as will be seen, major strides are taking place with regard to family planning, and there exists today continuing agitation to legalize divorce. Both of these factors are likely to have a major impact over time on the family organization and the life-style of family members.

Wife-Husband Roles

The central force in the family is the Filipino woman. Though not typically the major breadwinner, she holds the family purse strings. The husband gives his wife his earnings, apart from his pocket expenses. In a very real sense, she is the boss of the house; yet the image conveyed is that the man is the master. The author recalls being told, partially in jest but yet in all seriousness, that the reason no immediate decision is ever made at a political or business session is that the men must first check it out with their wives.

While the husband is recognized as chief breadwinner and head of the family, the wife has definite spheres of competence in which the husband accepts her leadership. This is particularly true in household chores and family expenditures. But women are also regarded as shrewd and energetic traders. Many engage in small, independent commercial ventures. At higher socioeconomic levels, maids are hired inexpensively to permit educated women to pursue commercial and professional opportunities. Annual maternity leaves make it possible for women to hold jobs even during the child-bearing years.

The Filipinas (female) starts off on a nearly equal educational plane with her male counterpart. More than one-third of college graduates are women. When unmarried, it is important that the female graduate get employment to earn money to be turned over to her mother, often as reimburse-

24. The crude birth rate (number per 1000 population) according to latest available data is 44.7 in the Philippines, 48.3 in Indonesia, 37.5 in Vietnam, and 42.8 in Thailand. This contrasts with a rate of 23.8 in Taiwan, a rate of 19.4 in Japan and a rate of 15.0 in the U.S. U.S. Bureau of the Census, *Statistical Abstract of the United States: 1975,* 96th ed. (Washington, D.C., 1975). No. 1392, p. 839.

ment for college and clothing expenses. Upon marriage, the female usually accedes to her husband's opinion as to whether or not she should continue working. Couples marry at an age similar to those in the United States. In 1968, Peter Smith placed the median age at marriage at 22.5 for males and 20.0 for females.[25]

Apart from the Muslim or tribal groups, monogamy is widely stressed as the appropriate form of marriage. Two exceptions to monogamous legal unions among Christian Filipino families are consensual marriages and the querida system. Consensual unions, often occurring among the poor who wish to avoid the wedding expense, are more or less permanent relationships between a man and a woman without the sanction of a marriage ceremony. The querida system is described in the section that follows.

The Querida System

One writer[26] claims that the Spanish influenced the family life of the Filipino in a number of ways. It strengthened the unity and solidarity of the family and encouraged self-sacrifice among the members. It stood for authoritarianism and thus strengthened parental authority. On the other hand, it relegated the woman to an inferior position which resulted in a double standard of morality. For example, a man could have extra-marital relations with another woman with only minor condemnation, but a wife who behaved similarly with another man would be severely condemned. One example of this is seen in the querida system.

The querida system involves a married man, usually of higher status, seeing, supporting, and possibly having children by a woman other than his wife. While a "mistress relationship" is frowned upon, the Civil Code provides for the maintenance of his illegitimate children. The double standard is seen in that equal privileges do not exist for the wife. He can separate from her for adultery on her part, but she cannot do likewise. Nor can the wife bring an action for legal separation against the husband unless he maintains his mistress in the same dwelling as his legitimate wife.[27] The wife can, of course, simply leave him or refuse to cohabit, which would be a separation *de facto*. But the former would simply create additional problems of support and custody of the children.

The frequency of this keeping of a "mistress," "second wife" (not le-

25. Peter C. Smith, "Age at Marriage: Recent Trends and Prospects," *Philippine Sociological Review* 16 (January-April 1968), p. 6.

26. Jacob S. Quiambao, "The Filipino Family and Society," in Amparo S. Lardizabal and Felicitas Tensuan-Leogardo, ed., *Readings on Philippine Culture and Social Life* (Quezon City: Bustamante Press, 1970), p. 89.

27. See Jorge M. Juco, "Fault, Consent and Breakdown—The Sociology of Divorce Legislation in the Philippines," *Philippine Sociological Review* 14 (April 1966), pp. 71–72.

gally), or querida, is unknown. John Carroll wrote that an informal survey of priests from twenty-two dioceses suggests that the percentage of men with queridas is about one or two, although in certain urban social strata it is probably much higher. He also noted that the census reports 47,520 more females than males claimed to be married, and 23,199 more females than males claimed to be divorced or separated, suggesting that at least 70,000 men or 1.5 percent of married men are keeping second "wives" or have "forgotten" their marriage obligations.[28]

The querida often represents a serious threat to a wife and children in diminishing their man's affection and support. Thus while wives may know about their husband's querida, they may pretend they do not. Hollnsteiner notes that as long as the man adopts some measure of self-control and fidelity, his morality is secure and his role adequately discharged. The wife in turn avidly participates in religious life and, in effect, prays for two, her piety making up for both her own and her husband's failings.[29]

Family Planning and Children

In a literal sense, the Philippines is a nation of children. Half of the population of more than 42 million people is under seventeen years of age. Six or seven children per family appears to be the average. The concern over population growth lead to an official plan to reduce the birth rate from an estimated 43.2 per 1000 in 1970 to 35.9 in 1977. This 1970 plan included: 1) limiting maternity-leave benefits to the first four deliveries, 2) provision of free family planning services for employees in all establishments employing 300 or more and maintaining a clinic, 3) development of incentive bonus schemes to encourage family planning among married workers, and 4) prohibition of the regulation that a woman be dismissed from employment once she married. Changes were made in 1974 to bring family planning to remote areas. These included the use of paramedical personnel (physicians, nurses, midwives, and field workers) for IUD insertion and distribution of orals, condoms, and diaphragms, establishment of village resupply points, and utilization of mobile teams. The 1976 government budget for family planning programs was 118 million pesos, up from 0.4 million in 1971. As a result, in 1975, more than 750,000 persons accepted government family planning services. While abortion was and is not an acceptable service, 51,000 women had IUD's inserted, 364,000 accepted oral contraceptives, 34,000 sterilizations

28. John J. Carroll, "The Family in a Time of Change," in John J. Carroll, et. al., *Philippine Institutions* (Manila: Sobdaridad Publishing, 1970), p. 11.

29. Mary R. Hollnsteiner, "The Filipino Family Confronts the Modern World," in *Responsible Parenthood in the Philippines*, edited by Vitaliano R. Gorospe (Manila: Ateneo Publications, 1970), p. 23.

were performed (up from 0 in 1973 and 1.4 thousand in 1974) and 301,000 accepted other program methods including rhythm.[30]

Children are highly valued in traditional Philippine society as economic assets, as insurance in old age, as a demonstration of male potency, as sources of enjoyment, as gifts from God, as extensions of themselves, and for many other reasons. Mounting evidence, however, indicates a desire for fewer children and a smaller family size. In one study of nearly 2500 students from eight universities, the average number of children perceived as ideal was 3.5. Less than 10 percent of the respondents mentioned six or more children as ideal while 15 percent said two or less was ideal.[31]

Filipino children are raised in an atmosphere of love and, in the younger years, of indulgence. The child is expected to be quiet and submissive rather than aggressive and domineering. Children are taught filial loyalty and obedience to elders. There is seldom a question as to who wields authority in the family. Father comes first, then mother, then the grandparents, then the uncles and aunts, and then those siblings older than themselves. Even among siblings, authority and responsibility are based on age. The older children look after smaller brothers and sisters. Aging parents are to be provided by for the children and, upon their death, the eldest son assumes the responsibility as head of the family.

Carroll[32] states that little pressure is put upon the child to achieve, and initiative in undertaking unfamiliar tasks is discouraged. A child who tries and fails is scolded for not asking assistance. It is assumed the child will learn naturally, by imitation and with the assistance of others. In school, being "the same as everyone else" is valued by the child more than excellence.

Several values appear to be of utmost importance for children to learn. Three of these are expressed in the concepts hiya, utang na loob, and pakikisama. *Hiya*, variously translated as shame, timidity, or shyness, is a desirable trait, especially among low-status persons in general and children in particular. Many times the author noted a small child hiding behind the leg of a parent, saying nothing and appearing shy and embarrassed. Another person would then remark with pleasure that the child was ashamed. Hiya is expressed in other ways as well. For example, if you help someone else, and later ask for help from that person, he or she cannot refuse without losing face and experiencing shame (hiya).

Children are also taught *utang na loob*, translated as a "debt of gratitude." Again, if something is done for someone, that person owes a debt of

30. Dorothy Nortman and Ellen Hofstatter, "Population and Family Planning Programs: A Factbook," *Reports on Population/Family Planning* (New York: Population Council, October, 1976), pp. 26, 37, 40, 55, 63.

31. J. Ross Eshleman, "Filipino Students Reactions to Fertility Control." Paper presented at the annual meeting for the Association for Asian Studies meeting, Washington, D.C., 1971 and summarized in *Philippine Sociological Review* 21 (April 1973), pp. 192–195.

32. Carroll, op. cit., p. 15.

gratitude, a repayment, or assistance in times of crisis or trouble. Utang na loob means to be aware of those from whom favors are received and to repay them in an acceptable manner. The repayment is often unquantifiable. How does one ever pay or express gratitude to parents for life, to friends for kindness, or to the elderly for their care and concern? To be aware of the debt and to give sporadic token gifts or services is to express utang na loob and avoid hiya.

A third important value to be taught children is known as *pakikisama*, translated as smooth interpersonal relationships (SIR). Good relationships are believed to enrich the spirit of the community. SIR is evidenced by the use of polite language, soft voice, gentle manner, and indirect approaches—like employing intermediaries—or ambiguous expressions that avoid directness and frankness. Children (and adults) must learn to avoid conflict or disagreement with persons in authority or the majority of the group. This value serves to avoid conflict and lead to concessions; however, several researchers have shown how it may distract an entrepreneur from taking the steps necessary to assure maximum success of a business enterprise. While good feelings and efficiency are not antithetical, an excessive concern over smooth interpersonal relationships leads one to tolerate inefficiency and poor performance.[33]

On many occasions, the author witnessed the employment of hiya, utang na loob, and pakikisama among students. To maintain smooth interpersonal relationships (pakikisama), students would often agree rather than offend the instructor. To not be shamed (hiya), students would sit quietly and nod approvingly rather than admit they don't understand. A graduate student to whom the author served as thesis advisor insisted that he join the group on an "outing," a visit with the family on a visit to the home province, and to this day sends gifts to express her debt of gratitude (utang na loob). It is the contention of Mina Ramirez that basic values and patterns of behavior such as hiya, utang na loob, and pakikisama are practiced by families to create security for self and family.[34] Among a people where socioeconomic conditions are poor, security exists in not offending, in having persons owe you a debt, in paying off debts where due, and in the avoidance of shame.

Extended Kinship Networks

Much has been written about the Filipino family network, the restriction the responsibility to extended family members places on individual achievement and getting ahead, and the comfort and security found among relatives. Barrio relatives may be more kin oriented, but urban families pos-

---

33. George M. Guthrie et. al., *The Psychology of Modernization in the Rural Philippines* (Quezon City: Ateneo de Manila University Press, 1970), p. 43.

34. Mina Ramirez, "A Phenomenology of the Filipino Family", *Saint Louis Quarterly* 6 (September-December 1968), p. 350–351.

sess in larger measure the resources needed to assist an extra relative looking for work or going to school. Take the situation that exists in Manila.

Manila is the urban center of the nation, being more than ten times the size of the second largest city, Cebu. In the U.S., it is generally assumed that rural families have more members and a larger household than do urban families. However, in the Philippines the extended-family responsibilities and the lack of low-cost housing combined with the greater job and educational opportunities in Manila lead to a situation of a disproportionate number of urban extended-family situations. Contrary to expectations, the percentage of households that include relatives other than the nuclear family of father, mother, and children increases in the Philippines with the level of urbanization.[35] Household size is larger in urban than in rural areas and the difference reflects the presence of extended kin.

Hollnsteiner shows how wealth and poverty are linked with kin support.[36] People living on a subsistence level, which many Filipinos are, become dependent on a traditional scheme of mutual responsibility among kinsmen. The businessman investing in a new corporate venture faces similar restrictions. The positions of treasurer, supply clerk, purchasing agent, manager, and general employees require trustworthy people. Relatives can generally be depended upon for loyalty and for working long hours with little pay. These are qualifications that may supersede skill. As a result, one researcher estimated that nearly 90 percent of all Filipino corporations are tightly held family corporations and 75 percent of all businesses are owned by single proprietors, usually the head of the family.[37] Another researcher found that kinship relations flourish and continually function in the lives of managers. Primary kin relations dominate kin involvement of managers, interaction with parents is frequent, relations with siblings are characterized by frequent contact, among secondary kin contact occurs more frequently with affines than with cousins or uncles or aunts—however, more cousins are interacted with because a greater number of cousins are available.[38]

Urbanization theory that suggests a disruption in the intensity or number of kin ties has little support in the Philippines. Several studies of urbanization, modernization, or industrialization in metropolitan Manila fail to find evidence of a severance of kin ties. Perhaps still active is the Tagalog (the national language of the Philippines) proverb that states: He who does not remember where he came from will not reach where he is going, or no matter

---

35. John J. Carroll, *Changing Patterns of Social Structure in the Philippines, 1896–1963.* (Quezon City: Ateneo de Manila, 1968), pp. 134–135.

36. Hollnsteiner, op. cit., p. 40; and William F. Skinner, "Urbanization and Household Structure in the Philippines," *Journal of Marriage and the Family* 39 (May 1977), pp. 377–385.

37. Richard P. Poethig, "The Philippine Urban Family," *Saint-Louis Quarterly* 6 (September-December 1968), p. 382.

38. Jesse A. N. Dizon, Jr., "Modern Filipino Kinship: The Manila Corporation Manager as a Case in Point," *Philippine Sociological Review* 21 (January 1973), pp. 37–50.

A Generalized Comparison of Selected Differences among Folk, Urban Filipino, and Western Family Systems

Primitive or Folk	Urban Filipino	Western
Either paternal or maternal dominance.	Facade of paternal dominance but bilateral kinship emphasis enhances power of wife.	Trend toward complete equality between husband and wife.
Family is the property holder and the source of labor.	Important in property holding, less effective as labor unit.	Economic role greatly diminished except as unit of consumption.
Little discipline of children who are socialized by environmental pressure.	Combination of discipline and indulgence in treatment of children.	Trend toward equality in parent-child relationship.
Romantic love secondary to economic and kinship considerations in marriage choice.	Romantic love exalted but subordinate to parental approval.	Romantic love all-important, with parental approval playing minor role.
Relatively free relationship with opposite sex before marriage.	Premarital associations, heavily chaperoned.	Little or no chaperonage and few taboos.
Society tends to approve fairly wide range of sex activity in both premarital and postmarital status. No commercialized vice or prostitution.	Double standard, with much latitude for men but little for respectable women. *Queridas*, consensual marriage, and prostitution increase opportunities for sexual activity.	Tendency to a single stand and for both sexes with fewer taboos for both. Prostitution plays minor role and mistresses are rare. Common-law marriage usually confined to lowest socio-economic group.
Divorce easy to obtain on many grounds. Usually no financial hardship on either party since land and property are merely divided.	No divorce. Legal separation without right of remarriage.	Divorce obtainable on many grounds but subject to legal restriction and financially burdensome.
Large family group including collateral relatives although older children often live in separate dormitory. High birth rate and high infant mortality.	Large family group, often including three generations and collateral relatives in same house. High birth rate. Infant mortality rate between Primitive and Western.	Small family includes only two generations and no collateral relatives. Low birth rate and low infant mortality.

Source: Socorro C. Espiritu, et. al., *Sociology in The New Philippine Setting* (Manila: Alemar–Phoenix Press, 1976), p. 173.

how high or far one travels he should keep in touch with those he left behind.[39]

THE MUSLIM FAMILY IN SOUTHERN PHILIPPINES

Muslim families, like lowland Christian or mountain province families, differ considerably from one area to another within the Philippines; yet they maintain certain practices in common as based upon the Koran and the Islamic religion. Most Muslim families in the Philippines are to be found in the most southern section of the country, which includes Mindanao and the Sulu Archipelago.

There are five main groups of Muslim Filipinos: Maranaos, Samals, Tausogs, Badjaoes, and Magindanaos. The Badjaoes and Samals are sea-faring and live mostly in vintas and houses constructed on poles over water along the seashore. The Maranaos are mostly tillers of the soil. While these groups show no noticeable differences in physical characteristics among each other or among Filipino Christians, they differ widely from the Christians in culture and social organization.

A Comparison of Muslim and Christian Filipinos

Rivera made the following observations on some of the differences in social and cultural characteristics of Muslims as compared to the Filipinos in general:

1. Male authority is more dominant in family and society generally.
2. A few wealthy men have several wives, but monogamous marriages prevail among them as among all Filipino elements.
3. Earlier marriage is encouraged.
4. The custom of dowry is observed in nearly all marriages, with the bride's parents generally receiving the property collected.
5. Divorce can be obtained more easily.
6. Segregation of the sexes is enforced more rigidly, especially after puberty.
7. The Maranao household is large, not because wives have more children each, but because several families often live in the same dwelling. (Several households of the sheiks, hadjis and datus contained twenty or thirty persons).

---

39. Ibid., p. 47.

8. The clan organization is stronger with elaborate ritual and hierarchy of functionaries.
9. The datus are more powerful politically than appointed or elected officials of the Philippine Government.
10. Religion probably plays a larger role in the daily behavior of Moslems than of Christians.
11. Formal education is valued less among the Maranaos than among Christian Filipinos, especially with reference to women.[40]

Gender Roles, Marriage, and Divorce

While it was noted that a double standard exists in the Filipino Christian family, it is even more pronounced among the Muslims. Among certain groups, women cannot leave their homes without the husband's permission. Many Muslim men speak fluent English, but one seldom finds a woman that speaks a language other than the native tongue. Close to the age of puberty, girls are usually taken from the public school and remain at home. Particularly among the higher class Muslims, women and girls are as much as possible secluded from the general public and cover their faces in public, while the poorer women go outside, do household tasks, and attend the marketplace. The male is the patriarch, the ruler, decision maker and head of the family. He handles the money, does the major buying, settles quarrels within the household, tills the soil or does the fishing, and if devoted prays five times a day facing Mecca. While women may attend the mosque, they sit in the rear or in a balcony out of view.

The double standard is most evident in marriage and divorce codes. A text of the Koran instructs men that if they "cannot act equitably toward orphans, then marry such women as seem good to you, two and three and four."[41] No such instruction is given to women. Divorce is an easy matter for the male as well. The husband simply announces, "I divorce you," three times to get it legalized. The Koran instructs the husband: "Ye may divorce your wives twice: Keep them honourably, or put them away with kindness."[42] If the husband divorces her a third time, it is not lawful for him to take her again until she shall have married another husband and is divorced by him.

While under the religion of Islam a man may have four wives if he is in a position to support and maintain them and the resulting children, the actual practice of polygyny is relatively infrequent. A second and subsequent wife entails the consent and approval of the first wife. The first wife is the head wife and has the first right to inherit the husband's property in case of

---

40. Generoso F. Rivera, "The Maranao Muslims in Lumbayao, Lanao," *Philippine Sociological Review* 14 (July 1966), pp. 127–128.
41. The Koran, Surah IV, vs. 3.
42. Ibid., Surah II, vs. 229.

> *Alex:*   *In Turkey, the role of the woman is really nothing. It's just that. Like my grandfather used to say, you can't do without them and you can't do with them either. You know, it's that type. You have to have women for housework, for households, for reproductive purposes, you know. She is a type of sex object, that's about it. Husbands never treat their wives as equals. Daughters the same way. The son is always treated better than the daughter. I was freer. I always got what I wanted, but my sister was brought up very strict, and she didn't have the same facilities that I had as far as schooling was concerned. She had to go to an all-girls school which was very strict.*
>
> *I'm an Orthodox Christian, but Turkey is basically Muslim. And as far as the Muslims are concerned, it's in their religion that women are supposed to be inferior. They do not go against it. It's known and accepted, no questions asked. Woman is inferior.*

death. The wives may or may not live together under one roof, depending on their relationship. If they have difficulty living together, separate houses may be necessary.

The taking on of a second wife is considered a sign of affluence and importance. It is also a way of sealing a much desired agreement of friendship or of acquiring needed capital for business or political purposes. A man who has wives in a number of districts draws support from those districts during elections or other occasions. In some instances, the first wife may prevail on the husband to take home another wife so she can be relieved of much of the household drudgery.[43]

Marriage customs are very well defined. For the male, marriage is an expensive affair. Among the upper classes, the bride's price runs to thousands of pesos plus some carabaoes (the work animal). In some instances heavy mortgages and borrowing from relatives may be necessary, for no legal marriage is effected until conditions are met. This is true among the poor as well, but the "price" of the bride is proportionately lower.

Among most groups, courtship is not considered important and the male-female marriage relationship is dominated by parental wishes. The couple are not allowed to speak to each other except in groups and, if they do, are closely watched. Espiritu and others[44] describe the case of Ali and Fatima:

> Shortly after the final arrangements were reached, the marriage was solemnized. The bride's dowry was delivered to Abdul's house a day before the

---

43. Rufino de Los Santos, "Moslem Values: A Challenge to Education," *Philippine Sociological Review* 14 (April 1966), p. 77.

44. Socorro C. Espiritu, Mary R. Hollnsteiner, Chester L. Hunt, Luis Q. Lacar, and Lourdes R. Quisumbing, *Sociology in the New Philippine Setting* (Manila: Alemar-Phoenix Press, 1976), p. 170.

wedding. Late in the afternoon of the next day, Ali was carried in a long procession to the house of Fatima. The marriage ceremony, consisting of the recitation of prayers in Arabic, then took place. Fatima was out of sight during the entire proceedings. The ritual was conducted with only the young man, the bride's father, and the religious *imam* (official) present since an Islamic marriage is principally a contract between the groom and the girl's father. Then the groom was led to the bride, whose forehead he symbolically touched to indicate his right to claim her as his wife.

Following the wedding, the couple start married life in the girl's family home. It is the duty of the girl's parents to train her to be a good wife. Later the couple move to the home of the husband.

As in the Christian family, children are highly valued, but unlike the Christian family, Muslim men can divorce a wife who does not conceive.

THE KALINGA IN THE MOUNTAINOUS NORTHERN PHILIPPINES

Kalinga is a subprovince in the Mountain Province of northern Luzon as well as the name of an ethnolinguistic people.[45] The province includes other minority groups such as the Bontoc, the Ibaloy, the Kankanay, the Apayas, and the better-known Ifugao with their renowned irrigated rice terraces thought to have been cut into the mountain side more than 4000 years ago. These groups were formerly marked by feuds, warfare, and frequent head-hunting forays. The head-taking has subsided, but occasional killings sparked by old feuds still occur. Today, the existence of peace pacts and the possibility of extensive travel has resulted in considerable exchange and generous hospitality.

While dwellings differ within and between villages, all houses are raised above the ground on posts, with steps or a ladder leading up to a single entrance. Generally, the houses are square single-room dwellings. The walls and floors are made of bamboo with the roofs pitched and made of reeds and grass. Each dwelling has a fire pit near the center that is filled with sand and accumulated ash. The newer style houses increasingly use hand-hewn boards with galvanized pitched roofs.

On a visit to the mountain province area, men, women, and children

---

45. This section is based primarily on Edward P. Dozier, *The Kalinga of Northern Luzon, Philippines* (New York: Holt, Rinehart and Winston, 1967). Some comments are based on observations of the author who visited Bontoc and Ifaguao villages in the Mountain Province.

are much in evidence. Babies are rarely put down but are carried in blanket slings passed over one shoulder and tied in front. The baby rides on the back or on either hip, supported by the blanket and easily slung to the front when it wishes to suckle. Women carrying babies go about their work transporting loads balanced on their heads, winnowing rice, cooking, weeding, or performing other tasks while the baby sleeps or enjoys the constant motion. Blanket slings, the wraparound skirts of the women, and the G-strings of the men are generally of a hand-woven, brightly colored cotton fabric. No shoes are worn and the upper body is often bare, although frequently tattooed. Beads and necklaces complete the costume. More recently, the influx of lowland Filipinos modified the traditional dress to trousers or shorts for men and blouses for women, particularly for the younger members of both sexes.

The Kalinga Household

The resident unit of the Kalinga is the household, occupied by a nuclear family and perhaps an aged grandparent. The number of children born is often as high as ten or fifteen, but seldom do more than half survive beyond the age of puberty. Pigs, chickens, and dogs roaming freely under the house contribute to the generally unsanitary conditions and pollution of the water. When disease epidemics hit a village, often the entire population is infected, since dwellings are clustered together and few precautions are taken.

The number of interacting households is partly dictated by the number of married daughters. Residence is predominantly uxorilocal (residence near the wife's parents), since the bride's relatives construct a home near the girl's parental home. The couple may live with the wife's parents (matrilocal) while their own house is constructed but leave upon completion. Families (including relatives) who cannot provide a home for their daughters are shamed. Kinship ties are strong, much visiting occurs among them, and each shares the pride or shame of the others. Members of a kinship group are required to support one another in all disputes and conflicts and are obligated to avenge any member who is killed or wronged. Marriage to kin is strictly forbidden through first cousins.

The importance of this kin network decreases the attention and focus on the nuclear unit. Grandparents are extremely important. They serve as caretakers of babies and children, as the source of learning ceremonial practices and beliefs, and as the key source of advice and counsel. Newborn infants are often given the name of a living or departed grandparent. This is related to beliefs that the attributes of its namesake are magically transferred to the child, and if the grandchild dies, the spirit of the child is taken by the named grandparent who serves as a guardian after death. Thus, great respect, attention, care, and affection are accorded to grandparents.

Child Rearing and Marriage

Child rearing may be characterized as indulgent and permissive. Parents seldom resort to whipping, but scold or frighten children into obedience. Strangers often become bogey men, and children may be told these men will carry them away if they do not behave. Until the ages of six or seven, children sleep with parents, but later the boys go to an *obog*, a vacant house used as a sleeping place, and girls sleep with age-mates in the homes of widows.[46] If an adolescent girl has sexual relations with a man not contracted to her in marriage, with a man already married, or with a man who has not promised to marry her, she will be whipped. The male escapes punishment unless he forced the girl into sexual relations, in which case he must pay heavy fines. This is not based on moral principles but on practical concerns of support and inheritance. For economic and inheritance reasons, most marriages are arranged. While the contract of an arranged marriage may be broken by the couple, parents make every effort to hold together a couple whose contract is considered a sound economic arrangement.

Marriage is the second of four stages in the Kalinga life cycle having social and ceremonial significance. The others are birth, sickness, and death. Birth is significant to a marriage in that a couple will separate if no children are born in order to try their luck with other partners. If in the second marriage no children are born, they separate again. As a result, the number of divorces is high among the Kalinga. Edward Dozier reported that as many as 50 percent of the men presently married in one region had been divorced at least once.[47] Such divorces are almost always because the woman did not conceive. A woman will keep trying to have children with different partners until the onset of menopause. In some cases a wife will permit her husband to have a mistress with the agreement among all three that if there are children, one of them will be raised as the married couple's own.

Factors that lead to the inability of a woman to have a child include 1) a disregard of bad omens at the time of marriage, 2) the activity of the *ngilin*, a water spirit who is believed to have the appearance of a human pigmy, and 3) an organic or physical defect in the reproductive organs of the woman. For the first two factors, the couple may pretend to separate to make the ngilin believe the couple gave up trying to have a child. This action will make the ngilin turn its attention elsewhere and, while it is distracted, the couple will conceive. As in most cultures, pregnancy is accompanied by a wide variety of superstition, myths, and rituals. For example, nausea during the wife's pregnancy is believed to have been brought on because the husband had eaten foods such as beef, frogs, and dog meat, prohibited during preg-

---

46. Among certain tribes this house is termed *ulog*. For example an insert in Chapter 12 describes an Igorot marriage folkway. Igorot is a slang term for the combination of mountain province tribes.

47. Ibid., p. 32.

nancy. Both husband and wife must avoid places such as streams and water-falls, because this is where the ngilin resides and the ngilin may devour or cause the death of the unborn. A pregnant woman must not eat eggs; the baby may be born blind. And the father must avoid playing the flute during labor or the child may become an incessant cry baby.

While variations exist from one region to another, it is not uncommon to engage children soon after birth. The boy's parents make the initial advances in selecting a man or two related to both parties to act as go-betweens. The mediators present the girl's parents with valuable beads and, if all goes well, a pig is killed and a feast is celebrated in the presence of the girl's relatives with the mediators as honored guests. Upon leaving, they are given a gift to deliver to the boy's parents. This is the first step of the contractual agreement.

When the boy is between twelve and fourteen, he is taken to the girl's house by his relatives. There he performs services such as hauling fuel or working in the fields. He may return home for a few days but generally remains with the family of the betrothed performing this form of bride service. When the boy is about the age of seventeen, he and certain relatives proceed through a series of events, feasts, and gift exchanges. After this gift exchanging the boy and girl sleep together. Five months later, the final exchange of gifts and the wedding feast take place. Carabaos are killed for the occasion, much wine is consumed, and relatives from both families through third cousins participate. At this feast, the couple receive a part of their share of the family inheritance—rice fields, jars, beads, and items that help the couple set up their own household. Up to this time, the couple lived with the girl's parents, but after the feast a separate residence is constructed for them and they participate fully as married adults in the work and life of the kin group and village. As indicated, children are essential for a stable and enduring marriage. Without children, separation or divorce is customary, gifts are returned or a settlement takes place between the families, and a new marriage is contracted. With children providing blood ties, Kalinga social and regional linkages are assured and kin obligations and privileges operate in full.

THE MANGYAN FAMILY IN CENTRAL PHILIPPINES

The primitive pagan tribes living in the mountains of the island of Mindoro are collectively referred to as the Mangyans.[48] Were it not for their distinctive attire, it would be difficult to differentiate these people from the

---

48. This section is taken primarily from Emeterio de la Paz, "A Survey of the Hanunoo Mangyan Culture and Barriers to Change," *Unitas* 41 (March 1968), pp. 3–63.

Kalingas, Muslims, or Christian Filipinos. They are a peaceful and shy people and, unlike the mountain province tribes who retaliate at the slightest provocation, the Mangyans retreat and give up their rights (including land) rather than fight for them. Certainly this was a factor contributing to their poverty-stricken situation. Mangyans are known to be polite and rarely quarrel with each other or outsiders. They are also extremely dirty. Rarely do they take a bath and, even if they do, the same unwashed G-string of the men and the rectangular piece of cloth wrapped around the women is put on again.

Sanitation is practically unknown. All kinds of excreta (from pigs, dogs, goats, chickens, children) are around the village. As a result of continuous betel nut chewing and frequent spitting, red splotches are seen everywhere. Adults and children are scantily dressed even in cold weather and, given these unsanitary conditions, respiratory, skin, and other diseases are frequent.[49]

Houses made from thatched grasses are elevated four to five feet from the ground and supported by bamboo posts. The house has no partition and is used for everything—sleeping, eating, workroom, and, in inclement weather, even cooking. There are no chairs, tables, or any other furniture, but several baskets hang from the rafters to hold personal belongings, food, and the like.

The Mangyans "earn a living" by hunting (wild birds, chickens, pigs, or deer), fishing, raising animals and grain, and gathering forest products such as rattan, vines, or bamboos. Frequently, after land has been cleared for rice, beans, or bananas, lowlanders come and claim the land for themselves. Ignorant of existing Philippine laws, having no written laws of their own, and wishing to live peacefully, they are continually driven deeper into the mountains and the islands interior.

Mangyan Marriage and Family Life

Most settlements are made up of families who are related to each other in some way. Elders are respected and recognized as heads. Children, when they get married, make their home either near the boy's or girl's parents, whichever they prefer. Most frequently they go to the girl's settlement, but visits to the boy's settlement are frequent. Seldom do marriages occur within the same settlement.

It is difficult to know the age at marriage. Ask any Mangyan his age and he will not know or be able to tell you, since they do not keep track of

49. The author visited a Mangyan village in 1969 with the family of a graduate student from the island of Mindoro. This family insisted he wear (carry) ginger in his pocket to protect him from sickness and the spirits of the Mangyan. (Apparently it worked; he didn't get sick.)

time. However, many a Mangyan girl is married before puberty, on occasion to an "elderly" man who takes over the responsibility of rearing her until she can bear him children. For the boy, the criterion for marriage is not age but his ability to support a family.

Courtship has been described as follows:

> If a young man wishes to court a girl, he has to learn many love songs, which they refer to as the *ambahan*. This *ambahan* is a general term used for all the love songs chanted on all occasions such as feasts and celebrations. In courting, the young man tries to catch the attention of the lady of his affections by singing the *ambahan*. Disguising his voice, he chants these love songs as he has learned them without any accompaniment. In between the recitations he plays his *subing* or *gitara*, a three-stringed guitar. He does not stop until the girl invites him inside the house. When invited, he lies down beside the girl. If the girl accepts him, he is allowed to stay the night. But if she refuses, he has to leave the house before the sun is up. Then he tries his luck again another time. This whole period of serenades is called a *pahagot*. Sometimes the boy is not deft in this area, in which case he asks others to do it for him. These people then are recompensed for this service in kind like loaning an instrument or a tool, a treat to some meal, a promise to help out in some project.[50]

If the girl accepts the boy for marriage, the parents of both come together to decide on the size of the bride payment. This may consist of a cow, number of pigs, rice, or ornaments. If the boy or his family is too poor to pay he may work for the girl's family for some time.

The actual wedding ceremony is short, but the celebration consisting of singing, dancing, eating, and drinking lasts "indefinitely," depending on the means of the boy. The finality of the marriage occurs when the girl bears a child. Inability to do so is cause for separation or desertion. Polygamy is unknown among the Mangyans as most are too poor to support several wives or many children.

As would be expected, given the lack of sanitary conditions and the absence of doctors, hospitals, and hygienic practices, the death rate of the newborn and in early life is very high although accurate data is not available. The mother in labor is left alone with her husband, who massages her abdomen. A midwife may be called to help in the delivery, but it is usually the husband who cuts the umbilical cord with a sharp bamboo stick and gives the mother a potion to drink prepared from boiled leaves, roots, and barks. After birth, the child is always with the mother until it is weaned, usually about one year. Similarly to the Kalinga, the mother carries the infant on a sling hung on her shoulders.

Mangyans, while considered pagan by the Christian, take great pride in their honesty, respect for property, hospitality, helpfulness and coopera-

---

50. Emeterio de la Paz, op. cit., p. 25.

tion, and sanctity of marriage. Houses are left open, borrowed articles are always treated with care and returned promptly, help is shared during planting and harvest, elders are respected, and infidelity is punishable in their unwritten laws with fines. Through contact with the lowland Christians, the Mangyans learned to chew tobacco, gamble, and to feel inferior to all others. The Christian lowlander, keenly aware of the Mangyan's shabby dress and illiteracy and recognizing them as a source of easy exploitation, has ridiculed, sexually abused, and cheated them and grabbed the untitled land. The very word "damuong" (lowlander) arouses feelings of fear, resentment, and hatred. The recourse of the Mangyan is to retreat. Even though laws have been passed to protect the rights of minority groups, ways have been found to circumvent the law. With the Mangyans, it is easier to do than with most.

Summary

This chapter on family life-styles in various cultures examined five family systems in two countries: Israel and the Philippines. In Israel, the kibbutz involves communal living, collective ownership of all property, and the rearing of children by nurses and teachers. The family is not a self-interested economic unit. Rather, both male and female work to support the community. The couple share a room or housing unit but their children, with few exceptions, live in children's houses. The kibbutz "family" system is clearly differentiated from nonkibbutz Israeli families. The latter are not examined here.

In the Philippines even more than in Israel a diversity of family lifestyles exist. This chapter focused on four family systems within that country: the predominant Filipino Christian family, the Muslim family in the southern part of the country, the Kalinga family in the mountainous north, and the Mangyan family in the central area.

The Christian Filipino family includes approximately 90 percent of all people in the country. The woman is the central force in the family unit as far as having the primary responsibility for the children, handling the money, and making most of the decisions. Yet the husband is recognized as the chief breadwinner and head. Marriages are monogamous but a married man may maintain a querida (mistress) as well. Only a small percentage of the population do so, however. Children play a significant role in the Filipino family, both in terms of numbers as well as importance, and families are very large. Selected basic values taught to children include "hiya," a sense of shyness and shame, "utang na loob," a debt of gratitude, and "pakikisama," meaning smooth interpersonal relationships.

The second major grouping in the Philippines consists of Muslims. In contrast to the Christian Filipino man to the north, the Muslim male is extremely dominant, he may have up to four wives, and he may easily divorce his wife. Certain Muslim groups live along the seacoast in houses built over the water on poles, earning a living primarily by fishing and trading. Others live inland and engage primarily in agricultural pursuits. While it may appear to many westerners that the double standard is extreme among the Christian Filipino family, it is much more so among Muslim Filipinos. Some women may not even leave their homes without the husband's permission. Courtship, while not considered important, is expensive to the family of the male.

The Kalingas, a tribal group, live in the mountain province northern part of the country. Their dress, housing units, children's sleeping quarters, uxorilocal residence structure after marriage, mate selection patterns, and the like stand in sharp contrast to the Filipino Christian family and in many ways in contrast to the Muslim or Mangyan family.

The Mangyan family, like the Kalinga, is considered by the outsider to be pagan. But the Mangyan are known to be a peaceful, honest, and cooperative people. Mangyans rarely bathe, and sanitation is generally ignored. They have no sense of time, thus age is less important than ability to care for one's family. Being illiterate, extremely poor, and valuing nonviolent action, the Mangyans have been exploited and driven into the mountain areas.

The next two chapters bring us to the United States, where the Amish and black families are examined. These family systems stand in sharp contrast to any family system examined thus far.

Key Terms and Topics

Discussion Questions

1. *In the previous chapter, the discussion on communes mentioned that many are short-lived and experience much strain and conflict. Explain how the kibbutz could exist for over seventy years?*
2. *What reasons exist for marriage among members of the kibbutz? Can you think of reasons for marriage even if no children are born?*
3. *What do the family and socialization practices in the kibbutz have to teach about "maternal instincts," wife-mother employment, sex roles, husband as the economic provider, parental discipline, peer group relationships, sex education, and other aspects?*
4. *What is to be gained by leaving the kibbutz for a year after high school?*

*Would you expect most youth to return to the kibbutz or stay outside?
Why?*

5. *What is to be gained by having students in the United States or Canada
study the family life-styles of tribes in a country such as the Philippines?*

6. *Divorce is not legally or socially accepted among the Christian Filipinos
and is a simple procedure among Muslim Filipinos. How can two family
groupings live in the same country and have such extreme norms?*

7. *What parallels exist between the Christian Filipino family and Christian
families anywhere else in the world? What differences can you identify?
How do you explain any similarities or differences?*

8. *Discuss the pros and cons of the querida system. How is it possible for this
system to exist in a sexually conservative, monogamous, Catholic country?*

9. *Three Filipino values termed "hiya," "utang na loob," and "pakikisama"
were described. What do they mean? Are there parallels to these in this
country? Describe some of the consequences of adherence to values such
as these.*

10. *Compare and contrast the Muslim and Christian family in the Philippines.*

11. *If a Muslim man can legitimately have up to four wives, why do so few
do so? Would you expect the first wife to strongly oppose the taking of additional wives? Why or why not?*

12. *The Kalingas and the Mangyans are both considered "pagan" minority
groups living in mountainous, remote interior areas of the Philippines?
What do these groups have in common with minority groups elsewhere
in the world with which you are familiar? Examine family factors such
as family size, husband and wife roles, courtship practices, role of kin
group, life expectancy, and the like.*

Further Readings

Bell, Norman W., and **Ezra F. Vogel.** *A Modern Introduction to the Family.* Rev. ed.
New York: Free Press, 1968. This book is basically a functional analysis of the
family system and includes articles on the kibbutz, Nayar, Russian, Tahitian, and
other families.

Carroll, John J., et. al. *Philippine Institutions.* Manila: Solidaridad Publishing House,
1970. A well-documented overview of findings about "lowland Christian" society
in the Philippines.

Criden, Yosef, and **Saadia Gelb.** *The Kibbutz Experience.* New York: Herzl 1974. Two
veteran kibbutzniks who left the U.S. in the forties to be among the earlier settlers
of Kfar Blum comment on life in the kibbutz.

Curtis, Michael, and **Mordecai Chertoff.** *Israel: Social Structure and Change.* New

Brunswick, N. J.: Transaction, 1973. Chapters 6–10 deal with the kibbutz today including one chapter on "The Family in the Kibbutz: What Lessons for Us?"

Dozier, Edward P. *The Kalinga of Northern Luzon, Philippines.* New York: Holt, Rinehart and Winston, 1967. A case study of a mountain province tribe in the Philippines giving an excellent account of the rituals and major events of the life cycle among these people.

Esperitu, Socorro C., Mary R. Hollnsteiner, Chester L. Hunt, Luis Q. Lacar, and Lourdes R. Quisumbing. *Sociology in the New Philippine Setting.* Manila: Alemar-Phoenix, 1976. A sociology textbook written for use in the Philippines. Chapter 10 on the family gives an interesting account of the Christian rural, middle-class Manila, and Muslim families.

Geiger, H. Kent, ed. *Comparative Perspectives on Marriage and the Family.* Boston: Little, Brown, 1968. A brief paperback including fourteen articles dealing with families and family topics from a cross-cultural and comparative perspective.

Goode, William J. *World Revolution and Family Patterns.* New York: Free Press, 1963. Deals with world changes in family patterns and has chapters on the West, Arabic Islam, sub-Saharan Africa, India, China, and Japan.

Gorospe, Vitaliano R., ed. *Responsible Parenthood in the Philippines.* Manila: Ateneo Publications, 1970. An examination of the family and the population issue from the approaches of behavorial science, philosophico-theological, and Christian experimental.

Lardizabal, Amparo S., and Felicitas Tensuan-Leogardo, eds. *Readings on Philippine Culture and Social Life.* Quezon City: Bustamante Press, 1970. In addition to a chapter on the Filipino family the book covers a wide range of topics about life in the Philippines: games, music, folk dances, architecture, literature, and the like.

Nimkoff, M. F. *Comparative Family Systems.* Boston: Houghton Mifflin, 1965. A book concerned with the major variations in the organization of the human family, describing twelve cases and presenting an interchange between society and the family.

Philippine Sociological Review. "Special Kinship Issue" 21 (January 1973); and "Special Population Issue" 21 (April 1973). Two special issues of the journal that include numerous articles on the Filipino family and kin network.

Queen, Stuart A., and Robert W. Habenstein. *The Family in Various Cultures.* 4th ed. Philadelphia: J. B. Lippincott, 1974. Chapter 6 deals with "The Minimum Family of the Kibbutz." This paperback book assembles comparable data about family systems around the world and indicates some of the historical origins of the family in the United States.

Spiro, Melford E. *Kibbutz: Venture in Utopia.* Cambridge, Mass.: Harvard University Press, 1956; and *Children of the Kibbutz.* New York: Schocken, 1958, 1965. Venture in Utopia presents the sociocultural setting within which the socialization and personality development occur as described in *Children of the Kibbutz.*

7   *Life-Styles among Amish Families:*
A Religious Subculture

7

Much of the census and research data on families in the United States, of necessity, overlook the wide range of family groups that neither fit the statistical norm nor are singled out for specific analysis. Any descriptive data, such as the census material presented in Chapter 1 on characteristics of families in the United States, the basic issues of change in Chapter 4, the variant marital and family life-styles in the previous chapter, and much of the material that follows in later chapters on mate selection, sexual behavior, parent-child relationships, or divorce are not applicable to an understanding of selected minority subcultural families. The theories and frames of reference in Chapter 2 or the explanations of family change in Chapter 4 should be applicable to family groups and systems irrespective of time or place.

In this chapter and the next, two diverse family systems are examined. The first, the Amish, is a religious subculture that attempts to maintain its ethnic and religious identity by remaining separate from "the world." The second, the black family, is a racial subculture that seeks entrance into the social and economic spheres of the larger society but faces many constraints in so doing.

The Amish and black families are among many that could be singled out for examination. Religious groups such as the Jews, Hutterites, Quakers, Shakers, or Mormons would serve as fruitful subcultures for analysis. The same is true for racial or ethnic groups such as the Indian, the Spanish-American, the Italian, the Chinese, or the Filipino. Each presents unique social structures and interpersonal processes that would be highly illustrative of variation in styles of family life. Each could assist in our understanding of family structures, functions, and change. The decision to select the Amish and the black family was somewhat arbitrary. Both should clearly show contrasting patterns of subcultural family systems, and both should serve to illustrate many concepts relevant to an understanding of family systems.

The Amish have a family organization that is monogamous and patriarchal. From the time of marriage until death of one spouse, marriages remain intact. Divorce is extremely rare, desertion is nonexistent, and legal separations are not a matter of awareness—much less of occurrence—among the Amish. These people are highly endogamous in their selection of mates. The birth rate is extremely high when compared with that of the non-Amish American family. Illegitimacy is unknown, due to the fact that a premarital pregnancy necessitates marriage. In short, it would appear that the Amish have one of the most stable and cohesive family systems in our society.

In one sense, the Amish provide an excellent look at the family of rural America in 1900. A study of this group illustrates the close links that existed between the family system and the religious, political, economic, and educational systems. This group shows the outcome of a resistance to change in a rapidly changing society and portrays some of the problems involved in attempts to maintain a cohesive way of life despite major conflicts with the larger dominant society. To understand the family of this religious subculture, let us briefly examine their history, their beliefs and practices, and their total way of life.

AMISH ORIGINS

The Amish, the most conservative branch of which is known as the Old-Order Amish, are an Anabaptist group that began in Switzerland prior to the 1700s.[1] A young Mennonite minister by the name of Jacob Amman felt that not all was well with the Mennonites of Switzerland and proposed to "restore the temple of God upon the old foundation."[2] The main charge against the church seemingly was its lack of discipline, especially its failure to apply the Meidung to excommunicated members.

The Meidung, also referred to as avoidance or shunning, was not new to the Dutch Anabaptists of Holland but had been unknown in the Swiss church. Amman, with several other converted ministers, set out upon a tour in 1693 through the various Swiss congregations in the interest of their new idea. Amman not only claimed that the church was lacking in discipline, but he also found fault with some of the new social customs and practices that had crept into the church at that time: fancy clothes, shaving of the beard, wearing long hair, and attending funerals in the state church.[3] As stated by

---

1. The Anabaptists are religious groups that believe in adult baptism. Three main Anabaptist groups in Europe were the Anabaptists of Holland, the Hutterian Brethren of Austria, and the Swiss Brethren. From this latter group in Switzerland came the Mennonites and from the Mennonites came the Amish. Although similar in religious doctrines, the Mennonites were and are today more "liberal" in behavior as seen by the use of automobiles and electricity, the shaving of beards, or the use of churches for religious services.

2. C. Henry Smith, *The Story of the Mennonites* (Newton, Kansas: Mennonite Publication Office, 1957), p. 129.

3. Ibid., pp. 129–130.

Ordnung (Rules)

Ordnung (Rules). *In the many communities of the North American Amish . . . No two of them are exactly alike, not to be alike do they wish . . . Each district, its own Bishops and preachers elects . . . No special training is required as in most all other sects.*

Each district decides separately what color their buggies to paint . . . Or how wide the brim on their hats that make 'em look so quaint . . . The Ordnung or rules are made up for only themselves by each group . . . And the Meidung or shunning sees to it that they jump through the hoop.

The men's hair in Ohio is worn shorter than here . . . And verboten are all alcoholic beverages, including beer . . . Our Amish here don't use cigarettes, but do smoke pipes and

cigars . . . Also forbidden of course, are electricity, telephones and cars.

Meidung (Shunning). Meidung is the Amish word for shun and shunning . . . And that is what an Amishman brings upon himself for sinning . . . And a sin can be the infraction of any of the Ordnung or rules . . . No matter how simple the infraction seems, the Amish are stubborn as mules.

When the Amisher is under Meidung, no one speaks to, and turns away from him . . . Even his wife and kids! That makes life for him very, very grim . . . He either comes around and repents, or joins a more progressive order . . . And in some cases, he even turns "English" and moves across the border.

Source: Carlton Lehman, *It Wonders Me* (New Wilmington, Pa.: Ara, 1968), p. 2. Reprinted by permission.

Smith, the whole movement was toward a strict observance of the older customs . . . and of suspicion of all innovations in the affairs of everyday living as well as in forms of church worship; an ever-present fear of the dangers of "worldliness."[4] The old was seldom discarded for the new in styles of dress as they changed during the centuries. And so hooks and eyes were used instead of buttons, buckles instead of shoestrings, and suspenders instead of belts, long after these once-common articles of wearing apparel had been discarded by the folks at large. Beards and long hair, once merely a common custom, acquired a religious significance and became the object of constant solicitude on the part of the church fathers.[5]

Apparently Amman and his group were not the only religious sect that was discontented with the social ills of their time. Hostetler cites a source that lists, among others, the Adamites, who ran naked in the woods; the Free-Livers, who had wives in common; the Weeping Brothers, who held highly emotional prayer meetings; the Blood-Thirsty Ones, who drank human blood; the Devil-Worshippers, who praised the devil ten times daily; and the Hypocritical Ones, who were indifferent to all liturgical ceremonies.[6] Unlike many

---

4. Ibid., p. 131.

5. Ibid., p. 131.

6. John A. Hostetler, *Amish Society*, rev. ed. (Baltimore: The Johns Hopkins Press, 1968), p. 24.

of these groups interested in fighting a national battle, the peaceful Anabaptists wanted simply to have freedom of religion and a voluntary church. The Anabaptists claimed that a true church could not depend on baptism administered in infancy. With peasant uprisings and many heretics subjected to the death penalty, the Anabaptists fled into the mountainous hinterlands of Europe, some to Prussia, Russia, and at a later date to the United States.

Just when the first Amish came to America is not known. Hostetler states that the Amish people came to Pennsylvania from Switzerland as early as 1727.[7] In America they found conditions favorable for growth and development: land was available in unlimited quantities,[8] and they could live adjacent to each other on family farms and maintain relatively self-sufficient and closely knit communities. Under these conditions, an integrated folk culture could develop and maintain its identity. So the Amish survived in the New World, emerging as distinctive, small, homogeneous, and self-governing communities.

Today, approximately 250 years after their earliest arrival in America, the estimated Amish population is close to 50,000. The largest number in any one state can be found in Ohio, although Lancaster County in Pennsylvania remains the best known and most publicized. States with Amish districts include Ohio, Pennsylvania, Indiana, Iowa, Illinois, Missouri, Kansas, Delaware, Michigan, New York, Maryland, Wisconsin, Virginia, Oklahoma, Arkansas, Tennessee, Kentucky, Florida, and Georgia. In addition, more than 1,500 Amish reside in Ontario, Canada.

Any growth in the Amish population is a result of a high rate of natural increase, that is, through large families. As reported by Hostetler, the average number of children per "completed" family as shown by several studies is from seven to nine.[9] These children are a valuable asset to the Amish farm economy heavily dependent as it is on manual labor for its operation, but they can and do present difficulty in accumulating the capital and land to assist them at the time of marriage.

THE AMISH WAY OF LIFE

The Amish family cannot be understood apart from the recognition that it is entirely rural oriented. Strong religious convictions, the use of a distinctive language and dress, and strong patriarchal authority have helped to preserve the Amish way of life.[10] Their subculture would be referred to by

---

7. Ibid., p. 38.
8. Ibid., p. 44.
9. Ibid., p. 82.
10. Ibid., p. 4.

Amish Stumped By New Milk Law

SHIPSHEWANA, Ind.—(AP)—Hundreds of Amish dairy farmers, unwilling to compromise their religious beliefs, are being forced out of business by a state regulation requiring them to cool their milk by modern means.

The regulation, which will go into effect March 1, requires that warm, fresh milk be cooled to 50 degress Fahrenheit within two hours after it leaves the cow, a process that can only be accomplished by refrigeration. The rapid cooling is intended to prevent growth of bacteria.

But the Amish are forbidden by their religion to use electricity, the source of power for most milk cooling systems. They have traditionally cooled their milk with cold water or ice, which can only cool milk to 70 degrees within two hours.

As a result, many Amish must sell their herds of dairy cows. Many are either planning to raise chickens or hogs. Others are seeking employment in the mobile home factories in the area.

Source: *Detroit Free Press*, January 3, 1977, p. 9-B. Reprinted by permission of The Associated Press.

sociologists as a Gemeinschaft.[11] The Gemeinschaft, like the "folk" society, is conceptualized as a small, isolated, traditional, simple, homogeneous society.[12] The folkways and mores are internalized from birth, and face-to-face oral communication retains a strong sense of togetherness. Customs, goals, and styles of life are not questioned as custom becomes sacred. The smallness, the homogeneous character, the self-sufficiency in economic life and the distinctiveness of the Amish people and community are the key features of this rural subculture in an urbanized American society.[13]

The Amish hold the Bible as a final guide in a changing world. Its teachings are accepted in simple faith. Most of the practices that seem strange or peculiar to those of us who are non-Amish can generally be explained by noting their interpretation of the scriptures. Long before the Korean or Vietnam War, the Amish refused to bear arms or go to war for "Whosoever shall smite thee on thy right cheek, turn to him the other also;"[14] "Recompense to no man evil for evil . . . live peaceably with all men;"[15] and "Be gentle unto all men, apt to teach, forebearing."[16] The Amish are reluctant to be photographed or painted for "Thou shalt not make unto thee any graven image."[17]

11. Gemeinschaft, as described by Ferdinand Toennies, can be found in C. P. Loomis, *Community and Society, Gemeinschaft and Gesellschaft* (East Lansing, Mich.: Michigan State University Press, 1957).

12. Robert Redfield, "The Folk Society," *American Journal of Sociology* (January 1947), pp. 292–308.

13. These four features are described in Chapter 1 of Hostetler, op. cit., pp. 9–22.

14. Matthew 5:39.

15. Romans 12:17–18.

16. II Timothy 2:24.

17. Exodus 20:4.

They refuse to go to law for "If any man sue thee at the law, and take away thy coat, let him have thy cloak also."[18] They refuse to buy life insurance or accept social security for "If any provide not for his own and especially for those of his own house, he has denied the faith and is worse than an infidel."[19] They refuse to send children to high schools and colleges for "Wisdom of this world is foolishness with God."[20]

In their worship services, the Amish meet in homes instead of churches, for "The Lord of Heaven and Earth dwelleth not in temples made with hands."[21] They engage in the practice of foot-washing, imitating the act of Christ when he "poureth water into a basin, and began to wash the disciples' feet."[22] The adult baptism and renunciation of infant baptism, which was part of the Anabaptist movement prior to the start of the Amish, is based on scriptures which say, "Repent, and be baptised every one of you;"[23] and "If thou believest with all thine heart, thou mayst (be baptised]."[24]

The Amish feel strongly that the scriptures teach a distinct separation between the church and the world. They believe it is impossible for a church to maintain its beliefs and values if its members associate freely with people who hold different values. This too is based on the scriptures, which teach that persons should not be "unequally yoked together with unbelievers,"[25] or should not be "conformed to this world."[26]

Because of teachings such as these, the Amish have not readily accepted many of the social and cultural changes that have been introduced into American society and termed "progress." Much of what you and I take for granted (neckties, airplane travel, perfumes, carpeting, wedding rings, musical instruments, etc.), is considered as "worldly" and therefore the work of the devil and not for their use or enjoyment—but all right for anyone else. This does not mean that all Amish avoid "worldly" things—some make and drink cider and beer and some smoke cigarettes. Although the Amish do not own automobiles, they do ride in them and frequently hire a neighbor to transport them. Although phones in the home are taboo, the use of a coin phone or that of a neighbor is common. Although certain changes are creeping into the Amish subculture, they are still driving horses and buggies, they speak an Americanized form of the German language often called Pennsylvania Dutch, they refuse to use electricity, bathroom fixtures, or oil furnaces, married men raise a beard but always shave the mustache, and, until recently,

---

18. Matthew 5:40.
19. I Timothy 5:8.
20. I Corinthians 3:19.
21. Acts 17:24.
22. John 13:5.
23. Acts 2:38.
24. Acts 8:37.
25. II Corinthians 6:14.
26. Romans 12:2.

The Amish

We're Amishmen, the men with the flat black hats and beard ... Our ways may seem queer to you, but that's the way we've been reared ... Now we don't care much for city ways, it's the country life for thee and me ... Lush meadows, tall corn, pigs, cows and chickens is what we like to see.

When we ride in cars, we go so fast we can't see the robin or the jay ... But by horse and buggy, we have time to see things along the way ... We know you English think we're backward, and with us sometimes fuss ... But what was good enough for our grandparents, is good enough for us.

We haven't radios or TV, with news everyday upsetting ... But we have other compensations, which to us are offsetting ... A man in this world usually gets what he deserves ... So we get a peaceful quiet life, which is easy on the nerves.

We don't have big fancy churches in which to kneel and pray ... Christ was a simple carpenter, and lived in a very simple way ... To us, our way seems more like Christ's way of life ... Getting along with our neighbors, and avoiding all strife.

We're not rushing here and there, seeking amusement, as many of you do ... You say we're queer; we think exactly the same about you ... Our clothes look funny, as some of you have said ... But in some of yours, WE WOULDN'T BE CAUGHT DEAD!

Source: Carlton Lehman, *It Wonders Me* (New Wilmington, Pa.: Ara, 1968), p. 1. Reprinted by permission.

buttons were not used on outer clothing. The shunning of outer buttons and mustaches, which were military symbols of the seventeenth century, represents an effort to register a pacifistic protest to war and militarism.

THE FAMILY SYSTEM

The Amish Home

The life of the Amish revolves around the home—work roles and the leisure activities that exist are centered around this location, child-rearing patterns are established around the home setting; until recently, babies were born in the home. "Courting" occurs in the home and religious services take place in the home, as do funerals and "get-togethers." The Amish leave this location very rarely, and when they do it is seldom beyond the local community except on special occasions or visits to other Amish communities.

To a non-Amishman who drives through Lancaster County, Pennsylvania, Holmes County, or Plain City, Ohio, or northern Indiana, the Amish home is often perceived to be a spacious farmhouse located on a picturesque rural lane. One or several buggies are located around the barn. No electric wires are seen. Plain blue or green cloth curtains are hung at the windows since lace or ruffled ones are taboo. The Amish barn (note the myth described in the footnote), frequently quite large, may encompass anything from cow, steer, and horse stables to a chicken house, a tobacco shed, a corn crib, and a storage place for machinery and hay.[27] Access to the upper level of the barn is gained by a gentle sloping bank of earth which serves as a driveway.

The Amish house is, to most outsiders, exceedingly modest. Since homes are without electricity no electric appliances are to be found; television sets, radios, stereo equipment, and musical instruments are taboo. Over-stuffed, colored modern furniture is absent. The floors are generally bare except for homemade hooked or braided rugs. The walls are devoid of pictures or paintings. It is likely that one would find brightly colored dishes, vases, glasses, quilts, and similar objects insofar as they have some use other than simply being decorative. But wallpaper and pictures or portraits are taboo since they are primarily items of decoration.

The home is heated by a central stove that is usually found in the kitchen. Heat is derived from coal or wood, and light is derived from kerosene or gasoline lamps. Water is pumped into the kitchen sink with power provided by a windmill or in some instances a waterwheel. The kitchen is often the largest room in the home and, since it contains the stove, it is also the warmest one. Thus, on cold winter evenings one would be likely to find the Amishman in the kitchen reading the Bible or *The Budget*.[28]

Since the Amish hold their church services in the home, the house is usually arranged in such a way that the doors separating the rooms on the first floor can be opened to form a space large enough to accommodate the members of the district congregation for a worship service.[29] If the house is too small, the barn or a toolshed may be used. Most Amish homes also have an "outside" or "summer kitchen" where most of the extensive food preparation is carried out. In the summer kitchen can be found the equipment for making sauerkraut, sausage, scrapple, apple butter, and other home-prepared food. Most Amish families preserve many hundreds of quarts of cherries, peaches, pears, and other fruits and vegetables, as well as jams and jellies.[30]

---

27. Several myths accompany the barns in Lancaster County and other areas of the "Dutch Country" in Eastern Pennsylvania. The most common myth is associated with the designs that are seen painted on various barns. They always have a star within a circle and are often referred to as "hex signs." They are supposed to prevent the devil from entering the barns to give the cows milk fever. One can purchase popular literature indicating that these "hex signs" are a continuance of very ancient tradition, according to which these decorative marks were potent to protect the barn, or more particularly the cattle, from the influence of witches. The hexafoos (witch foot) signs do not appear throughout the Amish community, although this myth has become deeply entrenched and widely disseminated today, especially to the tourist.

28. *The Budget* is a weekly newspaper put out by a non-Amish publisher in Ohio. It contains items such as visiting, births, weddings, illnesses, who was kicked by a horse, and other local or regional newsworthy items.

29. Elmer L. Smith, *Among the Amish* (Witmer, Pa.: Applied Arts Publishers, 1964), p. 30.

30. Ibid., p. 32.

It is of interest that although the Amish leaders frown upon smoking, tobacco is one of the major cash crops of the Amish farmer.

Husband-Wife Roles

The family's organization is centered around the father. This patriarchal structure can be seen by the extent to which his wife and children are subject to him. However, the line of authority is not rigid; the wife is consulted, particularly about child rearing, family problems, and decisions relating to home purchases. The children may also be consulted in planning farming matters. However, the husband's word is regarded as final.

The husband's way of life, as with most Amish behavior, stems from the scriptures. As stated in I Corinthians 11:3, "The head of the woman is the man." Thus both husband and wife are well aware that the husband is the head of the house, although age too is a significant status factor. The oldest male, or grandfather, is respected as the patriarch and his social status increases at least until he reaches the age where he simply moves into the *Gross Dawdy* (grandfather) house and the younger generation takes over.

The husband's major activities center around farming. He will purchase the equipment and livestock without seeking the advice of his wife. He will perform the majority of the farming activities with the assistance of his wife and children. Only on occasion would the husband assist his wife in household tasks.

An Amish wife is well aware of what is expected of her. She is subservient to her husband and generally her attitude is one of willing submission. As stated in I Timothy, a woman is not to teach, nor to usurp authority over the man.[31] The wife's duties include care of the children, cooking and cleaning, preparation of produce for market, making clothes for the family, preserving food, and gardening.[32] Generally women are not called upon to help with the heavier jobs in farming, but they do have the responsibility of keeping the inside as well as the outside of the house neat and clean in appearance.

Hostetler states that personal relationships between husband and wife are quiet and sober, with no apparent demonstration of affection.[33] Irritation between mates is expressed in a variety of ways and conditioned by informally approved means of expression: the tone of voice, a gesture, or a direct statement. The husband may express disapproval by complete silence at the dinner table and the wife is left to guess what is wrong.

Hostetler notes that the pattern of marital relationships among the

31. I Timothy 2:12.
32. Hostetler, op. cit., p. 150.
33. Ibid.. pp. 151–152.

An Amish Farmer's Day

In our locality, this is the typical day in the life of an Amishman ... Arise at dawn, feed horses, cows, calves, chickens and pigs; the day has begun ... Then the milking (by hand) of several cows and the cleaning of cans ... Breakfast comes next; his wife has ready bacon, eggs and taters in frying pans.

In winter, fried corn mush with honey or syrup is a favorite breakfast food ... With every meal, a silent prayer is offered to Him in gratitude ... It depends on the season, but most always, he's out in the fields ... Plowing, sowing or reaping; he's always striving for better yields.

Dinner's at noon and it's the biggest meal of the day ... That's after he's fed and watered his work horses, the sorrel and the gray ... Supper is usually light ("like our lunch") and comes after evening chores ... Most of their food is homemade or grown, not much comes from stores.

Oil lamps provide evening light, and wood's usually burned in the stove ... And it's stacked in piles, having been sawed down in the grove ... Bedtime is usually early, because dawn's light comes mighty soon ... With no radios or TV, they're luckier than we, because they're spared even ONE rock and roll tune.

You got yourself here on the dot,
So eat yourself full of what we got.

Source: Carlton Lehman, *It Wonders Me* (New Wilmington, Pa.: Ara, 1968), p. 5. Reprinted by permission.

Amish compares very favorably with Thomas and Znaniecki's description of the Polish pattern.[34] They say:

> The marriage norm is not love, but respect. The norm of respect from wife to husband includes obedience, fidelity, care for the husband's comfort and health; from husband to wife, good treatment, fidelity, nor letting the wife do hired work if it is not indispensible. Affection is not explicitly included in the norm of respect but is desirable. As to sexual love it is a purely personal matter, it is not and ought not to be socialized in any form; the family purposely ignores it and the slightest indecency or indiscreetness with regard to sexual relations in marriage is viewed with disgust and is normally condemned.[35]

Children

Within the Amish family and community, children are wanted. To the Amish they are seen as a gift of God and to the non-Amish they would generally be recognized as an economic asset. Families with six, ten, or fourteen children are common today. Smith says the average number of children

---

34. Ibid., pp. 152–153.
35. William I. Thomas and Florian Znaniecki, *The Polish Peasant in Europe and America*, vol. 1 (New York: Knopf, 1927), p. 90.

per Amish family is seven and one-half.[36] "Non-natural" means of birth control are generally not practiced.

According to Hostetler the first two years of life are undoubtedly the happiest.[37] The baby obtains what he wants and is given permissive care with great amounts of love from his parents, siblings, grandparents, uncles, aunts, and cousins. After these first two years, restrictions and exacting disciplines are continuously imposed upon the child. Of prime importance is being taught to respect the authority of parents and older persons.

Amish children do not receive regular allowances from their parents, but they do receive some farm animal such as a pig, sheep, or calf with the stipulation that the child take the major responsibility in caring for it. Needs of each child are met within the home, and the socialization process is effective enough to produce in the Amish insecure feelings when they go outside the Amish community.

Hostetler indicates that Amish children manifest resentments, as do all children, by pouting or by negative responses.[38] But when these manifestations are overt, "smackings" are sure to follow and may be given with the palm of the hand, a switch, a razor strap, or a buggy whip. Temper tantrums, making faces, name calling, and sauciness among youngsters are extremely rare; a child learns early that his reward for such a rebellion is a sound thrashing.

To the non-Amishman, the strict discipline by parents and the hard physical work required of children may appear to be exceedingly harsh treatment. However, treatment of the children is likely to be fair, with love and family solidarity a basic ingredient of the household.

The belief that Amish children from different families are subject to very similar patterns of child rearing led Witmer to question if the gamut of highly similar experiences shared by the children predetermine a basic personality pattern.[39] Thus, he investigated the differences in the variability of personality characteristics between twenty-five Old-Order Amish youth and twenty-five non-Amish youth from the same community. He found, as hypothesized, that the Amish group indicated more homogeneity and similarity of personality than did the non-Amish group.

As suggested, the home is the prime socializing agent. Children work long before they have physically matured or before they have finished any type of formal education. The life of the boys is patterned after that of the father and many, at the age of six or ten, can be seen in the fields working be-

36. Elmer L. Smith, *Studies in Amish Demography* (Harrisburg, Va.: Eastern Mennonite College, 1960), p. 18.

37. Hostetler, op. cit., p. 153.

38. Ibid., p. 157.

39. Joe Witmer, "Homogeneity of Personality Characteristics: A Comparison between Old-Order Amish and Non-Amish," *American Anthropologist* 72 (October 1970), pp. 1063–1068.

side an older brother or their father. Prior to his teen years a boy may be seen driving a harrow, husking corn, or distributing feed and bedding to the live-stock. The life of the girl is patterned after her mother's and she learns early the art of cooking and housekeeping. It is likely that each child in the home will have specific and regular work assignments that, depending on age, will involve setting the table, preparing meals, doing chores, gathering eggs, milk-ing cows, and a wide variety of other household or farm tasks.

These work responsibilities and the values taught in the home seem to conflict frequently with state education requirements. Most states enforce school attendance up to a specific age, but most public school systems are basically secular in their orientation. The Amish believe that their own youth should not be forced to enter public high schools or colleges. They prefer that the teacher understand their religious beliefs and teach accordingly. Since the demands of the Amish and the demands of the state are frequently at odds, there were newspaper accounts in the sixties about Amish fathers in Pennsyl-vania who were jailed for refusing to send their children to school, a Michigan teacher in an Amish school who had only an eighth-grade education and was thus violating the state teacher-certification requirements, and the widely publicized Amish settlement in Iowa where school authorities compelled the children to board a bus to attend the consolidated town school rather than the Amish private school.[40]

COURTSHIP PRACTICES

The choice of a marriage partner has to be endogamous. One must ob-tain a partner from within the Amish faith but not necessarily from the same community. Marriages within the primary family and extending to first cousins are taboo.

One main opportunity for young people to come in contact with each other is the Sunday evening "singing." Youth from several neighboring dis-tricts will get together for this occasion. It is said that young men dress to the hilt (or, at least, as far as church strictures permit them to), groom their horses, polish their buggies, and prepare to go to "singings" held on nearby farms.[41] There, under the watchful eyes of the owners of the farm, the young people gather noisily in the barn.

A "singing" is not regarded as a devotional meeting. Young people gather around a long table, boys on one side and girls on the other. The singing is con-

40. The Amish dispute is analyzed in detail in Harrell R. Rodgers, Jr., *Community Conflict, Public Opinion, and the Law* (Columbus, Ohio: Charles E. Merrill, 1969).

41. Vincent R. Tortora, *The Amish Folk* (Lancaster, Pa.: Photo Arts Press), p. 20.

ducted entirely by the unmarried. Only the fast tunes are used. Girls as well as boys announce hymns and lead the singing. Between selections there is time for conversation. After the singing, which usually dismisses formally about ten o'clock, an hour or more is spent in joking and visiting. Those boys who do not have a date usually arrange for a girl at this time.

Although there are other occasions when young folks get together, such as husking bees, weddings, and frolics, the "singing" is a regular medium for a boy-girl association. Both the boy and girl look upon each other as possible mates. Social activity is naturally arranged with marriage in view. A boy or girl may "quit" whenever they please, but limited selection also limits variation. The usual age for courtship, called rumspring (running around), begins for the boy at 16 and for the girl at 14 to 16.

Secrecy pervades the entire period of courtship and is seldom relaxed regardless of its length. If a boy is charged with having a girlfriend he will certainly be slow to admit it. Courting that cannot be successfully disguised becomes a subject for teasing by all members of the family.[42]

When a boy gets a "steady" girl, then in addition to the singing on Sunday evening he will see her on Saturday evening, and arrangements will be made with the girl prior to Saturday. On that night, he will dress in his best clothing and depart for the girl's home after he is assured that her parents are in bed. A flashlight is said to be standard equipment for the courting male. This is used to shine at the girl's window to indicate that he has arrived. Upon receiving this signal, she will quietly go down and meet him, and the couple may then visit together in the kitchen or sitting room until the early hours of the morning.

Bundling

Bundling is frequently associated with the Amish courtship system. A practice that was started in Northern Europe, brought to America, and practiced in the New England colonial family, bundling has been known to take several forms. The most common was using a bed with a "bundling-board." Under this arrangement a boy and a girl would lie on the bed without undressing. Second was the use of "bundling-bags." Under this system, the female got into a large sack with a wax seal at the neck. Obviously, this seal was supposed to remain unbroken. Third, there are also instances recorded where the female's ankles were tied together.

To understand bundling, it must be seen in the context in which it occurred. Among New England families and among the Amish, wood and candles were commodities that required much time and labor. To use these commodities throughout the evening hours would be a waste of materials.

---

42. Hostetler, op. cit., p. 159.

Amish Bundling

Many of you have heard of Amish bundling, well it's true, they do... Not having davenports, the young folks go to bed for the long night through... BUT they're supposed to keep their clothes on, and lie on it—not in it... All of them don't do as they're supposed to, don't think for a minute.

Because occasionally, a wedding is held in the good ol' summertime... When the usual time for Amish weddings is in Autumn or wintertime... The girl's mama or papa isn't supposed to know who their daughter is dating... Nor do they know for what groom she is eventually waiting.

Of a bachelor among the Amish, I don't know of a single one... There are a few old maids however, whose hearts have not been won... Bundling has been their get-acquainted custom for years and years... To them it's real sensible like and not as shocking as to you it appears.

Source: Carlton Lehman, *It Wonders Me* (New Wilmington, Pa.: Ara, 1968), p. 5. Reprinted by permission.

Also, where winters are cold, and distances of travel are sometimes great, bundling provided an opportunity for the male and female to visit alone without disturbing the rest of the family or using the heat and light commodities. One should also recognize that within the household were likely to be parents, six to fourteen children, and often grandparents and other relatives. Thus the sexual connotations that many people associate with it today were perhaps minimal. Add to this the rigid sexual codes that existed and one should get a relatively accurate picture of bundling in its social context. This subject has been widely exploited by the popular press; however, it is not known that bundling exists today among the Amish.

When the young couple are ready to establish themselves as an independent family unit, they begin to think of marriage. In preparation, the Amish youth has saved his money from wages he received as a hired hand or from his father since his twenty-first birthday. Prior to that age all the money he had earned on the farm went to his father, who in turn assisted him in getting the most essential equipment. For example, when the young man reached his sixteenth birthday, his father gave him a racy black open buggy, often called a courting buggy, and a horse of his own. Also, the girl will likely have accumulated a chest full of household linen.

The young couple continue their courtship in the assumption that no one else in the world knows, or should know, about it. If questioned by parents or friends about partners with whom they have frequently been seen leaving the "singings," both the young man and the young lady deny anything more than a passing interest. It is suggested that such white lies are traditional in the Amish family—the parents having done the same with their parents—and only serve to put everyone on guard.[43]

---

43. Tortora, op. cit., p. 25.

Age at Marriage

The age at marriage among the Amish is similar to the national standard. Studies of specific Amish communities in Ohio, Pennsylvania, and Illinois show that men marry from age twenty-two to twenty-four and women marry from twenty to twenty-two.[44] The comparable median age in the United States in 1974 was 23.1 for men and 21.1 for women. The disproportionate number of children per family between the Amish and non-Amish in the United States can thus scarcely be attributed to a younger age at marriage.

The Wedding

When the decision has been made to marry, the young man visits a deacon of the church. He confides in him and asks him to go as an intermediary to the father of the bride and ask permission for the marriage. From this time, the families take over the preparations for the wedding. As much as possible the plans are kept secret until the banns are published at a church meeting at least two weeks before the wedding.

> Signs of an approaching wedding provide occasion for joking and teasing. Since there is nothing among the Amish that corresponds to the engagement, other signs of preparation become indicative of a potential marriage. An overabundance of celery in the garden of a home containing a potential bride is said to be one such sign, since large quantities are used at weddings. Another cue may be efforts on the part of the father of the potential bridegroom to obtain an extra farm, or to remodel a vacant dwelling on one of his own farms.[45]

Most weddings take place in November and December, for in an agricultural community the harvest has by then been completed. The wedding itself will likely occur on a Thursday, or a Tuesday if there are conflicting dates with other marriages in the community. Sundays are generally not considered; this is the Lord's day and a literal day of rest, although the author, with a group of students, has attended a Sunday worship service during which a wedding took place (see insert). This, however, appears to be very infrequent. Why there is a Tuesday-Thursday limitation on weddings is somewhat unclear. It appears to be an Amish tradition that extends back several hundred years.

Prior to the wedding, large-scale preparations are in progress. Since no wedding invitations are mailed, the bridegroom personally invites the guests. After his wedding has been "published," the bridegroom lives at the bride's

44. Hostetler, op. cit., p. 85.
45. Ibid., p. 173.

On a Sunday in July, the author and a group of high-school teachers, who were participants in an NSF Institute in Sociology, attended an Amish worship service several miles east of Middlebury, Indiana. We were told to be there at 9:00 A.M. for the service. Arriving on time, we discovered that the Amish were seated and the service had begun. The horses had been placed in the barnyard, the buggies surrounded the house and barn, and the members were all seated on benches in a shed designed for the storing of implements. Several benches were reserved for us along the back wall on the side where the men were seated. All heads turned as we filed into the rows of backless benches. The children especially appeared very curious as to the nature of these outsiders. It is possible that some had never witnessed the peculiar garb of the religious sisters in our group nor ever had blacks worship with them.

This particular Sunday the attendance was somewhat larger than usual due to the wedding that was to take place between a woman from the local Indiana district and a man from Ohio. Some young boys were seated on a loft, and many young children were held by their fathers or mothers. The singing, which was occurring as we arrived, continued for at least one-half hour. The melody was sung without harmony or accompaniment and in German. Soon, several men who appeared and walked to the middle area separating the men and the women seated facing each other. Then one man preached for about forty-five minutes without notes, outline, or manuscript. Holding a Bible in one hand and making frequent gestures with the other, he gave a message ostensibly directed toward the couple to be wed but meant to remind all of the scriptural directions concerning the duties of husband and wife.

Several times throughout the service the whole assembly knelt in prayer. To some of us, unaccustomed to sitting on hard backless benches for lengthy periods of time, kneeling for prayer provided immediate positive fringe benefits beyond its intended spiritual purposes. More singing, praying, and another

sermon preceded the wedding ceremony. Finally, three men and three women walked to the center of the group and were seated facing one another. Since the dress of the bride and bridegroom was much like that of the other Amish, it was difficult to be certain who was about to be married. What could be termed a sermonette was given by the man who preached the first sermon. The marriage vows were taken and the couple left the building, the men walking in front of the women. A few announcements, prayer, and a hymn concluded the meeting almost four hours from the time of our 9:00 arrival. The young children left the service first, followed by the men and then by the women, who moved to the farmhouse to prepare the communal meal.

All of us were made to feel extremely welcome. They insisted we remain for the noon meal. While the tables were set, we talked. Amish men had many questions to ask us, and they answered freely any questions we raised. The children surrounded our two Catholic sisters and asked questions faster than they could be answered. When time came for the meal, we as guests and the adult men were to eat at the first serving. This pleased the teachers for, as they discovered later, the dishes and silverware we used were used by the next group without being washed.

Following the prayer for the food, all of us enjoyed the delightful experience of sharing in open discussion and eating the food served by the women. Between the bites of homegrown pickles, red beets, bread and jams, we asked questions about their beliefs and way of life. When I asked why the Amish groom always preceded the bride when walking together (which is generally opposite from that which occurs among non-Amish), a woman informed me that that is indicative of the many marital difficulties in "the world." Women don't know their place. The male should lead, the woman should follow. The men are the head of the house, women should be obedient and submissive to their husbands. Needless to say, I informed my liberated wife of my newly acquired bits of wisdom.

home until the wedding day, all keeping busy with the enumerable preparations that must be made. Walnuts and hickory nuts need to be cracked, floors scrubbed, furniture moved, silverware polished, and dishes borrowed.[46]

Wedding customs vary from one community to another; however the wedding day itself is generally a great occasion for the entire community. This day includes a three- or four-hour service in which the bride and groom are given instructions concerning the duties of marriage. Near the close of the service the bishop asks the couple to come forward. Without the aid of a book or written notes, he pronounces a blessing upon them. After taking their vows they are pronounced husband and wife.

The service is followed by an extensive dinner at the home of the bride, with much food provided and everyone expected to eat well. Singing, visiting, and eating continue until about five o'clock in the afternoon when many of the older people go home.

Presentation of wedding gifts is made at the home, and these, brought by each couple invited to the wedding, are displayed on the bed in an upstairs room. The gifts are likely to consist of dishes, bedspreads, towels, clocks, and various farm tools. In addition, the parents of the bride and groom also provide furniture, livestock, and other basic farm equipment when the couple moves into their home.

In the evening is a wedding supper where young people sit in couples. This may continue until about ten o'clock, after which many of the young folks go to the barn to play games until midnight.

The bride and groom spend the night at the bride's home. There is no immediate honeymoon, but what might be its equivalent is the practice of visiting uncles, aunts, and perhaps some cousins for a few weeks following the wedding.[47] Occasionally Amish newlyweds go on an extended tour for two weeks or more to other Amish communities.

FAMILY LIFE

After the post-wedding tour, the couple settle in the community and generally engage in farming. Estimates indicate that 50 percent of all Amish males are farmers and perhaps more than 80 percent are in farm-service occupations. An increasing number of men are accepting employment in industries such as processing plants or garment and trailer factories. Some men seek employment to supplement their farming activities, whereas others engage in cabinet making, carriage making, carpentry, blacksmithing, or masonry as full-time occupations independent of farming.

Since the Amishman often pays his bills promptly and in cash and keeps his farm and home neat, it is easy to accept the popular notion that the

46. Ibid., p. 174.
47. Ibid., p. 181.

Amish are a wealthy people. Hard work, saving, and thrifty spending patterns usually enable a man to support and "feed his family well." However, the wealth of the average Amishman is probably no greater than that of the average non-Amish farmer. This is not meant to imply that no Amishman is wealthy or to discount the stories heard by this writer about men who bought $100,000 farms and paid for them in cash. More significant than the amount of money is the manner in which it is spent. Since Amishmen are not large-scale owners or operators, they want no more land than is necessary to provide adequately for their families and, if possible, to provide land or a farm for each of their sons.

The Amish believe in and practice love and concern for all the members. Unlike the Hutterites and other groups that hold property in common, the Amish do not have a literal community of goods, but help each other voluntarily as the need arises. They feel the church is responsible for its own people and, accordingly, they do not accept government subsidies, welfare, or pensions.

Insurance comes in the form of assistance from the entire Amish community as needed. When fire or a tornado destroys the home or barn of an Amishman, his friends, neighbors, and relatives join forces to rebuild the structure at a "barn raising." In the spring of 1965 when a major tornado destroyed a large number of buildings in northern Indiana, buses loaded with Amish came from Ohio and Pennsylvania to assist in clearing away the debris and building new structures. The cost of all building materials was underwritten by the Amish themselves and all labor was donated.

A barn raising serves functions that go beyond the construction of a building. It is common to find the entire family making a contribution. Women serve the meals, refreshments, and drinks to the workers. Children assist in various tasks as needed. The occasion is a prime time to engage in fellowship as well as hard work, to hear the latest news (or gossip), and to reinforce in adults and children the value of the Amish way of life. Various activities throughout the year, such as women's quilting sessions, the attendance at cattle sales, the cooperative harvesting ventures, and of course the worship services and visiting patterns assist in the maintenance of primary-group relationships and a fellowship of believers.[48]

Members who violate the group norms are excommunicated and shunned (the Meidung). The Meidung, as mentioned, was crucial to Jacob Amman in his discontent with the church in Switzerland and is crucial to the Amish today. The Amish do not evangelize or proselyte outsiders but make great efforts to keep their own baptized members from accepting practices of "the world." A member who buys an automobile or becomes a drunkard or

---

48. A month-by-month account and explicit description of some of these activities can be seen in Charles S. Rice, *The Amish Year* (New Brunswick, N. J.: Rutgers University Press, 1956).

The Application of the Meidung

The application of the Meidung is clearly explained by an example given by Hostetler who takes the case of a young man he fictitiously names Joseph.

Joseph was raised in a very strict Amish home, under the guidance of parents who were known for their orthodoxy. He was baptized at the age of twenty. Three years after his baptism Joseph was excommunicated and shunned. Charges laid against him included the following: he had attended a revival meeting, begun to chum with excommunicated persons, bought an automobile, and begun to attend a Mennonite church.

Joseph was excommunicated with the counsel of the assembly and was informed in their presence. After being asked to leave the service he thought to himself: "It is strange to think that I am now to be 'mited.' I don't feel very comfortable." At home, the young man was shunned: he could no longer eat at the family table. He ate at a separate table, with the young children, or after the baptized persons were finished eating. Joseph was urged to

mend his ways, to make good his broken promise. His normal work relations and conversational pattern were strained. Several times he attended preaching services with his family. Since members may not accept services, goods, or favors from excommunicated members, he would not be allowed to take his sisters to church, even if he used a buggy instead of his offensive automobile, but they could drive a buggy and take him along. It was not long until Joseph accepted employment with a non-Amish person and began to use his automobile for transportation to and from work. When shunned friends came to his home for conversation, Joseph's parents met them at the gate and turned them away. It was not long until father and mother asked him to leave home. He explained: "I had to move away from home or my parents could not take communion. My parents were afraid that the younger persons in the family would be led astray. They didn't exactly chase me off the place, but I was no longer welcome at home."

Source: John A. Hostetler, *Amish Society*, rev. ed. (Baltimore: Johns Hopkins Press, 1968), pp. 63–64. Reprinted by permission.

an adulterer faces the threat of being excommunicated and shunned. It is a powerful means of social control—perhaps similar to having one's best friends reject you.

Within the family and community, the meidung or shunning is intended to show the wrongdoer his erring ways and to get him to repent. The punishment can be harsh and may last for life unless the offender makes peace with the church and reaffirms the promises made in the baptismal vows.

WHAT OF THE FUTURE?

As sociologists we should be able to make predictions as to the consequences of various forms of social organization. As persons from different systems interact, as changes in the material culture slowly occur, and as employment patterns change, so can we expect variations in the Amish life-style.

The Amish have shown an amazing resistance to change. However, in speaking to Amish parents, one becomes sensitive to their awareness and concern as to what is happening. Some Old-Order Amish leave for a more "liberal" religious group such as the "Beachy" Amish who have relaxed rules on automobiles and modern farm machinery. Others leave the group and join the Mennonites who encourage education but maintain many religious aspects of their Anabaptist heritage. Most members remain within the group, conform to the basic teachings, and gradually accept certain changes that occur.

These changes are most notable in material aspects: buttons instead of hooks and eyes, the use of diesel engines, hybrid seed corn, lights on buggies, bicycles, sewing machines, or the use of vitamins. However, the nonmaterial is changing as well: an increasing concern for professional Christians outside the local community, relief and mission work, new family names, or more youth attending high school.

It is possible that the future will see an increase not only in members who leave the community but also in outsiders coming in to adopt the Amish beliefs and practices. The past decade has included: pleas made for peace, an antimilitary orientation, a desire for assistance to the poor and elderly, a need for primary-group, personal, and intimate interrelationships, and a return to the "simple life." The Amish have stressed and lived this style of life for several centuries. For non-Amish to adopt this life-style would be a variation equally or more extreme than any described in the previous chapter.

Summary

Many subcultures with unique family structures and life-styles exist today in the United States. One of these is the Amish. They are an Anabaptist religious group that began in Switzerland about 300 years ago and first came to America nearly 250 years ago. Discontented with the many social "evils" of the larger society, the Amish sought a land where they could live and practice their religious beliefs without interference.

The home is the center of Amish life. Work roles, child-rearing patterns, mate-selection processes, and religious, wedding, and funeral services all occur at this location. Family life is organized around the father, with the wife and children obedient to his word. Work roles are clearly defined. Husband, wife, and children know what is expected of them. The husband's major activities center around farming or his job, the wife's major activities center around the house and her family, and the children assist their same-sex parent.

All Amish children are said to be wanted and are perceived as gifts of God. The young infant obtains what he wants and is given permissive care by his many siblings and extended kin. After the second or third year, discipline becomes strict and physical labor becomes common. At older ages, the child-labor factor often presents conflicting demands between state education requirements and family work requirements. It is not uncommon to read accounts of Amish fathers jailed for refusing to send their children to school.

Courtship practices are endogamous, that is, within the Amish community. Young people get together at Sunday "singings" and a male may escort a female to her home in his buggy. If the relationship becomes serious, the male may visit the girl's home on a Saturday night. Secrecy pervades this entire process. Bundling was a common practice in years past.

Marriage and the wedding itself are major events in the Amish community. After the man contacts a church deacon to serve as an intermediary to the father of the bride, preparation begins for the wedding itself. Prior to the wedding, banns are published and read at a religious service. After this time, the groom lives at the home of the bride until the wedding day, assisting in the extensive preparations. The wedding itself involves a three- or four-hour service, followed by dinner at the bride's home. Gifts of value in farming or housekeeping are presented to the newlywed couple. For the few weeks that follow, the bride and groom visit relatives and close friends.

Family life among the Amish incorporates the community as well. Religious activities, barn-raising affairs, quilting activities, and the harvest of various crops involve other community members. If a member violates the group norms and is shunned, his neighbors and friends as well as his own family will refuse to eat or work with him. Shunning is an effective means of social control.

The Amish have shown an amazing resistance to change. Although surrounded by "the world," major changes have been slow in coming. Major pressures from employment outside the Amish community itself and from non-Amish contacts are leading to the gradual acceptance of material goods and styles of life different from the recent past. In light of the explanations of change presented in Chapter 4, it will be of interest to note how social contacts and technological changes influence and modify Amish marital and family practices.

Key Terms and Topics

Amish Families	215	Husband-Wife Roles	223
Ordnung	217	"Singing"	226
Shunning or Meidung	217	Bundling	227
Gemeinschaft	219		

Discussion Questions

1. *In what ways does the Amish family system differ from the family system of rural America in 1900?*
2. *Can you cite other family groups or systems that desire to remain separate*

from "the world"? Upon what philosophy is their behavior based? How do they maintain internal cohesion and avoid external conflict?

3. To what extent should a minority group, or even a specific family group, be permitted to practice what they believe when it violates the laws of the land? Consider such Amish examples as their stand on war, education, transportation, social security, and so on.

4. Could the Amish family exist in Los Angeles or New York City? What social forces would operate against the maintenance of the group and their way of life?

5. Contrast the meidung with the means of social control in the United States.

6. How would you explain the larger family size among the Amish in contrast to most other rural groups in this country?

7. What are some of the pros and cons of bundling?

8. Interview several students who were born and raised in an ethnic subculture. What specific issues were of greatest concern to their families?

9. What social pressures operate on the Amish male and female that prevent them from leaving the community for employment or marriage? What factors encourage departure?

10. Given the explanations of family change presented in Chapter 4, make a prediction of the type of Amish family and community that will exist in twenty years.

11. Would it be possible for non-Amish couples to adopt this variant life-style? Why or why not?

Further Readings

Arons, Stephen. "Compulsory Education: The Plain People Resist." *Saturday Review* (January 15, 1972), pp. 52–57. A readable discourse on the resistance of the Amish to compulsory schooling. The basic argument focuses on Amish religious principles and their methods of child rearing versus mandates prescribed by the state.

Byler, Uria R. *School Bells Ringing.* LaGrange, Ind.: Pathway, 1969. Teachers especially will find this manual for Amish teachers and parents particularly interesting.

Hostetler, John A. *Amish Life.* Scottdale, Pa.: Herald, 1952. A 32-page pamphlet that summarizes the Amish way of life.

Hostetler, John A. *Amish Society.* Rev. ed. Baltimore: Johns Hopkins Press, 1968. The most complete, most authoritative account of the Amish available at this time.

Hostetler, John A. "Persistence and Change in Amish Society." *Ethnology* 3 (April 1964), pp. 185–198; also in J. Ross Eshleman, *Perspectives in Marriage and the Family.* Boston: Allyn and Bacon, 1969, pp. 168–185. An explanation of five elements of the Amish Charter (system of values).

Hostetler, John A. and **Gertrude Enders Huntington.** *Children in Amish Society: So-*

cialization and Community Education. New York: Holt, Rinehart and Winston, 1971. A paperback describing the Amish Community and its modes of education.

Kephart, William M. *Extraordinary Groups: The Sociology of Unconventional Life-Styles.* New York: St. Martin's, 1976. The first chapter of this book deals with the "Old-Order Amish."

Rice, Charles S. *The Amish Year.* New Brunswick, N. J.: Rutgers University Press, 1956. Each chapter of *The Amish Year* is a month-by-month journalistic type of account of activities central to the Amish.

Rodgers, Harrell R. *Community Conflict, Public Opinion and the Law: The Amish Dispute in Iowa.* Columbus, Ohio: Charles E. Merrill, 1969. A study of the Amish educational controversy in Iowa that lasted from 1962–1967.

Schreiber, William I. *Our Amish Neighbors.* Chicago: University of Chicago Press, 1962. An account of the Amish in Ohio studied by a non-Amish teacher of German who shared their language and their community.

Smith, Elmer L. *Among the Amish.* Witmer, Pa.: Applied Arts, 1959. A pictorial presentation in a 42-page paperback.

Staebler, Edna. *Sauerkraut and Enterprise.* Toronto: Canadian Publishers, 1966. One chapter of this very readable brief book describes the Old-Order Amish in Canada.

Tortora, Vincent R. *The Amish Folk.* Lancaster, Pa.: Photo Arts Press. A brief pictorial presentation of the Amish in Pennsylvania.

8 *Life-Styles among Black Families:*
A Racial Subculture

8

Anyone who has any interest in the area of race relations or, more specifically, in the black-white issue in American society, cannot afford to overlook the role of the family in this total, complex situation. In our society it is the family and more specifically the conjugal family that serves as the focal point for the accumulation of material resources by individuals; for the purchase, distribution, and consumption of those resources; for the development and formulation of personality; and for the formation of identity, where one has assigned to him a status and where one learns the basic values and norms of his particular society and subculture.

On the other hand, families are not isolated groups existing independently of the society of which they are a part. Therefore, if a disproportionate number of families of selected minority groups are poor, unemployed, or bitter, an understanding of these conditions must include the examination of the role played by the larger society. The family, the community, and the society are mutually interdependent. The husband-wife or the mother-son relationship is greatly influenced by the institutions and relationships that exist within the black community. Taverns, organized systems of hustling, barber shops, peer groups, churches, and neighborhood clubs, as well as business and employment opportunities, affect what happens to the family unit. These relationships are also greatly influenced by the nature of the national economy, the health, education, and welfare systems, or the general system of values that exist.

The black family is basically more similar than dissimilar to the dominant family forms that exist in the larger society, and the reader should be keenly aware of and should not overlook this. Note how for blacks or whites, social status is positively related to marital stability, children receive their basic identity and status subscription within the family context, and parents ascribe to the basic achievement and mobility values that exist within the larger society. On the other hand there are, of course, clear variations by social class, ethnicity, and religion, and in addition, unique historical experiences,

Notes on the Black Experience

The Black Experience is sitting in a predominantly white class and having the white professor teach directly at you.

The Black Experience is being congratulated because Willie Mays hit a home run.

The Black Experience is reading a news account of a murder and a rape with no thought for the victim, but rather, sending up a fervent prayer that the perpetrator is not black.

The Black Experience is going to the welfare department and having a white caseworker say that you are ineligible because you will not take your husband to court.

The Black Experience is going beyond that white caseworker to the black administrator who tells you the same thing.

The Black Experience is having to tell your four-year-old son that if he insists upon wanting to be white, when he will have to get himself a new set of parents.

The Black Experience is having to feel guilty and apologetic for being middle class.

The Black Experience is trying to decide whether or not you are black enough for blacks or too black for whites.

The Black Experience is having well-meaning whites look at you seriously and say, "I believe in equality, and therefore I cannot agree to preferential treatment for blacks."

The Black Experience is having the price of collard greens, pig feet, and chitterlings go sky-high simply because you decided to call them "soul food," thereby creating a gourmet market.

The Black Experience is listening to the Osmond Brothers and feeling that they robbed the Jackson Five.

The Black Experience is being called a thief and a con man when your white counterpart is referred to as an embezzler. It is being called militant when your counterpart is called liberal. It is being called a numbers racketeer when the white counterpart is called a Wall Street broker.

The Black Experience is being called a welfare recipient while the white counterpart is being called a Lockheed executive.

Finally the Black Experience is the perplexity you face when trying to answer the asinine question, "What is it the black man wants?"

Source: Gilbert L. Raiford, "Notes on the Black Experience," *Harpers Magazine* 244 (June 1972), p. 65. © 1972, by Minneapolis Star and Tribune Co., Inc. Reprinted by permission of the author.

such as slavery, legal and social segregation, and economic discrimination, have resulted in differences in life-styles and value patterns for blacks. These factors are discussed briefly in the sections that follow.

MAJOR TRANSITIONS OF THE BLACK FAMILY

There are various ways in which the black family is unique and different from the white family in American society. Andrew Billingsley and Amy Tate Billingsley describe six major social transitions (crises) that have affected or will affect the black family.[1] Two of these are securely in the past and four are in the process of occurring or have yet to take place. Although it could be argued that any one or two are of greater importance and significance than the others, the argument appears somewhat futile. Each indicates factors that should be recognized.

From Africa to America

Whereas Frazier tends to deemphasize the influence of an African heritage on black family life today,[2] Billingsley claims that three factors in the transition from Africa to America have profound relevance.[3]

First is color. It is this factor that is the most influential characteristic of the black person in society, and it is color that defines him as such. Blacks who can "pass" as whites are confronted with a totally different set of interaction patterns than are blacks who cannot "pass."

Second is cultural discontinuity: the system of behavior that was socially learned and shared by members of the African society was not applicable to the social conditions to be faced in America. It is perhaps difficult, if not impossible, to find any other group who came or was brought to America faced with such a disruption of cultural patterns.

Third is slavery. Again, unlike almost any others in America, the African did not choose to come. With few exceptions, *only* as slaves were Africans brought here. The impact of slavery on family patterns and norms at the time of slavery, as well as its significance for understanding the black family today, has become an issue of controversy. E. Franklin Frazier, and others[4] stress the extent to which slavery conditions disrupted the husband-wife bond, kin networks, and the continuity over time of family units. On the other hand, Herbert Gutman[5] vigorously attacks this "misdirected emphasis" on marital and family disruption by showing that most households (70 to 90 percent) had a husband or father present and had two or more members of a nuclear family unit. The matrifocal family was infrequent; unmarried black women under thirty lived with their parents, middle-aged black women lived with their husbands and children, elderly black women lived with their husbands or their married children, and subfamilies headed by single, widowed,

---

1. Andrew Billingsley and Amy Tate Billingsley, "Illegitimacy and Patterns of Negro Family Life," in Robert W. Roberts, *The Unwed Mother* (New York: Harper, 1966), pp. 133–149. Much of this material can also be found in Andrew Billingsley, *Black Families in White America* (Englewood Cliffs, N.J.: Prentice-Hall, 1968).
2. E. Franklin Frazier, *The Negro in the United States*, rev. ed. (New York: Macmillan, 1957).
3. Billingsley and Billingsley, op. cit., p. 135.
4. Frazier, op. cit.; Stanley M. Elkins, *Slavery: A Problem in American Institutional and Intellectual Life* (Chicago: University of Chicago Press, 1959), pp. 53–54; and Robert E. Park, "The Conflict and Fusion of Cultures," *Journal of Negro History* 4 (1919).
5. Herbert G. Gutman, *The Black Family in Slavery and Freedom, 1750–1925*, (New York: Pantheon, 1976), Chapters 1 and 10 in particular.

If You're Black, Stay Back

Although American Negroes come in all shades of black, white, and brown, historically light-skinned Negroes have dominated their communities, in a process that started with the preferred position of mulattoes in the slave economy. In a recent study of 250 Negro middle class families, Howard E. Freeman of Brandeis and J. Michael Ross, David Armor, and Thomas F. Pettigrew of Harvard have learned that color is still a potent factor in family status and attitudes (American Sociological Review, June 1966).

Education. Light Negroes were more likely to have had some college education (53.1 percent of light wives compared to only 28.8 percent of dark wives; 64.3 percent of light husbands compared to only 36.6 percent of dark husbands). Light Negroes were more likely to marry someone with a college education (63.3 percent of light wives compared to 34.9 percent of dark wives; 64.3 percent of light husbands compared to only 36.6 percent of the dark husbands).

Jobs. Light Negroes were more likely to have a white collar job (53.6 percent of the light husbands compared to 39 percent of the dark husbands).

Marriage. A Negro man is more likely to marry a lighter-skinned girl if he has a white collar job. Of 86 couples where the wife was lighter, 48 were white collar husbands, 38 blue collar. Of the 38 marriages where a blue collar husband had a lighter wife, 35 of the wives came from blue collar homes, only three from white collar backgrounds.

Attitudes. On most measures of attitude and personality, color did not seem nearly so relevant as the more usual status characteristics of income and education. But within each classification, the darker wives scored higher on anti-white attitudes than the light wives. For example, in the group with incomes of less than $6500, 75 percent of the dark wives scored above the median on the anti-white scale, compared to only 38 percent of the light wives. Also, the husband's skin color turned out to be more closely associated with a wife's attitudes than her own color—presumably it is the husband's color which marks the position of the whole family.

Source: "Roundup of Current Research," *Trans-Action* 4 (November 1966), p. 2. Reprinted by permission.

or abandoned mothers were incorporated into larger households. In brief, few young mothers lived alone with their children.

Persons on both sides of this controversy are likely to agree that slavery in America had a major impact. In the United States, slavery assumed inferiority. The slave had no legal rights, marriages were not licensed, many female slaves were sexually used and abused and miscegenation was frequent.[6]

From Slavery to Emancipation

Historical credence is given to the proclamation issued by President Lincoln in September, 1862, effective January 1, 1863, that freed the slaves in all territories still at war with the Union. At last the slave was free from servitude, bondage, and restraint—at least in theory. For thousands of Afro-

6. Miscegenation refers to marriage and interbreeding between members of different races, especially in the United States between whites and blacks.

Americans, however, emancipation brought with it a freedom to die of starvation and illness. In many ways this transition presented a crisis for many black families.

Billingsley and Billingsley state that three patterns of family life emerged from this crisis.[7] First, the majority of blacks remained on the plantations as tenants of their former owners with little or no wages for their labor. Second, families that had been allowed to establish common residence worked common plots of ground for extra food for the family. Families where the man was an artisan, preacher, or house servant made the transition with the least difficulty. The third pattern was perhaps the most disruptive of family life. In situations where only loose and informal ties held man and woman together, those ties were severed during the crisis of emancipation. This occurred despite the presence of children. In search of work, many men joined large bands of other homeless men who wandered around the countryside. This factor entrenched some females as the major productive and dependable family element.

Ann: *There's a slave of the mind and a slave of the body. Now if you ask me about enslavement of the body, it is not as relevant as slavery of the mind. If you notice, slaves overcame slavery because the mind was not enslaved, just the body. But you're working with a different kind of slavery now, and it's a slavery of the mind. If you can capture and enslave the mind, slavery will appear in another form.*

I feel it vaguely today but can't pinpoint it. For example, I never knew or was taught about black people, great black people. I went to a school that had all black students and all white teachers and administrators. Yes, I was very conscious about it. You are also conscious of the fact of how you're treated by a white teacher, a woman teacher. You learn right away of what white teacher is afraid of you and what white teacher is not afraid of you. You learn which one likes you and which one does not like you very early. You say a child does not notice? A child does notice.

Emancipation did offer some advantages for the black family. As stated by Billingsley:

> Although family members could be whipped, run out of town, or murdered, they could not be sold away from their families. Marriages were legalized and recorded. The hard work of farming, even sharecropping, required all possible hands—husband, wife, and children.

> Emancipation, then, was a catastrophic social crisis for the ex-slave, and reconstruction was a colossal failure. At the same time, there were some "screens of opportunity" which did enable large numbers of families to survive,

---

7. Billingsley and Billingsley, op. cit., p. 139.

some of to achieve amazingly stable and viable forms of family life, and a few to achieve a high degree of social distinction.[8]

Frank Furstenberg et al.[9] caution us against presenting a monolithic interpretation of slavery having only a destructive impact on the black family. They argue that the slave family was considerably stronger than has been believed, not patterned by instability, chaos, and disorder, but patterned by two-parent households. While a somewhat higher proportion of black families were headed by a female than was true for other ethnic groups, reasons other than slavery conditions explain it.

> In the first place, the great majority of black families were couple-headed. Second, ex-slaves were more likely to reside in couple-headed households. Third, when property holding among the different ethnic groupings was held constant, variations in family composition largely disappeared. Finally, we were able to show that economic status had a powerful effect on the structure of the black family because blacks suffered extremely high mortality and females with children faced difficulties in remarrying.[10]

From Rural to Urban Areas

As with the transition from slavery to emancipation, the transition from rural to urban areas brought both stabilizing as well as disintegrating factors. Very often, it was the men only who made the transition, tending to disrupt family life. Frequently, this meant a loss of the extended-family ties that may have existed. The urban areas lacked the religious norms that existed in rural areas. The cities were not only larger and more densely populated but also tended to be more impersonal and legalistic.

Today as well, the move to urban areas and its impact on black family structure can be traumatic for various reasons. Black males in particular bring with them aspirations for economic improvement which they expect to be fulfilled but which, for the great majority, are not. Unlike the white middle-class mobility patterns due to a "job offer," the black male is more likely to migrate because of current unemployment or an irregular work schedule.

On the other hand, the consequences of the shift from rural to urban areas that has occurred and is taking place today are not all negative. Many stabilizing factors and positive aspects have resulted. Although the city is often portrayed as a center of evil in our society, in a very real sense it has been the center of hope for the black family. As stated by E. E. LeMasters,

8. Billingsley, op. cit., p. 71.

9. Frank F. Furstenberg, Jr., Theodore Hershberg, and John Modell, "The Origins of the Female-headed Black Family: The Impact of the Urban Experience," *Journal of Interdisciplinary History* 6 (Autumn 1975), pp. 211–233.

10. Ibid., p. 232.

"The urban community actually offers many advantages: better school systems, with special classes for the handicapped child; better social welfare services, both private and public; better medical and public health facilities; more tolerance for racial and religious minorities; and greater chance for vertical social mobility."[11]

This transition from rural to urban areas and from nonmetropolitan to metropolitan areas is not complete. In 1960, 64.8 percent of all blacks lived in metropolitan areas. By 1974 this figure was up to 75.2 percent. Conversely, the corresponding figures for nonmetropolitan areas showed a decrease from 35.2 percent in 1960 to 24.8 percent in 1974.[12]

From Southern to Northern and Western Communities

The forces that led large numbers of black families to migrate from farm to urban areas were the same that moved large numbers of black families from the southern communities, to northern and midwestern industrial and commercial centers, and then to the West. In 1930 about four-fifths of all blacks lived in the South compared to slightly more than half (53 percent) in 1974.

In 1974 there were 23.5 million blacks in the United States and comprised 11.4 percent of the 211 million people in the United States. Geographically, they are overrepresented in the South (where they comprise 19 percent of the total population) and underrepresented in the other three regions (8.9 percent in the Northeast; 8.4 percent in the North Central; and 5.4 percent in the West).[13]

Generally, the black migration followed that of the general population; however, very few blacks have migrated to western states, with the exception of California. The migration of blacks from the South has been an important factor in the redistribution of the black population within the country. In 1970, about 45 percent of the blacks in the West and 34 percent of those in the North were born in the South, reflecting long-term migration patterns. In each of the last three decades, the South lost about 1.5 million blacks through net out-migration. Among the regions, the North received the largest number of migrants (284,000) from the South during the period 1965 to 1970.[14]

The significance of these migration patterns centers largely around

---

11. E. E. LeMasters, *Parents in Modern America* (Homewood, Ill.: Dorsey, 1970), pp. 198–199.

12. U.S. Bureau of the Census, *Current Population Reports*, Series P-23, no. 37, and Series P-23, no. 55, "Social and Economic Characteristics of the Population in Metropolitan and Nonmetropolitan Areas," (Washington D.C.: U.S. Government Printing Office, 1971 and 1975), Table 2, p. 20; and Table F, p. 6.

13. Ibid., Table 3, p. 30.

14. Ibid.

their selectivity: not all ages or complete families were caught up in the movement north, since the industrial pool there preferred young men. This had a tremendous impact both on the community left behind and on the community into which the black migrated. It affected family life by disrupting the nuclear family and by separating, geographically, extended-family ties, it affected the educational-occupational structure of both communities, and it had an effect on other factors such as housing, ghetto life, and patterns of discriminatory behavior.

These last two transitions have been occurring for the last sixty years or more and are still in process. In some ways these transitions produce a generation gap among blacks. On the one hand we have a sizable number of parents who were reared in rural Mississippi or Alabama in a highly segregated society and who were members of a lower-lower class. On the other hand we find an increasing number of children of these parents living in large urban centers who are partly integrated into the school system but who have aspirations and hopes for a high school or college education.

From Negative to Positive
Social Status

Some would argue that the single most important variable to understanding the black family today is social class. Generally, irrespective of race, the key to identifying, describing, and classifying family forms is by social class. Many family forms are more likely to be consequences of class than of either skin color or race. Major differences seem to exist within the black family if a distinction is made between the lower-lower substrata of the subculture and the "middle class" of the subculture. It is the black middle class that is seldom publicized. This is a stratum in which most of the marriages are stable two-parent units where husbands have a high school education or better and occupy positions in business, government, or our educational systems. These families are basically more similar than dissimilar to the dominant white-family form that exists in our society.

This shift from a negative to a positive social status includes a shift in the approach to and the interpretation of black families. The traditional and old model of the black family projected a negative stereotype, viewing the family as being one monolithic lower-class entity—as a social problem in itself, as a pathology of illegitimacy and broken homes, as centering around the female as a dominating matriarch, and as including males with low self-esteem.[15] The emerging or new model challenges these negative views, stress-

---

15. See Leonard Lieberman, "The Emerging Model of the Black Family," *International Journal of Sociology of the Family* 3 (March 1973), pp. 10–22; also note Warren D. Ten Houten, "The Black Family: Myth and Reality," *Psychiatry* 33 (May 1970), pp. 145–173.

ing the black family as a variety of types at different social-class levels, rejecting the social problem and pathology orientation as an expression of middle-class ethnocentrism, viewing the family as having strengths such as equalitarianism, self-reliant males, strong family ties, and high achievement orientations, and, finally, being worthy of study as forms of social organization in its own right. Diane Lewis,[16] for example, claims that "the hard black core of America is African" and that Afro-Americans share a unique and distinct subculture in American society.

The old model of the black family was vividly portrayed by Moynihan in his now classic "Moynihan Report."[17] It was his contention that there has been a serious weakening in the black social structure and that there is a trend away from family stability in lower socioeconomic levels. He concluded in his 1965 report that the structure of family life in the black community constituted a "tangle of pathology" and that at the heart of the deterioration of the fabric of black society is the deterioration of the family. The major block to equality centered around the matrifocal family. The implication is that young blacks grow and are reared in a mother-centered family without the helpful influence of both parents. This in turn, Moynihan argued, was a major reason why blacks were making only limited gains during the prosperous 1960s.

Billingsley,[18] Frazier,[19] and others disagree directly and strongly with Moynihan's central tenet. They contend that the black family is not a cause of the "tangle of pathology" but rather that it is an absorbing, adaptive, and amazingly resilient mechanism for the socialization of its children and the civilization of its society.[20]

More recent data[21] indicate that in terms of delinquency, aspirations, educational expectations, perceptions of the education desired by the parents, self-conceptions, and notions of appropriate gender role behavior of adults, the empirical evidence does not provide adequate support for the conclusions of the Moynihan Report. In fact, Alan Berger and William Simon suggest that even in the lower-class broken family, there is no indication that the black family is dramatically different from the white family in the way it treats its children and the results it produces. Billingsley adds a point made later in this chapter, that the majority of blacks live in two-parent nuclear families with

16. Diane K. Lewis, "The Black Family: Socialization and Sex Roles," *Phylon* 36 (Fall 1975), pp. 221–237.

17. Daniel P. Moynihan, *The Negro Family: The Case for National Action* (Washington, D.C.: U.S. Government Printing Office, U.S. Department of Labor, 1965).

18. Billingsley, op. cit.

19. Frazier, op. cit.

20. Billingsley, op. cit., p. 33.

21. Alan S. Berger and William Simon, "Black Families and the Moynihan Report: A Research Evaluation," *Social Problems* 22 (December 1974), pp. 145–161; and Roberta H. Jackson, "Some Aspirations of Lower Class Black Mothers," *Journal of Comparative Family Studies* 6 (Autumn 1975), pp. 171–181.

> *Ann:*   *I'm clearly aware that I'm a black in a white dominated society. But I feel like I'm a human being, and it does not bother me until you start to push, and then I will get hostile. I'm like any other person. I'm like you. If you had my back up against the wall, I would fight. At times it's quite natural to feel that you've been cheated, because you've not been able to live as if you were human, and if you were just as much man, just as much woman, like that white man or that white woman. But it's changing. A lot of it is still here but there's more cover up here than in South. You can't blame it on the South. It's here. It's all around. But if you deal with it and you say, hey, no, you cannot put me down.*
>
> *This is the thing that a lot of blacks didn't realize that Martin Luther King was trying to say. Hey, it can be done in a peaceful manner. Let's say, "I'm just as much man" or "just as much woman as you are, and I don't have to raise my hand to you." But you got to realize that you are black, accept it and be proud of it, and I do.*

the man gainfully employed and working every day but who is often unable to earn enough to pull his family out of poverty.

Let us examine if specific shifts have occurred from a negative to a positive social status as portrayed primarily by census data in regard to employment, income, and education. Note particularly, 1) the tremendous gains made in recent years in the United States for both black males and females and 2) the major disparities that still exist between black and white.

Employment

An increasing number of blacks are entering positions of leadership in the professions, in business, and in government. A *Wall Street Journal* article in 1970 stated that being black can mean getting a job rather than not getting one. In the early 1970s the job situation looked bleak; even those with master's and Ph.D. degrees were taking jobs they would not have taken in previous years. But the exception to that situation was said to exist among blacks.

> Black graduates are especially in demand due to increasing pressure on employers by the Federal Government to hire more minority-group members. The demand for black workers is heightened by the fact that some blacks are being wary of taking some offers because they seem too good to be true. They cannot comprehend that so many openings are available to them. They are wary and somewhat timid to take advantage of the opportunities.[22]

---

22. *The Wall Street Journal*, July 13, 1970, p. 3.

TABLE 8–1.   Unemployment Rates by Sex and Age: 1960, 1970, and 1974

(Annual averages)

Subject	Black and Other Races			White		
	1960	1970	1974	1960	1970	1974
Total	10.2	8.2	9.9	4.9	4.5	5.0
Adult Men	9.6	5.6	6.8	4.2	3.2	3.5
Adult Women	8.3	6.9	8.4	4.6	4.4	5.0
Teen-agers[a]	24.4	29.1	32.9	13.4	13.5	14.0

[a]"Teen-agers" include persons sixteen to nineteen years old.

Source: "The Social and Economic Status of the Black Population in the United States," *Current Population Reports*, Series P–23, no. 42, 1972. Table 37, p. 53; and no. 54 (1975), Table 39, p. 65.

In contrast to the availability of jobs for *certain* blacks is the widespread unavailability of jobs for the majority of them. For a number of years the unemployment rate among blacks was double the rate of the nation as a whole. That is, if the national unemployment rate was 5 percent, one could assume a 10 percent rate for blacks. In 1974, the annual average unemployment rate was 9.9 for blacks. This figure increased dramatically to 32.9 for black teen-agers (see Table 8–1). Opportunities for the lower educated, unskilled young blacks are not sufficient to meet the employment and income needs of this segment of our population.

Income

The economic gap that separates white and black Americans is, despite all the efforts of recent years, growing. There is no doubt that the urban black population of the middle class particularly has made substantial economic gains during the 1960s. These gains seem to exist whether one looks at occupation, education, or income. Yet, irrespective of absolute gains, the paradox is that blacks remain significantly deprived when compared to whites at the same status level. There has been considerable black advance—but there has been substantial white advance too. Thus when compared to whites, many blacks remain relatively deprived irrespective of class: they are still more than three times as likely to be in poverty, twice as likely to be unemployed, and three times as likely to die in infancy or child birth. In large cities, more than half of all blacks live in poor neighborhoods.[23]

23. "Recent Trend in Social and Economic Conditions of Negroes in the United States," *Current Population Reports*, U.S. Department of Labor, p. 23, no. 26, BLS no. 347 (July 1968), p. v.

TABLE 8–2.   Median Family Income of Negroes and Other
Races as a Percentage of White Family Income: 1950 to 1973

Year	White	Negro	Difference	Ratio: Negro to White
1974	$13,356	$7,808	$5,548	58
1973	12,595	7,596	4,999	60
1972	11,549	7,106	4,443	62
1971	10,672	6,714	3,958	63
1970	10,236	6,516	3,720	64
1968	8,937	5,590	3,347	63
1965	7,251	3,994	3,257	55
1960	5,835	3,233	2,602	55
1950	3,445	1,869	1,576	54

Source: Adapted from U.S. Bureau of the Census, *Current Population Reports*, Series P-60, no. 97, "Money Income in 1973 of Families and Persons in the United States," Washington, D.C.: U.S. Government Printing Office, 1975. Table 13, p. 30; and Series P-60, no. 99, Table 1, p. 5.

According to census data (Table 8–2) the dollar gap between blacks and whites actually grew in the last quarter century. In 1950, the median white-family income was $3,445; the median black-family income was $1,869—a dollar gap of $1,576. By 1974, after widely heralded social reforms, white income soared to $13,356 and black income rose to $7,808, showing an even greater dollar gap—$5,548.

The ratio of black to white income increased from fifty-four to sixty-four between 1950 and 1970 then decreased to fifty-eight by 1974. But ratios may mean very little when dollar amounts are insufficient to maintain families. In 1974, the poverty threshold for a nonfarm family of four was $5,038.[24] As one can see, this figure is only several thousand dollars less than the median family income of blacks in 1974. The seriousness of this becomes more intensified when linked with data already presented that more than half of all blacks live in central cities where life is more expensive, and the dollar gap means a lower standard of living.

Education

Transition from a negative to a more positive social status can also be seen by examining the percentages of the black population age 25 to 34 who have completed at least a high school education. In 1974 in this age category,

24. U.S. Bureau of the Census, *Current Population Reports*, Series P-60, No. 99, "Money Income and Poverty Status of Families and Persons in the United States: 1974." (advance report) (Washington, D.C.: U.S. Government Printing Office, 1975), p. 3.

67 percent of black males and 63.9 percent of black females had completed four years of high school or more. This is in contrast to the comparable 1970 percentages of 49.4 and 57.0 for males and females respectively and the 1960 percentages of 30.1 and 35.8.[25]

In just the past few years a significant change has taken place in the black male-female educational differential that would appear to have a major impact on black marital and family patterns. That is, as shown in the previous paragraph, traditionally a higher percentage of black females than black males completed high school. However, in 1974, a higher percentage of males than females had completed four years of high school or more. That a greater percentage of black men are completing high school combined with a greater percentage completing relative to women would indicate a major shift in employment opportunities for men, a shift in male-female decision-making patterns in marriage, a modification of the self-definitions and perceptions of men, and a general reorientation of male-female relationships in mate selection, sexual behavior, child-rearing patterns, or marital life-styles. This may be particularly true in a society that has traditionally operated on norms suggesting that the male should be the breadwinner and the major decision maker.

Frazier seems convinced that as the educational and economic position of blacks improves, there will develop a conformity to dominant family patterns.[26] It was his conviction that a black middle class would develop that would be made up of salaried professionals and white-collar workers. Has the family stability that Frazier predicted taken place?

It could be argued that it has and will continue to occur. For example, in 1970, at the upper-income level ($15,000 and over), about 94 percent of black families were headed by a man, about the same proportion as that for white families. In contrast, at the lower end of the scale ($3,000 and under) the proportion of black families headed by a man was 40 percent compared to 72 percent for whites.[27]

These data appear consistent with the propositions of both Goode[28] and Udry[29] who show (by use of census data) that as the social and economic position of blacks increases, marital dissolution decreases. Evidence seems to suggest a change in conditions among the black families from a submerged group at the bottom of the social-class structure to the development of a small, able

25. U.S. Bureau of Census, *Current Population Reports*, Series P-20, No. 274, "Educational Attainment in the United States: March 1973 and 1974," U.S. Government Printing Office, 1974, Table A., p. 1. The comparable figures for white males and white females were 82.3 and 81.0 respectively in 1974 and 59.3 and 62.8 in 1960.

26. Frazier, op. cit., p. 333.

27. *Current Population Reports*, op. cit., Series P-23, no. 42, p. 1.

28. William J. Goode, "Family Disorganization," in Robert K. Merton and Robert A. Nisbet, *Contemporary Social Problems* (New York: Harcourt, Brace, and World, 1971), pp. 493–494.

29. J. Richard Udry, "Marital Instability, by Race, Sex, Education, and Occupation; Using 1960 Census Data," *American Journal of Sociology* 72 (September 1966), pp. 203–209.

working class and the emergence of a larger middle class. Generally, as Goode and others suggest, as economic conditions improve, the incidence of family disorganization decreases, family life becomes increasingly stable, there are higher aspirations for children, and there is greater conformity to the sexual mores of society.[30]

From Negative to Positive
Self-Image

A basic tenet of social psychology states that we develop our selves, our identities, and our perceptions of our worth in interaction with others. As the black is the last to be hired and the first to be fired, as the black interacts in a white man's world, as the black child interacts in a society that encourages feelings of inferiority and degrades self-worth, he begins to believe what others say about him. The child who hears the policeman refer to his dad as "boy" and who lives in a system that teaches millions of black children to disrespect and despise their parents has been trapped in a self-fulfilling prophecy: a degraded person will oblige his detractors by believing and thus acting out the prophecies bestowed upon him.

Several writers have emphasized the extent to which black families must teach their children not only how to be human but how to be black.[31] They must learn to act out the role of the "inferior." This process of learning to be both human and black is not merely a historical event but a necessity of many black families in an attempt to exist in American society. The author recalls a recent conversation with a mother who had her child enrolled in a predominantly white elementary school. The very consciousness of color on the part of the other children served as a constant reminder to the child that she was different. To learn to achieve worth as a person included the necessity of accepting the worth of a darker skin color. It is doubtful that many white children face the same dual socializing experience in reference to skin color.

Black parents have to teach their children to act, think, and feel the black role. This is done by many families who are attempting to protect their children against the prejudice and discriminatory behavior that the outside world will provide to them as they approach adolesence and adulthood. Other parents are in the ambiguous situation of wanting to protect their children by

---

30. Note John H. Scanzoni, *The Black Family in Modern Society* (Boston: Allyn and Bacon, 1971).

31. Thomas Pettigrew, *Profile of the Negro American* (Princeton, N.J.: D. Van Nostrand Co., 1964), p. 4; Hylan Lewis, *Black Ways of Kent* (Chapel Hill, N.C.: University of North Carolina Press, 1955), p. 109; Claud Anderson and Rue L. Cromwell, "Black Is Beautiful and the Color Preferences of Afro-American Youth." *The Journal of Negro Education* 46 (Winter 1977), pp. 76–88.

isolating them from the white world but desiring to establish a sense of pride and worth in their children.

PATTERNS OF BLACK FAMILY LIFE

Billingsley and Billingsley describe three distinct patterns of black family life that have emerged from the six social transitions described.[32] They refer to these as the matriarchal pattern, the equalitarian pattern, and the patriarchal pattern. Although these refer primarily to the nuclear-family unit, they do not exclude other relatives. Not uncommon among nuclear families is the presence of nephews, aunts, grandparents, cousins, and other adult relatives. An estimated 25 percent of all black families have one or more relatives living with them. These extended-family units should not be overlooked or ignored when examining the three family patterns described. These extended kin, plus the many families with unrelated kin living in as roomers, boarders, or guests, exert a major influence in the life-style of black families. Emphasis is here given to 1) the wide range of family structures beyond the matriarchal, equalitarian, and patriarchal family patterns, and 2) the extreme resiliency of the black family institution. Neither mother-centered nor any other type families are necessarily "falling apart" but are capable of major adaptations to the historical and contemporary social conditions that confront them.

Matriarchal Family Pattern

The matriarchal family pattern, the least stable, is the one in which the female head is the dominant member. These families are most often characterized as "multi-problem families." Here is where we are most likely to find the "culture of poverty," the "lower-class subculture."

There were 7.5 million blacks and 16.3 million whites below the poverty or low-income level in 1974.[33] Low-income blacks comprised 31 percent of the black population, more than three times the comparable proportion of 9 percent for the white population.[34] Families with female heads comprise an

---

32. Billingsley and Billingsley, op. cit., pp. 149–156.

33. Families are classified as being above or below the low-income level by using a poverty index based on a sliding scale of income that is adjusted for such factors as family size, sex, and age of the family head, number of children, and farm-nonfarm residence. The low-income threshold for a nonfarm family of four was $5,038 in 1974, and $4,540 in 1973.

34. U.S. Bureau of the Census, *Current Population Reports*, Special Studies Series P-23, no. 54, "The Social and Economic Status of the Black Population in the United States" (Washington, D.C.: U.S. Government Printing Office, 1975), Table 23, p. 42.

increasing proportion of both black and white low-income families. However, such families are in the majority only among low-income black families. In 1970, about 56 percent of all poor black families were headed by women; by 1974, the proportion had grown to 67 percent. For whites in 1970 it was 30 percent, in 1974, 37 percent.[35]

Among the families headed by a female, the larger the family the more likely it was to have a low-income status. For example, if the family headed by a black female had only one child, 41 percent were in the low-income status. This jumps to 67 percent with three children and to 81 percent with five or more.[36] As might be expected, this relationship between the number of persons in the family and low-income status exists independent of race. Among white families headed by a female, one-fourth (25 percent) were families below the low-income level. If there was only one child in the family this figure was 28 percent, if there were three children it increased to 45 percent, and with five children or more it increased to 71 percent. It is a debated issue whether the incomplete family structure of the female-headed family explains its poverty or whether the poverty explains its structure. It is likely that each contributes to the other.

The matriarchal pattern may take several forms. One is the family in which there is no father. In this situation the child is given the surname of the mother, who lives in her own house or the house of her parents with her own children. Second is the family that has a temporary father or a series of temporary fathers. The father may appear when he has a job and live with his wife and then leave when the income ceases. A third subtype of the matriarchal pattern is one in which the father may be present but the mother is the dominant authority figure. These families would include those having fathers who cannot support a family and who cannot exercise the authority of parenthood.

If female-headed black families are any indication of a matriarchal family structure, it should be evident that this type of family is not the most frequent. Neither is it exclusive to black families, although it is considerably more prevalent than among any other ethnic group in America. In 1974, of the 5.4 million black families in the United States, 1.9 million, or 35.9 percent, were headed by a female (see Table 8–3). Of those black families with a female head, nearly one-third were separated, another third were widowed, one in six (16.7 percent) were divorced, and one in five were single.

An examination of Table 8–3 will show how these figures compare with white families for the same year. It can also be noted that the average

---

35. Ibid., Table 26, p. 45.
36. U.S. Bureau of the Census, *Current Population Reports*, Series P-60, no. 98, "Characteristics of the Low-Income Population: 1973, (Washington, D.C.: U.S. Government Printing Office, 1975), Table D, p. 6. The comparable figures for black families with a male head were 9.7 percent with one child, 15.4 percent with three children, and 37.2 percent with five or more children.

TABLE 8–3.   Selected Characteristics of Families: 1974

(Numbers in thousands)

Characteristic	White	Negro
All families	49,919	5,440
Female head	4,853	1,951
Percentage of all families	9.9	35.9
Average number of own children under 18 per family		
All families	1.13	1.41
Female head	1.10	1.71
Marital status of female head		
Total	100.0	100.0
Married, husband absent	18.9	33.0
Separated	14.7	29.4
Other	4.1	3.6
Widowed	39.7	29.7
Divorced	32.1	16.7
Single	9.3	20.5

Source: U.S. Bureau of the Census, *Current Population Reports* Series P–20, no. 276, "Household and Family Characteristics, March 1974," (Washington, D.C.: U.S. Government Printing Office, 1975), Table 7, p. 55.

number of children under eighteen per family is greater for black families headed by a female (1.71) than for all black families (1.41), whereas for white families headed by a female, the average number of children (1.10) is slightly less than for all white families (1.13).

In our society it has been assumed that adults cannot maintain family stability unless they are married and living with their spouses. Perhaps stability indicates factors other than the presence of both parents. An increase in income, a greater availability of housing, and the maintaining of kin ties with persons other than a spouse may permit more families to maintain a degree of stability that would be equal to or greater than that of families with a male present.

Saying that there can be stability in female-headed families is not to imply that these families have fewer problems than those with a male and female; however, it is meant to suggest that caution should be taken in assuming that families headed by a female are unstable and inadequate. This is frequently overlooked since the black female-headed family pattern is the one in which illegitimacy and other indices of unstable family life occur most frequently. These are the families most often and most commonly supported by public assistance and whose members are most alienated from the norms and values of the larger society.

To deal with the matriarchal pattern as one type of family structure among black families is in no way intended to support the idea of a female-dominated black subculture. Staples states that the myth of a black matriarchy is a cruel hoax adding injury to black liberation.[37] In his words:

> For the black female, her objective reality is a society where she is economically exploited because she is both female and black; she must face the inevitable situation of a shortage of black males because they have been taken out of circulation by America's neo-colonialist wars, railroaded into prisons, or killed off early by the effects of ghetto living conditions. To label her a matriarch is a classical example of what Malcolm X called the making the victim the criminal.[38]

The black woman has always occupied a highly esteemed place in black culture within American society. Under slavery conditions, many black fathers were forcibly deprived of the responsibilities and privileges of fatherhood. At that time and since, the power dimension within marriages is highly aligned along economic lines. And when a dominant white society continues to deny black males the opportunity to obtain the economic resources to assume leadership in the family complex, a large number of females are forced into a matriarchal role.

Establishing the matriarchal family pattern as the dominant one among blacks would be very difficult.[39] Census data, economic reports, and an increasing number of empirical studies verify that the role played by the black male in the family is a major and predominant one.

Equalitarian Family Pattern

The equalitarian two-parent family is the one most commonly found among blacks in our society. This is one in which the husband and wife are living together in their first marriage. Here we have two parents in distinctive but complementary and flexible roles. The husband is more likely to have stable employment and at least an operational level of education. Families of this type are more likely to be middle- or upper-lower-class families.

As of March, 1976, 73 percent of all ever-married black men (age fourteen plus) were living with their wives. The other 27 percent included 13.0 percent who were married without a wife present, 5.8 percent who were widowed, and 8.2 percent who were divorced. Of all ever-married black women

---

37. Robert Staples, "The Myth of the Black Matriarchy," *The Black Scholar* (January–February, 1970), pp. 8–16.

38. Ibid., p. 8.

39. Note arguments such as Ten Hauten, op. cit., pp. 145–173; Katheryn Thomas Dietrich, "A Reexamination of the Myth of Black Matriarchy," *Journal of Marriage and the Family* 37 (May 1975), pp. 367–374.

TABLE 8–4.   Marital Status by Race and Sex: March 1976

Marital Status	WHITE		NEGRO	
	Male	Female	Male	Female
Single	28.6	21.7	39.1	32.6
Married, wife—husband (present)	63.8	58.8	44.5	36.2
Married, wife—husband (absent)	2.0	2.7	7.9	11.7
Separated	1.2	1.9	6.9	10.3
Other	0.8	0.8	1.0	1.4
Widowed	2.2	11.8	3.5	12.8
Divorced	3.4	5.0	5.0	6.8
Total	100.0	100.0	100.0	100.0

Source: Adapted from U.S. Bureau of the Census, *Current Population Reports*, Series P-20, no. 306, "Marital Status and Living Arrangements: March 1976," (Washington, D.C.: U.S. Government Printing Office, 1977), Table 1, pp. 9–10.

(age fourteen plus) 53.7 percent were living with their husbands. The other 46.3 percent included 18.9 percent who were widowed, 17.3 percent who were married with the husband absent, and 10.1 percent who were divorced.[40] The data on the marital status of the total black population, including those single, can be seen in Table 8–4.

This majority pattern destroys the myths of the mother-present, father-absent black family. Clearly, the majority of blacks are in the status indicative of family stability. Most adults are currently married, most live with their spouses, most families are husband-wife families, and the majority of children are legitimate, and live with both parents.[41]

Despite its being in the majority, this equalitarian family pattern has been relatively neglected by most social scientists, in contrast to several excellent studies of the approximately one-fourth of black families characterized by the absence of the husband.[42] Perhaps the ignoring of this family pattern is due to the fact that these families are relatively stable, conforming, achieving, and cause few problems to anyone. Billingsley claims that social science

40. Percentages figured from data presented in Table 1, U.S. Bureau of the Census, *Current Population Reports*, Series P-20, no. 306, "Marital Status and Living Arrangements: March, 1976," (Washington, D.C.: U.S. Government Printing Office, 1977), Table 1, p. 10.

41. Reynolds Farley and Albert I. Hermalin, "Family Stability: A Comparison of Trends between Blacks and Whites," *American Sociological Review* 36 (February 1971), p. 15.

42. For instance, see Elliot Liebow, *Tally's Corner* (Boston: Little, Brown, 1967); and Lee Rainwater, "Crucible of Identity, The Negro Lower-Class Family," *Daedalus* 95 (1966), pp. 172–216.

has failed the black family, citing four factors that stand out as being paramount.

> The first is the tendency to ignore black families altogether. The second is, when black families are considered, to focus almost exclusively on the lowest income group of black families, that acute minority of families who live in public housing projects or who are supported by public welfare assistance. The third is to ignore the majority of black stable families even among this lowest income group, to ignore the processes by which these families move from one equilibrium state to another, and to focus instead on the most unstable among these low-income families. A fourth tendency, which is more bizarre than all the others, is a tendency on the part of social scientists to view the black, low-income, unstable, problem-ridden family as the causal nexus for the difficulties their members experience in the wider society.[43]

There seems to be a number of studies that would in large part escape the scathing criticisms Billingsley makes of white social scientists reporting on black family life in America. Since 1965 for example, Jessie Bernard,[44] Elizabeth Herzog,[45] Robert Coles,[46] P. Gurin and D. Katz,[47] and John Scanzoni[48] have completed studies that explode much of the mythology about black families, show their positive attributes, and present a more realistic appraisal of black family life.

An interesting study of stable black families in Indianapolis was completed by Scanzoni[49] who studied husbands and wives of black families who had lived together for five years or more. Using black interviewers, data were gathered from 400 households in an attempt to describe and try to analyze the urban black family system above the under class or lower class. A central hypothesis of Scanzoni's study was that an inextricable link exists between economic resources and black family structure. When dealing with the husband-wife relationship, a clear "drift" was found within black family structure toward a convergence with family patterns existing in the dominant society. In his words:

> The overwhelming majority of black Americans want to participate in the economic benefits of a modern society. As they increasingly enter into the dominant society economically, they also enter it conjugally. But owing to white

43. Andrew Billingsley, "Black Families and White Social Science," *Journal of Social Issues* 26 (1970), pp. 132–133.
44. Jessie Bernard, *Marriage and Family among Negroes* (Englewood Cliffs, N. J.: Prentice-Hall, 1966).
45. Elizabeth Herzog, *About the Poor: Some Facts and Some Fictions* (Washington, D.C.: U.S. Department of Health, Education, and Welfare, 1967).
46. Robert Coles, *Children of Crisis: A Study of Courage and Fear* (Boston: Little, Brown, 1967).
47. P. Gurin and D. Katz, *Motivation and Aspiration in the Negro College* (U.S. Department of Health, Education, and Welfare, Office of Education, 1966).
48. Scanzoni, op. cit.
49. Ibid.

discrimination which still hinders equal economic participation by blacks, black family patterns tend to diverge somewhat from dominant patterns. . . . In white marriages, "objective" resources such as husband's occupational status, education, and income tend to generate optimal attainment of these goals. Yet because blacks face discrimination in these three areas, we found it was more difficult for these kinds of factors to optimize desired marital goals. Other major differences between black and white family patterns centered on the meaning and consequences of wife employment, and on family authority and leadership.

These several differences, however, should not obscure the main point, i.e., there are more similarities than differences in black and white conjugal relations, and that if blacks are permitted to participate more fully in the economic system, any existing differences will probably diminish in significance.[50]

The inescapable conclusion of Scanzoni is that:

The black family in America, as much as the white family, is shaped by its relationship to the economic-opportunity structure. This relationship is mediated primarily via the occupation of the male head-of-household. Where he is not present, as is often the case in the lower class, this has certain negative consequences for the family. And where he is present, the degree of his integration with the opportunity system influences most, if not all, aspects of husband-wife and parent-child interaction.

That there is a "black community" and a "white community" reflects in part differential access to the economic rewards of the total society. That there are certain "black family patterns" which may differ somewhat from "white family patterns" reflects this same differential economic access.[51]

It is from families in which both husband and wife are present that most black leaders emerge. The role of the father as playmate, teacher, and disciplinarian to his children is less likely to take place in the matriarchal form of family organization when he is present and is impossible when he is not. In contrast, in the equalitarian pattern, the father plays a more dominant role, and the children develop a greater primary identification with the father. Billingsley and Billingsley state:

In spite of the richness of both the heritage and the potential contribution of the equalitarian family pattern, it is often vulnerable to falling into the matriarchal pattern. Remaining stable depends on a number of factors, including the vitality of its family tradition, employment of the father, development of a common family subculture, and the integration of the family in the life of the general community.[52]

Once again we return to the point made at the beginning of this chapter. Families are not isolated groups existing independently of the society of which they are a part. The success or failure of an equalitarian pattern or a

50. Ibid., pp. 264–265.
51. Ibid., pp. 309–310.
52. Billingsley and Billingsley, op. cit., pp. 154–155.

matriarchal pattern relates very closely to the opportunity structure which is provided to them.

Patriarchal Family Pattern

The patriarchal family pattern is heavily represented among upper-class blacks. Like the equalitarian family, this is a family in which the father is present. But here, the father makes most of the major decisions and is dominant in most respects.

Among the upper classes, the problems so often associated with the lower-class black family are almost totally nonexistent in the patriarchal family pattern. Endogenous marriages are highly encouraged. Much of a given generation's wealth is inherited from a previous generation. Upper-class blacks in large part tend to isolate themselves from the majority of black families. Many college graduates from this class background do not engage actively in black organizations, and their relationship to the rest of the black world is sometimes one of exploitation.

The patriarchal family pattern also exists among the middle and lower classes. In interviews with both the husband and wife of forty-three black working-class families in Ohio, it was found that both sexes perceived the power structure of the family to reside with the husband.[53] Specifically, only 2 percent saw the wife as dominant, 25 percent saw equality, and 73 percent saw the husband as dominant. These results differ profoundly from the popular stereotype of the matriarchal black family. They also differ profoundly from the earlier study by Blood and Wolfe in Detroit where 19 percent described the wife as dominant.[54] Both studies used the same family decision-making scale to measure the distribution of power in the family.

As stated by Billingsley and Billingsley, "The most noteworthy feature of this particular pattern of family life for our purposes is its stability and strict patterns of socialization and social control according to the values shared by the dominant group in our society."[55]

Summary

The black family in American society, like any family system, is not a uniform entity, nor is it isolated and separate from other social systems within the community and society. The basic structural patterns, the interpersonal

---

53. Jerry M. Lewis and Paul Sites, "Decision Making in Black Working Class Families," unpublished paper sent to the author.
54. Robert O. Blood and Donald M. Wolfe, *Husbands and Wives* (New York: Free Press, 1960), pp. 25 and 35.
55. Billingsley and Billingsley, op. cit., p. 156.

processes, or the personal value positions can only be understood within the context in which they exist.

In American society, black families have been and are affected by numerous major social transitions. The transition from Africa to America has relevance in understanding factors such as skin color, cultural discontinuity, and slavery. The transition from slavery to emancipation had a major influence on the emergence of multiple family forms, occupational patterns, kin relationships, and the forms of families that would result in the future. The transition from rural to urban areas, while presenting opportunities for better wages, schools, and health services also tended to disrupt family kin ties and community linkages. The transition from southern to northern and western communities, while still in process, closely paralleled the rural-urban movement. The transitions from negative to positive social status and from negative to positive self-images are in the process of occurring, and although major gains have taken place in income and education, the lag behind the white community is major and significant. In addition, the dual socializing experience of learning to be both black and human in a basically white society has a major significance in understanding black family organization and interpersonal relationships.

From these major social transitions, distinct patterns of black family life have emerged. The *matriarchal* and mother-headed family, while not the most prevalent type, is the one where multi-problems are most frequent. In these families a father may not exist, may be present temporarily, or may be present but unable to exercise authority. Those families headed by a female are most likely to be low-income families, have a greater number of children than white or other black families, and appear to face the greatest difficulties in meeting the daily demands of existence.

The *equalitarian* family, the most prevalent type, is one in which both husband and wife are living together and the spouses have distinctive and complementary roles. These families, often ignored in the social science literature, are relatively stable, conforming, and achieving. They desire to participate in the economic and social benefits of the larger society and tend to share the general values and goals of the larger society.

The *patriarchal* family pattern, although less common than the other forms of black families, is heavily represented among the higher socioeconomic levels of society. Here the father is present, makes most of the major decisions, and is dominant in most respects. Often these families tend to isolate themselves from the majority of black families. Noteworthy features of this pattern of family life are its stability and strict patterns of socialization and social control.

This chapter and the one preceding it focused on two subcultural family systems in the United States. The difference in the structure and interaction patterns within each family, the difference between the Amish and the black family, and the wide diversity between these families and the normative family type in the United States should have become clear. Shifting from an examination of family types based on religion and on race, we now turn to an examination of the diversity of family types based on social class.

Key Terms and Concepts

Discussion Questions

1. Is their a unique Afro-American family today?
2. Discuss the idea that black families are matricentric.
3. What black family characteristics of today can be traced directly to an African heritage? How does an understanding of slavery contribute to an understanding of patterns of black family life today?
4. Make a comparison of black and white families on dimensions such as family size, educational level, rural-urban residence, marriage rates, and others. How can these differences be explained? What differences exist if one controls for social class?
5. From the use of state census data, contrast the demographic characteristics by race of your county or state with national data. Explain similarities or differences that may exist.
6. Examine the "Moynihan Report." What data are presented that are subject to interpretations other than those given? Why did this report become an object of alarm and controversy?
7. What significance for families is attached to movements from south to north or from rural to urban residences? Are these factors any different for blacks than for whites?
8. Discuss the statement "The black problem in America is essentially a white problem."
9. What types of conditions, opportunities, or programs would be most beneficial in speeding the transitions from a negative to a positive social status and from a negative to a positive self-image?
10. What dangers lie in dealing with the black family as a homogeneous

grouping? Describe variations in life-styles and marital patterns within the black family.

11. *It has been claimed by several scholars that life for black families in the ghetto appears to be getting worse. Explain.*

12. *Discuss the unique role and status of the woman in the black family. How is it explained? Why or why not is it likely to change?*

Further Readings

Bernard, Jessie. *Marriage and Family among Negroes.* Englewood Cliffs, N.J.: Prentice-Hall, 1966. An extensive overview of the literature on black families and a discussion of two distinctive styles of adaptation: the acculturated and the externally adapted.

Billingsley, Andrew. "Black Families and White Social Science." *Journal of Social Issues* 26 (1970), pp. 127–142. A harsh and critical attack on the "white social science establishment" and its mistreatment of black families.

Billingsley, Andrew. *Black Families in White America.* Englewood Cliffs, N.J.: Prentice-Hall, 1968. A look at the black family as a complex institution within the black community, which is in turn highly interdependent with other institutions in the wider white society.

Frazier, E. Franklin. *The Negro Family in the United States.* Chicago: University of Chicago Press, 1939, 1948, 1966. First published as a research monograph in 1939 and giving a historical look at the black family, this book has been revised on several occasions to bring it up to date.

Gutman, Herbert G. *The Black Family in Slavery and Freedom, 1750–1925.* New York: Pantheon Books, 1976. An historical look at the black family that dispels the popular notions of the mother-centered, one-parent, disorganized, and pathological family conditions under slavery.

Hill, Robert B. *The Strengths of Black Families.* New York: Emerson Hall, 1971. The director of the research department of the National Urban League strips away many myths and stereotypes surrounding the black family.

Lewis, Diane K. "The Black Family: Socialization and Sex Roles." *Phylon* 36 (Fall 1975), pp. 221–237. A synthesis and reinterpretation of existing literature on sex role socialization in black families.

Liebow, Elliot. *Tally's Corner.* Boston: Little, Brown, 1967. A sensitive analysis of the life-styles of black men who hang out on a particular street corner in Washington, D.C.

Moynihan, Daniel Patrick. *The Negro Family: The Case for National Action.* U.S. Department of Labor, Government Printing Office, 1965. The "Moynihan Report," which created a major controversy by arguing that the structure of family life in the black community was increasingly unstable and was the fundamental source of weakness in the community.

Rainwater, Lee. *Behind Ghetto Walls: Black Family Life in a Federal Slum.* Chicago: Aldine, 1970. A book dealing with the intimate personal and family life of some 10,000 children and adults living in an all-Negro public housing project in St. Louis.

Scanzoni, John H. *The Black Family in Modern Society.* Boston: Allyn and Bacon, 1971. A developmental study of black urban famiiles characterized as conjugally stable and economically secure.

Staples, Robert. *The Black Family: Essays and Studies.* Belmont, Calif.: Wadsworth, 1971. A broad collection of readings that attempts to present a balanced view of the black family.

Staples, Robert. "Towards a Sociology of the Black Family: A Theoretical and Methodological Assessment." *Journal of Marriage and the Family* 33 (February 1971), pp. 119–138. A summary and analysis of research and theory on black families. Questions the validity of much past scholarly work. Excellent list of references up through 1970.

Stark, Carol B. *All Our Kin: Strategies for Survival in a Black Community.* New York: Harper, 1974. An anthropologist who lived in the flats, the poorest section of a black community in a midwestern city reports on men, women, kin, and domestic networks.

Willie, Charles V. *The Family Life of Black People.* Columbus, Ohio: Charles V. Merrill, 1970. A collection of twenty-six articles dealing with the central issue of stability and instability in family life.

Willie, Charles. *A New Look at Black Families.* Bayside, New York: General Hall, 1976. A detailed analysis of twelve case studies of black families from different income levels.

9 *Social Class Variations in Family Life-Styles*

The two previous chapters described the Amish family, a relatively homo-geneous religious system, and the black family, a widely diverse racial system. This chapter focuses attention on social class and the variations in family organization and behavior patterns at differing class levels. The point of departure for a discussion of social class and family life-styles is explicitly sociological. Two procedures are followed: 1) to take as given the existing social structure of class and trace its probable impacts on family behavior and attitudes; and 2) to take a particular family behavior and search for class variations. Both orientations illustrate the diversity of families along the class dimension in a pluralistic society. Most of this chapter uses the former procedure. Other chapters that include segments on the social-class dimension use the latter.

THE MEANING OF SOCIAL
CLASS AND SOCIAL STRATA

The concept of *social class* refers to an aggregate of individuals who occupy broadly similar positions on the scale of prestige. As even the most un-trained observer would note, some kinds of work, some styles of life, some types of homes, automobiles, or dress, are viewed as more prestigious than others. No person, family, or society fails to differentiate some roles and posi-tions as more important and socially more valuable than others. Generally, the persons who perform roles of a higher esteem are rewarded more highly. The process by which this ranking occurs in a more-or-less enduring hierarchy of statuses is known as *stratification*. This term, borrowed from geology, refers to a differential ranking of people into horizontal layers (strata) of equality and inequality.

Even children are conscious of differential ranking. Roberta Simmons and Morris Rosenberg conducted a study to examine children's perceptions of the stratification system and to consider the possible consequences of these perceptions for the larger social order.[1] From a sample of more than 1,900 black and white children from grades three through twelve in the Baltimore City School System, they found a clear awareness of occupational-prestige differences. This status consciousness appeared as early as the third grade (the youngest children interviewed). Furthermore, not only did children recognize an occupational-prestige hierarchy as early as the elementary-school stage, but children rated occupations in an order almost identical to that of high school pupils and, indeed, of adult samples. Although the majority of children did not believe in America as a land of equal opportunity for everyone and although the less privileged were less likely to expect high success, the researchers found that the majority of children at every combination of age, race, and socioeconomic level were fairly optimistic about their own personal aspects. The knowledge of the occupations that carry high rewards, combined with a belief that such occupations are possible to obtain, was thought to encourage high-mobility aspirations.

Whether children in all societies recognize the existence of an occupational-prestige hierarchy is not known. However, Kingsley Davis and others claim that all societies are differentiated or stratified into some kind of prestige ranking (an ordered arrangement along a scale of superiority-equality-inferiority according to some commonly accepted basis of valuation).[2] This universal feature fulfills the function of motivating men to do the different kinds of work that must be done in order for that society to continue to meet its needs. Generally, the work requiring the greatest training or talent and having the greatest importance for the society will receive the greatest rewards. The bat boy neither expects nor receives the money, applause, publicity, or favored treatment given the star pitcher. To have, or to have access to, the positions to which a society gives high value is to generally (but not always) receive greater rewards. These rewards are not only money but also power, recognition, or prestige.

Prestige is directly associated with one's occupation. Rankings of occupational prestige have shown a similarity over time as well as between countries. In a classic study by Alex Inkeles and Peter Rossi the ranking of occupations in six industrialized countries (United States, Great Britain, Soviet Union, Japan, New Zealand, and Germany) resulted in remarkable

---

1. Roberta G. Simmons and Morris Rosenberg, "Functions of Children's Perceptions of the Stratification System," *American Sociological Review* 36 (April 1971), pp. 235–249.

2. Kingsley Davis and Wilbert E. Moore, "Some Principles of Stratification," *American Sociological Review* 10 (April 1945), pp. 242–249; Kingsley Davis, *Human Society* (New York: Macmillan, 1949), pp. 364–366; and for a criticism of this idea, see Melvin W. Tumin, "Some Principles of Stratification: A Critical Analysis," *American Sociological Review* 18 (August 1953), pp. 387–393.

similarities.[3] The same was true over time. Occupational prestige scores of ninety occupations in 1947 and 1963 showed a correlation of .99.[4] Although systematic changes occurred over this period, the overriding conclusion is that occupational prestige is remarkably stable through time as well as space. It is persons who share a similar level of prestige who occupy a given social stratum or social class.

Consequences of Social Class

The real significance of the class structure stems from some of its consequences. In addition to influencing one's chances to live (which determine the likelihood of being born in the first place), of living through the first year, or of reaching retirement, social class influences our early socialization, the organization of society, the role expectations and role projections that we hold, the values that we stress, the types of behavior defined as deviant, and the likelihood of mental illness. In addition, class affects the likelihood of an education, its type, the motivation to get it, and the ends for which education is meant. It affects dropout rates, scores on intelligence tests, grades, occupational-vocational aspirations, and almost any other factor related to education.

The same is true with the family. Social class is related to the age at which one is likely to marry, the success of that marriage, the meaning attached to sexual behavior, the size of family, the recreation engaged in, the type of food eaten, the discipline and care given to children, sleeping arrangements, and, as suggested by Kinsey, the procedures followed in coitus.

Class differences exist even within a university community. In a study of the college adjustment of married students, variations existed by social class in terms of religious endogamy, courtship experience, aspirations and curriculum, educational status of the wives of married male students, effect of marriage on grades, planning of children, employment pattern of the male, parent and in-law relationships, participation in campus activities, patterns of wife employment, overall reactions to marriage, as well as in the adjustment of the parents to the presence of children.[5] Although a number of situations did not appear to be status linked, for most areas important differences existed by social-status background.

---

3. Alex Inkeles and Peter N. Rossi, "National Comparisons of Occupational Prestige," *American Journal of Sociology* 61 (January 1956), pp. 329–339.

4. Robert W. Hodge, Paul M. Siegal, and Peter Rossi, "Occupational Prestige in the United States, 1925–1963," *American Journal of Sociology* 70 (November 1964), pp. 286–302. A correlation of 1.00 indicates a perfect correlation or no difference. A correlation of 0 indicates no constant or patterned relationship. Thus the .99 correlation indicates a very similar ranking—almost identical—of prestige scores in 1947 and 1963.

5. J. Ross Eshelman and Chester L. Hunt, *Social Class Factors in the College Adjustment of Married Students* (Kalamazoo, Mich.: Western Michigan University, 1965).

Although it is true that there are no sharply defined boundaries from one class to another, a great many of the normal life experiences of certain people are highly similar to other people who share a similar class subculture. For example, where polygyny is practiced, it is the men of the higher social or economic position who are most likely to have a plural number of wives. Divorce rates go up as class level goes down. Birth rates increase as social-class levels drop. Upper-social-strata young persons are granted less freedom of choice of a mate than are lower-social-strata persons. In the western world particularly, the age of men at marriage rises with class position. If class lines are crossed in marriage, the woman is more likely to be upwardly mobile (hypergamy). The upper social stratum has more extended kinship networks than does the lower stratum. Upper-social-strata couples are more likely to begin using contraceptives when they are introduced than are lower-social-strata couples. One could continue indefinitely with a list of family variables that are highly related to class position. This list is not meant to be complete nor has each relationship been established to hold true cross-culturally. Also, it is extremely difficult to explain why or how all of these and other results occur. A key point is, however, that within a culture, as well as between cultures, significant regularities occur between a family's patterns and the class position it occupies. Although regularities occur within a given social class, major variations and differences occur between classes. In contradiction to the First Amendment, all men are not created equal.

In the class structure it is the family, not merely the individual, that is ranked. William Goode is not alone among sociologists in saying that the family is the keystone of the stratification system—the social mechanism by which it is maintained.[6] It is his contention that marriage, as the linking of two families, is the most complete expression of class equality and that homogamy in turn bolsters the existing class structure.

Consider for a moment the extent to which the school we attend, the friends with whom we associate, the occupation we choose, the qualities of a mate we desire, the recreation we enjoy, or any other personal attitudes and values we maintain are linked to our families and their position in the stratification system. Perhaps our "free choice" or our personal decisions are not so free or personal after all.

Determinants of Social Class

The determinants of social class, or the criteria used as bases, usually are related to the economic and value system of the community. If food is scarce and thus highly valued, as in many primitive tribes, high status will be given to the skillful hunter or courageous warrior. As communities or

---

6. William J. Goode, *The Family* (Englewood Cliffs, N.J.: Prentice-Hall, 1964), p. 80.

societies develop, the criteria by which individuals and families are ranked are likely to change. Ownership of land or cattle may be the criteria in agricultural societies. In urban-industrialized societies, the criteria used are likely to include occupation, education, wealth, source of income, type of dwelling, character of neighborhood, and self-identification.[7] In this type of society, the stratification system is more likely to include *achieved* criteria in conjunction with the *ascribed* statuses and thus results in a more open type of stratification system. That is, within limits, an individual can move up in the system if he meets the criteria used for assigning a higher rank. In contrast, where ascriptive criteria are the bases for class determination, there is relatively little social mobility, up or down. The result is a caste type of class system.

It is often assumed that the husband is the best single index of family ranking, since either 1) it is the occupational position per se rather than the individual that is ranked[8] or 2) the husband's occupation is a major (usually *the* major) component in the determination of the family's rank.[9] Ernest Barth and Walter Watson questioned the appropriateness of these assumptions and the underlying patriarchal model.[10] They hypothesized that 1) the work, occupational level, and income of a working wife have a major impact on family life-style and 2) in some instances the wife's occupation will be as good as or better than the husband's in predicting family behavior and life-style.

With the use of 1960 census data the authors showed that working wives earn, on the average, half as much as their husbands or, in other terms, the working wife's contribution to family income was the equivalent of a 50 percent pay raise for the husband. By 1971 this income was the equivalent of a 59.4 percent pay raise. This added income did affect the life-style (social class) of these families as evidenced by their ownership of more expensive homes, lower persons-per-room ratios, and more bathrooms and radios than families with nonworking wives.

Working wives affect life-styles in other ways. They have less time to invest directly in family activities, are more apt to be childless, and less apt to have two or more children. The wife's employment sometimes permits the husband to attend school. In brief, the data support both hypotheses: a wife's employment and income affect life-style and, according to certain indicators, the wife's occupation combined with the husband's serves as a better predictor

7. For a review of family research practice in operationalizing social class and social status see Luther B. Otto, "Class and Status in Family Research," *Journal of Marriage and the Family* 37 (May 1975), 315–332.

8. Davis and Moore, op cit., p. 242.

9. Bernard Barber, *Social Stratification: A Comparative Analysis of Structure and Process* (New York: Harcourt, Brace & World, 1957), p. 171.

10. Ernest A. T. Barth and Walter B. Watson, "Social Stratification and the Family in Mass Society," *Social Forces* 45 (March 1967), pp. 392–402. Also see Kathleen V. Ritter and Lowell L. Hargens, "Occupational Positions and Class Identifications of Married Working Women. A Test of the Asymmetry Hypothesis," *American Journal of Sociology* 80 (January 1975), pp. 934–948.

Highlights of Women's Employment and Education

Employment in 1974

Number. *About 36 million women were in the labor force in 1974. This was 46 percent of all women 16 years of age and over. Women accounted for 39 percent of the civilian labor force.*

Age. *The median age of women in the work force was 36 years—5 years less than it was in 1960. More than half of the women 18 to 64 years of age were in the labor force—53 percent.*

Marital Status. *Almost 3 out of 5 women workers were married (husband present). Of all married women (husband present) in the population, 43 percent were working.*

Family Status. *Almost 2 out of 5 women workers had children under 18 years of age. Of the 13.6 million mothers in the labor force, 4.3 million had children under 6 years. Working mothers had 25.7 million children, of whom 5.1 million were under the age of 6.*

Employment Patterns. *About 43 percent of women workers worked full time the year round. About 31 percent worked at least 35 hours a week but less than 50 weeks a year. The other 26 percent worked part time either part or full year.*

Occupations. *One third of all employed women were clerical workers. They included 4 million stenographers, typists, and secretaries. Twenty-one percent were service workers (except private household). Fifteen percent were professional and technical workers. They included 2 million teachers. Thirteen percent were operatives, chiefly in factories.*

Earnings in 1973

Median Earnings. *Half of the women who worked full time for 50 or more weeks in 1973 earned at least $6,488; this was only 57 percent of the $11,466 median earnings of fully employed men.*

Education in 1973

School and College Enrollment. *There were 28 million girls and women between 5 and 34 years of age enrolled in school in the fall of 1973. The 3.5 million women enrolled in college were 43 percent of all college students.*

Educational Attainment. *About 529,000 women earned college degress in 1972–73. The 25.5 million women workers 16 years of age and over who were high school graduates in March 1974 represented 72 percent of all women workers.*

Source: *1975 Handbook on Women Workers*, U.S. Department of Labor, Employment Standards Administration, Women's Bureau, Bulletin 297, 1975, pp. 3–5 and selected tables throughout the handbook.

of the family's life-style than does the husband's alone.

In determining social class, almost any criteria or prestige indicator (income, occupation, education, etc.) can be placed on a continuum and divided into any number of categories or strata. The Robert Lynd and Helen Lynd studies of Middletown, among the most famous community studies in sociology, used two classes: the business class and the working class.[11] Most

11. Robert S. Lynd and Helen Merrell Lynd, *Middletown* (New York: Harcourt, Brace and World, 1929); and *Middletown in Transition* (New York: Harcourt, Brace and World, 1937).

students may think in terms of three classes: upper, middle, and lower. The classical work by August Hollingshead titled *Elmtown's Youth* subdivided the community into five classes: upper, upper-middle, lower-middle, upper-lower, and lower-lower.[12] In Yankee City, Lloyd Warner and Paul Lunt discovered six separate social classes: upper-upper, lower-upper, upper-middle, lower-middle, upper-lower, and lower-lower.[13]

Following Warner and Lunt's classification, but not viewing each class as totally distinct and separate from the other classes, this chapter uses their six-class scheme to illustrate class differences in the American family. It should be made clear that the lines of demarcation are somewhat arbitrary. Who is to say that objectively there are two, six, or seventeen "classes"? And following the classification of Joseph Kahl, the classes described are set forth in "ideal-type" terms.[14] The classes are not precise descriptions of reality but are scientific constructs that indicate patterned relationships among variables; they hang together in a meaningful way.[15] The paradox of this six-class structure is that on the one hand, each class is clearly discernible, yet on the other hand, many families cannot be categorized accurately in this structure.

UPPER-CLASS FAMILIES

Upper-class families are frequently divided into two categories, based on the length of time the families have occupied an upper-class position. Most frequently the literature refers to these two categories as upper-upper class and lower-upper class. Hollingshead refers to them as established families, those that have been in the upper class for more than two generations, and new families, those that have achieved their position through the success of the present adult generation.[16]

The Established (Upper-Upper) Family

The established family group was noted not so much for what was achieved in one's own lifetime but for who one's ancestors were and who one's relatives are. To be an established family meant to be established to the class, not only to the community. Present members of this class were born

12. August B. Hollingshead, *Elmtown's Youth* (New York: Wiley, 1949).

13. W. Lloyd Warner and Paul S. Lunt, *The Social Life of a Modern Community* (New Haven: Yale University Press, 1941).

14. Joseph A. Kahl, *The American Class Structure* (New York: Holt, Rinehart and Winston, 1957).

15. W. Lloyd Warner, *Social Class in America* (New York: Harper, 1960), p. 16.

16. August B. Hollingshead, "Class Differences in Family Stability," *The Annals of the American Academy of Political and Social Science* 272 (November 1950), p. 40.

into it; the families into which they were born could trace their lineage through many generations. The wealth of the family, inherited from the husband's or the wife's side—and often from both—had been in the family for a long time. In New England, these families became the "400," "the Brahmins," and "the Hill-Streeters."

The upper-upper class was the smallest numerically of all social classes but had the highest prestige and influence. Unlike any other class, this class had great unity of culture. In some ways it formed a national and international elite.

Since this class was at the very top of the hierarchy, the members maintained their position by preserving symbols of status such as genealogies, autobiographies of ancestors, heirlooms, and records of ancestral achievement. They also maintained their position by carefully controlling the marriage choices of the young men. As stated by Hollingshead in 1950:

> Indeed, one of the perennial problems of the established family is the control of the marriage choices of its young men. Young women can be controlled more easily than young men, because of the sheltered life they lead and their passive role in courtship. The passivity of the upper-class female, coupled with sex exploitation of females from lower social positions by upper-class males that sometimes leads to marriage, results in a considerable number of old maids in the established upper-class families.[17]

The upper-upper-class girl was more closely watched than were the females of any other class. Dating outside the class was limited because the girls did not come into contact with boys from other social classes and because of the strong socialization provided by the family. The upper-upper-class boy was also socially controlled but not as rigidly as the girl. The patriarchal tradition gave the boy more freedom to interact with girls from different social classes. However, if the boys from this level got very serious with a girl from a lower social class, the family exerted exceedingly strong social pressure to keep him from marrying outside his class.

In this class, although few in number, children, especially sons, were very important for carrying on the family name and for providing for the continuation of a traditional profession or business. These children were educated in the camps, clubs, and colleges that provided a strong emphasis on the culture of the upper-upper class. The unity and the training that existed within this class tended to have a consequence of providing great personal and social security to the children. Economic security came from inherited sources. Professional and occupational security was provided by the family. Relationships with teachers, servants, and persons in the community provided a sense of self-worth and confidence.

Although upper-upper-class children were likely to commit many offenses similar to those of lower-class children, few were arrested and fewer

---

17. Hollingshead, op. cit., p. 40.

still ever got their names placed on police records. The influence of the family in the community led to a reluctance on the part of law enforcement agencies to arrest or convict anyone with high prestige and position in the community. Also, the kinship group itself was likely to serve as its own agency of control over its members. These controls and life-style of the upper-upper classes still seem to be in operation today.

It seems reasonable to assume that many changes would be taking place in upper-class families parallel to changes in the society in general. For example, since mid-century, the continuing push of egalitarian and democratic forces, the push for racial and class integration of private and Ivy League schools, the assumption by the middle classes of status symbols once associated only with the rich, and the like would cause one to assume the death of "high society." Yet in an interesting study of upper-class marriages, Paul Blumberg and P. W. Paul[18] found a major theme of continuity in these marriages over the last thirty years. They state:

> Although tremendous forces have shaken American society in the past generation, the upper class has maintained itself remarkably intact, and having done so, is perhaps the most untouched group in American life. . . . It is the upper-class territory of school, neighborhood, club, and blue book which remains the most racially segregated turf in America.[19]

Alex: *Well, my father happened to be wealthy, so what happened, he had all his relatives like his brothers, his sisters, would all live together. When I say together, this was like an apartment complex type of a deal. The house that we lived in everybody had their individual units where, you know, people had their privacy. But when it came to dining or sitting, the whole family was together, like we dined about thirty-five people at the same time.*

    You see my father is a jeweler and is quite a big landowner in Turkey. Our family is quite typical of upper-class Eastern families. The upper-class Eastern families would be the same way, where you would have a very big household; that means that the poorer side of the family lives with the richer side. They work for my father and he supports them.

The New (Lower-Upper) Family

In comparison with the established family just described, the new family lacks much of the security provided by the kinship groups. In fact,

---

18. Paul M. Blumberg and P. W. Paul, "Continuities and Discontinuities in Upper-Class Marriages," *Journal of Marriage and the Family* 37 (February 1975), pp. 63–77.

19. Ibid, p. 75.

many families who are new to this class have broken with their kin group as part of the price they pay for their upward mobility.

The lower-upper class more closely resembles the upper-upper class than does any other, but its members lack the long history of prestige and family lineage. In addition, they suffer from the reluctance of the top class to accept them as equals. Upper-upper-class members are likely to perceive the lower-upper class as the nouveau riche and as social climbers. As the upper-upper class loses members through low birth rates or through downward mobility, they are replenished by this upwardly mobile lower-upper class.

In comparison with the upper-upper class, the new families are less likely to inherit their wealth, exhibit less cultural unity, marry at a slightly earlier age, and have larger families (although still smaller than the classes below them). This class has a greater diversity of national backgrounds and their income, although it may be larger than in the upper-upper class, comes from earned rather than inherited sources and is likely to be spent in a different fashion. Whereas upper-upper-class members would spend their money for taxes, gifts, and education, the lower-upper class would spend more on conspicuous goods and products: automobiles, fashionable clothes, expensive recreation, or large houses. These conspicuous goods provide the lower-upper-class person with the status and recognition that are desired but cannot be provided by an old family home or various heirlooms. These new upper-class families know the power of money in the market place and often attempt to buy a high position in the status system.

Most marriages occur within the class and the preferred marriage is one that is upward. Marriage is generally viewed as stable, at least as indicated by a very low divorce rate.

In comparison with the upper-upper class, the lower-upper-class family tends to be nuclear, and the persons act independently of kin. The male, as head of the family, works to maintain and establish his economic position. The wife, whenever possible, attempts to associate herself with upper-upper-class women. Like the upper-upper-class wife, the lower-upper-class wife is relieved from many household duties by maids or part-time help and spends time in club life and community activities.

MIDDLE-CLASS FAMILIES

If American society is stratified into three general classes, the middle-class families form a balance wheel between the small but financially powerful upper-class families and the laboring strength of the lower-class families.[20]

---

20. Ruth S. Cavan, *The American Family*, 4th ed. (New York: Thomas Y. Crowell, 1969), p. 131.

Residing in a middle position, they have the possibility of moving upward or the threat of moving downward. One consequence of this appears to be that the class is very conscious of social values, involved in the major issues brought on by social change, very conservative, and relatively rigid in moral standards. Some middle-class families closely resemble upper-class families in their economic status and degree of influence. Other middle-class families vary little from the lower class in terms of their family patterns. Thus it would seem desirable to subdivide the middle class into upper-middle-class and lower-middle or blue-collar families.

The Upper-Middle Family

The upper-middle class and the two upper classes comprise what Warner calls the "level above the common man."[21] This class is comprised of a group of substantial businessmen and professionals who often serve as leaders in civic affairs. They live in comfortable homes in the better residential sections; however, their average income and house value is less than that of the upper classes. Since the professions are well represented in this class, many men had good educations. Income is generally sufficient to provide for travel during vacations, private lessons in dancing or music for the children, and support of local cultural projects.

Hollingshead states that the nuclear upper-middle-class family, composed of husband, wife, and two or three dependent children during the major years of the family cycle, is a very stable unit in comparison with the new upper-class family and the working-class family.[22] Divorce is rare, desertion by the husband or wife is most infrequent, and premature death rates are low.

This class does not have the cultural unity that exists in the upper classes. In many instances there is a deliberate "lack of tradition" and a permanent residence in the community of the kin. Being career oriented, most members of this class are college graduates and comprise the "solid, highly respectable" people in the community. Individualism and personal achievement are stressed. Although young children are not expected to work, vacation jobs are regarded as desirable. The reverence given to thrift and industriousness and the abhorrence of idleness leads to the employment of wives, which is rare in the upper classes. The emphasis on individual achievement increases the likelihood that husbands will take jobs in a community other than the ones in which they were born, raised, or educated.

Even though there is a prevalence of social and geographic mobility, family stability remains high despite the lack of extended kin to bring pressure on the family. Self-discipline, the demands of the job, and the moral

---

21. W. Lloyd Warner, *American Life* (Chicago: University of Chicago Press, 1953), pp. 55–56.
22. Hollingshead, op. cit., p. 42.

pressures exerted by friends and associates keep the nuclear family together.[23]

The nuclear family of the upper-middle class tends toward an equality of status between husband and wife. The husband is generally recognized as the head of the family, but his concern for the welfare of the nuclear unit is easily influenced by the other members' opinions and reactions. The roles of husband and wife are differentiated but strongly interlock. It is expected that the husband will be the major producer of a stable and dependable income, but he also has duties around the house, such as mowing the lawn and making repairs. The upper-middle-class wife may have a "cleaning woman," but the likelihood of a full-time maid is minimal. The home, the children, and the social activities of the family rest primarily in the hands of the wife and mother. Like her husband, she is likely to be sensitive to the family's social status in the community and will make deliberate efforts to fit herself into the business hierarchy.

The Lower-Middle Family

The lower-middle-class, the top of the common-man level, is made up of small businessmen, clerical workers, other low-level white-collar workers, and a few skilled workmen. Members of this class descend from the so-called old immigration, i.e., from northern and western Europe. Thus this class represents a wide variety of national backgrounds. Perhaps more than any other class, with the possible exception of the new upper-class families, an individual in this class has achieved his position through his own efforts.

Like those in the class above them, the families are relatively stable. Unlike the class above them, these families are faced with problems connected with the security of their economic positions and the education of their children. Although high educational aspirations may exist for their children, income limitations often compel them to obtain an education different from what they would choose and less than they would desire. Many state universities are comprised of a large proportion of students from this class background. Frequently students report the conflicts that exist between themselves and their parents. Many parents make major sacrifices to see their children receive formal education, with the result that the educational goals they set for their children train them in values that lead them away from the family. Thus a self-defeating prophecy is at work.

In the lower-middle-class family, the husband is clearly the head in that the wife accepts his decisions and caters to his wishes. However, the wife tends to control the personal and household expenditures.

Socially the kinship group is close. The major social activities take place with relatives from the husband's or wife's family. The nuclear families

---

23. Ibid., p. 43.

do not live as neighbors, but a large group of relatives and in-laws gather frequently at the home of one of the members. These nuclear families, although isolated geographically, function within a network of other nuclear families that provides services and help of all kinds.

A study in Cleveland of fifty-three lower-middle-class families indicated that within a one-month period preceding the interview, 100 percent of the middle-class families were considered to be actively involved in a network of interfamilial help by virtue of caring for children, financial aid, housekeeping, advice, valuable gifts, or help during illness.[24] The study found that 81 percent of lower-middle-class families have large family gatherings at least once a year. Ceremonial affairs such as Christmas, anniversaries, and other holidays were used largely for the gathering of kin who lived outside the neighborhood. It is this article that questions the notion that the nuclear family in modern society is the isolated unit it has often been reputed to be.

The middle-class parent places on the children a restrictive set of mores. They are taught by the parent not to fight, steal, or act out natural impulses. An open expression of interest in sex is forbidden. Unlike the lower-class child, the middle-class child rarely sees sexual activities by accident and only infrequently are matters of sex discussed in the home. However, since World War II, middle-class parents have become increasingly more permissive in child rearing than have lower-class parents. This trend may have been due to the better educated middle-class parents taking the advice of Dr. Spock, perhaps to the influence of the mass media, to seeking out professional advice, or to other reasons. In terms of discipline of children, this means that middle-class parents more likely use reason with the child, verbal threats, or withdrawal of rewards to punish or solicit the child's compliance. Lower-class parents are more likely to rely on physical punishment.

This difference was most explicitly established by Melvin Kohn.[25] He reasons that by virtue of experiencing different conditions of life, members of different social classes come to see the world differently, develop different conceptions of social reality, different aspirations, and different conceptions of desirable personality characteristics.[26] Middle class (white-collar) occupations in contrast with lower class (blue-collar) occupations require the individual to 1) deal more with the manipulation of ideas, symbols, and interpersonal relations, 2) be involved in work that is more complex, and requires greater flexibility, thought, and judgment, and 3) be less closely supervised. From these occupational differences come different values that are reflected in patterns of discipline. The middle-class values are likely to deal with self-

24. Marvin B. Sussman, "The Isolated Nuclear Family: Fact or Fiction," *Social Problems* 6 (Spring 1959), pp. 333–340.

25. Melvin Kohn, "Social Class and Parent-Child Relationships: An Interpretation," *American Journal of Sociology* 68 (January 1963), pp. 471–480; and Melvin Kohn, *Class and Conformity* (Homewood, Ill.: Dorsey, 1969).

26. Kohn, op. cit., p. 472.

direction, freedom, individualism, initiative, creativity, and self-actualization. Thus parents encourage in their children *internal* standards such as consideration, curiosity, and self-control. Discipline is based on the parents' interpretation of a child's motives for a particular act.[27]

These ideas of Kohn in regard to parent-child interaction by social class have received widespread attention and attempts at extension and replication.[28] Viktor Gecas and Ivan Nye,[29] in studying parents of third-grade children in the state of Washington, found modest support for the idea that middle-class parents paid greater attention to the child's intentions or motives than did lower-class parents. Gecas and Nye also found that in addition to class differences, sex differences were operative as well. Further, mothers more frequently used reason and request to get the child to do something and were more likely to be verbal (scolding and yelling) in their response to misbehavior. Fathers more frequently told the child what to do and relied more on physical punishment.

LOWER-CLASS FAMILIES

As with the upper and middle classes, the lower class is frequently divided into two: the upper-lower class, sometimes referred to as the working class or blue-collar workers, and the lower-lower class. The difference between these is probably greater than the difference between the lower-middle and the upper-lower classes. A brief description of each follows.

The Blue Collar (Upper-Lower) Family

Blue-collar, the "working class," or the upper-lower class is often difficult to distinguish from the lower-middle class. Nevertheless, the two classes do not represent one in most literature. The upper-lower class is made up of semiskilled workers in factories, service workers, and a few small tradesmen.

---

27. In contrast, lower-class or blue-collar workers deal more with the manipulation of physical objects, require less interpersonal skill, have more standardization of work, and are more closely supervised. This leads to values of conformity to *external* standards such as orderliness, neatness, and obedience. Discipline is based on the consequences of the child's behavior rather than on the interpretation of motive for the behavior.

28. James D. Wright and Sonia R. Wright, "Social Class and Parental Values for Children: A Partial Replication and Extension of the Kohn Thesis," *American Sociological Review* 41 (June 1976), pp. 527–537.

29. Viktor Gecas and F. Ivan Nye, "Sex and Class Differences in Parent-Child Interaction: A Test of Kohn's Hypothesis," *Journal of Marriage and the Family* 36 (November 1974), pp. 742–749.

In 1975 these workers constituted 45 percent of employed white persons and 63 percent of employed blacks.[30]

The job of a blue-collar worker generally requires some sort of manual skill.[31] The elite of the upper-lower class—electricians, plumbers, and other highly skilled operators—frequently earn more than members of the middle classes. For example, public school teachers, generally assigned to a middle-class position, are likely to average $3,000 to $4,000 a year less than do certain blue-collar workers. However, formal education beyond high school is not required for the manual skills necessary for the members of this class. Physical health is quite crucial to blue-collar workers, since many jobs are dependent upon an ability to perform heavy physical labor. These groups are generally represented by trade unions. A great amount of faith is placed in the unions to protect persons from those below them in the work hierarchy, to provide family medical expenses, and to prevent a dismissal from work.

Since members of this class are almost completely dependent on the swings of the business cycle in our wage-price-profits system, economic stability is lacking. Most income is received from wages earned by the hour, the piece, the day, or the week. To supplement the income of the husband, a considerable proportion of wives are employed outside the home. Unlike a sizable proportion of female workers from the middle and upper classes, the upper-lower-class wife takes a job more out of economic necessity than the desire for a "career." The strains associated with the uncertainties of many facets of life to members of this class present a high degree of family instability. Broken homes occur with such frequency that the majority of parents realize that they are a possibility.

It is the blue-collar more than any other class whose members conform to the traditional image of husband and wife roles.[32] The husband's role is to be a good provider and the wife's role, although she is often employed, is to do housework and care for the children. As the primary wage earner, the husband is the final authority and disciplinarian and, if necessary, is likely to use physical force to keep his wife and children in submission.

The wife and mother rears the children. If the family is broken by divorce or separation, it is with her that the children will remain. It is expected that she will remain faithful to her husband as long as he remains faithful to her. If these obligations are broken, the offended party is likely to separate or seek divorce.

Children are less important to families here than in the middle-class families even though there are more of them. Their role is definitely one of

---

30. U.S. Bureau of the Census, *Statistical Abstract of the United States*, 97th ed. U.S. Government Printing Office, 1976, no. 601, p. 373.

31. For a perceptive view of the meaning of work in the working class, see Lillian Breslow Rubin, *Worlds of Pain: Life in the Working-Class Family* (New York: Basic Books, 1976), Chapter 9, pp. 155–184.

32. Note in particular Rubin, ibid., Chapters 5–7, pp. 69–133.

subordination to the parents. Unlike middle-class parents who stress that children stay in school and who make major sacrifices to keep them there, the working-class families are more likely to expect that children will leave school after fulfilling the minimum legal requirements or at most after completion of high school. Boys and girls are taught to be self-sufficient, to be tough-minded, and to be able to compete for personal rights and privileges. Working-class boys begin their heterosexual experiences earlier and have them more frequently than do middle- and upper-class boys. Alfred Kinsey has commented that a boy from a working-class community who has not had sexual intercourse by the age of sixteen or seventeen is "either physically incapacitated, mentally deficient, homosexual, or earmarked for moving out of his community and going to college."[33] These class differences may be decreasing as the sexual mores of the middle classes become more permissive. It is in this class and in the lower-lower class, that children are most subject to the strains created between what the family teaches and what is taught through the mass media, the educational system, the churches, and the larger community.

The extended family, the neighborhood peer group, and the informal work group provide much social interaction for blue-collar families. As stated by Lloyd Warner:

> They have a feeling of family loyalty and obligation, even for distant relatives, and are likely to organize social and recreational activities within the extended family rather than with outside groups. Spending money on friends and relatives is a valued activity and necessary for the maintenance of status within the group. This involvement in primary groups protects the working-class man from the encroachment of an associational society with its impersonality and its stringent role requirements. At the same time, it lessens his ability to cope with modern complex society.[34]

Few studies present a glimpse into the life of upper-lower-class families equal to that found in Mirra Komarovsky's book, *Blue Collar Marriage*.[35] Using a case-study approach, fifty-eight "stable" families with children were interviewed. The respondents were chosen from a community the author termed Glenton that had a total population of about 50,000.

The families in Glenton illustrate how it is possible to live in a rapidly changing society and be relatively insulated from both change and cultural diversity. Husbands and wives knew what was expected of them and generally agreed about marital ideals. However, the role consensus or the clarity of role definition was not necessarily suited to the conditions of life under

---

33. Alfred C. Kinsey, Wardell B. Pomeroy, and Clyde E. Martin, *Sexual Behavior in the Human Male* (Philadelphia: Saunders, 1948), p. 381.

34. W. Lloyd Warner, "Democracy in Jonesville," in Jack L. Roach, Llewellyn Gross, and Orville Gursslin, *Social Stratification in the United States* (Englewood Cliffs, N.J.: Prentice-Hall, 1969), p. 180.

35. Mirra Komarovsky, *Blue Collar Marriage* (New York: Random, 1962).

which Glenton's families had to live. And a transition to new roles was often hindered by certain circumstances such as the poverty of some young couples, the poor occupational adjustment of the young unskilled workers, and the need to reside in the parental home after marriage. An illustration is given of a thirty-two-year-old husband which illustrates how unfavorable these circumstances can be.

> You keep thinking you can do almost anything and get away with anything when you're still young. There had been a couple of big layoffs when we got married, but work was still pretty good and I thought I could do anything and that I was going places and I was going to be somebody. Nothing was good enough for my wife, and we didn't think nothing of charge accounts and buying things. We hadn't been married long when I got my first layoff. They said I was young. They laid off others and they said they was old. We couldn't keep up our payments on the furniture, and we lost every stick of it, and she was pregnant. And I mean to tell you. We went and stayed at her ma's for a few days, and then up to my ma's for a while. There wasn't no room for us at her ma's and my ma had a spare room, and we must have stayed there about a month while I was looking for work and then I got it, and then we moved out again. And then this time, we got one thing by paying the whole money on it that we borrowed the money for. We borrowed it from people, and not the bank. And we bought a bed. We figured we could sit on that, and we had our cooking pots and could eat out of them. But we didn't want to think of sleeping on the floor anymore. It would have been all right if it was summer and she wasn't pregnant.[36]

The majority of men and women interviewed believed that the woman's place is "in the home." The great majority of the wives thought that men are more highly sexed than women, but there was no mistake in their feeling that ideally wives should also experience sexual enjoyment. Both sexes tended to think that friendship is more likely to exist between members of the same sex, whereas they saw the principal marital ties as sexual union, complementary tasks, and mutual devotion. Within this class, if one of the functions of modern marriage is to be friends, to share one's hurts, worries, and dreams with another person—a large number of couples fail to find such fulfillment.

The Family in Poverty
(Lower-Lower)

The lower-lower-class family is at the bedrock level of the social class system. To do justice to an understanding of this level, several chapters would be essential to explain the variations that one would find in rural or urban

---

36. Ibid., p. 47. Reprinted by permission.

1975 Census shows most poverty in 17 years

Washington—(AP)—More Americans slid into poverty last year than any time in the 17 years the government has been keeping track, the Census Bureau said Saturday.

The bureau blamed the 2.5-million increase in poverty-stricken people on the whipsaw effect of high inflation in the midst of recession, together with widespread exhaustion of unemployment benefits last year.

Despite an $818 increase in median family income, to $13,720 a year, inflation dragged the buying power of that income down to the lowest in five years.

For the number of people in poverty, it was the second increase in a row and only the third since the bureau began keeping such statistics in 1959. The increases last year and in 1970 were both about 1.3 million.

The Census Bureau said 25.9 million persons lived in families that were below the government-defined poverty level of $5,500 for a nonfarm family of four. The poverty level was up, due to inflation, from $5,038 in 1974.

The number of people in poverty was the largest since the 27.8 million in 1967, when the poverty level was $3,410.

The 1975 figure represented 12 percent, or nearly one out of every eight persons. That was up from 11.6 percent the year before and was the highest since the 12.6 percent in 1970.

The poverty income is set by computing the cost of a basic nutritionally adequate diet and multiplying that by three, based on the government finding that poor people spend one-third of their income on food. The 1975 level works out to $106 per week.

By comparison, the average wage of factory workers in mid-1975 was $163 per week. The minimum federal wage of $2.30 an hour represents $92 for a 40-hour week, and the average payment to retired workers on Social Security last year was $206 per month.

Source: *The Detroit News*, September 26, 1976, p. 2–B. Reprinted by permission of The Associated Press.

areas, in one part of the country as opposed to another, in black and white communities, or in various ethnic lower-class communities. Generally, common social characteristics of this lower-lower class include:

- Eight years or less of formal education
- Semi-skilled or unskilled occupation for the male
- Sporadic work, periods of unemployment
- Income of four or five thousand or less
- Large numbers of families on public assistance
- Residence in old homes or small apartments
- Crowded living conditions[37]
- Frequent location in slum areas of the city

About 24.3 million persons in the United States were below the low-income level in 1974, according to the results of a survey conducted by the

37. It is of interest that contrary to expectations, crowded living conditions were found to have little or no effect on family relations. See Alan Booth and John N. Edwards, "Crowding and Family Relations," *American Sociological Review* 41 (April 1976), pp. 308–321.

Bureau of the Census.[38] The low-income or poverty threshold—the income level that separates "poor" from "nonpoor"—was $5038 in 1974 for a non-farm family of four. At least 12 percent of the country's population falls below this poverty level. This includes about one-tenth of all white persons and one-third of blacks. It is estimated that over one-fourth of the nation's children and over half of its black ones live in conditions of poverty.

One study[39] indicated that the factors most highly associated with poverty are female-headed families, large family size, minority group status, age (children, youth, the aged), unemployment and underemployment, and lack of income from sources other than wages. While the number of female-headed families with children has been growing in all income groups in the population, 45 percent of these families are poor and the great majority of them are on welfare.[40]

Directly related to the poverty of the lower-lower class is the irregularity of employment; and since employment is irregular, income is irregular. Because income is irregular, a considerable amount of insecurity exists in re-

> *Alex:*   *See, in Turkey, we don't have welfare. If a husband leaves his wife, neighbors would take care of her. The community will take care of her. People take care of each other. Because you see back home it's a funny thing. You want to buy something, you don't have to pay. You say put it on my bill. Whether your credit is good or bad, or whether you ever pay or not . . . it's a different society. She'll live, no problem. Not like in America when you go to the supermarket.*

gard to food, clothing, shelter, transportation, and other essential items. Children may be forced or encouraged to contribute to the financial needs of the family, and few remain in school beyond the minimum legal age. These conditions contribute to and are highly related to other concerns. For example, the lower-lower class has the highest rates of divorce, psychoses, and physical disabilities, the least amount of dental and health care, the largest proportion of people on public welfare, the greatest rejection rate from the armed services, the highest crime rate, the largest number of children, the highest rates of venereal disease, the most unemployment, and, as perceived by many middle-class persons, "the most of the worst."

38. U.S. Bureau of the Census, *Current Population Reports*, "Money Income and Poverty Status of Families and Persons in the United States: 1974," U.S. Government Printing Office, Series P–60, No. 99, p. 1.

39. Catherine S. Chilman, "Families in Poverty in the Early 1970s: Rates, Associated Factors, Some Implications," *Journal of Marriage and the Family* 37 (February 1975), pp. 49–60.

40. Heather L. Ross and Isabel V. Sawhill, *Time of Transition: The Growth of Families Headed by Women* (Washington, D.C.: Urban Institute, 1975), p. 93; and Isabel Sawhill, "Discrimination and Poverty among Women Who Head Families," *Signs: Journal of Women in Culture and Society* 1 (Spring 1976), pp. 201–211.

Moving Families Out of the Poverty Cycle

Trying to move families out of the poverty cycle is like trying to get underdeveloped countries started on the road to industrialization, in the opinion of Alvin Schorr of the Office of Economic Opportunity. Both, Schorr states, need surplus capital to reach the "take off" point (*Social Security Bulletin*, February 1966). Specifically, Schorr suggests that there are five critical stages in the life cycle of the family at which an injection of surplus funds could prevent the decisions that lead to life-long poverty.

The Family Begins. Couples who marry in their teens, or whose first child is born at that time, are more likely to be poor all their lives than couples who put off marriage and parenthood. A 1960 survey of couples married for 20 years showed that when the wife had been less than 17 at the time of the marriage, the effects were lasting; the husbands in this group were the ones with the least education and the lowest level jobs.

Occupational Choice. The boys who marry young drop out of school and enter the labor market while they are still in their teens. They take the first job they can get (not an irrational choice, considering the high overall rate of unemployment in their age group) without regard for its long term potential; their work history is often chaotic, their earning capacity is meager.

Too Many Children. Women who have a first child while they are in their teens have more children altogether than women who can postpone the first birth. Poverty is directly related to the number of children in the family. Of all the poor families in the United States in 1963, only 12 percent had small families of one or two children; but 49 percent of these poor families had six children or more. At this stage of family development, what might once have been an adequate income is adequate no longer, and many once-solvent families fall into poverty at this point.

Family Breakdown. Early marriages tend to break up. Only half the women married at 17 or younger will still be living with the same husband 30 years later. About half the women who married at 17 will give birth to four children or more; these large families often create more pressure than a low income man can tolerate. Too often, he walks out. Neither the family headed by a woman alone, nor the already burdened second marriage that either spouse may make is likely to rise out of poverty.

The Cycle Begins Again. At the point where parents are entering the third or fourth stages, the children in the family are adolescent—just ready to embark on the first stage of the poverty cycle for themselves.

Source: "Roundup of Current Research," *Trans-Action* 3 (July-August 1966), pp. 2–3. Reprinted by permission.

These factors are so strongly intertwined that it becomes almost impossible to know what is cause and what is effect. Take for example the single factor of family size. Catherine Chilman notes that "contrary to much popular opinion, very poor people do not want large families; they simply have more difficulty in effective family planning."[41] Lee Rainwater relates the lack of effectiveness in family planning among the lower classes to the greater

41. Catherine S. Chilman, "Poverty and Family Planning in the United States," *Welfare in Review* 5 (1967), p. 12.

segregation in the conjugal role relationship.[42] A lack of communication exists between the husband and wife on family issues, and the husband is more likely to regard the whole question of family planning as his wife's business. This appears to be true in various cultures.[43]

It is difficult for most students and teachers to describe the life-style of the lower-lower class without imposing middle-class evaluations upon them. To even use a term such as "lower class" may be imposing a negative connotation and interpretation to persons who occupy the class level. As stated by Hyman Rodman,

> It is little wonder that if we describe the lower class family in terms of promiscuous sexual relationships, illegitimate children, deserting men, and unmarried mothers, we are going to see the situation as disorganized and chockfull of problems.[44]

To note conditions such as these may be necessary but hardly sufficient. In observing the social conditions of lower-class life from the perspective of a middle-class vantage point, caution must be taken not to become so busy looking at the "victims" that we fail to understand the reasons for the "problems." Perhaps it is more realistic to think of these conditions as consequences of, or in some instances, solutions to other issues faced by lower-class persons as they encounter the social, economic, political, and legal realities of life. Unlike many of the other variant life-styles described throughout this book, few people rationally and consciously choose or desire the styles of life most frequently associated with the lower-lower-class.

FAMILY MOBILITY: CHANGING CLASS LIFE-STYLES

One fundamental characteristic of families and class is the extent to which there is opportunity to move from one class to another. Although mobility is often thought to mean improvement, it can be upward, downward, or lateral. The first two types are referred to as vertical social mobility (upward or downward) and the latter is referred to as horizontal social mobility.

---

42. Lee Rainwater, *And The Poor Get Children* (Chicago: Quadrangle, 1960); and Lee Rainwater, *Family Design: Marital Sexuality, Family Size and Contraception* (Chicago: Aldine, 1965).

43. Lee Rainwater, "Marital Sexuality in Four Cultures of Poverty," *Journal of Marriage and the Family* 26 (November 1964), pp. 457–466.

44. Hyman Rodman, *Marriage, Family and Society* (New York: Random, 1965), p. 223.

The Likelihood of Social Mobility

The likelihood of vertical social mobility may be regarded as a function of three separate phenomena. First is the opportunity structure to which the individual has access. This is the organizational structure of a society that defines the ultimate achievement possibilities for the individual as well as the channels available to realize the achievements. Different opportunity structures apply to different individuals, groups, or subcultures within the same society. However, the structure of the society, including the presence or absence of jobs, the availability of educational and training programs, and other social characteristics, will in large part determine the extent to which mobility occurs.

The second component of the likelihood of vertical social mobility may be said to be the individual himself. In this regard, personality characteristics determine the individual's capacity for exploiting his opportunity structure and will influence the likelihood of mobility. These characteristics may include factors such as intelligence, motivation, motor skills, and value systems.

The third component of the likelihood of vertical social mobility may be termed the frictional factor. That is, two identically equipped individuals confronting the same opportunity structure may nevertheless attain disparate levels of mobility. These factors, inherent neither in the individual nor in the opportunity structure, may be referred to as chance, luck, or fortune.[45]

Bradley Schiller postulates that the family's economic circumstances are the key accessibility conditions for the various opportunity strata available to sons.[46] Thus each economic class confronts a separate and distinctive set of achievement opportunities. In comparing the pattern of socioeconomic achievement of children from welfare families with that of the general population, sharp differences are found. He suggests that the lack of achievement of poor children is largely due to the inequality of opportunity that exists along class lines. That is, a substantial portion of the underachievement of sons who grew up in families receiving Aid to Families with Dependent Children (AFDC) can only be explained by differential abilities or by the son's motivations or aspirations. The argument that the poor remain poor because they lack the motivation to rise above their origins receives little empirical support. In fact, several writers have assembled data that indicate similar motivations among poor and nonpoor and that suggest that aspirations for improving one's socioeconomic position may be even stronger among those individuals of poor origins.[47]

---

45. Bradley R. Schiller, "Stratified Opportunities: The Essence of the 'Vicious' Circle," *American Journal of Sociology* 76 (November 1970), p. 427.

46. Ibid., pp. 426–439.

47. Ralph Underhill, *Youth In Poor Neighborhoods* (Chicago: National Opinion Research Center, 1967); Allen B. Willson, "Residential Segregation of Social Classes and Aspira-

The Extent of Social Mobility

The American dream suggests that in this land of opportunity anyone can go from "rags to riches." The widespread belief is that with hard work and endurance, any motivation to get ahead will enable anyone who so desires to move upward on the social class ladder. Data do seem to suggest that social mobility in our society probably is increasing. However, social mobility and equality of opportunity have probably never been as widespread as Americans believe.

It has been estimated that one of every four or five persons moves upward at least one social class level during his lifetime.[48] It is in the lower-middle and the upper-lower-class levels that the greatest amount of upward mobility occurs. The least upward mobility is found in the upper-class levels.

Empirical studies of social mobility, particularly among males, suggest several general conclusions. One is that more sons will find themselves at the same level as their fathers than at any other level. Secondly, a substantial proportion of sons have experienced some mobility. Third, upward mobility is more prevalent than downward mobility. Fourth, when mobility does occur it is likely to mean a shift to class levels adjacent to those of the individual's father, that is, short-distance mobility is more frequent than long-distance mobility. A study by Peter DeJong showed similar mobility characteristics for females.[49]

Consequences of Social Mobility

It is unlikely that many of us would reject the opportunity for upward social mobility. With this opportunity we could envision a better job, higher income, heated apartments, a more luxurious home, a more prestigious neighborhood, opportunities to travel, better clothes, a new car, freedom from debt, and generally a more luxurious as well as refined life-style. And many, if not most of us who are reading this, believe that education is one means to obtain the rewards. Within our society with its fairly open class system and its increasing requirements for specialized and highly trained technicians and experts, brain power frequently means higher status. But a closer investigation of the open class system shows that not all consequences of mobility are posi-

tions of High School Boys," in Reinhard Bendix and S. M. Lipset, eds., *Class, Status and Power* (New York: Free Press, 1966); and Lola M. Irelan, *Low-Income Life Styles* (U.S. Welfare Administration, Publication #14, 1968), p. 5.

48. Carson McQuire, "Social Stratification and Mobility Patterns," *American Sociological Review* 15 (April 1950), pp. 195–204.

49. Peter DeJong, "Patterns of Intergenerational Occupational Mobility of American Females," unpublished M.A. thesis, Western Michigan University, Kalamazoo, Michigan, 1969.

tive. In various ways, the costs of upward social mobility may be great and its penalties quite severe.

Robert Stuckert studied several hundred white married couples in the Milwaukee area.[50] Wives who were upwardly mobile were compared with women who were nonmobile. It was found that the mobile identified less with their extended family than did the stable or nonmobile families: the mobile used the extended family less as a reference group or source of identity; the mobile expressed less neighborhood integration than did the stable in that they were less concerned about neighborhood unity and were less likely to view the neighborhood as a permanent residence; mobility was inversely related to contacts with the extended family. The conclusion was that for married women mobility tended to produce social isolation and was detrimental to extended family relations.

In checking cleavages and solidarities among kin as related to mobility, Bert Adams demonstrated that if siblings are mutually downwardly mobile, they are affectionally close but manifest affectional distance from their parents, particularly their mothers.[51] They are apparently drawn together by their mutual plight, while blaming their parents, or mothers, for their "failure." When only one child is downwardly mobile, he or she is affectionally distant from parents *and* the sibling.

Many students will discover, or may have already discovered, some disruptive effects of their increased education (a potential contribution to upward social mobility). The most obvious is likely to be an increasingly estranged relationship with parents. Particularly if parents are working-class people of limited formal education, many students will find that they are modifying their belief and value system in ways that may conflict greatly with those of their parents. The paradox of this situation is that these are frequently parents who make major sacrifices to provide a college education for their children with the painful consequence of having their children become socially distant from them.

There are instances in which marriage itself may be threatened by upward social mobility. The wife who works to assist her husband complete his education may find that his value system and life-style changes while hers remains more static. Success in business may encourage certain husbands to seek the friendship of more "sophisticated" females. Spouses may not be equally interested in mobility or may differ in their ability to readjust to the new requirements of a higher social status. These and many other examples of social mobility illustrate how this "desirable" phenomenon may disrupt husband-wife relationships.

Mobility as a disruptive process leaves persons isolated, detached,

50. Robert P. Stuckert, "Occupational Mobility and Family Relationships," *Social Forces* 41 (March 1963), pp. 301–307.

51. Bert N. Adams, "Occupational Position, Mobility, and the Kin of Orientation," *American Sociological Review* 32 (June 1967), pp. 364–377.

lonely, and emotionally distressed. In a review of empirical studies dealing with the emotional climate in the family, Kenneth Kessin reports that generally the data suggest stressful emotional relationships, tension, and parent-child estrangement associated with actual or anticipated mobility.[52]

Obviously, not all social mobility has negative consequences. In a relatively open class system, a high rate of social mobility may tend to stablize the social order by providing outlets to persons with particular skills or talents who are dissatisfied with their present social status. The possibility for upward social mobility may prevent the rebellious and revolutionary tactics that result from persons who are frustrated in their social position and have little opportunity for advancement. Families may receive new recognition and social prestige by their social climbing. Thus the question is not so much whether social mobility is good or bad, but rather what types of consequences to individuals and families result within societies that have closed or open class systems.

Summary

This book uses two procedures in dealing with social class. One, as in this chapter, is to take existing class structure and examine family patterns that are characteristic of a given social stratum. The second, as is done in other chapters, is to take particular subject areas such as sexual behavior, mate selection, or child rearing and note class variations.

The significance of the class structure stems from some of the consequences of being stratified. For example, social class is related to the age at marriage, success of the marriage, family size, patterns of sexual behavior, manner of rearing children, food eaten, movies seen, and the like. It is the family, not merely the individual, that is ranked within a given social stratum.

Frequently, reference is made to upper-, middle-, and lower-class families. For a more precise portrayal of these class levels, each of the three are separated into upper and lower classes. Thus the upper-class families are described as the established and new (upper-upper and lower-upper) families, the middle-class families are listed as upper-middle and lower-middle, and lower-class families are listed as blue-collar (upper-lower) and lower-lower.

The established upper-class family, while the smallest numerically, has the highest prestige and influence. Members of this class are born into it. Ancestors, lineage, and inherited wealth are important dimensions in understanding these families.

The new upper-class families lack the long history of prestige and family lineage of the established families. This stratum is occupied by the

52. Kenneth Kessin, "Social and Psychological Consequences of Intergenerational Occupational Mobility," *American Journal of Sociology* 77 (July 1971), p. 5.

nouveau riche, the social climbers, who may have as much money as those ranked above them but do not occupy the prestigious position within society. Extended-family kin are of less importance. Wealth is earned and conspicuously displayed in new homes, automobiles, and fashionable clothes.

Upper-middle-class families occupy the position above the "common man." Here are found the business and professional men who have better than average incomes, live in comfortable suburban homes, and represent the solid, respectable people of the community.

Lower-middle-class families occupy the top of the "common-man" level. Families are relatively stable but the economic security is less than exists at classes above them. Children are reared within a restrictive set of mores. Many rules of behavior are compulsive and ritualistic in nature.

Blue-collar families are often difficult to distinguish from the lower-middle class above them. These families are the working class, the semi-skilled factory workers, service workers, and small tradesmen. While income may be higher in many instances than in the class above them, the educational level is lower, economic stability is less, and physical health is more crucial for continued employment. This class represents the traditional image of husband-wife roles: husband as provider and final authority and wife as housewife and mother.

The lower-lower-class family is at the bedrock of the social-class system. This class has the lowest level of education, most unskilled jobs, lowest average income, poorest housing, highest rate of divorce, highest incidence of detected crime, most unemployment, largest number of children, highest rate of mental and physical illness, least amount of dental or health care, and the like. Often it becomes difficult to know whether conditions such as these cause poverty, or whether poverty causes these conditions.

What are the chances for and consequences of family social mobility? Social mobility does seem to be increasing and was probably never as widespread as has been widely believed. While seen as desirable by most persons, upward mobility may result in new recognition and social prestige or may bring rejection and social isolation. Clearly, extended-family cohesion is likely to decrease and lower levels of family participation are likely to result.

This chapter concludes Part II, which examined structural and subcultural variations in family life-styles. Part III examines premarital structures and processes and deals primarily with mate selection. In a general sense, the next eight chapters follow the marital and family life cycle, from the point of selecting a mate and premarital factors through marriage, parenthood, middle years and, finally, the later years. As you will note, a variety of frames of reference or theoretical approaches (structural-functional, exchange, conflict, psychoanalytic, behaviorist, symbolic interactional) are used in the examination of these organizational and processual patterns at various stages of the life cycle.

Key Terms and Concepts

Discussion Questions

1. In what ways is a sociologist's description of families by class different from that commonly found among laymen?
2. Discuss "all men (families) are created equal."
3. Make a stratification study of the families in your home community. Where do they live, work, and worship? Where do or will their children attend college (if at all)? What kind of cars do they drive, hobbies do they pursue? What are their family size, attitudes toward child rearing, and the like? Outline their style of living.
4. Discuss "when a college student from an upper-middle-class family takes a job in a factory, he becomes a member of the upper-lower class." Or "when the same student becomes unemployed he becomes a member of the lower-lower class."
5. Outline the predominant characteristics of the different social classes.
6. What parent-child differences in attitude and behavior are likely to result when a lower-middle- or upper-lower-class child gets a college degree and enters a professional occupation?
7. Discuss the role of children in families at different class levels.
8. What types of factors foster upward mobility? Downward mobility?
9. Why are many consequences of upward social mobility disruptive to kin and community ties?
10. Under what circumstances is marriage while in college an aid or a threat to upward social mobility?

Further Readings

Blumberg, Paul M., and **P. W. Paul.** "Continuities and Discontinuities in Upper-class Marriages." *Journal of Marriage and the Family* 37 (February 1975), pp. 63–77. A study of the social characteristics and changes in upper-class marriages.

Cavan, Ruth Shonle. *The American Family.* 4th ed. New York: Thomas Y. Crowell, 1969. Chapters 4 through 9 deal specifically with social classes, ethnic groups, and mobility.

Chilman, Catherine S. "Families in Poverty in the Early 1970s: Rates, Associated Factors, Some Implications." *Journal of Marriage and the Family* 37 (February 1975), pp. 49–60. An examination of frequency, implications, causes, and selected remedies for poverty in the United States.

Eshleman, J. Ross, and **Chester L. Hunt.** *Social Class Factors in the College Adjustment of Married Students.* Kalamazoo, Mich.: Western Michigan University, 1965. A study of the relationship between social-status background and the patterns of college marriage adjustment to campus life.

Glenn, Norval D., Jon P. Alston, and **David Werner.** *Social Stratification: A Research Bibliography.* Berkeley, Calif.: Glendessary Press, 1970. For those interested in social class, this book present an extensive listing of stratification sources classified into more than sixty categories including family structure, child rearing, sex standards, and family background and mobility.

Harrington, Michael. *The Other America: Poverty in the United States.* New York: Macmillan, 1962. Clarifies how the poor, who are without power, are physically and socially isolated from other groups in American society.

Komarovsky, Mirra. *Blue-Collar Marriage.* New York: Random, 1962. A case study of fifty-eight working-class families that provides a wealth of material on most aspects of married life.

Kriesberg, Louis. *Mothers in Poverty: A Study of Fatherless Families.* Chicago: Aldine, 1970. An attempt to explain the way of life of the poor and an exposition of various myths perpetuated about the culture of poverty.

Lundberg, Ferdinand. *The Rich and the Super-Rich.* New York: Bantam, 1968. A description of wealthy persons in America, their family links, the power they wield, and how their funds were and are obtained and used.

Rainwater, Lee, and **Karol K. Weinstein.** *And the Poor Get Children.* Chicago: Quadrangle, 1960. A study of the factors influencing the ways in which working-class people think about family planning and contraception.

Rubin, Lillian Breslow. *Worlds of Pain: Life in the Working-class Family.* New York: Basic Books, 1976. A subjective analysis of fifty working-class families and a comparison group of twenty-five professional middle-class families.

Tallman, Irving, and **Gary Miller.** "Class Differences in Family Problem Solving: The Effects of Verbal Ability, Hierarchical Structure, and Role Expectations." *Sociometry* 37 (1974), pp. 13–37. An empirical study showing and explaining why white-collar families perform better in solving problems than blue-collar families.

Part III

The Creation of the Marital Status: Premarital Structures and Processes

10

*Homogamy and Endogamy
in the Selection of Mates*

10

With this chapter we shift our discussion from family institutions, family change, and variations in family life-styles to premarital structures and processes in the creation of the marital status. This chapter examines five normative structures surrounding mate selection in the United States: age, residence, class, religion, and race. The terms generally employed to describe mate selection among those who share similar characteristics are homogamy and endogamy: homogamy denotes something about the likeness or similarity of married couples; endogamy refers to in-group marriages of almost any kind. That people marry those like themselves more often than could be due to chance is known as assortive mating. The "assorted" mates are matched on specific structural dimensions.

Homogamy and endogamy are critical factors in the continuity of the American family system (as well as of other social institutions). Homogamy functions to maintain the status quo and conserve traditional values and beliefs. These functions can be dysfunctional in that they reduce or eliminate contact with other people and cultures, restrict the free choice of a mate, or lead to the formation of that type of personality that is submissive to family and cultural control.[1] But as long as marriage is perceived to be an important and significant institution in the United States or in any society, it is not very difficult to understand why the same characteristics that are viewed as important in a society (age, race, religion, class) are also important in the selection of a mate.

It is common for students to operate on the idea that they are free to marry anyone they please. In reality, there is probably no society in which people actually choose their marriage partners on a completely individual basis. Only when persons consciously consider the socialization processes that

---

1. For a discussion of these ideas, see Ruth S. Cavan and Jordan T. Cavan, "Cultural Patterns, Functions, and Dysfunctions of Endogamy and Intermarriage," *International Journal of Sociology of the Family* 1 (May 1971), pp. 10–24.

lead them to prefer certain types of persons for marriage, consider the social pressures to marry certain types of persons, and investigate the extent of homogamy and endogamy within a given society, do they become aware of the limited freedom of choice that does exist.

Studies throughout the world report high rates of racial, religious, class, educational, and age homogamy. No society in the world leaves the selection

> Louise: *I really don't know what made him special before I married him. That's a big question. Definitely we had the same religious background, and he was also a very religious person and had very high ideals. He had very high ideals about what a family ought to be. I think we selected each other because we could see that we could build a good family together.*
>
> Mac: *For us to have a good relationship, we both have to work together, to help the other mate in times of trouble, give affection, give moral support. And not running out, not backing out in times of stress. My mate's different from other girls. She's got, can we say, charisma, she's got a unique personality. She's dominant in her role; she's strong, she works, she does work in the house when it needs to be done if we haven't done it already. She doesn't look for a crutch in life to say: "Hey, society, you owe me a debt." She . . . she's a very strong-minded person.*

of a marriage partner unregulated and indiscriminate. Whether the choice is by the persons getting married, by parents, relatives, delegated persons or groups, or by specific social agencies, it is always subject to regulation by social and cultural controls.

One should not be led into believing that endogamy and homogamy are the preferred or required norms in all respects. The most universal of all norms regarding marriage—the incest taboo—is an exogamous norm. Exogamy rules that members of a society marry outside their kin group. Thus all marriages are exogamous in that they are forbidden between members of the same nuclear-family unit. Generally, the same could be said for sex. Exogamy and heterogamy are often used interchangeably. However, technically speaking, exogamy *requires* differences whereas heterogamy *denotes* differences. If both heterogamy and exogamy are used to indicate marriage between persons of a different group, then no "purely" endogamous marriage exists.

Our discussion of homogamy and/or exogamy in the selection of mates will be confined to specific characteristics or groups that are culturally conceived as relevant to the choice of a spouse, particularly as exists within the United States. A marriage could conceivably be considered endogamous in regard to race, exogamous in regard to kin, heterogamous in regard to religion, and homogamous in regard to values and personality traits.

THE NATURE OF INTERMARRIAGE

Prior to discussing specific dimensions of mate selection such as age and race, several general characteristics of intermarriage need to be examined. Generally, these characteristics are applicable to a wide range of circumstances involving mixed marriages. One major difficulty centers around whom to exclude and whom to include. At what point is any characteristic homogamous or heterogamous? Rarely are the boundaries clear-cut and precise when it comes to determining just what is an endogamous or mixed marriage.

The Reporting of Rates of Intermarriage

In a research note it was suggested that several points should be put into writing in regard to the reporting and interpreting of rates of intermarriage. They are, in brief:

1. Let rates based on marriages always be distinguished from rates based on individuals.
2. Let group size be acknowledged as operating through mathematical necessity when it is found to be inversely related to intermarriage rates.
3. One should recognize inevitable differences between ethnic and religious intermarriage rates and evaluating the "triple melting pot" hypothesis.
4. When possible, let the ratio of a group's actual rate of intermarriage to its "expected" intermarriage rate be reported.[2]

First, most published rates of mixed marriage (or intermarriage) are based on the total number of a group's marriages. Sometimes they are interpreted as if they are based on the number of individuals who marry. Hyman Rodman indicated the ambiguity that was evident in the research literature and particularly in textbooks in failing to cite whether mixed-marriage rates were for marriages or for individuals.[3] A marriage rate refers to the percentage of marriages that are mixed of all marriages involving individuals in a specific category. A marriage rate for individuals refers to the percentage of married individuals in a specific category who enter a mixed marriage.

For example, if we have six homogamous Catholic marriages and four mixed Catholic marriages, we can speak of either a 40 percent or a 25 percent

---

2. Paul H. Besanceney, "On Reporting Rates of Intermarriage," *American Journal of Sociology* 70 (May 1965), pp. 717–721.
3. Hyman Rodman, "Technical Note on Two Rates of Mixed Marriage," *American Sociological Review* 30 (October 1965), pp. 776–778.

mixed-marriage rate. Four of the ten marriages, or 40 percent of the marriages involving Catholics, are mixed, but four Catholics out of 16, or 25 percent, are in mixed marriages.[4]

Unless none of the marriages or all of the marriages are mixed, the mixed-marriage rate for marriages is always greater than the mixed-marriage rate for individuals. Thus, if your objective is to prove that mixed marriages are occurring in greater frequency, you could use the mixed-marriage rate for marriages. If you wish to prove that the incidence of mixed marriage is not as great, you could use the mixed-marriage rate for individuals. Statistically, both figures would be accurate. Thus, one way to lie with statistics "honestly" is to use the rate that best fits your purpose or interest. For example, Harold Christensen and Kenneth Barber found that, in Indiana, 53 percent of all marriages involving Catholics were intermarriages; however, only 36 percent of all Catholic individuals married across faith lines.[5] Twelve percent of all marriages involving Protestants were interfaith, but 6.4 percent of Protestant individuals married across faith lines. Thus, is the interfaith rate for Catholics in Indiana one in two or one in three? Is the interfaith rate for Protestants one in eight or one in sixteen? The answer is both, depending on whether reference is made to the number of marriages that are mixed or to the number of individuals who enter mixed marriages.

The second point about intermarriage concerns the size of a group. Generally the larger the group, the lower its intermarriage rate. Or the smaller the group relative to the total population, the faster its rate goes up with each intermarriage. For example, Western Michigan University, a school with which the author has been affiliated, is overwhelmingly Protestant with a Catholic population of approximately 15 percent. The intermarriage rate for individuals, as seen from a study done by the author, was more than twice as high for Catholics as it was for Protestants.[6] That there is such a difference in the proportion of persons of differing religions who marry outside their religious grouping stems far less from the religious intensity of the persons who marry as from the opportunity for Catholics to meet and marry persons from a non-Catholic background.

The third point concerns the "triple melting pot" hypothesis, which proposes that ethnic lines were being crossed repeatedly in the United States while people continued to marry in their own religious groups, that is, within the three major religious groups in our country.[7] Paul Besanceney suggests that since a religious group is larger than any of the ethnic groups constituting it, it must be expected that these ethnic intermarriage rates will be larger than

4. Ibid., p. 776.
5. Harold T. Christensen and Kenneth E. Barber, "Interfaith vs. Intrafaith Marriage in Indiana," *Journal of Marriage and the Family* 29 (August 1967), p. 464.
6. J. Ross Eshleman and Chester L. Hunt, *Social Class Factors in the College Adjustment of Married Students* (Kalamazoo: Western Michigan University, 1965), p. 37.
7. Ruby J. R. Kennedy, "Single or Triple Melting Pot? Intermarriage Trends in New Haven, 1870–1940," *American Journal of Sociology* 49 (February 1944), pp. 331–339.

the corresponding religious intermarriage rates—from mathematical necessity.[8] He goes on to note that since identification with a religious denomination is at least in some degree a voluntary association, it is inappropriate to compare rates of religious intermarriage with those of ethnic intermarriage. Nationality or ethnic identification is based on an ascribed status—determined by birth and not by personal choice. Religious homogamy often is homogamous because husband and wife have the same preference, even though one of them has converted from another religion.

The fourth point concerns the ratio of "actual" to "expected" rates. The expected intermarriage rate is the percentage of people who would have selected a mate outside their own religion if they had chosen their marriage partners randomly, knowing the frequency distribution of the particular religious groups in the population. The actual rate refers to those marriages that do take place. The smaller the ratio of actual to expected intermarriages, the more cohesive the group and the smaller the number of marriages outside the group.

Factors Fostering Intermarriages

Actual rates of intermarriage are influenced by various factors, many of which center around the normative eligibility rules for mate selection, such as role compatability, value consensus, and similarity in age, class, religion, or race. However, apart from the normative rules are non-normative factors that favor endogamous marriages. For example, generally the larger the in-group, the greater the probability of an endogamous marriage. If the sex ratio is highly imbalanced, however, there is often a high rate of intermarriage, irrespective of the norms favoring in-group marriage. Larry Barnett, drawing from other studies, indicates that the following factors foster mixed marriage.

1. *Existence of the group as a minority.* In a community in which a group is a minority, its rate of intermarriage will be higher than in a setting in which the group is a majority.
2. *Unbalanced sex ratio.* In a community in which one sex outnumbers the other, traditional barriers are crossed with increased frequency as members of the more numerous sex seek mates.
3. *Development of cultural similarities.* As groups of different backgrounds come into contact, similarities in values and attitudes are developed. This encourages intermarriage, since people tend to marry those who are culturally similar to themselves.
4. *Disturbing psychological factors.* Rebellion against and feelings of rejection towards one's own group leads to an identification with and marriage into an out-group.
5. *Acceptance of certain cultural values.* The democratic ideal, the romantic

---

8. Besanceney, op. cit., p. 719.

complex, and the belief in the right of youth to choose their own mates without interference by family and community facilitate the crossing of group lines in dating and in marriage.

6. *Weakening of institutional controls over marriage.* The various religions, for example, are finding their members to be increasingly unwilling to accept church control over the selection of spouses.[9]

The following discussion examines the role of various social-structural dimensions as they affect interpersonal relations in the selection of a marriage partner. These include age, residence, social class, religion, and race. Obviously, this list is not, nor is it intended to be, inclusive of all social structures relating to the selection of a mate. However, it should give a clear indication of the extent to which endogamous marriages are predominant in the United States.

AGE AT MARRIAGE

Most couples in the United States are relatively homogamous in terms of the age at which they marry. Although a person is "free" to marry someone considerably older or younger (within legal limits), most single persons select a member of the opposite sex from a closely related age group. In 1976 the median age at first marriage was 23.8 for males and 21.3 for females, an age difference of 2.5 years (see Table 10–1).

An examination of Table 10–1 shows that the median age at first marriage as well as the age difference between males and females has changed considerably since the turn of the century. From 1890 until the mid-1950s the trend in the United States was toward an earlier age at marriage and a narrowing of the age difference between bride and groom at first marriage. Data for 1890 show the median ages at first marriage to be 26.1 years for males and 22 for females, an age difference of 4.1 years. In 1956, the median age at first marriage reached an all-time low (22.5 for men and 20.1 for women). Since that time there has been a gradual, though not continuous, increase in the median age at first marriage for both men and women.

Age Homogamy

Age homogamy is in itself a function of the age of marriage. Available data show the difference in the median age between male and female to be two and one-half years. Without exception, the median age at marriage for grooms is always higher than that for brides. It is estimated that in six of

---

9. Larry D. Barnett, "Research in Interreligious Dating and Marriage," *Marriage and Family Living* 24 (May 1962), p. 192.

seven marriages in the United States, the male is as old or older than his bride. Why is this so? Several explanations have been that the husband matures physiologically more slowly than does the wife; the husband as chief bread-winner of the family requires a longer time to prepare for this function; and there is a slight excess of males through about age 24 or 25.

Age differences in marriage are smallest at the younger ages and increase as the age goes up. Although it is the usual pattern for men to choose women younger than themselves, the difference in their ages increases as the age at first marriage for the male increases. This indicates that as men get older they increasingly marry younger women. A different pattern exists for women. As women get older they marry men who are more nearly their own age.

The reason for these seemingly contradictory data is that in the first case the median age of the bride is based on the actual age of the groom. In the latter case the median age of the groom is based on the actual age of the bride. There are considerable differences in average ages at marriage between previously married persons such as widows and divorcees, but the generalizations of differences in age at marriage seem to hold true regardless of age, sex, or previous marital status.

The Concern Over Young
Marriages

The majority of all Americans of both sexes marry at a relatively young age. The range for 75 percent of all first marriages is 21, plus or minus three or four years.[10] Marriage rates have either remained relatively stable or have increased since 1950. Yet teen-age marriage is a common occurrence. The great concern over marriages at these young ages centers around the high incidence of dropping out of school, the high unemployment rates among these persons, and the divorce rate (which for high school marriages is estimated at from two to four times that for marriages begun by persons after the age of 20).[11] A high proportion of these marriages involve a pregnancy at the time of marriage, and all data suggest a higher divorce rate among marriages begun with a pregnancy than among those where no pregnancy is involved.[12] the higher incidence of divorce among young marriages may be due as much to circumstances external to the marital relationship as to the age at marriage per se.

---

10. John Mogey, "Age at First Marriage," in Alvin W. Gouldner and S. M. Miller, *Applied Sociology: Opportunities and Problems* (New York: Free Press, 1965), p. 249.

11. Thomas P. Monahan, "Does Age at Marriage Matter in Divorce?" *Social Forces* 32 (October 1953), pp. 81–87; and Larry L. Bumpass and James A. Sweet, "Differentials in Marital Instability: 1970," *American Sociological Review* 37 (December 1972), p. 755.

12. The author's own data on young marriages showed a premarital pregnancy rate of 43 percent. See J. Ross Eshleman, "Mental Health and Marital Integration in Young Marriages," *Journal of Marriage and the Family* 27 (May 1965), p. 257.

TABLE 10–1.   Median Age at First Marriage, by Sex, for the United States, 1960 to 1976, and for Conterminous United States, 1890 to 1959

Year	Male	Female	Difference	Year	Male	Female	Difference
1976	23.8	21.3	2.5	1963	22.8	20.5	2.3
1975	23.5	21.1	2.4	1962	22.7	20.3	2.4
1974	23.1	21.1	2.0	1961	22.8	20.3	2.5
1973	23.2	21.0	2.2	1960	22.8	20.3	2.5
1972	23.3	20.9	2.4	1955	22.6	20.2	2.4
1971	23.1	20.9	2.2	1950	22.8	20.3	2.5
1970	23.2	20.8	2.4	1940	24.3	21.5	2.8
1969	23.2	20.8	2.4	1930	24.3	21.3	3.0
1968	23.1	20.8	2.3	1920	24.6	21.2	3.4
1967	23.1	20.6	2.5	1910	25.1	21.6	3.5
1966	22.8	20.5	2.3	1900	25.9	21.9	4.0
1965	22.8	20.6	2.2	1890	26.1	22.0	4.1
1964	23.1	20.5	2.6				

Adapted from U.S. Bureau of the Census, *Current Population Reports*, Series P-20, no. 306, "Marital Status and Living Arrangements: March 1976" (Washington, D.C.: U.S. Government Printing Office, 1977), Table A, p. 2.

Perhaps it is the pressure under which these marriages operate in the school, at work, and in religious and extended-family circles that make their success less probable.

Writing in 1926, Hornell Hart and Wilmer Shields concluded that marriages in which either party is nineteen or younger are from ten to 100 times as risky as are marriages at the ideal age—which to them was twenty-four for the bride and twenty-nine for the groom.[13] However, in studying divorce rates by age at marriage, Thomas Monahan in 1953 wrote that it is certain that the alteration in the pattern of age at marriage in the United States has been too small to account in any important way for the consistent rise in the divorce rate over the past fifty years.[14] Of itself, age at marriage does not appear to be a major point of difficulty in family life. Considering the upturn in the divorce rate in the latter half of the 1960s and the 1970s and considering the stabilization of ages at marriage, it is not likely that any rise in the divorce rate can be accounted for by age at marriage.

The Law and the Age at Marriage

The legal control of age, marriage, and divorce in the United States lies with the states rather than the federal government. Most state laws have two

13. Hornell Hart and Wilmer Shields, "Happiness in Relation to Age at Marriage," *Journal of Social Hygiene* 12 (1926), pp. 403–407.
14. Monahan, op. cit., p. 86.

provisions regarding age at marriage for men and women: one is the age at which young people may marry *without* the consent of their parents and the other is the age at which young people may marry *with* parental consent. If there is no applicable state statute on the subject, age under common law holds: 14 years for males and 12 years for females.[15] To be married *without* parental consent, most states require that the groom and the bride be 18 or older. In revising this text, it was interesting to note that thirty-three of the fifty states had made a change in the legal age at marriage between 1972 and 1976. The most frequent change (in twenty-five states) was in lowering the legal minimum marriage age without parental consent for men from 21 to 18. To be married *with* parental consent the minimum age is typically 18 years for grooms and 16 for brides (see Table 10–2). Since the laws regarding age at marriage are determined by the state there is some variation from one state to another in these ages. No state permits marriage for males or females without parental consent under age 18.

RESIDENTIAL PROPINQUITY

Well established in the sociology of the family literature is the idea that mate selection involves a "propinquity factor." A lengthy list of studies over the last thirty years seems to have established the general conclusion that the urban American tends to marry someone who lives within a fairly limited distance of his or her home. Evidence to support this idea usually takes the form of a frequency distribution or cumulative percentage of marriages in some community, classified by the distance separating the bride's residence from the groom's residence just prior to marriage.

Studies of Propinquity

Most studies take the lead of James Bossard who, in the early 1930s, checked 5,000 consecutive marriage licenses in which one or both applicants were residents of Philadelphia.[16] A tabulation was made of the distance between the residences of the couple. Of the total number of applicants, one in eight gave the same address, one in six lived less than a block from one another, one in four lived within two blocks or less, one in three lived within five blocks or less, and one in two lived within twenty blocks or less. The obvious point is that the percentage of marriages decreased steadily and

---

15. *Hugh Carter and Paul C. Glick, Marriage and Divorce: A Social and Economic Study*, rev. ed. (Cambridge, Mass.: Harvard University Press, 1976), p. 358.

16. James H. S. Bossard, "Residential Propinquity as a Factor in Marriage Selection," *The American Journal of Sociology* 38 (September 1932), pp. 219–224.

TABLE 10–2. Age at Marriage by State for Men and Women, with and without Consent. Blood Test and License Time Required

Marriage Information

Marriageable age, by states, for both males and females with and without consent of parents or guardians. But in most states, the court has authority, in an emergency, to marry young couples below the ordinary age of consent, where due regard for their morals and welfare so requires. In many states, under special circumstances, blood test and waiting period may be waived.

| State | With Consent | | Without Consent | | Blood Test | | Wait for License | Wait after License |
	Men	Women	Men	Women	Required	Other State Accepts		
Alabama[b]	17	14	21	18	Yes	Yes	None	None
Alaska	18	16	19	18	Yes	No	3 da.	None
Arizona	16²	16	18	18	Yes	Yes	None	None
Arkansas	17	16⁴	18	18	Yes	No	3 da.	None
California	(2)	(2)	18	18	Yes	Yes	None	None
Colorado	16	16	18	18	Yes		None	None
Connecticut	16	16q	18	18	Yes	Yes	4 da.	None
Delaware	(q)	16⁴	18	18	Yes	Yes	None	24 hrs.[c]
Dist. of Columbia	18	16	21	18	Yes	Yes	3 da.	None
Florida	18	16	21	21	Yes	Yes	3 da.	None
Georgia	18	16	18	18	Yes	Yes	None[b]	None[o]
Hawaii	16	16	18	18	Yes	Yes	None	None
Idaho	16	16	18	18	Yes	Yes	None[p]	None
Illinois[a]	(e)	15[e]	18	18	Yes	Yes	None	None
Indiana	17	17	18	18	Yes	No	3 da.	None
Iowa	16[e]	16[e]	18	18	Yes	Yes	3 da.	None
Kansas	(e)²	(e)²	18	18	Yes	Yes	3 da.	None
Kentucky	18	16	18	18	Yes	No	3 da.	None
Louisiana[a]	18	16	18	18	Yes	No	None	72 hrs.
Maine	16	16	18	18	No	No	5 da.	None
Maryland	18	16	21	18	None	None	48 hrs.	None
Massachusetts	(2)	(2)	18	18	Yes	Yes	3 da.	None
Michigan[a]		16	18	18	Yes	No	3 da.	None
Minnesota		16[e]	18	18	None		5 da.	None
Mississippi[b]	17	15	21	21	Yes		3 da.	None
Missouri	15	15	18	18	Yes	Yes	3 da.	None
Montana	(2)	(2)	18	18	Yes	Yes	5 da.	None
Nebraska	18	16	18	18	Yes	Yes	5 da.	None
Nevada	18	16	21	18	None	None	None	None
New Hampshire[a]	14[e]	13[e]	18	18	Yes	Yes	5 da.	None
New Jersey[a]		16	18	18	Yes	Yes	72 hrs.	None
New Mexico	16	16	21	21	Yes	Yes	None	None
New York	16	14	18	18	Yes	No	None	24 hrs.[h]
North Carolina[a]	16	16	18	18	Yes	Yes	None	None

TABLE 10–2—*Continued*

State	With Consent		Without Consent		Blood Test		Wait for License	Wait after License
	Men	Women	Men	Women	Required	Other State Accepts		
North Dakota[a]	(2)	15	18	18	Yes		None	None
Ohio[a]	18	16	18	18	Yes	Yes	5 da.	None
Oklahoma	16	16	18	18	Yes	No	None[i]	
Oregon	18[e]	15[e]	18	18	Yes	No	7 da.	None
Pennsylvania	16	16	18	18	Yes	Yes	3 da.	None
Rhode Island[ab]	18	16	18	18	Yes	No	None	None
South Carolina	16	14	18	18	None	None	24 hrs.	None
South Dakota	18	16	18	18	Yes	Yes	None	None
Tennessee[b]	16	16	21	21	Yes	Yes	3 da.	None
Texas	16	16	18	18	Yes	Yes	None	None
Utah[a]	16	14	21	18	Yes	Yes	None	None
Vermont[a]	18	16	18	18	Yes		None	5 da.
Virginia	16	16	18	18	Yes	Yes[r]	None	None
Washington	17	17	18	18	(d)		3 da.	None
West Virginia	18[2]	16	18	18	Yes	No	3 da.	None
Wisconsin	18	16	18	18	Yes	Yes	5 da.	None
Wyoming	18	16	21	21	Yes	Yes	None	None
Puerto Rico	16	16	21	21	(f)	None	None	None
Virgin Islands	16	14	21	18	None	None	8 da.	None

Many states have special requirements; contact individual state.

[a]Special laws applicable to nonresidents. [b]Special laws applicable to those under 21 years; Alabama; bond required if male is under 21, female under 18. [c]24 hours if one or both parties resident of state; 96 hours if both parties are nonresidents. [d]None, but male must file affidavit. [e]Parental consent plus court's consent required. [f]None, but a medical certificate is required. [g]Wait for license from time blood test is taken; Arizona, 48 hours. [h]Marriage may not be solemnized within 10 days from date of blood test. [i]If either under 21; Idaho, 3 days; Oklahoma, 72 hrs. [x]May be waived. [1]3 days if both applicants are under 18 or female is pregnant. [2]Statute provides for obtaining license with parental or court consent with no stated minimum age. [3]If either party is under 18, 3 days. [4]Under 16, with parental and court consent; Delaware, female under 18. [o]All those between 19 and 21 cannot ʋaive 3-day waiting period. [p]If either under 18, wait full 3 days. [q]If under stated age, court consent required. [r]Virginia blood test form must be used.

Source: *The World Almanac and Book of Facts* (New York: Newspaper Enterprise Association, Inc., 1977), p. 961. Compiled by William E. Mariano, Council on Marriage Relations, Inc., 110 East 42 St., New York, N.Y. 10017 (as of October 1, 1976).

Looking for a Mate?

NEW YORK—(UPI—The nation's supply of unmarried men is increasing. To meet one of them, the husband-hunter should go to New York, California or Alaska.

Or she should hit a big city, but avoid Minnesota, Pennsylvania and Ohio.

According to statisticians at Metropolitan Life, the number of eligible males has increased from 14.5 million in 1952 to 22.4 million in 1970.

More than a fifth of the unattached men —4 million of them—live in New York and California. And three-fourths of them live in cities.

The best odds for women, however, are in Alaska, where unmarried men outnumber single women 2 to 1, and in Hawaii, Nevada, and Rhode Island, where the ratio is about 6 to 5.

The hunting is poorest—and consequently best for men—in Minnesota, with 81 eligible men to every 100 women in the younger age brackets. Pennsylvania, Ohio, Iowa, West Virginia, and Utah also have more eligible women.

Source: *Detroit Free Press*, December 18, 1974, p. 2-C. Reprinted by permission of UPI.

markedly as the distance between residences of the contracting parties increased.

Since the work of Bossard, at least a dozen studies have been conducted that support an inverse relationship between mate selection and distance between contracting parties. Most have been concerned exclusively with proximity of addresses just before marriage, and their findings have been based on the records of marriage license applications.

Since most propinquity studies were completed two or three decades ago, it is difficult to determine whether place of residence is as significant a factor in mate selection today. One might also expect considerable variations among different groups such as rural residence, marriage among college students, or age. However, it is expected that people would tend to marry those who live near them.

Explanations of Propinquity

How can one account for the propinquity factor in mate selection? One attempt has been called the norm-segregation theory, which assumes that the marriage decision is normative. That is, the right to free choice is limited by the cultural considerations that identify persons who are eligible partners. In addition, each cultural group tends to be residentially segregated. This theory was first put to a test by Maurice Davie and Ruby Reeves in 1939.[17] One year later, S. A. Stouffer introduced the idea of "intervening opportunity."[18]

17. Maurice R. Davie and Ruby J. Reeves, "Propinquity of Residence before Marriage," *American Journal of Sociology* 44 (January 1939), pp. 510–517.
18. S. A. Stouffer, "Intervening Opportunities: A Theory Relating Mobility and Distance," *American Sociological Review* 5 (December 1940), pp. 845–847.

It was his hypothesis that the number of persons going a given distance is directly proportional to the number of opportunities at that distance and inversely proportional to the number of intervening opportunities. Opportunities could be seen as members who are potentially marriageable rather than members at large. Thus the more potential mates available close at hand, the less the likelihood of traveling a great distance to find a mate.

Another scheme to explain residential propinquity has been characterized as the interaction-time-cost theory. As stated by Alvin Katz and Reuben Hill the basic assumptions of this theory are as follows:

1. The marriage decision follows upon a period of courtship interaction. The greater the potential amount of courtship interaction, the higher will be the probability of marital choice.
2. The amount of potential interaction is inversely related to a time-cost function; the greater the cost, the less the potential interaction.
3. The time-cost function is directly related to the distance.[19]

This type of explanation does not contradict the cultural norm-segregation theory but rather adds the dimension of time and cost to the likelihood of a resulting marriage. Thus higher-status groups may be less propinquous than lower-status groups because they perceive the time-cost function differently. Higher-status groups may be willing to travel further and at greater cost than lower-status groups. Propinquity differences of occupational groups could then be ascribed to differential perception of the time-cost function.

William Catton and R. J. Smircich imply that normative factors in mate selection may not be overly important.[20] In a sample of Seattle marriages, Catton and Smircich found the usual propinquity pattern, but they suggest that distance gradients in patterns of human interaction may be interpreted as representing an economy of time and energy rather than competition between distance and intervening opportunities or a response to norms reflected in ecological segregation. They go on to state:

> This is not to say that human beings always economize with regard to time and energy in all their interactions. But since marriage rates seem to decline more nearly as a function of distance than as a function of intervening opportunities, we may infer that the number of *meaningful* "opportunities" for a person seeking a mate may be quite small. As the array of potential spouses physically present in the environment increases beyond a small number, the additional ones do not really constitute additional "degrees of freedom" in mate selection. The average person, no matter how many potential spouses may be "available" to him in terms of physical location and normative considerations

19. Alvin M. Katz and Reuben Hill, "Residential Propinquity and Marital Selection: A Review Theory, Method, and Fact," *Marriage and Family Living* 20 (February 1958), p. 31.
20. William R. Catton, Jr., and R. J. Smircich, "A Comparison of Mathematical Models for the Effect of Residential Propinquity on Mate Selection," *American Sociological Review* 29 (August 1964), pp. 522–529.

of exogamy and endogamy, can be intimately acquainted with only a few of them.[21]

An investigation of couples living in Oslo, Norway, revealed propinquity and homogamy to be totally independent.[22] The probability of marriage did vary directly with the degree of similarity in occupational status (a normative factor) and did vary directly with nearness of residence of the bride and the groom (propinquity). However, couples who lived very near one another before marriage were no more likely to be of the same occupational status than couples who lived at opposite sides of the city. Thus, in at least one urban setting, people married their equals in social status; they married their "neighbors," but the probability of neighbors being equals was virtually independent of the distance between their residences.

SOCIAL STATUS

Status endogamy, in our own society and around the world, is a desirable social norm, particularly for higher-status parents in regard to their children. Whether mates are selected by the individuals themselves, by parents, or by someone else, conditions supporting class endogamy are essential to preserve family lineage and status. On the other hand, persons from lower statuses have much to gain by marriage to persons of a higher standing. Irrespective of the desired or preferred circumstances, most marriages are endogamous.

Class Endogamy

Numerous studies in the past fifty years have found that both men and women marry persons from within their own class with a greater consistency than could be expected simply by chance. As early as 1918, an analysis of marriages in Philadelphia showed that intermarriage between men and women in the same industry was distinctly more common than chance expectancy, revealing something of an endogamous trend.[23] Later, data from marriages occurring in Massachusetts in the period of 1923 to 1927 were analyzed by Thomas Hunt to provide an estimate of the extent of occupational endogamy.[24] It was his finding that males and females of a particular socio-

21. Ibid., pp. 528–529.
22. Natalie Rogoff Ramsay, "Assortative Mating and the Structure of Cities," *American Sociological Review* 31 (December 1966), pp. 773–786.
23. D. M. Marvin, "Occupational Propinquity as a Factor in Mate Selection," *Publications of the American Statistical Association* 16 (1918–19), pp. 131–150.
24. Thomas C. Hunt, "Occupational Status and Marriage Selection," *American Sociological Review* 5 (August 1940), pp. 495–504.

economic status, as defined by occupation, have, with a few minor exceptions, married individuals of the same status more frequently than individuals of any other status. The same finding was produced by Richard Centers in 1949 when he analyzed marriages of various occupational strata from the position of the male, the female, and the parent.[25] In each case, the findings tended to confirm prior studies in showing a substantial amount of occupational endogamy.

More recently, in a study at Western Michigan University, endogamous norms were found to exist among married college students.[26] In extensive personal interviews with the married students living in university housing, it was found that men from high-status homes, where the father was a professional or a marginal professional, were most likely to marry women who had fathers in the same occupational strata. The same was true of the middle grouping of business, secretarial, and minor government occupations, as well as for the lowest grouping of skilled, unskilled, or farming occupations. The same pattern existed for married women.

Like occupational endogamy, educationally endogamous or homogamous marriages occur at levels higher than expected by chance. Richard Rockwell,[27] in examining marriage cohorts from census data, found that for virtually every marriage cohort, at least half of all marriages that *could* have been homogamous *were* homogamous. However, he did find that educational homogamy is lower now than at the beginning of the century. Nevertheless, both education and occupation remain as major factors in mate selection.

This intraclass pattern is often viewed by exchange theorists as a process in which individuals attempt to achieve the best possible bargain for themselves and their children by weighing marital resources and alternatives.[28] If this is true, it would be highly surprising if the endogamy pattern were not the most prevalent. It is at similar class levels where the marital resources would most likely be similar. If this is the case, what does a person of a lower social class have to trade with persons of a higher social status? Let us examine some of these patterns of marriage across class lines.

Mesalliance

Marriage with a person of an inferior position has been termed *mesalliance*. Special cases of mesalliance are *hypergamy*, denoting the pattern

25. Richard Centers, "Marital Selection and Occupational Strata," *The American Journal of Sociology* 54 (May 1949), pp. 530–535.
26. Eshleman and Hunt, op. cit., p. 32.
27. Richard C. Rockwell, "Historical Trends and Variations in Educational Homogamy," *Journal of Marriage and the Family* 38 (February 1976), pp. 83–95.
28. Exchange theorists view mate selection and other reciprocal interactions as a bargaining process. What is received is dependent upon what is available to give in return and vice versa (see discussion in Chapter 2).

wherein the female marries upward into a higher social stratum, and *hypogamy*, wherein the female marries downward into a lower social stratum.

With particular reference to the United States, a number of writers have concluded that hypergamy is more prevalent than hypogamy—women marry men of higher status more frequently than do men marry women of higher rank. On the basis of an exchange-theory argument, the social advantages of hypergamy seem to exist primarily for the low-status woman. For equity to occur, this type of exchange would require that the woman be exceptional in those qualities the culture defines as desirable. Depending on the society, qualities of women that determine status might include factors such as shade of skin color, facial and morphological features, and relative age. Glen Elder suggests that throughout history some women have been able to exchange their physical beauty for a young man's lineage, accomplishments, or mobility potential.[29] Typically, a woman is expected to use her attractiveness to gain certain legitimate ends such as recognition, status, and a husband.

American men rank physical attractiveness at or near the top among the qualities they desire in women, and this seems to be especially true of the upwardly mobile or strongly ambitious. Thus it would be expected that a male who achieves status through his occupation exchange his social rank for the beauty and personal qualities of the female. The idea that physical attractiveness is of great exchange value, particularly among women of working-class origin was one factor that Elder attempted to determine.[30]

Elder's basic hypothesis was confirmed.[31] Girls who became upwardly mobile through marriage were characterized by physical attractiveness, a desire to impress and control others, high aspirations for the future, and an avoidance of steady dating. Among women from the working class, physical attractiveness was more predictive of marriage to a high-status man than was educational attainment, while the relative effects of these factors were reversed among women of middle-class origins. Social ascent from the working class was also related to sexual restraint and a well-groomed appearance.

A number of researches confirm the idea that when a person marries outside his class, males will more frequently marry down than up. For example, Centers found that males of all groups, except the semiskilled and unskilled laborers, more frequently married down than up.[32] The higher the occupational stratum of the male, the more commonly he is found to have married down, and the lower the occupational level of the male, the more frequently he is discovered to have married up. For females, the trend is opposite to that for males; the lower the occupational level of the female, the less

29. Glen H. Elder, Jr., "Appearance and Education in Marriage Mobility," *American Sociological Review* 34 (August 1969), p. 520.

30. Ibid., pp. 519–533.

31. Taylor and Glenn reported findings consistent with Elder in regard to education but found the contribution of attractiveness to be almost nil: Patricia Ann Taylor and Norval D. Glenn. "The Utility of Education and Attractiveness for Females, Status Attainment through Marriage," *American Sociological Review* 41 (June 1976), pp. 484–498.

32. Centers, op. cit., p. 533.

predominant is marriage to a person of her own or a contiguous stratum. Generally speaking, for a majority of the strata, more females than males are discovered to be marrying up.[33]

Ronald Pavalko and Norma Nager suggest some factors that restrict and enhance women's access to high-status men:[34]

1. *Socioeconomic background* is a crucial factor in the opportunity that women have to meet men of their own or a higher class.
2. *Educational attainment* is another important means of access to "potentially" high-status men. The very fact of going to college places a young woman in a situation where the probability of meeting men destined for at least white-collar occupations is higher than it is for noncollege females. It appears to be a well-recognized function of our educational system to provide an area for mate selection for females.
3. *Occupational attainment* is a factor affecting access to high-status men. Women who attend college to prepare for careers in teaching, secretarial work, or dental hygiene, to mention a few, gain greater access to and contact with men in professional and higher-status occupations.
4. *Community size* appears to be a factor related to access to higher-status men. In terms of probabilities, women from urban areas have a better chance of meeting high-status men than do women from rural areas.

These four characteristics were developed by Pavalko and Nager in their "opportunity model" regulating women's access to men of high social status.[35] Using longitudinal data from two surveys of Wisconsin high school seniors in 1957 and 1964, their analysis focused on 296 women who selected nursing as their occupational choice. They hypothesized that those women who became nurses would be more likely to marry high-status men than those who did not. They also hypothesized that those who became nurses by attending college would be most likely to marry high-status men; those who became nurses but did not attend college would be next most likely to marry high-status men; and those who neither became nurses nor attended college would be least likely to marry men of high status.

Their hypotheses were generally supported. Women who became nurses more often married high-status men than those who did not become nurses and college-attending girls who became nurses were most likely to marry high-status men. Of the four variables (occupational attainment, educational attainment, socioeconomic background, and community size) suggested as defining this structure of opportunity, the data examined indicate that socioeconomic background is relatively more important than occupational attainment or community size. They conclude that the "opportunity-structure model" has considerable relevance to the question of how women

33. Ibid., p. 535.
34. Ronald M. Pavalko and Norma Nager, "Contingencies of Marriage to High-Status Men," *Social Forces*, 46 (June 1968), pp. 523–531.
35. Ibid., pp. 524–526.

gain access to high-status men and concomitantly to the upper levels of the stratification system.[36]

The Mating Gradient

As stated, when dating and marriage occur outside one's social class, men tend to date below their social levels, but women more often date above their class. This tendency has been called the "mating gradient." Most studies—although not all—support the notion that men marry downward more frequently than upward. In addition, the data suggest that men have a wider range of mate choice than do women except at the very top and bottom levels. As stated by Leslie:

> An interesting implication of the operation of the mating gradient is that it works to keep substantial numbers of the highest status women and the lowest status men from marrying. Women at the highest socioeconomic levels have a smaller pool of potential mates to begin with because it is not generally acceptable for them to marry downward. In addition, these high-status women must compete for high-status men, not only against one another but also against women from other status levels. To the extent that high-status men marry downward, they leave high-status women without partners. Among men, the reverse situation obtains. The lowest status men generally are not eligible to marry higher status women; yet higher status men may select lower status spouses. Thus, unmarried women may be, disproportionately, high-status women, and unmarried men may be, disproportionately, low-status men.[37]

The mating gradient also seems to operate in dating on college campuses. It is the freshman male and the senior female that have the smallest choice of probable dating partners. The freshman girl is the choice of college males at any class ranking, whereas the freshman male must, to a greater extent, limit his choices to the freshman females. At the other extreme, the situation is reversed. By the time the male and female are seniors, the male can select from any of the class rankings of females, whereas the female is more limited to senior or junior men.

RELIGION

All studies have found that marriage within one's religion is far greater than chance occurrence can explain. Carter and Glick, using census data, in-

---

36. Ibid., p. 531.
37. Gerald R. Leslie, *The Family in Social Context*, 3d ed. (New York: Oxford University Press, 1976), p. 506.

ferred that if all persons had completely disregarded religion as a factor in mate selection, 56 percent of married couples would have spouses of like religion and 44 percent would have spouses of different religions.[38] This inference is based on the assumption that the 70.4 percent of the Protestants in the United States would have married Protestants, that the 26 percent of Catholics would have married Catholics, and that the 3.6 percent of Jews would have married Jews. The sum of the squares of these three values equals 56.49 percent: the *expected* percentage of endogamous marriages. The *actual* percentage of all married couples with a spouse of the same religion was 91.4 for Protestants, 78.5 for Catholics, and 92.8 for Jewish.

These figures substantiate the major influences that religion, or at least religious affiliation, plays in the selection of a marital partner. Religion is probably second only to race in the segregation of males and females into categories that are granted approval or disapproval with respect to marriage.

The Determination of Interfaith Marriages

Determining what is within one's religion can be an extremely complex research problem. To even define, much less measure, a mixed religious or interfaith marriage involves problems that few persons have satisfactorily resolved. For example, if you were engaged in a research study to determine the frequency of interfaith marriage at your school or in your community, would you place a Methodist-Lutheran marriage in the intra- or interfaith category? Would a devout Catholic married to a person reared in the Catholic tradition but presently indifferent to religion make a mixed marriage? If an atheist marries an agnostic would they be marrying endogamously or exogamously? If a Protestant marries a Catholic and then the Protestant converts to Catholicism, is this an inter- or intrafaith marriage?

Most studies of interreligious marriage are limited to three broad categories—Catholic, Protestant, and Jewish—with only an occasional breakthrough to take account of finer classifications. Rarely are any divisions made in Catholicism. In Judaism, even though definite differences regarding interfaith and intra-Jewish marriages have been found to exist within the three major branches—Orthodox, Conservative, and Reform—it is relatively infrequently that studies distinguish among them.[39] The same is true among some of the major denominations of Protestantism: Methodist, Presbyterian, Lutheran, Baptist, and the like. This lack of differentiation is very unfortunate, for even the most untrained persons in religious thought recognize differences

---

38. Carter and Glick, op. cit., p. 141.
39. Ruth S. Cavan, "Jewish Student Attitudes towards Interreligious and Intra-Jewish Marriage," *American Journal of Sociology* 76 (May 1971), pp. 1064–1071.

in beliefs and practices *among* Protestant denominations to say nothing of those *within* denominations.

To deal with interfaith marriage solely on the basis of Catholic-Protestant, Catholic-Jewish, or Protestant-Jewish sets up an artificial distinction. However, it does provide general data that make possible the testing of hypotheses concerning the significance of religious endogamy within the major religious categories in the United States.

Frequency of Interfaith Marriages

The frequency of interfaith marriage is determined in most research studies by checking religious affiliation on public records or asking persons directly. From these studies, indications seldom exist as to the frequency of conversion or anticipated conversion of a spouse or interdenominational mixtures within religious groups. They do indicate that among Protestants, Catholics, and Jews in the United States, intermarriages are most common among Catholics and least common among Protestants and Jews.[40] Also, interfaith marriages are more frequent among the religiously less devout than among the religiously more devout.

Irrespective of religious affiliation, most marriages are endogamous.[41] However, the rates of religious endogamy vary greatly. For example, in Utah, marriages among Mormons are highly endogamous. But in Florida where Mormons constitute less than one percent of the population, it was ascertained that about two-thirds of the Mormons living there had married a non-Mormon.[42]

In the state of Indiana, Christensen and Barber used marriage records for the entire state to determine interfaith rates for marriages and interfaith rates for individuals.[43] For marriages, 12 percent involved Protestants, 53 percent involved Catholics, and 47.6 percent involved Jews. For individuals, percentages were 6.4 percent for Protestants, 36.4 percent for Catholics, and 31.2 percent for Jews. It was also observed that over a four-year period from 1960 to 1963, eight-ninths (88.9 percent) of the known-religion cases were intrafaith and only one-ninth (11.1 percent) were interfaith.[44]

It is interesting to note that endogamy is not merely the predominant pattern when the broad Protestant-Catholic-Jewish classification is used but is the denominational pattern with Protestantism as well. Data provided by Andrew Greeley from the 1957 *Current Population Survey of Religion* and

40. Jon P. Alston, William A. McIntosh, and Louise M. Wright, "Extent of Interfaith Marriages among white Americans," *Sociological Analysis* 37 (Fall 1976), pp. 261–264.

41. Recent national data placed this figure at 83 percent. Ibid., p. 264.

42. Brent A. Barlow, "Notes on Mormon Interfaith Marriages," *The Family Coordinator* 26 (April 1977), p. 148.

43. Christensen and Barber, op. cit., pp. 461–469.

44. Ibid., pp. 463–464.

from a national opinion research center study of June, 1961, college graduates, indicate that denominational homogeneity in marriage exists for at least three-quarters of the major religious denominations including the various groups within Protestantism.[45] Thus, not only are Protestants married to other Protestants, as previous studies have shown, but they are married to Protestants who share the same denominational affiliation. The ratio of mixed marriages does not vary much across denominational lines.

Characteristics of the Religiously Intermarried

Most religious groups in the United States oppose interfaith marriages among their membership. Several studies also indicate that a sizable proportion of the general population shares this opposition. Yet, many marriages occur among persons of different religious faiths.

Jerold Heiss tested certain hypotheses that indicate how it is possible for people to intermarry despite what appears to be a general disapproval of such marriages.[46] Drawing data from 1,167 people of the three major religious groups living in Manhattan, some general hypotheses were tested that compared the intermarried with the intramarried on early patterns of interaction between the married couple and their parents. In general, the intermarried as compared to the intramarried were characterized by nonreligious parents, greater dissatisfaction with parents when young, more early family strife, less early family integration, and greater emancipation from parents at the time of marriage. Although the data do not account for cases of intermarriage, they do suggest several internal and external controls that may tend to prevent marriage outside the group.

There seems to be some uncertainty as to which sex of which religion is most frequently involved in interreligious marriage. August Hollingshead noted that in New Haven, Connecticut, Jewish-gentile marriages most likely involved a Jewish male and a gentile female.[47] There was no consistent bias between sex and mixed Catholic-Protestant marriages; either partner was likely to be a Catholic or a Protestant. One consequence of Protestant-Catholic marriage in which sex did make a significant difference was in relationship to unwanted fertility. Bean and Aiken[48] found that couples in which the wife was Catholic and the husband Protestant had substantially higher unwanted

---

45. Andrew M. Greeley, "Religious Intermarriage in a Denominational Society," *American Journal of Sociology* 75 (May 1970), p. 949.

46. Jerold S. Heiss, "Premarital Characteristics of the Religiously Intermarried in an Urban Area," *American Sociological Review* 25 (February 1960), pp. 47–55.

47. August B. Hollingshead, "Cultural Factors in the Selection of Marriage Mates," *American Sociological Review* 15 (October 1950), pp. 619–627.

48. Frank D. Bean and Linda H. Aiken, "Intermarriage and Unwanted Fertility in the United States," *Journal of Marriage and the Family* 38 (February 1976), p. 67.

pregnancies than other combinations of couples. The consequences were virtually zero for couples in which the wife was Protestant and the husband Catholic.

Research by Lee Burchinal and Loren Chancellor, based on all marriages in Iowa from 1953 to 1957, showed that interreligious-marriage patterns were considerably more frequent among persons involved in remarriages than among persons entering first marriages.[49] An increment in interreligious-marriage rates between first marriages and remarriages was greater among Catholics than Protestants. The same study revealed a differential relationship between ages of marriage and interreligious-marriage rates, being greatest at the extreme ends of the age distribution used: sixteen or under and thirty or over.

The Success of Interfaith Marriages

The general opposition to interfaith marriages stems from the widespread belief that they are highly unstable and create a multitude of problems that intrafaith marriages do not experience. Frequent reference is made to the higher incidence of divorce and desertion as criteria for the success or failure of inter- versus intrafaith marriages. However, a study by Burchinal and Chancellor indicate virtually no differences between marital-survival rates of the denominationally homogamous Protestant marriage types and corresponding denominationally mixed Protestant marriage types.[50] In their study, the survival rate for the total population was 87.6 percent. Homogamous Catholic marriages had the highest survival rate; mixed Presbyterian, mixed Lutheran, and mixed Methodist had higher survival rates than did homogamous Methodist, Presbyterian, or Baptist.

The authors went on to indicate that the difference in survival rates among homogamous Catholics, homogamous Protestants, and Catholic-interreligious types were a function of age and social status.[51] In their words:

> In all religious affiliation types 1) survival rates were greater among the marriages involving the older as compared to the younger brides; and 2) survival rates increased directly with the occupational status levels.[52]

---

49. Lee G. Burchinal and Loren E. Chancellor, "Ages of Marriage, Occupations of Grooms and Interreligious Marriage Rates," *Social Forces* 40 (1962), pp. 348–354. Lee G. Burchinal and Loren E. Chancellor, "Social Status, Religious Affiliation, and Ages at Marriage," *Marriage and Family Living* 25 (May 1963), pp. 219–221.
50. Lee G. Burchinal and Loren E. Chancellor, "Survival Rates among Religiously Homogamous and Interreligious Marriages," *Social Forces* 41 (May 1963), pp. 353–362.
51. Ibid., p. 357.
52. Ibid., p. 357.

Religious intermarriage is no more likely than religious intramarriage to terminate in divorce. But Erich Rosenthal suggests that previous divorce is highly related to religious intermarriage.[53] This tendency is so pronounced that previous divorce must be considered a major contributing factor in the formation of religious intermarriages.

It is very easy to get caught in the assumption that success in marriage is equal to remaining together. It is true that most data would support lower divorce rates among Catholics and other religious groups, but many of these groups impose negative sanctions or express formal disapproval of divorce. It is questionable whether one can use divorce figures as indicators of unsuccessful marriages among churchgoers, irrespective of religious affiliation.

RACE

Of all the norms involving intermarriage, few are more widely held or rigorously enforced than in the area of race. Despite scientific findings and the removal of legal barriers, the restrictions concerning interracial marriages still remain the most inflexible of all the mate-selection boundaries.

Among most people of the world, interracial marriages are accepted both legally and socially. With the possible exception of the Republic of South Africa, few countries are as race conscious as the United States. The intermingling of people of different races is nothing new in world affairs. Based on historical and biological evidence, the idea of a "pure race" is totally inaccurate—race mixture has been going on throughout all of recorded history, and some evidence suggests that even in prehistory racial intermingling occurred. As there is no evidence to support a pure race, neither is there evidence to support the idea that racial mixtures result in biologically inferior offspring. Biologically there is nothing to prevent marriage of persons of different races.

Despite all the evidence disproving superiorities or inferiorities of certain racial groups, many people support this superior-inferior idea via their attitudes, values, and behavior. It is this factor of social definition—the attitudes, values, and resulting behavior—that makes interracial marriage significant. Just what is dubbed "mixed marriage" or intermarriage depends on what differences "make a difference" in the social definition. In the words of Sophia McDowell:

> If a Methodist marries a Baptist, a person whose father is a lawyer marries someone whose father is a doctor, or a blue-eyed individual marries a brown-

---

53. Erich Rosenthal, "Divorce and Religious Intermarriage: The Effect of Previous Marital Status upon Subsequent Marital Behavior," *Journal of Marriage and the Family* 32 (August 1970), pp. 435–440.

eyed one, we do not speak of "intermarriage," because we do not regard these denominations, occupations, or pigmentations as significantly different from each other. . . . The biological differences between blacks and whites have come to be regarded as terribly important, indeed, although there is no evidence of innate racial distinctions that could be relevant to marriage except those which have been created historically and institutionally.[54]

A removal of the legal prohibition to interracial marriage came in 1967 when the United States Supreme Court struck down as unconstitutional a 1924 Virginia law forbidding marriage between persons of different races. According to the court, a law of this type violates rights guaranteed to all persons under the fourteenth amendment to the Constitution. Irrespective of the Supreme Court's decision declaring such laws unconstitutional, the social mores and the disfavor placed on interracial marriage by all major racial, religious, and ethnic groups are so strong in most areas that relatively few marriages of this type take place.

The strength of the prohibition against interracial marriage, particularly black-white marriage, in itself increases the difficulty of obtaining the type of research evidence necessary to substantiate factors such as frequency, male-female differences, or the stability of marriages of this type. It must be noted and made clear that a discussion of race in relation to marriage is not independent of, or isolated from, age, residence, social class, religion, educational level, region of the country, whether the marriage is black-white or Oriental-Caucasian, whether it involves a marriage or a remarriage, or any other dimension. To deal with racial endogamy alone is impossible.

The Frequency of Black-White Intermarriage

Determining the frequency of black-white marriage is exceedingly difficult. As with religion, there is the matter of classification. If a black passes for white and marries a white is this an intermarriage or an endogamous marriage? If, as is on the law books of various states, a person is one-eighth or one-sixteenth black (an empirical impossibility), would it not be an intermarriage irrespective of which race one marries? Even if a categorization could be agreed upon and precisely determined, it could be argued that social sanctions against such marriages are so severe in most parts of the United States that the reported number of such marriages would be less than the actual number.

Information on interracial marriage has never been systematically collected in the United States. As a result, researchers have drawn upon case history materials, statistics published by specific localities or states, data pro-

---

54. Sophia F. McDowell, "Black-White Intermarriage in the United States," *International Journal of Sociology of the Family* 1 (May 1971), p. 57.

> *Louise:*   I would oppose my daughter marrying outside her religion on the
> same basis that I would oppose her marrying a very poor fellow who
> wasn't ever going to hold onto a steady job. Okay, whose religion is
> your family going to follow? Are you going to change? Is he going to
> change? Are you going to have a divided house or isn't religion going
> to be important to you? And I think it would be hard. If she asked my
> advice, I would caution her that she was adding another strain to a
> marriage and marriage has enough problems of its own. The same
> would be true for interracial marriage.
>
> *Alex:*   Here in America, when I date somebody, I usually try to stick to my
> own race. Since I am white I wanta date white girls; if I was black I
> would date black girls. It's not that I'm prejudiced, but it's just the
> way.
>
> *Ann:*   I could marry a white guy if I loved him. No problem if I don't have
> to live with anyone but him. I know you're wondering about what
> will neighbors think or how you would be accepted in society. As
> long as you don't harm me or mine, I don't care. I just don't care. I
> can take it if you let me live. If you do not put my back up against
> the wall, I can take it. I could live with a white man. It's not so
> frowned upon now. Used to be illegal. That's another thing. There
> are areas where you have your mixed families living. You gotta think
> about the children. Children are very cruel to each other. And a lot
> of us have not accepted the fact that the color of skin doesn't matter.
>
> *Mac:*   I think I could marry a black. I could live with myself and if other
> people could not accept it, you know, to hell with them, cause you're
> living for your mate, not for other people. I went out with this black
> girl who worked in a bar at the discotheque, but it was primarily for
> sexual reasons. We both talked about it and agreed.

vided on public records such as marriage applications, or counts taken from
population censuses. In 1960, for the first time, the U.S. population census
was tabulated to show the number of husbands and wives who had the same
or different racial backgrounds. However, serious problems exist in regard to
both the accuracy and the meaning of the census-assembled interracial figures.[55] For example, the data is collected by nonprofessional enumerators who
gather information from the person available, data is not independently
checked for its reliability or validity, data is based on self-identified "married"
couples not upon marriages, an undercounting of selected minorities is
known to result, and marriage and divorce forms are often not consistent from

---

55. See, for example, Thomas P. Monahan's letter to the editor, "Critique of Heer's Article,"
    Journal of Marriage and the Family 36 (November 1974), pp. 669–671.

state to state or over time. Since these are often the only available sources of data, extreme caution must be taken in assuming accuracy or in interpretation and analysis.

Concurrent with pressures from the civil rights movement, attempts have been made to exclude and/or remove the "race" item from many public records. For example, New York in 1965, Michigan in 1966, Maryland in 1970, Massachusetts in 1971, and the District of Columbia in 1975 had race or color removed from the marriage records by legislative or administrative action.

From marriage record data that was available from the National Center for Health Statistics covering forty-two states, Thomas Monahan[56] attempted to determine the extent of interracial marriage in the United States from 1963–1970. He estimated that when looked at as a whole, the proportion of all marriages of mixed race comprise less than three-fourths of 1 percent in any sample year. Of all marriages involving a black, 1.4 percent were mixed in 1963–1966 and 2.6 percent were mixed in 1967–1970.

Interracial marriage rates vary widely from one state to another. For example the percentage of black-white marriage reported for 1967–1970 was 1.94 in the District of Columbia, .73 in Massachusetts, and .45 or higher in Alaska, Hawaii, Maryland, New Hampshire, Rhode Island, Connecticut, and New Jersey. In contrast, North Carolina, Georgia, Tennessee, Alabama, Mississippi, and Louisiana had a percentage of black-white marriage under .09. The rates are much higher when all racially mixed marriages are considered. For example, combining white-other or black-other rates with the black-white rates, the percentages vary from 32.54 in Hawaii, 10.79 in Alaska, and 2.11 in Montana to .03 in Alabama and .07 in Mississippi.[57] The category "other" in census reporting includes Japanese, Chinese, Filipino, American Indian, Hawaiian, Eskimo or any not classified as black or white.

Various explanations exist to account for the tremendous variation in rates from one state to another. David Heer[58] in an article noting extreme differences in interracial marriage rates in four states he studied, Hawaii, California, Michigan, and Nebraska, gave several explanations. One, the propinquity factor, may be at work. Many areas have racial segregation and it is known that marriage occurs among partners who live in the same area or close to one another. Thus it is likely that the greater the racial segregation within an area, the lower the actual number of interracial marriages in relation to what one would expect by chance. Second, the social status of the black community relative to the white may be a major factor. Extreme differences in the status of blacks and whites tend to decrease the likelihood of any

56. Thomas P. Monahan, "An Overview of Statistics on Interracial Marriage in the United States, with Data on Its Extent from 1963–1970," *Journal of Marriage and the Family* 38 (May 1976), pp. 223–231.

57. Ibid., Table 5, p. 227.

58. David M. Heer, "Negro-White Marriage in the United States," *Journal of Marriage and the Family* 28 (August 1966), pp. 262–273.

marriages, racial or not. Third, the tolerance of the white community influences the rate. As a tolerance for black-white marriages increases, the incidence of marriages will increase.

Heer suggests that although marriages between blacks and whites are relatively infrequent in number, they are sociologically important because they serve as an indicator of the relationship between the two races. He hypothesizes that a low frequency of black-white marriage serves to reinforce the pattern of inequality between the two races. Several reasons for this are advanced.

> First of all, on a per-capita basis white persons hold a far higher share of the nation's wealth than do blacks and a low frequency of racial intermarriage makes it unlikely for a black to inherit wealth from a white. Secondly, blacks are by and large excluded from the many unionized manual jobs to which entrance is strongly determined by kin connections because existing jobs of this type are usually held by whites and black persons rarely have white kin. Thirdly, the lack of close relatives among whites affects the socialization of black youth. In particular, they cannot obtain an easy familiarity with the social world of whites and hence are inhibited from applying for jobs demanding such familiarity even when their technical qualifications are completely satisfactory. Finally, over the long run it may be surmised that prejudice against blacks on the part of white persons would be diminished if the proportion of whites with black relatives were substantial rather than negligible, as at present.[59]

Male-Female Intermarital Racial Differences

Most articles and books dealing with black-white marriages indicate that black males marry white females more frequently than white males marry black females. While some contradictory evidence exists, most research supports this black male-white female contention. In Monahan's data[60] 70 percent of the black-white marriages had a black male, about half of the states having 80 percent or more black males. Interestingly, in the white-other marriages, the opposite occurs: the male partner is more often white.

If Heer[61] is correct, the black male-white female pattern in intermarriage is increasing rapidly. He claims that during the decade of the sixties there was a 26 percent increase in the number of black-white marriages. This included a 62 percent rise in marriages involving a black husband and a white

---

59. David M. Heer, "The Prevalence of Black-White Marriage in the United States, 1960 and 1970," *Journal of Marriage and the Family* 36 (May 1974), p. 246.

60. Monahan, op. cit., pp. 229–230.

61. Heer, op. cit., 1974, p. 256.

wife accompanied by a 9 percent decline in the number involving a white husband and a black wife. It is possible, although not proven, that white male-black female relationships may more often be consensual unions.

There is a lack of consensus on the reasons for a differential incidence of interracial marriage by sex. The two most frequently cited are differences in socioeconomic status and differences in sexual norms. Let us examine these two reasons briefly.

The first, suggested by Kingsley Davis more than thirty years ago, was that if marriages between black men and white women largely involved black males of high social status and white women of low social status, then the groom could trade his class advantage for the racial caste advantage of the bride.[62] That is, an exchange process is in operation where the higher status black male offers his higher socioeconomic status for the preferred color status of the lower-class white female. The result is racial hypogamy and class hypergamy for the female. She marries down racially and up in social status or class, exchanging one for the other.

Several attempts to test the thesis of racial hypogamy-class hypergamy have not brought forth much support. This implies that for the female to marry up, she would generally have a lower level of education or lower status occupation than her husband. Neither Heer[63] nor Louis Carter[64] found the wives of black males to be of lower educational attainment.

The same lack of support based on occupation comes from Todd Pavela.[65] In an exploratory study of black-white marriage in Indiana, recorded data covering two years included ninety-five black-white marriages out of approximately 78,000 total marriages. Among these ninety-five, a relatively high proportion of black grooms married white brides (sixty-nine cases), as opposed to white grooms with black brides (twenty-six cases). But occupationally, the persons involved in black-white marriages showed a distribution similar to that of the entire state. There was no indication of a pattern of occupational dominance of one spouse over another, thus not supporting the contention that prosperous black men will marry economically inferior white women.

These results indicate that even if more black males are marrying white females than vice versa, the explanation of a socioeconomic exchange for color preference may be mythical.

The second frequently cited explanation for a preponderance of black male-white female marriage revolves around sexual norms. The argument is

---

62. Kingsley Davis, "Intermarriage in Caste Society," *American Anthropologist* 43 (July-September 1941), pp. 388–395.
63. Heer, op. cit., 1974, pp. 253–255.
64. Louis F. Carter, "Racial-Caste Hypogamy: A Sociological Myth?" *Phylon* 29 (Winter 1968), pp. 347–350.
65. Todd H. Pavela, "An Exploratory Study of Negro-White Intermarriage in Indiana," *Journal of Marriage and the Family* 26 (May 1964), p. 209.

that sexual norms allow white men to take sexual advantages of black women without marrying them.[66] Little research seems to support this argument either. It seems very probable that the sexual norms, at least on college campuses, may be actually the reverse of Davis's contention. That is, if the sexual norms are not equal, the black male may actually have greater sexual access to the white female than vice versa.

Characteristics of Interracial Marriages

There is some evidence that persons who marry across racial lines differ in such characteristics as age, previous marital status, occupation, residence, and integration with families from persons who marry within their own race. Census data show that brides and grooms marrying interracially are older than other brides and grooms. In addition, the median age difference between husbands and wives is significantly greater in interracial marriages than in racially endogamous marriages. In addition to being older, interracially married couples are more likely to come from the divorced population, particularly the bride. Relatively fewer interracially married persons were from the widowed population.[67]

In checking trends in Hawaiian interracial-marriage rates by occupation, Robert Schmitt reports high negative correlations with income levels.[68] In comparing 1956–1957 and 1967–1968 data, it was found that all occupational groups recorded increased interracial-marriage rates. Interracial-marriage rates for both periods were highly (and negatively) correlated with median earnings. But even though rates have increased in all occupational groups, wide differences related to occupational status have persisted. Mixed marriages are still far less common among professional and managerial grooms than among service workers and laborers.[69]

White persons who marry interracially are more likely to be from urban rather than rural areas and to be native-born white women or foreign-born white men. More than twenty-five years ago, St. Clair Drake and Horace Cayton suggested that the following types of blacks from Chicago tended to intermarry more frequently with whites: intellectuals and bohemians who are not responsive to social restrictions; members of cults that include disregard

---

66. Davis, op. cit., pp. 388–395.

67. "Marriages: Trends and Characteristics: United States," U.S. Department of Health Education and Welfare, Series 21, number 21 (September 1971), p. 20.

68. Robert C. Schmitt, "Recent Trends in Hawaiian Interracial Marriage Rates by Occupation," *Journal of Marriage and the Family* 33 (May 1971), pp. 373–374.

69. Ibid., p. 374.

of racial differences as part of their social philosophy; and lower-class blacks without pride of race.[70] Probably the same would be true today.

The Success of Interracial Marriages

Do black-white marriages succeed? As stated by Pavela, in many respects, black-white marriages studied contradict their picture in the public mind and even in much sociological literature.[71] It would appear that such intermarriage now occurs between persons who are, by and large, economically, educationally, and culturally equal and who have a strong emotional attachment, be it rationalization or real. The external pressures faced by interracial couples are often great but certainly do not appear to be overwhelming.

A generally accepted view is that those who enter a racially mixed marriage are more likely to get divorced. Analyzing a set of data on the state of Iowa covering almost thirty years, Monahan infers that blacks, both males and females, have contributed almost twice as many divorces to the picture as one would expect from their proportion of marriages. But when the divorce rate of mixed marriages of blacks with whites is examined, Monahan finds that in Iowa the mixed marriages are more enduring (i.e., less likely to divorce) than are black-black marriages in Iowa. Aa a whole, black-white marriages would appear to have a greater stability than do marriages where both parties are black in Iowa, and intermarriages of black males with white wives are more enduring than marriages of whites with whites.[72]

Monahan found a somewhat similar pattern in Hawaii by examining the rates of divorce.[73] To determine the interracial-divorce pattern, the divorces granted in the five-year period, 1958–1962, were divided by marriages contracted in the preceding seven-year period, 1956–1962. He concludes that whatever the explanation, interracial marriage does not necessarily lead to a weakening of family ties. Despite the considerable increase in interracial marriages in Hawaii, the divorce rate has stabilized at a level lower than in previous decades, and, as a whole, the mixed-race marriages are only moderately less successful than are the same-race marriages.

Recognizing that Iowa and Hawaii may be unique cases, recognizing that interracial marital success depends upon which races are intermarrying and the circumstances surrounding the marriage, and recognizing different methodological and research problems, the findings of Monahan should cer-

---

70. St. Clair Drake and Horace R. Cayton, *Black Metropolis* (New York: Harcourt, Brace, and World, 1945), pp. 137–139.

71. Pavela, op. cit., p. 211.

72. Thomas P. Monahan, "Are Interracial Marriages Really Less Stable?" *Social Forces* 48 (June 1970), pp. 464 and 469.

73. Monahan, op. cit., pp. 40–47.

Interracial Adoption

"White families who adopt black children must make up their minds that they must become part of the black community and be 'black,'" says a pioneer in the field of trans-racial adoptions.

Margaret Edgar is a Canadian who founded the Open Door Society in Montreal in 1950, over 12 years before the first attempts at trans-racial adoptions were made in the United States. In addition, she has six adopted children of her own: three white, one Japanese and two black.

Mrs. Edgar was in Washington last week to meet with the Council on Adoptable Children, a citizens group formed in the metropolitan Washington area to promote the adoption of hard-to-place children. Many members are white parents of black children.

"The hardest thing is for members of the adoptive white family to think of themselves as black or of the black community, and this is very necessary so that they can teach the black child how to survive in a racist society."

This does not mean that the white family has to give up its white identity. Instead it should develop an additional one; a specific knowledge of what being black is all about. The family could, for example, participate in seeing black plays, visiting black friends and taking part in black festivals. "After all, blacks have always had dual identities," she noted.

While Mrs. Edgar says she is not an advocate of trans-racial adoption ("The ideal is to place a black child in a black family,") she believes that when this is impossible, finding the right white family is the next step. "I'm interested in what is best for the child."

She said that one criterion for judging the "right" white family for a black child is whether the couple has an already established relationship with black families; "a sincere friendship." "Trans-racial adoption should not be used for liberal causes."

"You have to watch for those whites who want to raise a 'little white child in a brown skin.' This is a naive concept. The world isn't made like that." She has been made aware of the many problems by raising her own multiracial family who range in age from 23, the oldest, to 10, the youngest.

Black critics of trans-racial adoption fear that the black child in a white family loses his sense of black heritage and suffers an identity crisis. But this need not happen.

In Montreal, for instance a black cultural school was opened for both adopted children and black children born to black families. Because Canada has a very small minority of blacks and they are not concentrated in any sort of ghetto, there is a lack of real black "community." "Most black Canadians go through an identity crisis."

Although the same prejudices and racism exist in Canada, "American families are more vocal in their opposition to trans-racial adoption." She said she only places black children in black families in the United States.

On the other hand, she said, Canadians either over-react or ignore the situation. Children face the brunt of discrimination when they go to school. "And that's why the parents must have a total commitment to the black child as a black human being."

Karen Mitchell, a member of the Council on Adoptable Children and a white parent of two black children, essentially agrees with Mrs. Edgar. She said the council recruits black families to adopt black children and encourages white families to consider adopting the white handicapped and older "hard-to-place" children.

Three years ago, however, the black child numbered among the unadoptable. That was when Karen and Robert Mitchell adopted Mark, now 3. "More black families are adopting children now, so the council is concentrating on finding homes for the older child, (over 2 years) and the handicapped child.

"We're also supporting the idea of subsidized adoption that would enable more black families to adopt."

The Mitchells live in an integrated suburb in Maryland. Their youngest child is 22-month-old Kim. Mrs. Mitchell says the problems that Mark faces are similar to those encountered by black children in middle-class black families who live in the suburbs. "He sees there are differences (between black and whites) but he knows who he is, which is a positive attitude for any child.

"I agreed that it's important that the white adopting family learn to 'think black,'" Mrs. Mitchell said. "How else can they understand what the child is going through?

"When a couple specifies that they want only a 'biracial child' (who had one black and one white parent) we try to steer them away from adopting a black child. After all, a 'biracial' child is black and you can't make him into two people.

"A biracial child is no different than any other black child. He has the same problems. If you can't accept him as black you shouldn't consider trans-racial adoption at all."

Source: Angela Terrell. "Interracial Adoption," *The Washington Post*, December 10, 1972, pp. L1, L2.

tainly lead to a serious questioning of the negative aspects of interracial marriage. The question then follows: What about the children? Larry Barnett, quoting Drake and Cayton, states:

> At least in Negro-White marriages, contrary to what might be expected, children are not a special problem. They are considered to be Negroes by both White and Negro communities. The youngsters generally make an adequate adjustment to the Negro community, and thus their problems are the same as those of the children of two Negro parents.[74]

A child born of a black-white couple will be lighter than the black partner. Joseph Washington indicates that:

> A light child has always had the best of it in the black community because of the feeling that being the light child is nearest to the majority group and therefore has advantages which do not accrue to the darker child. . . . The chances are also better for a light child to gain acceptance by his white grandparents. . . . Since the child is considered black in this society, from the child's perspective there is no more difficulty getting along with children than experienced by a black child of black-black parents. By the time the child enters college or is ready for work, the color of his skin has been a definite advantage to him which he may or may not wish to use. Thus, whether on the family, personal, or social level, the child of a black-white marriage has all the disadvantages of being black mitigated by some of the advantages of being light or white.[75]

Whether dealing with husband-wife, parent-child, or employer-employee relationships, the success of the relationship depends upon the total

---

74. Larry D. Barnett, "Research on International and Interracial Marriages," *Marriage and Family Living* 25 (February 1963), p. 107.

75. Joseph R. Washington, Jr., *Marriage in Black and White* (Boston: Beacon, 1970), p. 296.

situation and not merely upon the fact that one partner is black and the other is white. Interpersonal relationships of any sort are affected by external forces as well. Thus parents, kin, neighbors, local politicians, or society in general lend support or opposition with varying degrees of pressure and influence on the marriage, family, or job situation. Success is relative, extending far beyond the boundaries of any two persons—with skin color alike or different.

The Trend in Intermarriage

Generally, there seems to be widespread agreement that the trend in interracial marriage is upward, although the incidence is still so low that these marriages will probably have very little effect in accomplishing racial integration. As suggested by Heer, it is hard to imagine a set of conditions under which black-white marriage rates would increase so rapidly as to achieve any large intermingling within the next 100 years.[76] It is likely that interacting forces are at work. For example, if schools become integrated, if educational opportunities become available to blacks, if job opportunities increase, then it is likely that the incidence of interracial marriage will increase. And if black-white marriages increase, this is likely to play some role, albeit small, in bringing blacks nearer to equality with whites.

Summary

Homogamy and endogamy refer to the extent of intermarriage among people who share similar characteristics or are of like groups. This chapter examined the nature of intermarriage and five normative structures surrounding mate selection in the United States: age, residence, class, religion, and race. The choice of a mate along these and other structural dimensions has significant consequences for the society, the marriage, or the persons involved.

The reporting and interpreting of any type of intermarriage has its difficulties. The boundaries of race, class, or religion are rarely clear-cut and precise. Rates for individuals are often confused with rates for marriages, and rates from small groups are relatively higher than rates from large groups. Actual rates of intermarriage vary according to numerous social conditions, such as an unbalanced sex ratio, size of the group, the development of cultural similarities, psychological factors, acceptance or rejection of certain cultural values, and the institutional controls over the marriage.

Most couples in the United States are relatively homogamous in the age at which they marry. Since the turn of the century, the tendency has been for the male-female age difference at the time of marriage to narrow. Recently

---

76. Heer, op. cit., p. 273.

this difference has shown an increase. Age at marriage as well, decreased for both sexes between 1890 and the mid-1950s. Since then there has been a slight increase.

Mate selection involves a "propinquity factor." Studies seem to conclude that persons choose mates who live within a fairly limited distance of their own homes. This has been explained by a norm-segregation idea in which eligible partners who share class, religious, ethnic, or racial characteristics tend to reside close to one another. It has also been explained by an interaction-time-cost idea in which interaction patterns differ by available time and resources available to travel greater distances.

Status endogamy appears to be a desirable and a widely practiced norm with both men and women tending to marry within their own class background far more than would be expected to occur simply by chance. When marriage occurs with someone from a lower position (mesalliance) it may denote hypergamy or hypogamy. The former involves the marriage of a female into a higher position, thus the male marrying downward, and the latter involves the male marrying upward and the female downward. Hypergamy appears to be more prevalent than hypogamy. The general tendency for men to date and marry downward more frequently than upward has been termed "the mating gradient."

Religious endogamy, although less rigid than racial endogamy, remains an important factor in mate selection. Precise data on the frequency of intermarriage are difficult to determine since most research fails to differentiate between belief and practice or between groups within Protestantism and Judiasm, to say nothing of the differentiation within any particular denomination. Consensus seems to exist that the religiously devout marry endogamously in greater frequency than the religiously less devout. It is widely believed that marital-success rates are higher among those couples religiously devout as well as those couples who marry endogamously, but the data and the interpretations of the data vary considerably.

In the United States, racial endogamous norms are more rigorously enforced than any others described in this chapter. Findings suggest that black males marry white females more frequently than white males marry black females. Evidence does exist to indicate that persons who marry across racial lines differ from those in endogamous marriages in such characteristics as age, previous marital status, occupation, residence, and integration with families. They tend to be older, more frequently previously married, of a lower occupational level, urban, and less integrated with their families. The success of these marriages tends to contradict public opinion. While the trend in interracial marriage is upward, the incidence is low and the number will, in all probability, have little effect on an integration of the races.

In general, intermarriage of all types appears to be on the increase, but endogamous marriages continue to occur in frequencies far greater than one could expect to occur by chance alone. The next chapter continues to concentrate on mate selection, but a general shift occurs from a structural orientation to more of a processual and interactional orientation. What are the explanations of choosing one mate over another? What are the processes followed in moving from meeting to marriage? These and related issues follow.

Key Terms and Concepts

Discussion Questions

1. Differentiate between endogamy, homogamy, exogamy, heterogamy, and a mixed marriage.
2. What factors operate most strongly to prohibit mixed marriages?
3. What trends do you predict in regard to age at marriage, place of residence, social class, religion, and race? What factors operate to increase or decrease rates of marriages within or outside of a particular category?
4. What are the laws in your state regarding age at marriage? Do differentiations exist for male and female as to the age at marriage? Why is this? What legal changes do you think would be advisable?
5. Explain what is meant by and the reasons for residential propinquity. Can you think of situations and/or circumstances that would decrease the influence of residence on the choice of a mate? What are various consequences of marriage to the "guy next door" as opposed to someone 2,000 miles away?
6. Discuss hypergamy and hypogamy—their likelihood, their explanation, and some consequences of their occurrence.
7. Does the mating gradient occur in your school? Why or why not? Is the basic pattern likely to change in ten years?
8. Take a brief survey among your friends as to the importance of religious endogamy in dating or marriage.
9. Why would religious endogamy be stressed within groups of Protestants and Jews as well as between them?
10. To what extent is an exchange theory adequate in explaining interclass or interracial marriages? What are the factors offered in exchange? How are exceptions handled?

11. *List the objections to interracial marriage. How many of them would be supported by empirical research?*
12. *Discuss the idea: With the integrating of our schools, jobs, and neighborhoods, soon everyone will be marrying anyone.*

Further Readings

Bossard, James H. S., and **Eleanor S. Boll.** *One Marriage, Two Faiths.* New York: Ronald, 1957. Drawing from case histories gathered over a quarter of a century of teaching, the authors attempt to meet the questions and problems of people concerning interfaith marriage.

Carter, Hugh, and **Paul C. Glick.** *Marriage and Divorce: A Social and Economic Study.* Rev. ed. Cambridge, Mass.: Harvard University Press, 1976. Presents a systematic documentation of important trends and variations in demographic aspects of material behavior in the United States during recent decades.

Cavan, Ruth S., and **Jordan T. Cavan** (Guest Editors). *International Journal of Sociology of the Family* 1 (May 1971). A special issue on intermarriage in a comparative perspective covering religion, caste, and race in addition to articles on theories of intermarriage.

Christensen, Harold T., and **Kenneth E. Barber.** "Interfaith versus Intrafaith Marriage in Indiana." *Journal of Marriage and the Family* 29 (August 1967), pp. 416–469. A statewide analysis of marriages in Indiana from 1960 to 1963 using public records to determine intra- and intermarriage rates.

Gordon, Albert I. *Intermarriage.* Boston: Beacon, 1964. A study, review of literature, and interpretation of interfaith, interracial, and interethnic marriages.

Heer, David M. "The Prevalence of Black-White Marriage in the United States, 1960 and 1970." *Journal of Marriage and the Family* 36 (May 1974), pp. 246–258. An analysis of change in black-white intermarriages in the United States throughout the sixties.

Larsson, Clotye M. *Marriage across the Color Line.* Chicago: Johnson, 1965. Contains twenty-six stories or cases taken from *Ebony, Negro Digest,* or *Tan* involving interracial marital and family situations.

Lenski, Gerhard. *The Religious Factor: A Sociological Study of Religion's Impact on Politics, Economics and Family Life.* Garden City, N.Y.: Doubleday, 1961. A study completed in Detroit attempting to discover the impact of religion on secular institutions including the family.

McDowell, Sophia F. "Black-White Intermarriage in the United States." *International Journal of Sociology of the Family* 1 (May 1971), pp. 49–58. An overview of interracial marriage in the United States showing the barriers, problems in researching, prevalence, and trends of black-white marriage.

Monahan, Thomas P. "An Overview of Statistics in Interracial Marriage in the United States, with Data on Its Extent from 1963–1970." *Journal of Marriage and the*

Family 38 (May 1976), pp. 223–231. One of the more recent attempts to examine frequency and change in interracial marriage rates.

Pavalko, Ronald M., and **Norma Nager.** "Contingencies of Marriage to High-Status Men." *Social Forces* 46 (June 1968), pp. 523–531. An investigation of factors that restrict and/or enhance women's access to marriage with men of a higher status.

Washington, Joseph R., Jr. *Marriage in Black and White.* Boston: Beacon, 1970. An analysis of racial intermarriage presenting a very readable overview of the black-white marriage situation in the United States.

11

Mate-Selection Processes

11

As should have become very clear from reading the last chapter, mate selection is not simply a matter of preference or choice. Despite the increase in freedom and opportunities that young people have to select "anyone they please," many factors that are well beyond the control of the individual severely limit the number of eligible persons from whom to choose. The taboo on incest and the restrictions placed on age, sex, marital status, class, religion, race, and others in most societies narrow considerably the "field of eligibles." A sizable volume of research suggests that all societies have systems of norms and sometimes specific rules about who may marry whom. Although some of the norms and rules may be violated, they do tend to make highly predictable the likelihood that certain persons will marry.

ARRANGED MARRIAGE VERSUS FREE CHOICE OF A MATE

The processes followed in the selection of specific marital partners vary widely from one society to another. On an ideal-type continuum, these methods may vary from totally arranged marriages at one extreme to a totally free choice of mate at the other. Where marriages are arranged, the couple have nothing to say about the matter. The selection is usually, but not always, made by parents or kin. The other extreme, totally free choice, is so rare that to discuss it would be simply conjectural. The United States is, however, one of the few societies of the world that approaches this end of the continuum. In its extreme form, parents and kin are not consulted and in some instances not even informed of the impending marriage. Between these two extremes are various combinations of arranged–free choice possibilities. Parents may arrange and give their son or daughter a veto power. The son or daughter may

Freedom to Choose

Below is a discussion which David and Vera Mace had with a group of ten Indian girls. After describing to these girls how young people in the West are free to meet each other and have dates, how a boy and a girl will fall in love, and how, after a period of going steady, they become engaged and then get married, the following conversation took place.

"Wouldn't you like to be free to choose your own marriage partners, like the young people do in the West?"

"Oh no!" several voices replied in chorus. Taken aback, we searched their faces.

"Why not?"

"For one thing," said one of them, "doesn't it put the girl in a very humiliating position?"

"Humiliating? In what way?"

"Well, doesn't it mean that she has to try to look pretty, and call attention to herself, and attract a boy, to be sure she'll get married?"

"Well, perhaps so."

"And if she doesn't want to do that, or if she feels it's undignified, wouldn't that mean she mightn't get a husband?"

"Yes, that's possible."

"So a girl who is shy and doesn't push herself forward might not be able to get mar-

ried. Does that happen?"

"Sometimes it does."

"Well, surely that's humiliating. It makes getting married a sort of competition in which the girls are fighting each other for the boys. And it encourages a girl to pretend she's better than she really is. She can't relax and be herself. She has to make a good impression to get a boy, and then she has to go on making a good impression to get him to marry her."

Before we could think of an answer to this unexpected line of argument, another girl broke in.

"In our system, you see," she explained, "we girls don't have to worry at all. We know we'll get married. When we are old enough, our parents will find a suitable boy, and everything will be arranged. We don't have to go into competition with each other."

"Besides," said a third girl, "how would we be able to judge the character of a boy we met and got friendly with? We are young and inexperienced. Our parents are older and wiser, and they aren't as easily deceived as we would be. I'd far rather have my parents choose for me. It's so important that the man I marry should be the right one. I could so easily make a mistake if I had to find him for myself."

make his or her own selection and give the parents the veto power. One of the persons to be married, usually the son, may select the bride with his parents. Regardless of the method of mate selection, every society has a set of norms to prescribe the appropriate procedure.

Where mate selection is arranged, the family is generally the chief and only source of employment; marriage, rather than establishing a new family, is a means of providing for the continuity and stability of the existing family. Arranged marriage has the effect (functions) of providing the elders with control over the younger family members and control over who from the outside enters and becomes part of the family unit. In addition, it preserves family property, furthers political linkages, protects economic and status concerns,

Wanted: Suitable Match

Wanted Handsome Boy, Sikh *Hindu, employed Central Services, doctor, businessman, for beautiful, fair, slim Sikh girl 22 years, M.A., convent educated, well versed in domestic affairs. Decent marriage. Write . . . .*

Wanted Two Beautiful Brahmin *brides, M.B.B.S., for two handsome Brahmin boys, M.B.B.S., P.C., M.S. Age 26, 24-1/2 yr., height 173 cms, 170 cms, in govt. service. All are M.B.B.S. Write . . . .*

An Attractive Proposition. *Matrimonial correspondence invited from genuinely interested parties preferably Gujeratis for handsome young educated well-settled son 26 years owning own posh flat Bombay of highly educated cultured parents both of whom enjoy all Indiawide reputedly high position and status. Advertisement purely for widest possible contacts. Write with fullest details in complete confidence. . . .*

Wanted Extremely Beautiful *tall pretty Sikh girl for Sikh Arora bachelor 32 years, 180 cms. Employed foreign collaborated firm, emoluments 1900/monthly. Write . . . .*

Source: *The Times of India,* August 8, 1976.

and keeps the family intact from one generation to another. As a result, almost without exception, the chosen partners must share similar group identities. Racial, religious, and particularly economic statuses must be similar. Arranged marriages, rather than being based on criteria such as romantic love, desire for children, loneliness, or sexual desire, will likely include factors such as the size of the bride's price, the reputation of the potential spouse's kin group, levirate and sororite obligations, and traditions of prescribed marriage arrangements.[1]

An example of an arranged marriage between the groom and the bride's parents is provided by John Peters, who spent eight years in the jungles of northern Brazil. He describes mate selection among the Shirishana as follows:

> The female has no choice in the selection of her spouse. Any person who is in the *Wanima* kinship relationship to the potential bride and who is acceptable to her family could be her mate. The selection is generally made when the female is three years of age and the male 14 to 20 years of age. (In several instances the male has been an estimated 34 years.) The selection may be initiated by the mother of the male, but more commonly is done by the male himself. On occasion a male has asked the family of a pregnant woman that the unborn child become his wife, should it be a girl.[2]

---

1. For some courtship patterns associated with freedom of choice of spouse, see Paul C. Rosenblatt and Paul C. Corgby, "Courtship Patterns Associated with Freedom of Choice of Spouse," *Journal of Marriage and the Family* 34 (November 1972), pp. 689–695.

2. John Fred Peters, "Mate Selection among the Shirishana," *Practical Anthropology* 18 (January–February 1971), pp. 20–21. See also John Fred Peters, "The Effect of Western Material Goods upon the Social Structure of the Family among the Shirishana," unpublished doctorial dissertation (Kalamazoo: Western Michigan University, 1973).

Arranged marriages result in a commitment among the selected partners that is, in many instances, as binding as the marriage itself. Since the marriage exists primarily to fulfill social and economic needs, concerns such as incompatibility, love, or personal need fulfillment are not at issue. As a result, divorce is practically unknown or occurs only infrequently. Instances where marriages must be terminated frequently bring a great sense of shame and stigma to the entire family and kin group.

Evidence suggests that as traditional cultures are exposed to "western" models of modernization and as they industrialize and adopt new technology from the outside world, those segments of cultures with the greatest exposure to these influences tend to increasingly depart from an arranged marriage pattern to one of increasing "free" or "love" matched marriages.[3]

As suggested, totally free choice is practically nonexistent anywhere in the world. This would imply freedom to choose a person for marriage without regard to the wishes of anyone else, certainly not the wishes of parents or kin groups. Also, it would imply that instrumental considerations such as money, power, social rank, occupation, education, age, incest, family ties, or even sex would not be major considerations in the choice. To refer to limited free choice takes these factors into consideration and permits a choice of a mate by the spouses themselves within the limits of the permitted social groupings. Given this choice, then, love and prestige ratings become significant as do the processes of getting to know one another and of moving the relationship toward increasing commitment. Personal needs and values also become significant. Thus our attention is turned to the premarital dyad and to various theories and processes that explain mate selection.

INDIVIDUALISTIC EXPLANATIONS OF MATE SELECTION

With a decrease in kinship control over mate selection, particularly in western societies, has come a freedom that has brought about an enormously complex system. It would seem obvious that this process occurs long before the first "date." Since in the United States it is possible to have more than one mate (although legally only one at a time), for many, the mate-selection process never ends. Most psychological and other "individualistic" theories ex-

3. Greer Litton Fox, "Love Match and Arranged Marriage in a Modernizing Nation: Mate Selection in Ankara, Turkey," *Journal of Marriage and the Family* 37 (February 1975), pp. 180–193; and Nathan Hurvitz, "Courtship and Arranged Marriages among Eastern European Jews Prior to World War I as Depicted in a Briefensteller," *Journal of Marriage and the Family* 37 (May 1975), pp. 422–430.

plaining this choice are based on a wide range of experiences, along with a variety of subconscious drives and needs.

Instinctive, Innate, or Biological

One of the oldest, and perhaps most radical, explanations of mate selection suggests that what guides a man to a woman is instinct (rarely was it thought to be the other way around). Instinct is established by heredity and deals with unlearned behavior. To this author there is no such thing as a human instinct, but to many biologists and psychologists instincts are basic to human behavior. For example, Flynn sees identification and individuality as two distinct yet inseparable instinctual forces.[4] He asserts that human behavior reflects basic instincts, and, among others, that the sexual instinct is of major importance in the control of behavior and contributes to the quality of maturity.

Fletcher, too, believes that instinctual experience and behavior are discernible and are of the utmost importance in the nature of man. He states:

> The development of the sexual instinct becomes of the utmost importance in human life. The early instincts of hunger, thirst, and defecation have erotic components that became separated from these specific activities, and become sources of excitation in their own right, being subsequently involved in the further development of the sexual instinct and in the development of love-attachments.[5]

As far as is known, no one has ever discovered any instinctive, unconscious, or purely biological determinants for mate selection. Of course, the fact that they are unconscious or innate makes them difficult, if not impossible, to discover. However, to attribute explanations of selecting a mate to the unconscious adds little more to our understanding of basic processes involved in mate choice than does explaining it by spirits, fairies, or supernatural powers.

Parental Image

Closely related to the instinct theory is the psychoanalytic idea of Freud and his followers suggesting that a person tends to fall in love with and marry a person similar to his opposite-sex parent. This too is generally un-

---

4. John T. Flynn, *Identification and Individuality: Instincts Fundamental to Human Behavior* (New York: Beekman, 1970), pp. 1–2.

5. Ronald Fletcher, *Instinct in Man* (New York: International Universities Press, 1957), pp. 296–299.

conscious and centers around the *Oedipus complex*. To a male child, early in life his mother becomes his first love object. But the presence of his father prohibits him from fulfilling his incestuous desire, and, as a result, the male infant develops an antagonism toward his father for taking his love object from him. This in turn results in an unconscious desire to kill his father and marry his mother. The male infant's desire for his mother and fear of his father is so great that he develops a fear of castration or, as Freud called it, castration anxiety—a fear that his father wants to emasculate him by removing the penis and testes. But since the father is also protective, helpful, and respected by the mother, a great amount of ambivalence exists, which is resolved only by a primary type of identification with the father. The Oedipus complex is thus temporarily resolved for the male, but the repressed love for his mother remains. By adolescence, when the male is free to fall in love, he selects a love object that possesses the qualities of his mother.

The opposite, but parallel, result occurs for the female. She at an early age becomes aware of lacking a male sexual organ and develops penis envy. Feeling castrated, her feelings are transformed into the desire to possess a penis, especially the father's. These feelings for the forbidden object remain repressed thorughout childhood, but her love for her father, known as the *Electra complex*, culminates in marriage when she selects a mate with the qualities of her father. Both the Oedipus complex and the Electra complex are discussed more fully in Chapter 15.

Although it seems very reasonable to believe that young people, in selecting a mate, would be keenly aware of the qualities of their parents and the nature of their marriage, no clear evidence has been produced to support the hypothesis that the boy seeks someone like his mother and the girl seeks someone like her father. There are times when very close resemblances seem to exist between a man's wife and his mother; however, these occur hardly more frequently than they would merely by chance.

Complementary Needs

The theory of complementary needs in mate selection has been developed and enhanced by Robert F. Winch. It was his belief that although mate selection is homogamous with respect to numerous social characteristics such as age, race, religion, ethnic origin, residential propinquity, socioeconomic status, education, or previous marital status, when it comes to the psychic level and individual motivation, mate selection tends to be complementary rather than homogamous. The idea grew out of a modified and simplified version of a need-scheme theory of motivation;[6] but rather than the needs being similar, they will tend to complement one another.

---

6. H. A. Murray, et al., *Explorations in Personality* (New York: Oxford University Press, 1938).

Winch states:

> The basic hypothesis of the theory of complementary needs in mate selection is that in mate selection each individual seeks within his or her field eligibles for that person who gives the greatest promise of providing him or her with maximum need gratification. It is not assumed that this process is totally or even largely conscious.

> It follows from the general motivation theory that both the person to whom one is attracted, and the one being attracted, will be registering in behavior their own need patterns. Many second hypotheses follow from the first— that the need pattern of B, the second person or the one to whom the first is attracted, will be complementary rather than similar to the need pattern of A, the first person.[7]

To test his hypothesis of mate selection, Winch subjected to intensive study twenty-five husbands and their wives. In each of three early papers, Winch claims that the bulk of the evidence from these couples supports the hypothesis that mates tend to select each other on the basis of complementary needs.[8] Conversely, in each of these three papers, he claims that support is not available for the conflicting hypothesis that spouses tend to be motivationally similar.

Several years later, Winch published his book on mate selection.[9] For mate selection to take place on the basis of the love, that is, due to complementary needs, it is understood that both man and woman must have some choice in the matter. The theory would not be operative in settings where marriages are arranged (as by parents, marriage brokers, or others). Thus love will likely only be an important criterion under cultural conditions where 1) the choice of mates is voluntary, 2) the culture encourages premarital interaction between men and women, and 3) the marital relationship is culturally defined as a rich potential source of gratification.[10] Since love is defined in terms of needs, the general hypothesis is that where people marry for love, their needs will be complementary.

Reports by Winch and his colleagues led to a constant flow of articles attempting to retest the complementary-needs hypothesis.[11] The results were

7. Robert F. Winch, Thomas Ktsanes, and Virginia Ktsanes, "The Theory of Complementary Needs in Mate Selection: An Analytic and Descriptive Study," *American Sociological Review* 19 (June 1954), p. 242.

8. Ibid., pp. 241–249; Robert F. Winch, "The Theory of Complementary Needs in Mate Selection: A Test of One Kind of Complementariness," *American Sociological Review* 20 (February 1955), pp. 52–56; and Robert F. Winch, "The Theory of Complementary Needs in Mate Selection: Final Results on the Test of the General Hypothesis," *American Sociological Review* 20 (October 1955), pp. 552–555.

9. Robert F. Winch, *Mate Selection* (New York: Harper, 1958).

10. Ibid., p. 71.

11. Charles E. Bowerman and Barbara R. Day, "A Test of the Theory of Complementary Needs as Applied to Couples during Courtship," *American Sociological Review* 21 (October 1956), pp. 602–605; James A. Schellenberg and Lawrence S. Bee, "A Reexamination of the Theory of Complementary Needs in Mate Selection," *Marriage and Family Living*

basically negative, failing to provide empirical support to the idea that people tend to choose mates whose needs complement their own.

> One reason can be that the theoretical considerations concerning complementarity are incorrect. Another reason may be that the theory of complementarity is correct in principle but that it is much too little specified. A third reason may be that the measurement of needs is not in agreement with the theory.[12]

Any or all of these reasons may be correct. What is clear is that relatively little empirical support exists for the theory of complementary needs as originally formulated. In fact, most research attempting to explain mate selection on the basis of personality traits, whether similar, different, complementary, or some combination thereof, seems to have bogged down into a morass of conflicting results. Most findings suggest the probable futility of further pursuit of personality match.[13] In spite of the research, unsupported theories—whether instinctive, mother-images, complementary needs, or personality traits—die hard and further research on these ideas is sure to follow.

SOCIOCULTURAL EXPLANATIONS OF MATE SELECTION

Age, residential propinquity, class, religion, and race are sociocultural factors that influence mate selection. Any factor in which social norms and endogamous factors play a part in who marries whom falls into this category. Roles and values, although basic to norms of endogamy, can also be viewed as interaction processes that explain the choice of a mate.

Role Theory

Role theory, at least to this author, appears to be conceptually more justifiable as an overall explanation of marital choice than any of the previous

22 (August 1960), pp. 227–232; John A. Blazer, "Complementary Needs in Marital Happiness," *Marriage and Family Living* 25 (February 1963), pp. 89–95; Jerald S. Heiss and Michael Gordon, "Need Patterns and Mutual Satisfaction of Dating and Engaged Couples," *Journal of Marriage and the Family* 26 (August 1964), pp. 337–339; R. G. Tharp, "Psychological Patterning in Marriage," *Psychological Bulletin* 60 (March 1963), pp. 97–117; Bernard I. Murstein, "The Complementary Need Hypothesis in Newlyweds and Middle-Aged Couples," *Journal of Abnormal and Social Psychology* 63 (1961), pp. 194–197; Bernard I. Murstein, "Empirical Tests of Role, Complementary Needs in Mate Selection," *Journal of Marriage and the Family* 29 (November 1967), pp. 689–696.

12. Jan Trost, "Some Data on Mate-Selection: Complementarity," *Journal of Marriage and the Family* 29 (November 1967), p. 738.

13. See, for example, J. Richard Udry, "Personality Match and Interpersonal Perception as Predictors of Marriage," *Journal of Marriage and the Family* 29 (November 1967), pp. 722–724.

explanations or theories. All social humans or, more specifically, all marriage-able persons, have expectations regarding the behavior desired by themselves and by their prospective mates. One perception of role, as described in Chapter 2, refers to a set of social expectations appropriate to a given status: husband, wife, male, female, single, and the like. These expectations, implicit or explicit, have been internalized and serve to direct and influence personal behavior as well as the behavior desired in a prospective marriage partner. Basically, we tend to desire (internalize) the roles defined by our society, subculture, and family.

Roles and personality needs differ in a very important respect. With role, the focus of attention is on behavior and attitudes appropriate to a situation irrespective of the individual, whereas with personality needs, the focus is on behavior and attitudes that are characteristic of the person or individual irrespective of the situation. The difference is crucial. One idea focuses upon definitions, meanings, and social expectations. In regard to mate selection, individuals select one another on the basis of role consensus, role compatibility, or on the basis of courtship, marital, and family-role agreement.

Role consensus or agreement, widely and successfully used as an indicator of marital success or adjustment, has been applied relatively infrequently to mate selection. However, similar processes could be expected to be as operative prior to marriage in the selection process as after marriage. Where role discrepancies exist, marriage is less likely to occur in the first place. Would Joe, who expects a wife to care for children, cook meals, and clean the house, marry Mary, who expects to be a career woman? Or reciprocally, would Mary want to marry Joe if that is what he expects of her? It is theoretically possible that the question of why Joe expects certain things from Mary and Mary certain things of herself could well be a matter of personality needs acted out in roles. But this is speculative and at the moment appears to lack empirical support.

Disparity in role agreement can be obtained by listing series of expectations associated with various statuses and comparing the responses of the couple. The expectations of the couple on any given dimension can be used: decision making, recreation, sex, church attendance, care of children, employment, and the like. A given role expectation is less crucial than the agreement of the persons involved. For example, if Joe expects that sleeping on the Sabbath is more important than church attendance, no conflict exists if Joe's spouse holds a similar expectation or attaches little importance to the expectation. The role itself is not as important as the consensus of the partners in regard to the role. Also the role expectation itself may change as the situation changes. Maybe Joe's spouse thinks Joe should attend church on the Sabbath but does not expect him to do so when out of town or on vacation.

In brief, the couple likely to marry is the male and female who share similar role definitions and expectations. This assumes, of course, that forces such as an existing marriage, age, parents, money, schooling, or other sociocultural factors do not hinder or prevent it.

Value Theory

A value theory of mate selection suggests that interpersonal attraction is facilitated when persons share or perceive themselves as sharing similar value orientations. Values define what is good, beautiful, moral, or worthwhile. They are the criteria or conceptions used in evaluating things (including objects, ideas, acts, feelings, and events) as to their goodness, desirability, or merit. Values are not concrete goals of action but are criteria by which goals are chosen.

A value theory of mate selection suggests that when persons share similar values, this in effect validates oneself, thus promoting emotional satisfaction and enhancing the means of communication. When a value is directly attacked or is ignored under circumstances that normally call it to attention, those who hold the value are resentful. Thus it is Robert Coombs's contention that because of this emotional aspect it seems reasonable to expect that persons will seek their informal social relations with those who uncritically accept their basic values and thus provide emotional security.[14] Such compatible companions are most likely to be those who "feel" the same way about "important" things, i.e., those who possess similar values. This accounts for the tendency to marry homogamously and explains why friendships (homophily) and marriages involve people with similar social backgrounds.

Of values, Coombs says:

> 1) Values seldom or never stand as absolutes but are relative to other values and sometimes seem to be arranged on a linear scale from high to low. Thus we speak of "value systems." 2) We may refer to both positive and negative values since there are some situations which people seek and others which they avoid. 3) Values are so meaningful to those who hold them that they are accepted without question and are thought to be desirable for other persons as well as for oneself. 4) Values are not innate but rather are internalized in the human personality through the process of socialization i.e., learned through social experience. Since a great deal of learning is cultural, many values are shared by the general population. However, since all people within a culture do not have exactly the same experiences, each person forms a somewhat unique system of values. Thus we may speak of both "personal" and "cultural" values.[15]

In brief, the theory posits that 1) persons with similar backgrounds learn similar values, 2) the interaction of persons with similar values is re-

---

14. Robert H. Coombs, "A Value Theory of Mate Selection," *The Family Life Coordinator* 10 (July 1961), p. 51. Coombs's attempts to test his theory empirically can be seen in Robert H. Coombs and William F. Kenkel, "Sex Differences in Dating Aspirations and Satisfaction with Computer-selected Partners," *Journal of Marriage and the Family* 28 (February 1966), pp. 62–66; and Robert H. Coombs, "Value Consensus in Partner Satisfaction among Dating Couples," *Journal of Marriage and the Family* 28 (May 1966), pp. 166–173.

15. Ibid., p. 51.

warding, resulting in effective communication and a minimum of tension, and 3) rewards leave each person with a feeling of satisfaction with his partner and thus a desire to continue the relationship.

It is Coombs's contention that the theory of value consensus helps explain the findings that exist dealing with homogamy, endogamy, propinquity, parental image, complementary needs, or ideal-mate conception. Sharing values brings people together, both spatially and psychologically. Thus a person may want to marry a member of the same religious denomination, for example, because this might be a very important value in and of itself, or, secondly, because persons who share similar social backgrounds will likely be socialized under similar conditions and consequently develop similar value systems. The same would hold true for other explanations, such as parental image. Since it is parents who are major socializing agents for most children, it could be expected that a relationship would exist between personal values and values of parents as well as between values desired in a mate and values of parents. Thus it is perhaps not parent image that influences marital choice but rather parent-image influence via the internalization of a set of values.

Exchange Theory

Exchange theory was described briefly in Chapter 2. Also, as mentioned in several instances in the previous and current chapters, the idea of some type of exchange is basic to the mate-selection process. Whether it is an exchange of higher economic status for a preferred color status, an exchange of athletic prowess for beauty, or an exchange of sex for money, the central idea is that some type of transaction and bargaining is involved in the mate-selection process. Prior to 1940, a major contribution of Willard Waller's treatise on the family was his analysis of courtship conduct as bargaining and/or exploiting behavior. In his words: "When one marries he makes a number of different bargains. Everyone knows this and this knowledge affects the sentiment of love and the process of falling in love."[16]

Today it is doubtful that "everyone knows this." The criteria he used for exchange have since come under attack, but the fact that bargaining takes place in the mate-selection process has received further investigation and support.

Numerous articles lend support to mate selection as a process of social exchange.[17] They suggest that few people get something for nothing. And although bargaining may not always take place, some type of social exchange

16. Willard Waller, The Family: A Dynamic Interpretation (New York: Cordon, 1938), p. 239.

17. Michael M. McCall, "Courtship as Social Exchange: Some Historical Comparisons," in Bernard Farber, ed., Kinship and Family Organization (New York: John Wiley, 1966); and John N. Edwards, "Familial Behavior as Social Exchange," Journal of Marriage and the Family 31 (August 1969), pp. 518–526.

High Cost of Wives

The high cost of wives is arousing many modern Africans.

Government price controls have been suggested to curb inflated prices. Many want to abolish the auction-like atmosphere surrounding marriage arrangements.

The bride price is a hallowed tribal custom which demands a down payment from prospective husbands and additional installments in exchange for permission from the bride's family to marry.

In Nigeria the fee is usually cash, payable before the marriage. Kenya custom sometimes permits payment in goods such as livestock, lumber and bicycles. The dowry in Kenya can be the equivalent of five years of the groom's income.

A Nigerian schoolteacher commented:

"Even when the price is reasonable it takes away the money a man needs to set up a home, unless of course he is just adding a new wife to an old household."

Africa remains a masculine stronghold. Male offspring are pampered while small girls are set toiling in the fields or put out as petty traders as soon as they can count.

Often the only important occasion a girl's family has to make her subject to celebration is upon arrangement of a profitable marriage. Losing a daughter, they may gain a herd of goats.

Angry young men in Nairobi formed a dowry reformation movement to protest payment for brides to greedy fathers.

"Love should make the decision of matrimony—not money," says the movement's president, Melody Omegoroh.

A new civil code adopted in the Ivory Coast abolished contract marriages along with polygamy, but there are no signs it is being enforced.

Source: Kenneth L. Whiting, *Kalamazoo Gazette*, December 5, 1965.

will. The difference between bargaining and exchange is that bargaining implies a certain purposive awareness of the exchange of awards. Bargaining entails the knowledge of what one has to offer and what the other person can get, whereas under a simple exchange this awareness is not always readily apparent.

John Edwards states that the behavior of socialized persons is purposive or goal-oriented and not random. Implicitly this indicates that behavior is rewarded and intended to avoid nonrewarding situations. It also indicates that each party in a transaction will attempt to maximize gains and minimize costs. Over the long run, however, in view of the principle of reciprocity, actual exchanges tend to become equalized. If reciprocity does not exist—that is, nothing is given in return—the relationship will likely terminate.

There are perhaps few areas where social exchange appears more evident than in the research dealing with dating and mate selection. Even though most dating behavior is overtly intended for the specific purpose of marriage, transactional processes are in operation. In dating, for example, the male may consider sexual intercourse as a desired goal and highly valued reward. To achieve this reward he may have to offer in exchange flattery (my how beautiful you look tonight), commitment (you are the only one I love), goods (I thought you might enjoy these flowers), and services (let me get you a drink).

The social-exchange approach as applied to the family may be termed "interstitial."[18] Its underlying presuppositions about familial behavior are neither as basic as those embodied in the interactional framework nor as macroscopic and highly abstract as those in which the institutional approach is based. The social-exchange approach neither explains how interaction arises nor describes the larger social environment but rather seeks to explain why certain behavioral outcomes take place.

Sequential Theories

Up to this point it should be evident to the reader that, although single factors were stressed as significant in the process of mate selection, most explanations take into account factors implied in other explanations. Several writers consciously and intentionally combine or place in sequence selected single factors: role, values, needs, exchanges, and the like. Three of these ideas are considered briefly: the "filtering" idea of Alan Kerckhoff and Keith Davis,[19] the process idea of Charles Bolton,[20] and the SVR idea of Bernard Murstein.[21]

Kerckhoff and Davis introduce a longitudinal perspective during the mate-selection period. They hypothesize that 1) the degree of value consensus is positively related to progress toward a permanent union, and 2) the degree of need complementarity is positively related to progress toward a permanent union.[22]

To test these hypotheses the authors conducted a longitudinal study of college students who were engaged, pinned, or "seriously attached." The authors considered the degree of consensus in family values, the degree of need complementarity, and the movement of the couple toward a permanent union. They found that value consensus was significantly related to progress in the relationship for only the short-term couples, whereas complementarity was significant for only the long-term couples. They interpret the finding to indicate a series of "filtering factors" operating in mate selection. Early in the relationship social attributes such as religion, education, and the occupation of the father are in operation. As the relationship continues, a consensus of values becomes significant. Still later in the relationship, complementary

---

18. Ibid., p. 525.
19. Alan Kerckhoff and Keith Davis, "Value Consensus and Need Complementarity in Mate Selection," *American Sociological Review* 27 (June 1962), pp. 295–303.
20. Charles Bolton, "Mate Selection as the Development of a Relationship," *Marriage and Family Living* (August 1961), pp. 234–240.
21. Bernard I. Murstein, "Stimulus-Value-Role: A Theory of Marital Choice," *Journal of Marriage and the Family* 32 (August 1970), pp. 465–481.
22. Kerckhoff and Davis, op. cit., p. 366.

needs play an important part. They suggest that the complementary factor is seen later in the relationship due to the unrealistic idealization of the loved ones in the early states of the relationship.

Bolton sees mate selection as a development of a relationship. Rather than basing mate selection on the personal or social attributes of the specific individuals involved, mate selection is viewed from the perspective of the development process itself. Like many other explanations of mate selection, endogamous or homogamous factors are included, but unlike many other explanations, mate selection is herein viewed as a developmental process wherein the interpersonal transactions have their own course of events and one interaction tends to shape another. In Bolton's words:

> Perhaps mate selection must be studied not only in terms of variables brought into the interaction situation but also as a process in which a relationship is built up, a process in which the *transactions between individuals* in certain societal context are determinants of turning points and commitments out of which marriage emerges.[23]

This perspective parallels very closely that of the symbolic-interaction frame of reference described in Chapter 2. At that point, role was viewed in two ways: 1) as a package of behavioral expectations attached to a status, and 2) as the relationship between what we do and what others do with the roles or expectations developed in the interaction process. Mate selection is seen to occur in much the same manner as in the second view. That is, the outcome of the interaction of individuals involved is not mechanically predetermined, but rather, it is the end product of a sequence of interactions characterized by advances and retreats along the paths of available alternatives. In short, the development of love relations is problematic because the product bears the stamp of what goes on between the couple as well as what they are as individuals.[24]

A third sequential explanation of mate selection is provided by Murstein.[25] He sees mate selection as a three-stage sequence involving stimulus-value-role (SVR). These three stages refer to the chronological sequence in the development of the relationship. Social exchange theory is used within each to explain the dynamics of interaction and attraction.

SVR theory holds that in a relatively "free-choice" situation, as exists in the United States, most couples pass through three stages before deciding to marry. In the stimulus stage an individual may be drawn to another based on his perception of his own qualities that might be attractive to the other person. Because initial movement is due primarily to noninteractional cues

---

23. Bolton, op. cit., p. 235.
24. Ibid., p. 236.
25. Murstein, op. cit., pp. 465–481.

not dependent on interpersonal interaction, these are categorized as "stimulus" values.[26]

If mutual "stimulus" attraction has occurred between a man and a woman, they enter the second stage of "value comparison." This stage involves the appraisal of value compatability through verbal interaction. They may compare their attitudes toward life, politics, religion, sex, and the role of men and women in society and marriage. If, as they discuss these and other areas, they find that they have very similar value orientations, their feelings for one another are likely to develop. Bolton suggests that couples may decide to marry on the basis of stimulus attraction and verbalized value similarity. But for most persons it is important that the couple be able to function in compatible roles, but this ability is not as readily observable as are verbalized expressions of views on religion, politics, and the like. For this reason Murstein places the role stage last in his three-stage time sequence leading to marital choice.

The role stage requires the fullfillment of many tasks before the couple is ready to move into marriage. They must increasingly confide in each other and become more aware of each other's behavior. They must measure their own personal inadequacies and those of their partner since, for example, moodiness, inability to make decisions, dislike of the self, and neuroticism may be hard to bear in the marriage situation. Finally, they must attain sexual compatibility whether by achieving a good sexual relationship in practice or by agreement as to the degree of sexuality that will be expressed during the "role" stage prior to marriage.[27]

Murstein's own data provide considerable support for his theory. In time, replication studies will likely be made and alternative models will be offered to further explain mate selection.

PROCESSES OF STATUS CHANGE: SINGLE TO MARRIED

The mate-selection process is the manner in which an individual changes status from single to married. All human societies have some socially approved and structured procedure to follow in getting married. They vary from one society to another and, particularly in industrialized societies, include a wide range of variance within a society. A mate-selection process that involves the individuals themselves only exists where there is some degree of personal choice in marital partners. Where marriages are "arranged,"

---

26. Ibid., p. 466.
27. Ibid., p. 470.

the process generally occurs between kin groups. In any case, it is rare for mate-selection processes to exist independently of other institutions such as schools, churches, or business.

In the United States, the mate-selection process, particularly for first marriages, is highly youth centered and competitive. It involves a wide range of social relationships prior to marriage that involves an increasing degree of commitment. Writers use different terminology to describe this process but generally it involves a series of stages that may include group dating, casual random dating, going steady, being pinned, pearled, chained, or lavaliered, cohabiting, engaged to be engaged, engaged, or some other type of classification indicating a more binding relationship or a marriage commitment. The flexibility of the system permits this process to be followed once or many times prior to marriage, covering a time span of days to years, and including or omitting one or several of those stages.

Perhaps the mate-selection process in the United States can be compared to a male-female game, which has rules, goals, strategies, and counterstrategies.[28] In one sense, playing the game is voluntary since it is not mandatory that everyone play, but it is probably more difficult to avoid than to achieve. In elementary school (or before) parents inquire about boyfriends or girlfriends. As children mature, the pressure from parents, peers, and, usually by now, an internalized self-concept, all encourage getting involved. The goals of the game (see functions of dating in the next section) may simply involve enjoyment, affection, group approval, learning to play better, or getting a mate. Since a double standard exists, females have a different set of rules, norms, and goals than do males.

The social norm for the male in the United States implies that his basic goal in this game is to move the relationship toward sexual intimacy. Even before the first "date" or meeting, a key question is "Will she or won't she?" The extent to which direct or "rapid" approaches are used to answer the question will depend on a wide range of social and interpersonal factors: previous marriage, age, social class, income, religion, beauty, friends, and so on.

The social norm for the female in the United States implies that her basic goal in this game is to move the relationship toward commitment. Even before the first date, key questions might be "Will he ask me out again?" or "Is he a potential husband?" To get the commitment, the female has the responsibility to regulate the progression of the intimacy goal of the male. To get intimacy (sex is a more accurate term at this point), the male must convince the female that she is not like all other girls but is different, unique, and special.

These two norms work reciprocally. Progress toward one calls for prog-

---

28. The idea is an expansion of Waller and Hills' "courtship bargains" and "courtship barter." See Willard Waller (revised by Reuben Hill), *The Family: A Dynamic Interpretation* (New York: Holt, Rinehart and Winston, 1951), pp. 160–164.

ress toward the other. They work together. As commitment increases, intimacy increases and vice versa. Most communication in this game is likely to be in the form of nonverbal cues, signs, gestures, and other symbolic movements. But were the communication verbal, the conversation might go something like this:

He: Say, how about it?
She: How about what?
He: Oh, moving a bit closer.
She: Why?
He: I enjoy being near you.
She: Is that better?
He: Mind if I kiss you?
She: Why I hardly know you.
He: I knew you were the girl for me the moment I first saw you.
She: I suppose one kiss would be O.K.
He: Goodness, no one ever kissed me like that before.
She: You're so kind.
He: And your voice is like music to my ears.
She: Are there other girls?
He: No longer, you are the only one for me.
She: You mean, really, it's just the two of us?
He: It's just us. How I long to touch you.
She: But I shouldn't.
He: But I love you.
She: Well in that case.
He: Shouldn't we talk over our wedding plans with your parents?
She: Oh, how I need you. Please do. Take all of me, etc., etc., etc.

Although sexual or commitment progression is rarely this rapid, a process somewhat parallel to that seems to take place.[29] Suppose the rules are not followed—the male makes no moves toward intimacy or the female makes no moves to halt the intimacy or get a commitment. The female, after one date, may say to herself or others, "What a nice guy, he really is a gentleman," or the like. Suppose after two, four, or eight dates, he still makes *no* moves toward intimacy. Now the female is likely to ask questions such as "What's wrong with him?" or "What's wrong with me?" Suppose the female makes no moves to stop or slow down the intimacy moves of the male, or, as is occurring

29. Numerous sources in the U.S. as well as Australia tend to support this idea. See, for example, John K. Collins, Judith R. Kennedy, and Ronald D. Francis, "Insights into a Dating Partner's Expectations of How Behavior Should Ensue during the Courtship Process," *Journal of Marriage and the Family* 38 (May 1976), pp. 373–378; and John K. Collins, "Adolescent Dating Intimacy: Norms and Peer Expectations," *Journal of Youth and Adolescence* 3 (1974), pp. 317–327.

with increasing frequency, she makes the intimacy moves. The game may continue to be played but it is unlikely the goal will be a marriage-oriented one—separate from a longitudinal courtship process involving various stages of progression toward marriage.

Viewed primarily from the perspective of the middle classes, dating, going steady, and getting pinned and engaged will be viewed briefly. More extensive analyses of these criteria can be found in most "functionally oriented" marriage textbooks.

Dating

One form of behavior experienced by most adolescents in the United States is dating. Of all the stages of the courtship process, dating is the one that carries the least commitment in continuing the relationship. Dating has been defined as an American invention that emerged after World War I among college students and other young adults. In most of the world where parents have an extensive involvement in the selection of marriage partners, dating is not a relevant factor to be considered. However, as shifts occur away from family control over the selection of a marriage partner, an increasing amount of emphasis is placed on establishing social structures that permit the persons themselves to interact and get to know one another. In America, dating is one of these structural patterns, although certainly not the only one established for purposes of male-female interaction.

Usually dating is stereotyped as a romantic, exciting, interesting, and valuable experience in and of itself. Although it may be problematic and filled with frustrations, the general view of it is positive and optimistic. Writers agree that dating fulfills various functions for the individual:

1. Dating may be a form of recreation. It provides entertainment for the individuals involved and is a source of immediate enjoyment.
2. Dating may be a form of socialization. It provides an opportunity for individuals of opposite sex to get to know each other, learn to adjust to each other, and to develop appropriate techniques of interaction.
3. Dating may be a means of status grading and status achievement. By dating and being seen with persons who are rated "highly desirable" by one's peer group, an individual may raise his status and prestige within his group.
4. Dating may be a form of courtship. It provides an opportunity for unmarried individuals to associate with each other for the purpose of selecting a mate whom they may eventually marry.[30]

The primary reasons for dating and the functions the date fulfills influence the dating role. In other words, it could be expected that persons who

---

30. James K. Skipper, Jr., and Gilbert Nass, "Dating Behavior: A Framework for Analysis and an Illustration," *Journal of Marriage and the Family* 28 (November 1966), pp. 412–413.

> *Louise:* I started dating when I was a senior in high school. I graduated in 1939. The pattern then was quite different than it is now. Few young people had cars. So we rode the street cars or buses or walked. It also meant our contacts were centered around the school we went to. I went to a parochial school so I only knew the kids that went to that school. And also, it was like a small town. Although we lived in Detroit, the boundaries of the parish sort of represented the town. And our families all knew each other. So we rarely went with strangers. A lot of our boy-girl parties were group things. In fact, I met my husband in a group situation. A group of us girls went out with a group of fellows. And the fellows had very little money for dates. So there were picnics or house parties, parish dances, and that kind of thing. And as far as going steady, my mother was definitely against it because she wanted me to go on to school and definitely did not want me to marry early. I had other goals. I thought it was awfully stupid to get married as soon as you got out of high school. You just never saw the world. Never got to know other people. I always wanted to move outside of that circle although it was very comfortable.
>
> *Alex:* My parents found a girl for me once. That's why I had a problem with my father. The first time I met this girl I didn't know what they were arranging. I just thought we were invited over to her house as a guest or whatever. I didn't know that they had an engagement in mind. I mean, you see I wasn't told. I have a very rebellious nature, especially when it comes to something like that. So I said, hey look, I'm not going for that. When we came home my father was very displeased about the way I acted.
>
> *Mac:* My dating really didn't start until junior high when I was sixteen years old. Then I only dated one chick and took her to the show. I more or less kissed her a few times, but I felt funny kissing her. As a matter of fact, she was in my art class and I never forget that the following Monday she was in class. I said "hi," very afraid of showing my emotions to her.

date for recreation will behave differently than those who date for socialization, status achievement, or mate selection. Clyde McDaniel tested out selected relationships between dating roles of females and reasons for dating.[31] He found that girls who date primarily for the purpose of recreation are more likely to be assertive—to take the initiative or act as aggressor in dating activities. Girls who date primarily for the purpose of anticipatory socialization are more likely to be receptive—to be responsive in most instances to male

31. Clyde O. McDaniel, Jr., "Dating Roles and Reasons for Dating," *Journal of Marriage and the Family* 31 (February 1969), pp. 97–107.

initiative. Girls who date primarily for the purposes of mate selection are more likely to be assertive-receptive—to alternate between assertiveness and receptivity. The role patterns also changed by progression in the courtship process. Girls who were randomly dating were most likely to date for recreational purposes, those who were going steady were most likely to date for purposes of mate selection, and those who were pinned or engaged were most likely to date for the purpose of anticipatory socialization.

Winch refers to dating as the "window-shopping" period—it carries no commitment to buy the merchandise on display.[32] Random dating fulfills a *dalliance* type of relationship for many couples; the relationship exists for *recreation*, play, or "something that's fun to do" with no future commitment or obligation on the part of either party. The date exists as an end in itself.

Skipper and Nass suggest that in any dating relationship the individual's primary motivations may be placed on a continuum ranging from completely expressive (dating as an end in itself) to completely instrumental (dating as a means to some larger goal).[33] The individual's emotional involvement in the dating relationship may also be placed on a continuum ranging from no emotional involvement to complete emotional involvement. The motive that an individual has for dating will determine his place on these two continuums. For example, if the primary motivation in dating is mate selection, this individual is likely to have both a strong instrumental orientation and a strong emotional involvement. If the primary motivation is either socialization or status seeking, the individual is likely to have both low instrumental orientation and low emotional involvement. However, the individual whose primary motivation in dating is recreation is likely to have a strong expressive orientation and low emotional involvement.

The authors go on to suggest that individuals dating each other will have a desire to continue their relationship if either the emotional involvement or the instrumental orientation to one another is high. Where there is a disparity between the emotional involvement and/or the instrumental orientation, the likelihood is great that conflict and distress will occur. Also if there is a disparity between these two factors, the individual with the greater emotional involvement and/or instrumental orientation will suffer the greater distress and will have the least control over the relationship.

This idea is somewhat similar to that suggested by Waller more than thirty-five years ago, in what he termed *the principle of least interest*.[34] He observed that seldom are both persons in a dating relationship equally interested in continuing the relationship. Since both parties are not equally emotionally involved, if the dating were terminated, it would be more traumatic for one than for the other. Thus, essentially, the principle of least interest

---

32. Robert F. Winch, *The Modern Family* (3rd Edition). New York: Holt, Rinehart, and Winston, Inc., 1971, p. 530.
33. Skipper and Nass, op. cit., p. 413.
34. Waller, op. cit., p. 275.

says that the person who is less interested in continuing the dating relationship is in a position to dominate, and possibly exploit, the other party.

A test of the "principle" found some support for it by sex.[35] Females exerted significantly greater effort to maintain their dating associations, whereas
males were less interested and emotionally committed to continuing their
current dating relationships. If this is true, the principle of least interest suggests that males can best dictate the nature of the relationship.

This principle may also suggest a factor involved in the continuation
or breakup of a relationship. If an imbalance or unequal interest exists, it
would suggest difficulty in continuation and further development of a relationship. Research evidence seems to support this idea. In a two-year study of
over 200 couples in the Boston area, only 23 percent broke up in which both
members reported that they were equally involved in a relationship. In contrast, 54 percent of those couples in which at least one member reported that
they were unequally involved subsequently broke up.[36]

Steady Dating, Going with Someone, Pinned, or Lavaliered

In the courtship process, it is highly typical that most adolescents make
the move from an uncommitted relationship to a premarital relationship that
involves some commitment to one another and an exclusion of others. Irrespective of the term used, whether going steady, steady dating, going with
someone, pinned, pearled, lavaliered, or any other, societies that permit the
individuals themselves to choose their spouses need some device for individuals to lessen the open competition with others and at the same time provide
anticipatory socialization for the marital role. Opportunities are needed to
focus in on the "field of eligibles," to get to know what is expected of self and
others, and to get to know someone better without a major commitment or
norm of permanence attached to the relationship. Steady dating or "going
with someone" fills the gap between recreational or dalliance dating and engagement or marriage.

The functions filled by this form of interaction are highly similar to
those described under dating. They may provide recreation, socializing experiences, status achievement, or selection of a mate. The specific patterns of
activity or meanings attached to the relationship may vary considerably from
one context to another.

On college campuses, at least in the 1960s, a series of terms (pinned,

---

35. Kenneth N. Eslinger, Alfred C. Clarke, and Russell R. Dynes, "The Principle of Least In-
    terest, Dating Behavior and Family Integration Settings," *Journal of Marriage and the
    Family* 34 (May 1972), pp. 209–272.
36. Charles T. Hill, Zick Rubin, and Letitia Anne Peplau, "Breakups before Marriage: The
    End of 103 Affairs," *Journal of Social Issues* 32 (1976), p. 153.

pearled, lavaliered, etc.) and a variation of meanings were available to categorize relationships as perhaps more serious than steady dating but with less commitment than engagement. Perhaps the best known of these arrangements was that of pinning. The custom involved a gift of the male's fraternity or dormitory pin to the coed. The pin was considered a temporary gift and was returned to the male in case the pair broke up. Pinning was one means of publicly announcing to the campus community that the couple had a commitment to one another. In many instances the commitment may have been little more serious than steady dating, whereas others may have defined it as similar to engagement.

Very little research data are available on this mate-selection structure. Perhaps the undefined nature of this type of relationship permits the male the "best of all worlds." The female may say that she is "engaged to be engaged." Her mother may say her daughter is engaged and wedding plans should be in progress. The male's friends may operate on the assumption that she is engaged but he is not, and the male himself may be convinced that he is definitely not engaged. He has made no financial investment for a ring and no social investment as a result of formal announcements, pictures in local newspapers, and the like. The female, who is practically engaged, is assured of the commitment that accompanies pinning or being lavaliered. Thus, in the courtship game that involves the exchange of intimacy and commitment, the female who has the commitment also shares the intimacy. As a result, many males may find that to be pinned or in a similar arrangement is the most ideal situation to be in, particularly if he is dating a girl whose sexual permissiveness is directly related to her love for, and marriage commitment to, the male.

Engagement

Engagement in some form has existed in almost every society in the world. Since marriage is seldom taken lightly, most societies have provided some social structure to instill an awareness in the couple and the community that the relationship is a serious one and that marriage will likely occur. In many societies engagement is considered extremely important and much more binding than it is in the western world today. Since it implies the final transition in the courtship process of changing status from single to married, and since it involves a transfer from dating availability to dating exclusiveness, various rituals, gifts, and interactions occur to implant in the minds of the couple and the public the importance of the relationship.

Engagement serves a variety of functions for both the couple and society. For the couple, it provides a clear indication that marriage is about to occur. Due to the exclusive nature of the relationship, personal and interpersonal testing can continue with less threat from competitive forces. A more thorough awareness of marital role expectations, value consensus or dissensus,

Wedding Announcements as Fillers?

Connubial Copy. *Many women's editors across the country would like to copy the L.A. Times and a few other big-city dailies that now use wedding announcements as fillers, if at all. It becomes almost an ideological issue, because these announcements, except in small communities, can only cover the children of the affluent. The usual yardstick at the L.A. Times, says one staffer, is "Yes to the daughter of the owner of the International House of Pancakes chain; No to the daughter of the owner of a single House of Pancakes franchise." But* L.A. Times *Associate Editor James Bellows is realistic about why his paper can move away from marriage items, while smaller papers cannot: "If you live in a town like Charleston, S.C., where everybody has*

lived for 100 years, you could not pull out the brides because everybody wants to read about each other."

Even the New York Times *still runs yards of connubial copy, mostly on Sunday, when the brides break up acres of retail advertising. Nevertheless, since "Family/Style" Editor Charlotte Curtis took over, the tone of 4-F page—"family, food, fashions, furnishings"—has changed drastically. She is bored with social chitchat but fascinated with sociology. Says Curtis: "To look at current phenomena —the geodesic dome, plastic furniture and the family—that's where the big revolution is happening. The basic overturning of the family is just as important as the overturning of Lyndon Johnson."*

Source: *Time Magazine*, March 20, 1972, p. 48. Reprinted by permission from TIME, The Weekly Newsmagazine; Copyright Time Inc.

and future aspirations can be examined. It provides the final opportunity prior to the legal union for the couple to understand self in relation to the partner. It is likely that many couples view an engagement as a kind of trial marriage, including total sexual intimacy, the sharing of certain financial obligations, and in some instances living together.

Engagement also provides the function of making public the plans of the couple. This can best be seen by the placement of the female's picture in community newspapers. In colonial days the announcement was accomplished by the posting of *banns*. A number of days or weeks prior to the marriage, a public notice of intent to marry would be published, posted at key locations in the community, and announced in the churches. In the smaller gemeinschaft-like communities, the word traveled quickly and the community served as a key force in the binding of the relationship. Today, in our urbanized societies, it could be questioned how significant the formal newspaper announcement is in making public the plans and applying community pressures upon the couple.

An engagement ring, like a public announcement, serves the purpose of enabling the female to publicly and continuously display her symbol of commitment. The ring, which involves a financial commitment on the part of the male (and many times on the part of the female), symbolizes the seriousness of the relationship and the intent of a forthcoming marriage. In a

Philippine Courtship Folk Beliefs

If on the day of their betrothal either the groom or the bride gets sick, it is a sign that their married life will not last long.

The bride should not fit her wedding dress or her wedding will be cancelled; or one of the party may die and the wedding not consummated.

And when a maiden weds let the older women instruct her well. And on the day of the wedding she is not to see the groom, not until at the altar. Else, the wedding might not go through or an accident might happen to either the bride or the groom. As soon as the ceremony is over let her rise ahead of the groom and lean on his shoulder. Thus, she will always be able to make him do as she wishes and not have an over-bearing husband.

If the wedding dress is torn before the wedding it is a bad omen; if it is wet, somehow, it is also bad.

During the wedding ceremony, the two candles that are lighted in front of the couple mean the length of their lives, and if the candle near the girl is brighter than that of the boy, that means that the girl will live longer than the boy.

For a bride to be sad on her wedding day means bad luck. For a bride to be late at her wedding means bad luck. For a bride to sleep soundly and awake cheerful indicates eternal happiness.

After the wedding, if the girl walks ahead of the man and groom, she will rule the husband.

Source: Francisco Demetrio y Radaza, S. J., ed., *Dictionary of Philippine Folk Beliefs and Customs* (Cagayan de Oro City: Xavier University, Book III, 1970), pp. 633, 635, 637, 639, 642, 644.

day of calling for equality between sexes, perhaps the time is near when the male will expect an engagement ring as well.

LOVE: ITS STRUCTURAL IMPORTANCE, FUNCTION, AND DEVELOPMENT

Perhaps love—basically a psychological and emotional element—like human reproduction—basically a biological phenomenon—has little place in a sociology textbook. However, love, like reproduction, can be viewed from a wider perspective by focusing upon the structural patterns by which societies control it.

William Goode notes that the printed material on love is immense.[37] He classifies it into several categories:

1. The poetic, humanistic, literary, erotic, and pornographic. By far the largest body of all literature on love use it as a sweeping experience. Writers within this category arouse our sympathy and empathy, permit readers to watch the

---

37. William J. Goode, "The Theoretical Importance of Love," *American Sociological Review* 24 (February 1959), pp. 38–40.

> *Alex:*   Back home we don't use that word "love." That's a taboo because love usually relates to sex. So when you ask if my father loves my mother I'm sure he does but he would never admit it. Here I often see this guy come home and kiss his wife. God, I never saw my father sit even three feet close to my mother in public.
>
> *Ann:*   I did not love my husband when I married him, that is true fact. At the time, I was having problems at home, and I was living with my brother. My husband asked me to marry him. And I . . . we put it off, honestly. I rejected the marriage at first for about two or three weeks and he just insisted, so one night, we just went and got married. I didn't think it would work at the time. I really didn't. But a lot of people say you cannot grow to love somebody and I grew to love him. I really did.
>
> *Mac:*   The most important thing is the money situation. Then love. We gotta watch our budget. We don't have enough money for now and this creates a hardship. We're just skimping on what's coming in the door and that's a source of conflict.

intimate lives of others, and provide how-to-do-it books in terms of exciting oneself or one's sexual partner.

2. The structural importance of love. A group of writers have presented propositions pointing to the functions of love and the conditions under which love relations occur. These propositions would include statements such as, "Love as a common prelude to and basis of marriage is rare," "Love is aim-inhibited sex," "In societies where very close attachments between parents and children prevail, a love complex is necessary in order to motivate the child to free him and his attachments to his parents," and so on.

3. Cross-cultural work of anthropologists. In general anthropologists have ignored love as a factor of importance in kinship patterns. The implicit understanding is that the nature and functions of love are confined primarily to western societies.

Since strong love attachments apparently can occur in any society, and since love is frequently a basis for and prelude to marriage, it is Goode's contention that love must be controlled or channeled in some way.[38] If the potentially disruptive effects of love were not kept in check, the stratification and lineage pattern would be weakened greatly. Since mate choices have consequences for the family and society, and since love may affect mate choice, both mate choice and love must be controlled, and since both issues are too important to be left to children, it becomes crucial that institutional patterns exist by which this control is achieved.

---

38. Ibid., p. 42.

Professor Thinks We Discharge Auras

New London, Conn.—(AP)—The faith healer's aura may be more than a phenomenon perceived—only by those who believe in his power, says a Connecticut College psychology professor.

Dr. Bernard Murstein says he has found physical proof that humans emit auras related to their feelings.

Through an electrophotographic process, Dr. Murstein and a graduate student, Serge Hadjolian, have found that people who like one another emit strong auras and those disliking one another have no emissions.

"Here is a measure that seems to go beyond any verbal disguises," Dr. Murstein said in an interview."

"It might be of help in determining how much people are attracted to one another. Sometimes people are confused whether or not they really like someone."

In experiments, Dr. Murstein has paired subjects place their fingertips on a photo-graphic plate and passes an electrical current through the plate.

If the subjects liked one another as determined in a preexperimental questionnaire, bright and wide rings appeared around the fingerprint imprint on the developed picture, Dr. Murstein said. In cases where the subjects disliked one another the converse was true, he said.

"It must be some kind of feeling of relaxation or comfort that might be analogous to a cat purring," the professor said. "The body knows when it feels comfortable and reacts accordingly."

He added that he believed the auras were formed by the body's response to the buzzing electrical discharge from the photographic plate but he had no proof of this.

"Nobody knows what in particular causes it. We do know it has something to do with degree of attraction," he said."

Source: *The Detroit Free Press*, July 12, 1975, p. 13-B. Reprinted by permission of The Associated Press.

The Social Control of Love

The social control of love can occur in several ways.[39] First, child marriage can eliminate any opportunity to interact intimately as an adolescent with other children or to have any resources with which to oppose the marriage. Second, kinship rules can define rather closely a class of eligible future spouses. Here the major decision, made by elders, is when the marriage is to occur and what classes and groups are eligible as future spouses. Third, by socially and physically isolating young people from potential mates, whether eligible or ineligible as spouses, love can be controlled. If young people see one another infrequently or not at all, love is not likely to develop. Fourth, close supervision by duennas or close relatives, but not actual social segregation, can serve. In this instance love is permitted before marriage, but only between eligibles. Except for marital love, there is no encouragement for love to appear at all, and in the courtship process close supervision sustains female chastity

---

39. Ibid., pp. 43–45.

and prohibits love as play from developing. And fifth, love can be controlled by permitting love relationships, with the only source of social control being the individual's own teen-age companions, peers, or the parents of both the boy and the girl. Parents seek to control love relationships by influencing the informal contacts of their children: moving to appropriate neighborhoods and schools, giving parties and helping to make out invitation lists, and making their children aware that certain individuals have ineligibility traits (race, religion, manners, taste, clothing, and so on).

Goode's conclusion is that:

> Love is a universal psychological potential, which is controlled by a range of five structural patterns, all of which are attempts to see to it that youngsters do not make entirely free choices of their future spouses. Only if kin lines are unimportant, and this condition is found in society as a whole, will entirely free choice be permitted. Some structural arrangements seek to prevent entirely the outbreak of love, while others harness it. Since the kin lines of the upper strata are of greater social importance to them than those of the lower strata are to the lower strata members, the former exercises a more effective control over this choice. Even where there is almost a formally free choice of mate, this choice is guided by peer group and parents toward a mate who will be acceptable to the kin and friend grouping. The theoretical importance of love is thus to be seen in the socio-structural patterns which are developed to keep it from disrupting existing social arrangements.[40]

Within this framework established by Goode, it is clear that several factors operate to control love in the United States, with primary emphasis upon the fifth pattern. Most people in our society believe that love is important for marriage. Less recognition is given to marriage for reasons other than love: money, escape from home life, social prestige, or similar reasons. Even if one does not marry for love, it become essential for most young people to convince themselves they are "in love."

It is Greenfield's contention that love in American society fulfills the function of motivating individuals to do irrationally that which they would not do if the choice was truly a rational one—namely, marry.[41] Since nearly everything from food to sex can be purchased in the market place, many individuals would not marry if the choice was truly a rational one; getting married may be considered an irrational choice of action.[42] Some inducement is necessary to get people to behave emotionally and irrationally and to desire and occupy the positions of husband and wife. It is at this point that the romantic-love complex plays its important part. The function of romantic

---

40. Ibid., p. 47.
41. Sidney M. Greenfield, "Love and Marriage in Modern America: A Functional Analysis," *Sociological Quarterly* 6 (Autumn 1965), pp. 361–377.
42. This idea is seriously questioned by Martha Baum, "Love, Marriage and the Division of Labor," *Sociological Inquiry* 41 (Winter 1971), pp. 107–117.

love in American society appears to be to motivate individuals to occupy the positions within the nuclear family that are essential to maintain the existing arrangements for distributing and consuming services and to keep the social system in working order.

For purposes of this section, no attempts will be made to differentiate or define the wide variety of terms used to describe love: romantic love, infatuation, conjugal love, Eros, agape, and others. Also, no differentiation will be made between "true" or "real" love and the other forms of love often viewed as inferior in quality to the "true" type. Whatever love is, it never exists independently of social and cultural norms and controls. It is a phenomenon that is learned in interaction with others and is greatly influenced by the social and cultural situation.

The Development of the Love Relationship

One sociologist attempted to describe the interpersonal processes involved in the development of the heterosexual love relationship.[43] At the beginning of a relationship, two people become aware of the presence or absence of a feeling of *rapport*. If they share certain social and cultural backgrounds, they may feel quite at ease and be willing to talk about themselves and learn more about each other. If cultural backgrounds differ in some particular way, although they may still be compatible, they may feel quite ill at ease and watch the clock until the evening ends. If the feeling of rapport is not present as a first step, the development of a heterosexual relationship stops.

Concomitant with rapport is a second process that Ira Reiss labels *self-revelation*.[44] When one feels at ease in a social relationship, he is more likely to reveal intimate aspects of his existence. He is, under such conditions, more likely to tell of his hopes, desires, fears, and ambitions, and is more likely to engage in sexual activities. Again, the social and cultural background of each person will help determine whether petting is acceptable, whether talking about one's personal ambitions is proper, or whether discussing religion is right.

Following self-revelation, a third process occurs, the *development of mutual dependencies* or, more technically put, of interdependent habit systems.[45] One becomes dependent on the other person to fulfill one's own habits, e.g., one needs the other person to tell one's ideas or feelings to, to joke with, or to fulfill one's sexual desires. When these expectations are not fulfilled, loneliness and frustration are experienced. Again, the types of habits

---

43. Ira L. Reiss, "Toward a Sociology of the Heterosexual Love Relationship," *Marriage and Family Living* 22 (May 1960), pp. 139–145.
44. Ibid., p. 142.
45. Ibid., p. 142.

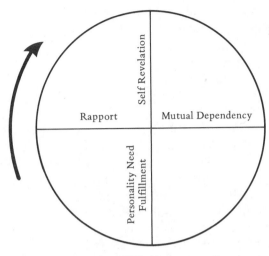

FIGURE 11–1.

Graphic Presentation of the Wheel Theory of the Development of Love. From Ira L. Reiss, "Toward a Sociology of the Heterosexual Love Relationship," *Marriage and Family Living* 22 (May 1960).

that are experienced are culturally determined in large measure.

Finally, a fourth process is involved, that of *personality need fulfillment*.[46] These needs, as with mutual dependencies, self-revelation, and rapport, will vary with cultural background.

These four processes are in a sense really one and have been labeled by Reiss as the "wheel theory."[47] When one feels rapport, he reveals himself and becomes dependent, thereby fulfilling his personality needs. The circularity is seen in that the needs being fulfilled were the original reason for feeling rapport. The "wheel" can turn in a negative direction and "unwind," lessening self-revelation, rapport, and the like, or it can turn in a positive direction and increase the intensity of each process.[48] (See Figure 11–1.)

It is Reiss's contention that romantic love, sexual love, rational love, or other varieties can be explained theoretically as developing via the wheel processes of rapport, self-revelation, mutual dependency, and personality need fulfillment. He believes that these four processes occur universally in any primary relationship: friendship, parent-child, male-female, and so forth. They do not depend on the truth or falsity of the complementary-need or homogamy conception of mate selection but are compatible with these and other major theoretical ideas and research findings.

46. Ibid., p. 143.
47. Ibid., p. 143.
48. Borland suggests the wheel be viewed as a "clockspring" which winds and unwinds, illustrates depth or degrees of a relationship, represents varying time and speed, and can even be overwound. Delores M. Borland, "An Alternative Model of the Wheel Theory," *The Family Coordinator* 24 (July 1975), pp. 289–292.

UNMARRIED COHABITATION
OR LIVING TOGETHER

Is it possible that much of what is written in this chapter is a picture of mate selection processes prior to 1970? Is it possible that mate selection in the late 1970s and after is not marriage oriented, is not oriented toward a single partner, and does not stress permanence? Is it possible that a decrease in a double sexual standard will totally eliminate the male-female sex game described earlier? Is it possible that dating, pinning, and engagement are premarital structural arrangements only significant as historical phenomena? Is it possible that love is no longer structurally or developmentally important? Or are we simply witnessing major modifications in, and additional alternatives to, the explanations of mate-selection processes provided?

An alternative to marriage and an increasingly prevalent nonmarital arrangement is seen in unmarried or premarital cohabitation, living together, "shacking up," live-ins, unmalias, or consensual unions. These involve a situation where a man and a woman who are not married to each other, neither by ceremony nor by common law, occupy the same dwelling. The arrangement—particularly prevalent on college campuses—may or may not be marriage oriented, may be the beginning of a long-range life-style or be for short-term convenience, may or may not involve intimate unrestricted sexual union, and may or may not include the knowledge of parents.

Prevalence of Unmarried
Cohabitation

How prevalent is living together? Paul C. Glick[49] using census data reports a spectacular eight-fold increase in the 1960s in the number of household heads who were reported as living apart from relatives while sharing their living quarters with an unrelated adult "partner" (roommate or friend) of the opposite sex. Between 1970 and 1976, this number approximately doubled. As a result, in 1976, 1.3 million persons lived in the 660,000 two-person households in which the household head shared the living quarters with an unrelated adult of the opposite sex.[50] To maintain a proper perspective, it should be noted that among all primary individuals in 1976, 89 percent

---

49. Paul C. Glick, "A Demographer Looks at American Families," *Journal of Marriage and the Family* 37 (February 1975), p. 24.

50. U.S. Bureau of the Census, *Current Population Reports*, Series P-20, No. 306, "Marital Status and Living Arrangements: March, 1976" (Washington, D.C.: U.S. Government Printing Office, 1977), Table F, p. 5.

lived alone, 9 percent lived in two-person households and the rest lived in three or more person households. Thus, unrelated adults of the opposite sex sharing living quarters as a household represent about 4 percent of all primary individuals and about 1 percent of all household heads. The percentage of unrelated adults of the opposite sex living together increases with age, which led Glick to suggest that older couples likely include a substantial proportion of widowed persons living in this manner to avoid losing survivor benefits through remarriage.[51]

In a nationwide sample of 2,510 young men, Richard Clayton and Harwin Voss[52] reported that 18 percent of the respondents had lived with a woman for six months or more outside the bonds of matrimony, but at the time of the interviews only 5 percent were cohabiting. The variable that yielded the greatest difference in cohabitation was ethnicity. Twenty-nine percent of the blacks had cohabited in comparison with 16 percent of the whites.

Unmarried cohabitation is not unique to the United States. Jan Trost,[53] while focusing primarily on Sweden, refers to the practice in Mexico, Denmark, Finland, Norway, and Iceland. In Sweden as of 1975, 53 percent of cohabiting couples under age twenty-five were unmarried (20 percent for age twenty-five to thirty-four and 3 percent for those over age fifty-five).

Clearly, as shown, not all unmarried heterosexual "living-together" arrangements occur in the U.S., among young people and/or college students; however, most of the research concentrates on these groups. As could be expected, the extent of cohabitation varies considerably from campus to campus. Charles Cole reviewed ten cohabitation surveys to assess the prevalence on American college campuses.[54] The percentages ranged from lows of 9 and 12 percent at a small liberal arts college and a large state university both in the Midwest to highs of 31, 33, and 36 percent at two universities in the Northeast and one in the Southwest. The male/female ratio for cohabitation was consistently higher for males.

A study of over 1,000 students at Pennsylvania State University[55] reported nearly identical cohabiting experiences for men and women (33.4 percent of the men, 32.3 percent of the women). As expected, the percentages increased with class standing (freshmen, 19 percent; sophomores, 25 percent;

51. Glick, op. cit., p. 24.

52. Richard R. Clayton and Harwin L. Voss, "Shacking Up: Cohabitation in the 1970s," *Journal of Marriage and the Family* 39 (May 1977), pp. 273–283.

53. Jan Trost, "Married and Unmarried Cohabitation: The Case of Sweden, with Some Comparisons," *Journal of Marriage and the Family* 37 (August 1975), pp. 677–682.

54. Charles Lee Cole, "Cohabitation in Social Context," in Roger W. Libby and Robert N. Whitehurst, *Marriage and Alternatives: Exploring Intimate Relationships* (Glenview, Ill.: Scott, Foresman, 1977), Table 2, p. 68.

55. Dan J. Peterman, Carl A. Ridley and Scott M. Anderson, "A Comparison of Cohabiting and Noncohabiting College Students," *Journal of Marriage and the Family* 36 (May 1974), p. 347.

juniors, 34 percent; seniors, 47 percent. Lura Henze and John Hudson[56] found that 29 percent of the males and 18 percent of the females at Arizona State University had cohabitated. Of those who had not, 71 percent of the males and 43 percent of the females responded Yes to the question "Would you want to cohabit?" This would indicate the likelihood of greatly increased cohabitation percentages, given the opportunity and the appropriate person.

Characteristics of Unmarried Cohabitors

A master's thesis by Sheryl Lautenschlager described selected characteristics of college students who had at some time lived in a consensual union.[57] She found that although the majority expressed a preference for an organized religious faith, the attendance factor was low. The majority preferred the

---

56. Lura F. Henze and John W. Hudson, "Personal and Family Characteristics of Cohabiting and Noncohabiting College Students," *Journal of Marriage and the Family* 36 (November 1974), p. 723.
57. Sheryl Y. Lautenschlager, "A Descriptive Study of Consensual Union among College Students," unpublished M.S. thesis, California State University, Northridge, California, 1972.

For God and Country: Marry

Washington—President Carter last week said in a visit to one of his many bureaucracies: "Those of you who are living in sin, I hope you will get married."

It was a stunner to many unmarried people in Washington who didn't realize that because they were sharing the same apartment their president thought they were living in sin.

Broombaker was the first to call. "I don't know what to do. Nora says we have to get married."

"That's ridiculous," I said. "How long have you been living together?"

"Three years," he replied.

"Isn't she sort of pushing things?" I asked.

"That's what I told her. I said we had a good thing going and asked her why she wanted to louse it up."

"What did she say?"

"She said she didn't care one way or the other. But Carter wanted it that way."

"I didn't even know she voted for Carter."

"She didn't. She voted for Ford, but she said now that Carter is her president, she feels she owes him her full loyalty."

"Did you tell her that the president just suggested people stop living in sin? He didn't make it an executive order."

"I went further than that. I told her he made the suggestion to the Housing and Urban Development Department and he was only talking to them. Nora's in Rural Electrification and they're not covered by HUD."

"What did she say to that?"

"She said the president meant ALL government employes should get married."

"It didn't strike me that way," I said. "The way I saw it on TV, the president had probably been briefed beforehand that the HUD employes were a pretty wild crowd, and he just decided that he didn't want people involved with low-cost housing to be messing around."

"That's exactly what I told Nora," Broombaker said. "I told her that if the president was worried about sin in the Rural Electrification Administration he would have made a special trip over there to tell them."

"She didn't buy it?"

"Nope. She said it was our patriotic duty to get married. Every American should ask not what her country can do for her but what she can do for her country. She said that if the president of the United States wants us to get hitched he must have a reason."

"What reason?" I yelled. "Did you ask her that?"

"Sure I did. I pointed out that three presidents of this country had led us blindly into a war in Vietnam. Why should we believe a president who wants to lead us blindly into marriage?"

"Good for you! That must have really got to her."

"It did," Broombaker said. "She told me to get out of the apartment."

"For how long?"

"For good. She said it's impossible now for her to have the same relationship with me under Carter that she did under Nixon and Ford."

"You poor guy. Where are you going to go?"

"Well, I called up this girl I met at a party about a year ago. She said to give her a jingle if I ever got tired of Nora."

"That was good thinking," I said.

"She asked me what I had on my mind, and I told her I thought we might go out a couple of times and if it worked out we could keep house together."

"And?"

"She said that would be a sin."

"The president's only been here a month," I said, "and he's wrecked this town."

"I can't figure him out," Broombaker said. "He pardons draft dodgers and at the same time he insists that single people who are serving their country have to be punished."

Source: Art Buchwald, *Detroit Free Press*, February 24, 1977, p. 19-A. Reprinted by permission of Art Buchwald.

Democratic party, viewed themselves as liberal in their political views, accepted legal abortion, and approved of the standard that men and women should be free to decide for themselves about premarital and extramarital intercourse. Over two-thirds of the respondents said their parents were aware of their consensual union and very few hid their relationship from their friends. The vast majority claimed to love their partner and have the love returned. Most of the females neither feared nor wanted a pregnancy. The females were more marriage oriented than the males, with education the obstacle most often preventing legal marriage. Compared to a nonconsensual union group, those living in a consensual union expressed less guilt about their sexual experiences, were less likely to view their parents' marriages as very happy, considered their parents restrictive or very strict, and had more difficulty communicating with family members.

> **Louise:** *My third child who is studying medicine had spent a summer living with his wife before he married her. They traveled all over. This created a very serious rift between us and resulted in a very serious division in our family. I definitely did not approve. It caused a lot of strain, a lot of anxiety. The saving thing I guess was that he was far away from home.*
>
> *From where I come from sex belongs in marriage. It's a commitment that you make for life and I do not endorse trial marriages which is I suppose what you would call this just trying it out. I view it as one or the other using the other person with the option to walk off if it doesn't work out.*
>
> **Mac:** *I've been living with my mate for two years; we've been going together for three. I pushed for marriage but she doesn't want to. So, we both want to be darned sure that we're ready for marriage, specifically the legal part. It costs five dollars to get married. To get divorced it costs three or four hundred. I've learned from experience, in the immediate family and friends, that you should know your partner to the maximum, and the only way you're going to do that is by living day to day with them.*
>
> **Alex:** *Live with? In my country you couldn't even bring girls home. You were ashamed. Your father would hang you by your ears. Anyway, I think its immoral. That's my reason. If that's what they want in America, that's alright, but I wouldn't.*

Macklin[58] found that most cohabiting relationships involved a gradual drifting into staying together, first overnight or a weekend, later on a more regular basis. They did so out of rejection of the superficial "dating game," the loneliness of a large university, and the emotional satisfaction that comes from having someone to sleep with who cares about you. Marriage, to many of these students, appeared to have negative connotations, limiting freedom and growth as well as assuming traditional husband-wife roles.

Two studies previously mentioned compared cohabiting and noncohabiting college students. Peterman et. al.[59] found little difference in the two groups on family and community background or on their levels of intellec-

---

58. Eleanor D. Macklin, "Heterosexual Cohabitation among Unmarried College Students," *The Family Coordinator* 21 (October 1972), pp. 463–472. Macklin is one of the leading researchers and coordinators of work underway in cohabitation. As of April 1976, she had issued five lengthy newsletters reporting on current writing and work in progress. The last issue included a bibliography of approximately 150 theses, papers presented, and publications on nonmarital cohabitation.

59. Peterman et. al., op. cit., pp. 349–350.

tual and emotional functioning. The likelihood of cohabitation was greatly increased if the students lived off-campus. Henze and Hudson[60] found that major differences between the two groups were in church attendance, life style, and drug use. Cohabiters tended to be nonchurchgoers, to label themselves as liberals, and to be users of both marijuana and hard drugs. Like the other study, family characteristics did not distinguish cohabiters from noncohabiters.

Two other studies compared unmarried cohabiting with legally married couples. The first found major differences in territoriality and privacy.[61] The unmarried were far more likely to have an area for being alone. Whereas marriage norms oppose physical separateness and promote togetherness, unmarried couples were likely to maintain rights to another residence as well as to have places within the residence for being alone. Based on this privacy factor, the authors conclude that unmarried cohabitation is not an accurate portent of what a married relationship would be like.

The second, in a matched sample of fifty cohabiting and fifty married couples, revealed that cohabiting couples were less church oriented, more antiestablishment, more pessimistic, more fearful of close ties, more withdrawn, more likely to experience internal conflicts, more restless, and more impulsive. In general, cohabitors tended to be more discouraged and less well adjusted than marrieds.[62]

Consequences of Unmarried Cohabitation

Is unmarried cohabitation a cure-all for traditional sex or gender role inequality, for successful long-term relationships, for lowering divorce or marriage rates, and the like? Apparently not exactly. Rebecca Stafford et. al.[63] studied the division of labor in household tasks using matched samples of married and cohabitating college men and women. Both cohabiting groups of the "now" generation are still dividing housework along traditional lines with the women bearing the brunt of the labor. Compared to their parental generation, the young men are sharing the dishes and laundry more and the young

60. Henze and Hudson, op. cit., pp. 723–724.

61. Paul C. Rosenblatt and Linda G. Budd, "Territoriality and Privacy in Married and Unmarried Cohabiting Couples," *The Journal of Social Psychology* 97 (October 1975), pp. 67–76.

62. James W. Crooke, James F. Keller, and Edward Markowski, "A Comparison of Sociocultural Characteristics and Personality Traits of Cohabiting and Legally Married," *International Journal of Sociology of the Family* 6 (Spring 1976), pp. 87–98.

63. Rebecca Stafford, Elaine Barkman, and Pamela Dibona, "The Division of Labor among Cohabiting and Married Couples," *Journal of Marriage and the Family* 39 (February 1977), pp. 43–57.

Sadie Hawkins Day Revisited

Popular myth has it that women are always trying to trap men into marriage, while men are interested in anything but tying the knot—like Daisy Mae chasing Li'l Abner on Sadie Hawkins Day. And it appears that this myth does have some basis in fact. According to the findings of a study by Keith Davis of Rutgers University, Milton Lipetz of the University of Colorado and Judith Lynees of Purdue University (Fort Wayne), unmarried women living with men are much more interested in marriage than their male counterparts (Journal of Marriage and the Family, May 1972).

The study involved 49 unmarried couples recruited from the Boulder, Colorado, community. Of these, 18 were living together and 31 were dating steadily. The couples in both groups had gone together for about eight or nine months and had similar middle-class backgrounds. Yet there were significant differences in the orientations of the two groups toward marriage.

The going-together couples had more traditional orientations toward each other, with both partners being equally committed to marriage. And the living-together females were only slightly less committed to marriage. The living-together males, however, showed very little interest in marriage—only three of the 18 voiced any marital commitment. While the women in this group seem to want the security of marriage, the men view living together as an alternative life style.

As would be expected, living-together men were significantly more satisfied with their sexual arrangements than going-together men. Yet all groups reported happiness with the arrangement to be at a high level. Therefore, whether or not the sexual arrangements were satisfactory, they were not an important aspect of the positiveness of the relationships. Instead, happiness was related to need, respect, involvement and trust, and here there were important differences between the two groups.

Trust and involvement were generally high in all cases. But the living-together men reported less need and respect for their partners than did any other group, important variables in terms of marriage. Indeed, the findings indicate that to a large extent, the living-together couples did not reciprocate these important feelings while the going-together couples did.

"In view of the fact that more living-together women were thinking seriously about marriage" than living-together men, the authors feel that "the low degree of respect and need reported for these women may indicate an awareness of this motivation and a rejection of it by the males." So take heed, Daisy Mae: the best way to lose a man is to let him know he's being chased.

Source: "Roundup of Current Research," Trans-Action 10 (January–February 1972), pp. 15, 17. Reprinted by permission.

women are sharing the lawn mowing and home repairs more. But women in both the married and unmarried groups still take most of the responsibility for and perform most of the household tasks. Apparently unmarried cohabitation is not a cure for gender inequality.

Another study of living together considered two major questions: the degree to which a sample of living-together couples could be considered to contribute to a predicted decline in marriage rates by adopting the arrangement as a long-term life-style; and 2) the degree to which a basis for a successful long-term relationship had been established by the living-together couples.[64]

These questions were examined by comparing living-together, unmarried couples with going-together (conventional, seriously dating) couples. It was found that the going-together couples held traditional orientations toward each other with a commitment to marriage forming a strong part of this orientation. The living-together couples appeared to come to their arrangement with varied expectations. The living-together women seemed to desire security through eventual marriage, whereas the men indicated that the arrangement was more likely to be an alternative to marriage.[65] Had the women come to the situation with motivations similar to those of the men, this living-together group would be expected to have very low marriage rates. If the females' desires to be married are fulfilled, the rates could be unchanged or only slightly depressed. Thus the answer to the first question dealing with living together as a factor in declining marriage rates appears to be "yes" for men and "no" for women.

The second question was to what degree the living-together couples established a basis for a successful long-term relationship. It was found that, to a very striking degree, living-together couples did not reciprocate the kinds of feelings (need, respect, happiness, involvement, or commitment to marriage) that one would expect to be the basis of a good heterosexual relationship.[66] The authors indicate that whether such a lack of reciprocity is typical of such relationships, or whether it is merely typical of those who volunteered for the research, cannot be conclusively answered from their data. A further analysis of their data can be seen in the insert.

While unmarried cohabitation may not be a cure-all for heterosexual or marital problems, it would appear that it has definite functional value. Among other factors, for many couples it provides a financially practical condition, a warm homelike atmosphere, more privacy than a dormitory or co-operative housing arrangement, easy access to a sexual partner, an intimate interpersonal relationship, a nonlegal, nonpermanent, nonbinding union, and a form of trial marriage. At this point it appears to be an extension of the courtship process and an institutionalized alternative life-style.

Summary

The processes followed in mate selection vary widely from one society to another, ranging from totally arranged marriages to limited "freedom of choice." The difference is centered in who is making the choice.

64. Judith L. Lyness, Milton E. Lipetz, and Keith E. Davis, "Living Together: An Alternative to Marriage," *Journal of Marriage and the Family* 34 (May 1972), pp. 305–311.
65. Ibid., p. 305.
66. Ibid., p. 310.

A range of explanations exists as to who selects whom and why. At one extreme are individualistic explanations with the answers rooted in instincts, needs, drives, parental-images and complementary needs. In contrast are sociocultural explanations with the answers rooted in norms, roles, values, and social exchanges.

Sociocultural explanations operate at a more conscious level, are more readily testable, and have greater research support than individualistic explanations. These, too, are not fully adequate to explain mate selection, but they do appear to be more fruitful. One sociocultural theory involves roles—the internalized, learned, social expectations as to what attitudes and behavior are appropriate or inappropriate in the selection of a mate. In brief, the couple likely to marry is the male and female who share similar role definitions and expectations.

Closely related to role theory is the idea that interpersonal attraction is facilitated when persons share or perceive themselves as sharing similar value orientations. This sharing of values, in effect, validates one's self and thus promotes emotional satisfaction and enhances the means of communication.

Exchange theorists view mate selection as a bargaining or social-exchange process. While not explaining how interaction arises, the theory does explain the behavioral outcomes. The mate-selection choice is based on the selection of persons who share equivalent resources, each having something to offer that is desired by the other.

Some writers see mate selection as resulting from several of these processes operating simultaneously or sequentially. One explanation involves a series of "filtering factors." Another sequential explanation sees mate selection as a developmental process of interactions between individuals, the outcome of which is not mechanically predetermined but is the end product of a sequence of events along the paths of available alternatives. A third sequential explanation involves a three-stage chronological sequence involving stimulus, value, and role (SVR). Noninteractional cues get the couple together (stimulus), followed by an appraisal of compatability through verbal interaction (value), and resulting in confiding, measuring, and testing one another's adequacies or inadequacies (role).

The mate-selection process is the manner in which an individual changes his status from single to married. The process involves all sorts of strategies and counterstrategies, rules and roles applicable to male-female interaction. Generally, it involves a series of types of dating that lead to increasing degrees of commitment.

Love, as a factor in mate choice, must be controlled or channeled. This is done throughout the world by child marriage, by kinship rules that define rather closely a class of eligible future spouses, by socially isolating young people from potential mates, by close supervision by duennas or close relatives, or by permitting love relationships with the source of control internalized in the person and supported by peers, parents, or others. The development of the love relationship has been described as circular, involving first the establishment of rapport, followed by self-revelation, the development of mutual dependencies, and finally personality need fulfillment.

Final consideration in the chapter was given to unmarried cohabitation, living together, or consensual unions. Descriptive data were provided to indicate prevalence, selected characteristics of the persons involved, and selected consequences. Unmarried cohabitation may serve as an extension of the courtship process for some and as an alternative life-style for others.

This chapter and the previous one provided an overview of selected structural characteristics, functions of, and processes involved in the selection of mates. Examined were selected types of endogamous and exogamous marriages as well as various explanations as to why certain mate choices occur. Although the male-female sexual relationship is generally an important dimension to consider in understanding mate selection, only minimal attention was given to it. Sexual relationships, of significance to marriage and the family throughout the world, are more fully analyzed and described in Part IV. Chapter 13, on premarital sexual standards and relationships, further enhances an understanding of this and the previous chapter on mate selection. Attention is now directed to sexual norms and relationships.

Key Terms and Concepts

Discussion Questions

1. *Would there be any advantages for young people to have their marriage arranged for them? Would the consequences in marriage be different? How?*
2. *To what extent was or is your mate likely to be a result of instincts, innate drives, parental image, or complementary needs?*
3. *In spite of the logical and rational basis of the theory of complementary needs, why is there so little empirical support for it?*
4. *In what ways is role theory consistent or inconsistent with homogamy, value, and sequential theories?*

5. *List a number of role expectations that you hold for yourself and your spouse. Have a dating partner do the same. Then on a rating scale of one to five indicate whether you agree or disagree with the expectations. Compare and discuss the results. Examples: I expect the male should do the laundry. I expect the female to see that the children get religious training. Both the husband and wife should be employed full time.*

6. *What do you value most? Could you marry anyone who did not share these values? Why?*

7. *To what extent is the portrayal of the male-female game in the courtship process an accurate one?*

8. *Recall your own past love affairs or those of your friends. Is the "principle of least interest" applicable? How was it manifest?*

9. *What variations in the courtship process take place by social class, religious orientation, ethnic group, or age?*

10. *What difference, if any, would you expect to result from education in mate-selection or courtship processes?*

11. *Inquire among your friends as to how many would marry if "not in love." Inquire as to what love means to them and how they think it changes with time and/or marriage. How are love relationships controlled?*

12. *How do you explain the frequency of premarital cohabitation? In what ways is or is not cohabitation a trial marriage? What advantages or disadvantages exist for males, females, or both?*

Further Readings

Bell, Robert R. *Marriage and Family Interaction.* 4th ed. Homewood, Ill.: Dorsey Press, 1975. Chapter 4 on the dating-courtship process, Chapter 5 on love, and Chapter 6 on mate selection present a sociological analysis of these areas.

Blood, Robert O., Jr. *Love Match and Arranged Marriage.* New York: Free Press, 1967. A comparison of 1) the old and new systems of mate selection in Tokyo and 2) the similarities of internal and external forces on marriage in Tokyo and Detroit.

Burgess, Ernest W., and **Paul Wallin.** *Engagement and Marriage.* Philadelphia: J. B. Lippincott, 1953. One of the most extensive longitudinal studies ever completed on engagement and the early years of marriage. Most of this book is based on an intensive analysis of 1,000 engaged couples and a follow-up with 666 married couples.

Clayton, Richard R. and **Harwin L. Voss,** "Shacking up: Cohabitation in the 1970's," *Journal of Marriage and the Family* 39 (May 1977), pp. 273–283. Using a nationwide sample of young men, the authors present data on prevalence and correlates of cohabitation.

Eckland, Bruce. "Theories of Mate Selection." *Eugenics Quarterly* 15 (June 1968), pp. 71–84. A paper devoted to a review and clarification of theories of mate selection appropriate to both biological and social scientists.

Eshleman, J. Ross and **Juanne N. Clarke,** *Intimacy, Commitments and Marriage: Development of Relationships.* Boston: Allyn and Bacon, Inc., 1978. A look at the process of becoming a human being, the development of relationships, and variations in commitments throughout the life cycle.

Goode, William J. "The Theoretical Importance of Love." *American Sociological Review* 24 (February 1959), pp. 38–47. An analysis of love as an element of social structure. Five principal types of "love control" are described.

Kline, Arthur F., and **Morris L. Medley.** *Dating and Marriage: An Interactionist Perspective.* Boston: Holbrook, 1973. A collection of twenty-five readings focusing upon the dyadic relationship between men and women.

Moss, J. Joel, Frank Apolonio, and **Margaret Jensen.** "The Premarital Dyad during the Sixties." *Journal of Marriage and the Family* 33 (February 1971), pp. 50–69. One of the decade review articles covering three aspects of the premarital dyad: courtship development, dating behavior, and mate selection.

Murstein, Bernard I. "Stimulus-Value-Role: A Theory of Marital Choice." *Journal of Marriage and the Family* 32 (August 1970), pp. 465–481. A three-stage sequential theory of mate selection moving from an initial stimulus, to value compatibility, to role "fit."

Peterman, Dan J., Carl A. Ridley, and **Scott M. Anderson.** "A Comparison of Cohabiting and Noncohabiting College Students." *Journal of Marriage and the Family* 36 (May 1974), pp. 344–354; and Lura F. Henze and John W. Hudson. "Personal and Family Characteristics of Cohabiting and Noncohabiting College Students." *Journal of Marriage and the Family* 36 (November 1974), pp. 722–727. Two studies, one at Pennsylvania State University and the other at Arizona State University comparing unmarried students who cohabit with those who do not.

Waller Willard. *The Family: A Dynamic Interpretation.* New York: Holt, Rinehart and Winston, 1938. Revised by Reuben Hill, 1951. One of the classical early textbooks on the family taking a look at the personal interactive aspects of marriage and the family.

Winch, Robert F. *Mate Selection: A Study of Complementary Needs.* New York: Harper, 1958. On the basis of twenty-five upper-middle-class undergraduate married couples, Winch presents his support for his theory of complementary needs.

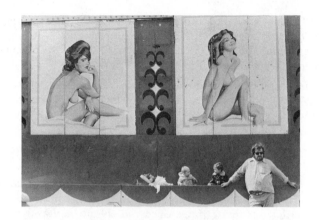

Part IV

Sexual Norms and Relationships

12

Sex in a Social Context

12

In the last half-century, the significance of sex in American life has moved from backstage to the spotlight, from an unmentionable topic to an issue of almost obsessive public concern. Few topics occupy as much widespread attention and thought as do matters relating to sex, both as a social and as a personal phenomenon. The increasing significance of sex in modern life is evidenced by the recent controversies centering around abortion, gay liberation, women's movements, education in the public schools, pornographic literature, X-rated movies, the availability of contraceptives, coed housing, "swinging," and the general concern over sexual identity and male-female roles, to mention a few.

Obviously, all issues cannot be discussed in two or three chapters on sexual relationships. However, what is perhaps obvious should be reemphasized—namely, that sex is inseparable from the rest of our living, being, and entire social order.

Although this chapter deals primarily with the social and cultural aspects of sex, there is no conscious intent to minimize the complexity of this issue. The chapter will not include pictures and discussions of male-female anatomies and physiological processes, but it is recognized that no singular process can be taken alone or accepted as the only factor that controls and determines sexual behavior and relationships. Few would argue that biology is not important or that people should not be aware of the physiological processes of conception and birth. However, it is doubtful that the real issues of sexual behavior today derive from a lack of knowledge of these processes. Thus the premise of this chapter is that biological and physiological processes are necessary, but not sufficient in themselves, for an understanding of sex in a pluralistic society, particularly as it relates to our courtship, marriage, and family system.

Source: *The San Diego Union*, January 22, 1975.

SEX AS PLAY AND WORK

Nelson Foote, Anna and Robert Francoeur, and others have indicated in writing what many people have been thinking for a long time, namely, that sex is fun,[1] cool,[2] and pleasurable.[3] The many facets and forms of sex make it the favorite form of play for millions of persons. It has been suggested that it is this very factor of fun and play that produces guilt on the part of persons who were reared in a tradition of work as good, play as evil. As with any kind of play, rules are generated and each player assists the others in the enforcement of the rules. Granted the rules will vary widely from one social situation to another but, without their observance, the play and the fun will not continue. Outsiders may like to impose a different set of rules, but to do so

1. Nelson N. Foote, "Sex as Play," *Social Problems* 1 (April 1954), pp. 159–163.
2. Anna K. Francoeur and Robert T. Francoeur, *Hot and Cool Sex: Cultures in Conflict* (New York: Harcourt Brace Jovanovich, 1974); and Robert T. Francoeur and Anna K. Francoeur, "The Pleasure Bond: Reversing the Antisex Ethic," *The Futurist* 10 (August 1976), pp. 176–180.
3. William H. Masters and Virginia E. Johnson, in association with Robert J. Levin, *The Pleasure Bond* (Boston: Little, Brown, 1975).

may bring negative reactions. And a lack of knowledge of the rules of the game may bring total rejection and complete ostracism.

Foote clarifies this point with the example of a male student who spent a year doing academic work in Sweden.[4] The young man had learned that in that country the double standard is almost extinct, and women both permit and are permitted the same liberties as men in premarital relations. This knowledge excited in him the hope of sexual gratification as other college males only dream of. After a series of frustrating and bewildering encounters with some young Swedish women, he found himself disgraced and outcast. He had not played the game correctly nor had he realized how strictly its rules are enforced in that country.

The fun of sex is also evidenced in the small proportion of coitus, either in or out of marriage, that is consciously undertaken to effect reproduction. The vast market for contraceptives among both the single and married, the increasing number of sterilizations (particularly vasectomies among males), the appearance of massage parlors, the frequency of abortion, and the attention given to swinging, unmarried cohabitation, or homosexual relationships certainly bear out this point. Writing in the early 1950s, Kinsey and his colleagues indicated that most intercourse was not engaged in for purposes of pregnancy and that the probability of a pregnancy from any particular act of coitus was an estimated one pregnancy from each 1,000 nonmarital copulations.[5] Even then, they felt the pregnancy figure was high considering the effectiveness of the condom or diaphragm.

Today, with increased reliability, availability, and awareness of contraceptives, it can be stated with assurance that the incidence of pregnancy per 1,000 nonmarital copulations is considerably lower. Keep in mind that sex as fun and play involves conformity to certain rules of the game. Few persons, and perhaps no subculture, grants approval to sex with anyone, at any place, at any time. Not only do the rules suggest what should not be done, but they indicate certain behaviors that should be followed. The lower-class male in American society who does not display his masculinity by means of physical prowess, aggression, and visible sexual success may be given "second-string" status by his peers. All play has rules; to violate the rules of the group or to violate personally internalized rules and norms will most certainly diminish "the fun of being close."

Sex can also be work. Not all sex, even that which is given group sanctions, is play. It has been observed that the play of many Americans has become a laborious kind of play, a duty to be performed. The play tends to be measured by standards of achievement. Am I a winner? Am I doing as well as I could or I should? In other words, consumption becomes production. By focusing on fifteen popular marriage manuals, Lionel Lewis and Dennis Bris-

---

4. Foote, op. cit., p. 162.
5. Alfred C. Kinsey, Wardell B. Pomeroy, Clyde E. Martin, and Paul H. Gebhard, *Sexual Behavior in the Human Female* (Philadelphia: W. B. Saunders, 1953), p. 327.

sett show how sex, an area of behavior not usually thought of as involving work, has been treated as such.[6] They emphasize how general work themes are presented as an essential part of sexual relationships and how the public is advised to prepare for sex just as they are advised to prepare for a job.

In their analysis of the fifteen manuals, the work theme became evident without getting beyond the cover page or chapter titles. These included themes such as "The Marriage Art," "Modern Sex Techniques," "How to Manage a Sex Act," "The Fourth Key to Soundly Satisfying Sex: A Controlled Sexual Crescendo," and others. They note that the female is particularly cautioned to work at sex—since being naturally sexual appears to be a trait ascribed only to the male. Many of the manuals place a central importance on experiencing orgasm. So important is it to reach orgasm—to have a product— that "all the other sexual activities of marriage are seen as merely prosaic ingredients or decorative packaging of the product."[7]

Like job training, marital sex is said to necessitate a good deal of preparation if it is to be efficiently performed. Thus it involves a good deal of study, practice, and open discussion. To not prepare is to lead to "mistakes at work" and such cannot be tolerated.[8] Particular attention is paid to the other partner's physiology, the methodology of marital sex, and the mastering of specific techniques.

The authors go on to note that, as in most work activities, the activities of marital sex are highly scheduled performances. Like a three-act play, there are phases or stages that must be followed to satisfactorily perform intercourse. All of these stages should be fitted into the total activity; none should be missed and none should be prolonged to the exclusion of others. All of this, according to the authors, seems to support the notion that play, at least sexual play, has indeed been permeated with dimensions of a work ethic. The paradox of play as work may be said to be an outcome of the peculiar condition of American society where play must be justified. In times past, leisure was something earned, a prize that was achieved through work. In brief, if you are going to play, work at it.

TOWARD A THEORY OF SEXUAL NORMATIVE MORALITY

The extent to which sex is a right or a duty, work or play, sinful or nonsinful, good or bad, right or wrong, is often viewed in terms of absolutes.

---

6. Lionel S. Lewis and Dennis Brissett, "Sex Is Work: A Study of Avocational Counseling," *Social Problems* 15 (September 1967), pp. 8–18.
7. Ibid., p. 12.
8. Ibid., p. 13.

Premarital sexual relationships are viewed as permissible or not permissible. Oral-genital contacts are viewed either as "dirty" and sinful, or non-dirty and appropriate. Masturbation may be viewed as harmful or beneficial. The sociologist, however, would state that the appropriateness, rightness, or goodness of sexual matters must be viewed in relation to their cultural setting. Morality and immorality are terms commonly used to designate behavior that is considered right or wrong, but what is right in one context may be wrong in another.

Sociologists use the term "cultural relativism" or "cultural relativity" to illustrate that traits or behavior patterns are neither good nor bad in themselves but are relative to the cultural setting in which they occur. In American society premarital pregnancy is viewed negatively, the mores condemn it, and few arrangements exist for the care of illegitimate children. On the other hand, among the Bontocs in the Philippines, premarital pregnancy was viewed as good since it established the fertility of the female and made her a highly desirable marriage partner. In our society, two males walking down the street with hands clasped or arms around one another's shoulders causes double glances and amused, if not negative, reactions. In rural areas of the Philippines, identical behavior is relatively common and granted social approval. As stated by William Graham Sumner, "The mores can make anything right." This idea of cultural relativism challenges the notion of absolute standards of judgement to be applied uniformly regardless of time or place.

How then, does the social scientist approach questions of sexual morality? If premarital pregnancy is approved among the Bontocs, should it not be approved in Salt Lake City? Is everything relative? Is nothing sacred? Philosophical questions of ultimates and absolutes lie outside the realm of the social scientist, and, thus, determining "moral" or intrinsically right behavior cannot be done. But the social scientist can determine the extent to which behavior is consistent or inconsistent with the norms of the group and can examine the consequences that stem from various types of behaviors. The social scientist cannot affirm a moral system but can determine antecedents and consequences, or cause-and-effect relationships, which are of assistance in selecting criteria for moral decisions.

Harold Christensen examined the extent to which sex patterns showed regularities and variabilities in three cultures and moved toward a theory of normative morality.[9] He defined normative morality as any code of right and wrong that is founded upon the operations of normative systems. He attempted to put science in place of polemics and to see questions of right and wrong in terms of the measurable and variable consequences of the behavior involved.

It is his contention that:

_____

9. Harold T. Christensen, "Scandinavian and American Sex Norms: Some Comparisons, with Sociological Implications," *The Journal of Social Issues* 22 (April 1966), pp. 60–75.

Standards of Sexual Behavior and Privacy

From one society to another, standards of sexual behavior are very different. There are islands in the Pacific where unmarried adolescents engage in sexual relations without disapproval from the community—even when some of the girls get pregnant. And, of course, there are societies like our own, where sex before marriage is frowned upon, but frequently practiced. For some time Robert J. Maxwell of Cornell University has been looking for some characteristic trait that would help an anthropologist in sorting societies into those that are either permissive, variable, or quite strict about premarital sexual behavior. Apparently he has found such a characteristic—of all places, in the walls of houses (Cornell Journal of Social Relations, Spring 1967).

The point of departure for Maxwell's thinking about sex and walls was sociologist Erving Goffman's thesis that "restrictions placed upon contact, the maintenance of social distance, provide a way in which awe can be generated and sustained in the audience." If this is generally true, it should follow that, in societies where sex is private and hidden, it generates awe. And in such societies, strict codes of sexual behavior could—and would— be enforced.

Now, Maxwell assumed that sex was most likely to be private if the houses in a society have walls of stone, brick, clay, or anything else that no one can see through. Sex is most likely to be casual and observable if people live in houses made of latticework or grass, or with open walls.

With these assumptions, Maxwell was in a position to make a cross-cultural check of his theory. He used the Ethnographic Index—which, quite conveniently, has information about both wall material and norms of premarital sex behavior for 93 different societies. When the wall types and sex standards are condensed into three categories, these are the correlations:

Wall Material	Sex Norms		
	strict	middling	permissive
opaque	18	16	6
intermediate	3	2	4
transparent	3	15	26

The possibility that correlations like this would occur by pure chance are one in a thousand.

Source: "Roundup of Current Research," Trans-Action 5 (June 1968), p. 4. Reprinted by permission.

If everything were regular, that is, generalizable across cultures, one could look to these universals as bases for a uniform morality; or, if everything were culture bound, one could conclude that nothing is fixed and morality is entirely relative. The truth of the matter seems to lie between these two conditions.[10]

Regularities in Sexual Norms

A number of Christensen's findings were not relative to a particular culture but were found to apply in each of the three cultures he studied:

10. Ibid., p. 71.

Danish, midwestern United States, and Mormon. Among others, these included:

1. Most sexual intimacy and reproductive pregnancy occur within the institutional bounds of marriage.
2. The modal timing of first *postmarital conception* is approximately one month after the wedding.
3. Patterns of sexual behavior are strongly correlated with personal attitudes and social norms; permissive thinking tends to beget permissive behavior and restrictive thinking, restrictive behavior.
4. Approval of nonmarital coitus, as applied to the premarital period, increases with each specified advance in involvement and/or commitment between the couple; but, as applied to the postmarital period, the reverse is true.
5. Females are more conservative in sexual matters than are males, almost without exception and regardless of the measure used or whether it measures attitudes or behavior.
6. Females who engage in premarital coitus are more likely than males to do so because of pressure or felt obligation, and also more than males to have as a partner either a "steady" or a fiance(e).
7. There is a suggestion—though the testing was inconclusive—that persons who have premarital coitus are disproportionately low on satisfaction derived from their courtships.
8. Premarital pregnancy couples subsequently experience higher divorce rates than the postmaritally pregnant.
9. Of the premarital pregnancy couples, higher divorce rates are found for the "shotgun" type, that is, those who wait for marriage until just before the child is born, than for those who marry soon after pregnancy.
10. Of the postmarital pregnancy couples, higher divorce rates are found for the early conceivers than for those who wait a few months before starting their families.
11. Premarital pregnancy is greater among young brides and grooms in contrast to older ones, among those who have a civil wedding in contrast to a religious one, and among those in a laboring line of work in contrast to the more skilled and professional occupations.[11]

These regularities, which are suggestive of cultural universals, appear to be the types of things one would expect to be functional to either personality or social systems per se. That is, reproduction is generally confined to marriage; beliefs and practices are reasonably aligned; females are more conservative in sexual matters than males; and divorce rates are higher among the premarital pregnancy couples.

Relativism in Sexual Norms

Many sexual acts and their consequences are highly dependent on the cultural milieu in which they occur. Thus cultural relativism in regard to

---

11. Ibid., pp. 68–69. Reprinted by permission of The Society for the Psychological Study of Social Issues.

Igorot Marriage Folkway

Among several mountain tribes in Igorot land high up in the Mountain Province, a kind of trial marriage exists.

As soon as a girl reaches the age when her elders consider her as ready for marriage, she begins to sleep in the ulog, the village sleeping-quarters for such young girls of marriageable age and where she continues to sleep until she gets married.

If the young girl loves a boy and the boy

loves her in return, he is invited to sleep with her in the ulog. The Igorot belief is that the procreation of children is the only reason for marriage, so if the young girl gets pregnant, there is rejoicing. Only then do they get married. Actual betrothal follows an exchange of special gifts—usually through an intermediary —generally betel-nut in a special container, or sometimes a beautifully decorated hat.

Source: Francisco Demetrio y Radaza, S.J., ed., *Dictionary of Philippine Folk Beliefs and Customs* (Cagayan de Oro City: Xavier University, Book III, 1970), p. 629.

sexual matters exists both in degree and kind. For example, the Danish respondents, in comparison with the two American samples:

1. Gave greater approval to both premarital coitus and postmarital infidelity.
2. Approved earlier starting times, in relation to marriage, of each level of intimacy—necking, petting, and coitus.
3. Thought in terms of a more rapid progression of intimacy development from its beginnings in necking to its completion in coitus.[12]

In regard to behavior, the Danish students, more than others:

1. Participated in premarital coitus.
2. Went on to coitus from petting: that is, fewer of them engaged in terminal petting.
3. Confined premarital coitus to one partner and had first experience with a "steady" or fiance(e); hence, were less promiscuous.
4. Gave birth to an illegitimate child.
5. Conceived the first legitimate child (postmarital birth) premaritally.
6. Postponed further conception following the wedding; hence, showed a low proportion of early postmarital conceptions.[13]

Christensen's view of normative morality, in terms of behavioral consequences, recognizes that there are both functional and dysfunctional practices within cultures. But when something is recognized as dysfunctional, the judgment is not ultimate but is only in reference to the normative system in which it exists. Sexual practices in the United States must be viewed against our sexual norms, and sexual practices in any other part of the world must be

12. Ibid., p. 62. Reprinted by permission of The Society for the Psychological Study of Social Issues.
13. Ibid., p. 63. Reprinted by permission of the Society for the Psychological Study of Social Issues.

The Signs of Sodom and Gomorrha

"EVEN AS SODOM AND GOMORRHA AND THE CITIES ABOUT THEM IN LIKE MANNER, GIVING THEMSELVES OVER TO FORNICATION AND GOING AFTER STRANGE FLESH."   Jude 7

Are we on the brink of judgment? Are we going to allow America to become like Sodom and Gomorrha?

The civilization in America is living on the brink of moral disaster through the Sensitivity Training classes and Sex Education classes that are moving into our schools and churches of America. If these programs are allowed to continue there will be chaos in America. This chaos will be so great that the moral fibre will decline to a state of amorality.

These programs have the endorsement of the N.E.A. and SIECUS in America from the pit of HELL and are SATANIC Devised. They are rotten to the core as they seek to endorse legalized sin.

Every Christian has the responsibility to exalt righteousness and produce a righteous environment for their children. It is my prayer that the following information will awaken the Christians of America to action that would bring revival.

"AWAKE TO RIGHTEOUSNESS, AND SIN NOT; FOR SOME HAVE NOT THE KNOWLEDGE OF GOD: I SPEAK THIS TO YOUR SHAME."   I Corinthians 15:34

Source: Distributed mimeograph prepared by the Citizens Committee for Christian Action, Buchanan, Michigan, 1969.

seen within their normative context. If practices become more permissive and the norms remain relatively conservative, there will be an increase in strain (dysfunction) within the personality systems. When practices and norms coincide, there will be fewer negative consequences of behavior. Denmark, which had the greatest amount of sexual permissiveness, showed the least negative effects from both premarital coitus and premarital pregnancy: guilt and kindred feelings were at a minimum, there was little pressure to advance the wedding date, and the influence of these intimacies upon subsequent divorce was relatively small.[14] Conversely, negative effects were in each instance greatest in the most restrictive culture (Mormon); the more moderate culture (midwestern) showed in-between effects. Thus behavior is not good or bad, per se, but must be viewed as relative to the cultural context in which it occurs. Christensen states:

> It should be clear that normative morality, though relativistic, is different from sexual freedom justified on the ground that "anything goes" since in some part of the world it is practiced. Normative morality is based, not so much on the fact that practices vary, as on the fact that certain consequences adhering to acts are relative to time, place, and circumstances. It is a responsible ethic or morality.[15]

14. Ibid., p. 66.

15. Harold T. Christensen, "Normative Theory Derived from Cross-cultural Family Research," *Journal of Marriage and the Family* 31 (May 1969), p. 222.

THE CONTROL OF
SEXUAL RELATIONSHIPS

All societies control in some manner both the relationship between the sexes and the expression of sexual behaviors. The social control of sex is a universal cultural characteristic. Only rarely does this regulation hinge on the fact of sex itself. That is, to the overwhelming majority, the point of departure for the regulation of sex is not sexual intercourse per se, but one or more other social phenomena with respect to which sex is important, notably marriage, kinship, social status, reproduction, and ceremony.[16]

The incest taboo and marriage appear to be the opposite extremes of sexual control: the incest taboo forbids sexual relationships between certain members, marriage requires sexual relationships between certain members. Without doubt, these controls vary widely from one society to another: first-cousin marriages and sexual expression is taboo in some, preferred in others; premarital coitus is expected and proper in some, deviant in others; extramarital sex, masturbation, homosexuality, illegitimacy, and the general how, when, who, and where of sexual practices vary both within our own society and around the world.[17] Variations occur in place, in time, in practice, and in the ideal as well as in the real.

The Incest Taboo

A universal avoidance of intercourse between certain family members, particularly those within and closest to the nuclear family, is provided by the incest taboo. Murdock, in drawing data from 250 societies, set forth eight empirical conclusions concerning incest taboos.[18] These can be seen in the insert.

Explanations of the Incest Taboo

How can incest be explained? One theory attributes the incest taboo to the recognition by primitive man of the dangers of close inbreeding.[19] However, it is doubtful that early societies were aware of the genetic effects or the

---

16. George P. Murdock, *Social Structure* (New York: Macmillan, 1949), p. 263.

17. This is illustrated excellently in Gwen J. Bronde and Sarah J. Greene, "Cross-cultural Codes on Twenty Sexual Attitudes and Practices," *Ethnology* 15 (October 1976), pp. 409–429.

18. Ibid., pp. 284–289.

19. Melvin Ember, "On the Origin and the Extension of the Incest Taboo," *Behavior Science Research* 10 (June 1975), pp. 249–281.

Conclusions Concerning Incest

1. With the exception of married parents, incest taboos apply universally to all persons of opposite sex within the nuclear family. The data reveal not a single instance in which sexual intercourse or marriage is generally permissible between mother and son, father and daughter, or brother and sister.

2. Incest taboos do not apply universally to any relative of the opposite sex outside of the nuclear family. Though nowhere may a man marry his mother, his sister, or his daughter, he may contract matrimony with . . . his paternal aunt . . . his maternal aunt . . . his half-sister by the same mother . . . his half-sister by the same father . . . either parallel cousin . . . his sororal niece . . . and his fraternal niece.

3. Incest taboos are never confined exclusively to the nuclear family. Universally they apply to at least some secondary and tertiary relatives.

4. Incest taboos tend to apply with diminished intensity to kinsmen outside of the nuclear family, even though they are designated by the same kinship term as primary relatives. Our data reveal no instance where a relative outside the nuclear family is more stringently tabooed than one within it.

5. Incest taboos, in their application to persons outside the nuclear family, fail strikingly to coincide with nearness of actual biological relationship. Regulations vary widely in different cultures; relatives with whom intercourse and marriage are strictly forbidden in one society are often privileged or preferred mates in another.

6. Incest taboos are highly correlated with purely conventional groupings of kinsmen. They tend to apply, for example, to all relatives called by a classificatory kinship term which includes sexual tabooed primary relatives. . . . The tendency of incest taboos to be associated with those relatives who are called "mother," "sister," or "daughter" is expressed by a coefficient of association of +.94.

7. Incest taboos and exogamous restrictions, as compared to other sexual prohibitions, are characterized by peculiar intensity and emotional quality. . . . In none of the societies surveyed, we believe, do taboos against adultery or fornication exceed in strength the strictest incest taboos prevalent in the same society, and rarely if ever do they equal or even approach the latter in intensity.

8. Violations of incest taboos do occur. Despite the strength of cultural barriers and their internalization in the consciousnesses of individuals, sporadic instances of incestuous intercourse are reported in most of our sample societies.

Source: George P. Murdock, *Social Structure* (New York: Macmillan, 1949), pp. 284–289. Copyright 1949 by the Macmillan Co. Reprinted by permission.

principles of heredity. Even if they were, it seems logical that it would have been used to produce a higher quality man such as has since been widely adopted with animals. Furthermore, these variable taboos do not coincide with biological nearness, thus discounting the idea that incest rules have their basis in biological or genetic factors.

A second explanation attributes incest prohibition to instinct. But if it were instinctive, avoidance of incest would be automatic and if it were instinctive, how would one explain the diversity of the taboos and their lack of correlation with actual consanguinity?[20] It is a fallacy to attempt to explain social phenomena that vary widely from one society to another on the basis of a relatively stable biological factor, and thus instinctive interpretations of social phenomena are rarely seen in the social sciences.

Edward Westermarck[21] and Havelock Ellis[22] regard prohibition of incest as habits formed during childhood. It is suggested that habits of avoidance result from the dulling of the sexual appetite through prolonged associations. This idea suggests that to grow up in the same household with a person of the opposite sex eliminates that person as a sexual or marital partner. However, as Murdock suggests, this theory does not harmonize with cases where marriage with a housemate is actually favored, is inconsistent with the widespread preference for levirate and sororate unions, is contradicted by the enduring attachments between husband and wife that occur in most societies and, above all, overlooks, and even inverts, the vast body of clinical evidence showing that incestuous desires are regularly engendered within the nuclear family and are kept in restraint only through persistent social pressure and individual repression.[23]

Freud's explanation of the incest taboo relates to the Oedipus and the Electra complexes. His idea, like many others, does not account for the variation and extension of such taboos beyond the immediate nuclear family. Nor does it suggest why they are so regularly a part of culture, receiving the approval of society and incorporated everywhere in sanctioned cultural norms.

Murdock suggests that no unitary theory of incest taboos appears capable of accounting for all their aspects. For his explanation, he draws upon psychoanalysis, sociology, cultural anthropology, and behavioristic psychology. According to Murdock:

> It thus appears that a complete scientific explanation of incest taboos and exogamous roles emerges from a synthesis of the theories of four separate disciplines that deal with human behavior. *Psychoanalytic theory* accounts for the peculiar emotional quality of such taboos; for the occurrence of violations, which neither an instinct hypothesis nor Westermarck's theory of acquired aversion explains; for the diminished intensity of taboos outside of the nuclear family; and for the universal occurrence of incest avoidance tendencies which serve as a basis for cultural elaboration. *Sociological theory* demonstrates the social utility of both intra-family and extended incest taboos and thus accounts for the universality. *Psychological behavior theory* reveals a mechanism by which extension occurs and that by which social utility becomes translated into custom, thus supplying an essential part of the reasons for both the uni-

20. Ibid., p. 290.
21. Edward Westermarck, *The History of Human Marriage*, vol. 2 (New York: Allerton, 1922), p. 192.
22. Havelock Ellis, *The Psychology of Sex: A Manual for Students* (London: Emerson, 1934), p. 80.
23. Murdock, op. cit., p. 291.

versality and the variety of extended taboos. *Cultural anthropology*, finally, contributes to our explanation of the varied conditions of social structure and usage which channelize generalization or produce discrimination, and thus accounts for the differential incidence of exogamous rules and extended incest taboos, for their correlation with conventional groupings of kinsmen, and for their lack of correspondence with actual biological relationship.[24]

It would be difficult to imagine the nature of the full system of rules within the family and between families if there were no prohibitions against sexual relations and marriage between members of the same nuclear family. Take simply the confusion of statuses that would result should inbreeding

---

Mac: *My first sexual experience was with my mother. I was fourteen. She was, and always has been, in a stupor state of drunkenness. It was in the summertime, and she came home and more or less seduced me. And being a virgin, I encountered sex for the first time. What I'm saying right now only about two or three people know. I don't remember if I was fully aware of what was happening. I was emotionally excited and erotic and it was the erotic stage that overwhelmed me. It was like a power manipulating me that said, "yes," "yes," "yes," and I pursued it.*

About a year later, after the intercourse, she used this as a threat, to dehumanize my character, you know. She has done it often since then. I think it was last year, that my mate and me were over in the kitchen at my brothers. We all were having drinks, and my mother said, "If you say that, I'll tell something about you." I knew what she was referring to, what she was saying, and felt this as being dehumanized.

This experience might have been a detriment to my character because I've kept it secret. I kept it repressed even though it was like a cancer eating me up inside. Only recently have I been willing to talk about it with anyone.

---

occur. "The incestuous male child of a father-daughter union . . . would be a brother of his own mother, that is, the son of his own sister; a step-son of his own grandmother; possibly a brother of his own uncle; and certainly a grandson of his own father."[25]

Some writers, citing Russell Middleton,[26] T. Shroeder,[27] and others,

---

24. Ibid., p. 300.
25. Kingsley Davis, "Legitimacy and the Incest Taboo," in Norman W. Bell and Ezra F. Vogel, eds., *A Modern Introduction to the Family* (Glencoe, Ill.: Free Press, 1960), p. 401.
26. Russell Middleton, "Brother-Sister and Father-Daughter Marriage in Ancient Egypt," *American Sociological Review* 27 (October 1962), pp. 603–611.
27. T. Schroeder, "Incest in Mormonism," *American Journal of Urology and Sexology* 11 (1915), pp. 409–416.

argue that the incest taboo is not universal and in certain instances is highly dysfunctional. The cases most frequently mentioned are those of brother-sister marriages among the Incas, the Hawaiians, and the ancient Egyptians. However, for our basic purposes, isolated instances such as these rarely pertain to a society as a whole but only to limited groups of high prestige where maintenance of status takes precedence over other factors. Exceptions to the taboo on incest are sanctioned primarily among the royalty and rarely for commoners.

Sexual Control Through Marriage

In contrast to the incest taboo on sexual relationships between specified persons, marriage, almost universally, creates a condition in which specified persons are granted complete social approval to engage in coitus. In some instances, sexual relationships within marriage are obligatory. The most widely approved source of sexual gratification and the most legitimate context to begin a family is via marriage. To found a family outside the marital relationship, or even to engage in sexual relationships with persons other than one's spouse, is generally taboo. As with incest, the taboos on adultery are very common. Of the 148 societies in Murdock's sample for which data were available, 120 of them had a taboo on adultery.[28] He points out, however, that these figures apply only to sex relations with an unrelated or distantly related person. Sex in marriage and extramarital relations are discussed in Chapter 14.

Other Means of Controlling Sexual Behavior

Sexual behavior is controlled in numerous other ways. Some societies attempt to enforce norms of chastity by secluding single girls. Some provide escorts or duennas when girls are with the opposite sex in public. Ethnic and subcultural differences regulate sexual matters by a lifelong process of instilling sexual norms into the consciousness of the members within that ethnic group. The stratification system also serves to regulate sexual expression. Class and caste systems operate both to separate groups geographically as well as to define appropriate or inappropriate sexual partners. Sex is also highly regulated by the statuses we occupy. Males may behave differently than females in many situations, priests behave differently than school teachers, divorcees behave differently than married persons, and grandparents behave differently than grandchildren.

Most societies use the reproductive cycle to regulate sex. Taboos may

---

28. Murdock, op. cit., p. 265.

be placed against sexual intercourse during pregnancy, during the menstrual period, immediately following childbirth, or through the period of lactation. Special events also serve to regulate sex. Intercourse may be required or forbidden during times of certain festivities, religious ceremonies, weddings, harvest time, or the like. Quite clearly, there are no societies which do not use various means to regulate and control the sexual behavior of its members.

Sexual control may be indicated by the forms of sexual outlets granted social approval and/or availability to members of a given society. Certain societies display pornography openly, whereas others prosecute those who sell or display this type of literature. Some societies have burlesque movie houses; others forbid them. Whereas the most approved sexual outlet occurs in marriage, most societies indicate instances of prostitution, rape, child molesting, bestiality, voyeurism, masturbation, homosexuality, group sex, and the like. Let us examine two of these: masturbation and homosexual contacts, particularly as they exist within the United States.

AUTOEROTICISM

Premaritally, maritally, or postmaritally, a common source of sexual outlet is self-manipulation of the genitals, known as masturbation. It is possible that for both sexes there is no sexual outlet that provides as good a measure of sexual interest and intrinsic capacity as does masturbation. It could well be asked, "Is masturbation not an individualistic, personal, and psychological phenomenon, and if so, should it be included in a sociology book? Stated simply, it is included because the act and effects of masturbation are bound up with the way the act is defined within a given group, subculture, or society. It is doubtful that masturbation or any type of sexual behavior can be understood solely in terms of overt behavior. To ignore, or overlook, the internal symbolic processes (as most behavioral theorists do) is to ignore the integrative and organizing phenomenon in human behavior. In regard to masturbation, the internal symbolic processes include the imagery that has been learned to be erotic. The erotic imagery accompanying the act of masturbation does not differ in any essential detail from that attending heterosexual coitus.

Kinsey notes that before and during masturbation, erotic literature and pictures are occasionally used by Americans of the better educated classes; and he adds that "nearly, but not quite, all males experience sexual fantasies during masturbation. . . . The fantasies are heterosexual when the primary interests of the individual are heterosexual, homosexual when the individual's overt experience or psychic reactions are homosexual.[29] The experiences a

---

29. Alfred C. Kinsey, Wardell B. Pomeroy, and Clyde E. Martin, *Sexual Behavior in the Human Male* (Philadelphia: W. B. Saunders, 1948), p. 510.

person has had will accompany and facilitate masturbation. Masturbation, for the male or female, will be inhibited or facilitated by factors such as social class, age, religion, race, and marital status, to mention a few.

> *Louise:*   *Masturbation is definitely overplayed. If that was a person's orientation to sex, it would be, you know, a very sad substitute. To take a plastic coin for the real thing or cuddling a doll for a real baby, you know, I think it would be a very sad, sad situation.*
>
> *Alex:*   *In Eastern countries masturbation is introduced to people as a sickness, as a mental disease. They say if you masturbate there is something wrong with you. But from my experience I found out that if you don't masturbate there is really something wrong with you. I figure a normal human being should have a biological sex drive, and if he can't satisfy it, there will be something wrong with him. That was my conclusion. So as far as I was concerned, masturbation is all right.*
>
> *Mac:*   *I think masturbation is healthy. If you can't have your polygamy, the next best thing is to pick up Playboy. Personally, it's very acceptable and I like it.*

Because masturbation involves a symbolic partner or partners and is usually a solitary form of sexual outlet, it is subject to less moral condemnation than the pair types of sexual outlet. Education in the schools and mass media appear to be greatly reducing the many myths that surrounded masturbation in the past, for example, the belief that masturbation leads to moral degeneration, feeble-mindedness, adult sterility, or complexion problems. Despite there being no physical danger in masturbation, it still provokes guilt and anxiety feelings, particularly among many adolescent boys. It is possible that this very guilt and anxiety give the sexual experience the intensity of feeling that is often attributed to sex itself. Simon and Gagnon report:

> Guilt and anxiety do not follow simply from social disapproval. Rather, they seem to come from several sources, including the difficulty the boy has in presenting himself as a sexual being to his immediate family, particularly his parents. Another source is fantasies or plans associated with masturbation—fantasies about doing sexual "things" to others or having others do sexual "things" to oneself . . . and, of course, some guilt and anxiety center around the general disapproval of masturbation. After the early period of adolescence, in fact, most youths will not admit to their peers that they did or do it. Nevertheless, masturbation is for most adolescent boys the major sexual activity, and they engage in it fairly frequently. It is an extremely positive and gratifying experience to them.[30]

---

30. William Simon and John Gagnon, "Psycho-sexual Development," *Trans-Action* 6 (March 1969), p. 13.

In 1953 Kinsey reported that, by the time of marriage, 41 percent of females and 94 percent of males had engaged in masturbation to the point of orgasm.[31] Among a random sample of university students at three schools in the New York City area, Ibtihaj Arafat and Wayne Cotton[32] found the occurrence of masturbation to be 89 percent for males and 61 percent for females. In addition to the time difference (1953 and 1973) the later study reports on student responses of "present" activity whereas Kinsey reports on adult responses of "ever" masturbatory activity. Most people begin masturbating between the ages of nine and sixteen, but a high percentage of females begin between the ages of 17 and 21.[33]

Predictably, the greatest change in masturbation has occurred and will likely continue to occur among females. The rationale for this is that the rate of masturbation for males is high at all class and education levels, whereas among females a significant change is related to higher educational levels as well as to a sexual awakening of females as to the acceptance and enjoyment of sexual activities. Thus, as an increasing proportion of females graduate from high school and college, as an increasing proportion enter the work force, and as an increasing proportion gain "liberation" from traditional conceptions of sex, there is an increased likelihood of masturbation. Referring to general sexual experience—and not merely to masturbation—Robert Bell writes:

> The higher-educated female is more apt to engage in sexual behavior for several reasons. First, she tends more often than the lower-educated female to set the belief that women are equal to men in the area of sexual rights. Second, she is less subject to social control through fear, superstition and a belief in sin. Third, because she marries later, she has more opportunity to indulge in premarital sexual behavior than the lower-educated female.[34]

Although a greater percentage of males than females engage in masturbation, the range of variation in sexual activity is far greater for the female than for the male. Kinsey found that among those females who had masturbated, some had not had such experience more than once or twice a year. Most, however, masturbated from once a month to once a week. At the extreme were females who had regularly masturbated to the point of orgasm several times in immediate succession, and there were some who had masturbated to orgasm as often as ten, twenty, and even one hundred times within a

31. Kinsey *(Female)*, op. cit., p. 520.
32. Ibtihaj S. Arafat and Wayne L. Cotton, "Masturbation Practices of Males and Females," *The Journal of Sex Research* 10 (November 1974), pp. 293–307.
33. Ibid., p. 299.
34. Robert R. Bell, *Premarital Sex in a Changing Society* (Englewood Cliffs, N. J.: Prentice-Hall, 1966), p. 94.

Contrasts in Legislating Sex

Two news items in the mid-1970s present an interesting picture of contrasts in legislating sex.

The West German Bundesrat (upper house) passed legislation permitting homosexuality and the swapping of marital partners among consenting adults. Taking effect in 1975, the law also permits the sale of pornography to anyone eighteen years of age and over. The West German Minister of Justice explained the legislation as an attempt to pro-gress from the attitudes of the nineteenth century.

Dade County voters in Florida on June 7, 1977, repealed a gay rights ordinance that barred discrimination against homosexuals in jobs, housing, and public accommodations. Anita Bryant, who actively campaigned for repeal with the support of her church-based Save Our Children organization, said that if homosexuality were the normal way, God would have made Adam and Bruce.

single hour.[35] Among all types of sexual activity, masturbation is the one in which the female most frequently reaches orgasm. The Masters-Johnson research reported that masturbatory frequency in their male group ranged from once a month to two to three times a day.[36]

Despite the evidence that masturbation is not harmful, the teachings of many parents, schools, and others continue to portray it as a "less-than-desirable" type of behavior and one not to be discussed openly. Thus problems associated with masturbation result not from self-stimulation but from the internalized meaning that has been learned and exists before masturbation occurs. It is not amazing how the joys or sorrows of what is generally perceived as a personal, psychological, and (generally) private matter are molded and influenced by the groups and subsystems of which we are a part?

HOMOSEXUAL RELATIONSHIPS

Whereas masturbation involves only a symbolic partner or no partner at all, homosexuality involves a partner of the same sex for purposes of sexual gratification. The sociological significance of homosexuality takes on meaning only when it is recognized that some of the strongest sexual norms are those defining permissible sexual partners. Frequently, the concern is less with what is done than with whom it is done. In the Old Testament, homosexuality is mentioned twice, both times in Leviticus. One source states that "you shall not be with a man as with a woman, it is an abomination."[37] The

35. Kinsey (Female), op. cit., p. 146.

36. William H. Masters and Virginia E. Johnson, *Human Sexual Response* (Boston: Little, Brown, 1966), p. 201.

37. Leviticus 18:22

other states that "if a man lie with a man as with a woman, both have done an abomination; they shall surely be put to death, their blood is upon them."[38] Both Levitical condemnations prescribe capital punishment for homosexuality. In contrast, lesbianism is not even mentioned.[39]

Even today, although generally deplored as a mode of sexual behavior in American society, sanctions against homosexuality are more stringent for men than for women. Lesbianism is usually not legislated against at all, and legislation against male homosexuality is usually confined to specific sexual acts such as public indecency or the corruption of minors. Even though laws dealing with homosexuality may be permissive or nonexistent, public attitudes are generally negative.

Janis Kelly[40] advances the idea that all heterosexual relationships are corrupted by the imbalance of power between men and women in that men are by definition important and in conquest. For love, mutual openness, and trust to develop, a balance of economic and social power must exist that for women is only possible among other women. Lesbianism, according to Kelly, is emotionally, intellectually, physically, and interpersonally superior to heterosexuality in that it has no power struggles, is less likely to disassociate mind and body, and contains the conditions for learning to love fully and without fear.

One study,[41] in looking at female homosexuals who establish a relatively permanent quasi-marital union, attempted to determine if roles will be differentiated so that one will perform a male sex role and the other a female sex role. It was found that homosexuals organize themselves internally into subgroups stratified by conduct, age, education, and income. In general, the homosexual subculture contains many elements closely resembling the heterosexual courtship and marriage systems. The person assuming the male role ("butch") initiates the interaction (leads on the dance floor, lights the partner's cigarette, holds the coat, opens doors), repairs things around the house, is likely to be older, is likely to have a higher income, and has less desire to bear children.

How widespread is homosexuality and how does one identify a homosexual? First, homosexuality is not identifiable by simple visual indicators, and second, homosexuality is not a dichotomous dimension. That is, it is false to assume that a person either is or is not a homosexual. Only the human mind invents categories and tries to force facts into separate pigeonholes. Kinsey and his co-workers established that there are degrees of sexuality. They de-

38. Leviticus 20:13
39. William Orbach, "Homosexuality and Jewish Law," *Journal of Family Law* 14 (1975–1976), p. 369.
40. Janis Kelley, "Sister Love: An Exploration of the Need for Homosexual Experience," *The Family Coordinator* 21 (October 1972), pp. 473–475.
41. Mehri Samandari Jensen, "Role Differentiation in Female Homosexual Quasi-Marital Unions," *Journal of Marriage and the Family* 36 (May 1974), pp. 360–367.

vised a seven-point scale, ranging from exclusive heterosexuality to exclusive homosexuality. Between these two points were five degrees of heterosexuality-homosexuality. They found that 28 percent of the females and 50 percent of the males had at some time or other had an overt homosexual experience, and 4 percent of the males and 1 percent of the females had been exclusively homosexual throughout their lives.[42]

Although the exact proportion of the population that is exclusively homosexual is unknown, most estimates indicate that the rates are surprisingly low. Surprisingly in that much, if not most, of our human interaction occurs with members of the same sex. Our public schools, churches, athletic events, restaurants, bars, dormitories, jails, and a wide variety of other places encourage same-sex interaction. Despite the widespread social opportunities for same-sex stimulation, few persons become emotionally committed to homosexuality as a source of sexual outlet. As long as our, or any, society provides rewards contingent on normal heterosexual relations and punishments or negative evaluation on homosexual relations, the incidence and frequency

Alex:	*In Arabia or mostly Islamic countries, homosexuality is a big problem. A lot of poor people don't even know how they got that way. Since you can't discuss anything even with parents, there is nobody to guide them. Some of my friends feel very threatened by homosexuals. They don't exactly threaten me. But there again, back home, we didn't have homosexuals that present themselves like they do in America. We didn't have gay liberation or gay bars or nothing like that. If a person was homosexual, probably no one would ever know about it.*
Mac:	*I think that physical intimacy with a male is dehumanizing and one loses one's masculinity. I have thought I'd like to see my mate having sexual relations with a woman. If it were a threesome, I wouldn't mind it, with me included. I haven't done it and, yeah, I'd like to, but I know reality.*

of homosexuality is not likely to increase very greatly. Most contacts that do or will occur will have to remain hidden—out of sight from public view.

What about the future of the homosexual or gay community and the future of marriage between persons of the same sex? Neither are likely to gain much headway. Members of the gay liberation movement are arguing vehemently for treatment equal to that received by the heterosexual—to be treated as a human being and not to be shown discrimination in employment or other social interactions. They assume that if the public is educated and informed, prejudice will decrease and homosexuality will become accepted as a "natural" form of sexual behavior. At present, there appears to be little evidence

42. Kinsey *(Female),* op. cit., pp. 474, 487; *(Male),* op. cit., p. 651.

Who Do You Dream About?

If you're a male who at night dreams mostly about males, then we've got some news for you: You're probably a homosexual. At least, this is the connection turned up by researchers at Utah State University.

The researchers wanted to find out if male homosexuals dream differently from heterosexual males. They do. The researchers report that homosexuals' dreams resemble those of women in a number of respects. That is,

settings are usually indoors rather than outdoors. Also, homosexuals' dreams tend to be less aggressive than those of heterosexuals.

Homosexuals generally have far more warm and friendly interactions in their dreams than do heterosexual males. And women are not entirely excluded from homosexuals' dreams. The dreams of homosexual men reveal a pronounced interest in males, but women make an occasional appearance.

Source: *Sexology* 39 (December 1972), p. 55. Reprinted by permission.

that public opinion is abandoning its antipathy to the homosexual. The widespread negative opinion toward homosexual relationships may, in large part, account for the instability of homosexual relationships, not so much because they are homosexual but because they are not reinforced by other social bonds and networks.

It is probable that much of the opposition to homosexuality exists because of its incompatibility with the family and the sexual bargaining system. If sex is defined as existing primarily for procreation, homosexuality is totally ruled out. If sex is defined as a love relationship between partners who are oriented toward a marriage, then homosexuality becomes inconsistent with the norms surrounding a marital relationship. If sex is defined as purely an instrumental matter, that is, simply a means of sexual relief, homosexuality conflicts with the seriousness attached to sexual matters. When sex occurs among persons who are isolated from the opposite sex, such as in prisons or logging camps, these acts may be defined as situational and not as a "homosexual way of life" and for that reason be only mildly censored. However, even these acts are not encouraged or granted social approval, for they somehow tend to separate sexual feelings and behavior from acceptable types of social relationships and sentiments.

It has been widely maintained among psychotherapists that the major reason for widespread opposition to homosexuality stems from an underlying fear within each of us of our own homosexual tendencies. Their argument is that persons who do not feel threatened by any homosexual leanings within themselves are likely to be more understanding of homosexuality in general, whereas those who are most threatened by their own homosexual leanings frequently are vociferously abusive in their attacks against homosexuality. Although this argument may find support in specific case studies, it is likely that for societies in general this speculative and theoretical argument exceeds empirical support.

Summary

As should have become clear in reading this chapter, sexual attitudes, behavior, norms, and values cannot be fully understood apart from the social context in which they occur. Although, cross-culturally, few sexual regulations are as universally disapproved as incest and as universally approved as marriage, all societies place various types of taboos, restrictions, or sanctions on sexual outlets.

Sexual behavior has been portrayed as both play and work. It is play in that it is seen as enjoyable, has specified players, and follows definite rules. Sex is also seen as work. For some, it has become a duty to be performed, involving study and effort to successfully complete various tasks.

Whether sex is viewed as work or play, enjoyable or malicious, harmful or beneficial is often relative to the social and cultural context in which it occurs. The theory of sexual normative morality indicates that sex patterns show both regularities and variabilities, and behavioral consequences are functional or dysfunctional only with reference to the normative system in which they exist. Acts are relative to time, place, and circumstance.

No society fails to place controls on the sexual behavior of its members. The most universal control is the incest taboo, which prohibits sexual intercourse between certain kin, always at least within the nuclear family and usually beyond it. In contrast to the incest taboo, which restricts sexual relationships, is marriage, which often demands sexual relationships or at least grants complete social approval to them. Other controls include secluding women or single girls, separating people by class or location, socializing members to appropriate sexual norms, and the like. Practices, norms, and controls may differ, but sexual behavior will be regulated in various ways in all societies.

The range of sexual outlets varies from self-autoeroticism to group activities. It may involve the same or opposite sex, children or aged, married or single, forced activity or willing interchanges, and economic or noneconomic exchanges, to mention a few. This chapter examines masturbation and homosexuality as two sexual outlets. Masturbation may well provide as good an index of sexual interest and intrinsic capacity as any other type of sexual activity. It occurs among nearly all men and increasingly among women. Masturbation can only be understood in light of the internalized symbolic processes that result from interactive experiences in the home, school, and with others.

Unlike autoeroticism and masturbation, which involve a symbolic partner of either sex, homosexuality involves a partner of the same sex. Frequently, public concern is greater over who the partner is than what is done, and homosexual males are of greater concern than are lesbians. The rates of homosexuality are unknown but appear to be surprisingly low since most of our social relationships occur with same-sex persons. Opposition to homosexuality may exist because of its incompatibility with the family and the sexual bargaining system. It cannot produce children and is viewed as inconsistent with the norms of love and permanence surrounding marriage.

This chapter was intended to place sex within a social context and to indicate selected ways in which societies operate to control sexual activity. Certain sexual behaviors may bring praise and rewards whereas others may bring ridicule and punishment. The relative nature of these factors indicates the extent to which the time, place, and norms surrounding any given activity influence the consequences of that activity. This becomes clear in the next two chapters. Social approval is granted to a wide range or heterosexual activities when they involve the unmarried prior to marriage and the married within the marital context. The next chapter focuses on premarital sexual standards and relationships.

Key Terms and Topics

Discussion Questions

1. What changes have occurred in sexual norms and values in the last fifty years? How can you tell?
2. In your opinion, which is more important to understanding sexual behavior: biological needs, drives, hormones, and the like or norms, values, attitudes, and so on? Explain.
3. Are males and females inherently different in sexual socialization? In what ways does society contribute to the difference?
4. Examine sex manuals and determine ways in which sex is perceived as work. Compare the difference in instructions given to males and females.
5. What methodological problems exist in studying the sexual norms of a given society? How can these problems be minimized?
6. Discuss ways in which our society operates to control sexual relationships. Why is this so?
7. Discuss in regard to sex, "The mores make anything right."
8. Compare the sexual codes portrayed by the Catholic Church, selected Protestant groups, soap operas on TV, Playboy magazine, the law, nudists, men in the armed services, or topless bar girls.

9. *Which explanations for the universality of the incest taboo can you accept? Are there possible explanations other than those given? What are they?*

10. *List the possible ways and sources for sexual outlets. Which receive social approval and which are less approved? What factors make the difference in the acceptability given to having intercourse with one's spouse, one's brother or sister, someone of the same sex, a prostitute, or a dating companion?*

11. *In what ways is masturbation beneficial or harmful. Why is masturbation less frequent among females? Among the lower educated? Do you predict any major changes in attitudes or behaviors in this area in the next ten years?*

12. *What constitutes homosexuality? Under what social conditions is it most likely to occur? Why will it or will it not gain widespread social acceptance in the next twenty-five years? In what ways do homosexual relationships in quasi-marital situations parallel heterosexual marital situations?*

Further Readings

Bell, Robert R., and **Michael Gordon.** *The Social Dimension of Human Sexuality.* Boston: Little, Brown, 1972. A collection of seventeen readings covering the areas of premarital, marital, and extramarital sex, female sexuality, homosexuality, and commercialized sex.

Broderick, Carlfred B., and **Jessie Bernard.** *The Individual, Sex and Society.* Baltimore: Johns Hopkins Press, 1969. A collection of articles oriented toward the pedagogical aspects of sex education.

Edwards, John N., ed. *Sex and Society.* Chicago: Markham, 1972. Very similar in size and content to the Bell and Gordon book, the seventeen articles here include incest and postmarital coitus in addition to premarital, marital, and extramarital coitus, homosexuality, and prostitution.

Gagnon, John H. *Human Sexualities.* Glenview, Ill.: Scott, Foresman, 1977. An examination of the range of human sexualities including gender roles, sexual response, masturbation, homosexuality, bisexuality, offenses and offenders, therapies, and other topics.

Gagnon, John H., and **William Simon.** *Sexual Conduct: The Social Sources of Human Sexuality.* Chicago: Aldine, 1973. A valuable addition to the sexual literature, tracing various ways in which sexuality is learned and expressed.

Hite, Shere. *The Hite Report.* New York: Dell, 1976. The responses of more than 3,000 women (from more than 100,000 questionnaires distributed) who describe in their own words their feelings about masturbation, orgasm, intercourse, clitoral stimulation, lesbianism, and the sexual revolution.

Humphreys, Laud. *Tearoom Trade: Impersonal Sex in Public Places.* Chicago: Aldine, 1970. A study of male homosexual behavior in public restrooms. Data was gained by the author posing as a participant lookout.

Kinsey, Alfred C., Wardell Pomeroy, and **Clyde Martin.** *Sexual Behavior in the Human Male.* Philadelphia: W. B. Saunders, 1948; *Sexual Behavior in the Human Female* (with Paul Gebhard). Philadelphia: W. B. Saunders, 1953. The classical Kinsey studies presenting an intensive analysis of male and female sexual behaviors ranging from sexual activities to male-female comparisons of the anatomy, physiology, psychology, and neural mechanisms of sexual response.

McCary, James Leslie, and **Donna R. Copeland.** *Modern Views of Human Sexual Behavior.* Chicago: Science Research Associates, 1976. A collection of readings giving a broad overview of various aspects of human sexuality.

Murdock, George P. *Social Structure.* New York: Free Press, 1965. Although recommended reading for a general and excellent cross-cultural perspective on family structures, the book also extensively analyzes sexual patterns and incest.

Safilios-Rothschild, Constantina. *Love, Sex and Sex Roles.* Englewood Cliffs, N.J.: Prentice-Hall, 1977. An examination of the dynamics of women-men relationships with a focus on love, friends, sex, and change within a social context.

Seaman, Barbara. *Free and Female.* Greenwich, Ct.: Fawcett, 1972. A paperback dealing with the sexual role of women as viewed by a feminist. Many mottos, customs, and assumptions about women are questioned in an attempt to liberate women to explore and affirm their own sexuality.

Verene, D. P., ed. *Sexual Love and Western Morality: A Philosophical Anthology.* New York: Harper, 1972. Drawing upon writers such as Plato, Aristotle, Augustine, Aquinas, Luther, Nietzsche, Freud, Hegel, Fromm, DeSade, Russell, and DeBeauvoir, this anthology examines sex in western thought and contemporary society.

Weinberg, S. Kirson. *Incest Behavior.* New York: Citadel, 1963. An extensive study of interfamily sexual relationships based on interviews with approximately two hundred individuals who had been involved in an incestuous relationship.

Wiseman, Jacqueline P. *The Social Psychology of Sex.* New York: Harper, 1976. A symbolic interactionist analysis of sexual interaction, drawing upon readings of studies of actual social behavior in the sexual realm.

13

Premarital Sexual Standards and Relationships

13

In our own society, as well as in virtually all others, the primary and most pervasive sexual interest is with heterosexual behavior and relationships, both marital and nonmarital. These relationships generally refer to far more than coitus or sexual intercourse. They may include overt acts such as kissing, petting, and the like but also are likely to include attitudes, social values, and norms appropriate to the acts.

Many distinctions can be made in classifying heterosexual relationships. Most often they involve one male and one female but multiple partners are at times involved. They may involve persons who are not married but whose relationship is marriage oriented (premarital). They may involve persons who are not married and to whom marriage is not a factor (nonmarital). They may involve a husband and wife (marital). They may involve a married person with a partner other than the spouse (extramarital). They may involve a sexual exchange of married partners (swinging or wife/husband swapping). They may involve divorced or widowed persons who were once married but are currently socially and legally single (postmarital). This chapter will examine selected sexual standards and relationships that exist prior to marriage.

PREMARITAL SEXUAL STANDARDS

In his book, *Premarital Sexual Standards in America*, Ira Reiss states that logically there can be three major types of sexual standards: one stating that premarital sexual intercourse is wrong for both sexes; one stating that premarital intercourse is right for both sexes; and one stating that premarital intercourse is right for one sex but wrong for the other.[1] Empirically, America

---

1. Ira L. Reiss, *Premarital Sexual Standards in America* (Glencoe: Free Press, 1960), p. 82.

has sexual standards that fit all three possibilities: a single standard of abstinence, a single standard of permissiveness, and a double standard. The second standard, that intercourse is right for both sexes, often subdivides people into two groups: 1) those who accept intercourse only when there is a stable relationship with engagement, love, or strong affection present, and 2) those who accept intercourse when there is a mutual physical attraction, regardless of the amount of stability or affection present.[2]

Although many people have tendencies toward more than one standard, most Americans can be classified as adhering predominantly to one or another. In summary they are: 1) *abstinence*—premarital intercourse is wrong for both men and women regardless of circumstances; 2) *permissiveness with affection*—premarital intercourse is right for both men and women under the conditions that there is a stable relationship with engagement, love, or strong affection present; 3) *permissiveness without affection*—premarital intercourse is right for both men and women regardless of the amount of affection or stability present, providing there is physical attraction; and 4) *double standard* —premarital intercourse is acceptable for men but is wrong and unacceptable for women.[3] Let us examine each briefly.

Single Standards of Sexual Behavior

Abstinence for both sexes is a single standard closely tied in with religious beliefs. Norms of abstinence include: 1) petting without affection, 2) petting with affection, 3) kissing without affection, and 4) kissing with affection. Some men and women who accept abstinence feel that as long as coitus is avoided, they can pet heavily with most people who physically attract them or when strong affection or love is present. To adherents of this standard, premarital chastity technically means that a person has not engaged in behavior involving the penetration of the vagina by the penis. Reiss makes reference to "promiscuous virgins" who engage in genital apposition, mutual masturbation, and mutual oral-genital stimulation, all of which avoids sexual intercourse, but in a technical sense only.[4]

The second single standard, *permissiveness with affection*, permits sexual intercourse under certain specified conditions. This standard is perceived to be person centered in that the particular person with whom the act is being performed is highly emphasized. Accordingly, love and affection are prerequisites for intercourse. It is Reiss's contention that this standard is seriously neglected by much of the present-day literature on sex.

2. Ibid., p. 83.
3. Ibid., pp. 83–84.
4. Ibid., p. 203.

Wear Stars and Simplify Sexual Communication

Brash British teen-agers have started wearing stars—a new system for advertising just how far they'll go in their sex life.

A one-star girl or boy won't neck.

A five-star wearer will stop at nothing.

Star-wearing broke out two weeks ago at the big railroad engineering town of Swindon. It's reported to be spreading.

Said three-star Jane Phillips, 19:

"It's a good idea. Boys who wear three stars like I do seem to get on well with me. I don't feel let down when I date a three-star boy."

Commented four-star Graham Tanner, 20:

"I don't date girls with more or less stars than I have. Courting is now a real pleasure. Both the girl and I date and I know exactly where we stand. You don't hurt anybody's feelings this way."

Said two-star Mary Hicks, 18:

"I draw the line at two stars, and I like to know in advance what the boys I go out with are like."

A social worker who spends much time with young people—and who asked not to be identified by name—said:

"They're wearing these stars all right. But I've never found anybody yet modest enough to wear one star, or promiscuous enough to wear five."

The teen-agers have even composed a verse to explain the system:

One Star—must ask ma.
Two Star—ah, ah, ah.
Three Star—ha, ha, ha.
Four Star—not too far.
Five Star—stop the car.

Source: *Detroit Free Press*, October 29, 1963. Reprinted by permission of The Associated Press.

The third single standard, that of *permissiveness without affection*, suggests that as long as male and female are attracted physically, premarital intercourse is appropriate. The adherents of this standard place a very high value on physical pleasure. The two main kinds of believers in this standard are 1) orgiastic—those who seek highly promiscuous coitus with precautionary measures of secondary importance, and 2) sophisticated—those who seek physical pleasure in a more controlled and careful way.[5] The orgiastic people aim at pleasure in an open and all-consuming fashion and direct much of their behavior toward persons who occupy an inferior class or occupational status. The sophisticated people are those who accept sexual relations without affection as right and proper because they feel it is "natural." Since men and women desire sexual intercourse, there is no reason why it should not occur; it is viewed as natural and necessary, akin to eating and breathing. Permissiveness without affection is considered by Reiss to be a body-centered relationship in that the accent is placed on the physical aspects of the act. Many adherents to this position insist that body-centered coitus is actually better than person-centered coitus because it lacks personal obligations and is thus

5. Ibid., p. 118.

Women and Sex in Sweden

Many American women blame their inadequacies on the inequality of the sexes. If women weren't burdened by a double standard of sexual morality and a fear of pregnancy, they argue, they would be free to develop their talents and enjoy productive careers like men. Now, there are countries where women have the sexual freedom that these American women long for. In Sweden, contraceptive techniques are taught in the schools and diaphragms, loops, or pills are prescribed for any woman who wants them. And yet, according to Inger Becker, Swedish women don't make any better use of their freedom than women in more traditional societies (New Society, Sept. 7, 1967).

Swedish conventions about sex, marriage, and feminine respectability are freer than those in our society. Sexual intercourse before marriage is condoned; men do not expect a virgin bride; babies born outside of marriage are so acceptable that some mothers announce these births in the local newspapers.

There is, then, no sexual double standard that excuses the Swedish girls who take easier courses in school than boys take, or the many women who have stop-gap jobs but no long-term careers. In fact, Miss Becker charges, Swedish girls do just what girls have always done: They use their bodies as their primary means of support. They entrap young men into marriage by allowing themselves to become pregnant (50 percent of the children born in Sweden are unplanned, and, in one-third of the marriages, children are born before the marriage is eight months old).

Why has the sexual emancipation of Swedish women failed to make men and women there "fellow human beings"? The predatory relationship continues, Miss Becker charges, because women are just lazy. It is still much easier to marry a doctor than to become one—and the rewards in status and income are the same. Swedish girls are also encouraged to continue this kind of dependency by a social climate that tends to romanticize out-of-wedlock pregnancy, and by a social and legal situation where a man must support any child he fathers (his salary is attached, if necessary.)

The author suggests that it is time the law caught up with the realities of modern contraception—the techniques are reliable and under the woman's control. If men were no longer forced to help support children they didn't want, perhaps women would become careful about contraception. But whether a change in the law would do much to change the habits of Swedish women is problematical. What is clear from this essay is that feminine habits of dependency involve more than sexual inequality.

Source: "Roundup of Current Research," *Trans-Action* 5 (April 1968), p. 7. Reprinted by permission.

a "purer" form of pleasure.[6] This standard has never been widespread in the U.S. or Canada.[7] Perhaps we are only beginning to see the day when a single standard of permissiveness without affection becomes widespread. At least up to the 1970s, western culture has stressed female subordination and restriction and has not allowed women and men equal sexual privileges.

6. Ibid., p. 121.

7. Charles W. Hobart, "The Social Context of Morality Standards among Anglophone Canadian Students," *Journal of Comparative Family Studies* 5 (Spring 1974), pp. 26–40.

The Double Standard of
Sexual Behavior

The *double standard*, so termed because it entails using one standard to evaluate male behavior and another standard to evaluate female behavior, makes it possible for a man and a woman to be judged quite differently for the same behavior. This sexual standard is the dominant one in American society, although it is likely that a high proportion of both sexes would not view it as the ideal. As emphasized by the women's movement, the double standard has become relevant to far more than just sexual behavior and is applied in business, politics, religion, education, and most spheres of social life.

One characteristic of the double standard is that it is self-contradictory. It supposedly allows sexual freedom to men but not to women. How is such opposed behavior possible? A man cannot have sexual freedom unless he has a woman with whom to exercise this freedom. But the double standard holds that no woman should engage in premarital coitus—and thus no man is able to either; a paradoxical situation is thus brought about.[8] This contradiction was resolved historically by prostitutes, who would engage in sexual activity with a wide variety of men. Men have resolved it by selecting women from groups that are thought of as inferior or as "different." This includes girls from lower income classes, different racial groups, or members of a different religion—some of the social criteria for finding potentially "bad" girls.[9] Some double-standard men do not limit themselves to certain types, and they try to have coitus with all the women they see socially in order to discover which girls are "bad."[10]

The arguments for the double standard, which suggest that "that's the way men are," "boys will be boys," or "men 'need' coitus more than females," have little basis in fact. The author has yet to see a death, hospitalization, or illness rate for sexual abstinence. Findings of the Masters-Johnson research indicate that women have as definite an orgasm as do men and that, in general, women have a greater potential for sexual responsiveness than do men, since they tend to respond faster, more intensely, and longer to sexual stimulation. Aside from obvious anatomical variants, men and women are homogeneous in their physiologic responses to sexual stimuli.[11] Kinsey came to the same conculsion almost fifteen years earlier when he reported:

> The anatomic structures which are most essential to sexual response and orgasm are nearly identical in the human male and female. The differences are

---

8. Ibid., p. 98.
9. William F. White, "A Slum Sex Code," *American Journal of Sociology* 49 (July 1943), pp. 24–31.
10. Reiss, op. cit., pp. 100–101.
11. William H. Masters and Virginia E. Johnson, *Human Sexual Response* (Boston: Little, Brown, 1966), Chapter 17 and p. 285.

relatively few. They are associated with the different functions of the sexes in reproductive processes but they are of no great significance in the origins and development of sexual response and orgasm. If females and males differ sexually in any basic way, those differences must originate in some other aspect of the biology or psychology of the two sexes. They do not originate in any of the anatomic structures which have been considered here.[12]

In brief, the justification for a double standard, based on the innate needs or drives of men being basically different from those of women, has little if any empirical support. The differences that exist—and certainly many do—are basically social, learned differences. Since they are learned, any differences that exist can be relearned to equalize the situation and correct the imbalance of accepting male indulgence and condemning female indulgence.

Reiss contends that the double standard today is an ancient sex code in a modern society.[13] And, indeed, many of the recent changes in social organization and culture are opposed to the double standard and accentuate its conflicts and contradictions. But although the double standard is thought to have been weakened by the feminist movement (with its platform of equality), the development of contraception (with its removal of much of the fear of pregnancy), and the industrial revolution (which gave women greater economic opportunities), the double standard is still very much a part of American society, as will be shown later in the chapter.

PREMARITAL PETTING AND PHYSICAL INTIMACY

A widespread sexual outlet for nearly all males and females is petting or necking, which generally refer to a heterosexual physical contact that does not involve a union of the genitalia but does involve a deliberate attempt to effect erotic arousal. Although most acts of coitus are preceded by petting, petting is here used as a source of erotic arousal and sexual outlet as an end in itself. Among many young people it serves as a substitute for coitus and is engaged in for pleasure.

Premarital petting offers several advantages for both sexes. It is a means of gaining sexual experience, even to the point of orgasm, while still "technically" remaining a virgin; it is less severely condemned than coitus; it eliminates the possibility of pregnancy; and it does provide the sensual pleasure that accompanies sexual activities. Certainly, this activity is not new

---

12. Alfred C. Kinsey, Wardell B. Pomeroy, Clyde E. Martin, and Paul H. Gebhard, *Sexual Behavior in the Human Female* (Philadelphia: W. B. Saunders, 1953), p. 593.
13. Reiss, op. cit., p. 115.

to the present generation, although the terminology may have changed. If there is anything unique in the petting behavior of American youth, it is more likely in the incidences or frequencies rather than in its occurrence or the techniques that are employed. It may also differ in the frankness in which it is discussed and in the significance it plays in sexual activity.

Frequency of Petting Activities

The widespread incidences of petting activities in the United States is clearly documented by Kinsey,[14] Reiss,[15] Winston Ehrmann,[16] and others. Kinsey noted that 40 percent of the females in his sample had had heterosexual petting experience by fifteen years of age and nearly 100 percent of those who had married had had some sort of petting experience prior to marriage. For males, the figures are highly similar except that more boys (57 percent) had done some petting by age fifteen. Petting to the point of orgasm was engaged in by nearly one-third of both sexes,[17] and the proportion of those who petted to the point of orgasm increased with each decade of birth.

Distinct correlations exist between the frequency of petting and educational attainment. Males with the lowest educational level pet the least, men of the middle group are next, and the men of the higher educational groups pet most of all. Specifically, petting to the point of orgasm occurred among 59 percent of the college males, 30 percent of the high school males, and 16 percent of the grade school males. Interestingly, the average frequencies of petting to the point of orgasm were markedly uniform for the females of all educational levels represented in Kinsey's sample.[18] There was, however, a greater acceptance of the socially more taboo petting techniques in the better educated groups of females. This was particularly true with oral-genital contacts.

According to Kinsey, it is petting, rather than home, classroom, or religious instruction, lectures or books, classes in biology, sociology, or philosophy, or actual coitus, that provides most females with their first real understanding of a heterosexual experience. It was the first source of arousal for about 34 percent and the first source of orgasm for about one-quarter (24 percent).[19]

---

14. Kinsey, op. cit., pp. 227–281; Alfred C. Kinsey, Wardell B. Pomeroy, and Clyde E. Martin, *Sexual Behavior in the Human Male* (Philadelphia: W. B. Saunders Co., 1948), pp. 531–546.

15. Reiss, *The Social Context of Premarital Sexual Permissiveness* (New York: Holt, Rinehart and Winston, 1967).

16. Winston Ehrmann, *Premarital Dating Behavior* (New York: Bantam Books, 1959).

17. Kinsey (*Female*), op. cit., pp. 233 and 267.

18. Ibid., pp. 240–241.

19. Ibid., p. 264.

Consequences of Premarital Petting

The consequences of premarital petting for marital sexual adjustment, at least as noted by Kinsey, are highly positive. As a socializing agent, premarital petting was of considerable significance for the females studied. It introduced them to the physical, psychological, and social problems that are involved in making emotional adjustments to another individual, and it provided an opportunity for them to learn to adjust emotionally to various types of males. Specifically, Kinsey noted:

> It is sometimes said that premarital petting may make it difficult for the female to be satisfied with coitus in marriage. The statement has never been supported by any accumulation of specific data, and we have not seen more than three or four such cases. On the other hand, we have the histories of nearly 1,000 females who had done premarital petting and who had then responded excellently in their marital coitus.[20]

Reiss, using a national probability sample of students in American high schools and colleges, measured premarital sexual standards on a twelve-item scale of increasing degrees of sexual permissiveness. His research focused on two basis purposes: 1) to develop and test Guttman scales to measure premarital sexual permissiveness and 2) to examine the sociocultural correlates of premarital sexual permissiveness.[21]

For purposes of his study physical acts were divided into three categories: kissing, petting, and coitus. Conditions of affection were divided into four categories: engagement, love, strong affection, and no affection. Each of the three physical conditions was qualified by each of the four affection-related states, making a total of twelve statements that the respondent was asked to agree or disagree with either strongly, moderately, or slightly.[22] Four of the twelve items pertained to petting being acceptable before marriage when 1) the person is engaged to be married, 2) is in love, 3) has strong affection for the partner, and 4) has no particularly affectionate feeling toward the partner. The percentage of the respondents agreeing with these petting items can be seen in Table 13–1.

It can be noted that petting is given most approval under conditions of engagement, strongly followed by conditions of love. The least agreement concerns petting where there is no particular affection felt toward the partner. Generally, students are more accepting of petting than are white or black adults. Black adults are generally more accepting of petting than are white adults except where there are no feelings of affection. Interestingly, the least acceptance of petting comes not from the adults but from the female student

---

20. Ibid., pp. 266–267.
21. Reiss, op. cit., p. 13.
22. Ibid., p. 21.

TABLE 13–1.   Percentage Agreeing with Petting in Reiss's Male and Female Premarital Permissiveness Scale (by Race)

Petting Condition	Adult Sample White	Adult Sample Black	Student Sample Total Percent Black and White
Male			
1. When engaged	60.0	67.6	85.0
2. When in love	58.5	66.9	80.4
3. When feels strong affection	54.0	56.8	67.0
4. Even if no feelings of affection	28.7	28.1	34.4
Female			
1. When engaged	55.2	63.9	81.8
2. When in love	51.3	63.9	75.2
3. When feels strong affection	44.3	56.9	56.7
4. Even if no feelings of affection	19.7	22.9	18.0

Adapted from Tables 2.8 and 2.10 in Ira L. Reiss, *The Social Context of Premarital Sexual Permissiveness* (New York: Holt, Rinehart and Winston, 1967), pp. 29 and 31. Copyright © 1967 by Holt, Rinehart and Winston, Inc. Adapted and reprinted by permission of Holt, Rinehart and Winston, Inc.

sample under conditions of no particular feelings of affection felt for the partner. In premarital petting, as in all areas of sexual behavior, more approval is generally given to the male's activity than to the female's. This condition is most pronounced where there are no feelings of affection and is least adhered to under conditions of love or engagement.

Antecedents of Sexual Behavior

Simple logic would seem to indicate that a major antecedent or preceding factor in explaining or understanding premarital sexual behavior would be parental influence in the sexual socialization process. For example, is it not logical to assume that individuals brought up in sexually conservative homes will have less premarital heterosexual involvement than those from more liberal home environments? In other words, homes in which parents do not openly display affection, have a rigid and concerned attitude toward nudity, never discuss sex openly, and never have books or pamphlets available on sexual subjects would be expected to produce or lead to more conservative behavior or less sexual involvement by their children. This hypothesis was put to a test in a national probability sample of nearly 1,200 college students.

Interestingly, the findings showed no significant relationship for males or females between parental sexual conservatism and premarital sociosexual involvement.[23] This seems to indicate that perceived parental sexual conservatism leads neither to increased or decreased premarital sexual activity.

This finding is explained in several ways.[24] First, it is possible that children might not interpret the presence or absence of sexual behavior on the part of parents as having any sexual significance because they are not yet capable of conceptualizing these behaviors in the same way parents do. These forms of parental behavior turn out to be insignificant when compared to other sexual socializing influences. Second, while parents may be extremely influential in general socialization, they may be less influential than significant others outside the home, particularly peers, in sexual socialization.

In addition to the impact of parental influence, Graham Spanier examined other antecedents to premarital sexual behavior, using data gathered from the same national sample of 1,200 students. Spanier[25] hypothesized a positive relationship between perceived sex knowledge, exposure to eroticism, dating experiences, and premarital sexual behavior. That is, the more knowledge, the greater the exposure to erotic materials, and the greater the dating frequency of students, the more premarital heterosexual involvement the individual will report having. Each of these relationships was supported. While a causative relationship should not be inferred, there does seem to be a two-way interactive process in which sex information leads to increased sexual involvement, and increased sexual involvement leads to increased acquisition of sex knowledge.

In another publication, Spanier[26] indicates that sex knowledge gained through formal sex education (school classes and programs) has little if any influence on premarital sexual behavior; however, exposure to informal education, peer group interaction, mass media publications, and the like explains considerable variation in behavior. However, both formal and informal sex education experiences were found to be weaker predictors of sexual behavior than were religiosity and dating frequency.

Reiss contends that the degree of acceptable premarital sexual permissiveness in a courtship group varies directly with the degree of autonomy of the courtship group and the degree of acceptable premarital sexual permissiveness in the social and cultural setting outside the group.[27] Anything that promotes autonomy from adults for young people should promote higher levels

23. Graham B. Spanier, "Perceived Parental Sexual Conservatism, Religiosity, and Premarital Sexual Behavior," *Sociological Focus* 9 (August 1976), pp. 285–298.

24. Ibid., pp. 295–296.

25. Graham B. Spanier, "Perceived Sex Knowledge, Exposure to Eroticism, and Premarital Sexual Behavior: The Impact of Dating," *The Sociological Quarterly* 17 (Spring 1976), pp. 247–261.

26. Graham B. Spanier, "Formal and Informal Sex Education as Determinants of Premarital Sexual Behavior," *Archives of Sexual Behavior* 5 (1976), pp. 39–67.

27. Reiss, op. cit. (1967), p. 167.

of sexual permissiveness. Close involvement with peers, not going to church, falling in love, active participation in the dating courtship game, and the like promote independence and increased autonomy. Likewise, if the family, and educational, political, or religious institutions, as well as the social setting in the culture and community, accept high degrees or sexual permissiveness, fewer counteracting forces are available to restrain sexual permissiveness. As indicated elsewhere, religion appears to be the most obvious adult institutional restraint on sexual permissiveness in or out of marriage.[28]

Interrelating Beliefs, Reported Behavior, and Perceptions of Others

The author, in some of his own research, was interested in finding the relationship between sexual beliefs, reported sexual behavior, and perceptions of others' sexual behavior. He hypothesized that people are most conservative in what they believe to be proper, more permissive in what they say they do (or have done), and most permissive in what they perceive others to be doing. It was believed that this would hold true at all stages of the courtship process, for males and females, and in different cultures.

To test this hypothesis, data were gathered from 1,660 students at Western Michigan University in 1966, from 2,258 students at eight colleges in the Philippines in 1969, and from a randomly selected group of 436 single students at Western Michigan University in 1971.

Eight items of increasing degrees of sexual permissiveness, ranging from no physical contact to intercourse, were distributed to the Michigan students and six items of increasing degrees of sexual permissiveness were distributed to the Filipino students. Philippine culture, where premarital sexual codes are more conservative, required a revision in the items. Given the eight or six items, the respondents simply had to write the number that corresponded most closely to what they believed to be proper behavior, what they said they do or have done, and what they perceive others to be doing. This was done for marriage and for four stages of the courtship process: random dating, going steady, pinned or some equivalent, and engaged. Not surprisingly, most consensus of response for all respondents related to marriage, since, as stated previously, marriage legitimizes coitus. Thus it was hypothesized that where persons have a choice in mate selection (where love is a conditional factor for marriage) and the closer one gets to marriage, the more permissive the belief, reported behavior, and perception of others.

Without exception, in all three samples, for both males and females,

28. For example, in Reiss's study only 6 percent of white females who were high on measures of religiosity accepted premarital coitus, compared to 53 percent who were low on religiosity. Ibid., p. 43.

Alex: Yes, I've had sex in my home country. But I couldn't go out and have a relationship with a Christian person, because mostly they believe in remaining a virgin till they get married. Same with the Moslem girls. Now, being a Christian, we wouldn't fool around with the Moslem because we're the minority. We could get into deep trouble that way. So, Constantinopole, being a very touristic city, you would always have a relationship with some kind of a tourist, whether it's an American, or German, or French.

I haven't gone to any, but prostitution is legal and houses are established by the government. It's just like a big hospital. You go into the reception room. They'll tell you about the prices, and what services you get for each price. The people that work in the prostitution houses are clean. They get inspected every three or four days by government doctors. It's a legal thing. You can just go in there and pay the money You don't have to be old.

Ann: I recall my first sexual experience. There wasn't much to it. I didn't enjoy it. To me it was very disgusting. Well, you know, your parents don't tell you anything, so you're listening to the other girls around you. You're supposed to be so free, right! I thought it was the worst damn thing that ever happened to me. I say, you call that great! They don't tell you about the pain.

the level of intimacy (beliefs, behavior, and perceptions of others) increased as one got closer to marriage. Petting was clearly the norm, particularly in the United States studies, if there was any degree of commitment. This factor, however, was of secondary interest to the central concern: the relationship between what a person believes, what a person does, and what a person perceives his friends and peers to be doing.

It was the author's contention that socialization practices in Judeo-Christian cultures led to the internalization of sexual beliefs that were relatively restrictive. Thus beliefs about proper behavior were expected to be more conservative than behavior or perception of others' behavior.

As a person gets involved in the courtship process, as going steady and a commitment type of relationship take place, the behavior will be beyond the boundaries of what is believed to be proper. After engaging in the behavior, the belief toward that behavior is likely to change in the direction of greater permissiveness. An interaction process is at work. More permissive behavior modifies the belief. Thus, while interrelated, it was expected that the behavior of unmarried persons involved in the courtship process would remain equal to or be more permissive than their belief as to proper behavior.

There are several reasons for the greater permissiveness of actual behavior than of belief as to proper behavior. It is likely that traditional values continue to be applied even when the behavior has changed. Also, it is possible that premarital sexual behavior is subject to more rapid social change than are attitudes. Robert Karen, as well as Robert Bell and Leonard Blumberg, found behavior while dating to exceed the limits the participants had previously set.[29, 30] This value-behavior conflict may produce guilt. Although numerous researchers[31] found a proportion of their respondents reporting guilt feelings, it is interesting that Reiss found that guilt did not inhibit sexual behavior.[32] A tendency exists to continue guilt-producing behavior until it is accepted.

The third factor that was likely to influence both behavior and personal belief was the perception of the behavior of peers (a reference group). If "all my friends are doing it" (whatever "it" may be), then I too had better get "with it." It was expected that 1) others' behavior is perceived to be more permissive than one's own, and 2) this expectation will lead to a more permissive behavior, which in turn leads to a more permissive belief as to what is proper. The causes of the differences mentioned above are not supported or rejected by the data but the basic hypothesis is supported. That is, students in Michigan in 1966 and 1971 and students in the Philipines in 1968–1969 were most conservative in what they believed, more permissive in what they said they did (behaviorally), and most permissive in what they perceived others to be doing.

PREMARITAL HETEROSEXUAL INTERCOURSE

Premarital sexual intercourse indicates that at least one of the partners is single and has not been previously married. It is premarital in that the person has never been married, not in the sense that the relationship is confined to the person one will marry. In American society premarital coitus usually involves two single persons, although one person may be married.

Cross-culturally, many societies permit sexual intercourse before marriage. In *Social Structure*, Murdock reports:

> Non-incestuous premarital relationships are fully permitted in 65 instances, and are conditionally approved in 43 and only modally disapproved in

---

29. Robert L. Karen, "Some Variables Affecting Sexual Attitudes, Behavior and Inconsistency," *Marriage and Family Living* 21 (August 1959), pp. 236–237.

30. Robert R. Bell and Leonard Blumberg, "Courtship Intimacy and Religious Background," *Marriage and Family Living* 21 (November 1959), p. 358.

31. Reiss, op. cit., pp. 118–119; Robert R. Bell and Leonard Blumberg, "Courtship Stages and Intimacy Attitudes," *Family Life Coordinator* 9 (March 1960), p. 62; Kinsey (*Male*), op. cit., pp. 316–319; and Ernest W. Burgess and Paul Wallin, *Engagement and Marriage* (New York: J. B. Lippincott, 1953), p. 374.

32. Reiss, op. cit., pp. 111–121.

Russian Revolution: A Sexual One

It may be that the major revolution in Russia is not one of class conflict but one of sexual behaviors. Parade (August 3, 1975) reported some results of a survey conducted by a Soviet magazine Nash Sovremennik. They discovered that university students overwhelmingly approved of premarital sex. More than half of the men had had their first sexual experience before age eighteen and nearly two-thirds of the women had had their first experience before age twenty-one.

In Leningrad, a majority of the women interviewed admitted they were on the lookout for extramarital affairs and were not in love with their husbands.

Other data from Russia suggest that unmarried cohabitation is common. Illegitimacy is increasing, while the total birthrate is decreasing. The incidence of divorce, premarital sex, and adultery all seem to have risen dramatically. Possibly the Soviet Union is in the midst of a marital and sexual revolution.

6, whereas they are forbidden in only 44. In other words, premarital license prevails in 70 percent of our cases. In the rest the taboo falls primarily on females and appears to be largely a precaution against child-bearing out of wedlock rather than a moral requirement.[33]

It should be recognized that many of Murdock's societal cases are relatively small ones, not the most populous Western societies. The actual proportion of the population that meet these criteria may be small. However, taking his figures at face value, the United States, at least traditionally, would fall within one of the more restrictive societies in regard to premarital sexual relationships. The United States, as in other instances, would place a greater taboo against the female, largely as a prevention of pregnancy out of wedlock. Thus, perhaps the crucial question, particularly for females, is not whether premarital intercourse will be permitted, but whether unmarried motherhood will be allowed. It is likely that a commitment to norms of chastity lessens as a separation of premarital intercourse from pregnancy becomes possible. Thus, if contraceptives, sterilization, abortion, or other social arrangements exist to prevent or terminate a pregnancy, premarital sexual permissiveness will increase.[34]

American society appears to be in a minority for not encouraging and granting social approval to premarital coitus among unmarried adolescent and teen-age youth, at least as a normative condition. In American society there are mixed attitudes concerning heterosexual coitus: there is widespread agree-

---

33. George P. Murdock, *Social Structure* (New York: Macmillan, 1949), p. 265.

34. Indirect support for this hypothesis was found by Delcampo and others who reported a positive relationship between knowledge of contraceptive devices and premarital sexual permissiveness. Robert L. Delcampo, Michael J. Sporakowski, and Diana S. Delcampo, "Premarital Sexual Permissiveness and Contraceptive Knowledge: A Biracial Comparison of College Students," *The Journal of Sex Research* 12 (August 1976), pp. 180–192.

ment that it is the most desirable, most mature, and socially most acceptable type of sexual outlet but, at the same time, religious and legal codes condemn it when it occurs outside of marriage and thereby negate all the claims concerning its desirability. According to Kinsey,

> Such conflicting appraisals of similar if not identical acts often constitute a source of considerable disturbance in the psycho-sexual development of American youth. These disturbances may have far-reaching effects upon subsequent adjustments in marriage. Our case histories show that this disapproval of heterosexual coitus and of nearly every other type of heterosexual type of activity before marriage is often an important factor in the development of homosexual activity.[35]

Frequency of Premarital Intercourse prior to 1965

The difference between the "ideal" and the "real" norm is significant: the ideal norm portrays what ought to be; the real norm portrays what is. Also significant is the difference between incidence and prevalence. Incidence is the occurrence or nonoccurrence of an experience. Generally, one has or has not had intercourse, is or is not a virgin, has or has not experienced orgasm. Prevalence is a different matter. Premarital intercourse may have occurred once or a thousand times. It may occur infrequently or on a regular basis. Thus the incidence rate (number who have or have not) differs considerably from the prevalence rate (frequency). Robert Bell states that probably few findings of the Kinsey reports were more shocking and upsetting to the American population than that showing that about 50 percent of all the married women studied had had premarital coitus (incidence).[36] Few findings so sharply illustrate the disparity between the values of premarital virginity and actual sexual behavior (prevalence). It should be noted that a considerable proportion of the premarital coitus had occurred in the year or two immediately preceding marriage, with a portion of it confined to the period just before marriage. In fact, among the married females who had premarital coitus, 87 percent had had at least a portion of it with men they subsequently married. Some 46 percent had confined coitus to their fiancé.[37]

In summarizing the incidence of premarital intercourse as indicated from approximately twenty different studies completed prior to 1955, Ehrmann noted that the incidence for males ranged from 32 to 73 percent and for

---

35. Kinsey (*Female*), op. cit., p. 285.
36. Robert R. Bell, *Premarital Sex in a Changing Society* (Englewood Cliffs, N.J.: Prentice Hall, 1966), p. 98.
37. Kinsey, (*Female*), op. cit., p. 292.

females from 7 to 47 percent.[38] At the time of his writing, there had been considerable unanimity of opinion that the percentage of college women engaging in premarital coitus ranged from 15 to 25 percent. Virtually all analyses up to that time and ten years later appeared to be in accord with Bell's (1966) conclusion:

> On the basis of the available evidence, it appears that the greatest changes in premarital coitus for the American female occurred in the period around World War I and during the 1920's. There is no evidence that the rates since that period have undergone any significant change. Probably the most important change in female premarital sexual behavior in more recent decades has been an increase in premarital petting.[39]

Frequency of Premarital Intercourse since 1965

Since the middle of the 1960s, many social forces have appeared on the American scene that have led to behavioral changes regarding premarital coitus and have the potential for producing further changes. In the last decade, a large number of youth has rejected many aspects of the major institutions in American society. A highly influential proportion of college students has been deeply involved in the civil rights movement and later in the protest over the Vietnam War. On most university campuses, the birth control pill became available and acceptable for personal use to a large number of unmarried co-eds. In addition, around the mid-1960s, sexual candor became increasingly legitimized in the mass media, even by one of the most conservative of the media—television. The result of these social forces developing in the latter half of the 1960s has led to a rapid increase in the rejection of many traditional values and in the development of increasingly important patterns of behavior common to a general youth culture. In 1970, three separate articles appeared in *Journal of Marriage and the Family* suggesting an increased rate of premarital coitus among college women along with less feelings of guilt about these experiences.

In February of 1970, Robert Bell and J. B. Chaskes reported on a 1968 replication of a 1958 study of premarital sexual behavior and attitudes.[40] The two groups of co-eds used were alike in social-class background (as measured by the education and occupations of their father), in age, in class standing, in religious background, and in the mean age of their first date. There were

---

38. Ehrmann, op. cit., pp. 41–42.
39. Bell, op. cit., p. 57.
40. Robert R. Bell and J. B. Chaskes, "Premarital Sexual Experience among Co-eds, 1958 and 1968," *Journal of Marriage and the Family* 32 (February 1970), pp. 81–84.

some significant changes from 1958 to 1968 in regard to premarital intercourse. The number of women having premarital coitus when in a dating relationship went from 10 percent in 1958 to 23 percent in 1968, and the coitus rates while going steady went from 15 percent in 1958 to 28 percent in 1968. While there was some increase in the rates of premarital coitus during engagement, 31 percent in 1958 to 39 percent in 1968, the change was not as striking as for the dating and going-steady stages. The data suggest that the decision for having intercourse in 1968 was much less dependent upon the commitment of engagement and more a question of individual decision regardless of the level of the relationship. To put it another way, if, in 1958, a co-ed had premarital coitus, it most often occurred while she was engaged. But in 1968, women

---

Bedding the Unwed

Sally Trull and Herb Clinch drive up to your rose-covered cottage in his old Volks and start unloading their bags for a weekend visit. Herb works with you at the recording studio. Sally went to school with your wife. They met a month ago at your apartment and have been seeing a lot of each other ever since. Where do you put their bags?

Together, in the guest room? Wait a minute, why are you assuming right off the bat that they want to sleep together? In separate rooms, then? But if they do want to sleep together, should you inflict this inconvenience on them, just for the sake of appearances? How in the world are you going to handle this situation without asking a very personal question you would probably not ask under any other circumstances?

The best solution is to put those bags in the front hall and dodge the issue for a minute. And if Herb is as clever as you've always thought, he'll seize the opportunity and say: "I'll put these bags in your guest room. Can you show me where it is?"

Or Sally might offer a cue to solitary slumber by saying: "I might as well unpack. Where do you want me to sleep?"

It really is Herb's responsibility or Sally's to resolve the big quandary. After all, it's their

secret—and they can't keep it past bedtime anyway.

None of this artful dodging would be necessary, of course, if you had cleared this all up with Herb at the time you invited him (or your wife could have done it with Sally). This does involve a prying question, but you can muffle it by saying: "We've only got one extra bedroom, but the couch folds out, if you don't mind."

The point is to make the guests decide and to let you know what they have in mind. Don't do what I did once in an excess of would-be liberated hosting and install two platonic friends, willy-nilly, in the same bed. They felt too awkward to come out and say they weren't making it and wanted separate quarters. And so they spent a chaste night together, and it was several weeks before one of them finally confided that our well-intentioned hospitality had gone a bit too far.

If, on the other hand, you are one of those people who feel strongly against and will not permit illicit cohabiting to go on under your roof, you may end up losing some friends. Forcing lovers apart purely for the sake of appearances is small-minded and, ultimately, impolite.

Source: Raymond Sokolov, "The New Etiquette," *Saturday Review of the Society* 55 (January 1973), p. 34.

were more often likely to have their first sexual experience while dating or going steady.[41] As stated by the authors in their summary:

> The most important finding of this study appears to be that the commitment of engagement has become a less important condition for many co-eds engaging in premarital coitus as well as whether or not they will have guilt feelings about that experience. If these findings are reasonably accurate, it could indicate the first significant change in premarital sexual behavior patterns since the 1920's.[42]

A second report on change in sexual behavior of college students came from Kaats and Davis in August of 1970. They state:

> In marked contrast to pre-1962 data on sexual behavior of college women were our findings in the spring of 1967 at the University of Colorado of a reported premarital coital rate of 41 percent—a figure about twice as high as that which has traditionally been reported at other universities. . . . Conversely, the figure for males, 60 percent, was nearly identical with that which has been reported since the turn of the century. If the findings could be replicated they may suggest that this university is much more "liberal" in this area than most or that we are experiencing a marked shift in the behavior of college women.[43]

The authors note a converging of sexual behavior (sexual equalitarianism) between males and females. Yet, despite this convergence and despite their relatively liberal sexual behavior, considerable evidence was found among men and women alike for the existence of a strong double standard. Both male and female respondents considered virginity for the female more important than for the male. Sisters, more than brothers, would be encouraged by their siblings not to engage in premarital intercourse. Respondents would lose more respect for females who engage in premarital intercourse without love than for males and felt that premarital coitus was more injurious to a girl's reputation than to a boy's.

Kaats and Davis indicate:

> It becomes clear that even in this liberal sample the majority of both men and women held a double standard. In this sample where barely more than half of the females were still virgins, 45 percent of the men wanted to marry a virgin. What this may suggest is that, while male attitudes may be changing, they may not be changing as rapidly as the sexual behavior of college women. Consequently, this discrepancy may result in male attitudes which are out of step with changes in the behavior of college women and point to an area which will cause some difficulty and conflict between the sexes.[44]

---

41. Bell and Chaskes, op. cit., pp. 82–83.
42. Ibid., p. 84.
43. Gilbert R. Kaats and Keith E. Davis, "The Dynamics of Sexual Behavior of College Students," *Journal of Marriage and the Family* 32 (August 1970), p. 390.
44. Ibid., p. 395.

Girls rated high on physical attractiveness were found to have higher premarital coital rates. In spite of not differing from the less attractive women in most of the attitudinal measures nor on background items (such as age, semester in college, family background, birth order, strength of religion, dating status, sorority membership, reasons for abstaining from or indulging in premarital coitus, and frequency in experiencing sexual urges), girls rated high on physical attractiveness were more likely to hold a favorable self-picture, rated themselves as physically attractive, had more friends of the opposite sex, believed that more of their friends had had intercourse, dated more frequently, had been in love more often, had had more petting experience, and had a higher rate of experience with intercourse. In the view of the authors:

> Data on the relationship between sexual behavior and physical attractiveness of women provided evidence for a "meaningful opportunity" interpretation of being physically attractive. . . . In our view, the more attractive girl is the target of more, more sincere, and more persistent romantic interactions.[45]

The third study, appearing in the *Journal of Marriage and the Family* in 1970, was written by Harold Christensen, who has devoted several decades to studying sexual behavior cross-culturally.[46] His study involved behavior as well as attitudes, studied males as well as females, compared three separate cultures, and measured identical phenomena in the same manner in the same populations at two different points in time.

In 1958, Christensen administered questionnaires to college samples in three cultures differing on a restrictive-permissive continuum: the highly restrictive Mormon culture in the western intermountain region of the United States; a moderately restrictive midwestern culture in central United States; and the highly permissive Danish culture which is a part of Scandinavia. The study was repeated in 1968 using the same questionnaire and administered in the same three universities.

Attitudes concerning premarital coitus were found to have liberalized considerably during the decade for both sexes (especially for females) in both the Danish and the two American cultures studied. Females still had more restrictive attitudes than males, but the difference was less than formerly. Premarital coital behavior, on the other hand, increased less dramatically or (in the case of American males) not at all. The authors note that the relatively more rapid change in attitudes has meant a decline in the discrepancy between values and behavior. The relatively greater liberalization of females has meant an intersex convergence of both attitude and behavior.

---

45. Ibid., p. 398.
46. Harold T. Christensen and Christina F. Gregg, "Changing Sex Norms in America and Scandinavia," *Journal of Marriage and the Family* 32 (November 1970), pp. 616–627.

A considerable amount of research, in addition to the studies cited, supports recent changes in premarital sexual behavior. Richard Udry et al.[47] examined trends in premarital coitus by cohort analysis of samples of white and black women living in sixteen U.S. cities. Their data suggest 1) increases in premarital coitus for each successive cohort, with the most rapid increase appearing for those age fifteen to nineteen in the late 1960s; 2) these increases were not attributable to changes in socioeconomic status; and 3) lower rates of premarital coitus among whites than blacks for all cohorts, regardless of socioeconomic status.

Ira Robinson et al.[48] found a liberalization in the sexual behavior of the college-educated female between 1965 and 1970. The change was most pronounced in petting behavior. Arthur Vener and Cyrus Steward[49] studied fourteen- and fifteen-year-olds in the same school system from 1970 to 1973. For both males and females they found significant increases in coitus over the three-year period. Interestingly, they found at this age level that sexual behavior was related to delinquency in general: car theft, vandalism, soft and hard drug use, smoking, and alcohol consumption.

Rebecca Vreeland, in reporting on sex at Harvard, states that both freshmen and seniors are experiencing much more sexual intimacy than they were a decade ago.[50] She claims that the social forces behind this increase seem to be the pill, which allays fears of unwanted pregnancy, opportunity for uninterrupted privacy brought on as the restrictions concerning opposite-sex visitors in student rooms have been dropped, a view of achieving climax via heavy petting as both hypocritical and unsatisfactory, and a general shift in morals away from the Victorian idea that sex is a sin, to be endured for the propagation of the species.

Karl Bauman and Robert Wilson,[51] comparing students in 1968 and 1972, reported 1) more permissive attitudes toward premarital sexual behavior (for both men and women), 2) fewer differences in attitudes between men and women, and 3) less adherence to the double standard. Roberta Nutt and William Sedlacek[52] found that 77 percent of the freshman males and 69 per-

47. J. Richard Udry, Karl E. Bauman, and Naomi M. Morris, "Changes in Premarital Coital Experience of Recent Decade-of-birth Cohorts of Urban American Women," *Journal of Marriage and the Family* 37 (November 1975), p. 783–787.

48. Ira E. Robinson, Karl King, and Jack O. Balswick, "The Premarital Sexual Revolution among College Females," *The Family Coordinator* 21 (April 1972), pp. 189–194.

49. Arthur M. Vener and Cyrus S. Stewart, "Adolescent Sexual Behavior in Middle America Revisited: 1970–1973, *Journal of Marriage and the Family* 36 (November 1974), pp. 728–735.

50. Rebecca S. Vreeland, "Sex at Harvard," *Sexual Behavior* 2 (February 1972), p. 9.

51. Karl E. Bauman and Robert R. Wilson, "Premarital Sexual Attitudes of Unmarried University Students: 1968 vs. 1972," *Archives of Sexual Behavior* 5 (1976), pp. 29–37; and Karl E. Bauman and Robert R. Wilson, "Sexual Behavior of Unmarried University Students in 1968 and 1972," *The Journal of Sex Research* 10 (November 1974), pp. 327–333.

52. Roberta L. Nutt and William E. Sedlacek, "Freshman Sexual Attitudes and Behavior," *Journal of College Student Personnel* (September 1974), p. 347.

cent of the freshman females at the University of Maryland in 1974 believed in sexual intercourse before marriage.

In a 1971 national probability sample of 4,600 females aged fifteen to nineteen, Melvin Zelnik and John Kantner[53] found that 28 percent were non-virginal (23 percent of the white teen-agers and 54 percent of the black teen-agers). Among nineteen-year-olds, 46 percent (40 percent of the white and 80 percent of the black) had premarital intercourse.[54] While numerous other results could be cited,[55] one factor appears clear: major changes have occurred in sexual attitudes and behavior, particularly among females, over the past two decades.

Changes in the Double Standard

Data on premarital sexual norms for both males and females come from the author's own studies completed at Western Michigan University in 1966 and 1971. As shown, major changes have taken place in this five year interval for males and females, with both sexes becoming increasingly more permissive. The results do not suggest promiscuity (indiscrimate sexual intermingling) but do suggest a widespread acceptance in attitude and behavior toward intercourse under conditions of "love," a marriage orientation, or a relationship of commitment.[56]

But what about the double standard? Is it decreasing? That is, are the sexual patterns and responses of males and females becoming more identical? Are male-female attitudes and behaviors less different than previously?[57] These questions can be partly answered by comparing the male-female re-

53. Melvin Zelnik and John F. Kantner, "Sexuality, Contraception and Pregnancy among Unwed Females in the United States," in the United States Commission on Population Growth and the American Future, *Demographic and Social Aspects of Population Growth* 1 (Washington, D.C.: Government Printing Office, 1972), p. 360.

54. John F. Kantner and Melvin Zelnik, "Sexual Experience of Young Unmarried Women in the United States," *Family Planning Perspectives* 4 (October 1972), pp. 9–18.

55. Morton Hunt, *Sexual Behavior in the 1970's*, Chicago: Playboy Press, 1974; Robert Sorensen, *Adolescent Sexuality in Contemporary America* (New York: World Publishing, 1973); Daniel Perlman, "Self-Esteem and Sexual Permissiveness," *Journal of Marriage and the Family* 36 (August 1974), pp. 470–473; and Robert H. Walsh, Mary Z. Ferrell, and William L. Tolone, "Selection of Reference Group, Perceived Reference Group Permissiveness and Personal Permissiveness Attitudes and Behavior: A Study of Two Consecutive Panels (1967–1971, 1970–1974), *Journal of Marriage and The Family* 38 (August 1976), pp. 495–507.

56. This finding is consistent with numerous other studies. Note in particular Robert A. Lewis and Wesley R. Burr, "Premarital Coitus and Commitment among College Students," *Archives of Sexual Behavior* 4 (1975), pp. 73–79.

57. Ferrell et al. found that attitudinally there was general support for a single standard of sexual permissiveness; however, behaviorally there was general support for a sexual double standard. Mary Z. Ferrell, William L. Tolone, and Robert H. Walsh, "Maturational and Societal Changes in the Sexual Double Standard: A Panel Analysis (1967–1971, 1970–1974)," *Journal of Marriage and the Family* 39 (May 1977), pp. 255–271.

sponse scores of 1966 with the male-female response scores of 1971. If the double standard is decreasing, the 1971 differences should be less than the 1966 differences.

The results can be seen in Table 13–2. What do they indicate? First, of the twelve mean-score differences for 1966 and 1971, six are greater in 1971 than they were in 1966 and six are smaller. Thus the double standard has both increased and decreased. Second, note where the increases and decreases in male-female differences occurred: five of the six increases exist at random dating and going steady, and five of the six decreases exist at pinned and engaged. This would indicate that in this five-year period, differences in beliefs and behavior between males and females increased under conditions of no or slight commitment. Under conditions of a greater commitment (pinned and engaged) the male-female differences (double standard) decreased. Third, in both 1966 and 1971, there was a general pattern of less male-female difference as one approached marriage. Although there are several exceptions, the least difference existed at engagement and the greatest difference at random dating and going steady. Thus, "love" tends to equate the sexual expression of males and females, resulting in a decrease in a double sexual standard between the sexes.

Summary

Premarital sexual relationships are generally thought to include a wide variety of sexual activities performed by those who have never been married. Nonmarital may be a more accurate and all-encompassing concept with the reference to any type of sexual activity occurring outside of the marital context. Sexual activity may include coitus, but in a more general sense, it includes a wide variety of touching, kissing, and caressing activities.

Three major types of heterosexual standards are possible in regard to coitus. One states that premarital intercourse is wrong for both sexes (a single standard of abstinence), a second states that premarital intercourse is right for both sexes (a single standard of permissiveness), and the third states that premarital intercourse is right for one sex but wrong for the other (a double standard). America has sexual standards that fit each logical possibility, but most are variations of basic types.

Serving as a preliminary to, or a substitute for, coitus is the widespread practice of petting. Distinct differences exist in petting activities by educational attainment for men, but not for women, although the better-educated females are more likely to accept the socially more taboo petting techniques. Petting, in addition to erotic response, fulfills functions relating to socialization and heterosexual adjustment. It has the greatest acceptance and approval under conditions of love and orientation toward marriage.

It was hypothesized and supported that people are most conservative in what they believe to be proper sexual behavior, more permissive in what

TABLE 13–2.   Male-Female Differences in Mean Scores of Sexual Permissiveness
at Various Stages of the Courtship Process

	Personal Belief	Personal Behavior	Perception of Others
1966			
Random dating	.83	1.42	.56
Going steady	1.00	1.07	.70
Pinned, lavaliered	1.02	.60	.63
Engaged	1.07	.30	.46
1971			
Random dating	1.13>	1.95>	.88>
Going steady	1.15>	1.20>	.59<
Pinned, lavaliered	.88<	1.83>	.27<
Engaged	.65<	.21<	.14<

they do, and most permissive in what they perceive others to be doing. This was tested in two countries and at two different times in the United States.

Premarital heterosexual intercourse is the specific sexual activity that has attracted the most attention. Widespread agreement existed among studies completed prior to the middle of the 1960s that rates of premarital coitus had not undergone any significant change since the 1920s, except for an increase in premarital petting among females.

Since the middle of the 1960s, many social forces have appeared on the American scene that have led to major behavioral changes. Agreement again seems to exist that significant changes have taken place (particularly among females on college campuses where the most research has been conducted) in the incidence, frequency, and acceptance of coitus. Interestingly, among coeds this change includes a decreasing importance of a commitment to marriage or conditions of engagement as a prerequisite for premarital coitus. Despite these changes, the existence of a strong double standard remains. Both males and females consider virginity for the female more important than for the male.

Has the double standard decreased between 1966 and 1971? Yes and no. It appears to have increased under conditions of no or slight commitment (dating and going steady) and decreased under conditions of a greater commitment (pinned and engaged). Whether this pattern will continue remains to be seen.

This chapter, following a chapter on sex in a social context, examined sex specifically in a premarital context. It included discussions on premarital sexual standards, premarital petting, and premarital heterosexual intercourse. In the next chapter our attention turns to sex in a marital context.

Key Terms and Topics

Discussion Questions

1. What are the pros and cons of the maintenance of a premarital sexual standard of 1) abstinence, 2) permissiveness with affection, 3) permissiveness without affection, 4) a double standard?
2. Discuss the statement, "Males deserve greater access to premarital coitus than do females and females who violate this standard are to be considered abnormal and unsuitable marriage partners."
3. In what ways are premarital sexual standards changing? Are these changes more likely among males or females? Why?
4. Discuss arguments for and against premarital sexual freedom.
5. What constitutes a premarital sexual relationship: glances, holding hands, touching noses, oral-breast manipulation, intercourse? Explain.
6. What social factors are related to the likelihood of petting activities? Consider age, social class, religions, and male-female statuses among others.
7. In what way does premarital petting or intercourse contribute to or hinder sexual adjustment in marriage? How could it affect general marital adjustment?
8. Does a "generation gap" exist in regard to premarital sexual behavior? If so, why? How can the gap be decreased?
9. To what extent do you think sexual norms in your school or community are similar to or different from the norms described in this chapter? Why?
10. Examine reasons as to why people are most conservative in what they believe to be proper, more permissive in what they do, and most permissive in what they perceive others to be doing.

Further Readings

Bell, Robert R. *Premarital Sex in a Changing Society.* Englewood Cliffs, N. J.: Prentice-Hall, 1966. A sociological analysis, based on available scientific research, of sexual attitudes and behavior in the United States.

DeLamater, John D. "Methodological Issues in the Study of Premarital Sexuality," *Sociological Methods and Research* 3 (August 1974), pp. 30–61. Methodological issues are examined in studies of premarital sexuality: variation in gender terms, variation in the order of measures of behavior, the sex of the interviewer, data from males versus females, and others.

Ehrmann, Winston. *Premarital Dating Behavior.* New York: Henry Holt, 1959. A study of the premarital heterosexual activities of over 1,000 male and female college students.

Gagnon, John H., and **William Simon.** *The Sexual Scene.* Chicago: Aldine, 1970. An interesting collection of articles on various aspects of sexual behavior that originally appeared in *Trans-Action* magazine.

Hunt, Morton. *Sexual Behavior in the 1970's.* Chicago: Playboy Press, 1974.

Juhasz, Anne McCreary. *Sexual Development and Behavior: Selected Readings.* Homewood, Ill.: Dorsey, 1973. An interdisciplinary collection of readings that attempts to address the problem of choosing a sexual life-style in harmony with self-concept, value system, ideals, and goals.

Kirkendall, Lester. *Premarital Intercourse and Interpersonal Relationships.* New York: Julian, 1961. From a study of young men on the meanings attached to premarital intercourse, an interpersonal framework is suggested as a basis for moral decision making.

Reiss, Ira L. *Premarital Sexual Standards in America.* Glencoe, Ill.: Free Press, 1960. A sociological investigation of the relative social and cultural integration of American sexual standards.

Reiss, Ira L. *The Social Context of Premarital Sexual Permissiveness.* New York: Holt, Rinehart and Winston, 1967. A systematic sociological study of premarital sexual attitudes with an integration of six basic propositions into one theory of sexual behavior.

Sorenson, Robert. *Adolescent Sexuality in Contemporary America.* New York: World, 1973. Interviews with 393 adolescents based on a national sampling of households.

Spanier, Graham B. "Perceived Parental Sexual Conservatism, Religiosity, and Premarital Sexual Behavior," *Sociological Focus* 9 (August 1976), pp. 285–298; "Formal and Informal Sex Education as Determinants of Premarital Sexual Behavior." *Archives of Sexual Behavior* 5 (1976), pp. 39–67; and "Perceived Sex Knowledge, Exposure to Eroticism, and Premarital Sexual Behavior: The Impact of Dating." *The Sociological Quarterly* 17 (Spring 1976), pp. 247–261. Three research reports drawing data from a national probability sample of 1,177 American college students.

14

Sexual Relationships in a Marital Context

14

Were it not for the legal and social norms pertaining to sex, there would be very little reason for differentiating marital sex from premarital, nonmarital, extramarital, postmarital, or any other type of sexual relationship. This is why, although both married and unmarried men and women were included in the research population of the Masters-Johnson studies, no controls were made for marital status. Early in their investigation, a nonmarried group provided the opportunity for comparison-controlled studies with established marital groups. However, in their words:

> The unrehearsed physiologic and anatomic response patterns of the unmarried were recorded and contrasted to the mutually conditioned and frequently stylized sexual response patterns of the marital units. This technique for experimental control was abandoned as soon as it was established unequivocally that there is no basic difference in the anatomy and physiology of human sexual response regardless of the marital status of responding units.[1]

The legal and social norms regarding sex in American society make coitus between husband and wife the one totally approved type of heterosexual activity. And, for most persons in American society, marital coitus provides throughout their lifetime a larger proportion of their total sexual outlet than any other activity. Cross-culturally, as well as in the United States, it is recognized as the most important of all sexual outlets because of the significant role it plays in the maintenance of the family system.

SEX AND MARRIAGE

Few would deny the importance of sexual intercourse to marriage. It is the one factor that, normatively at least, differentiates the marital relation-

---

1. William A. Masters and Virginia E. Johnson, *Human Sexual Response* (Boston: Little, Brown, 1966), pp. 16–17.

ship from any other social relationship. The relative importance of the sexual aspects of a marriage as compared with nonsexual aspects of a marriage will differ by sex, social class, and other factors. Let us examine first some selected results of the Kinsey studies, then turn our attention to recent changes in marital sexual activity and to other factors related to sex within a marital context.

Selected Results of the Kinsey Studies

In any discussion of sexual behavior in the United States, Kinsey's findings cannot be overlooked. In his study of American females, the incidences and frequencies of marital coitus had reached their maximum in the first year or two after marriage. From that point, they had steadily dropped into minimum frequencies in the oldest age groups. There is no other activity among females to show such a steady decline with advancing age.[2]

Kinsey notes that these declines in the incidences and frequencies of marital coitus, and of coitus to the point of orgasm, do not provide any evidence that the female ages in her sexual capacities. In fact, there is little evidence of the aging of the sexual capacities of the female until late in life. The decline is likely related to, and controlled by, the male's desires and it is primarily his aging rather than the female's loss of interest or capacity that is reflected in the decline.

One tragic finding for a number of marriages in Kinsey's studies was that many of the husbands reported that early in their marriages they had wanted coitus more often than their wives, and the younger married females reported that they would be satisfied with lower coital rates than their husbands wanted. On the other hand, in the later years of marriage, many of the females expressed the wish that they could have coitus more frequently than their husbands were then desiring it. Over the years most females become less inhibited and develop an interest in sexual relations that they may then maintain until they are in their fifties or even sixties.[3]

There were surprisingly few differences between the frequencies of marital coitus among females of the several educational levels represented in Kinsey's sample. Men provide an interesting contrast. In the lower educational groups, about 80 percent of the total outlet in the early years of marriage is provided by marital coitus, and the incidence for this group increases to 90 percent as the marriage is continued. For the college-educated man, marital coitus provides 85 percent of the total outlet during the early part of marriage, but by the time he reaches the age of 55, only 62 percent of his total

---

2. Alfred C. Kinsey, Wardell B. Pomeroy, Clyde E. Martin, and Paul H. Gebhard, *Sexual Behavior in the Human Female* (Philadelphia: W. B. Saunders, 1953), p. 348.

3. Ibid., p. 353.

sexual outlet is provided by marital coitus. At no time in their lives do college-bred males depend on marital intercourse to the extent that lower-level males do throughout most of their marriages.[4]

Kinsey suggests that only the upper-level males become increasingly interested in extramarital relations as they grow older.[5] Why is this so? It may be that the increased frequency of extramarital intercourse is due to 1) a conclusion that the early restraints on their sexual lives were not justified, 2) a conclusion that extramarital experience should be secured before old age has interfered with the capacity to do so, 3) an increasing dissatisfaction with the relations with restrained upper-level wives, or 4) a preoccupation of the educated male with the professional or business affairs of his life leading to a decrease in marital intercourse—and perhaps increased nonmarital opportunities. It should be noted that 19 percent of the total sexual activity, aside from marital coitus, is not in homosexual contacts or extramarital intercourse, but rather is from such solitary activities as masturbation and nocturnal emissions.[6]

The frequency of marital coitus, again according to Kinsey, decreases with age, dropping from an average of 3.7 times per week during the teens to about 2.7 at the age of thirty, 1.4 at the age of forty, and 0.8 at the age of sixty.[7] Male and female estimates are highly comparable although females tend to estimate the frequencies of their marital coitus higher than males estimate them. Females who desire less coitus than they have are likely to overestimate, whereas males who wish for more than they obtain are likely to underestimate.

The precoital techniques in marriage were quite the same as those found in the premarital petting that may or may not have led to coitus. In Kinsey's sample:

> Simple lip kissing between the spouses had almost always (99.4 percent) been an accompaniment to the marital coitus. In order of descending incidences, the other techniques which were used at least on occasion had included the manual stimulation of the female breast by the male (in 98 percent); the manual stimulation of the female genitalia by the male (in 95 percent); the oral stimulation of the female breast (in 93 percent); the manual stimulation of the male genitalia by the female (in 91 percent); extended oral techniques in deep kissing (in 87 percent); and finally the oral stimulation of the female genitalia by the male (in 54 percent) and of the male genitalia by the female (in 49 percent).[8]

---

4. Alfred C. Kinsey, Wardell B. Pomeroy, and Clyde E. Martin, *Sexual Behavior in the Human Male* (Philadelphia: W. B. Saunders, 1948), p. 567.

5. Ibid., 568.

6. Ibid.

7. Kinsey (*Female*), op. cit., p. 77.

8. Ibid., p. 361.

Secrets of a Trim, Attractive Body

Do you want to achieve or maintain a good-looking, sleek body? A New York doctor, Abraham I. Friedman, recently reported that "sex is the ideal substitute for the gratification of emotional overeating."

Dr. Friedman, who for 25 years has worked exclusively on weight control problems, said that increased sexual activity can help overweight people lose as much as four to five pounds a month in addition to the loss from regular dieting. He said the cause of many of his patients overeating was emotional and that most of them had sexual difficulties. "They were substituting food for sex and love."

Dr. Friedman reported that the center of sexual response is in the same area of the brain that contains the center of appetite control. So, aside from the calories burned up (about 200) in the physical activity of lovemaking, "it is very likely that the increased activity of one center—sex—may have a dampening effect on the other—appetite."

Psychologically, there is a close link between our basic needs for food and sex. "When people are deprived of love and sex," said Dr. Friedman, "they often turn to food and overeat." Conversely, pounds and inches can be lost by sensibly substituting one basic need for another. The doctor said that "for every three times you substitute sex for a 700-calorie snack, you'll lose more than one pound."

Moral: Next time you feel the urge to reach for a peanut-butter-and-banana sandwich, now you know what you really should be reaching for.

Source: *Sexology* 39 (November 1972), p. 69. Reprinted by permission.

How do Kinsey's data compare with more recent research? Note selected similarities and differences in marital sexual activity reported by Kinsey at the middle of the century with reported activity today.

Change and Factors Related to Marital Sexual Activity

Some of the changes in frequency of sexual activity mentioned in the chapter on premarital sexual behavior appear to be paralleled in marriage. Charles Westoff,[9] reporting on data from national probability samples of married women of reproductive age in 1965 and 1970, showed an increase in the overall coital frequency (see Figure 14–1). The increase is slightly higher among women in their twenties than among older women, but the increase appears among women at all ages studied. This rise in reported coital frequency between 1965 and 1970 was found to exist almost regardless of method

9. Charles F. Westoff, "Coital Frequency and Contraception," *Family Planning Perspectives* 6 (Summer 1974), pp. 136–141.

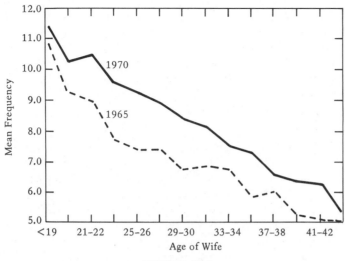

FIGURE 14–1.

Mean Coital Frequency in Four Weeks Prior to Interview, by Age, 1965 and 1970. Source: Charles F. Westoff, "Coital Frequency and Contraception," *Family Planning Perspectives* 6 (Summer 1974), Figure 2, p. 137. Reprinted by permission.

of contraceptive used and even where no method was used. Thus it is not accurate to attribute the increase in coital frequency entirely to the increase in the proportion of women using the pill. On the other hand, the author notes that it seems reasonable to infer that the greater use of more reliable methods decreased anxiety about unintentional pregnancy and, therefore, relaxed some of the constraints on sexual expression (or perhaps on the willingness to talk about it).[10]

Since there remains an increase in coital frequency over and above that accounted for by types of exposure to risk, how can this increase be explained? In addition to the influence of modern contraceptive technology, the availability of legal abortion could be said to further reduce anxiety about unwanted pregnancy. Other factors likely include the increase in openness about sex since the mid-1960s, the exploitation of sexual themes by the mass media, the developing emphasis on the woman's right to personal fulfillment, a shift from the traditional passive sexual role to more assertive behavior among women, and the viewing of sex itself as a more natural, less taboo topic.

Figure 14–1 shows what other studies indicate in regard to the relationship between coital frequency and age: a decline in frequency of coitus as age increases. This should not be interpreted to mean that sex becomes unimportant in marriage after age forty. But it may call for a redefining of aging sexual behavior and the development of values that maximize the sexual relation-

---

10. Ibid., p. 138.

ship of aging couples. This may include the elimination of a stereotype that
only links sex with youth and the early years of marriage. This may include
viewing sexual activity as more than "performance" oriented, more than
genitally or intercourse oriented, and more than orgasm oriented. Other forms
include nongenital sexual pleasuring and oral and digital manipulations that
may or may not result in actual physiological orgasm and/or ejaculation.[11]

Many factors other than contraceptive usage and age have been found
to be highly related to marital sexual activity. John Edwards and Alan Booth[12]
indicate that the more severe the marital strain, the lower the frequency of
marital coitus. They suggest that the sexual behavior of both males and females is largely contextual, determined to a greater extent by present circumstances (like marital strain) than past background.

Westoff reports that coital frequency increases with the amount of education of the wife, is higher among women who work in paid employment
than those who do not work (highest among career-motivated women), and is
positively associated with the effectiveness of contraception.[13] The highest
frequencies are reported by women who are using the pill or the IUD or whose
husbands have had vasectomies. The lowest frequencies are associated with
the use of the rhythm method and the douche.

The one exception to the positive correlation between coital frequency
and effectiveness of contraception was with the sterilized women.[14] Women
electing tubal ligations are drawn disproportionately from the poorest, least
educated strata and are likely to have had more children than couples in
which the husband elects to have a vasectomy.[15]

As has been noted elsewhere, sexual activity (premarital, petting, masturbation, oral-genital, and so on) varies considerably by educational and social class background. Again, the same pattern occurs within marriage. One
prime example is indicated by Lee Rainwater in a report on marital sexuality
in four cultures of poverty: Mexico, Puerto Rico, England, and the United
States.[16] The central sexual norm among the "culture of the poor" is that sex
is a man's pleasure and a woman's duty. Women are believed not to have sex-

---

11. Martha Cleveland, "Sex in Marriage: At 40 and Beyond," *The Family Coordinator* 25
    (July 1976), pp. 233–240.

12. John N. Edwards and Alan Booth, "Sexual Behavior in and out of Marriage; An As-
    sessment of Correlates," *Journal of Marriage and the Family* 38 (February 1976), pp.
    73–81.

13. Westoff, op. cit., pp. 139–140.

14. Ibid., p. 140.

15. H. B. Presser and L. L. Bumpass, "Demographic and Social Aspects of Contraceptive
    Sterilization in the United States: 1965–1970," in U.S. Commission on Population
    Growth and the American Future, *Demographic and Social Aspects of Population
    Growth*, edited by C. F. Westoff and R. Parke, Jr., vol. 1 of *Commission Research Re-
    ports*, U.S. Government Printing Office, 1972, p. 505.

16. Lee Rainwater, "Marital Sexuality in Four Cultures of Poverty," *Journal of Marriage
    and the Family* 26 (November 1964), pp. 457–466.

ual desires at all, and those who do are referred to as "loca" (crazy) in Mexico or immoral in the other three cultures. Generally, husbands in this subculture don't expect their wives to be demanding or passionate. A large proportion of the wives dwell on the negative aspects of sex, speaking of submitting to their husband's "abuse" because it's their obligation.

Rainwater's explanatory hypothesis to account for the pattern of marital sexuality in cultures of poverty relates to the degree of segregation in the role relationship. He suggests that in societies where there is a high degree of role segregation of husbands and wives, the couple will tend not to develop a close sexual relationship, and the wife will not look upon sexual relations with her husband as sexually gratifying.[17] Thus where husbands and wives are likely to segregate work and recreational or domestic activities, this is likely to influence the nature of their sexual relationship as well.

Autoeroticism in Marriage

In the chapter on sex in a social context, masturbation or autoeroticism was mentioned as a common sexual outlet. One would assume and expect that if masturbation is considered a substitute for intercourse, the frequency of masturbation would be low among the married who have daily sexual access to a partner. This hypothesis was not borne out. J. S. Greenberg and F. X. Archambault did not find significant differences between frequencies of masturbation and intercourse,[18] and Hessellund found that while there was a significant difference in intercourse frequency among married and unmarried subjects, there were no significant differences in frequency of masturbation between married and unmarried subjects.[19]

In or out of marriage, more men than women masturbate and do so more frequently. Hessellund tentatively concludes that for men masturbation functions more as a supplement to sexual life, while for women it is to a greater extent a substitute for intercourse.[20] Gagnon and Simon attribute the continued masturbation of men after marriage—and not only when their wives are absent—to continuation of the acting out of sexual fantasies that first developed in early adolescence.

For women, it could be predicted that as gender role training includes the development of sexual imagery, an increase in masturbatory activity, for both married and single women, would follow. Masturbation permits independent and autonomous control of pleasure, producing an orgasm that fe-

17. Ibid., pp. 465–466.
18. J. S. Greenberg and F. X. Archambault, "Masturbation, Self-Esteem and Other Variables, *Journal of Sex Research* 9 (February 1973), pp. 41–51.
19. Hans Hessellund, "Masturbation and Sexual Fantasies in Married Couples," *Archives of Sexual Behavior* 5 (1976), pp. 133–147.
20. Ibid., p. 139.

males particularly find to be more intense physiologically than occurs from intercourse. This may result from the fact that the masturbator does not have to regulate his or her own sexual pleasure to the sequence or routines of another person and thus inhibit the power of self-gratification.[21]

SEXUAL ADJUSTMENT

Sexual adjustment has been highlighted by certain writers as the keystone to marital adjustment. However, it is highly unlikely that adjustment of any sort is a dichotomous either/or phenomenon. Within any marriage, there are certain times and situations in which sex is "better or worse" than other times or situations. Also, to assume that frequency of intercourse, attainment of female orgasm, or an uninhibited sex life is equal to sexual adjustment is both misleading and false. It is very difficult to separate sex from the total complex of interaction that constitutes married life. Sexual adjustment may be one indicator of general marital adjustment, but it is doubtful that sexual adjustment alone will maintain an otherwise "poor" relationship. Dissatisfaction in a marriage is likely to be reflected in the frequency and performance of marital coitus, and conflict in sexual coitus may be symptomatic of other tensions within the marital relationship. What appears to be significant in sexual adjustment in marriage is that both husband and wife be mutually satisfied.

Masters and Johnson estimate that 50 percent of all marriages in the United States have some form of sexual inadequacy, such as primary or secondary impotence, vaginismus, premature ejaculation, orgasmic dysfunction, unequal levels of response, or others.[22] This may be a partial explanation for the popularity of sex manuals.

Marriage-Sex Manuals

An indirect indication of the desire for sexual adjustment in marriage may stem from the sale of marriage manuals. This assumes, perhaps falsely, that the purchases are made 1) primarily by married persons and 2) for purposes of improving sexual relations within marriage. Nevertheless, the wide circulation of some of these manuals is astounding. By 1977, one volume[23] in its fifty-fifth printing had sold over 670,000; a second[24] had "been read

---

21. John H. Gagnon and William Simon, *Sexual Conduct* (Chicago: Aldine, 1973), p. 65.
22. William H. Masters and Virginia E. Johnson, *Human Sexual Inadequacy* (Boston: Little Brown, 1970), pp. 351–369.
23. Hannah M. Stone and Abraham Stone, *A Marriage Manual* (New York: Simon and Schuster, 1953).
24. Eustace Chesser, *Love Without Fear* (New York: The New American Library, 1947).

Rape in Marriage

If rape means sexual intercourse by force and without the consent of the other person, nowhere is rape more common than in marriage. But legally, rape cannot occur between husband and wife since in many areas the wife is technically "property" owned by and responsible to the husband. In South Australia, this may be changed. Legislation proposed by the labor government would permit wives to charge their husbands with rape.

by" 3,500,000; and a third[25] advertises on its cover "over a million and a half copies in print." One national bestseller[26] claims to be a "gourmet guide to love making." Whether these books are read, the advice is followed, or the relationship is affected is another issue. Sales alone, however, indicate the widespread interest.

Unfortunately, many popular manuals, magazines, and journals, in fulfilling a basic function of educating and informing men and women about sex, have also contributed to a fear of sexual performance. To be informed about the average number of coital experiences per week among married couples, multiple orgasms, or coital positions may be very interesting but may also lead to serious questioning and doubts about one's own performance. The male and female whose sexual practices do not conform to the social norms may seriously question their own adequacy or "normality." If other couples are having intercourse three or four time a week and we are engaging in coitus once a month, is something wrong? If other women during orgasm turn blue, hear bells chime, or pant and scream ecstatically, am I less of a woman if I quietly experience a pleasant sensation? Masters and Johnson state that these grave self-doubts and usually groundless suspicions are translated into fears of performance.

> It should be restated that fear of inadequacy is the greatest known deterrent to effective sexual functioning, simply because it so completely distracts the fearful individual from his or her natural responsivity by blocking reception of sexual stimuli either created by or reflected from the sexual partner.[27]

The Masters-Johnson Program

Probably no therapy program for dealing with sexual inadequacies has ever been undertaken with as solid a research base and as great an instance of success as that of the Reproductive Biology Research Foundation under the directorship of Masters and Johnson. One of many exciting aspects of

25. John E. Eichenlaub, *The Marriage Art* (New York: Dell, 1961).
26. Alex Comfort, ed., *The Joy of Sex* (New York: Simon and Schuster, 1972).
27. Masters and Johnson, op. cit., pp. 12–13.

Louise: *All my views aren't that clear-cut. I suppose I could come off as the wisest in the world if I had clear-cut views on what the place of sex is in an adult life. Through our married life, it definitely had a place. It definitely was tied in with procreation. But I was not real fruitful, because I said that we did not use any contraceptives and I became pregnant only five times. I miscarried once. If I had become pregnant twelve times, perhaps I would have shifted my views on it too. I realize that it's reality, but I do think . . . well, even the joy of it was heightened during pregnancy.*

Ann: *Sex is important, it's part of marriage. To me it's part of any important relationship. And, it's like anything else. You have to work at it, you know. You've heard the old cliche that blacks are really great at it. That's not really so; they have to work at it like everyone else. That means you just can't, hey, jump into it and have sex and say, oh wow, it was satisfying because he's such a great guy. You know, that's not so. I like foreplay and my husband doesn't. At first, we used to have foreplay, and then after we were married for awhile, he just, you know, right in there, right out . . . sleep, you know. I don't know. I think it's something you have to work at, it's an art.*

Mac: *I like to experiment with life and polygamy with a group or sexual encounters, but there's a problem. In general, I'm still the aggressor in bed and there has been occasion where she starts to aggress me and I become impotent. Psychologically, I've gotta get this out of the front of my mind because she is equally . . . uh . . . she has just as much right to my body as I do hers. Our general pattern is to try anything with each other.*

their therapy program is that marriages, or "units," are treated and are a focus of the treatment. If one person has a problem, the other person can not claim to be "uninvolved."

> Isolating a husband or wife in therapy from his or her partner not only denies the concept that both partners are involved in the sexual inadequacy with which their marital relationship is contending, but also ignores the fundamental fact that sexual response represents (either symbolically or in reality) interaction between people. The sexual partner ultimately is the crucial factor.[28]

Secondly, all treatment in the therapy program is by a dual-sex therapy team (one man, one woman) from separate professional disciplines (one from the biological sciences and one from the behavioral sciences). It is their belief that a dual-sex team avoids the potential therapeutic disadvantage of inter-

---

28. Ibid., p. 2. Reprinted by permission.

preting patient complaints on the basis of male or female bias, contributes a "reality factor," helps in communication, increases honesty, and discourages transference, that is, an identity with a therapist rather than the partner or spouse.

A third significant aspect of their therapy that cannot be overlooked is their overall success rate of 80 percent as checked five years after the treatment. Their initial failure rate for males and females regardless of the type of sexual inadequacy was 18.9 percent.[29] An evaluation five years after termination of the treatment program showed a failure rate of 20 percent. To the authors it is clear that once the sexual inadequacies of primary impotence, premature ejaculation, ejaculatory incompetence, and primary and situational orgasmic dysfunction are reversed during the rapid-treatment phase of the therapy program, these inadequacies rarely return to distress the person previously handicapped.[30]

The purpose of the treatment program is to restore sex to its natural context so it functions like breathing, that is, without conscious effort and with spontaneity. The types of dysfunctions they attempt to correct include primary (total) and secondary (partial) impotence, premature ejaculation, and ejaculatory incompetence on the part of the male; orgasmic dysfunction and vaginismus on the part of the female; and dyspareunia (painful intercourse) and the aging process on the part of both sexes.[31]

Three concepts that appear particularly significant to the behavioral scientist are what they term the "spectator role," the "sexual value system," and their emphasis on "sensate focus."[32]

The spectator role involves learning to eliminate the negative effect of self-consciously trying to produce certain sexual results. It attempts to eliminate the deliberate placing of the mind on what is desired rather than on a "natural response." In reference to the spectator role of the impotent husband, the authors note:

> As sex play is introduced and mutual attempts made by marital partners to force an erective response, the impotent husband finds himself a spectator to his own sexual exchange. He mentally is observing his and his partner's response (or lack of it) to sexual stimulation. Will there be an erection? If and when the penis begins to engorge, how full will the erection become? When

---

29. Ibid., p. 361.
30. Ibid., p. 366.
31. Here, dysfunction refers to a sexual malfunction, usually social and psychological in origin. Primary impotence refers to the inability to ever achieve or maintain an erection sufficient for intercourse. Secondary impotence refers to failure at some times, success at others. Premature ejaculation refers to ejaculation before, immediately upon, or shortly after penetration. Orgasmic dysfunction refers to the inability and failure of the female to reach orgasm. Vaginismus refers to the psychosomatic illness that affects a woman's ability to respond sexually by virtually closing the vaginal opening to male entry. Dyspareunia refers to painful intercourse.
32. Ibid., pp. 65–66, 25–26, 67–75.

erection is obtained, how long will it last? The involuntary spectator in the room demands immediate answers for these questions from the anxious man in the bed, so intensely concerned with his fears of sexual performance. Rather than allowing himself to relax, enjoy sensual stimulation, and permit his natural sexual responsivity to create and maintain the erective process, he as a spectator demands instant performance. In the spectator role, a dysfunctional man completely negates any concept of natural sexual function. He cannot conceive of involuntary sexual responsivity sustaining an erection as a natural physiological process on the same natural plane as that of his involuntary respiratory responsivity sustaining his breathing mechanism.[33]

The problem is compounded because the wife too is operating in the spectator role. In her attempt to provide her husband with an erection, she too may be questioning what she is doing wrong in assisting him to perform adequately. Again in the author's words:

> Neither partner realizes that the other is mentally standing in an opposite corner, observing the marital bedding scene in a spectator role. Both partners involuntarily distract themselves in their spectator roles, essentially uninvolved in the experience in which they are involved, to such an extent that there is no possibility for effective sexual stimuli to penetrate the impervious layers of performance fear and involuntary voyeurism.[34]

The "sexual value system" termed SVS by the authors refers to those sensory experiences an individual has had under circumstances that he or she finds pleasurable on the one hand and, on the other, not offensive to the values he or she has learned from society (e.g., family, church, school, peer group, or other). Physiologically, male and female sexual response are very similar, but where the female differs radically is in her sexual value system— her psychosocial aspect of sexuality.

> It is obvious that man has had society's blessing to build his sexual value system in an appropriate, naturally occurring context and woman has not. Until unexpected and usually little understood situations influence the onset of male sexual dysfunction, his sexual value system remains essentially subliminal and its influence more presumed than real. During her formative years the female dissembles much of her developing functional sexuality in response to societal requirements for a "good girl" facade. Instead of being taught or allowed to value her sexual feelings and anticipation of appropriate and meaningful opportunity for expression, thereby developing a realistic sexual value system, she must attempt to repress or remove them from their natural context of environmental stimulation under the implication that they are bad, dirty, etc. She is allowed to retain the symbolic romanticism which usually accompanies these

33. Ibid., p. 65. Reprinted by permission.
34. Ibid., p. 66. Reprinted by permission.

sexual feelings but the concomitant sensory development with the symbolism that endows the sexual value system with meaning is arrested or labeled—for the wrong reasons—objectionable.[35]

In many ways society prohibits the female in American society from developing a positive sexual value system. Whereas the male may often be praised or honored in his sexual performance, the reality of the female's sexual function today still carries many implications of shame and misbehavior—neither of which contributes to high levels of marital sexual harmony. Many women are reared in our society to believe that "nice girls don't involve themselves," "sex is for reproductive purposes," or "sex is a man's privilege." As Lehrman notes in his explanation of the Masters and Johnson studies:

> As an example of a negative value, most women in this society are offended by the idea of being sexually stimulated in a nonprivate setting. So, if the couple attempted sex play or intercourse where there was a danger of interruption and exposure, the part of the female partner's brain that sends out sexual signals to the body would probably hold those signals back: she'd fail to be stimulated (even though everything else in that particular setting was acceptable to her). There are many other negative values commonly affecting females in our society such as taboos relating to premarital sex, touching the genitals, etc.
>
> An example of the positive value might be the familiar one of romantic music with the lights low, or the memory of a favorite male caressing her neck, or a penchant for dark-haired men deriving from her feelings for her dark-haired father or a dark-haired first date, etc. The list is infinitely variable, depending on who the woman is and how she grew up in society.[36]

The core of the relearning process centers around the sense of touch (sensate focus). Sensate focus involves one partner serving as "the giver of pleasure" and the other partner delegated to "get pleasure."

> Sensate focus, the dimension of touch, was chosen to provide the sensory experience most easily and appropriately available to marital partners as a medium for physical exchange in reconstituting natural responsivity to sexual stimuli. The sense of touch is not only a primary component of psycho-sexual response but it is also considered a most meaningful form of psycho-social communication in this and many other societies. The familiarity with which touch is customarily, often spontaneously, used to greet, show affection, comfort, reassure, etc., gives this medium of sensate expression exceptional value for bridging the chasm of physical restraint in, or actual withdrawal from, sexual interchange so often present between marital partners contending with sexual dysfunction.[37]

---

35. Ibid., pp. 215–216. Reprinted by permission.
36. Nat Lehrman, *Masters and Johnson Explained* (Chicago: Playboy Press, 1970), p. 37.
37. Masters and Johnson, op. cit., p. 76.

Gripes About Sex, Italian Style

A survey among married Italian women has unleashed a barrage of complaints about married Italian men.

Sex in marriage, many of them lamented, is a household chore, for the convenience and pleasure of husbands only. A quarter of the women interviewed said they have been unfaithful to their husbands, and half the faithful ones said they remained so only because they didn't have the chance to do otherwise.

The wives' complaints are outlined in a recent book by Lieta Harrison, a Sicilian writer who surveyed the sex habits of 1,056 married women. Miss Harrison interviewed an equal number of mothers and their married daughters, posing the same questions to ascertain changing attitudes.

"Within a generation," the writer concluded, "Italian society has changed radically. The married daughters have discovered 'sex.' They believe that sex is not 'shameful.' They have also found out their 'right to orgasm.'"

The elder mothers—42 per cent of them —even accept that their husbands should be more passionate with their mistresses than with their wives. Only 3.5 per cent of the young married ones agree with that.

Sixty-six per cent of the young married women consider sex the most important factor in marriage. Only 8 per cent of their mothers think so.

Yet the mothers and their married daughters agree on one thing: disappointment with their husbands.

"My husband considers our home a hotel," complains one wife, 34. "He comes home, demands food, sleeps alone and goes away."

Miss Harrison writes: "Italian men are disappointing as lovers, overbearing as husbands, phantom fathers. They are also negligent and unprotecting—and adulterers."

Between a quarter and 30 per cent of the wives interviewed said they are aware of their husbands' extramarital affairs. But, according to the survey, more than a quarter of the young housewives retaliate in the same manner, double from the figure a generation ago.

"With no reason, he stopped loving me," a wife was quoted in the survey. "But I am young, 28, and I have the right to a normal life. That's why I have a lover."

Said one faithful Roman wife, "I haven't betrayed him because I am stupid."

Another said, "I'm always pregnant, that's why."

Source: *The Washington Post*, January 4, 1973, p. C-8. © *The Washington Post*. Reprinted with permission.

The authors state that, for many couples, sensate-focus sessions represent the first opportunity to "think and feel" sensuously without pushing for an orgasm, explaining sensate preferences, demanding personal reassurances, or sensing a need to "return the favor." Early in the training, one partner may touch anything but genitals and breasts while the other partner tries to relax and envelop himself in sensory pleasure. Later treatment includes touching the genitals and other sensate-focus activities.

As noted, Masters and Johnson indicate that the greatest overall cause of malfunction is fear. It is fear that makes a person overly conscious of what he is doing—fear of failure, fear of not pleasing the other person, and so on that lead to sexual difficulty. If Masters and Johnson and their therapy team are correct, as their success rate seems to indicate, their research and program could reorient sex education programs from doctors, nurses, and health[38] to an increased role for the social and behavioral scientist.

EXTRAMARITAL COITUS

A chapter on sexual relationships in a marital context may well be incomplete without a look at sexual relationships among married persons with other persons (married or single). The family in a pluralistic society is not without sex in plural and diverse patterns and relationships.

The term extramarital coitus or adultery refers to nonmarital sexual intercourse between a man and a woman, at least one of whom is married at the time to someone else. Almost without exception in the United States, adultery is legally punishable. And although actual prosecution is rare, the moral condemnation that accompanies extramarital coitus is, in general, much stronger than that directed at premarital or postmarital coitus. It is widely held that adultery is condemned in practically all western cultures because of the threat it poses to the family unit. Secondly, it is assumed (and sometimes falsely so) that marriage provides a socially approved legitimate sexual partner, and thus sexual deprivation is minimized.

Most societies recognize the legitimacy of some extramarital coitus under certain conditions, but all societies have placed certain limitations on extramarital coitus and have developed certain means for enforcing the restrictions. Robert Harper says that the reasons for the restrictions in most preliterate groups, ancient societies, and even recent civilizations have not been because of sexual restrictions per se or even because of morality. Rather, "Adultery has most often been considered a threat to the economic stability of society; most specifically, male property rights."[39]

The double standard is widespread in regard to adultery. Much greater concern centers around the extramarital behavior of the wife than that of the husband. Kinsey notes that most societies permit or condone extramarital coitus for the male if he is reasonably circumspect about it and if he does not carry it to extremes that would break up his home, lead to the neglect of his family, outrage his in-laws, stir up public scandal, or start difficulties with the husbands or other relatives of the women with whom he has his relationships.[40] On the other hand, such extramarital activity is much less frequently

---

38. SIECUS, The Sex Information and Education Council of the United States, from its inception, defined sex as a "health" entity. This orientation is perhaps explained by the founding of the organization by an M.D. and the major role given to physicians in its operation.

39. Robert A. Harper, "Extramarital Sex Relations," in Albert Ellis and Albert Abarbanel, *Encyclopedia of Sexual Behavior* (New York: Hawthorne, 1961), p. 384.

40. Kinsey (*Female*), op. cit., p. 414.

> *Alex:*   Don't believe that sex doesn't occur outside of marriage in my coun-
> try. I'll tell you that sexual relationships occur, but it's such a shame
> that it's always covered up. See, in America a man goes out and does
> anything he likes the night before, right? Then he comes back to his
> friend at work the next day and brags about it. Now that's another
> thing that I was very surprised about. Sins are the same sins; it's
> just that in America people take pride in doing those sins. They brag
> about it. Back home we don't brag about it. You don't tell people
> what you will do tonight, or whenever.
>
> *Ann:*   Do I believe in a one man-one woman marriage or relationship? For
> me, no. But for others just starting out, I say give it a chance. And I
> think this is the way to be if you want to make it. If you don't, then
> do what you want. See who you want. But I'm very, well . . . I used
> to really just get upset by the fact that someone's cheating on me. It
> used to bother me a lot. I would honestly get very upset. I would not
> let a husband bring a woman in my home, and I knew his wife, you
> know.
>
> My husband's first cousin did this to me. We had a very bad argu-
> ment about it, and he left home because of it. I said to my husband,
> well, why would you want him to bring some other woman to my
> home when you know his wife comes here? I said, I think it's very
> wrong and very unfair to her. I'm sitting there laughing with her,
> and ha-ha-ha, how're you doing, and I know this is going on. I said,
> I feel wrong, I wouldn't tell her about it, no. But I still feel guilty
> about the fact of letting this happen or go on in my home.

permitted or condoned for the female. And when it is permitted, it usually
occurs on special occasions or with particular persons (such as at certain orgiastic ceremonies, for the new bride as part of the marriage ceremony, or, in
a few instances, as a means of entertaining the husband's guests.)

Even though a double standard exists in the United States, it is far less
pronounced than in many countries that provide and permit considerable
freedom for the male with harsh restrictions and taboos placed on the female.
For example, Japan prior to World War II could be considered a "man's
world." Asayama[41] reporting on Japan notes that all Japanese husbands enjoyed some form of sexual contact outside of marriage. In contrast, infidelity
by a wife was condemned as a crime from both a legal and moral point of
view. Since World War II, the social and economic conditions for women improved, changing the situation radically. However, sexual freedom for women
does not approach the same level as for men. Even today, it is felt that Japa-

41. Shin'ichi Asayama, "Adolescent Sex Development and Adult Sex Behavior in Japan,"
    The Journal of Sex Research 11 (May 1975), p. 107.

nese men openly enjoy more sexual freedom than do Americans and probably European men. American women enjoy more freedom than Japanese women, but American women seem to be less tolerant than Japanese women about their husbands' extramarital sexual relations.[42]

A unique feature of extramarital sex involving Japanese women is their emotional involvement with their partner. While Japanese women may not approve of extramarital sex, once exposed to the opportunity, they are inclined to be emotionally involved. American women, in contrast, are less likely to be pushed into an extramarital relationship by an unhappy marriage but rather are pulled or drift into the relationship.[43] In the absence of restrictive cultural norms regarding sexual activity, American women who engage in extramarital sex approve of it, but their commitment to it is weak. This is consistent with Johnson's findings that 60 percent of adulterous wives had high marital adjustment (compared to 30 percent of the husbands), showing a low association between extramarital sex and marital dissatisfaction for wives.[44]

Like any other sexual outlet, it is impossible to know with any high degree of accuracy how frequently adultery takes place. Kinsey figures indicate that by age forty, 26 percent of the females and 50 percent of the males had experienced extramarital coitus.[45] Maykovick found that 32 percent of middle-class American women aged thirty-five to forty had experienced extramarital sex at least once.[46] Bell, with a sample of women younger than those in the Kinsey study found that 26 percent of the women had extramarital coitus and predicts that ultimately the rate of extramarital coitus for the women thirty years of age and under will be somewhere between 40 and 50 percent.[47] Johnson noted that 69 percent of the husbands and 56 percent of the wives in his study indicated a positive inclination to interact with a person of the opposite sex when their spouse was out of town. This does not mean coitus would result from such interaction but it does indicate potential given the opportunity.[48]

What factors account for or are highly related to extramarital coital experience? Of all the factors that Kinsey examined, religious devoutness, more than any other, affected the active incidences of extramarital coitus, particularly for the females. The lowest incidences of extramarital coitus had

---

42. Minako K. Maykovich, "Attitudes versus Behavior in Extramarital Sexual Relations," *Journal of Marriage and the Family* 38 (November 1976), p. 693.

43. Ibid., pp. 696–698.

44. Ralph E. Johnson, "Some Correlates of Extramarital Coitus," *Journal of Marriage and the Family* 32 (August 1970), p. 454.

45. Kinsey (*Female*) op. cit., p. 437.

46. Maykovick, op. cit., p. 695.

47. Robert R. Bell, "Changing Aspects of Marital Sexuality," in Sol Gordon and Roger W. Libby, *Sexuality Today and Tomorrow* (Belmont, Calif.: Wadsworth, 1976), pp. 217–218.

48. Johnson, op. cit., p. 452.

occurred among those who were most devoutly religious and the highest incidences among those who were least closely connected with any church activity. This was true of all the Protestant, Jewish, and Catholic groups in the sample.[49]

Kinsey noted that premaritally experienced females were somewhat more inclined to accept coitus with males other than their husbands after marriage. Perhaps it is not that premarital coitus leads to (or causes) extramarital coitus but rather perhaps the females who were inclined to accept coitus before marriage were also the ones more inclined to accept coitus after marriage with someone other than their husbands. The persons who objected more seriously to extramarital coitus were males and females who had never had such experience.[50] Those who have had experience are more likely to indicate that they intend to have more. Among the married females in Kinsey's sample who had not had extramarital experience, some 83 percent indicated that they did not intend to have it, but in a sample of those who had had extramarital experience, only 44 percent indicated that they did not intend to renew their experience.[51]

Like Kinsey, Singh et al. indicate that premarital sexual permissiveness is highly related to extramarital sexual permissiveness.[52] Other studies tend to emphasize different dimensions of primary significance. Edwards and Booth indicate that extramarital coitus is positively related to marital strain and a negative perception of the marriage but is not significantly related to background factors such as occupation, education, religiosity, or urban residence.[53] Whitehurst found extramarital sex among males to be related to a sense of alienation and powerlessness.[54] Bell and others found the variables most predictive of extramarital sex for women to be a low rated marriage, sexually liberal as indicated by the acceptance of fellatio (oral stimulation of the penis) or oral intercourse, and a liberal life-style.[55]

Swinging

A specific type of extramarital coitus is that of "swinging," "consensual adultery," "mate swapping," "wife swapping," "co-marital mate sharing,"

49. Kinsey (Female) op. cit., p. 424.

50. Ibid., p. 430.

51. Ibid., p. 431.

52. B. Krishna Singh, Bonnie L. Walton, and J. Sherwood Williams, "Extra-marital Sexual Permissiveness: Conditions and Contingencies," Journal of Marriage and the Family 38 (November 1976), pp. 701–713.

53. Edwards and Booth, op. cit., pp. 79–81.

54. Robert N. Whitehurst, "Extramarital Sex: Alienation or Extension of Normal Behavior," in John N. Edwards, ed., Sex and Society (Chicago: Markham, 1972), pp. 236–248.

55. Robert R. Bell, Stanley Turner, and Lawrence Rosen, "A Multivariate Analysis of Female Extramarital Coitus," Journal of Marriage and the Family 37 (May 1975), pp. 375–384.

Please Reply in Confidence

Chicago West Suburbs—Happily marrieds, 26 and 33, white, would like to hear from social minded marrieds for fun evenings and good times. Phone and photo please.

Pontiac Area Marrieds—Attractive, would like to hear from other similar-minded adults for dining, nights out, and games. Not necessarily in that order.

Texas Marrieds—Late 30's, attractive, Latin, would like to hear from other Latin or Anglo marrieds for adult fun and friendship. Answer all. Phone and photo please.

Florida Marrieds—Liberal minded, affectionate, attractive, late 20's, would like to hear from other similar qualified marrieds. We can travel. Phone, photo and address if possible.

Jersey Marrieds—White, 29 and 30, happily married, discreet and liberal-minded. Would like to hear from other liberal-minded marrieds who enjoy photography and correspondence. Age and race no barrier. Photo please with phone will bring prompt reply.

Northern Calif. Marrieds—Attractive, white, liberal-minded. Would like to hear from other marrieds for adult fun. Discretion assured. Will answer all who include phone and photo.

Southern N.Y. Area—Attractive and happily marrieds, 28 and 25, white, would like to hear from other liberal-minded marrieds. Phone and photo and must be discreet.

Source: "Very Confidential," *National Informer* 23 (February 25, 1973), p. 19.

or group sexual activities. Swinging is having sexual relations (as a couple) with at least one other individual. It also involves a willingness to swap sexual partners with a couple with whom the spouses are not acquainted and/or to go to a swinging party and be willing for both spouses to have sexual intercourse with strangers. Brian Gilmartin[56] refers to swinging as "co-marital sexual mate sharing" because it involves only a temporary exchange of partners for sexual activities and not the broader spectrum of marital activities. The term "wife swapping" at times refers to the same activity, although this term may be objectionable to groups sensitive to sexual inequality. One rarely hears of "husband swapping" although that occurs with equal, if not greater, frequency.

Gilbert Bartell, an anthropologist, and his wife used the participant-observation approach for generating data to study 280 white middle-class suburban swingers from the metropolitan Chicago area.[57] The swingers ranged from ages eighteen to seventy with an estimated median age of twenty-nine for the women and thirty-two for the men. All respondents said they were

56. Brian G. Gilmartin, "Some Social and Personal Characteristics of Mate-sharing Swingers," in James R. and Lynn G. Smith, eds., *Co-Marital Sex: Recent Studies of Sexual Alternatives in Marriage* (Boston: Little, Brown, 1972). See also Brian C. Gilmartin, "Swinging: Who Gets Involved and How?" in Roger W. Libby and Robert N. Whitehurst, *Marriage and Alternates: Exploring Intimate Relationships* (Glenview, Ill.: Scott, Foresman, 1977), pp. 161–185.

57. Gilbert D. Bartell, *Group Sex: An Eyewitness Report on the American Way of Swinging* (New York: New American Library, 1971).

Protestant, Catholic, or Jewish with none admitting to atheism or agnosticism. Nearly 90 percent of the couples had two or three children. Topics such as politics and religion were seldom discussed since they proved to be sensitive subjects to individuals trying to put their "best foot" forward.

Swingers were said to swing to help relieve the boredom with marriage and the alienation and loneliness of the suburbs. For men, it helped to fulfill the need of acting out sexual needs based on fantasies retained from adolescence. Most persons first became aware of swinging through a friend or acquaintance, saw an article about it, or saw a swingers' magazine. The magazines were important in getting people together via advertisements (note insert). Partners were also obtained at bars or clubs established for swingers, by personal reference, or by personal recruitment.

The first meeting or contact is usually without sexual involvement. In letters or phone conversations, couples seldom expressed what they liked to do but often specified what they did not like or would not do. The call usually terminates when a time and a neutral meeting place has been agreed upon. Later meetings usually occur at a motel or at the home of one of the couples. Stag films are often shown to stimulate sexual activity. This is followed by open or closed swinging, the latter meaning the two couples exchange partners and then go separately to private areas.

Bartel goes on to report that male swingers are extremely concerned with their ability to satisfy a female, especially by cunnilingus (oral stimulation of the vulva or clitoris). They report that one of the most intriguing findings of the entire study was the frequency of ambisexual relationships between women. Nearly two-thirds of all female informants openly admitted to sexual relationships with other female swingers.[58] Men frequently watched this activity both as a sexual stimulus and as a way of conserving their own sexual energy.

Swinging activity may continue for varying lengths of time. It appears that after eighteen months to two years, many swingers drop out entirely or curtail their activity severely. Some couples complain that swinging takes too much of their time and energy. Others became concerned about contracting venereal disease, got tired of meeting the same people, discovered (as Bartell's data confirmed) that many suburban swingers were racists and held fascist views completely alien to their own life-style, recognized in diminution of their self-images and self-esteem, or found their fantasies were better than the real thing.

A study of marriage counselors[59] who worked with swingers who dropped out reported problems of jealousy, guilt, threat to the marriage, development of outside emotional attachments, boredom and loss of interest,

---

58. Ibid., p. 104.
59. Duane Denfeld, "Dropouts from Swinging," *The Family Coordinator* 23 (January 1974), pp. 45–49.

disappointment, divorce or separation, wife's inability to "take it," and fear of discovery.

What about the consequences of swinging on the marriage itself? One publication suggested that the family that swings together clings together.[60] Is that possible? Bartell indicates: "Our observations have convinced us that it is possible that marriages can—contradictory as it may appear—benefit from the group sex experience."[61] For many swingers there was an increased sexual interest in the mate or partner, with the majority of the respondents reporting that swinging created for them a better relationship both socially and sexually.[62]

Research reported by Charles Palson and Rebecca Palson[63] as well as by Charles Cole and Graham Spanier[64] suggests that marital cohesion may be as strong, if not stronger, among swingers than among monogamous couples who refuse to consider participating in swinging (monogymites). The explanation advanced is that value consensus between the husband and wife is the crucial factor that will determine whether co-marital sexual mate sharing will be detrimental or supportive of the husband-wife relationship. Problems arise if one of the spouses does not accept the value orientation and normative code of mate sharing and enters co-marital sexual mate sharing only to please the spouse.

The number of writers, teachers, or counselors who share the view of the "healthfulness" of swinging are clearly in the minority. This may be based on traditional norms stemming from a Judeo-Christian culture, but it may also be based on certain social and psychological principles pertaining to interpersonal relationships, primary groups, basic learned needs of exclusiveness, jealousy, security, and permanency, not to mention the possible influences on children, kin, and others' or one's own definition of self.

This is not to deny that extramarital sex occurs in both "good" and "bad" marriages, nor does it assume that because coitus occurs outside the marriage relationship, "my spouse no longer loves me" or "I have failed as a marriage partner." It does suggest increasingly complex patterns of primary-group interactions and major redefinitions of marital and extramarital role expectations. Rather than viewing extramarital coitus or swinging as right or wrong, good or bad, it may be more beneficial to examine the conditions under which it takes place and the consequences that result, whether negative

---

60. Duane Denfeld and Michael Gordon, "The Sociology of Mate Swapping: Or the Family That Swings Together Clings Together," *The Journal of Sex Research* 6 (May 1970), pp. 85–100.

61. Bartell, op. cit., p. 114.

62. Ibid., p. 210.

63. Charles Palson and Rebecca Palson, "Swinging in Wedlock," *Society* 9 (February 1972), pp. 28–37.

64. Charles L. Cole and Graham B. Spanier, "Comarital Mate-sharing and Family Stability," *The Journal of Sex Research* 10 (February 1974), pp. 21–31.

or positive. This view is consistent with the "theory of sexual normative morality" described in Chapter 12.

Swinging, group sex, mate swapping, key clubs, and such may well become a recognized alternate sexual style for married couples in our pluralistic society. It involves a single standard of sex—what is sexually right for the husband is also sexually right for the wife. It is different from most instances of adultery, which frequently involve only one marital partner, secrecy, guilt, and dishonesty rather than fun and recreation. Robert Bell reports that most swingers are conventional middle-class individuals who show no social aberration other than their propensity to swing.[65]

Edward Hobbs argues that, from a theological perspective, there can be no justification for continued insistence on the forms of marriage we have inherited, at least not simply because we have inherited them. We have inherited a form that insists on permanence and sexual exclusiveness. He claims that we are in the process of abandoning the permanence of marriage while maintaining (in law and principle, even if less in reality than ever before) its sexual exclusiveness. We may seriously ask whether something approaching a reversal of these two attitudes toward marriage might not promote a healthier and happier model for American family structure.[66]

POSTMARITAL COITUS

Compared to the subjects of premarital, nonmarital, marital, or extramarital coitus, relatively little attention has been given to the subject of coitus after the dissolution of marriage through death, separation, or divorce. An intense interest exists in the sexual activities of the young prior to marriage and the importance of coitus in marriage. But after marriage, the importance of coitus enters into a state of limbo between an activity that is vital and necessary to psychological and emotional health and an activity that contradicts the conventional morality of confining coitus to marriage. Gebhard states that the escape from this dilemma is to ignore and minimize the problem as much as possible, but if forced to take a position to condemn publicly and condone privately.[67] This dilemma between the public and private norms as they relate to postmarital coitus indicates a social permissiveness insofar as publicity is kept minimal. It may also contribute to the low level of available information

---

65. Robert R. Bell, "Swinging: The Sexual Exchange of Marriage Partners," *Sexual Behavior* 1 (May 1971), pp. 70–79.
66. Edward C. Hobbs, "An Alternate Model from a Theological Perspective," in Herbert A. Otto, ed., *The Family in Search of a Future* (New York: Appleton-Century-Crofts, 1970), pp. 25–41.
67. Paul Gebhard, "Postmarital Coitus among Widows and Divorcees," in Paul Bohannan, ed., *Divorce and After* (Garden City, N. Y.: Doubleday, 1970), pp. 81–96.

as well as the high level of curiosity about the sexual activity of formerly married persons.

Styles of Postmarital
Sexual Activity

In a report on the world of the formerly married, primarily about the middle class, Morton Hunt discerned three major styles of sexual activity within the broad range of behavior extending from total celibacy to compulsive promiscuity.[68]

The *abstainers* comprise the small minority of persons who never, or very rarely, engage in postmarital coitus. Some of these persons have chastity thrust upon them by circumstances such as physical illness, old age, impotence, or geographical isolation, but most choose celibacy deliberately for one reason or another: fear of failure, negative feelings toward sex, disinterest, or perception of sex as sinful, immoral, disgusting, meaningless, or other reasons. The relative rarity of the abstainer is further substantiated in the sections that follow.

The *user*, who comprises the largest number of the three categories, needs sex, uses it as a means of gaining important goals, but is not ready or willing to commit himself to a permanent love relationship. Sexual activities are not promiscuous nor are they meaningless. They are casual or uninvolved sexual liaisons significant to the process of redefining the self and rediscovering the meaning of one's manhood or womanhood. The user, particularly if a woman, approaches first sexual experiences with anxiety, but after meeting someone, becoming aware of a mutual attraction, revealing experiences, and so forth, develops rapport quickly, and sexual exchanges advance rapidly toward coitus. Most of these experiences, although lacking exclusiveness or permanence, are successful, meaningful, and important in changing self-images and restoring confidence in oneself as a desirable, capable, and sensual partner.

The user, who seeks coitus without love and permanency, does face drawbacks. Some fear an erosion of their own ability to love, sense an element of promiscuity, fear potential pregnancy, or worry that the relationship may develop into an unwanted deep emotional involvement. In Hunt's words, the formerly married user is caught between two cultures:

> While they permit themselves their present conduct and justify it, they also have a nagging residual feeling that it is not really proper, and do not want their children to emulate them. They remain only partly freed from the stan-

---

68. Morton M. Hunt, *The World of the Formerly Married* (Greenwich, Conn.: Fawcett, 1966), pp. 120–138.

dards of the conventional world, and retain dual citizenship, since they mean eventually to quit the new world and make their way back to the one they left. Casual sex experiences help them toward that goal by restoring self-esteem and rebuilding sexual identity, yet at the same time threaten to misdirect them by breaking down the synthesis of sex and love and by conditioning them to enjoy uncomplicated and primitive desire. Until they solve this dilemma, they vacillate between self-love and self-contempt, between bursts of sensuality and periods of self-denial, between delight in their way of life and despair at not living another and presumably better way.[69]

The *addict* is the third type of person who engages in postmarital sexual activity. He views sexual liberation as a healthful end in itself and a permanently desirable way of life. Partners are used as conveniences, not people. A deep analysis of self, feelings, and relationships is not the goal. The goal is a momentary sense of importance, achievement, and sexual encounter. Bars, cocktail lounges, and other market places are used to find new partners. Liaisons are casual and fleeting. Love and sex become antithetical. Many counselors would view the addict as a person who needs constant reaffirmation of worth, is low in self-esteem, and possesses a deep-rooted neurosis. These same feelings, which likely contributed to the failure of many of their marriages, exist to prevent them from remarrying and to habituate them to casual sex.

The Incidence of Postmarital Coitus

It is generally assumed, as the evidence already presented suggests, that all, if not most, previously married men and women engage in coitus. Based on questionnaires, interviews, and direct observations, plus consultations with psychologists and social scientists who have studied the matter, Hunt writes:

> Of all the people one might meet in the World of the Formerly Married at any given moment, almost none of the men and only about one-fifth of the women have had no sexual intercourse at all since their marriages broke up. Obviously, time plays a part in this: the longer a person remains an FM, the greater the likelihood that he or she will have begun having postmarital sexual activity. But most people start very soon; five out of six FMs begin having sexual intercourse within the first year, most of them with more than one partner.[70]

The data given refer to incidence, not frequency. That is, almost all of the male and about 80 percent of the female formerly marrieds had coitus. Reporting on the incidence of postmarital coitus based upon interviews with 632 white females, the Institute for Sex Research, with which Kinsey was as-

69. Ibid., p. 134.
70. Ibid., p. 119.

TABLE 14–1. Age-Specific Incidence of Postmarital Coitus for Women

| Age-period | DIVORCED | | WIDOWED | |
	Percent	Total	Percent	Total
21–25	73.4	177	42.1	19
26–30	70.3	236	54.8	42
31–35	78.3	207	47.2	53
36–40	77.9	154	35.8	53
41–45	68.6	118	34.7	49
46–50	59.0	61	26.5	49
51–55	39.4	33	26.3	38
56–60	42.9	14	23.5	34

Source: Paul Gebhard, "Postmarital Coitus among Widows and Divorcees," in Paul Bohannan, ed., *Divorce and After* (Garden City, N. Y.: Doubleday, 1970, p. 84. Copyright 1970 by Paul Bohannan. Reprinted by permission of Doubleday and Company, Inc.

sociated, found major differences between the postmarital sexual behavior of the widowed and the divorced. Eighty-two percent of the divorced had had such coitus compared to 43 percent of the widowed.[71] At all ages the divorced have substantially more women having coitus than have the widowed. The age-specific incidence of postmarital coitus can be seen in Table 14–1. During their twenties and thirties, roughly two-thirds to three-quarters of the divorced were having coitus in contrast to one-third to one-half of the widowed. In their forties the divorced widen their lead: about three-fifths to two-thirds of them experiencing coitus, as opposed to roughly one-quarter to one-third of the widowed. After age fifty the differences are lessened as age exerts its leveling influence, but they are still very marked.

Gebhard says that the enormous differences between the widowed and the divorced seem to derive from several interrelated factors,[72] one of which was religion with the critical matter proving to be the degree of devoutness rather than the denomination. In the various age-periods, from 30 to 40 percent of the widowed were labeled devout on the basis of church attendance, as opposed to 15 to 29 percent of the divorced. There was a moderate tendency for both groups to become more devout with increasing age. A second factor was prior experience in coitus outside of marriage. If one has had premarital or extramarital coitus one is more likely to engage in postmarital coitus. No great differences existed in premarital coitus (28 percent widowed, 37 percent divorced) but greater differences existed in extramarital coitus (8 percent widowed, one-third divorced). The divorced had a "head start" on the widows in that 31 percent were having coitus in their final year of marriage. A

71. Gebhard, op. cit., p. 84.
72. Ibid., p. 86.

third factor may center around the type of relationship desired. Although there may be no lack of men available to the widow, she may be more interested in an emotional rather than a purely sexual relationship. Emotional relationships take longer to develop than do sexual ones. A fourth factor may be the trauma of being widowed. Even after the initial phase of acute grief has ameliorated, the widow may find it difficult to find a mate who measures up to the image of her deceased husband, an image which tends to benefit from selective memory. A fifth factor may relate to remarriage. Divorcees are more likely to engage in coitus. That is, many women who would ordinarily avoid coitus for moral (or other) reasons will have it when marriage seems impending. A curious phenomenon is noted by Gebhard.

> Once a woman begins postmarital coitus she is extremely likely to have it with more than one man. This generalization applies to both the divorced and widowed, and may be the basis for the stereotypical concepts of the "merry widow" and "gay divorcee" as being somewhat promiscuous. Whereas a high proportion of never-married women have premarital coitus only with the fiance whom they subsequently married, relatively few women with postmarital coitus confine it to one fiance. Of course nearly all of the women, widowed or divorced, who remarried and who had postmarital coitus had a portion of that coitus with their future husbands.[73]

Frequency of Postmarital Coitus

The frequency of postmarital coitus is derived from the study of 632 white females mentioned earlier. This study showed that the average frequency of coitus among the twenty- to forty-year-old divorced who had coitus varied from 64 to 73 times per year, an average (mean) frequency ranging from 1.23 to 1.4 per week.[74] In the early forties the frequency dropped rather sharply.

The frequency for the widowed averaged less than once a week from age twenty to forty with sharp declines after that time. Thus the pattern is similar for the divorced and widowed but the frequency is less for the widowed. The reasons for the divorced-widowed differences are likely similar to the reasons explaining differences in incidence: greater prior experience in premarital and extramarital coitus, greater religious devoutness of the widows, and the like. An additional factor stems from an unproven impression of Gebhard:

> Widows as a whole are less sexually motivated than the divorced. The widowed seem to have a larger proportion of women who could figuratively

---

73. Ibid., p. 88.
74. Ibid., p. 89.

"take sex or leave it." This attitude has no necessary relationship to orgasmic capacity: such a woman can have marital coitus with orgasm for years, be widowed, and then live years of abstinence with little or no sexual frustration. This is incomprehensible to most males.[75]

The reason for the sharp decline in the early forties may in part be attributable to the beginning of menopause. Kinsey reports the average age of onset as 46.3.[76] A number of women experience menopausal symptoms prior to this age and these symptoms may have a depressant effect.

It is perhaps surprising to note that when the coital-orgasm rate in the postmarital period is compared to that of the previous marriage, both the widowed and divorced have a greater orgasmic response in postmarital life. Of those having coitus, 57 percent of the divorced and 48 percent of the widowed had a higher percentage of orgasm during their postmarital life than in their former marriage.[77] This may be attributable to the greater proportion of postmarital women who decide whether or not coitus will occur. It may also be attributable to the newness and the happier emotional relationships of the postmarital situation. Particularly for the divorced, one can generally assume unhappiness in the terminal years of the marriage. And it has been demonstrated that marital unhappiness is associated with a lower orgasm rate for wives.[78] A third factor accounting for the higher postmarital orgasm rate may relate to the relaxation of inhibition that accompanies age, experience, and maturity. It could be assumed that different partners and new experiences would result in learning-educational benefits.

Thus, in dealing with coitus after marriage, it can be seen that most persons have coitus relatively soon after the marriage with an average frequency that declines with age and an orgasm rate that exceeds marriage rates.

Summary

Marriage legitimizes the sexual relationship. The social norms that surround sex and marriage are the key factors in differentiating marital sex from premarital, extramarital, or any other circumstance outside the marital relationship. Coitus within marriage comprises a larger proportion of the total sexual outlet than any other type of heterosexual activity and is recognized cross-culturally as important in the maintenance of the family system.

As was true in the previous two chapters, one key source of data on sexual behavior is provided by the Kinsey studies. These indicate that the in-

---

75. Ibid., p. 90.

76. Kinsey (*Female*), op. cit., p. 736.

77. Gebhard, op. cit., p. 92.

78. Paul Gebhard, "Factors in Marital Orgasm," *The Journal of Social Issues* 22 (April 1966), p. 90.

cidence and frequency of marital coitus reach their maximum in the first year or two after marriage, with a steady decline from that time on. The decline is more related to and controlled by the male's desires and his aging than to the female's loss of interest or capacity.

As in premarital coitus, marital coital rates showed an increase during the latter part of the 1960s. A variety of explanations account for this shift including a decrease in exposure to the risk of pregnancy and an increased societal openness about sexual matters. Coital frequency in marriage has been found to be related to age, contraceptive usage, social class, and a variety of other variables.

Sexual adjustment is one factor in marital adjustment, but it is doubtful that this factor alone would maintain an otherwise "poor" marital relationship. Sexual inadequacies, according to Masters and Johnson, occur in 50 percent of all marriages in the United States. One indication of the desire for sexual adjustment—or at least a desire for literature about sexual matters—can be seen in the widespread sale of marriage-sex manuals. It is possible that some of these manuals provide a major disservice to sexual adjustment by providing advice that operates negatively against adjustment, failing to see sex in a total social context of values and norms, failing to take into consideration the wide range of differences in sexual drive and interest, focusing on techniques, and engendering feelings of inadequacy in not being able to meet the expectations given. It is this fear of inadequacy that appears to be the greatest known deterrent to effective sexual functioning.

One of the most extensive, research-based programs for dealing with sexual inadequacies is the Reproductive Biology Research Foundation under the directorship of Masters and Johnson. Their program treats marriages rather than individuals and has a five-year success rate of better than 80 percent. Three concepts of significance to the social scientist include the spectator role, the sexual value system, and sensate focus. Fear was cited as the greatest overall cause of malfunction.

As clearly indicated, not all heterosexual coitus of married persons occurs with the spouse. Extramarital coitus appears to be widespread with major differences between males and females and across cultures. Extramarital coitus appears to be highly related to premarital permissiveness, to marital strain, to alienation and powerlessness, and to sexual liberalism in general.

Of more recent public interest is swinging—having sexual relations as a couple with at least one other individual or the swapping of sexual partners with another couple. Swinging, group sex, mate swapping, key clubs, and such may well become widely recognized alternate sexual styles for married couples in our pluralistic society. Without a doubt they are receiving increasing attention.

Another context in which sexual relationships occur is the postmarital. The sexual norms relating to the world of the formerly married are different from the premarital, marital, or extramarital. Three major styles in postmarital sexual activity are described: the abstainer, the user, and the addict. Nearly all men and the large majority of women engage in coitus at some time after marriage. Major differences exist among women between the divorced and the widowed in the incidence of coitus.

This chapter could fit within the framework of Part V, as well as serve as the third and concluding chapter of this section on sexual norms and relationships. It examined sexual relationships in a marital context by reviewing key findings, discussing sexual adjustment in marriage, describing aspects of the Masters-Johnson program, and concluding with extramarital and postmarital coitus. All are significant to marital interaction. Continuing within a premarital and marital life cycle sequence, attention is directed in the following chapter to marital structures and processes.

Key Terms and Topics

Sex and Marriage	433	Spectator Role	443
Kinsey Studies	434	Sexual Value System	444
Autoeroticism in Marriage	439	Sensate Focus	445
Sexual Adjustment	440	Extramarital Coitus	447
Marriage—Sex Manuals	440	Swinging	450
Masters-Johnson Studies	441	Postmarital Coitus	454

Discussion Questions

1. *Examine the two volumes of the Kinsey studies. What do you perceive to be their most significant findings? To what extent are their findings influenced by their samples, their methods of gathering data, and their interpretation of the data? How applicable are these findings today?*

2. *In what ways is marital coitus likely to be influenced by employment of husband and/or wife, income, religion, number and/or presence of children, age, and other factors? How do you explain changes that have taken place?*

3. *What, in your estimation, constitutes "good" sexual adjustment in marriage? Is it possible to have "good" sexual adjustment and "poor" marital adjustment? Is the opposite possible?*

4. *Make a list of sexual difficulties in marriage. Are some of them unsolvable? What factors are most likely to lead to these difficulties? What factors are significant in resolving them?*

5. *Review five leading sex manuals. Do they contain contradictory advice? To what extent are social norms and values discussed? In what ways might they be helpful/harmful to marital sexual relationships?*

6. *Describe husband-wife and male-female differences in sexual response through the life cycle. How are these differences explained?*

7. *Read* Human Sexual Response *and* Human Sexual Inadequacy *by Masters and Johnson. In what ways are those books alike or different? Are the extensive technical terminology of the first and the nontechnical program description of the second intended for different reading audiences and for different purposes? What are the major findings of each?*

8. *What are the arguments for and against extramarital sex, swinging, or mate swapping? How can they be disruptive to or improve marriage?*

9. *In what ways is postmarital coitus different from marital or premarital coitus? In what ways would you expect similarities or differences between the sexual behavior and activity of the divorced versus the widowed?*

10. *Discuss the pros and cons of sex education. What are some "worthy" goals of a program at various levels of our educational system?*

Further Readings

Bartell, Gilbert D. *Group Sex: An Eyewitness Report on the American Way of Swinging.* New York: New American Library, 1971. A study by Dr. Bartell who, with his wife, answered ads for swinging, attended parties, and interviewed swinging couples.

DeLora, Joann S., and **Carol A. B. Warren.** *Understanding Sexual Interaction.* Boston: Houghton Mifflin, 1977. An overview of the current knowledge concerning human sexuality. Examines the common sexual patterns for persons from infancy to old age.

Cuber, John F., and **Peggy B. Harroff.** *The Significant Americans: A Study of Sexual Behavior among the Affluent.* New York: Appleton-Century, 1965. A research study by the authors through interviews with 437 American men and women who were designated as elites, top influentials, or upper middle class.

Francoeur, Robert T., and **Anna K. Francoeur,** (eds.), *The Future of Sexual Relations.* Englewood Cliffs, N.J.: Prentice-Hall, 1974. A collection of readings concerned with predicting the future of sexual relations based upon present realities and identifiable tendencies.

Gordon, Sol, and **Roger W. Libby.** *Sexuality Today and Tomorrow.* Belmont, Calif.: Wadsworth, 1976. A book of readings presenting a range of ideas related to sexual life-styles and value systems.

Hunt, Morton M. *The Affair.* Cleveland: World, 1969. A study of in-depth interviews with persons or their partners involved in extramarital affairs.

Hunt, Morton M. *The World of the Formerly Married.* Greenwich. Conn.: Fawcett, 1966. A description of the life of the separated and divorced in middle-class America including their sexual activity.

Libby, Roger W., and **Robert N. Whitehurst.** *Marriage Alternatives: Exploring Intimate Relationships.* Glenview, Ill.: Scott, Foresman, 1977. Like their earlier book, *Renovating Marriage,* this book breaks from tradition in looking at alternatives to marriage for sexual and intimate relationships.

Libby, Roger W., and **Robert N. Whitehurst.** *Renovating Marriage.* Danville, Calif.: Concensus, 1973. The reader should find this collection of articles extremely thought provoking, as it examines emerging sexual life-styles and questions the notions of monogamy and the confinement of sex after marriage to marital partners.

Masters, William H., and **Virginia E. Johnson.** *Human Sexual Inadequacy.* Boston: Little, Brown, 1970. The second major work in their series of clinical studies of sexual behavior. Unlike the first volume, this volume can be more readily understood by the nonphysician.

Masters, William H., and **Virginia E. Johnson.** *Human Sexual Response.* Boston: Little, Brown, 1966. The pioneer volume of the already classic Masters-Johnson clinical research efforts of an eleven-year investigation into the anatomy and physiology of human sexual response.

Neubeck, Gerhard. *Extra-Marital Relations.* Englewood Cliffs, N.J.: Prentice-Hall, 1969. One of the most comprehensive, nonjudgmental books on extramarital relations. Consists of a series of papers by sociologists and psychologists.

Reuben, David R. *Everything You Always Wanted to Know About Sex, But Were Afraid to Ask.* New York: David McKay, 1969. A highly popularized book written by a psychiatrist that attempts to answer questions asked about sex.

Part V

Marital and Family Relationships: Patterns of Interaction throughout the Life Cycle

15

The Marital System

15

Although this chapter concentrates more exclusively on marriages, with particular emphasis on the dominant husband-wife patterns and roles in the United States, each previous chapter included discussions of selected aspects of the marital system. The first chapter included census data on marriage and issues within American marriages. Subsequent chapters differentiated marriages from families, presented a wide range of variant marital life-styles including those with multiple spouses, dual careers, and androgynous role relationships, provided information on Amish and black marital practices, social-class differences, interfaith and interracial situations, structures, and processes in the selection of a mate, and sexual relationships in a marital context. Included within this chapter are data on the functions of marriage, marriage trends and characteristics, a discussion of conjugal power, and some factors associated with marital adjustment.

FUNCTIONS OF MARRIAGE

Today marriage is popular. Despite conflict, divorce, and a changing marital scene, most Americans marry. Normative expectations include marriage as an appropriate and desirable state and with rare exceptions this end is accomplished. Despite the complex tasks of mastering the mate-selection games, celebrating the rituals and ceremonies that accompany the act of marriage, and fulfilling the requirements of domestic life, few avoid these rounds of activity and remain unmarried. Obviously, marriage fulfills various functions for the individual and society.

Marriage, as an institutionalized relationship within the family system, fulfills many functions attributed to the family in general. As suggested in earlier chapters, family functions include a wide range of consequences, such as basic personality formation, status ascriptions, nurturant socializa-

Marriage Vows: Before and After

He married her because among other things, her hair looked so beautiful.

He divorced her because she spent so much time fixing her hair.

She married him because his muscles rippled so when he swam.

She divorced him because he spent more time in the bedroom doing setting-up exercises than anything else.

He married her because she was such an adept conversationalist, never at a loss for a word.

He divorced her because she never got off the telephone.

She married him because he loved to take her dancing.

She divorced him because he was "tired" most of the time.

He married her because she was so "vivacious."

He divorced her because she was too restless.

She married him because he could support her in lavish style.

She divorced him because he had too firm a hold on the purse-strings.

He married her because their families shared a common background.

He divorced her because her family kept interfering in their affairs.

She married him because he had a robust masculine appetite and appreciated her cooking.

She divorced him because he never wanted to take her out to eat.

He married her because she was quick, neat and intelligent.

He divorced her because she had absolutely no patience with the children, who were sometimes slow, slovenly, and stupid.

She married him because he was a "real sport."

She divorced him because he refused to give up the sporting life.

He married her because they shared the same intellectual and political beliefs.

He divorced her because she wasn't interested in anything but the house and the kids.

She married him because he was so courteous and attentive in all the little things that matter so to a woman.

She divorced him because he was so punctilious about little things, and so oblivious to important things.

He married her because all the other men were so impressed with her magnificent figure.

He divorced her, after the third child, because she had "let herself go."

Source: Sidney Harris, *Detroit Free Press*, November 21, 1966, p. 15-A. Copyright Publishers-Hall Syndicate. Reprinted by permission of the author.

tion, tension management, replacement of members, economic cooperation, reproduction, stabilization of adults, and the like. Many of these functions, while not requiring marriage for their fulfillment, are enhanced by the marital system.

The functions of marriage differ as the structure of marriage differs. For example, where marriage is specifically an extension of the kin and extended-family system, procreation, passing on the family name, and continuation of property become a basic function. Thus, to not have a child or, more specifically, to not have a male child, is sufficient reason to replace the present wife or add a new wife. In the United States, while most children are born of a married couple and while most married couples want children, to not have children is rarely a sufficient reason to remarry. Nor is the impossibility of having a child, as with sterile persons or older women, a sufficient reason for not marrying. Thus why marriage?

The chapter on mate-selection processes mentioned that, for arranged marriages, important factors include the bride's price, the reputation of the potential spouse's kin group, levirate and sororate arrangements, and traditions of prescribed marriage arrangements. Where marriage is based on "free choice," individualistic factors are accorded greater significance. Thus in the United States, marriage has many functions and involves many positive as well as negative personal factors: establishment of a family of one's own, children, companionship, happiness, love, ego support, economic security, an approved sexual outlet, avoidance of the stigma attached to the unmarried, affection, escape, elimination of loneliness, pregnancy, ad infinitum. The greater the extent to which the perceived needs of marriage are met, and the fewer the alternatives in the replacement of the unmet needs, the greater the likelihood of marriage and the continuation of that marriage. Why marriage? At a personal level, any perceived reason may explain marriage; but at a social level all societies sanction certain reasons and renounce others. Thus personal factors operate within the confines of social boundaries; the functions that marriage performs are determined and qualified by the social and cultural context.

The social and cultural context of the United States is currently witnessing variant forms to monogamy for the fulfillment of individuals' perceived needs. A familiar pattern is sequential or _serial_ monogamy: the marriage, divorce, remarriage, divorce pattern. Another familiar pattern is _adultery_, the maintenance of the marriage with a secret satisfaction of sexual and emotional needs outside the conjugal relationship. A new form of joint adultery, known as _swinging_ or _swapping_, involves both husband and wife engaging in sexual relationships with other couples—with the consent of everyone involved. _Nonmarital cohabitation_, a relatively common practice today, involves a male and a female sharing a common residence. _Communes_, where several persons live together and pool their labor and resources, are another alternative to the fulfillment of personal and social needs. These alternative forms have been examined previously. In the United States as around the world, marriage or some alternative exists to fulfill basic functions generally attributed to the husband-wife relationship.

MARRIAGE TRENDS AND CHARACTERISTICS

In the United States the number of marriages has increased significantly since the end of the Civil War. They doubled between 1867 and 1900 and more than doubled between 1900 and 1940. From 1940 to 1975 they in-

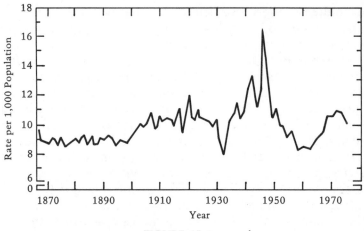

FIGURE 15–1.

Marriage Rates: United States, 1867–1970. [Source: "Marriage: Trends and Characteristics, United States," U.S. Department of Health, Education and Welfare, Vital and Health Statistics, Series 21, no. 21 (September 1971), p. 2; and *Statistical Abstract of the United States: 1976*, 97th ed. (Washington, D.C., 1976). no. 97, p. 68.]

creased by about 25 percent.[1] The marriage rate as well, relating all marriages to the total population, has varied widely over the past 100 years (see Figure 15–1). This rate has fluctuated under the influence of wars, changing economic conditions, sex ratio of the marriageable population, and the number of potential brides and grooms present in the general population. Characteristically, the marriage rate has risen at the outset of a major war, declined during the course of the conflict, and increased sharply in the immediate post-war years. This was the experience for World Wars I and II and was probably true during the Civil War.[2] Economic recessions and depressions generally have had an inhibiting effect on marriages, as have shifts in the age distribution of the population resulting in a smaller proportion of the population at the young-adult ages.

Again referring to Figure 15–1, note that from 1867 to 1900, a period of reconstruction and rapid industrial and urban growth, the marriage rate was relatively stable, staying within the bounds of 8.6 and 9.6 per 1,000 population. Early in the twentieth century the marriage rate pushed upward, showing wider fluctuations at a higher level until the stock market crashed in 1929.[3] During the 1930s and 1940s fluctuations in the marriage rate became

1. "Marriage: Trends and Characteristics, United States," U.S. Department of Health, Education, and Welfare, Vital and Health Statistics, Series 21, no. 21 (September 1971), p. 1; and *Statistical Abstract of the United States: 1976*, 97th ed. (Washington, D.C.: 1976), No. 68, p. 51.

2. Ibid., p. 1.

3. Ibid., p. 2.

more pronounced. In 1932, at the depth of the depression, the rate plunged to a low of 7.9, probably unprecedented in this country except perhaps during the Civil War.[4]

The impact of World War II is unparalleled in the history of marriage rates in the United States. Just before and immediately after the United States' entry into the war, the rate rose sharply as young men sought to avail themselves of the deferred status granted to married men or simply wanted to marry before going overseas. The end of the war and the return of millions of men to civilian life precipitated an upsurge in marriages. In 1946 the marriage rate reached 16.4, an unprecedented and to date unsurpassed peak. By 1949 the rate had returned to the pre-World War II level, dropping as rapidly as it had climbed. This marked the end of twenty years of the most frequent and pronounced fluctuations in the history of United States marriage rates.[5]

During the 1950s and 1960s, the marriage rate was quite different from that of earlier years. During this period, unmarred by economic depression but plagued by two limited wars, the marriage rate did not exhibit the stability of the late nineteenth century nor the sharp fluctuations of the twentieth century. It changed from a downswing in the 1950s to an upswing in the late 1960s. However, the change was gradual, with small year-to-year differences, since the effect of the Korean conflict on the marriage rate was minor when compared with the effect of World War II.

The conflict in Vietnam, the longest war ever fought by the United States, is believed to have exerted only a minor measurable effect on the annual marriage rate. From 1963 to 1967 the marriage rate increased continuously due to the large number of young people maturing to marriageable ages. Since 1968, the marriage rate has varied between 10.5 and 10.9 per 1,000 population, ending the increase of the 1960s. Most recent data from the mid-1970s shows another decline in the marriage rate.

Season and Day Variation in Marriage Rate

In the United States, marriages have a distinct seasonal pattern: it appears that a higher percentage of marriages occur in June (12.2 percent) than in any other month, with August (10.3 percent) and September (10.2 percent) as the next most popular. The seasonal low for marriages occurs during the first part of the year. January, February, and March (6.0, 5.9 and 6.1 percent respectively) regularly have fewer marriages than any other month. These monthly variations are also greatly affected by holidays, the ending and be-

---

4. Paul H. Jacobson, *American Marriage and Divorce* (New York: Rinehart, 1959).
5. "Marriage: Trends and Characteristics," op. cit., pp. 2–3.

ginning of school years, climatic conditions, and religious holy days such as
Lent. Marriages are less frequent among some religious groups during Lent
with upsurges just before and after the Lenten season. Interestingly, the favorite month for marriages also varies by age group: teen-age brides and grooms
prefer June, brides aged thirty to thirty-four and grooms aged forty-five to
fifty-four more frequently choose December, and brides thirty-five to fifty-
four and grooms fifty-five to sixty-four tend to select July.[6]

Marriages also vary widely by day of the week. Over half of all marriages take place on a Saturday (55 percent). More than three times as many
marriages were performed on Saturday than on Friday, the next most popular
day, and more than ten times as many as on Tuesdays, Wednesdays, and
Thursdays, the least popular days.[7]

Geographic Variation in Marriage Rate

Marriage rates in the United States consistently show distinct differences by geographic regions. The West has the highest rate, followed closely
by the South. The Northeast has the lowest rate and the North Central the
second lowest. Within regions, however, there is wide variation among states,
particularly in the West. In 1974, rates for the western states ranged from
180.3 per 1,000 population in Nevada to 7.7 per 1,000 in California.[8]

Marriages are reported by, and subject to laws of, the state where the
ceremony is performed. Lenient marriage laws attract couples from out of
state, particularly if the adjoining states have more restrictive laws. A high
marriage rate for a state is generally associated with a high proportion of
marriages in which both bride and groom live outside the state. The major
attractions are laws that permit marriages at young ages without parental
consent, laws that do not require a waiting period between the date of application for a license and issuance of the license or between license issuance
and the ceremony, or laws that do not require a medical examination.[9]
These factors have a two-pronged effect—they lower the rates of the states
from which the couples are drawn and raise the rates of the states to which
they are attracted.

When dealing with marriage rates by states, Nevada stands in a class
all by itself with a rate of nearly 190 marriages per 1,000 resident population.
In 1973, it reported 4.5 percent of all marriages in the nation and recorded a
rate of almost ten times the figure for the next highest state (South Carolina)
and twenty-five times the figure for the lowest state (Delaware).

6. Ibid., p. 8.
7. Ibid., p. 8.
8. "Statistical Abstract, 1976," op. cit., no. 102, p. 70.
9. "Marriage: Trends and Characteristics," op. cit., p. 10.

For a WEDDING of DISTINCTION
In Unequaled Splendor

If you cannot afford the price of a wedding, pay what you can; we refuse no one.

$25.00

Includes bride's corsage and 8 x 10 wedding portraits

WEDDING
Chapel

OPEN 24 HOURS

The Most Beautiful Chapel In Las Vegas Performing Weddings At Prices You Can Afford. Every Service Available • Honeymoon Suites • Flowers • Tapes • Banquet Facilities • Rings • Music • Transportation • Photos • Dressing Rooms • Champagne •

Religious or civil ceremonies in luxurious surrounding that you and your bride will always remember. We can furnish any and everything you may desire for your wedding.

Married Couples: Repledge Your Vows. All Facilities Available And You Receive A Beautiful Certificate.

Source: *Las Vegas Panorama*, August 22–28, 1975, p. 7.

A few years ago, Nevada was the only state that required neither a medical examination nor a waiting period. It was also the only state where suit for divorce could be filed after residence of only six weeks, or less under certain circumstances. In addition, the parties could remarry immediately after the final decree.[10]

POWER IN CONJUGAL RELATIONSHIPS

One important aspect of the marital system is the power positions of husband and wife—as individuals and in relation to each other. There ap-

10. Ibid., p. 11.

pears to be considerable agreement that power refers to the ability to influence others and affect their behavior. Conjugal power would refer to the
ability of the husband and wife to influence each other. It is often measured
by determining who makes certain decisions or who performs certain tasks.

Power involves the crucial dimensions of authority and influence.
Social norms determine who has authority, in that the culture designates the
positions that have the "legitimate" and prescribed power (authority). In
some societies, authority is invested in the husband; in others, it rests with
the oldest male in extended-family situations, and in some it goes to the
mother-in-law. Other family members can *influence*, that is, exert pressure
upon, the person with authority. The President of the United States has the
prescribed authority to make a wide range of decisions, but he can be influenced by the press, the public, or his own family, none of whom are given
the authority to make political decisions. The husband may have authority
over his wife and children, but he is greatly influenced by them.

Characteristics of Conjugal Power

Mary Rogers[11] makes several key points about power. *First,* she argues that power is a capacity or an ability to influence others, *not* the exercise
of that ability. Ability does not denote social action. The perceived or real
ability to influence can affect outcomes even when the exercise of that ability
is not undertaken. *Second,* an individual's power must be viewed relative to
specific social systems and the positions (statuses) a person occupies within
a given social system. Note that power is not inherent within a person.
Power must be viewed in dynamic terms; one must note that the power of
individuals to influence others is linked to the social statuses and social roles
they occupy and perform within special social systems. *Third,* if power is an
ability to influence others, resources are the primary determinants of that
ability. A resource is "any attribute, circumstance, or possession that increases the ability of its holder to influence a person or group."[12] Attributes
might include age, sex, race, health, and level of energy; circumstances might
include location, friendships or acquaintances, flexibility, or access to information; possessions may include money, land, property, goods, and so on.
The contention is that persons with greater resources have an advantage over
those without those resources. In a social-exchange perspective, they can bargain with others from a position of strength.

Ronald Cromwell and David Olson[13] delineate three domains of fam-

---

11. Mary F. Rogers, "Instrumental and Infra-Resources: The Base of Power," *American Journal of Sociology* 79 (May 1974), pp. 1418–1433.

12. Ibid., p. 1425.

13. Ronald E. Cromwell and David H. Olson, eds., *Power in Families* (New York: John Wiley,
1975).

> Louise: Our marriage was pretty much along the traditional line. The home
>   and the children were primarily my responsibility. Because he trav-
>   eled, it was really very necessary that I, you know, was able to as-
>   sume a lot of responsibility. He was definitely the wage earner, the
>   provider. He managed the money; he made the major decisions and
>   it was that way because he was very good at it. I was very happy with
>   him assuming that role.
>
> Alex: Men usually consider themselves with business affairs and that's
>   about it. My mother has maids to do the housework and cooking and
>   things like that. But my mother does cook sometimes and I think
>   she's a better cook than the maids.
>
> Ann: I don't think the wife should do everything in the household. Most
>   married men feel they are the head of the house and half of them
>   don't know a darned thing to do in the house. Even if he earns the
>   bread and she spreads it out—O.K. But it should be worked out so
>   they both know what to do. You never know when she'll get sick
>   and can't do everything by herself.
>
> Mac: Our relationship, we like to say, is an equalitarian one. I do the
>   dishes at the home, the kitchen, the maintenance work at the house,
>   whereas she works to bring in the income. This is a tentative thing
>   till I reach my goal and get a job.

ily power: bases of family power, family power processes, and family power
outcomes. The *bases* of family power consist primarily of the resources an
individual possesses. In addition to those already mentioned, an individual
may have the ability to provide information, rewards, or punishment, may
be identified with or attractive to others, may have authority (legitimate
power) over others, or may have general resources such as education, income,
or occupation. Family power *processes* focus on the interaction of family
members. It includes processes occurring during general family discussions,
decision making, problem solving, conflict resolution, or crisis management.
Family power *outcomes* include who makes the decisions and who wins.

Processes of Conjugal Power

The processes in the use of power within marriage are dimensions
often overlooked. Since marriage involves two or more people, and since
social power involves the ability of one person to influence others, it becomes necessary to ask questions that involve persons in relation to each
other. For someone to influence, someone else must be influenced. And in
being influenced, how does this affect the use of power of the influencer?

Jetse Sprey[14] indicates that in any reciprocal power relationship, compliance itself must be considered a potential source of influence. If there is total compliance by one spouse to the demands of the other, such an event must be seen as part of a reciprocal exchange of power from which it is not logically possible to determine who is the more powerful. For example:

> A wife may threaten her husband with divorce unless he stops his heavy drinking. If we assume that she has the ability to carry out her threat, the fact remains that it is up to her spouse to accept or reject her demand. By refusing to comply, he will force her to either carry out the threat or to retreat. In both instances her conduct would be influenced by his. If he decides to stop his drinking she indeed did influence his conduct, but his decision to comply in turn determines her course of action. There is an additional aspect to this case: In a marriage, a threat to divorce affects *both* its sender and its receiver, since each must face the consequences if it is carried out. Both spouses presumably are aware of this and can be expected to perceive a threat of this nature within this shared context. To interpret, therefore, the outcome of the above confrontation as a mere "win" for the wife, and to code it as an indication of her "power," seems rather unrealistic, to put it mildly.[15]

This illustration and others that could be given clearly demonstrate the complexity of understanding power processes. The use of power is often indirect; the outcome may have no "winner" or finality, and the nature of the interaction will vary from one group and system to another and from one social context to another.

Conjugal Power and Decision Making

One of the ways in which conjugal power has traditionally been measured was to determine which spouse made major decisions and how the husband and wife decision-making patterns varied by area of concern. One of the most widely cited studies and one that served as a major stimulant to many studies that followed was that of Robert Blood and Donald Wolfe.[16] In an attempt to measure the balance of power between husbands and wives, they interviewed 731 city wives in metropolitan Detroit.

They selected eight situations that they felt would include both masculine as well as feminine decisions about the family as a whole. These included: 1) what job the husband should take, 2) what kind of car to get, 3)

---

14. Jetse Sprey, "Family Power and Process: Toward a Conceptual Integration," in Ronald E. Cromwell and David H. Olsen, eds., *Power in Families* (New York: John Wiley, 1975).

15. Ibid., p. 68.

16. Robert O. Blood, Jr. and Donald M. Wolfe, *Husbands and Wives: The Dynamics of Married Living* (Glencoe, Ill.: Free Press, 1960), p. 20.

TABLE 15–1. Allocation of Power in Decision-Making Areas
(731 Detroit Families)

WHO DECIDES?	DECISION (in percent)							
	Hus-band's Job	Car	Insur-ance	Vaca-tion	House	Wife's Work	Doctor	Food
(5) Husband always	90	56	31	12	12	26	7	10
(4) Husband more than wife	4	12	11	6	6	5	3	2
(3) Husband and wife exactly the same	3	25	41	68	58	18	45	32
(2) Wife more than husband	0	2	4	4	10	9	11	11
(1) Wife always	1	3	10	7	13	39	31	41
N.A.	2	1	2	3	1	3	3	3
Total	100	99	99	100	100	100	100	99
Husband's mean power	4.86	4.18	3.50	3.12	2.94	2.69	2.53	2.26

Source: Robert O. Blood, Jr., and Donald M. Wolfe, *Husbands and Wives: The Dynamics of Married Living* (Glencoe, Ill.: Free Press, 1960), p. 21. Reprinted by permission of the Macmillan Company. © 1960 by The Free Press, a Corporation.

whether or not to buy life insurance, 4) where to go on a vacation, 5) what house or apartment to take, 6) whether or not the wife should go to work or quit work, 7) what doctor to have when someone is sick, 8) and how much money the family can afford to spend per week on food.

The wives' answers to the eight questions are shown in Table 15–1 with the items arranged in order of decreasing male participation. Two decisions are primarily the husband's province (his job and car), two are primarily the wife's province (her work and food), while all the others are joint decisions in the sense of having more "same" responses than anything else. Even the wife's working turns out to be quite a middling decision from the standpoint of the mean score, leaving only the food expenditures predominantly to the wife.

Perhaps the responses of the wives to these eight decision-making questions are not surprising. Both legally and socially in the United States, it is expected that the male is responsible for the economic support of his wife and children. His job and his work are his primary exertions in both time and energy. Factors related to automobiles might also be expected to be primarily the concern of the husband; although most wives in our society have operators' licenses, when the husband and wife travel together it is likely to be the husband who does the driving. Traditionally, it has also been the husband who cares for repairs and upkeep of the automobile.

Whether or not to buy life insurance, where to go on a vacation, and what house or apartment to take are decisions that are more likely to be shared equally by husband and wife than by either spouse separately. It could be assumed that both have equal competencies in these choices as well as because these areas affect both partners more equally than do the other decision-making areas.

The decisions the wife always makes are most clearly related to whether or not she should go to work, what doctor to have, and the money to be spent on food. It is interesting to note, however, that the husband is much more involved in the decision on the wife's work than is the wife involved in what job the husband should take. Only on the decisions regarding whether or not the wife should go to work and on the amount of money that the family can afford to spend per week on food, do a greater percentage of wives always make the decision when compared to joint decision making or husband decision making.

The theoretical explanation of why husbands make certain decisions, wives make others, and there is joint involvement in still others is based on resource availability. That is, the source of authority and power lies in the comparative resources each spouse has available. The balance of power is weighted toward the partner who has the greater resources as perceived by the spouse.

Richard Centers et al. raise several research questions posed by the Blood and Wolfe study cited.[17] First, they question the representativeness of the sampling of eight decision areas, which include an overrepresentation of areas traditionally or normatively within the male domain and competence. Second, they question the possibly distorted picture of conjugal-power balance, which might be created by eliciting the responses of wives only. Several other studies have shown that husbands report less power for themselves than their wives claimed for them,[18] that wives tend to overestimate the power of their husbands,[19] and that discrepancies exist in husbands' and wives' reports about their respective roles in decision making.[20] Third, they question the applicability of the results to geographic areas other than Detroit. Finally, they question the explanation of power solely as a function of the resources commanded by the interacting parties and the failure to examine other factors.

---

17. Richard Centers, Bertram H. Raven, and Aroldo Rodrigues, "Conjugal Power Structure: A Re-examination," *American Sociological Review* 36 (April 1971), pp. 264–278.
18. David M. Heer, "Husband and Wife Perceptions of Family Power Structures," *Marriage and Family Living* 24 (February 1962), pp. 65–67.
19. William F. Kenkel, "Influence Differentiation in Family Decision-Making," *Sociology and Social Research* 42 (September–October 1957), pp. 18–25.
20. William F. Kenkel and Dean K. Hoffman, "Real and Conceived Roles in Family Decision Making," *Marriage and Family Living* 18 (November 1956), pp. 311–316.

To answer these questions, Centers et al. interviewed 776 husbands and wives in the Los Angeles area regarding their relative power in fourteen decision areas.[21] These areas included the eight used in the Blood and Wolfe study plus 1) who to invite to the house or go out with, 2) how to decorate or furnish the house, 3) which TV or radio program to tune in, 4) what the family will have for dinner, 5) what clothes will be bought, and 6) what type of clothes the spouse will buy.

In the decision-making areas that were identical in the Detroit (Blood and Wolfe) and Los Angeles (Centers et al.) studies, the results showed remarkably close agreement, but when the six new items were added the husband's mean power dropped. Thus, the answer to the first question did indicate that the balance and distribution of power will differ as different decision areas are examined. Second, there was essential agreement in the reports of husbands and wives, thus strengthening confidence that the phenomena Blood and Wolfe described were not merely the creatures of wifely vanity or timidity.[22] This factor does, however, conflict with other studies previously cited that show considerable discrepancies between the answers of husbands and wives about prevailing decision making and also conflicts with the cross-cultural data of Constantina Safilios-Rothschild.[23] She found in both America and Greece a consistent incongruence between husbands' and wives' perceptions of decision making. This incongruence she explains as follows:

> The incongruence between husbands' and wives' perceptions of decision-making may be due to one or both spouses' need to dominate the family power structure or to adhere to equalitarian norms. Thus, a spouse, for whom it is very important to be predominant in the decision-making, may perceive only these cues which permit him (or her) to see himself as the most powerful member of the family. The analysis of the Greek data, for example, showed that when husbands or wives perceive that they prevail in the decision-making, they are satisfied with their marriage; while the opposite is true when they perceive the decision-making as rather equalitarian.[24]

The third question concerned the applicability of results in Detroit to results in Los Angeles. As stated previously, the results showed remarkably close agreement. The fourth and final question concerned the explanation of power, particularly the resource-control theory, which holds that the more a partner controls resources of value to himself and his mate, the greater his relative power. Centers et al. state:

> Unfortunately, our data are not as clearly supportive of the valued-resources approach. We did find that husband's power increased with his level of occu-

21. Centers et al., op. cit., p. 266.
22. Ibid., p. 275.
23. Constantina Safilios-Rothschild, "Family Sociology or Wives' Family Sociology? A Cross-Cultural Examination of Decision-Making," *Journal of Marriage and the Family* 31 (May 1969), pp. 290–301.
24. Ibid., p. 301.

pational prestige and income. However, we did not find that his power decreased if the wife was employed. Husband's power increased with his level of education, which tended to be correlated. Our results with regard to power as a function of length of marriage, initially parallels Blood and Wolfe's—husband's power is greatest during the honeymoon period (first four years). However, contrary to Blood and Wolfe's study, husbands in our sample of families did not show a further decline in husband power thereafter. Further, the Blood and Wolfe interpretation of the age differences—greater wife dependence upon husband for satisfaction of affectional needs—is not supported in our data on individual differences in needs.[25]

The Theory of Resources Issue

Sprey[26] makes several interesting points in regard to the "resource" argument. One, he questions how individuals without authority or other resources manage to influence the family process. Housewives in patriarchal families and children in most households fit into this category. Second, he suggests that while the availability of a given resource will be a necessary condition for its use, the *absence* of a resource among other members may serve to limit, or even neutralize, its usefulness for those who have access to it. A child, for example, may use ignorance or lack of knowledge to counteract a parent's expertise in a given dispute. Third, he suggests that the distribution of resources is relative: defined and guided by the rules and role prescriptions of the system in question. Yet, while systems provide boundaries and rules, they do not determine outcomes. Outcomes, influenced by resources as related to the system involved, are a result of reciprocal influencing.

The "theory of resources," previously described and criticized, provides the conceptual core around which many of the later studies have been built. Several authors have stressed that power is not merely based on an individual's resources but on the comparative contributions (resources) and exchange processes of the husband and wife relative to each other. Most of these studies were done outside the United States and stress, in addition, the cultural context in which the interaction occurs.[27] Hyman Rodman, for example,[28] developed a "theory of resources in a cultural context" that takes

25. Centers et al., op. cit., p. 276.

26. Sprey, op. cit., pp. 76–78.

27. Christine Oppong, "Conjugal Power and Resources: An Urban African Example," *Journal of Marriage and the Family* 32 (November 1970), p. 676–680; Constantina Safilios-Rothschild, "A Comparison of Power Structure and Marital Satisfaction in Urban Greek and French Families," *Journal of Marriage and the Family* 29 (May 1967), pp. 345–352; Marie LaLiberte Richmond, "Beyond Resource Theory: Another Look at Factors Enabling Women to Affect Family Interaction," *Journal of Marriage and the Family* 38 (May 1976), pp. 257–266.

28. Hyman Rodman, "Marital Power in France, Greece, Yugoslavia, and the United States: A Cross-National Discussion," *Journal of Marriage and the Family* 29 (May 1967), pp. 320–

into account the "theory of resources," the "theory of exchange," the comparative contributions of both husband and wife, and the cultural context in which the interaction occurs.

In a study of power in Turkish marriages, it was noted that the husband's absolute power diminishes when either the husband or the wife comes from a background that evinces increasing contact with the world of modern ideas as channeled through education, experience in urban centers, and nonagricultural occupations.[29] Results suggest that, for wives, increasing amounts of those attributes (resources) that provide her with a greater store of skills and experience enhance her ability to participate in decisions and to counteract her husband's power to forbid. For the husband, however, the increase in resources probably operates to introduce him to alternatives to the traditional patriarchal mode of husband-wife interaction. In other words, the contributions of both spouses, relative to each other, affects the pattern and outcomes of conjugal power relationships.

In an attempt to develop a theory of power relationships in marriage, Boyd Rollins and Stephen Bahr suggest:[30] 1) that it is important to focus on comparative power of husband and wife rather than the amount of individual power either may have, 2) that relative authority, relative resources, and relative power do not exist independently of the perceptions of the marriage partners, 3) that power and control are relative constructs in marriage only when conflict exists between the goals of the marriage partners, and 4) relative power and relative control may vary from one area of marriage to another. With the exception of the third point, the other issues have been discussed previously. The logic of the importance of conflict is based on the idea that the influence of one person on another is somewhat meaningless if the other person behaves in the same manner even if the influencer were absent.

The power dimension of marriage is too complex and vast to cover adequately in a portion of one chapter. Interested persons may want to examine further the references mentioned in this section, particularly the Cromwell-Olsen work[31] and the review article on power provided by Safilios-Rothschild.[32]

324; Hyman Rodman, "Marital Power and the Theory of Resources in Cultural Context," *Journal of Comparative Family Studies* 3 (Spring 1972), pp. 50–69.

29. Greer Litton Fox, "Another Look at the Comparative Resources Model: Assessing the Balance of Power in Turkish Marriages," *Journal of Marriage and the Family* 35 (November 1973), pp. 718–730.

30. Boyd C. Rollins and Stephen J. Bahr, "A Theory of Power Relationships in Marriage," *Journal of Marriage and the Family* 38 (November 1976), pp. 619–627.

31. Cromwell and Olsen, op. cit.

32. Constantina Safilios-Rothschild, "The Study of Family Power Structure: A Review, 1960–1969," *Journal of Marriage and the Family* 32 (November 1970), pp. 539–552; Note also Constantina Safilios-Rothschild, "A Macro- and Micro-Examination of Family Power and Love: An Exchange Model," *Journal of Marriage and the Family* 38 (May 1976), pp. 355–361.

ADJUSTMENT AND
CONFLICT IN MARRIAGE

The second chapter included a section on a social conflict frame of reference. It was indicated that the most basic assumption of this frame of reference is that conflict is natural and inevitable in all human interaction. Definitely, this is true of marital interaction as well. To write about "power," as was just done, is to alert the reader to differences, bargaining, unequal resources, exchange, game playing, competition, cooperation, and conflict. To write about marital adjustment is to alert the reader and focus attention on two (or more) individuals who must define and redefine their relationship to one another, who must make rules, and who must carry out role expectations.

This process of defining, making rules, and performing role expectations leads to inevitable sources of conflict: conflict over one's work, over children, over criticism, over in-laws, over expenditures, over sex, and, as stressed in popular literature, even over where one squeezes the toothpaste. Thus the issue is not whether conflict exists but how conflict is managed in a way that is mutually satisfactory to the marriage partners. This is basically what is meant by marital adjustment.

Marital adjustment is probably the most frequently studied dependent variable in the marriage and family field.[33] Many attempts have been made to assess the quality of marital relationships, using such concepts as marital adjustment, success, satisfaction, stability, happiness, consensus, cohesion, adaptation, integration, role strain, and the like. Sometimes these terms are used interchangeably, other times each denotes something different. Sometimes the terms are used in a psychological sense, referring to the state of one of the marital partners, sometimes they are used in a social-psychological sense, referring to the state of the relationship, and sometimes they are used in a sociological sense, referring to the state of the group or system. In addition, there are times the terms are used to refer to the achievement of a goal and other times they are used to refer to a dynamic process of making changes. All the concepts emphasize a dimension that contrasts with maladjustment, dissatisfaction, instability, unhappiness, and so forth.

The adjustment of married mates is unlike any other human relationship. It may share many conditions of friendship groups, peer groups, work groups, or religious groups, but the role of relationships of husbands and wives differ. Marriage, involving two sexes in physical propinquity, is public and binding in nature. Being publicly sanctioned, marriage becomes more difficult to break. Being binding, the members must act as a unit and cooperation becomes essential. Every decision made must take into account the de-

---

33. Graham B. Spanier, "Measuring Dyadic Adjustment: New Scales for Assessing the Quality of Marriage and Similar Dyads," *Journal of Marriage and the Family* 38 (February 1976), p. 15; and Graham B. Spanier and Charles L. Cole, "Toward Clarification and Investigation of Marital Adjustment," *International Journal of Sociology* 6 (Spring 1976), pp. 121–146.

Meaningful Conversation and Marriage

484

At a party the other evening, people were discussing marriage. Marilyn turned and looked at her husband lovingly (as if she had just popped a Geritol tablet) and said, "Dan and I have a good marriage because we have meaningful conversations with one another."

I couldn't get it off my mind. On the way home I asked my husband, "Have we ever had a meaningful conversation?"

"I don't think so," he said.

"That's hard to believe," I persisted. "In 26 years we've never had one?"

"Not that I can remember."

We drove along in silence for about 20 minutes. Finally I said, "What is a meaningful conversation?"

"You're kidding! You actually don't know?"

"No. What is it?"

"Well," he said, "it's a conversation with meaning."

"Like the oil embargo and Paul Harvey?"

"Exactly."

"What about them?" I asked.

"What about who?"

"The oil embargo and Paul Harvey."

"It doesn't have to be a conversation about the oil embargo and Paul Harvey," he

said. "It could b[...]
your daily sche[...]

"I shaved my [...]

"That is not pertine[...] you."

"Not really. I was using your razo[...]

"If you read the paper more," he said, "your conversations would be more stimulating."

"Okay, here's something meaningful I read just yesterday. In Naples—that's in Italy—police were searching for a woman who tried to cut off a man's nose with a pair of scissors while he was sleeping. What do you think of that?"

"That's not meaningful," he said.

A few minutes later I offered, "Suppose it was the American Embassy and the woman was a spy, and the nose belonged to Henry Kissinger which held secret documents about an oil embargo between Saudi Arabia and Paul Harvey?"

He drove in silence. "How long have Dan and Marilyn been married?"

"Twelve years," I said.

"They must pace their meaningful conversations."

From *At Wit's End* by Erma Bombeck. Reproduced through the courtesy of Field Newspaper Syndicate.

sires and wishes of the spouse. These forces determine the level of adjustment and the nature of the marital relationship.

Dimensions of Marital Adjustment

From the introductory statement it should be clear that marital adjustment is a varied concept that lacks a general consensus of definition. A general concept is likely to include a relative agreement by husband and wife on issues perceived to be important, sharing similar tasks and activities, and showing affection for one another. Marital success, as distinguished from marital adjustment, generally refers to the achievement of one or more goals: permanence, companionship, fulfilling the expectation of the community, and so forth. Marital happiness, distinguished from either adjustment or success, is an emotional response of an individual. Whereas happiness is an individual phenomenon, marital success and adjustment are dyadic achievements or states of the marriage.

Jessie Bernard states that the major dimensions of any human adjustment problem are 1) the degree or extent or nature of the differences between or among the parties involved, 2) the degree or extent or nature of the communication between or among the parties, and 3) the quality of the relationship between or among them—that is, its positive or negative affectivity, friendliness, or hostility.[34]

Differences may be a matter of degree or they may be categorical: no expectations, no leeway. Often matters of principle are categorical and thus the most difficult to resolve. Thus "we will never miss Mass," or "premarital sex is wrong," if taken categorically, does not permit flexibility in dealing with a mate or spouse who feels differently. On the other hand, differences of degree permit give-and-take, bargaining, and negotiation.

Communication, of necessity, involves interaction. Communication is an extremely complex factor in marital relationships: it may be verbal or nonverbal, explicit or tacit, it may clarify or mislead, draw relationships closer together, or tear them apart. To not talk at all, to talk constantly, to order, to nag, to scold, to praise may each be used to convey a certain message. It is Bernard's contention that communication between spouses is often honestly blunted because of sex differences.[35] "I just can't understand women" or "I just don't know what he or she expects of me" are complaints heard frequently.

The quality of the relationship is a third major dimension of adjustment. A friendly and loving spouse does not automatically mean adjustment, but it makes accommodation easier. Making sacrifices or changes in plans becomes easier when spouses have a love and genuine concern for one another. If the quality of the relationship is affection, results are far different than if it is hatred or hostility. These three dimensions—differences, communication, and quality of the relationships—are each important for understanding the process of adjustment.

The Evaluation of Marital Adjustment

The measurement of marital adjustment in a serious way began in the late 1920s.[36] Ten years later, comprehensive studies were conducted to de-

---

34. Jessie Bernard, "The Adjustment of Married Mates," in *Handbook of Marriage and the Family*, Harold T. Christensen, ed. (Chicago: Rand McNally, 1964), p. 690.
35. Ibid., p. 692.
36. Gilbert V. Hamilton, *A Research in Marriage* (New York: Albert and Charles Boni, 1929).

termine personality factors associated with marital adjustment[37] and to predict marital success.[38] The latter study on prediction was the beginning of a
much larger longitudinal study published more than a decade later.[39] Both
studies by Ernest Burgess on marriage and engagement measured adjustment
by concentrating primarily on five areas: agreements and disagreements, common interests and activities, demonstration of affection and sharing of confi-
dences, dissatisfaction with the marriage or engagement, and feelings of
personal isolation and unhappiness. Other criteria that have been applied in
attempting to evaluate marital relationships include how well a marriage
meets the needs and expectations of society, its permanence or endurance,
the degree of unity or consensus developed between the members, and the degree to which it facilitates personality development. Different weights are
applied to specific criteria depending on the researcher and the society.
Bernard claims:

> It is universally preferred that husbands and wives be fond of one another,
> that they live without quarreling and bickering, and that they find satisfaction in
> their relationship; but if a choice has to be made between this desideratum and
> stability, stability is given precedence in some societies, marital happiness and
> satisfaction in others.[40]

Bernard goes on to make a significant point for evaluating a marital
relationship. She says a criterion should be set up in terms not of the best
imaginable relationship but of the best possible one.[41] Thus a marriage may
be said to be successful to the extent that it provides the highest satisfaction
possible, not the highest imaginable. However unsatisfactory it may be in
terms of happiness, it may still be judged better than the alternatives.

From this relativistic and exchange point of view, a marital relationship is successful if 1) the satisfaction is positive, that is, if the rewards to both
partners are greater than the cost, and 2) if it is preferable to any other alternative. Two examples follow:

> 1) A and B do not like one another; they get on one another's nerves; the costs
> of remaining married are great in frustration and loneliness. But the rewards
> are great also; together they can afford a lovely home; they have high status
> in the community; the children are protected from scandal; the church ap-
> proves of them; etc. This relationship is "successful" or "good," not because
> it is the best imaginable, but only because it is the best possible in the sense
> that the satisfactions are greater than the costs.

---

37. Lewis M. Terman, *Psychological Factors in Marital Happiness* (New York: McGraw-Hill,
1938).
38. Ernest W. Burgess and L. S. Cottrell, Jr., *Predicting Success or Failure in Marriage* (New
York: Prentice-Hall, 1939).
39. Ernest W. Burgess and Paul Wallin, *Engagement and Marriage* (Philadelphia: J. B. Lippincott, 1953).
40. Bernard, op. cit., p. 730.
41. Ibid., p. 732.

2) An example in which a marital relationship is successful only because it is better than any alternative would be the marriage of a dependent woman to, let us say, an alcoholic, in which the costs in misery were much greater than the rewards in security or status; but the spread between costs and satisfactions would be much greater if she left him. She would then be alone; she would not have the protection of the status of marriage; she would not even have the occasional sober companionship of a husband, etc. Bad as it is, therefore, her marriage seems better to her than any alternative she has.[42]

Many statistical studies have been geared to find factors associated beyond chance with marital adjustment.[43] But often the findings quoted in texts and popular literature are those that support the opinions of the writer, and contradictory evidence is frequently discounted or ignored completely. Most researchers are prone to a Pollyanna-like view of marriage characterized by a tendency to view consistently nonargumentative discussions, agreements, similarity, and the like as good or positive and conflict, anger, disagreements, or differences as negative. Conflict is generally viewed in the context of divorce and not as inevitable to a marriage. The literature lacks research data on conflict management as an aspect of marriage (note conflict theory in Chapter 2). In addition, nearly every family text published since 1960 quotes findings of marital studies done in the first half of the century and bases current training and "advice" on that literature. Thus, the points made by Reuben Hill more than twenty-five years ago in all likelihood hold true today and suggest caution in the wholesale acceptance of many studies of marital success and adjustment:

1. Because of the criteria used, the studies "stack the cards" in favor of a conventionality and conservatism of behavior better suited to the Victorian bourgeois family situations of the day before yesterday than to those of today.

2. The factors asserted to be most highly associated with success in marriage are unconfirmed for the most part by more than two or three studies and are questioned by other studies.

3. The factors, if valid, are probably valid only for the early years of marriage.

4. The findings are limited in application to the white, urban, middle class, from which they were drawn.

5. The coefficient of determination of the best associations is still small; roughly 75 percent of the factors that count for marital success are left unaccounted for.[44]

---

42. Ibid., pp. 732–733.

43. For a bibliography of 114 sources of research done prior to 1962 concerning success in marriage, refer to Clifford Kirkpatrick, *The Family as Process and Institution*, 2d ed. (New York: Ronald, 1963), pp. 673–678. A description of various measures of marital competence are summarized in Murray Straus, *Family Measurement Techniques* (Minneapolis: University of Minnesota Press, 1969).

44. Willard Waller, *The Family: A Dynamic Interpretation*, revised by Reuben Hill (New York: Holt, Rinehart and Winston, 1951), p. 353.

> *Louise:*   If I had to use one word to describe my marriage it would be "good."
> It had its ups and downs definitely, but there were a lot more ups
> than downs.
>
> *Alex:*   I don't think I'll be married for awhile, because I figure I'm still
> young. When you're young you want to meet a lot of people, you
> want to have your fun. I think it would be kinda hard. That's why
> I don't want to get married. If you can't be devoted to one person,
> why get married, you know?
>
> *Ann:*   Yes, I'm married but it isn't a good one. It didn't work out between
> us. We've been separated for five years. My husband is here in the
> city though, and I see him quite regularly you know. And I call him
> if I need something for the boys. But he doesn't support any of us on
> a regular basis. Only when I am in very dire need does he kind of
> help out.
>
> *Mac:*   I would say that in the future we will be married. We want to know
> each other as much as possible. I want to be darned sure that I'm
> ready for the marriage institution.

In general, by 1960 the following had all been delineated as variables correlating positively with marital happiness: higher occupational statuses, incomes, and educational levels for husbands; husband-wife similarities in socioeconomic status, age, and religion; affectional rewards, such as esteem for spouse, sexual enjoyment, companionship; and age at marriage.[45]

Between 1960 and 1970, more than one hundred research studies were published on marital happiness and stability.[46] Since 1970, studies using more sophisticated methodological procedures[47] and many studies following the patterns of earlier research have been conducted. Selected areas of this and earlier research are summarized below.

Role Expectations, Congruence, and Marital Adjustment

The role concept is often used in a structured perspective to refer to the social expectations associated with a given status. At this point the status of concern is marriage and its component statuses of husband and wife. A per-

45. Mary W. Hicks and Marilyn Platt, "Marital Happiness and Stability: A Review of the Research in the Sixties," *Journal of Marriage and the Family* 32 (November 1970), p. 555.
46. For a bibliography of these studies, see ibid., pp. 569–574. See also Judith Long Laws, "A Feminist Review of Marital Adjustment Literature: The Rape of the Locke," *Journal of Marriage and the Family* 33 (August 1971), pp. 483–516.
47. See, for example, Brent C. Miller, "A Multivariate Development Model of Marital Satisfaction," *Journal of Marriage and the Family* 38 (November 1976), pp. 643–657.

son who is aware of what to expect in a recurring situation and can respond with an appropriate set of responses is "adjusted" to the role involved. This adjustment is perceived as essential to success in the marital situation.

There are several sources of difficulty in the achievement of, and adjustment to, marital roles.[48] First, unlike many societies, the United States does not provide, and often resists providing, systematic training in what to expect in marriage. Perhaps traditionally, formal systematic training was not essential since the informal kin and community network fulfilled this function. With the breakdown of traditional patterns of authority, kin ties, work roles, and the like, it becomes increasingly essential for married couples to develop their own norms and expectations appropriate to their situation. One husband may assist in household tasks, while another holds them inappropriate to his male-husband status. One wife may get up to fix her husband's breakfast, while another assumes her husband is sufficiently capable of getting his own. Marital training provided in the United States in high school and college courses is often taken primarily by girls in courses titled family life, home economics, or health education.

A second source of difficulty in adjusting to marital roles arises from cultural discontinuities. That is, a lack of continuity exists in what is learned from observing parents and what is emphasized during adolescence among peers. What is first learned must later be unlearned. Mate-selection roles, sex roles, or work roles have meanings for many teen-agers that differ considerably from those held by parents.

A third source of difficulty arises when husband and wife have learned different expectations as to the nature and content of marital roles. This difficulty may be minimal if the spouses share similar ethnic, religious, class, and other endogamous backgrounds. Even when the backgrounds are similar, peer and educational experiences may lead to shifts in expectations stemming from the ethnic or class subculture. If the expectations differ, a problem of role adjustment occurs, and the greater the diversity of expectations the greater the potential for conflict.

A. R. Mangus hypothesized that the integrative quality of a marriage is reflected in degrees of congruence or incongruence between the way each partner sees his own role in the marriage and the way that role is perceived by the other partner.[49] He also assumed that the integrative quality of a marriage is reflected in degrees of congruence between what a spouse expects in a mate and what he actually perceives in the one he married. In other words, the degree to which the partner's role expectations are fulfilled or frustrated is a measure of marital integration. Finally, Mangus hypothesized that the

---

48. Robert F. Winch, *The Modern Family*, 3d ed. (New York: Holt Rinehart and Winston, 1971), pp. 552–554.
49. A. R. Mangus, "Role Theory and Marriage Counseling," *Social Forces* 35 (March 1957), pp. 200–209.

The Sense in Humor

A cartoon strip by Jules Feiffer expresses this outlook succinctly. It shows a housewife musing:

By the time George told me he was leaving on a business trip for a month I had lost all feeling for him. . . . Each dinner when he'd come home I'd try to rekindle the flame, but all I could think of as he gobbled up my chicken was: "All I am is a servant to you, George." . . . So when he announced he had to go away I was delighted. While George was away I could find myself again! I could make plans! . . . The first week George was away I went out seven times. The telephone never stopped

ringing. I had a marvelous time! . . . The second week George was away I got tired of the same old faces, same old lines. I remembered what drove me to marry George in the first place. . . . The third week George was away I felt closer to him than I had in years. I stayed home, read Jane Austen, and slept on George's side of the bed. . . . The fourth week George was away I fell madly in love with him. I hated myself for my withdrawal, for my failure of him. . . . The fifth week George came home. The minute he walked in and said, "I'm back, darling!" I withdrew. . . . I can hardly wait for his next business trip so I can love George again.

Source: Harvey Mindess, "The Sense in Humor," *Saturday Review*, August 21, 1971, p. 11.

integrative quality of a marriage is reflected in the degree to which the role expectations that one partner has of the other are consistent with the other's expectations of himself.

Eleanore Luckey has reported a number of studies that associate marital satisfaction with the perceived personality characteristics of self and spouse.[50] She selected eighty-one couples at the University of Minnesota from a much larger subject-pool in order to provide two groups highly differentiated on a standardized marital-happiness scale. Also, she had an interpersonal checklist of 128 descriptive-adjective phrases completed by each subject for self, spouse, ideal self, mother, and father. By comparing the self rating with each "significant other," she could estimate the degree of congruence or divergence of perceptions. The results indicate that satisfaction in marriage is related to the congruence of the husband's self-concept and that held of him by his wife. The relationship did not hold for concepts of wives. Happiness was related to self-other congruence for both husbands and wives.

When the relationship between marital satisfaction, perception of self and spouse, and number of years married was investigated, it was found that the longer the couples were married, the less favorable personality qualities

---

50. Eleanore B. Luckey, "Marital Satisfaction and Its Concomitant Perceptions of Self and Spouse," *Journal of Counseling Psychology* 11 (1964), pp. 136–145; "Marital Satisfaction and Personality Correlates of Spouse," *Journal of Marriage and the Family* 26 (May 1964), pp. 217–220; "Marital Satisfaction and Congruent Self-Spouse Concepts," *Social Forces* 39 (December 1960), pp. 153–157; "Marital Satisfaction and Its Association with Congruence of Perception," *Marriage and Family Living* 22 (February 1960), pp. 49–54.

they saw in their mates.[51] As the average marriage length was 7.7 years, the older couple was not adequately represented. Among these couples, overall marital satisfaction was negatively related to the number of years married, a finding consistent with those reported below under "Marital Satisfaction over the Life Cycle."

Conclusions similar to Luckey's were reached by Robert Stuckert.[52] He found the dominant factor associated with marital satisfaction for the wives to be the extent to which their perception of their husband's expectations correlated with the husband's actual expectation. For the husbands, the actual similarity between their own role concepts and expectations and those of their wives was the most important factor. Chadwick et al.[53] also found that adequacy of role performance of both self and spouse and spouse's conformity to expectations emerged as strong predictors of marital satisfaction.

Marital Satisfaction over the Life Cycle

The development concept as applied to adjustment in marriage has stimulated interest in changes over the life cycle. This approach, which deals with changes over time or with differences at varying stages of the life cycle, stands in contrast to the attempts previously described in this chapter at finding factors or dimensions relating to marital satisfaction.

Studies of marital satisfaction over the life cycle show mixed results, but a general pattern indicates a decline in satisfaction over the first ten to fifteen years of marriage. This seems to be more true for wives than for husbands. One of the earlier and frequently cited studies by Peter Pineo deals with disenchantment in the later years of marriage. Four processes appeared to dominate his data:

1. There is a general drop in marital satisfaction and adjustment, which we conceptualize as a process of disenchantment.
2. There is a loss of certain intimacy. Confiding, kissing, and reciprocal settlement of disagreements become less frequent; more individuals report loneliness. This loss of intimacy appears to be an aspect of disenchantment.
3. Personal adjustment and reports of personality characteristics are relatively unaffected by the process of disenchantment or loss of intimacy.
4. Certain forms of marital interaction are found to change as the frequency of

51. Eleanore B. Luckey, "Number of Years Married as Related to Personality Perception and Marital Satisfaction," *Journal of Marriage and the Family* 28 (February 1966), p. 47.

52. Robert P. Stuckert, "Role Perception and Marital Satisfaction—A Configurational Approach," *Marriage and Family Living* 25 (November 1963), p. 419.

53. Bruce A. Chadwick, Stan L. Albrecht, and Phillip R. Kunz, "Marital and Family Role Satisfaction," *Journal of Marriage and the Family* 38 (August 1976), pp. 431–440.

sexual intercourse diminishes and the amount of sharing of activities drops, without any major link to disenchantment.[54]

It was Pineo's belief that disenchantment was derived from romanticism in mate selection plus the discovery of aspects of a mate that could not possibly have been known to the individuals at the time of marriage. Thus perfect mating could occur only with some element of luck. It is these unforseen changes in situation, personality, or behavior that contribute most to the disenchantment in the early years of marriage. If this analysis is correct, a decrease in marital satisfaction, at least in the first five or ten years, could be expected to result wherever mates are selected on the basis of personal choice. Some additional support for this idea comes from studies in France and Japan, both of which indicate that marriages tend to deteriorate over time.[55, 56]

What happens to marital satisfaction over the life cycle when the time span extends beyond five or ten years? Using an eight-stage family life cycle similar to that developed by Duvall as described in Chapter 2, Boyd Rollins and Harold Feldman traced the pattern of general and specific aspects of marital satisfaction.[57] Separate questionnaires were obtained from husbands and wives in 799 middle-class families. The results suggest that husbands and wives are influenced in different ways by stage or family life-cycle experiences. In general, family life-cycle experiences were associated with marital satisfaction more for wives than husbands. Especially in this subjective area of feelings about marital interaction, the dependent-children stages of the family life cycle were associated with negative evaluations of the marriage by the wife.

The pattern of "general marital satisfaction" for wives steadily declined from the "beginning" (Stage I) to the "school-age" stage (Stage IV), then leveled off with a rapid increase from the "empty-nest" (Stage VII) to the "retired" stage (Stage VIII) of the family life cycle (see Figure 15–2). For the husbands there was a slight decline from the "beginning" to the "school-age" stage, a slight increase to the "empty-nest" stage, and then a rapid increase to the "retired" stage. The amount of change for husbands, though statistically significant, was found by the authors to be less than that for the wives.

The authors, in attempting to determine the satisfaction with the present stage of the family life cycle, found a curvilinear pattern for both husbands and wives (see Figure 15–3). Particularly for wives, there was a substantial decrease in general marital satisfaction and a high level of negative

54. Peter C. Pineo, "Disenchantment in the Later Years of Marriage," *Marriage and Family Living* 23 (February 1961), pp. 3–11.

55. French Institute of Public Opinion, *Patterns of Sex and Love* (New York: Brown, 1960), pp. 166–172.

56. Robert Blood, *Love Match and Arranged Marriage* (New York: Free Press, 1967).

57. Boyd C. Rollins and Harold Feldman, "Marital Satisfaction over the Family Life Cycle," *Journal of Marriage and the Family* 32 (February 1970), pp. 20–28.

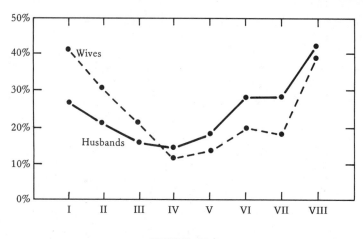

FIGURE 15–2.

Percentage of Individuals at Each Stage of the Family Life
Cycle Reporting their Marriage Was Going Well "All The
Time." (Stage I, beginning families; Stage II, child-bearing
families; Stage III, families with preschool children; Stage
IV, families with school-age children; Stage V, families with
teen-agers; Stage VI, families as launching center; Stage VII,
families in the middle years; Stage VIII, aging families.)
[Source: Boyd C. Rollins and Harold Feldman, "Marital Satisfaction over the Family Life Cycle," *Journal of Marriage
and the Family* 32 (February 1970), p. 25. Reprinted by
permission.]

feelings from marital interaction during the child-bearing and child-rearing
phases until the children were getting ready to leave home. After the child-
rearing phases, both the husband and the wife had substantial increase in
marital satisfaction through the "retirement" stage.

The Rollins-Feldman data suggest that the experiences of child bearing and child rearing have a rather profound and negative effect on marital
satisfaction for wives, even in their basic feelings of self-worth in relation to
their marriage.[58] For the males, the most devastating period of marriage appears to be when they are anticipating retirement. Marital satisfaction might
be influenced more by occupational experience for husbands than the births
and developmental levels of children in their families.

A later study by Boyd Rollins and Kenneth Cannon[59] provides some
precautionary notes to the data just presented. First, while consistent variation from stage to stage is found in several studies, the amount of change is
neither as great nor as significant as is often implied in textbooks such as this.

---

58. Ibid., p. 27.
59. Boyd C. Rollins and Kenneth L. Cannon, "Marital Satisfaction over the Family Life Cycle:
    A Reevaluation," *Journal of Marriage and the Family* 36 (May 1974), pp. 271–282.

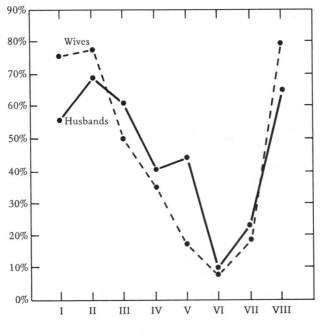

FIGURE 15–3.

Percentage of Individuals in Each Stage of the Family Life Cycle Reporting their Present Stage of the Family Life Cycle As Very Satisfying. (Stage I, beginning families; Stage II, child-bearing families; Stage III, families with preschool children; Stage IV, families with school-age children; Stage V, families with teen-agers; Stage VI, families as launching center; Stage VII, families in the middle years; Stage VIII, aging families.) [Source: Boyd C. Rollins and Harold Feldman, "Marital Satisfaction over the Family Life Cycle," *Journal of Marriage and the Family*, 32 (February, 1970), p. 26.]

Second, while male-female differences are found in most studies, these differences too tend to be overplayed. Graham Spanier et al.[60] followed up this same issue and provided further precautionary notes to the curvilinearity aspect of marital satisfaction over the life cycle. From three coordinated studies in Iowa, Ohio, and Georgia they found a decline in marital adjustment from Stage 1 to Stage 3 of the family life cycle, but only in Ohio was the curvilinear relationship evident. The Georgia and Iowa relationships were not significantly curvilinear for males or females. Thus, the question of curvilinearity is not yet settled.

60. Graham B. Spanier, Robert A. Lewis, and Charles L. Cole, "Marital Adjustment over the Family Life Cycle: The Issue of Curvilinearity," *Journal of Marriage and the Family* 37 (May 1975), pp. 263–275.

Criticisms of Adjustment Studies

The studies mentioned, and many others, have been criticized on a number of general points. First, *what was the researcher investigating?* That is, what was the central concept under study and was this concept synonymous with other concepts or variables used interchangeably? When the dependent variable of one investigator is marital adjustment, it may or may not be synonymous with other variables such as success or happiness. For example, whereas older people were found to be better "adjusted" than young people, they were also less "happy."[61]

Second, *how was the variable measured?* The conceptualization and hence operationalization of terms is one fundamental criticism of marital-adjustment and prediction studies.[62] Stability as a proxy for marital success often means the marriage has not ended. In this sense, many nonterminated marriages, although stable, are not necessarily "happy, successful, or adjusted." Perhaps it is warranted to infer that marriages that were terminated were not "happy, successful, or adjusted," but to infer the obverse is less justifiable. Thus the absence of divorce or separation should be treated lightly in determining marital adjustment.

In addition, caution should be taken in using the verbal response of "happily married" as an accurate assessment of the quality of a marriage. Most studies of marital adjustment to date have tended to rely heavily on self ratings of marriage via interviews, questionnaires, self-rating instruments, and other paper-and-pencil techniques. Subjects' statements taken at face value ignore the distortions effected by the need to meet society's expectations with regard to happiness in marriage.

Third, *is the self, the spouse, or the couple being measured?* This factor has a number of significant aspects connected with it. In some instances, marriages are assessed on the response of one spouse. The book *Husbands and Wives* was written from data supplied by wives.[63] In this study of 909 spouses interviewed, not one was a male.

This type of assessment is likely to produce a bias in that a wife with a vested interest describes her husband as though she were her spouse. Her description is, of course, based on her beliefs about him. These statements may or may not be consistent with his beliefs about himself. In other instances, marriages are assessed by the use of criteria that may be applicable to either one spouse, both spouses separately, or the marriage as a unit. Happi-

61. G. Gurin, J. Veroff, and Sheila Feld, *Americans View Their Mental Health* (New York: Basic Books, 1960).
62. To "operationalize" is to define concepts of a nonanalytic nature in terms of identifiable, measurable, and repeatable criteria.
63. Blood and Wolfe, op. cit.

ness can apply to one, both, or neither spouse. The same is true for measures such as "marrying the same person again if they could do it over," satisfaction with the marriage, and the absence of regret over the marriage. The criticism at this point centers around the unit used for analysis: husbands, wives, marriages, husbands talking about wives, and so forth.

Fourth, *does marital adjustment simply measure conventionalization?* Marital conventionalization is seen as the extent to which married persons distort the appraisal of their marriages in the direction of social desirability. In other words, are couples who are classified as high on marital adjustment those that meet the criteria of social desirability and conservatism?

Vernon Edmonds and others indicate that marital-adjustment scales in general are heavily contaminated by subjects' tendencies to distort the appraisals of their marriages in this way.[64] Persons have a tendency to deceive themselves and others that their marriages are "better" than they really are. This marital conventionalization was found to be much greater and much more variable in noncollege than in college populations.[65] Indicators of conservative orientations included measures of traditional family morality, religious activity, ascetic morality, premarital sexual abstinence, and general conservative ideology. Each variable correlated highly with marital conventionalization. But when marital conventionalization was held constant via partial correlation techniques, no significant correlations remained between marital adjustment and the conservative indices of traditional family morality, religious activity, ascetic morality, church attendance, or premarital sexual abstinence. A negative correlation did emerge between marital adjustment and general conservative ideology. This indicates that, with the exception of a general conservative ideology (which is associated negatively), no significant relationship exists between marital adjustment and the conservative indices when marital conventionalization is held constant.

Fifth, *how can adjustment be measured or predicted on the basis of static factors when marriage is a dynamic, changing, developing relationship?* The length of acquaintance, the age at marriage, the number of brothers and sisters, church membership, educational level, order of birth, place of marriage, employment of the wife, place of residence, and the like are static factors. Is it not likely that, with time, these factors become more or less significant in relationship to the spouse? People change. Love changes. Interests change. Farber refers to marriage as a "pair of mutually contingent careers."[66] Foote speaks of the "matching of husband and wife in phases of develop-

---

64. Vernon H. Edmonds, Glenne Withers, and Beverly Dibatista, "Adjustment, Conservatism, and Marital Conventionalization," *Journal of Marriage and the Family* 34 (February 1972), pp. 96–103.

65. Ibid., p. 101.

66. Bernard Farber, *Family: Organization and Interaction* (San Francisco: Chandler, 1964), pp. 334–338.

ment.''[67] Thus, critics suggest that rather than measuring and defining marital adjustment in terms of momentary assessment, it should be evaluated in terms of development, processes, and changing relationships.

Finally, of more recent origin has been a criticism of studies referred to in one report as *The Rape of the Locke.* In reviewing the marital-adjustment literature from the approach of a feminist, Judith Laws presented evidence that ''normative definitions of marriage act to suppress female sexuality; that the child-bearing complex acts to reduce the wife's feelings of efficacy and even her relative power within the family; that damaging conflicts and powerful sanctions are set up to divorce the wife from the exercise of her talents and assertion of her personhood in the world outside the family.''[68] A self-fulfilling prophecy results when the questions researchers ask or fail to ask reflect traditional prejudices. This is evident in the portrayal of husband-wife roles. The wife's role is conceived as being dictated by biological capabilities in conception, child bearing, and lactation. A sexual division of labor is justified by supernatural, highly abstruse premises. These factors, often not consistent with observable facts of women's life cycles in the present world of work, sexual behavior, and leadership positions, are used to justify the expectation that a wife's primary responsibilities center around the home. Thus research has been criticized as reflecting traditional stereotypes of women and marriage, and adjustment as being determined by the actualization of these stereotypes.

Considering the criticisms of adjustment and prediction studies, research in the future could be expected to take a different approach. Prediction studies of marital success, which came close to a complete halt in the 1960s, may or may not be revived. But it could be expected that future research would deviate in many ways methodologically, would pay increasing attention to the nature and measurement of adjustment, and would concentrate to a greater extent on the life span, the effect of conventionalization, the marital unit rather than the person unit, and the dynamic processual aspects of relationships.

Summary

The marital system fulfills many functions that differ as the structure of marriage differs. Where marriage is an extension of the kin-group or the extended-family system, individualistic factors become relatively unimportant. In

---

67. Nelson Foote, ''Matching of Husband and Wife on Phases of Development,'' *Transactions of the Third World Congress of Sociology* 4 (London: International Sociological Association, 1956), pp. 24–34.

68. Judith Long Laws, op. cit., pp. 483–516.

contrast, where marriage exists primarily for the individual and the conjugal relationship, the functions that marriage fulfills for the kin group decrease in importance. In either case, the functions that marriage performs will, to a large extent, be predictable on the basis of the social and cultural context that surrounds marriage.

In the United States, marriage rates have increased significantly since the end of the Civil War. These rates fluctuate under the influences of war, changing economic conditions, sex ratio of the marriageable population, and the number of potential brides and grooms present in the general population. The rate of marriage varies by season, day of the week, and region of the country.

An important and widely researched area of marriage deals with the power positions of husband and wife as individuals and in relation to each other. Power refers to the ability to influence others and to affect their behavior. Power, often measured by determining who makes certain decisions, includes the crucial dimensions of authority (legitimized power) and influence.

The major domains of family power have been delineated as bases, processes, and outcomes. The bases of power have centered primarily around the resources an individual possesses. The processes of family power focus on the interaction and dynamic aspects of decision making or conflict management. The outcomes of family power deal with the product, decision, or results of the process.

Studies of decision-making outcomes indicate that certain decisions are made primarily by the husband, others primarily by the wife, and others jointly. Who makes which decision has been widely explained by a theory of resources—the one with the information, education, income, and so forth. This theory has been the topic of considerable debate and criticism but has led to a further development of resource exchange, resources in a cultural context, or a theory of comparative resources.

As with power, many attempts have been made to measure adjustment in marriage. Although lacking a general consensus of definition, adjustment generally includes relationships that are high in husband-wife agreement and high in the sharing of activities, tasks, and affection. Only infrequently has conflict been viewed as a basic aspect of marriage, the management of which is crucial in adjustment. Generally, it has been found that the greater the congruence of role perception and role performance, the higher the level of satisfaction.

When marital adjustment and satisfaction are examined throughout the life cycle, satisfaction appears to be highest at the beginning of marriage, with low points coming when families have school-age children and teenagers. The results are mixed on what happens at later stages of the life cycle. Some studies indicate a curvilinear relationship throughout the life cycle; the beginning and the end of marriage are points of highest satisfaction. Other studies cast doubts as to the extent of upturn in satisfaction and adjustment in the later stages of the life cycle.

Marital adjustment studies have been criticized on a number of points. Concepts are not always adequately defined, variables are not always adequately measured, failure often exists in the differentiation of the unit of analysis, frequently marital adjustment simply measures conventionalization, many studies fail to account for change, and a more recent criticism has focused on the asking of "loaded" questions, which lead to findings that perpetuate traditional stereotypes and prejudices.

Generally, it is the marital system that precedes and is basic to the parental system to which we direct our attention in the chapter that follows.

Key Terms and Topics

Discussion Questions

1. *List a number of marriage functions. Are any universal? Which functions are most prevalent in the United States?*

2. *What are some explanations for the popularity of marriage? What factors are likely to increase or decrease the number and rate of marriages over time?*

3. *Check marriage rates in your state or community. How do they compare with other states and with national data? What variations occur by month and day of week?*

4. *Differentiate power, authority, and influence. How can each be determined and measured?*

5. *Make a list of ten decision-making areas. Take a brief survey among friends to determine whether their father, mother, or both jointly made these decisions. Are certain decisions consistently made by one or the other sex?*

6. *What is your theory of conjugal power? Can you think of instances where the person with the greatest resources does not have the most power? Are there instances where persons with very few resources still have a high degree of power?*

7. *Women's movements are striving for more power. What types of power issues relate to the roles of wives, mothers, and marriage? What are some recommended changes and means of attaining these changes?*

8. *Describe the nature of marital success, i.e., what is it? How can it be measured? Is success the same as adjustment, happiness, and compatibility?*

9. *Select two or three of the most "ideal" marriages of which you are aware. What factors tend to make those marriages "ideal"? Do the same features exist in each marriage?*

10. *What factors indicate conventionality and conformity? Is the conventional marriage the "adjusted" or "successful" marriage?*

11. *You are asked to be a judge at the "Marriage of America Pageant." After dispensing with the "highly significant and informative talent, bathing suit and gown competition" what criteria would you use to select the five finalist couples?*

12. *Why are role expectations important to marital adjustment? What are some sources of difficulty in the achievement of, and adjustment to, marital roles?*

13. *How would you explain the curvilinear relationship—if it exists—between marital adjustment and the family life cycle?*

14. *Are the criticisms of marital adjustment studies justified? Design a study that would not be subject to these types of criticism.*

Further Readings

Albrecht, Ruth E. and **E. Wilbur Bock.** *Encounter: Love, Marriage and Family.* Boston: Holbrook, Second Edition, 1975. A collection of readings focusing on eight issues: change, dating, premarital sex, intermarriage, laws, marital adjustments, marital problems, and parenthood.

Bernard, Jessie. "The Adjustments of Married Mates," in Harold T. Christensen, ed. *Handbook of Marriage and the Family.* Chicago: Rand McNally, 1964, pp. 657–739. One of the most comprehensive discussions of the dimensions and models of marital adjustment available.

Blood, Robert D., and **Donald M. Wolfe.** *Husbands and Wives.* Glencoe, Ill.: Free Press, 1960. A study of 731 urban and suburban wives and 178 farm wives attempting to understand the dynamics of American marriage.

Crosby, John F. *Illusion and Disillusion: The Self in Love and Marriage.* Belmont, Calif.: Wadsworth, 1976. An attempt by a marriage counselor and clergyman to explain the disillusionment couples often experience in marriage.

Cromwell, Ronald E., and **David H. Olson, eds.** *Power in Families.* New York: John Wiley, 1975. An interdisciplinary focus on power, stressing major conceptual, theoretical, methodological, and substantive issues.

DeLora, Jack R. and **Joann S. DeLora.** *Intimate Life Styles: Marriage and Its Alterna-*

tives. Pacific Palisades, Calif.: Goodyear, Second edition, 1975. A collection of approximately fifty sources covering mate selection, sex, the contemporary family, voices of protest, current alternatives to traditional marriage, and future intimate life-styles.

Hunt, Richard A. and **Edward J. Rydman.** *Creative Marriage.* Boston: Holbrook, 1976. A look at couple relationships with the intent of making them more exciting and creative.

Kammeyer, Kenneth C. W. *Confronting the Issues: Sex Roles, Marriage, and the Family.* Boston: Allyn and Bacon, 1975. A collection of readings built around controversies within marriage and the family. Section I deals with attacks, defenses, and alternatives to marriage as an institution.

Lopata, Helena Z. *Occupation: Housewife.* New York: Oxford University Press, 1971. A study of suburban Chicago women who perform the social role of housewife and within their life cycle combine this role with that of wife, mother, and neighbor.

Rausch, Harold L., William A. Barry, Richard K. Hertel, and **Mary Ann Swain.** *Communication, Conflict and Marriage.* San Francisco: Jossey-Bass, 1974. An addition to the literature on marital interaction using comparative and longitudinal methods and based on an attempt at integrating communication and conflict theories.

Roleder, George. *Marriage Means Encounter.* Dubuque, Iowa: Wm. C. Brown, 1973. The aim of the book is to expose six areas of encounter common to all marriages: premarital sex, marital sex, marital roles, parenthood, the new marriage, and marital failure. The thirty-three selections come from a wide variety of popular magazine and text-like sources.

Safilios-Rothschild, Constantina. *Toward a Sociology of Women.* Lexington, Mass.: Xerox, 1972. While not focusing on marriage, this book on a sociology of sex roles has much to say about conjugal relationships, motherhood, and the married professional woman.

Wells, J. Gipson. *Current Issues in Marriage and the Family.* New York: Macmillan, 1975. A collection of readings dealing with the following issues: to marry or not, what form of marriage, roles of men and women, children or not, divorce, marital fidelity, and the future.

Wiseman, Jacqueline P., ed. *People as Partners,* 2d ed. San Francisco: Canfield, 1977. An examination of the family from the perspective of partners: role, mate selection, sex, children as junior partners, and the like.

16

The Parental System

16

The parental system centers primarily around the interrelated statuses of parents and children. All societies have normative restrictions on appropriate and inappropriate behavior for both, and all societies have sets of role expectations accorded to the parent and child statuses. Some of the parent-child norms are near universal, whereas others are relatively unique to a particular society or subculture. For example, no society is known to place the primary responsibility for the rearing of children on men; no society is known in which the young children customarily are dominant over the father; and almost all societies place restrictions and taboos on the eating of certain foods by pregnant women. On the other hand, American birth customs are unusual for the relative absence of supernaturalism.[1]

Wide variations occur from one society to another in family size, methods of child rearing, extended family sharing in child-related tasks, illegitimacy rates, and the like. On the other hand, certain similarities exist in the norms and consequences of particular structural patterns within the parental system. Lower classes rear children differently than do the higher classes. Illegitimate children do not begin life on an equal footing with legitimate children. First-born children appear to differ from later born children in a wide variety of adult activities. The parental system and selected structural patterns are the focus of description and analysis in this chapter. The next chapter, while dealing with some organizational characteristics, focuses more on interactional and social-psychological dimensions of the parent-child relationship.

---

1. Several of these are discussed in William N. Stephens, *The Family in Cross-Cultural Perspective* (New York: Holt, Rinehart and Winston, 1963).

PARENTS IN MODERN
AMERICA

Parenthood cannot be evaluated apart from the society in which it functions. Although there is considerable variation in parental roles and behaviors by racial, ethnic, religious, or class subcultures, there appear to be some common threads of parental roles in the United States. E. E. LeMasters, in a sociological analysis of parents, lists thirteen characteristics of the role of parent in the United States.[2]

These are summarized briefly as follows:

1. The role of parent in modern America is not well-defined. It is often ambiguous and hard to pin down.
2. The role is not adequately delimited. Parents are expected to succeed where even the professionals fail.
3. Modern parents are not well-prepared for their role as fathers and mothers.
4. There is a romantic complex about parenthood. In some ways this complex is even deeper and more unrealistic than that relating to marriage.
5. Modern parents are in the unenviable position of having complete responsibility for their offspring but only partial authority over them.
6. The standards of role performance imposed on modern parents are too high. This arises from the fact that modern fathers and mothers are judged largely by professional practitioners such as psychiatrists and social workers rather than by their peers—other parents who are "amateurs" and not professionals.
7. Parents are the victims of inadequate behavioral science. They have been told repeatedly . . . that nothing determines what the child will be like but the influence of the parents. . . . This is obviously not true.
8. Parents do not choose their children unless they are adoptive parents.
9. There is no traditional model for modern parents to follow in rearing their children. The old model has been riddled by critical studies, yet no adequate new model has been developed. Instead, we have had a series of fads and fashions in child rearing based on the research of the moment. . . . Educators have been unconsciously presenting their middle-class values for all parents to emulate.
10. Contrary to what some may think, parenthood as a role does not enjoy the priority one would expect in modern America. The needs of the economic system in particular come first.
11. Other new roles have been assumed by modern parents since World War I that are not always completely compatible with the role of parent. The clearest and most striking example of this would be the occupational roles assumed by millions of American mothers.
12. The parental role is one of the few important roles in contemporary America from which one cannot honorably withdraw. Most of us can escape from our jobs if they are too frustrating; many of us escape from our

2. E. E. LeMasters, *Parents in Modern America*, rev. ed. (Homewood, Ill.: Dorsey, 1974), pp. 50–53.

parents when we marry; and a considerable number of husbands and wives manage to withdraw with some honor from marriages that they no longer find enchanting.

13. And last but not least, it is not enough for modern parents to produce children in their own image: the children have to be reared to be not only different from their fathers and mothers but also better.

Parents in modern America operate in a social context of rapid change, and frequently the results are neither anticipated nor desired. Increasing industrialization and urbanization have brought with them numerous problems for parents.[3] For some, the pluralistic nature of the city means that parents have to function in close proximity with other parents of diverse ethnic, religious, and racial backgrounds, which often creates a source of conflict. For some, the increased leisure of urban living means that, unlike the farm situation, children cannot always be kept busy. The school year was not designed for urban parents. For some, the increased leisure time and close physical proximity in the city contribute to a youth peer group that develops norms of behavior and loyalties that challenge the power and influence of parents. For some, the impersonality and anonymity of the city create conditions in which parents in the urban community do not really know with whom their children are associating nor do they know the parents of these children. For some, the pervasiveness of urban mass media, as evident in the press, television, movies, and radio, promotes ways of life in which parents may or may not believe. And for some, the urban ghetto, with its crowded conditions and substandard housing, creates problems for children far different from those faced by the affluent families in the suburbs.

Obviously, not all social change effects parents negatively. For many, the trend toward industrialization and urbanization brings opportunities that are unknown in rural America. With these changes come jobs, higher incomes, educational opportunities, improved legal and public health facilities, a greater tolerance in many areas for minority groups, and recreational as well as "cultural" opportunities that were not available to parents in rural America thirty or fifty years ago. Despite the innumerable difficulties and hardships, most parents are successful in the fulfillment of their parental responsibilities.

THE TRANSITION TO PARENTHOOD

What is involved in the transition to parenthood? What must be learned and what readjustments of roles must take place in order to move smoothly from a childless married state to parenthood? What is the effect of parenthood on the adult? In what ways do parents, and in particular mothers,

---

3. Ibid., pp. 175–176.

change as a result of their parental experiences? These two closely related questions were of central concern to Alice Rossi in her analysis of the parental role.[4]

Unlike most writers on parent-child relationships, those who focus on the child, Rossi focuses on the adult parent. This perspective was preceded by several developments in the behavioral sciences. One has been the idea that personality is a constantly changing phenomenon, not a stable one, and that individuals change along the life cycle as they live through such critical experiences, as becoming a parent. This transition is part of the heightened contemporary interest in adult socialization. A second development has been the growing concern of behavioral scientists to comprehend adequately social and individual phenomena and to build theories appropriate to a complex social system.[5] Anthropologists, sociologists, and psychologists have joined theoretical forces to answer questions about culture and personality. The subculture, the family, and the social context have become important in understanding both the adult and the child.

Rossi's discussion on the impact of parenthood follows a comparative approach by asking in what basic structural ways the parental role differs from other primary adult roles such as the marital and occupational.[6] She concentrates on four unique and salient features of the parental role.[7] First, for women, there is cultural pressure to assume the role. Whereas men have freedom of choice where work is concerned, the cultural pressure for a young woman is to consider maternity necessary for her fulfillment as an individual and to secure her status as an adult. Perhaps today, this cultural pressure has decreased with the declining birth rate, the emphasis on zero population growth, and the stress on two-child or childless families.

Second, the parental role is not always a voluntary decision. Unlike engagement, pregnancy may be the unintended consequence of a sexual act that was recreative in intent rather than procreative. Also, unlike engagement, the termination of a pregnancy is less socially sanctioned.

Third, the parental role is irrevocable. To give birth to a child is always to have a child. It is possible to have ex-spouses and ex-jobs but it is not possible to have ex-children. Once the birth occurs, there is little possibility of undoing a commitment to parenthood except, of course, in instances of abandonment or placing the child for adoption.

Fourth, the parental role is unique in the preparation American couples bring to it. Rossi says there is 1) paucity of preparation, 2) limited learning during pregnancy, 3) abruptness of transition, and 4) lack of guidelines

---

4. Alice S. Rossi, "Transition to Parenthood," *Journal of Marriage and the Family* 30 (February 1968), pp. 26–39.

5. Ibid., p. 27.

6. Ibid., p. 29.

7. Ibid., p. 30.

Educating Future Parents

All happy families are alike, Tolstoy believed, but the misery of unhappy families is never alike. One of the problems when families discover that it is a rough road to harmony is the realization by the father and mother of how unprepared they were for parenthood. Often they came into marriage guided by no other compass than one pointing to the enjoyment of "togetherness." But this happy destination is not arrived at automatically. The lack of preparation for marriage often means that, when the hard days of sacrifice and responsibility come, the individuals may be taken by surprise. America spends large amounts of time and money preparing our young to be soldiers, workers or whatever, but hardly a thought is given to preparation for parenthood; ironically, it is the one career that can be the most demanding and perplexing.

The ideal solution is for parents themselves to prepare their own young to be parents. But, as W. Stanley Kruger of the Office of Education points out, it "is probably fair to say that being a good mother or father is more difficult today than it was 50 years ago, and more difficult still than 100 years ago. Family life has increasingly become less in-

timate, less organized, less bound by precepts and standards and the iron command of parents over children. Sons, daughters, fathers and mothers are not impelled to spend most of their time together, working as a team to keep the household going. Through the children of those previous generations may have found the situation painfully confining, they did get a solid grounding in what being a father or a mother was all about. No longer, or at least not as universally."

Some help may be on the way. Last year, the Office of Child Development and the Office of Education began a program in a small number of schools. The program, Education for Parenthood, was designed to instruct young men and women—particularly teen-agers—in the techniques and responsibilities of motherhood and fatherhood. For the school year beginning this fall, Education for Parenthood programs are expected to be in some 500 public school districts. If ever a program had a potential for not only helping to head off later problems but also helping to create positive attitudes about the most important human relationship, it is Education for Parenthood.

Source: *The Washington Post,* May 31, 1973, p. A18.

to successful parenthood.[8] The paucity of preparation is witnessed by our educational system's teaching of subjects in science and mathematics but not in areas relevant to family life: sex, home maintenance, child care, interpersonal competence, empathy, and the like. The limited learning during pregnancy makes adjustment to parenthood potentially more stressful than marital adjustment, whereas during the engagement period preceding marriage, couples have opportunities to share social experiences, engage in sexual experimentation, and the like in preparation for their marriage, there is a lack of any realistic training for parenthood during the anticipatory stage of pregnancy. The abruptness of transition occurs when a new mother starts out im-

8. Ibid., p. 35.

mediately on twenty-four-hour duty. The birth of a child is not followed by any gradual taking on of responsibility, as in the case of a professional work role. Finally, the lack of guidelines to successful parenthood stems from an inability to be able to say just what parental role prescriptions have what effect on the adult characteristics of the child.

Parenthood as Crisis

"Everybody" loves a newborn infant. Some love them more when they belong to someone else. But what effect does that "lovable" newborn and later the young child have upon parents? Several decades ago, E. E. Le-Masters began what was to result in a series of studies by hypothesizing that the birth of a couple's first child is a critical event.[9] He claimed that parents in our society have a romantic notion about child rearing and that they tend to suffer from a process of disenchantment after they become parents. In his study of forty-six middle-class couples, he reported evidence that supported his hypothesis of disenchantment: 83 percent of the couples reported an "extensive" or "severe" crisis in adjusting to the birth of their first child.

Several years later, Everett Dyer did a study, "Parenthood as Crisis: A Restudy," to determine if it is true that the arrival of the first child constitutes a "crisis" or "critical event." Would the addition of this new member of the family system constitute a structural change that would force a drastic reorganization of statuses, roles, and relationships in order to reestablish an equilibrium in the family system?[10] The findings of the second study tended to support the main hypothesis that the addition of the first child constituted a crisis event for these middle-class couples to a considerable degree, forcing each couple to reorganize many of their roles and relationships. A majority of couples experienced extensive or severe crisis. This study went on to report that "the degree to which the event of the first child represents a crisis event appears to be related to 1) the state of the marriage and family organization at the birth of the child, 2) the couple's preparation for marriage and parenthood, 3) the couple's marital adjustment after the birth of the child, 4) certain social background and situational variables such as the number of years married, planned parenthood, and the age of the child.[11] It is interseting to note that following a difficult period of several months most of the couples appeared to have made a satisfactory recovery.

Unconvinced that the two studies just cited were truly representative of parenthood—since they studied middle-class parents—Daniel Hobbs pub-

---

9. E. E. LeMasters, "Parenthood as Crisis," *Marriage and Family Living* 19 (November 1957), pp. 352–355.

10. Everett D. Dyer, "Parenthood as Crisis: A Restudy," *Marriage and Family Living* 25 (May 1963), pp. 196–201.

11. Ibid., p. 201.

Oh, Those Summer Vacations

Don't get me wrong. I dearly love my children. In fact, I even like them at times. It's just that after (roughly) 81 days, 14 hours, and 37 minutes of summer holiday, I was beginning to think that if I had it to do over again, I should have raised dahlias instead of children.

While dahlias may not give you blue papier mâché napkin rings on Mother's Day, neither are they noted for wearing the same socks for a week, getting bloody noses, giving bloody noses, or whining, "What's there to do?" for 81 straight days.

Now I'm not alone in my sentiments. After all, I wasn't the only mother outside at 8 in her bathrobe throwing rose petals in front of the school bus, although I admit that perhaps I did go too far in kissing the driver on both cheeks. I just hope that he didn't recognize me with my chin strap on.

The school bus finally got on its way, but returned in five minutes to bring back the two-year-old twin boys that some crafty Mom snuck aboard while I was distracting the driver.

The first thing I did after the school bus left was to pour myself a second cup of black coffee. I sat and sipped it for 15 minutes, glorying in the absolute silence. Nobody asked me for string. Or tape. Or more French toast. Or a baby sister.

Next I went into the bathroom with a magazine—without even locking the door.

After that I did 20 minutes of Bend and Stretch and 10 Deep Knee Bends without hearing one single snicker.

One of these days I'm going to get around to cleaning the raspberry jam off the stereo. And I haven't forgotten that there are all those fingerprints to scrub off the kitchen ceiling. But you see, it's been quite a long summer and I'm just starting my winter holiday.

Source: Nancy Stahl, "Kids or Dahlias," *Detroit Free Press*, September 5, 1971. Copyright, 1971, Universal Press Syndicate.

lished, "Parenthood as Crisis: A Third Study."[12] Findings of the Hobbs study diverge rather sharply from those of LeMasters and Dyer, both in the distribution of couples according to the degree of difficulty reported and with regard to variables differentiating couples who have little difficulty with the first child from those who have greater difficulty. Even the middle-class couples in the Hobbs study reported little difficulty with the first child.

These three studies were followed by others[13] that further questioned the advisability of labeling the arrival of the first child as a "crisis." Writers noted that a crisis perspective places the emphasis on negative outcomes and overlooks the positive and gratifying aspects of parenthood. Over several de-

---

12. Daniel F. Hobbs, Jr., "Parenthood as Crisis: A Third Study," *Journal of Marriage and the Family* 27 (August 1965), pp. 367–372.

13. Daniel F. Hobbs, Jr., "Transition to Parenthood: A Replication and an Extension," *Journal of Marriage and the Family* 30 (August 1968), pp. 413–417; Arthur P. Jacoby, "Transition to Parenthood: A Reassessment," *Journal of Marriage and the Family* 31 (November 1969), pp. 720–727; Candyce Smith Russell, "Transition to Parenthood: Problems and Gratifications," *Journal of Marriage and the Family* 36 (May 1974), pp. 294–302.

Violence and Pregnancy

Considerable research has been reported on parenthood as crisis, but there may be a crisis of pregnancy that often leads to physical violence. Richard Gelles, in a study on violence between husbands and wives, made the startling discovery that a number of wives reported that they were physically attacked while they were pregnant.

Interviews with women who were beaten during their pregnancy gave some insight into the causes behind the association between being pregnant and being beaten by one's hus-

band. The major factors appeared to be 1) sexual frustration of the husband, 2) family transition, stress, and strain, 3) irritability and depression of the wife, 4) prenatal child abuse, and 5) defenselessness of the wife.

The examination of this issue suggests that violence during pregnancy is much more common than anyone has suspected. This violence may not be just an individual aberration of aggressive husbands but may grow out of usual family stresses that are compounded by the stress of a pregnancy situation.

Source: Richard J. Gelles, *The Violent Home: A Study of Physical Aggression Between Husbands and Wives* (Beverly Hills: Sage, 1974); Richard J. Gelles, "Violence and Pregnancy: A Note on the Extent of the Problem and Needed Services," *The Family Coordinator* 24 (January 1975), pp. 81–86.

cades the emphasis shifted from crisis to difficulties to transition. A 1976 study[14] found only slight amounts of difficulty in adjusting to the first child, with mothers reporting significantly greater amounts of difficulty than did fathers. The conclusion was that it is more accurate to refer to beginning parenthood as a transition rather than a crisis.

Whether it should be termed crisis or not, there is little doubt that when a dyad (husband and wife) becomes a triad (parents and child) a major reorganization of statuses, roles, and relationships takes place. The effect of the birth of a child and the preschool years of the children on the adjustment of the parents seems fairly well established. As noted in the previous chapter, general marital satisfaction of couples tends to decrease after the birth of their children through the preschool and school years until the children are getting ready to leave home. The experiences of childbearing and child rearing appear to have a rather profound and negative effect on marital satisfaction, particularly for wives, even in their basic feelings of self-worth in relation to their marriage.

The Value of Parenthood

Apparently not all children are problematic, produce a crisis situation, or are viewed negatively. In spite of unplanned pregnancies, a decreasing birth rate, a decrease in the average family size, and an increase in childless

14. Daniel F. Hobbs, Jr., and Sue Perk Cole, "Transition to Parenthood: A Decade Replication," *Journal of Marriage and the Family* 38 (November 1976), pp. 723–731.

marriages (all discussed elsewhere in the book), women continue to want and to voluntarily have children. Thus, it must be assumed that children fulfill basic functions for society and satisfy certain needs for individuals.

Lois Hoffman[15] lists basic values that incorporate the many satisfactions children provide in various cultures. The first is the idea that having children satisfies a need for attaining adult status and a social identity. Particularly for females, parenthood establishes a person as a truly mature, stable, and acceptable member of the community. For many women, it is defined as their major role in life and the fulfillment of womanhood.

A second value relates to an expansion of the self, a tie to a larger entity, and an attaining of a kind of immortality. The "carrying on of the family name" and the establisment of a continuity between the past and the future are basic to this value. A third value of children is to help to expand the parents' self-conception by evoking new, previously untapped dimensions of personality. Motherhood may be seen as synonymous with virtue. A good father may bring self-respect.

A fourth value of children relates to primary group ties and affection. Hoffman found that two-thirds of the respondents in a nationwide sample of married women under forty with at least one child indicated that children satisfied their desire for love and the feeling of being in a family.[16] Ranked close to this was a fifth value of stimulation and fun, stated by 60 percent of the respondents. This included statements such as, "they keep you young," "they bring a liveliness to your life," or "they're fun."

Other values include a feeling of achievement and competence, power, social comparison, and economic utility. Some of these values are more prevalent in cultures outside the U.S.[17] Power, for example, is a significant value in certain villages in India where the new bride moves into the household of her husband's family where she lives in a subservient role to her mother-in-law. By having sons, she gains some control over her own life and over her childless sisters-in-law. Eventually, when her sons bring home brides, she becomes the powerful and dominating mother-in-law.[18] In the U.S., power can be seen in the control and influence parents hold over other human beings—their children. A value like economic utility tends to have greater significance in rural areas or in certain countries. Children provide inexpensive labor and, in addition, are often viewed as important to care for parents in their old age.

15. Lois Wladis Hoffman, "The Value of Children to Parents and the Decrease in Family Size," *Proceedings of the American Philosophical Society* 119 (December 1975), pp. 430–438.

16. Ibid., p. 433.

17. See James T. Fawcett et al., *The Value of Children in Asia and the United States: Comparative Perspectives*, papers of the East-West Population Institute 32 (July 1974), pp. 1–69.

18. T. Poffenberger and S. B. Poffenberger, "The Social Psychology of Fertility Behavior in a Village in India," in J. T. Fawcett, ed., *Psychological Perspectives on Population* (New York: Basic Books, 1973), pp. 135–162.

> *Mac:*   *I don't know for sure if I have any children or not. Well, let's go back to when I was 17 and 18, in that puppy love stage. I was courting with a young lady at that time and she was the type of character who was ambitious with her mates. She wanted me but yet another one too. So I had competition and I knew to my knowledge that I had competition from her old boyfriend. And we got all set, and she came up pregnant. Well I made the offer that I would like to marry her, but she viewed me as unstable as far as a job. At that time I was working at a gasoline station. So she said no, that she didn't want to marry me, but she wanted to marry her old boyfriend. So I'm not positive if the child is mine or not but I often feel that yes it is mine.*

The Concern over Young Parenthood

Chapter 10 had a brief subsection titled, "The Concern over Young Marriages." The concern over young parenthood—primarily teen-age parenthood—is directly linked to the concern over young marriage, with premarital pregnancy as a primary factor in leading to marriage, and as directly related to marital disruption. Census data indicate a general pattern of greater stability of marriage, both black and white, among women who are not premaritally pregnant and less stability among women who had children before marriage.[19]

In a study of 400 young adolescent mothers, their partners, progeny, and parents, Frank Furstenberg explored when, how, and why childbearing before the age of eighteen jeopardizes the life prospects of the young mother and her child.[20] Four or five of the adolescent mothers became pregnant within two years following the onset of intercourse, which typically occurred at age fifteen. Fewer than one in four of the teen-agers' mothers admitted that they had known that their daughters were having sexual relations prior to the pregnancy. While most of the adolescents had some limited knowledge of birth control, they tended to be most aware of those forms to which they had the least access, and their control was confined largely to "getting the boy to use something." Contraception was much more likely to be practiced by couples who had a stable romantic relationship.

As might be expected, the pregnancies were greeted by both adolescents and parents with astonishment. Three-quarters of the expectant mothers

19. U.S. Bureau of the Census, *Current Population Reports*, Series P-23, No. 63, "Premarital Fertility," U.S. Government Printing Office, 1976, p. 19.

20. Frank E. Furstenberg, Jr., "The Social Consequences of Teen-age Parenthood," *Family Planning Perspectives* 8 (August 1976), pp. 148-164. The data presented in this section came from this report.

wished they had not become pregnant and half could not tell their parents for several months. Those women who married were more likely than those single to indicate positive feelings toward the pregnancy. Of those who married, more than one-third had done so by the time of delivery, three-fifths by one year, and three-quarters within two years after delivery.

Furstenberg's results, consistent with other studies, found that premarital pregnancy greatly increased the probability of eventual marital dissolution. A comparison group of classmates who married but had not conceived premaritally had a probability of the marriage breaking up after two years only half of that for the adolescent mothers. Although the pregnancy may not *cause* the breakup of the marriage, the unplanned pregnancy is an important link to a weak economic position of the male who fathers a child out of wedlock. Most of the men—young, inexperienced and unskilled—had a low earning potential before they wed. Again, like other studies, economic resources are strongly linked to marital stability.

The problems of young parenthood are further compounded by additional unwanted pregnancies. Estimates vary, but Furstenberg indicates that most published studies show that at least half of teen-age mothers experience a second pregnancy within thirty-six months of delivery. In his sample, one-fourth of the women became pregnant within twelve months of the birth of the first child, and by three years, half of the women with two children had become pregnant a third time.

Pregnancy and/or marriage was a principle reason for leaving high school. One-fourth of the adolescents never returned and half never graduated. This compared to 18 percent of the classmates who did not graduate.

One-quarter of the respondents had obtained most, if not all, of their income from working. Welfare barely edged out income from spouse as the second most common source of support. Welfare was not, however, a contributing factor in the encouragement of childbearing out of wedlock. The welfare mother was not significantly more likely to become pregnant after she went on relief than the young mother who was not receiving support. In any case, nearly half of all adolescent mothers were living below the poverty level. The median annual per capita income of the classmates who had not conceived before marriage ($1,000) was two-thirds greater than that of the young mothers ($600).

The presence of one or more children made holding a full-time job very difficult. Most of the women who worked had another individual to share the responsibilities of caring for the child. Few of the mothers could be classified by any standard as rejecting parents.

Five years after the initial delivery, more than three-fifths of the fathers were maintaining relations with their children. While only one-fifth were actually living with their children, another fifth saw the children at least once per week and the remaining one-fifth visited their children on an irregular basis. The absence of the father was not found to influence adversely the mother's adaptation to parenthood.

Furstenberg argues for social programs that are preventive rather than reactive. These would include educational, vocational, medical, or contraceptive programs that continue to provide services for as long as the need for service exists and are geared to the client rather than to the professional. As stated by Furstenberg, early parenthood destroys the prospect of a successful economic and family career but not because most young parents are determined to deviate from accepted avenues of success or because they are indifferent to, or unaware of, the costs of early parenthood. The principle reason that so many young mothers encounter problems is that they lack the resources to repair the damage done by a poorly timed birth."

The concern over young parenthood is associated with social isolation, less schooling, lower income, increased poverty and dependency, and increased levels of childbearing, much of which is unwanted and out of wedlock.[22]

LEGITIMACY AND ILLEGITIMACY

Closely related to the concern over young parenthood is the issue of legitimacy. Legitimacy is basic to the human family only, since no other animal grouping has regulations that define who has the right to procreate and rear a fully accepted member of society. It is the family and marital system that universally fulfills the function of giving legal status and social approval to the birth of a child. Legitimacy is acquired by being born into a family. To be born into a family defines who the infant is, his relationships with other family members, and his ascribed positions to be held within society.

To be born outside the family is to be illegitimate. Illegitimacy refers to a birth occurring to any women while she is unmarried or to a birth occurring as a result of an incestuous or adulterous relationship. Generally, illegitimacy has been viewed as an economic burden and a social problem. Whether these views change over the next few decades remains to be seen.

The Concern over Illegitimacy

Bronislaw Malinowski is credited with enunciating the Principle of Legitimacy, which asserts that every society has a rule that each child should

21. Ibid., p. 164.

22. The reader may want to note H. Theodore Groat, Arthur G. Neal, and Lynn Mathews, "Social Isolation and Premarital Pregnancy," *Sociology and Social Research* 60 (January 1976), pp. 188–198; and T. James Trussell, "Economic Consequences of Teen-age Childbearing," *Family Planning Perspectives* 8 (July/August 1976), pp. 184–190.

Pregnancy Out of Wedlock

To hear the guardians of morality tell it, girls who "get in trouble" (unmarried and pregnant) are "bad" (promiscuous). This is a notion that respectable people find comforting, because it relegates all the discomforts of out-of-wedlock pregnancy to some hinterland inhabited by "bad" girls—good girls needn't worry. But Hallowell Pope of the University of North Carolina has conducted a study of 387 white and 552 Negro unwed mothers, and is convinced that unwed mothers are very much like other girls of their age. (Journal of Marriage and the Family, August 1967).

In the first place, the girls in this study were not, by any reasonable standard, promiscuous. The majority (60 percent of the white girls and 78 percent of the Negro girls) were dating the father of their child, exclusively, for at least six months before the pregnancy. Many were planning on marriage (41 percent

of the whites, 32 percent of the Negroes). And most of them believed that they were in love (84 percent of the whites, 74 percent of the Negroes).

These girls were not led astray by "older" men, or men who were strangers to the girls' parents and friends. Most of the fathers were the same age as the girls, give or take two or three years; their social and educational backgrounds were generally similar. Only 18 percent of the sexual partners of the white girls and 9 percent of the partners of the Negro girls were unknown to the girls' parents; the great majority of the sexual partners (72 percent of the whites, 86 percent of the Negroes) were among the girls' regular group of friends.

The women in this study, Pope concludes, are deviant because they became pregnant, not because they engaged in a sexual relationship outside of marriage.

Source: "Roundup of Current Research," *Trans-Action* 5 (March 1968), p. 5. Reprinted by permission.

have a legitimate father to act as its protector, guardian, and representative in the society.[23] Like all rules, this one is violated. To strongly enforce the rule results in low rates of illegitimacy; to not enforce it results in high rates. But why a concern over legitimacy at all?

The answers to this question are varied. In 1939 Kingsley Davis provided a functional explanation of attitudes toward illegitimacy by theorizing that the function of reproduction (i.e., the preservation of society) can be carried out in a socially useful manner only if it is performed in conformity with institutional patterns.[24] Only by means of an institutionalized system can individuals be organized and taught to cooperate in the performance of this long-range function. This function (reproduction) must be integrated with other social functions. It is the family that constitutes the social machinery for creating new members of society. The birth of children in ways that do not fit into this machinery must necessarily receive the disapproval of society.

23. One such statement is to be found in his "Parenthood, the Basis of Social Structure," in V. F. Calverton and Samuel D. Schmalhausen, eds., *The New Generation* (New York: Macaulay, 1930), pp. 137–138.
24. Kingsley Davis, "The Forms of Illegitimacy," *Social Forces* 18 (1939), pp. 77–89.

A family unit requires someone to assume the roles of sociological father and sociological mother. Even though some degree of premarital sexual license exists in about 70 percent of the societies for which information is available, childbirth outside marriage is not approved in those societies. The suggestion is that marriage bestows legitimacy on parenthood more than on sex. That is, most societies are more concerned with illegitimacy than with sexual intercourse outside marriage.

The focus on the absent father in most instances of illegitimacy is directly related to his lack of ties with the child. The mother, tied to the child from inception, is provided a "natural" link in her assuming the responsibility and role obligations of parent.

The question posed by Davis can again be asked: "Why does society not solve the problem of illegitimacy by requiring the use of contraceptive methods and, when these fail, abortion?"[25] His answer is that to break the normative relations between sexuality and the family, so that adults would as a matter of course decide rationally whether they would enjoy sex within or outside the family, would also reduce the strength of the motive to marry and found a family. The radical changes necessary to eliminate illegitimacy would very likely come close to eliminating the family system too. If this is the case, the concern over legitimacy and illegitimacy is well understood.

Goode suggests that disapproval of illegitimacy seems to be correlated roughly with the amount of disruption created by the illegitimacy and also depends both on who the offending parties are and who judges them.[26] The upper social strata do not disapprove much of illegitimacy occurring among the lower classes, but they disapprove intensely if one of the offending parties is an upper-class woman.

One central element in understanding illegitimacy is the placement of the child. Thus, it could be expected that illegitimacy among the lower classes would be of less concern to a society than would illegitimacy among the higher classes. With less property to protect or to inherit and with lineage and family honor less a focus of attention in the lower classes, families have less to lose if illegitimacy occurs. Thus one expected result would be higher illegitimacy rates among the lower classes.

Among the higher classes, since property and family name is at stake to a greater degree, some expected results of illegitimate births are likely to include pressure on the couple to marry, turning over the child to an adoption agency, or leaving home to bear the child. Births can be avoided altogether via abortion, which is more accessible to the educated and financially able.

---

25. Kingsley Davis, "Illegitimacy and the Social Structure," *American Journal of Sociology* 45 (September 1939), pp. 221–222.

26. William J. Goode, *The Family* (Englewood Cliffs, N. J.: Prentice-Hall, 1964), p. 24.

TABLE 16–1. Illegitimate Live Births, by Race and Age of Mother: 1950 to 1974

In thousands, except as indicated. Prior to 1960, excludes Alaska and Hawaii. Includes estimates for states in which legitimacy data were not reported. No estimates included for misstatements on birth records or failures to register births]

Race and Age	1950	1955	1960	1965	1970	1972	1974
Total	141.6	183.3	224.3	291.2	398.7	403.2	418.1
Percent of all births	3.9	4.5	5.3	7.7	10.7	12.4	13.2
Rate	14.1	19.3	21.8	23.4	26.4	24.9	24.1
White	6.1	7.9	9.2	11.6	13.8	12.0	11.8
Negro and other	71.2	87.2	98.3	97.6	89.9	86.9	85.1
By race of mother							
White	53.5	64.2	82.5	123.7	175.1	160.5	168.5
Negro and other	88.1	119.2	141.8	167.5	223.6	242.7	249.6
Percent of total	62.2	65.0	63.2	57.5	56.1	60.2	59.7
By age of mother							
Under 15 years	3.2	3.9	4.6	6.1	9.5	9.9	10.6
15–19 years	56.0	68.9	87.1	123.1	190.4	202.3	210.8
20–24 years	43.1	55.7	68.0	90.7	126.7	119.6	122.7
25–29 years	20.9	28.0	32.1	36.8	40.6	41.2	44.9
30–34 years	10.8	16.1	18.9	19.6	19.1	19.0	18.6
35–39 years	6.0	8.3	10.6	11.4	9.4	8.6	8.2
40 years and over	1.7	2.4	3.0	3.7	3.0	2.7	2.3

Source: U.S. Bureau of the Census, *Statistical Abstract of the United States: 1976*, 97th ed. (Washington, D.C., 1976), Table 81, p. 58.

Illegitimacy Rates

At the very time that birth rates are steadily declining and reaching all-time lows (see next section in this chapter), the illegitimacy birth rate is showing a dramatic increase. The number of illegitimate live births exceeded 418,000 in 1974 (Table 16–1). This represents a 295 percent increase in the number of illegitimate births since 1950. Even more dramatic is the change in the percentage of all births that are illegitimate. In 1950, the percentage was 3.9. By 1974, the same figure was 13.2, an increase of 338.

The rate varies widely by race, with much of the difference explained by social class. The differences in stigma attached to illegitimacy, the likelihood of reporting, and the access to, and use of, contraceptives and abortion account for a major proportion of the white-nonwhite difference. The incidence of illegitimate live births by age of mother indicates that nearly half of the total occurs between the ages of 15 and 19 (210,800 of the 418,100). This age breakdown can be quite profound when one considers the social dysfunctions of illegitimacy in terms of the necessity for the mother to drop out of school to deliver the child and her ability to rear and care for her child.

Does Illegitimacy Make a Difference?

Again we return to the question relating to the concern over illegitimacy. Does it really make a difference that more than 418,000 births each year are outside of wedlock? Do illegitimate children experience more social, economic, and health handicaps than legitimate children? Is the presence of both a male and a female parent essential to the growth and development of a child? Does the unmarried mother face increased emotional and economic difficulties that seriously affect both the mother and the child? Some of these specific questions are discussed elsewhere (note chapters on social class, variant forms, black family, and parent-child socialization in particular); however, several research studies are worthy of consideration here.

Empirical research indicates that illegitimacy does have an impact on the child, the parent, and society, both in the U.S. and elsewhere. In Great Britain, the National Child Development Study showed that by age seven, children born out of wedlock fared considerably worse than legitimate children on a number of social, economic, and health measures.[27] Differences persisted even after social class was taken into account. In Brazil, the bearing of an illegitimate child was found to have important consequences for the mother's social mobility.[28]

Similar findings exist in the United States as evidenced in studies completed in California[29] and North Carolina.[30] Information from a sample of two-year-old legitimate and illegitimate children in California indicated that despite significant social changes, illegitimate children continue to face poorer life chances than legitimate children. They were found to have a higher infant mortality rate, and the unadopted illegitimate children fared quite poorly on a number of measures including school performance. Unmarried mothers were less likely to marry within three years than the general popula-

---

27. This research is discussed in E. Crellin, M. L. Kellmer Pringle, and P. West, *Born Illegitimate: Social and Educational Implications* (London: National Foundation for Educational Research in England and Wales, 1971).

28. Sugiyama Icitaka, E. Wilbur Bock, and Felix M. Berardo, "Social Status, Mobility, Illegitimacy and Subsequent Marriage," *Journal of Marriage and the Family* 37 (August 1975), pp. 643–654.

29. Beth Berkov and June Sklar, "Does Illegitimacy Make a Difference? A Study of the Life Chances of Illegitimate Children in California," *Population and Development Review* 2 (June 1976), pp. 201–217.

30. C. Allen Haney, Robert Michielutte, Carl M. Cochrane, and Clark E. Vincent, "Some Consequences of Illegitimacy in a Sample of Black Women," *Journal of Marriage and the Family* 37 (May 1975), pp. 359–366.

tion of unmarried women and were more likely to separate from their husbands if they did later marry. It was of interest to note that adopted illegitimate children did as well or better than legitimate children. It would appear from the data in this study that despite a decrease in the degree of stigma attached to illegitimacy and the proliferation of services and programs for illegitimate children and their mothers, these children do not begin life on an equal footing with legitimate children, and their handicaps persist beyond the hazards of infancy.[31]

In North Carolina, meaningful differences were found by legitimacy status for number of children desired, attitude toward pregnancy, and attitude toward marriage. The authors suggest that it is the absence of a legal spouse rather than the definition of a birth as illegitimate that exerts the most important effect on these attitudes.[32]

As shown, in American society both young parents and the unwed mother have difficult personal adjustments to make. Little toleration is extended to the young unwed mother who wishes to keep her child as her own, although greater toleration does exist in the lower-class strata where the commitment to the norm of legal marriage is less and where the punishments for deviation and the rewards for conformity are lower. In 1935, the U.S. Congress established a national policy of providing financial aid to a mother and her children when they did not have financial support. This Aid to Families with Dependent Children (AFDC) program enabled a mother to keep her children with her. Programs such as these receive constant protests from taxpayers who argue (falsely) that mothers want more children to increase their aid. While the increased aid is seldom a central motivational factor in the birth of additional children, this is not to deny that for younger women, larger welfare payments may be associated with higher illegitimacy rates.[33] This may be related to the failure of the welfare system to include poor, male-headed households.

Mothers who do not keep their children sometimes place them in foster homes until they can be located in adoptive homes. But this too raises the question of financial support and the acquisition by the child of a social position. In a series of studies of unmarried mothers, Clark Vincent has found that those who placed their child for adoption had more education, higher socioeconomic status, a lower proportion of broken parental homes, fewer siblings, and fewer unhappy and mother-dominated homes than did those who kept their children.[34] The extent to which a father is needed in the home is examined in the next chapter.

---

31. Berkov and Sklar, op. cit., p. 215.
32. Haney et al., op. cit., p. 365.
33. Barbara S. Janowitz, "The Impact of AFDC on Illegitimate Birth Rates," *Journal of Marriage and the Family* 38 (August 1976), pp. 485–494.
34. Clark E. Vincent, *Unmarried Mothers* (New York: Free Press, 1961).

FAMILY SIZE AND
RELATED FACTORS

Birth Rates and Birth Expectations

Most married couples want, have, or expect to have children. In 1975, there were 3.15 million births in the United States, a rate of 14.8 births per 1,000 population.[35] The same year, 18.6 percent of all ever-married women aged fifteen to forty-four, either by choice or circumstances, were childless.[36] However, the salient characteristic of fertility in the United States since the late 1950s has been the precipitous decline in the birth rate for both white and black women. In addition to the decline in actual fertility, there has also been a decrease in the average number of lifetime births expected by currently married women.[37]

The birth rate is one of the best documented series of descriptive social data available today. Census data show quite clearly the increase and decrease in number of births and birth rates in the United States between 1910 and 1975. In 1910 the birth rate was 30.1 per 1,000 population, decreasing to 19.4 in 1940, increasing to 25 in 1955 and steadily decreasing since 1957 to the present time. In the 1970s, the total fertility rate for American women dropped about 27 percent between 1970 and 1975. This decline was especially sharp in 1971 to 1973 but is a continuation of the drop in the level of fertility since the peak year of the baby boom in 1957.

One of the most intriguing contrasts between women now in their forties and women in their twenties is the wide difference in the size of families these women have or expect. Over one-third of the women of all races forty to forty-nine years old in 1975 already had borne four or more children. However, less than one woman in ten currently in her twenties expects to have four or more children.[38]

In 1976, the average number of lifetime births *expected* by wives in the eighteen to thirty-nine-year age span was 2.4, a decline from a 3.1 average

35. Bureau of the Census, *Statistical Abstract of the United States: 1976*, 97th ed., Washington, D.C., 1976. Table 68, p. 51.

36. Ibid., Table 75, p. 56. Comparable figures for 1940 were 26.5; 1950, 22.8; 1960, 15.0; and 1970, 16.4 percent.

37. Canada as well experienced a sharp decline in its birth rate, dropping from 26.1 births per 1,000 population in 1961 to 16.2 in 1971. Reasons for this can be seen in D. Ian Pool and M. D. Bracher, "Aspects of Family Formation in Canada," *Canadian Review of Sociology and Anthropology* 11 (November 1974), pp. 308–323.

38. U.S. Bureau of the Census, *Current Population Reports*, Series P-20, No. 288, "Fertility History and Prospects of American Women: June 1975," U.S. Government Printing Office, 1976, p. 3.

> Louise: *In a way we planned our children. We planned about six or eight of them, so in other words we really never had all the children that we had wanted to have.*
>
> Ann: *Plan children! I only have two but my husband, God! Oh, Wow . . . to my knowledge he must have eight or ten. I'm only his second wife. The rest of the children are just spread out. His first wife, at the time we were married, only had one child. Since we've been married, she's had three others by him.*
>
> *That's a major reason why we're separated. I couldn't deal with the fact that he's still having children and we are married. Part of the reason we broke up is because I was pregnant, and so was his first wife by him, you know, and I thought, well, hey . . . you gotta have one or the other . . . not both.*
>
> Mac: *I think an unwanted child shouldn't be on earth because it's going to be treated with apathy from the parents.*

reported in a similar survey in 1967.[39] A comparison of the average number of lifetime births expected by currently married women and by single women indicates that single women have a slightly lower expected average of births per woman than do wives (1.9 versus 2.1 in the eighteen to twenty-year age group). The difference in lifetime birth expectations between married and single women increases with age, indicating both a reduction in the remaining number of reproductive years and a decrease in marriage prospects at later ages for single women. If women now in their late teens and twenties live up to their expectations for the future, the number of persons who come from "large" families will eventually be a much smaller proportion of the population than at the present time.

There seems to be widespread agreement that the number of children and family size will continue its downward trend or perhaps level off at no more than two children. Due to factors such as improved methods of birth control, liberalized abortion laws, and increased acceptance of birth planning by Catholics, we might anticipate a decrease in the number of unplanned and unwanted births. But, as Hoffman suggests, when we go in to predict how many children people will want in the future, we are on a very shaky ground.[40]

Although we have a fairly good understanding of what has happened to birth rates over our national history, our understanding of what determines

---

39. U.S. Bureau of the Census, *Current Population Reports*, Series P-20, No. 300, "Prospects for American Fertility: June 1976," U.S. Government Printing Office, 1976, pp. 1–2.
40. Hoffman, op. cit., p. 430.

the variations in these rates is less adequate. Birth rates can be explained by factors such as the value attached to children and procreation, the nature of the economy, the type of family structure (such as extended or nuclear), and a whole series of "intermediate variables" such as age at marriage, proportion of adults married, use of contraceptives, practice of abortion, and the like. Economic optimism could change the current attitude toward a small family size. A decrease in the attention given to conception control or overpopulation by the mass media could influence the desire for more children.

Hoffman questions whether people are not having as many children as previously because whatever needs are involved in wanting children are satisfied in some other way.[41] For example, jobs and careers for women appear to be an alternative to children or result in a choice for few children, particularly if adequate rewards for participation are made available to women.[42]

A wide variety of variables have been found to be related to marital fertility: socioeconomic status, religion, race, education, urbanization, female income, female labor force participation, gender roles, and others. Even the size of the family of origin (number of brothers and sisters) appears to have a modest influence on marital fertility. This influence was found to be greater among first-born women, women who maintained life-styles similar to their mothers, and women who were satisfied with their parental family.[43]

Effects of Large or Small Families

There is little doubt that the number of people in a group influences the interaction and behavior of the members of that group. If you have one roommate and you agree, a decision is unanimous. If you have two roommates, both of whom agree with each other but differ from you, you have the unhappy choice of accepting their decision, trying to change the decision of at least one, or going your own way. Clearly, the number of interactions, the probability of dissensus, the attention given to any one person, and the like are influenced by the number of members in the group. The same factors hold true within a family system. One-child families are conducive to certain patterns of life that differ from two-, three-, or four-child families.

To perceive a family as large or small is relative. In the United States

41. Ibid., p. 430.

42. Elizabeth Maret Havens and Jack P. Gibbs, "The Relation between Female Labor Force Participation and Fertility," *Sociological Methods and Research* 3 (February 1975), pp. 258–290; John Scanzoni, "Gender Roles and the Process of Fertility Control," *Journal of Marriage and the Family* 38 (November 1976), pp. 677–691; and Lois W. Hoffman, "Employment of Women and Fertility," in L. W. Hoffman and F. I. Nye, eds., *Working Mothers* (San Francisco: Jossey Bass, 1974), pp. 81–101.

43. Nan E. Johnson and C. Shannon Stokes, "Family Size in Successive Generations: The Effects of Birth Order, Intergenerational Change in Lifestyle and Familial Satisfaction," *Demography* 13 (May 1976), pp. 175–187.

Fallout From Excess Kids

Since 1968, there has been a dramatic increase in big families. Today 48 percent say 2.1 children is the ideal family.

Where does that leave me? Somewhere between the propagation of the faith, the population explosion and 1.1 surplus kid at my dinner table.

And don't think I haven't paid dearly for my 1.1 overflow. To begin with, he fouled up the family vote. We used to vote even, at two-all, which left some room for persuasion. Since he arrived, my husband and I haven't won a decision in 15 years. Whether it is a vote on a vacation site, what TV show we are going to watch, or whether or not parents are to be impeached, the vote is always the same: Kids, 3—Parents, 2.

I am not being dramatic when I say this is a two-child-geared society. If the Good Lord had meant for people to have more than two children, he would have put more than two windows in the back seat of the car. We once threatened to put one on the front fender and the other two cried because they each wanted one.

A popsicle can only be divided two ways. There are two pairs of shoelaces in a package, so that one child always goes around with gym shoes that flop off his feet when he walks. There are only four chairs to a dinette set (so that one never matches) and four breakfast sweet rolls to a package.

We always had one too many for a rowboat, and when we rode the Ferris wheel, it was two to a seat and the odd one always rode alone like an only child.

Few people realize this, but did you know that a No. 2 can of fruit cocktail contains only two maraschino cherries? This means when you divide two maraschino cherries between three children, two are happy and the other one runs right out and retains F. Lee Bailey to fight a cherry custody suit.

Chores are geared toward twos—one washes dishes and the other dries, but what does the third child do? He becomes a useless bum and grows up to steal hubcaps.

Bunk beds come in twos. There are two sinks to a bathroom, two Hostess Twinkies to a package and free circus tickets come in pairs.

I mentioned this to the kids the other night and half-kiddingly said, "You know what this means, don't you? One of you has to go. Just for kicks, let's take a vote on it."

When the votes were counted, it was 4–1. I had been phased out of the family.

Somehow, I expected more from a full-grown man who has his own car window.

From *At Wit's End* by Erma Bombeck. Reproduced through the courtesy of Field Newspaper Syndicate.

four or more children may be viewed as a "large family." In many countries, and perhaps in the United States at the turn of the century, a family of four would lead to a reaction such as "only four"? Irrespective of the cutoff point as to what is a large or small family, a small family is such for one of two primary reasons: either the parents wanted a small family and achieved their desired size or they wanted a large family but were unable to attain it. In both cases, there is a low probability of unwanted children. In contrast, a large family is such because the parents achieved the size they desired or because they had more children than they in fact wanted. The probability is therefore greater that larger families include unwanted or unloved children.

Particularly in large families, last-born children are more likely to be unwanted than first- or middle-born children. This idea is consistent with what is known of abortion patterns among married women. That is, married women are most likely to resort to abortion when they have achieved the number of children they want or feel they can afford to have.

Wray presents a substantial body of evidence concerning the relation between family size or number of children and factors relevant to health.[44] He found no studies that showed significant health benefits associated with large families, although there were a few studies that showed no effect, either positive or negative.

The effects associated with family size on the well-being of individuals, primarily the children, are varied but serious:

> Increased illness, including malnutrition, serious enough in younger children to increase mortality rates; less satisfactory growth and intellectual development; increased illness in the parents; as well as clear-cut economic and emotional stresses. Family size is not the only cause of these effects, but it is clearly implicated as an important element in the interacting network of causal factors.[45]

A study by Bossard was conducted to obtain broad comparisons between the systems of two-child families and families with six or more children. A summary of some of the differences he found included:

1. Differing child-rearing patterns with greater patriarchy among the large families and greater matriarchy among the small families. Large families were more prone to physical means of punishment as well as greater regimentation in children's job assignments.
2. Large families were more vulnerable to economic hardship and family breakup—not by divorce but by desertion, death of a parent, or alcoholism.
3. While more vulnerable, parents of large families experienced less anxiety over children.
4. Security in the children of large families came from siblings. In the small families, security came from parents.
5. The members of large families reported the family group to be a source of cohesiveness to be maintained for the good of all. Members of small families saw the family more as a launching pad to the outside world.
6. Problems of parent-child relationships differed. Children of large families were more likely to feel that parents did not have enough time to satisfy each child. Children of small families remarked about the intensity of the relationship and the competition for affection.[46]

---

44. Joe D. Wray, "Population Pressure on Families: Family Size and Child Spacing," *Reports on Population Family Planning* (New York: Population Council 9 (August 1971), pp. 403–461.

45. Ibid., p. 454.

46. James H. S. Bossard, "Large and Small Families—A Study in Contrast," *Journal of the American Society of Chartered Life Underwriters* (Summer 1959), pp. 222–240; James H. S. Bossard and Eleanor S. Boll, *The Sociology of Child Development*, 4th ed. (New York: Harper, 1966), pp. 38–42.

These contrasts in family systems indicate certain quite different influences on the children growing up within them. The emphasis is on the group rather than the individual in the large family, whereas in the small family, the overriding emphasis is on developing the full potential of the individuals.[47]

It should be emphasized that it is not family size per se that creates varied systems of family living. Rather, it is the life factors and personal values that arise in relation to a certain size of group. Large families heighten the complexity of intragroup relations, pose additional problems in the fulfillment of family needs, and are likely to influence the amount of parental comfort or praise available per child. But the nature of the complexity, the types of problems, or the frequency of parental expression vary by factors such as the sex of the children and the class status of the parents.

Birth Order

Birth order (sibling position) has been found to have a major influence on a wide variety of behavioral and attitudinal phenomena. Associating with adults has been found to be more characteristic of first borns[48] and associating with peers more characteristic of last borns.[49] Last-born girls tend to visit with friends more frequently, are more likely to be members of clubs, make use of the media, engage in social activities, and be consistently more traditional than older siblings.[50]

A study of college students shows that first-born girls (as compared with later-born girls) are more traditionally oriented toward the feminine role, have more traditional beliefs about female personality traits, are more likely to choose marriage over graduation from college, and are more likely to describe themselves as religious.[51] In general, the findings support the proposition that first-born children are "conservers of the traditional culture."

The only child, like later-born children in a multiple-child family, was found to score higher on sexual permissiveness.[52] The only child was said to be high on permissiveness because his solitary position in the family tends to

47. Ibid., p. 42.

48. E. Singer, "Adult Orientation of First and Later Children," *Sociometry* 34 (September 1971), pp. 328–345.

49. Aida K. Tomeh, "Birth Order and Friendship Association," *Journal of Marriage and the Family* 32 (August 1970), pp. 360–369.

50. Aida K. Tomeh, "Birth Order and Familial Influences in the Middle East," *Journal of Comparative Family Studies* 2 (Spring 1971), pp. 88–100; and Aida K. Tomeh, "Birth Order, Club Membership and Mass Media Exposure," *Journal of Marriage and the Family* 38 (February 1976), pp. 151–164.

51. Kenneth Kammeyer, "Birth Order and the Feminine Sex Role among College Women," *American Sociological Review* 31 (August 1966), pp. 508–515.

52. Ira L. Reiss, *The Social Context of Premarital Sexual Permissiveness* (New York: Holt, Rinehart and Winston, 1967), pp. 152–154.

give him more attention and special privileges, which promotes permissiveness. It was speculated that having an older sibling of the same sex encourages permissiveness because it sets up a role model that the younger sibling can follow and thereby initiates him into sexual sophistication at an earlier age than the individual who is oldest in the family. The oldest also has the greatest likelihood of responsibility for other children and this may give him more self-discipline and more concern for possible consequences, thereby restricting his permissiveness. Like the only child, the youngest child has no responsibility for other siblings.

Sex Control and Gender Preference

An interesting question to ponder at the end of a chapter dealing with the parental system is "What will be the consequences when parents can control whether to have a boy or a girl (sex control) and can choose a male or a female (gender preference)?" It is likely that within the foreseeable future, parents will be able to choose the sex of their children with either of two basic procedures: 1) by controlling the type of sperm that will fertilize the egg, or 2) by prenatally determining the sex of an embryo and then aborting it if it is of the undesired sex.[53]

Gale Largey has reacted to a number of projected societal consequences of sex control.[54] How would you react? One, will sex control result in an unbalanced sex ratio? It has been estimated that choosing the sex of the child will increase the proportion of male births by 7 to 10 percent. Also, a series of research reports seems to indicate that boys are preferred over girls in much of Africa, Asia, and the Middle East, among the Swiss, Belgians, and Italians in Europe, and among Jews and Catholics in the United States to mention a few. If this excess of males was to occur, would it increase the number of males who never marry, delay their age at marriage, force an increase in homosexuality and prostitution, or even force the introduction of polyandry?

Second, would a consequence of choosing the sex of a child be a reduction in the birth rate because some parents would not have to bear additional children in order to have one or another of a particular sex? Studies indicate that the desire for more children is closely correlated with the number of sons. Third, would a consequence be an increased proportion of first-born males? Some of the consequences of birth order have already been shown. Thus, the result may be children who have more friends, are more conservative, or are more eminent scholars. Finally, would a consequence of choosing a boy or a girl be improved family relationships by avoiding births

---

53. Gale Largey, "Sex Control and Society: A Critical Assessment of Sociological Speculations," *Social Problems* 20 (Winter 1973), p. 310–311.

54. Ibid., pp. 310–318.

of the undesired sex, by having fewer resented or rejected children, or by the elimination of gender role confusion?

We are living in a "biological revolution" of which sex control is one aspect, yet such control is one biological "advancement" that could have a far-reaching social impact on the parent system in the United States and around the world.

Summary

The previous chapter examined various aspects of the marital system. Continuing through the life cycle, children follow shortly after the beginning of most marriages. This chapter examines structural factors relating to the parental system: a system of interrelated statuses of parents and children.

In the United States the role of parent is often ambiguous and inadequately delimited. Parents operating under a romantic notion about children are often ill prepared for the tasks they must perform. This is complicated by the lack of a traditional model to follow and an absence of precise scientifically established guidelines. This transition to parenthood includes cultural pressure to assume a role that is irrevocable and often involuntary. To some, parenthood is a crisis event, requiring a major reorganization of statuses, roles, and relationships. However, not all children are problematic but rather fulfill basic functions for parents and satisfy a range of needs for the individuals involved.

Young parenthood is an issue of specific concern, both in terms of the parents and the children. Parents are often at a disadvantage in terms of the marriage, education, income, employment, and training in general. Many children are born outside of the marital system and are reared in one-parent situations. Illegitimacy does appear to make a difference in the ability to get started on an equal footing with legitimate children and to avoid disadvantages after infancy as well. While the legitimate birth rate is dropping, the illegitimate birth rate is increasing sharply.

Most married couples want and have children. Only about one in six, either by choice or by circumstance, is childless. Since the middle of the 1950s, the birth rate has decreased steadily as has the average number of births expected by wives. There has been a substantial movement in the birth expectations of young wives toward the two-child or less family and away from the three-or-more-child family. The slogan "stop at two" appears to be coming true in fact.

Family size does make a difference. Small families were found to differ from larger ones in a number of ways. In small families, children were more likely to be planned, health benefits were likely to be greater, less regimentation appeared in task assignments, and less vulnerability existed as to economic hardships. On the other hand, in large families certain kinds of anxiety over the children were less, security was found in siblings rather than parents, and familism (family emphasis over individual emphasis) was greater. It is not family size per se, however, that is crucial but rather the life factors and complexity of intragroup relations that result from differing family size. As with size of family, many differences exist by order of birth. First-borns appear to be more traditionally oriented, less sexually permissive, more achievement oriented, and differ from later-born children in a wide variety of ways.

Key Terms and Topics

Parents in Modern America	504	Birth Rates and Birth Expectations	520
Parenthood as Crisis	508		
Young Parenthood	512	Effects of Large and Small Families	522
Legitimacy and Illegitimacy	514		
Rates and Consequences of Illegitimacy	517	Birth Order	525
		Sex Control and Gender Preference	526
Family Size	520		

Discussion Questions

1. *Discuss the likely effects of the following structural dimensions on parents: age of parents, length of marriage, number of children, spacing of children, and sex of children.*
2. *In what ways do urbanization and industrialization effect parental roles in American society? Would these factors not occur irrespective of urbanization and industrialization?*
3. *How does the parental role differ from marital and occupational roles? Do these differences assist or deter the fulfillment of the parental role?*
4. *What conditions are likely to increase the probability that parenthood will be a "crisis" event?*
5. *In an examination of the birth-rate data presented, explain: 1) why the birth rate dropped sharply in the 1930s, 2) how it was accomplished without the pills, abortions, and sterilizations more prevalent today, and 3) the gradual drop in the birth rate since 1955 and the reasons for it.*
6. *Discuss the implications of the slogan "stop at two" in regard to family size. Why two? What if everyone had two? What means should be used to accomplish this if it is perceived as a desirable goal?*
7. *Why is illegitimacy considered a "social problem"? If it is a social problem, why does not society make available birth control, abortion, sterilization, and the like for the unwed male or female?*

8. *Visit a planned-parenthood center and examine its literature. How does it convey the family-planning idea to lower-class families? Who are its clients by race and social class? What role does the father play in method of control, visits to the center, or decision making about family planning?*

9. *Itemize advantages and disadvantages of large and small families. Differentiate by sex and social class. How do older children differ from younger ones?*

10. *If sex of the fetus could be determined accurately within a few weeks following pregnancy, what effect, if any, would this have on birth rates? Would most parents in the United States choose boys, girls, or have no preferences? What about other countries, particularly outside of the Western World?*

Further Readings

Benson, Leonard. *Fatherhood: A Sociological Perspective.* New York: Random, 1968. An attempt to bring together the scattered materials about paternity and place them in a coherent framework.

Bernard, Jessie. *The Future of Motherhood.* New York: Penguin, 1974. An examination of the way our society institutionalizes the bearing and rearing of its children and the technological, political, economic, and ethical forces that shape its operation.

Bernard, Jessie. *Women, Wives, Mothers: Values and Options.* Chicago: Aldine, 1975. A collection of papers by Bernard sketching the life patterns of women: sex differences, young women, wives, and mothers.

Fawcett, James T., et al. *The Value of Children in Asia and the United States: Comparative Perspectives.* Papers of the East-West Population Institute 32 (July 1974), pp. 1–79. A comparative research study of the value of children in six countries: Japan, Korea, Taiwan, Philippines, Thailand, and the United States.

Fein, Greta G., and Alison Clarke-Stewart. *Day Care in Context.* New York: John Wiley, 1973. A thorough treatment of the complex issues that bear upon the formulation and implementation of day-care programs. Day care is examined from historical, social, psychological, and educational perspectives.

Hawke, Sharryl, and David Knox. *One Child by Choice.* Englewood Cliffs, N.J.: Prentice-Hall, 1977. An examination of the single child and the parents of the single child.

LeMasters, E. E. *Parents in Modern America.* Rev. ed. Homewood, Ill.: Dorsey, 1974. A focus on what happened to "normal" parents in the child-rearing process. One of the most comprehensive sociological approaches to parenthood in American Society.

Rainwater, Lee. *And the Poor Have Children.* Chicago: Quadrangle, 1960. A study of contraceptive behavior and attitudes viewed within the context of sexual behavior and attitudes among the lower classes.

Rainwater, Lee. *Family Design: Marital Sexuality, Family Size, and Contraception.* Chicago: Aldine, 1965. Using social class, conjugal role organization, and religion as control variables, this study undertaken for the Planned Parenthood Federation examines in detail role concepts of husband and wife, sexual relations, cultural determinants, family size norms, and contraceptive practices as related to family planning.

Roberts, Robert W., ed. *The Unwed Mother.* New York: Harper, 1966. Fifteen articles on illegitimacy and the unwed mother that present a theoretical overview and an examination of cross-cultural, psychological, and sociological perspectives with a presentation of alternate solutions available.

Scanzoni, John H. *Sex Roles, Life Styles and Childbearing.* New York: Free Press, 1975. An examination, based on over 3,000 interviews, of the effect that gender role norms have on the decision to have or not have children.

17   *Parent-Child Interaction
and Socialization*

17

The previous chapter examined selected structural arrangements of the family system: norms and values surrounding parenthood, young parenthood, legitimacy and illegitimacy, birth rates and birth expectations, effects of large or small families, birth order, and the like. This chapter as well looks at selected social structural patterns such as father absence and gender (male-female) differences, but it focuses primary attention on interactional and social psychological patterns in parent-child relationships. Of central concern are theoretical frames of reference that vary in their explanations of the socialization process and an examination of sex role socialization.

THE SOCIALIZATION OF PARENTS AND CHILDREN

The helplessness of infants is perhaps unequaled among newborn. They cannot walk, feed themselves, know where danger lies, seek food or shelter, or even roll over. Babies may grow up to be criminals, teachers, or athletic superstars, but first they must learn to have basic needs cared for, learn to interact with other humans, and learn what behavior is expected and accepted. In short, they must learn to be human.

The process of acquiring these physical and social skills to become a social being and a member of society is called socialization. Socialization, the central concept of this chapter, is a never-ending process of developing the self and of learning the ways of a given society and culture. While the focus of attention in the socialization literature is generally upon the newborn and young child, teen-agers, and middle-aged and older people as well are in a continual process of learning skills, developing the self, and becoming a participant in the groups and social systems of society. Parents too need to be socialized to parenthood. Parents not only influence and shape the behavior of children, but children do the same to parents.[1]

Socialization, particularly of the young infant, may be the single universal function of the family.[2] There may be others—such as social placement —but every society appears to link people by affinal or consanguineous ties to the nurturant socialization of persons. This does not imply that families do not fulfill other functions, that socialization only occurs among infants, or that the family is the only socializing agent. Rather, the key implication is that the basic function of the family in all societies is nurturant socialization.

Preconditions for Socialization

Frederick Elkin and Gerald Handel state that there are three preconditions for adequate socialization: first, there must be an ongoing society; second, the child must have the requisite biological inheritance; and third, the child requires a human nature.[3]

First, the newborn enters an existing society that has rules, norms, values, attitudes, ways of behaving, and a wide variety of social structures that are highly regular and patterned but in constant change. The unsocialized infant has no knowledge of these changes, structures, or processes. The patterns of thinking, feeling, and acting of that society are what the socializing agents must pass on to the newcomer. This is the task of socialization.

The second precondition for socialization is a biological inheritance that is adequate to permit learning processes to occur. Thus a brain, a digestive system, and a beating heart are clearly prerequisites for socialization. These prerequisites, however, while necessary, are not sufficient. A "perfect" biological system, while influencing the socialization process, will not be the determinant of what is internalized mentally. Factors such as brain damage, deafness, extreme tallness or shortness, shape of nose and chin, or a wide variety of other physical conditions may hinder or influence interaction and socializing processes. But it should be made extremely clear that the biological inheritance, while influencing learning processes and necessary for their occurrence, are never sufficient conditions for socialization. Certain needs such as food, drink, and sleep are basic to survival, but they can be satisfied in a wide variety of ways. And while temperaments and intelligence may be basically biological, the development or direction that they take is influenced and modified by the society in which the infant exists. In brief, while bio-

---

1. Joy D. Osofsky, "The Shaping of Mother's Behavior by Children," *Journal of Marriage and the Family* 32 (August 1970), pp. 400–405.

2. Ira L. Reiss, "The Universality of the Family: A Conceptual Analysis," *Journal of Marriage and the Family* 27 (November 1965), pp. 443–453.

3. Frederick Elkin and Gerald Handel, *The Child and Society: The Process of Socialization*, 2d ed. (New York: Random, 1972), p. 9.

The Adjustment of Older Adopted Children

According to most guides to child-rearing, the first years of life are the crucial ones. If a child is not properly cared for by loving parents during infancy, his prospects for later adjustment are supposed to be very poor. Because most child-welfare workers believe this theory, they don't hold much hope for older adopted children who have been treated badly in early childhood. Now Alfred Kadushin of the School of Social Work of the University of Wisconsin has done a study of older adopted children that offers a serious challenge to this view (Social Work, October 1967).

Kadushin and his associates interviewed the adoptive parents of 91 children, all placed for adoption when they were already 5 years old or older. The children had been removed from their parents by court order, which—in view of the reluctance of courts to take a child away from all but the most destructive parents—meant that all had been seriously neglected or mistreated. Yet when social workers questioned the adoptive parents of these children, they found that the great majority (70 to 80 percent) felt that the adoption had turned out quite well. Clearly, these children were not so damaged by their early experiences that they were unable to fit into their new homes.

What's more, Kadushin can cite a number of other studies of people who had very difficult childhoods and still grew up into successful, well-adjusted adults. When Anne Rose and Barbara Burks, for example, looked up 36 young adults who had been removed from their own homes in early childhood because of their parents' chronic alcoholism, they found that most of the 36 were married, were leading satisfactory lives, and had adequate personal and community relationships.

Victor and Mildred Goertzel, looking back over the lives of 400 eminent people, found that only 58 had come from the recommended type of warm, supportive, relatively untroubled home; the others came from homes that "demonstrated considerable pathology."

Evidence of this sort, Kadushin believes, ought to move child-welfare workers to revaluate their theories. He suggests two facts that can help explain the strange recovery of these children from early trauma. First, detailed observation of the behavior of newborns is making it quite clear that children differ right from the moment of birth. Because they are inherently so different, some may be psychologically destroyed by early trauma while others, emotionally tougher, are not.

Second, if you believe that behavior is malleable and is shaped by the rewards and punishments in the environment, then it is not surprising that a child who behaves one way in a deprived household with abusive parents learns to behave quite differently if he is moved to a stable, middle-class environment with attentive parents. For these children, adoption is psychotherapy. And for many of them, the therapy seems to be remarkably effective.

Source: "Roundup of Current Research," *Trans-Action* 5 (May 1968), p. 6. Reprinted by permission.

logical requisites are necessary for adequate socialization, they alone are not determinants of socialization.

The third precondition is human nature. Here human nature refers to certain factors that are universal among humans and yet distinctive to humans as compared to other animals. Within the symbolic-interaction frame of reference, human nature would include the ability to take the role of the other, the ability to feel as others feel, or in general the ability to symbolize. To symbolize is to give meaning to abstractions, to recognize words, sounds, and gestures, and to attach meaning to them. The wink of an eye, the shake of a fist, or the nod of a head take on meaning in terms of man's ability to symbolize. As far as is known, this is a nature unique to humans.

THEORIES OF SOCIALIZATION PROCESSES

As previously defined, socialization refers to the processes by which the infant and adult learn the ways of a given society and culture and develop into participants capable of operating in that society. A number of relatively comprehensive theories have been developed to explain various aspects of this process.[4] Let us examine a number of these.

A Learning-Behavorist Frame of Reference

Learning theory, also recognized as reinforcement theory, stimulus-response theory, and behaviorism, assumes that the same concepts and principles that apply to lower animals apply to humans. Thus it is logical and rational to spend time in the laboratory experimenting with rats, cats, dogs, pigeons, monkeys, or other animals to learn more about humans. Although there are many variations of learning theory, as with the psychoanalytic theory that follows, basic assumptions and common lines of agreement do exist.

Learning, or socialization as applied to the newborn infant, involves changes in behavior that result from experience. (This is opposed to changes in behavior that result from physiological maturation or biological conditions.) Learning involves conditioning that may include classical conditioning or instrumental (operant) conditioning. Classical conditioning links a response to a known stimulus. Most students are already familiar with Pavlov's dog experiment, which provides a good example of classical conditioning. The hungry dog, placed in a soundproof room, heard a tuning fork prior to receiving meat. When repeated on several occasions, the dog salivated upon hearing the tuning fork prior to receiving, or even without receiving, the meat. The tuning fork, a conditioned stimulus, produced the response (salivation). In the classical conditioning experiment, the focus of attention is largely on

---

4. For a comprehensive review of the socialization literature see David A. Goslin, ed., *Handbook of Socialization Theory and Research* (Skokie, Ill.: Rand McNally, 1969). A paperback reader to consider is Edward Z. Dager, ed., *Socialization* (Chicago: Markham, 1971).

Meatloaf Gambit

It is true enough that virtually all of the world's great chefs are men—but it is also true that most men are the world's worst cooks. Teaching a husband to cook, laudable though that feminist goal may be, can create frightening strains in a marriage—not to mention the gastrointestinal system. However, Suzanne Prescott, 29, a Chicago rock musician, has suggested a painless and sinisterly Skinnerian strategy for transforming husbands into expert meat-loaf makers.

"The first week," she says, "you call home and say you've got to work late but the meatloaf is ready to go so why doesn't he just put it in the oven? Next week you call home and tell him you've left all the ingredients out on the counter and suggest he stir them together and put the loaf in the oven. The third week you call and say that everything is in the refrigerator and he knows how to put it together from last week. The fourth week you ask him to go to the store and buy the ingredients, and you've arrived.

"Trouble is that you end up eating meatloaf all the time."

Source: *Time Magazine*, March 20, 1972, p. 57. Reprinted by permission from TIME, The Weekly Newsmagazine; Copyright Time Inc.

the stimulus. If this works with dogs, the same principle should hold true with an infant upon hearing his mother's approaching footsteps. The footstep stimulus, with repeated occurrences, should elicit a response from the child.

Instrumental conditioning, or what Skinner calls *operant* conditioning, places the focus of attention on the response. The responses are not related to any known stimuli but rather they function in an instrumental fashion. We learn to make a certain response on the basis of the consequences the response produces. It is the response, rather than the stimulus, that is correlated with reinforcement. Let us return to the example of the hungry dog. Under classical conditioning the dog salivated upon hearing the tuning fork, the stimulus. Under operant conditioning, the hungry dog may sniff, paw, and chew whatever is around. If upon pawing, the dog opens a door behind which is food, the sniffing and chewing will soon decrease and the pawing on the door will occur whenever food is desired. Thus instrumental conditioning is a response followed by a reward (reinforcement).

How does this apply to an infant? Suppose the infant utters sounds like "da-da-da." Father, who is convinced he is saying daddy, rewards the child by picking up, feeding, or rocking him. As a result, the response (da-da-da) soon becomes used by the infant all day long. The infant has learned to make a certain response on the basis of the consequence or result the response will produce; hence it is the response that is correlated with reinforcement.

These same general principles, refined by behaviorists with reference to intermittent reinforcement, partial reinforcement, negative and positive reinforcement, discrimination of stimuli, differentiation of response, and the like are said to apply in the learning of any kind of behavior. Socialization results from stimulus-response conditioning and from positive and negative reinforcements. The conditioning stimuli (classical conditioning) and the consequences of responses (operant conditioning) are both external to the animal or human.

Many of these processes are most readily observed in early childhood when parents use rewards and punishment as deliberate techniques for teaching the child approved forms of behavior. As individuals mature, sanctioning becomes increasingly complex, and candy, weekly allowances, spanking, or other forms of rewards and punishments lose their ability to either eliminate undesirable or increase desirable behavior.

Within the learning-theory, behaviorist framework, symbols, language, reasoning, internalized meanings, and other internal processes play a minimal role, and this is in sharp contrast to the symbolic-interaction framework (described in Chapter 2 and later in this section) where the socialized being can create his own stimuli and responses, can define and categorize, can distinguish between self and nonself, can separate inner and outer sensations, and can take the role of the other. As a result, this basically mechanistic approach to socialization is rejected by most sociologists to whom the self, roles, reference groups, and symbolic processes are viewed as central to an understanding of human behavior. Although learning theory has been extremely illuminating in research with animals and infants, it has been less successful in explaining social situations, group norms, or the learning of language itself.

From the biased perspective of this author, it is largely a waste of time, effort, and expense to attempt to understand the behavior of socialized man, capable as he is of dealing with symbolic processes, reasoning, shared meanings, and the like, by studying nonhuman forms. Behaviorism does, however, add greatly to our understanding of the human who 1) has not learned to share meanings—the infant, the isolate, or the severely retarded—or 2) has once learned but no longer has the capacity to share meanings—the more severe cases of aphasia or the extreme cases of schizophrenia where words may exist but the meanings are not shared with others.

This brief, minimal treatment of learning theory may seem unfair to the disciples of behaviorism.[5] The same can be said for the minimal treatment of the psychoanalytic theory that follows. Both are intended to illustrate some contrasting views on the nature of socialization.

---

5. For a full treatment of this theory of learning, see for example: B. F. Skinner, *The Behavior of Organisms: An Experimental Analysis* (New York: Appleton-Century-Crofts, 1938); B. F. Skinner, *Walden Two* (New York: Macmillan, 1953); B. F. Skinner, *Contingencies of Reinforcement: A Theoretical Analysis* (New York: Appleton-Century-Crofts, 1969); and B. F. Skinner, *Beyond Freedom and Dignity* (New York: Random, 1971). Students may also want to examine Ernest R. Hilgard and Gordon H. Bower, *Theories of Learning*, 3d ed. (New York: Appleton-Century-Crofts, 1966); John T. Doby, *Introduction to Social Psychology* (New York: Appleton-Century-Crofts, 1966); or Albert Bandura and Richard Walters, *Social Learning and Personality Development* (New York: Holt, Rinehart and Winston, 1963).

A Psychoanalytic
Frame of Reference

The classical psychoanalytic theory, developed by Sigmund Freud and his adherents, stresses the importance of biological drives and unconscious processes. Both are in sharp contrast to the behaviorist theory just described. The process of socialization, according to this framework, consists of a number of precise though overlapping stages of development. What happens at these stages from birth to age five or six, although unconscious, becomes relatively fixed and permanent. These stages are referred to as the oral, anal, and phallic, followed later by a period of latency and a genital phase. Attention is focused around three principle erogenous zones—the mouth, the anus, and the genitals, which are the regions of the body where excitatory processes tend to become focalized and where tensions can be removed by some action such as stroking or sucking. Each region is of extreme importance in the socialization process because they are the first important sources of irritating excitations with which the baby has to contend and upon which the first pleasurable experiences occur.

The first stage of development, the *oral*, occurs during the first year of the child's life. The earliest erotic gratifications come from the mouth and, as a result, the child forms strong emotional attachments to the mother who supplies the source of food, warmth, and sucking. During this first year, the child is narcissistic in that he derives gratification for himself via the oral source, namely the mouth. The modes of functioning of the mouth include taking in, holding on, biting, spitting out, and closing, all prototypes for ways of adjusting to painful or disturbing states. They serve as models for adaptations in later life. For example, Hall indicates:

> Taking in through the mouth is a prototype for acquisitiveness, holding on for tenacity and determination, biting for destructiveness, spitting out for rejection and contemptuousness, and closing for refusal and negativism. Whether these traits will develop and become a part of one's character or not depends on the amount of frustration and anxiety which is experienced in connection with the prototype expression.[6]

The *anal* stage of development follows and overlaps with the oral stage. This phase is so called because the child experiences pleasure in excretion and because toilet training may become a major problem. At this point, two functions become central: retention and elimination. Since the mother is still the predominant figure, her methods of training the child and her attitudes about such matters as defecation, cleanliness, and control are said to determine the impact that toilet training will have upon the development of the person. Carried to the extreme, the mother who praises the child for a large

---

6. Calvin S. Hall, *A Primer of Freedom Psychology* (New York: World, 1954), p. 104.

bowel movement may produce an adolescent who will be motivated to produce or create things to please others or to please himself, as he once made feces to please his mother. On the other hand, if the mother is very strict and punitive, the child may intentionally soil himself and, as an adolescent, be messy, irresponsible, disorderly, wasteful, and extravagant. As Hall states, "Strict toilet-training procedures may also bring about a reaction formation against uncontrolled expulsiveness in the form of meticulous neatness, fastidiousness, impulsive orderliness, frugality, disgust, fear of dirt, strict budgeting of time and money, and other overcontrolled behavior. Constipation is a common defense reaction against elimination."[7]

The *phallic* stage is the period of growth during which the child is preoccupied with the genitals. Prior to this stage, the first love object of both the boy and girl is the mother. But with the arrival of this stage, the sexual urge increases, the boy's love for his mother becomes more intense, and the result is jealousy of the father who is his rival. The boy's attachment to his parent of the opposite sex is widely known as the Oedipus complex. Concurrently, the male becomes fearful that his father will remove his genitals and develops a fear known as *castration anxiety*. This anxiety increases upon observation of the female who has, in his unconscious mind, "already been castrated." A similar or reverse process is in operation for the female. She forms an attachment to her father, the Electra complex, but has mixed feelings for him because he possesses something that she does not have. The result is *penis envy*. According to traditional Freudian psychology, penis envy is the key to feminine psychology. Located here are the roots of male dominance and female submissiveness, male superiority and female inferiority.

The oral, anal, and phallic stages taken together are called the pregenital period and occupy the first five or six years of one's life. These are the important years when the basic personality patterns are established and fixed. Following this time, for the next six or seven years until the onset of puberty, the male and female egos go through a latency phase when the erotic desires of the child are repressed and he forms attachments to the parent of the same sex.

Finally, with the arrival of puberty, the genital phase of development begins. This period is less a stage than the final working out of the previous stages, particularly the oral, anal, and phallic that occurred during the pregenital period. At this time, group activities, marriage, establishing a home, developing vocational responsibilities, and "adult" interests become the focus of attention. Given the importance of the early years, one can readily understand why factors such as bottle or breast feeding, nursing on a regular or self-demand time schedule, weaning abruptly or gradually, bowel training early or late, bladder training early or late, punishment or nonpunishment

---

7. Ibid., p. 108.

for toilet accidents, or sleeping alone or with one's mother, serve as crucial items of attention to the psychoanalyst.

The claims of the Freudians regarding the importance of infant training to personality adjustment have received mixed empirical support. The support that has been received has, in general, been derived from clinical studies of emotionally disturbed individuals. Other studies show different results. For example, one attempt to test empirically the crucial role of infant discipline in character formation and personality adjustment was published more than twenty years ago and has since become a somewhat classical article on the subject.[8] That study set up a series of null hypotheses concerning the relationship of specific infant disciplines to subsequent personality adjustments. The general hypothesis was that the personality adjustment and traits of children who had undergone varying infant-training experiences would not differ significantly from each other. These infant-training experiences included the self-demand feeding schedule, gradual weaning, late bowel training, and similar factors. The results indicated support for the null hypothesis, that is, there were no significant differences in the personality adjustment of children who had undergone varying infant-training experiences. Of 460 Chi-square tests, only 18 were significant at or beyond the .05 level.[9] Of these, 11 were in the expected direction and 7 were in the opposite direction from that expected on the basis of psychoanalytic writings. Such practices as breast feeding, gradual weaning, demand schedule, bowel training, and bladder training, which have been so emphasized in the psychoanalytic literature, were almost barren in terms of their relationship to personality adjustment as measured in this study.[10]

Child Development
Frames of Reference

The ideas of Erik Erikson and Jean Piaget are of interest in dealing with the socialization issue. Both, like Freud, focus their attention primarily on stages of development. Both, unlike Freud, extended their stages beyond the early years and place more importance on social structure and reasoning.

Erikson, one of Freud's students, was a psychoanalyst who saw socialization as a lifelong process, beginning at birth and continuing into old age. He developed and is well known for his eight stages of human development.[11]

---

8. William H. Sewall, "Infant Training and the Personality of the Child," *The American Journal of Sociology* 58 (September 1952), pp. 150–159.

9. The .05 level means that these relationships would occur simply by chance less than 5 times in 100.

10. Sewall, op. cit., p. 158.

11. Erik K. Erikson, *Childhood and Society* (New York: Norton, 1950).

Each stage constitutes a crisis brought on by physiological changes and the constantly changing social situation. In infancy, during the first year, the crisis centers around *trust* versus *mistrust*. Being totally dependent on adults, the feelings of the child are developed in response to the quality of maternal care as dependable or undependable, accepting or rejecting. In early childhood or the first two to three years, the issue centers around *autonomy* versus *shame and doubt*. Again the feelings of the child are developed in response to the actions of parents who allow the child to accomplish new things and govern himself (autonomy) or receive constant supervision, indicating he cannot reach, walk, control his bowels, and the like without ridicule and shame.

The play stage, at ages four or five, involves the issue of *initiative* versus *guilt*. As children master their own bodies, as they play and fantasize and act out adult roles, they develop feelings of self-worth. Ridicule and disinterest lead to guilt feelings, while encouragement to explore may lead to personal initiative. By school age and up to adolescence, the issue centers around *industry* versus *inferiority*. Parents become less the focal point as the school and the community take on greater importance. Recognition is received by achieving success in physical and mental skills and producing things (industry), while failure in school, disapproval of race or family background, and inability to achieve may be negative experiences that result in feelings of inferiority.

By adolescence, the issue becomes one of *identity* versus *role confusion*. Identity, the focal concern of Erikson,[12] is being able to achieve a sense of continuity about one's past, present, and future. An inability to integrate the many and varied roles into a clear identity leads to role confusion. Peers at this point are of prime importance.

Young adulthood, another major turning point in life, involves the issue of *intimacy* versus *isolation*. Friendships, love affairs, and intimacy requires the risk of rejection, losing the friend or lover, and being hurt. Only with a clear sense of ego identity and an ability to trust can one avoid isolation. In young adulthood and middle age the issue centers around *generativity* versus *stagnation*. People can feel they are making contributions to society, working creatively, rearing children for the next generation, and in general being productive, or they may find life as boring, painful, and dull. Childish self-absorption and "early invalidism, physical or psychological, are signs that a person has not found generativity."[13] Old age, the last stage of development is one of reflection and evaluation and focuses on the issue of *integrity* versus *despair*. Integrity involves coming to terms with life and death. Despair involves seeing life as a series of missed opportunities and realizing it is too late to start over.

Erikson sees the social order as resulting from and in harmony with

12. Erik K. Erikson, *Identity: Youth and Crisis* (New York, Norton, 1968).
13. Erikson, op. cit., p. 267.

these eight stages of development. As people work out solutions to these developmental concerns, the solutions become institutionalized in the culture.

Piaget, a Swiss social psychologist, spent more than thirty years observing and studying the development of intellectual functions and logic in children.[14] His work has stimulated an interest in maturational stages of development and in the importance of cognition in human development. Differing dramatically from the views of the learning and psychoanalytic frames of reference, Piaget sees development as an ability to reason abstractly, to think about hypothetical situations in a logical way, and to organize rules (which Piaget calls operations) into complex, higher order structures. Children invent ideas and behaviors that they have never witnessed or had reinforced.

Piaget believes that there are four major stages of intellectual development: sensorimotor (zero to eighteen months), preoperational (eighteen months to age seven), concrete operations (age seven to twelve), and finally formal operations (age twelve onward). The stages are continuous and each is built upon and is a derivative of the earlier one.

The *sensorimotor stage*, further differentiated into six developmental stages[15] involves for the child a physical understanding of himself and his world. The unlearned responses such as sucking and closing one's fist become repetitive but with no intent, purpose, or interest in the effect this behavior has on the environment. Later activities in this first stage become more intentional. A child may kick his legs to produce a swinging motion in a toy hung on his crib. A child may knock down a pillow to get a toy behind it. A primary cognitive development at this stage is the discovery of object permanence: toys and mother do not dissolve when they are not visible. Early development includes the coordination of simple motor arts with incoming perceptions (sensorimotor arts).

The *preoperational stage* involves language and its acquisition. Objects are treated as symbolic of things other than themselves. Dolls may be treated as babies or a stick may be treated as a candle. At this stage, overt actions and the meaning of objects and events are manipulated, but the child has difficulty taking the point of view of another child or adult. Unlike the next (operational) stage, the child does not have a mental representation of a series of actions. For example, a child may be able to walk to a store several blocks away but cannot draw the route on paper. Nor can the child at this stage grasp the notion of relational terms (darker, larger), reason simultaneously

---

14. A comprehensive interpretation and summary of Piaget's works can be found in J. McV. Hunt, *Intelligence and Experience* (New York: Ronald, 1961), pp. 109–307. See also Jean Piaget and Barbara Inhelder, *The Psychology of the Child* (New York: Basic, 1969); and Piaget's theory in P. H. Mussen, ed., *Carmichael's Manual of Child Psychology*, 3d ed. (New York: Wiley, 1970), pp. 703–732.

15. These stages Piaget refers to as reflexes, primary circular reactions, secondary circular reactions, coordination of secondary reactions, tertiary circular reactions, and internal experimentation. Jean Piaget, *The Construction of Reality in the Child* (New York: Basic, 1954).

Louise: *I could write volumes about this foster child we've raised. When he came to us he was two years and four months old and was really a basket case. I had read about children from deprived backgrounds, but I had never seen one. It was really a cultural shock for all of us. Not only for my husband and for me, but for our older children and for the neighbors. The child didn't seem to know what people were for. He could ignore a person like he ignored a piece of furniture. He apparently had never had any interpersonal relations with another human. It was so total we just sort of struggled with it and didn't know what we were struggling with. He did not want anybody near him and he was only two years old. Our way was to hold our children, cuddle them, tell them bedtime stories and carry them around. The older children played with him but he had no idea of what they were doing. Everything terrified him. It was a lot more than I miss my mother. In fact, he did not know the words mama, daddy. He didn't miss anybody cause he didn't know what anybody was for. He had no language in that he didn't understand like our two-year-olds understood everything. He had no understanding of the difference between yes, go ahead and do it, or no, you can't do that. No was a concept he never heard.*

Apparently he never sat at a table and ate a meal. He was, more like an animal. I really hate using that word when we are talking about humans, but. You could not sit him at a table; he didn't know what it was for. I recall the first meal we had—that he had with us. Like the first breakfast he had with us. He drank orange juice for as long as I gave it to him. Like he had four or five glasses of orange juice. He gobbled up toast and ate huge bowls of cereal. First I thought, "Gee, the kid is starved." But then I realized that he ate like that probably because that's his pattern. You eat all you could get when you could get it because you didn't know when the next meal was coming from. But we ate three times a day. It was years, and I mean years, before he could really sit at the table with us, eat a meal, and then leave without creating a major disturbance. By major, I mean he thought he could get his jollies by just sweeping everything off the table or grabbing the table and making things spill or taking his own food and throwing it around. You would think that in a few weeks this will all go away. But it didn't and we started bringing him around to psychologists and the agency was very helpful. They scheduled him for appointments where he was seen by neurologists and psychologists and he had EEGs, intelligence tests, and he had all of the support that seemed to be available in the community. They would all just say that as far as they could see he had no brain damage; his intelligence was maybe low normal.

For a long time he was as rigid as a door. He would not bend an inch. Like here's an example of what I mean. At our house the chil-

dren play outside in the summer. We have playground equipment in the back yard and the children have bikes. I raised a bunch of kids who really love the outdoors. But I don't think he had ever been outside his little apartment or whatever it was they lived in. So, I would put him outside in the morning and his hands would go up to his eyes like he couldn't stand the light. I'd stay out there with him, but unless I was holding his hand, he would spin right around and go into the house again. So I'd take him out and put him outside again. We actually had to physically hold him out there. You could not walk him. You couldn't put him in the sandbox. He didn't know what a sandbox was for. He didn't know what toys were for. He had no idea what you did with a toy. We had to very patiently teach him all of this.

Eventually he began to show that it became important to him that he start pleasing us. But now this didn't happen until he was almost school age. Prior to that he couldn't care less whether he pleased us or pleased anybody else. He had not been socialized that way and I think that kind of socialization happens really early. I'm even more aware of it with my own grandchildren. They're sensitive. They cry if they are corrected. He never cried. We still laugh about the time I broke the pingpong paddle on him and he got up and said, "That didn't hurt." He went back and started doing exactly the same thing he was spanked for. I just had to take a deep breath and sit back and let him do it. Or I would have killed him that day, I'm sure I would have.

about part of the whole and the whole, or arrange objects according to some quantified dimension such as weight or size.

The *operational stage* involves the ability to do things such as those mentioned in the preoperational stage. Children learn to manipulate the tools of their culture. They learn that mass remains constant in spite of changes in form. They learn to understand cause and effect, to classify objects, to consider the viewpoints of others, and to differentiate between dreams and real things. By approximately age twelve the child enters the adult world and the stage of formal operations.

The *formal operations* stage includes the ability to think in terms of abstract concepts, theories, and general principles. Alternate solutions to problems can be formulated. Hypothetical propositions can be formulated and answered. Preoccupation with thought is the principal component of this stage of development.

Piaget's insights into cognitive development are unsurpassed. His stages take into account both social and psychological phenomena. Like Freud, Piaget has a specific conception of the goals of maturity and adulthood. Like Freud, Piaget believes that the child passes through stages. But where Freud

emphasized emotional maturity and the unconscious as of extreme importance, Piaget emphasizes reasoning and consciousness. Whereas Freud focused
on bodily zones, Piaget focuses on the quality of reasoning.

Of the frames of reference covered up to this point, they can be summarized by suggesting that the learning theorists are concerned with overt
behavior, the Freudians with motives and emotions (often unconscious and
rooted early in childhood), and the child developmentalists with motor skills,
thought, reasoning processes, and conflicts. Let us now turn our attention to
a symbolic interaction frame of reference that shares many assumptions of
Erikson and Piaget in the importance given to language, reasoning, and societal influences.

A Symbolic-Interaction
Frame of Reference

Contrasting considerably with the learning and psychoanalytic frames
of reference is the symbolic-interaction frame of reference. Within this framework, although the first five years are important, personality does not become
fixed; socialization becomes a lifelong process. Within this framework,
although mother is an important figure, so too are fathers, siblings, grandparents, teachers, and many others who are perceived as significant to the child
or adult. Although internal needs and drives are important as energy sources
and motivating devices, greater significance comes from interactions with
others and the internalized definitions and meanings of the world in which
one interacts. Although erogenous zones may be sources of pleasure and gratification, the significance of these zones depends on the learned internalized
meanings attached to them. Whereas unconscious processes may be at the
core of socialization (purely speculative), conscious processes relating to perceptions of self and others take on prime importance. Whereas rewards and
punishments influence behavior, these can only be understood in the light of
the meanings attached to them. Whereas conditioning (classical or operant)
is significant and basic to learning, internal processes cannot be ignored. To
understand socialization as explained within a symbolic-interaction frame of
reference (see Chapter 2), it is necessary to review in more detail the basic assumptions and meaning of key concepts such as social self, significant others,
and reference groups.

Basic Assumptions of
Symbolic Interactionism

As summarized in Chapter 2, the interactionist frame of reference,
when applied to the study of the family and to an understanding of socializa-

tion, is based on several basic assumptions. Four of these have been delineated by Stryker.[16]

The initial assumption is that *humans must be studied on their own level.* Symbolic interactionism is antireductionistic. If we want to understand socialization, infant development, and parent-child relationships among humans, then we must study humans and not infer their behavior from the study of nonhuman or infrahuman forms of life.

The basic difference between human and infrahuman is not simply a matter of degree but a basic difference of kind. The evolutionary process involves quantitative differences in species, not merely qualitative ones. The human-nonhuman difference centers around language, symbols, meanings, gestures, and related processes.

Thus, to understand a person's social development and behavior, relatively little can be gained by observing chimpanzees, dogs, pigeons, or rats. Social life, unlike biological, physiological life, or any nonhuman form, involves sharing meanings, communicating symbolically. Due to language and the use of gestures, human beings can respond to one another on the basis of intentions or meanings of gestures. This assumption is in direct contrast with the behaviorist assumption, which suggests that humans can best be understood by studying forms of life other than humans. Psychologists who assume that the difference between human and animal is one of degree have relatively good success in explaining and controlling those who do not share meanings or communicate with one another at a symbolic level: infants, extreme psychotics, isolated children, the severely retarded, the brain damaged, people with more severe forms of aphasia, and the like. To the interactionist, the possession of language has enabled humans alone to deal with events in terms of the past, present, or future and to imagine objects or events that may be remote in space or entirely nonexistent.

The differences between socialized human beings and the lower animals, or between human families and nonhuman families, may be summarized by saying that the lower animals do not have a culture. They have no system of beliefs, values, and ideas that are shared possessions of groups and are symbolically transmitted. They have no familial, educational, religious, political, or economic institutions. They have no sets of moral codes, norms, or ideologies. Much stress and emphasis is placed on similarities between the animal and human worlds, but an equal amount of emphasis needs to be given to understanding and focusing on that which is different in humans. Recognizing these differences, the symbolic interactionists assume that to un-

---

16. Sheldon Stryker, "Symbolic Interaction as an Approach to Family Research," *Marriage and Family Living* 21 (May 1959), pp. 111–119; Sheldon Stryker, "The Interactional and Situational Approaches," in Harold T. Christensen, ed., *Handbook of Marriage and the Family* (Chicago: Rand McNally, 1964), pp. 134–136; and Sheldon Stryker, "Symbolic Interaction Theory: A Review and Some Suggestions for Comparative Family Research," *Journal of Comparative Family Studies* 3 (Spring 1972), pp. 17–32.

derstand humans one must study humans. Thus very little can be learned about socialization, husbands, wives, children, in-laws, grandparents, or family life-styles of the upper class, the American Indians, or the Amish by studying nonhuman forms.

A second assumption is that *the most fruitful approach to social behavior is through an analysis of society.* One can best understand the behavior of a husband, wife, or child through a study and an analysis of the society and subculture of which they are a part. Personal behavior is not exclusively or even primarily an individual phenomenon but is predominantly a social one. The assumption is not made that society is the ultimate reality, that society has some metaphysical priority over the individual, or that cultural determinism explains all behavior. Neither does it exclude biogenic and psychogenic factors as important in explaining or understanding behavior. However, these factors are not salient variables. They are viewed as constants in a social setting and as random variables in a personality system.

Being born into a given society means that the language one speaks, the definitions one gives to situations, and the appropriateness or inappropriateness of any activity are those learned within a social and cultural context. Thus the behavior of couples from rural areas in the Philippines, who would not be seen holding hands in public, or the behavior of an American couple kissing and necking in a public park can only be understood by analyzing the society in which these behaviors take place.

A third assumption is that *the human infant at birth is asocial.* Original nature lacks organization. The infant is neither social nor antisocial (as with original sin in certain religious organizations or the id within the psychoanalytic scheme). The equipment with which the newborn enters life does, however, have the potential for social development.

It is the society and the social context that determine what type of behavior is social or antisocial. A newborn infant does not cry all night to punish or displease his parents nor does he sleep all night to please them. Only after these expectations become internalized do social or antisocial acts take on meaning. Although the newborn infant has impulses—as does any biological organism—these impulses are not channeled or directed toward any specific ends. But the human infant, having the potential for social development, can, with time and training, organize these impulses and channel them in specific directions. This process, by which the newborn infant becomes a social being, is the main concern of social psychologists, who are interested in the process of socialization, and of family sociologists, who are interested in child rearing.

A fourth assumption is that *a socialized human being,* meaning one who can communicate symbolically and share meanings, *is an actor as well as a reactor.* This does not simply mean that one person acts and another person reacts. The socialized human being does not simply respond to stimuli

from the external environment. Rather, humans respond to a symbolic environment that involves responses to interpreted and anticipated stimuli.

That humans are actors as well as reactors suggests that investigators
cannot understand behavior simply by studying the external environment
and external forces—they must see the world from the viewpoint of the subject
of their investigation. Humans not only respond to stimuli but select and
interpret them. As a result, it becomes crucial and essential that this interpretation and meaning be known. It is this assumption that most precisely differentiates symbolic interactionists from the positivists in sociology and the
behaviorists in psychology.

The assumption that humans are both actor and reactor suggests that
humans alone can take the role of the other—that is, they can view the world
from the perspective of the other person. Thus we can put ourselves in the
"shoes of another person." We feel sad over the misfortune of a friend, we
share the joys of our children even though the experience did not happen to
us. A professor can take the role of the student and anticipate the response
to a three-hour lecture or a certain type of exam without giving either the
lecture or the exam. A wife can anticipate the response of her husband to an
embrace or inviting friends to dinner. The responses of the professor and the
wife may be inaccurate but the perception and the meaning or definition attached to the situation will influence and direct behavior. In short, a person's
behavior is not simply a response to others but is a self-stimulating response: a
response to internal symbolic productions.

The Development of a Social Self

Self is a key concept in understanding socialization and personality.
Self, although often seen in psychological and personal terms, is a social
phenomenon. It is developed in interaction with others. The process of socialization, a primary concern of child rearing, and that which makes humans
social beings is the development of a social self: the organization of internalized roles.

A woman may occupy the statuses of wife, mother, sister, student, executive, Methodist, and many others. Each status has expectations (roles)
assigned to it. A person must know how each role is related to the others. All
these roles need to be organized and integrated into some reasonable, consistent unity. This organization of internalized roles is the *social self*.

This organization of roles and the internalization of them occurs in
interaction with others; the social self is never fixed, static, or in a "final"
state. George Herbert Mead used *self* to mean simply that people are the objects of their own activities; they can act toward themselves as they act toward

Self-Image and the Role of the Disturbed Child

As children grow up and construct the identity they will have as adults, they try on a whole wardrobe full of roles: they tuck up the hem of this one, discard that one as unbecoming, use a part of one they like but throw away the rest. One of the roles a developing child may try on, say Michael Schwartz, Gordon F. N. Fearn, and Sheldon Stryker of Indiana University, is that of the emotionally disturbed child. There is a danger that he may find that this part has its own rewards, and choose it for life (Sociometry, September 1966). If this idea of role selection is valid, it should follow that among children hospitalized for emotional disturbances those who are pleased with themselves as they are will be least likely to recover. As a test, the authors asked 87 children, institutionalized because of their aggressive or violent behavior, to choose the adjective in each of these pairs that described how they felt about themselves: cruel-kind, honest-dishonest, bad-good, clean-dirty, beautiful-ugly, pleasant-unpleasant, gentle-violent, unimportant-important, awful-nice, stupid-smart. Then the children's answers were checked against their therapists' predictions about their futures. It turned out that those children with the most positive self-images (kind, honest, good, and so on) were more likely than the others to have a poor or very poor prognosis. By asking the children to choose adjectives "as you feel your mother [father, best friend, therapist] sees you," the researchers found that self-images of the good prognosis patients was positively correlated with their idea of what their friends thought of them, and not particularly in tune with the opinions they attributed to parents or to therapists. The poor prognosis patients, on the other hand, very strongly rejected the images of their peers and their self-images showed a very strong positive correlation with the image they believe their therapist held. The authors suggest that the good prognosis patients, the ones who will shed the role of "disturbed child" after a while, are somewhat anxious about themselves. (They have not-so-positive self images.) They are attuned to the reflections of themselves coming back from people who aren't playing the "disturbed" game with them—the "best-friends" or non-therapeutic personnel (nurses' aides, janitors) they "tune into" in the hospital.

Source: "Roundup of Current Research," *Trans-Action* 4 (March 1967), p. 3. Reprinted by permission.

others.[17] Thus we can talk to ourselves, be proud of ourselves, be ashamed, or feel guilty.

It does not take much imagination to assess the central role a grandparent, parent, spouse, or sibling, that is, the family, plays in the development of a social self. Who we are, how we feel, what we want, and so on constitute our social self. The animals, infants, and other forms of life who have neither language nor any internalized role definitions have no social self. They cannot take the position of others and cannot view themselves as objects. Neither can they judge past, present, or prospective behavior. Among humans, where the potential exists for sharing meanings, a social self can develop.

17. George Herbert Meade, *Mind, Self and Society* (Chicago: University of Chicago Press, 1934).

*The Significance of Significant Others
and Reference Groups*

Significant others and reference groups are of central importance in understanding the development of the child and the modification of the social self. Not all persons or groups are of equal importance to us. Certain persons and groups, again in processes of interaction, come to be perceived as more important, as more significant, and as a source of reference. These persons and groups with which we psychologically identify are termed respectively, *significant others* and *reference groups*.

To most infants and young children, "mother" is a significant person, that is, an object of emotional involvement, especially in the child's development. However, the mother is not the only significant other, as is seen in the influence of the father, siblings, peers, teachers, athletes, or movie stars. These are persons who are important and with whom one psychologically identifies. To identify with them is to attempt to conform to the expectations one perceives of their having toward oneself. An attempt is made to please and receive approval from those others who are significant.

Louise:	*I think the greatest gift you can give a child is another brother or sister. I've seen it in my own children. It is far better than a room full of toys or endless trips. They entertain each other. A lot of socializing goes on at a peer level. It isn't mother teaching, or mother imposing restrictions on behavior. It's the children monitoring each other, and I've seen it work just beautifully with our foster child. I think the greatest thing we did for the foster child was to bring him into a family where he now has two brothers and two sisters. It is far better than any material things any of our children could have.*
Mac:	*I try to love the two kids of my mate. I'm not their biological father and they can see that. We play together a lot. We work together to keep the house clean, too.*

There are two essential ways in which significant others present themselves: 1) by what they do, and 2) by what they say and how they say it. The doing and saying is organized in terms of roles. Mothers (traditionally at least) change diapers, cook meals, clean houses, offer tenderness, and the like. Fathers leave home for work, read newspapers, complain about bills, watch football games, and so on. As a child or an adult interacts with others, he or she becomes interested in some, attached to others, and shares certain expectations and behaviors with them. Significant others are perceived as role models. Personal behavior and thinking is patterned on the conduct of these persons. Uncle Pete the pilot, Sally the movie star, or Marcia the teacher, as a significant other, may each play a decisive part in the socialization and development of our social self. A brother[18] or the television comedian may too become a role model, a significant other, and a person with whom we psychologically identify.

In addition to persons who are viewed as significant, groups (real or imaginary) are used as a frame of reference with which a person psychologically identifies. These groups are generally termed *reference groups*: any group from which an individual seeks acceptance or uses as a source of comparison. A church, a club, or a company may serve as a point of reference in making comparisons or contrasts, especially in forming judgments about self. In some instances a person may attempt to gain membership or acceptance in the group, although this is not always the case. These groups, like significant others, serve as standards for conduct, as bases for self-evaluation, and as sources of attitude formation.

To most adolescents, peers rather than parents are said to be key groups of reference. They serve many functions once fulfilled by parents. Peers, who understand the adolescent and share his world, become his reference set for sizing up his own problems, strivings, and ambitions. Behavior defined as deviant by parents may be given social approval by peers. Drugs, alcohol, premarital sex, interracial dating, political liberalism, and the like may be conforming behavior to peers. The antisocial behavior of adolescents, as viewed by parents, may simply mean that the adolescent is "in step with a different drummer" (peers). In Chapter 13, a reference-group framework was used to explain an increase in personal sexual permissiveness when the behavior of friends is viewed as permissive. Ira Reiss[19] and James Teevan[20] both noted that the peer reference group is an important determinant of sexual attitudes and that as permissiveness of the peer group increases, sexual permissiveness also increases. Thus reference groups serve as sources of comparison and as influential source of behavioral and attitudinal change for children, youth, or adults.

Socialization Stages and Interaction Processes

The importance of the early years cannot be denied. Very early experiences provide the infant with his first sense of himself, other persons, and social relationships. It is usually the mother who becomes the first, primary, and most significant other. But rather than specific priorities such as breast

---

18. See, for example; Jane H. Pfouts, "The Sibling Relationship: A Forgotten Dimension," *Social Work* 21 (May 1976), pp. 200–204.

19. Ira Reiss, *The Social Context of Premarital Sexual Permissiveness* (New York: Holt, Rinehart and Winston, 1967), p. 139.

20. James J. Teevan, Jr., "Reference Groups and Premarital Sexual Behavior," *Journal of Marriage and the Family* 34 (May 1972), pp. 283–291.

or bottle feeding, or toilet training early or late, the significant dimensions in the socialization process become attention, love, and warmth, or their absence. More important, the nature of the social relationships with mother and others influences the image that the infant or child has of himself. Scolding, slapping, pampering, or praising may not be crucial per se but their repetitive nature leads to the internalization of a sense of self-worth and an image of one's self. Although "mother" is crucial in the development of these images, so are father, siblings, other kin, and friends. Although mother carries out most of the infant-care functions, the socialization experiences of most infants include interaction with other members of the nuclear family, extended family, and others. Since relationships with different persons signify statuses and roles in relation to kin, each provides a unique and different contribution to the socialization process. Each contributes to what Erikson claims is the first issue facing the helpless newborn: that of trust versus distrust.[21]

In the development of the self, Mead postulated that children go through three continuous stages of observation: preparatory, play, and game.[22] In the preparatory stage, children do not have the ability to view their own behavior. Actions of others are imitated. As described under the learning frame of reference and also under the interaction frame of reference, certain sounds like "da-da-da", bring attention and a response from others. This operant conditioning leads the child to repeat and learn the sounds.

The second stage, overlapping with and a continuation of the preparatory stage, is the play stage. At this point, children take the roles of others, that is, they play at being the others whom they observe. They may sweep the floor, put on their hat, and pretend to read a book. Elkin and Handle describe the four-year-old "playing daddy" who put on his hat and coat, said "goodbye," and walked out the front door only to return a few minutes later because he did not know what to do next.[23]

Later, children enter the game stage. At this point, they do not merely play or take the role of another; they now participate in games involving an organization of roles, involving the development of the self. At this point they have to recognize the expected behavior of everyone else. This involves a process of responding to the expectations of several other people at the same time. This is termed the *generalized other*.

> In playing baseball or football, the child must be aware of the possible actions of each of the players. Out of the concrete roles of the particular persons, the child abstracts a composite role for himself. The child, in effect, asks what

---

21. Erikson, op. cit.

22. George H. Mead, *Mind, Self and Society* (Chicago: University of Chicago Press, 1934), p. 150. For a comparison of Piaget and Mead regarding play and games, see Norman K. Denzin, "Play, Games and Interaction: The Contexts of Childhood Socialization," *The Sociological Quarterly* 16 (Autumn 1975), pp. 458–478.

23. Elkin and Handle, op. cit., p. 51.

is expected of him and of others from the generalized standpoint of the team and the game. The same principle applies to any rituals or common tasks which involve collaboration or a division of assignments. Thus on the basis of his group relationships and expectations, he comes to view himself from the position of the group, from what Mead calls the *generalized other*.[24]

The concept of generalized other enables us to understand how given individuals may be consistent in their behavior even though they move in varying social environments. We learn to see ourselves from the standpoint of multiple others who are either physically or symbolically present.

In light of this perspective of socialization, it should be recognized that any behavior results less from drives or needs, less from unconscious processes, and less from biological or innate characteristics than from interaction processes and internalized meanings of self and others. As a result the behavior appropriate to whites or blacks, royalty or outcasts, Jews or gentiles, or male or female is dependent less upon skin color, genital makeup, or biological facts than upon the internalized meanings and definitions that result from interaction with others.

THE SINGLE PARENT AND SOCIALIZATION

In 1974, there were 56.4 million white and 9.5 million black persons under age eighteen in the United States. As can be seen in Table 17–1, 86.7 percent of white and 50.7 percent of black persons were living with both parents. Ten percent of white and 38 percent of black persons were living with mother only. The others were living with the father only (1.2 percent white; 1.8 percent black) or were living with neither parent (1.7 percent white; 9.7 percent black).

While the number of persons in this age group increased slightly between 1960 and 1970 and since 1970 has decreased, the percentage of persons living with mother only has increased sharply for both black (19.8 in 1960; 29.3 in 1970; and 37.8 in 1974) and white (6.1 in 1960; 7.8 in 1970; and 10.4 in 1974). Similar increases have not taken place in the percentages of persons living with father only; however it is of interest that these father-child families have only recently come to the attention of researchers at all. The mother was always the focus of attention, since she gave birth to the child, was primarily responsible for the nurturant socialization responsibilities, was more likely to be a widow than was the husband likely to be a widower, and was generally given legal custody of the children by the courts in cases of divorce and separation. Thus as could be expected, most literature on this topic deals

24. Ibid., p. 35.

Table 17–1. Persons Under Eighteen Years Old, by Presence of
Parents and Whether Living with Mother Only,
by Marital Status of Mother, for the United States: 1974, 1970, and 1960

Presence of parents and marital status of mother	1974		1970[1]		1960	
	White	Negro	White	Negro	White	Negro and Other
All persons under 18[2]—						
thousands	56,437	9,526	59,026	9,483	55,586	8,724
percent	100.0	100.0	100.0	100.0	100.0	100.0
Living with both parents	86.7	50.7	89.2	58.1	90.6	66.6
Living with mother only	10.4	37.8	7.8	29.3	6.1	19.8
Separated	2.8	16.3	1.7	13.6	1.3	9.0
Other married, husband absent	0.8	2.1	1.1	2.6	1.2	2.4
Widowed	1.9	4.9	1.7	4.2	1.7	4.0
Divorced	4.6	6.7	3.1	4.6	1.8	2.4
Single	0.4	7.8	0.2	4.4	0.1	2.0
Living with father only	1.2	1.8	0.9	2.2	1.0	2.0
Living with neither parent	1.7	9.7	2.2	10.3	2.1	11.7

Source: U.S. Bureau of the Census, Current Population Reports, Series P-20, No. 266, "Household and Families, by Type: March, 1974" (Wahington, D.C.: Government Printing Office, 1974), Table 3, p. 4.

1. Revised using population controls based on the 1970 census.
2. Excludes persons under eighteen years old who are heads and wives of heads of families and subfamilies.

with the mother-child unit. Even this literature, rather than dealing with the mother who is present, deals with the father who is absent: the fatherless family. And following an institutionalized sex bias, studies are more likely to be centered on boys than girls in fatherless families. Very little research has been concerned with the effects on the female from the father-absent home. Let us turn our attention briefly to these two single-parent situations: the mother-child family (the father-absent family) and the father-child family (the mother-absent family).

The Father-absent Family

In 1974 nearly 7,000,000 children were in homes without a father present and the number increases yearly. Concurrent with this factor is the widely held view of the American middle class that every child needs a social father. Recently, however, a number of considerations have increased doubts

> *Louise:*   *I think a child needs two parents. Two parents are really very important. When I was growing up, I don't think I knew any single person keeping the child. The child was given up for adoption. That is all that I ever knew. Later, I became aware that there were other ways of doing it, like it's extremely rare for a black family to give up the child. They do seem to be able to raise the child and socialize the child. But again, I also pick up as you move into reasons for truancy, reasons for delinquency, or reasons for serious emotional problems in children, that you go back to the family. And many children never form an identity or know for sure who they are. In other words, I see a gap here. The black culture is saying we can raise our children and do a good job of it, but then as you move along you see that they do have a lot of serious social problems. You go back to the fact that the boy never had a man for a model. In other words, he never had a father, earning a living, acting as a head of a household, making the decisions, doing the things the man does. So the boy never learns how to act as a man.*
>
> *Ann:*   *No, a child must not have two parents. That's not necessary. Where the conflict comes in is where you've got two people living together who are constantly arguing and fussing with each other, this is what causes the problem with the kids. But if it's broken off and he has visiting rights and the children see daddy and the children see mommy and you explain to them what's going on, then they're a lot better by it. It is harder though to make a living.*

that a husband-father is indispensable for the rearing of a child. Among others are included the following:

1. An increasing tolerance regarding extramarital sex relations seems to have led to a reduced condemnation of the illegitimate sexual relationships and its issue.
2. An increasing proportion of mothers in the labor force correspondingly increases the proportion of children whom mothers can maintain and to whom they can confer societal positions.
3. The studies on father-absent families have led to no clear conclusion that fathers are needed for the adequate socialization of children.
4. Increasingly militant advocates of women's rights have denounced sex role differentiation as enslaving women and hence as immoral.[25]

In spite of these doubts about the need for a father in the home, the trend toward more female-headed families remains a matter of national con-

---

25. Robert F. Winch, *The Modern Family*, 3d ed. (New York: Holt, Rinehart and Winston, 1971), pp. 197–198.

cern.[26] Heather Ross and Isabel Sawhill[27] state that these concerns focus on 1) the precarious financial status of female-headed families, almost half of whom are poor, spend some time on welfare, and run a high risk of living under conditions of poverty; 2) the possible effect on children of not having an adult male influence in the home; and 3) the lack of clarity about how public policy has contributed to these changes and the role it could play with respect to this type of family structure.

In regard to the precarious financial status of female-headed families, census data indicate that in 1975 the median money incomes of families with a female head was $6,844. Families with a male head had a median income of more than twice that amount—$14,816.[28] Using the "poverty index" developed by the Social Security Administration, more than one-third (35.3 percent) of all families with a female head were below the low income level—classified in poverty.[29] The social concern about female-headed families increases when it is noted that most of these families are at the poverty level, a majority of female-headed families are on welfare, and women with unstable sources of income feel less able to plan for their lives (fate control).[30]

What happens to children in female-headed families? In a review of studies published during the last two decades, which focused directly on children from fatherless homes, Elizabeth Herzog and Cecilia Sudia examined a core group of sixty studies to check on the assumption that research consistently shows adverse effects associated with fatherless homes. The following statements come from their conclusion section.[31]

The authors raise the basic question as to whether fatherless boys are more prone than others to the problems widely attributed to them and if so, why. They examine three areas in some detail: juvenile delinquency, school achievement, and masculinity. Concerning juvenile delinquency, they said that it seems likely that even if all sources of bias were adequately controlled —including bias in apprehension and treatment of boys from low-income homes—these boys would be somewhat overrepresented among juvenile delinquents. However, it also seems likely that the differences would be dwarfed

26. An excellent treatment of the mother and family unit headed by a woman can be seen in Ruth A. Brandwein, Carol A. Brown, and Elizabeth Maury Fox, "Women and Children Last: The Social Situation of Divorced Mothers and their Families," *Journal of Marriage and the Family* 36 (August 1974), pp. 498–514.

27. Heather L. Ross and Isabel V. Sawhill, *Time of Transition: The Growth of Families Headed by Women* (Washington, D.C., Urban Institute, 1975), pp. 3–4.

28. U.S. Bureau of the Census, *Statistical Abstract of the United States*, 1976, 97th ed. (Washington, D.C., 1976), no. 657, p. 408.

29. Ibid., no. 676, p. 417.

30. Sally Bould, "Female-Headed Families: Personal Fate Control and the Provider Role," *Journal of Marriage and the Family* 39 (May 1977), pp. 339–349.

31. Elizabeth Herzog and Cecilia Sudia, *Boys in Fatherless Families* (U.S. Department of Health, Education, and Welfare, Youth and Child Studies Branch (Washington, D.C., 1970).

by other differences, especially those relating to socioeconomic status and home climate. Differences that did exist could not be directly contributed to father absence: stress and conflict within the home, inability of the mother to exercise adequate supervision, depressed income and living conditions, and community attitudes toward the boy and the family.

With regard to academic performance, it appeared unlikely that father absence in itself showed significant relationship to poorer school achievement if relevant variables (including type of father absence and socioeconomic status) were adequately controlled.

The evidence surrounding masculine identity was found to be so fragmented and so shaky that it was difficult to achieve or to claim judicious perspective. Their efforts yielded a negative conclusion: that the evidence so far available offers no firm basis for assuming that boys who grow up in fatherless homes are more likely, as men, to suffer from an inadequate masculine identity. They state:

> Two conclusions apply to all the areas considered:
>
> 1. The perceptible impact on a boy of growing up in a fatherless home is determined as least as much by elements that are present before and after separation from the father as by father absence in and of itself.
> 2. The impact of father absence on a boy is mediated and conditioned by a complex of interacting variables and probably cannot be explored fruitfully as a discrete critical variable in itself. Two corollaries are:
>   a) That the number of parents in the home is probably less crucial to a child's development than the family functioning of remaining members —which is far harder to determine.
>   b) That family functioning is determined not only by the individual characteristics and interactions of its members, but also by the circumstances and environment of the family unit.[32]

Caution should be taken in determining the importance or influence of the father by studying the outcome in father-absent families. In other words, to conclude that outcomes such as higher delinquency rates, poorer school achievement, or suffering from an inadequate masculine identity can *not* be attributed directly to father absence does not justify the conclusion that fathers are unimportant or do not contribute to the development of the child. Pedersen notes that the father's absence may influence the child directly, and it is likely that his absence influences the mother-child relationship. But it would be impossible to unscramble his relative contribution in the two areas simply from a study of the outcome.[33]

---

32. Ibid., p. 62.
33. Frank A. Pedersen, "Does Research on Children Reared in Father-absent Families Yield Information on Father Influences?" *The Family Coordinator* 25 (October 1976), p. 459–464.

The Mother-Absent Family

The father-child family, like the mother-child family, is usually a result of widowhood, divorce, separation, nonmarriage, and more recently single-parent adoption. Fathers represent about 10 percent of the single-parent population. But studies of this population may prove to be more insightful into child development than mother-child studies in light of the extreme importance placed upon mothers as key agents of socialization. A number of studies have been completed in recent years dealing with this structural arrangement. Let us examine several of them.

In Greensboro, North Carolina, twenty single-parent fathers were interviewed to determine the successes and strains they experience in child rearing, in using compensatory services, and in their own adult life-style.[34] Unlike the poverty-status conditions reported for many mother-child units, the fathers in this study had an average annual income exceeding $18,000. They received custody of their children because their former wives did not want or were unable to care for their children (desertion, mental illness, drug and alcohol abuse, and the like). Almost all of the fathers felt capable and successful in their ability to be the primary parent of their children. Little evidence was found to support the idea of a significant problem with role strain and adjustment. While they expressed concern over their ability to be a nurturing parent, these concerns appeared similar to those of most parents.

In southern California, thirty-two single fathers were interviewed to determine their attitudes, feelings, and conflicts about their experiences.[35] Their mean income was $12,500 with only three families with income below the poverty threshold. Although the majority of the fathers hired others to supervise their preschool children, many no longer did so when the children began to attend school. There was a notable lack of help from the extended family. Most of the fathers regularly cooked, cleaned, shopped, and managed their own homes. The adjustment of these fathers to their role appeared to be directly related to whether the father initially had chosen to become a single parent or whether it was forced upon them. Those who did not want to assume the role had severe problems in their relationship with the children.

While both the size and the lack of representativeness of the samples raise serious questions about the two studies just cited, it would appear that single fathers have access to greater resources and perhaps adjust better than single mothers to the one-parent situation. Whether this would be supported in other studies is not known. A third study indicated that difficulties in

34. Dennis K. Orthner, Terry Brown, and Dennis Ferguson, "Single-parent Fatherhood: An Emerging Family Life Style." *The Family Coordinator* 25 (October 1976), pp. 429–437.

35. Helen A. Mendes, "Single Fatherhood," *Social Work* (July 1976), p. 308–312; and Helen A. Mendes, "Single Fathers," *The Family Coordinator* 25 (October 1976), pp. 439–444.

home management as single parents appeared to stem more from the over-burdening of roles than from unfamiliarity with the tasks facing them.[36]

Too few studies exist at this point on mother-absent families to come to definite conclusions; however, it does seem clear that just as a two-parent family does not guarantee happiness, adjustment and well-behaved children, neither does a one-parent family signify the opposite. Nor are the findings reported meant to imply that the absence of a father or a mother has no effect whatever. Paul Glasser and Elizabeth Navarre, for example, note some of the structural problems of the one-parent family.[37] Such families are much less flexible in providing for physical, emotional, and social needs of the family. There are definite limitations on time and energy for the fulfillment of various tasks. In addition, the communication structure is modified consider-ably. Since children see much of the adult world through the eyes of their parents, the loss of one parent is likely to produce a structural distortion. In regard to the power structure, with one parent it is impossible for the child to play one adult against the other. This situation may also create certain prob-lems in adjusting to the parent of the opposite sex. In terms of affectional support, the danger of the one-parent family is that the demands of one to fulfill the needs ordinarily met in marriage by two may prove intolerable to the solitary parent, with the result being physical and emotional exhaustion. It is not only the one-parent family, however, that produces structural dis-tortions. Note the effect of the two-parent family and the mass media on sex role socialization.

GENDER IDENTITY AND SEX ROLE SOCIALIZATION

Who would deny there are physical differences between males and females? Probably none. But who among us would argue that differences in the behavior of males and females are rooted in the genes, in the innate, in the hormones, in the biological, or in the anatomy? Probably some would, others wouldn't be so sure, and still others would deny it forcefully. Maybe all three groups are partially correct. For centuries, it was assumed that male-female differences in behavior were inborn or "natural." Females had "ma-ternal instincts" and were submissive; males were aggressive and dominant. More recently, certain social scientists—particularly anthropologists who dis-covered societies where men are passive and women domineering—ques-tioned any relevance of biological factors in behavior. They argued that all

36. Rita D. Gasser and Claribel M. Taylor, "Role Adjustment of Single Parent Fathers with Dependent Children," *The Family Coordinator* 25 (October 1976), pp. 397–401.
37. Paul Glasser and Elizabeth Navarre, "Structural Problems of the One-parent Family," *The Journal of Social Issues* 21 (January 1965), pp. 98–109.

Brother Becomes Sister; The Alteration of Masculine-Feminine Behavior

A young rural couple took their identical twin boys to a physician to be circumcised. During the first operation, performed with an electric cauterizing needle, a surge of current burned off the baby's penis. Desperate for a way to cope with this tragedy, the parents took the advice of sex experts: "Bring the baby up as a girl." The experiment has apparently succeeded. Aided by plastic surgery and reared as a daughter, the once normal baby boy has grown into a nine-year old child who is psychologically, at least, a girl.

This dramatic case, cited by Medical Psychologist John Money at the Washington meeting of the American Association for the Advancement of Science, provides strong support for a major contention of women's liberationists: that conventional patterns of masculine and feminine behavior can be altered. It also casts doubt on the theory that major sexual differences, psychological as well as anatomical, are immutably set by the genes at conception. In fact, say Money, there are only four imperative differences: women menstruate, gestate and lactate; men impregnate. Many scientists believe that crucial psychological imperatives follow from these biological facts, limiting the flexibility of sexual roles. Money, however, is convinced that almost all differences are culturally determined and therefore optional. The Johns Hopkins psychologist further spells out his views on sex-role learning in a book titled: Man & Woman, Boy & Girl.

In the normal process of sexual differentiation, Money explains, if the genes order the gonads to become testes and to produce androgen, the embryo develops as a boy; otherwise it becomes a girl. Androgen not only shapes the external genitals but also "programs" parts of the brain, so that some types of behavior may come more naturally

to one sex than to the other. For instance, both men and women can mother children— the necessary circuits are there in every brain —but the "threshold" for releasing this behavior is higher in males than in females. The same phenomenon is demonstrated by laboratory animals. If a mature female rat is put into a cage with newborn rats, she begins mothering them at once. In a similar situation, a male rat does nothing at first, but after a few days he too begins to display maternal behavior.

Money believes that hormones secreted before and after birth have less effect on brain and behavior in human beings than the "sex assignment" that takes place at birth with the announcement: "It's a boy!" or "It's a girl!" This exultant cry tells everyone how to treat the newborn baby, and sets off a chain of events, beginning with the choice of a male or female name, that largely determines whether the child will behave in traditionally masculine or feminine ways.

Money's evidence for this familiar thesis comes largely from cases in which accidents before or after birth made it impossible to raise children according to their genetically determined sex. In each of his examples, youngsters learned to feel, look and act like members of the opposite sex.

For the little boy who lost his penis, the change began at 17 months with a girl's name and frilly clothes. An operation to make the child's genitals look more feminine was done, and plans were made to build a vagina and administer estrogen at a later age. The parents, counseled at the Johns Hopkins psychohormonal research unit, began to treat the child as if he were a girl. The effects of the parents' changed attitude and behavior were marked. "She doesn't like to be dirty," the mother told the clinic in one of her periodic *reports. "My son is quite different. I can't wash his face for anything. She seems to be daintier. Maybe it's because I encourage it. She is very proud of herself when she puts on a new dress, and she just loves to have her hair set."*

The experience of two hermaphrodites, from different families, further bolsters Money's view. Each was born with the female chromosome pattern, and each had internal female organs but a penis and empty scrotum outside. One set of parents believed they had a boy and raised their child accordingly; the

other set assigned their offspring as a girl. (Surgery and hormones made the youngsters' appearance conform to the chosen sex.) According to Money, the children's "antithetical experiences signified to one that he was a boy and to the other that she was a girl." The girl therefore reached preadolescence expecting to marry a man; in fact, she already had a steady boy friend. The boy, by contrast, had a girl friend and "fitted easily into the stereotype of the male role in marriage," even though "he and his partner would both have two X chromosomes."

Source: *Time Magazine,* January 8, 1973, p. 34. Reprinted by permission from TIME, The Weekly Newsmagazine. Copyright Time Inc.

behavior was learned. While this author tends to lean more toward the latter position, the most accurate answer probably lies between the two positions and is far more complex than suggested by a nature or nurture, biology or culture argument.

The argument for the biological is deeply rooted in a number of theories of socialization including the psychoanalytic frame of reference discussed earlier in this chapter. It is further enhanced by research into hormones (such as progesterone and estrogen secreted by the ovaries in females and testosterone and the androgens secreted by the testes in males) that initiate sexual differentiation in the fetus and later at puberty activate the reproductive system and the development of secondary sex characteristics. Research has shown that if a female fetus is given testosterone, she will develop male-like genitalia. If a male is castrated (testes removed) prior to puberty, he will not develop secondary sex characteristics such as a beard. But do these chemical substances known generally as hormones influence behavior?

The strength of cultural factors is overwhelming in our understanding of gender identity and sex role socialization. One prime example comes from cross-cultural data that has shown great diversity in the attitudes, values, and behavior of both men and women. Margaret Mead's classic study of three primitive tribes in New Guinea found both men and women among the Arapesh to be cooperative, mild-mannered, gentle, and unaggressive (sex-typed feminine behavior). Among the Mundugumor, both men and women were hostile, aggressive, combative, individualistic, and unresponsive (sex-typed masculine behavior). Among the Tchambuli the typical sex roles found in the western cultures were reversed: women dominant, powerful, and impersonal; men emotionally dependent and less responsible.[38] If it can be assumed

---

38. Margaret Mead, *Sex and Temperament in Three Primitive Societies* (New York: Morrow, 1935; Mentor, 1950).

that the biological makeup and hormonal balance of men and women in these three tribes and men and women in the western world are similar, then how is the behavior difference explained?

Another, and even more convincing line of research comes from studies of hermaphrodites, persons who possess complete sets of both male and female genitalia and reproductive organs. Infants who were assigned one sex at birth and were later found to belong biologically to the opposite sex, behaved as they were assigned and taught. Biological females, defined and reared as males, grew up developing fantasies of males, enjoyed sports assigned generally to males, fell in love with girls, and the like. Biological males, defined and reared as females, had the "maternal instinct," preferred marriage over a career, and were oriented toward dolls and domestic tasks.[39] Thus when socialization contradicts the biological, hormonal, or genetic, the learned and interactional experiences prove to be powerful determinants of current gender roles (see "Brother Becomes Sister" insert).

As each frame of reference described earlier would suggest, socialization to gender (male-female) roles begins at birth and continues throughout ones lifetime.[40] As Weitzman indicates "from the minute a newborn baby girls is wrapped in a pink blanket and her brother in a blue one, the two children are treated differently."[41] From that point on, socialization as to appropriate roles for males and females constitutes one of life's most important learning experiences. The decade of the 1970s brought with it a renewed urgency in the study of gender roles with the central theme that socialization of both sexes into fixed roles occurs at great cost to individual needs.

There is little doubt that children learn about gender roles very early in their lives, certainly long before they enter school. One study reported that by the time boys and girls are four, they realize that the primary feminine role is housekeeping while the primary masculine role is wage earning.[42] Another study by the same author indicated that eight-year-old boys described girls as clean, neat, quiet, gentle, and fearful, while they described adult women as unintelligent, ineffective, unadventurous, nasty, and exploitative.[43] A third study by Joan Aldous indicated that low-income white and black preschool children have a knowledge of conventional adult sex assignment despite father absence and role reversals in their own families. The cost of this knowledge of adult

39. John Money, *Sex Research: New Developments* (New York: Holt, Rinehart, 1965).
40. Orville G. Brim Jr., "Socialization through the Life Cycle," in *Socialization after Childhood* (New York: Wiley, 1966), pp. 3–49; Rhoda E. Estep, Martha R. Bunt, and Herman J. Milligan, "The Socialization of Sexual Identity," *Journal of Marriage and the Family* 39 (February 1977), pp. 99–112.
41. Lenore J. Weitzman, "Sex-Role Socialization," in Jo Freeman, ed., *Women: A Feminist Perspective* (Palo Alto, Calif.: Mayfield, 1975), p. 108.
42. Ruth E. Hartley, "Children's Concepts of Male and Female Roles," *Merrill-Palmer Quarterly* 6 (1960), pp. 83–91.
43. Ruth E. Hartley, "Sex-Role Pressures and the Socialization of the Male Child," *Psychological Reports* 5 (1959), pp. 457–468.

sex assignment is clearly seen in her study.[44] That is, discrepancies resulted between the expectations—that father should be the breadwinner—and the reality—that restricted job opportunities prevented the unemployed father from living up to these expectations. Aldous claims that the roots of parent-child and marital conflict in lower-class life lie in the very early socialization learnings of children.[45]

A niece of the author theorized and supported empirically the idea that American society sex-types dependent behavior in girls and independent behavior in boys.[46] Simultaneously promoted was the greater probability of more males internalizing a self-defined identity and of more females being totally "other-defined"—that is, of females who identified themselves primarily by the dependence relationships (for example, "wife of, mother of . . ."). The American female was seen as a product of a "generalized-dependency socialization," wherein she was not particularly encouraged to grow into leadership, responsibility, and decision-making roles of great consequence. More often, she was nurtured and mentally "conditioned" throughout childhood and adolescence to eventually emerge submissively with the traditional other-defined female role. Thus socialization for generalized dependency hindered the achievement of identity defined exclusive of others. Whether or not the female even perceived the attitude of such an external influence nurturing her other-dependence, she was, as a general rule, exposed to such an environment.

The socialization of sexual roles follows the same general processes of socialization. In interaction with others, in words, deeds, films, and books, the child is taught what behavior is appropriate for each sex. As one writer indicated, "We throw boy babies up in the air and roughhouse with them. We coo over girl babies and handle them delicately. We choose sex-related colors and toys for our children from their earliest days. We encourage the energy and physical activity of our sons, just as we expect girls to be quieter and more docile. We love both our sons and daughters with equal fervor, we protest, and yet we are disappointed when there is no male child to carry on the family name.[47] In regard to relative status, boys are more highly valued than girls. In regard to personality differences, most boys are active and achieving whereas most girls are passive and emotional.

Lenore Weitzman and others concentrated on one aspect of sex-role

---

44. Joan Aldous, "Children's Perceptions of Adult Role Assignment: Father-Absence, Class, Race and Sex Influences," *Journal of Marriage and the Family* 34 (February 1972), pp. 55–65.

45. Ibid., p. 64.

46. Suzanne Eshleman, "Sex Differences in the Relationship of Maternal Socialization to Adolescent Dependency and Achievement Behaviors," unpublished M.A. thesis, Cornell University, 1971, pp. 2–3.

47. Florence Howe, "Sexual Stereotypes Start Early," *Saturday Review* (October 16, 1971), p. 76.

Sex Stereotypes Hurt

Richmond, Va.—(UPI)—Researchers at Virginia Commonwealth University have concluded that one reason boys underachieve in elementary school may be due to sexual stereotypes and the predominance of women teachers.

Dr. Joseph J. Crowley, director of the school's psychological services center, and Dr. Sally B. Canestrari said sexual stereotypes may prevent male children from associating with feminine words and concepts.

While boys and girls score equally well on IQ tests, educators and researchers have found that boys do not learn as quickly or as much as girls in elementary school.

Crowley said the difference is frequently written off by educators as evidence that boys do not mature as quickly as girls. He said, however, that in non-English speaking countries there is no noticeable difference in achievement between the sexes. He said there are as many male teachers in European elementary schools as there are women teachers.

The two researchers made their conclusions from a study conducted last spring in which 72 children in grades one through three were tested on the speed with which they learned words having feminine, masculine and neutral connotations.

Crowley said the girls in the test group learned the words quickly without differentiating between the categories. The boys learned the masculine words easily, but had trouble learning the feminine words.

"This suggests that boys in the early years don't learn things that remind them of femininity," Crowley said. "This is a real handicap since children seem to associate school with women, probably since most elementary schools are primarily staffed by women."

Crowley said boys are more strictly confined to their sexual roles than little girls.

"For instance, girls can get away with being tomboys and still be considered feminine," he said. "They can play baseball or they can play with dolls. They can wear slacks or they can wear dresses. Boys, on the other hand, can only be boys."

Crowley said he believes that because the male role is so narrowly defined for little boys, "they shun feminine things, and we think, based on our research, this includes school."

Source: *Detroit Free Press*, November 5, 1976, p. 6-C. Reprinted by permission of UPI.

socialization: the socialization of preschool children through picture books.[48] They chose eighteen children's books identified as "the very best": the winners of the Caldecott medal, given by the Children's Service Committee of the American Library Association for the most distinguished picture book of the year. Their analysis was concentrated on winners and runners-up for the past five years. To ensure representativeness of the study, the authors examined three other groups of children's books: the Newberry award winners, the Little Golden Books, and the "prescribed behavior or etiquette books." Their findings make interesting reading. They note that it would be impossible to

---

48. Lenore J. Weitzman, Deborah Eifler, Elizabeth Hokada, and Catherine Ross, "Sex-Role Socialization in Picture Books for Preschool Children," *American Journal of Sociology* 77 (May 1972), pp. 1125–1150.

And What Do You Want To Be When You Grow Up?

The only academic area that boys call their own is science. Science is their "thing," they say, and girls tend to agree. Reading, music and art, however, are for girls, and both sexes agree on that too. Social studies are for both.

Such, at any rate, seems to be the general opinion of more than 400 boys and girls in grades 4–6 at a suburban New York public school. This gross sex-typing of academic subjects by children is the discovery of Carol Bobbe who published her findings in a doctoral thesis at Yeshiva University in New York this year.

Mrs. Bobbe gave the children a list of activities, or things children do, "getting good marks in arithmetic" for example. Under each item the children were asked to circle one response: "B" for "boys usually do it," "G" for girls, and "BG" for both.

The children's preferences were also plumbed. If, for example, a child liked to "do arithmetic examples," he or she would circle the letter "L," if not, the letter "D." Mrs. Bobbe found that "children tended to prefer those areas [they judged] to be sexually appropriate." However, after comparing the children's actual performance in these sex-typed areas with their preferences, she found no correlation at all.

Incidentally, the only subject on which the girls and boys disagreed as to which sex it was "for" is arithmetic. The boys said it was for girls and boys; the girls said it was for themselves. Perhaps gallantry isn't dead after all.

Source: "Roundup of Current Research," *Trans-Action*, 8 (September 1971), p. 20. Reprinted by permission.

discuss the image of females in children's books without first noting that, in fact, women are simply invisible. They found females underrepresented in the titles, central roles, pictures, and stories in every sample of books examined. Most children's books were about boys, men, and male animals, and most dealt exclusively with male adventures. Where there were female characters, they were usually insignificant or inconspicuous.

What were the activities of boys and girls in the world of picture books? Weitzman et al. found that not only were boys presented in more exciting and adventuresome roles, but they engaged in more varied pursuits and demanded more independence.[49] In contrast, most of the girls in the picture books were passive and immobile. Girls were more often found indoors than were boys. The girls in the stories played traditional feminine roles directed toward pleasing and helping their brothers and fathers.

Most books clearly implied that women cannot exist without men. That is, the role of most of the girls was defined primarily in relation to that of the boys and men in their lives and was not defined primarily in relation to girls working or playing together.

What about adult role models? Weitzman's study found the image of the adult women to be stereotyped and limited.[50] Again, the females were

49. Ibid., pp. 1131–1138.
50. Ibid., pp. 1139–1144.

passive while the males were active. Men predominated the outside activities and women the inside ones. While inside, the women performed almost exclusively service functions, taking care of the men and children in their families. When men lead, women follow. When men rescue others, women are the rescued.

One interesting finding was that not one woman in the Caldecott sample had a job or profession. Motherhood was presented in the picture books as a full-time, lifetime job, despite the reality that about 90 percent of the women in this country will be in the labor force at sometime in their lives and that the average woman has completed the main portion of her child rearing by her mid-thirties. Most of the stories portrayed the woman as a mother or a wife, although she also played the role of fairy, fairy godmother, or underwater maiden. The roles that men played were highly varied: storekeepers, housebuilders, kings, spiders, storytellers, gods, monks, fighters, fisherman, policeman, soldiers, adventurers, fathers, cooks, preachers, judges, and farmers.[51]

The authors suggest that not only do narrow role definitions impede the child's identification with his same-sex parent, but these rigid sex role distinctions may be harmful to the normal personality development of the child. They discourage and restrict a women's potential and offer her fulfillment only through the limited spheres of glamour and service. In the authors' view, the simplified and stereotyped images in these books present such a narrow view of reality that they violate the child's own knowledge of a rich and complex role.[52]

SOCIALIZATION IN ADOLESCENCE AND AFTER

Most books on socialization, most chapters on child rearing, and the greatest public interest in both, focus generally on the young child. Perhaps this is readily understandable since, to the newborn child, the entire world is new. Even the most common and routine events must be learned. But if socialization is role learning, if socialization refers to learning the ways of a given society and culture, and if socialization means the development of members who are capable of operating in society, then how can anyone argue that socialization is complete after five or six years of life? Particularly in a rapidly changing society such as exists in the United States, persons are newcomers to unfamiliar events almost daily. Without a doubt, early socialization experiences will have a major influence and impact on the types of events and

51. Ibid., pp. 1140–1141.
52. Ibid., p. 1147.

experiences that are acceptable or unacceptable. But socialization is a continuous process, and learning experiences after the early years not only mean incorporating the new but discarding much of the old.

It is a rare society in which the individual can be prepared during childhood for the complex roles that are essential to know at a later time. This in no way denies the fundamental importance of socialization experiences in the childhood years but only asserts that role learning is a continuous process. The emphasis placed on education at the junior high, high school, and college levels represents formalized attempts at changing adolescents' perceptions about the world in which they live.

James Coleman's study of adolescents in ten high schools clearly documents the extent to which key socializing agents shift from the home to "outsiders."[53] Peers rather than parents become important reference figures for high school youth. During the teen years, the school and the peer group are powerful and pervading forces in the socialization of the adolescent. Learning processes similar to those in early childhood are in operation. The adolescent is actively engaged in sex role identification, learning the norms and expectations of the opposite sex, participating in new and different types of social activities, gaining insights and skills for the future occupational world, attempting to become emancipated from parents, and developing a new sense of self-reliance. Many studies indicate clearly the significance of socialization during the adolescent years.[54]

Socialization does not end at adolescence, but when attention shifts from adolescent to postadolescent socialization, the available data drop considerably. In comparison with the data on infants, school-age children, and adolescents, the available research data on adult socialization, even at a descriptive level, are minimal. The next chapter examines the family during the middle and later years and includes a brief selection on the socialization of the aged.

Summary

The central concept in dealing with parent-child relationships is socialization —the process by which the infant and adult learn the ways of a given society and culture and develop into participants capable of operating in that society.

53. James S. Coleman, *The Adolescent Society* (Glencoe, Ill.: Free Press, 1962).

54. See for example, Coleman, op. cit., David Gottlieb and Charles Ramsey, *The American Adolescent* (Homewood, Ill.: Dorsey, 1964); Elizabeth Douvan and Joseph Adelson, *The Adolescent Experience* (New York: Wiley, 1966); Edgar Friedenberg, *The Vanishing Adolescent* (New York: Darrell, 1959); and Jesse Bernard "Teen-age Culture," *Annals of the American Academy of Political and Social Science* 338 (1961), entire issue; and "American Adolescents in the Mid-Sixties," *Journal of Marriage and the Family* 27 (May 1965), entire issue.

Socialization of the young infant may be the single universal function of the family. Preconditions for socialization include an ongoing society, biological inheritance, and human nature.

Several frames of reference are examined to explain various aspects of socialization: a learning-behaviorist, a psychoanalytic, two child development, and a symbolic-interactionist. Learning or reinforcement theory assumes that the same concepts and principles that apply to lower animal forms apply to humans. The conditioning processes may be classical or operant. The former links a response to a known stimulus, the latter links a response to the consequence produced by the response. Child-rearing and socialization processes result from conditioning and positive or negative reinforcements.

The classical psychoanalytic theory contrasts sharply with the behaviorist theory. Internal drives and unconscious processes are of central importance. Socialization takes place according to precise, though overlapping, stages of development. These include the oral, anal, and phallic, followed later by a period of latency and genital phase. What happens in these early stages from birth to age five or six, although unconscious, becomes relatively fixed and permanent, serving as the basis for responses in later life.

Child development theories focus on the individual and the manner in which motor skills, thought, and reason develop. Erikson described eight stages of human development, each constituting a crisis brought on by changing social situations as the individual moves from infancy through old age. Piaget focused more on the cognitive development of the child and described four major stages of intellectual development.

The symbolic-interaction theory contrasts considerably with all theories described. Infants, who are not born social, develop through interaction with other persons. As interaction occurs, meanings are internalized and organized and the self develops. The social self enables a person to consciously and purposively represent to himself what he wishes to represent to others. A social being can take the role of others, can interpret and define, and can have and use symbols. In interaction with others, the child learns to define himself and the world in certain ways. These definitions and meanings in turn predispose him to behave in ways consistent with these self-concepts. Interaction, the social self, significant others, reference groups, the generalized other, and other central concepts are basic to the socialization process.

Interaction patterns are also basic to understanding the single parent and socialization. It is not the biological two-parent situation per se that appears to be so crucial but rather available socializing agents or models who can represent the missing parent. This may help explain why a review of studies over two decades on children from fatherless homes showed little effect on juvenile delinquency, school achievement, or masculinity. Far less frequently studied but equally significant is an understanding of the mother-absent family.

In dealing with sex-role socialization, studies leave little doubt that children learn at an early age what roles are appropriate to their sex. Females learn to be dependent on others, to be housekeepers, and to perceive males as leaders and wage earners. Males internalize similar expectations as perceived by the females and view females much as the female views herself. The world of children's picture books illustrates clearly the ways in which our society stereotypes sex roles. This sex-typing may have negative consequences for the normal personality development of the child.

Socialization does not end in childhood. At every age and stage of the life cycle, new expectations and norms must be learned and old ones modified. This idea is further examined in the following chapter as we continue our progression through the family life cycle. Next, a glimpse at families in the middle and later years.

Key Terms and Topics

Discussion Questions

1. *Discuss ways in which parents need to be socialized. What role does the infant play in this process?*
2. *Review the preconditions for adequate socialization. What would happen if any of them were absent? Would socialization be possible? Why or why not?*
3. *What do you perceive to be the most important factors in the producing of stable, healthy adults?*
4. *Contrast the learning-behaviorist, the psychoanalytic, the child development, and the symbolic-interaction frames of reference in regard to socialization. What are the contributions each makes. What are some of the drawbacks of each?*
5. *Take a pencil and paper to a nearby park, a preschool setting, or somewhere where you can observe the interaction between adults (preferably a parent) and children. Record what is said and done for a five- or ten-*

minute period. What inferences can you draw about social class, language patterns, child-rearing practices, discpline, and the like?

6. *Interview three mothers of preschool children. Find out whether the arrival of their first child was a crisis; whether they toilet-trained their babies early, breast-fed or bottle-fed them, etc., and whether they believe it makes any difference; what means of punishment they use; what role the father plays in child rearing; how other children assist or hinder the socialization process; and so forth.*

7. *In what ways and areas are you being socialized? To what extent are you a victim of early childhood experiences, a father-absent family, a lower-class background, or a home with marital conflict? When will you be "fully" socialized?*

8. *How do you explain the minimal overall negative effects of the father-absent family? Does this mean fathers are unimportant? What advantages and disadvantages exist in a father-child family over a mother-child family?*

9. *Reviewing variant marital and family life-styles of earlier chapters, discuss the effect of these styles on child rearing, for example, communes, plural spouses, dual-career marriages, affiliated families, and others.*

10. *Is gender identity important? Is it possible to rear a child to become "human" without an emphasis on maleness or femaleness?*

11. *Examine ways in which literature (magazines, newspapers, novels, and others) sex-type males and females. Do the same for TV shows, commercials, or movies. Is it possible to eliminate or even change this practice? How?*

12. *Examine elementary textbooks and storybooks. What type of "family life education" is offered? How are male and female roles portrayed? Analyze the occupational roles, family roles, and authority patterns of each.*

Further Readings

Chafetz, Janet Saltzman. *Masculine/Feminine or Human?* Itasca, Ill.: F. E. Peacock, 1974. A paperback designed for undergraduates that attempts to delineate the parameters of the sociology of sex role field.

Dager, Edward Z., ed. *Socialization.* Chicago: Markham, 1971. Paperback of ten articles covering socialization and social control, socialization theory and research, and change and resocialization.

Davis, Kingsley, "The Sociology of Parent-Child Conflict." *American Sociological Review* 5 (August 1940), pp. 523–535. Although published several decades ago, this classic paper on parent-child conflict is still widely reprinted today.

Duberman, Lucile. *Gender and Sex in Society.* New York: Praeger, 1975. Chapter 2 in particular deals with socialization; however, the entire book examines gender roles in a race, class, employment, and a cross-cultural perspective.

"Ecology of Child Development." *Proceedings of the American Philosophical Society* 119 (December 1975). An issue containing five key articles on childhood and human development in a familial and social context.

Elkin, Frederick, and **Gerald Handel.** *The Child and Society: The Process of Socialization.* 2d ed.: New York: Random, 1972. A coherent treatment, from a sociological standpoint, of how children are socialized into modern society.

Eshleman, J. Ross, and **Juanne N. Clarke.** *Intimacy, Commitments, and Marriage: Development of Relationships.* Boston: Allyn and Bacon, 1978. Part II—"Becoming a Human Being"—includes chapters on gender identity and development, sex role socialization, and socialization and child-rearing patterns.

"Fatherhood." *The Family Coordinator* 25 (October 1976). A special issue of twenty-two articles dealing with fatherhood, including an extensive bibliography of literature related to roles of fathers.

Lindesmith, Alfred R., Anselm L. Strauss, and **Norman K. Denzin.** *Social Psychology.* 4th ed. Hinsdale, Ill.: Dryden Press, 1975. One of the major social psychology textbooks that approaches socialization and interaction quite exclusively from the symbolic-interaction frame of reference.

Lynn, David B. *The Father: His Role in Child Development.* Belmont, Calif.: Wadsworth, 1974. A comprehensive examination of the father role. Part I looks at father in a cultural context. Part II looks at fathers in relation to mothers, sex roles, child rearing, and their absence.

Ross, Heather C., and **Isabel V. Sawhill.** *Time of Transition: The Growth of Families Headed by Women.* Washington, D.C.: Urban Institute, 1975. An extensive analysis of families headed only by a female parent, showing their unprecedented rate of increase potential of an absent father, and the role public policy has played.

Stoll, Clarice Stasz. *Female and Male: Socialization, Social Roles, and Social Structure.* Dubuque, Iowa: Wm. C. Brown, 1974. A brief paperback dealing with sexism, becoming, being, and coping with being female and male and the politics of gender.

Tomeh, Aida K. *The Family and Sex Roles.* Toronto: Holt, Rinehart and Winston of Canada, 1975. A paperback attempting to bring together cross-cultural studies in sex role behavior, women, and family structures.

Walters, James, and **Nick Stinnett.** "Parent-Child Relationships: A Decade of Research." *Journal of Marriage and the Family* 33 (February 1971), pp. 70–111. An interdisciplinary review of approximately 200 studies from 1960–1970.

18

*Marriage and the Family in the
Middle and Later Years*

18

Chapter 16 and 17 examined some selected aspects of the family with children. But marriage and family life do not end when children enter adolescence or, in later adolescence, when the children leave home for marriage, employment, school, military service, or some other reason. Family structure, interactions, and life-styles change considerably at this period of the family life cycle: the second half. A prime example of this change was shown in Chapter 15 in dealing with marital satisfaction over the life cycle. Studies indicated a process of disenchantment and a decrease in satisfaction at this time, followed by increases in the later years.

It is the intent of this chapter to examine two major periods in the life cycle: the middle years from approximately age forty to retirement and the later years from approximately age sixty or sixty-five. This includes general descriptions of families at these periods plus a consideration of the employed wife, grandparents, retirement, socialization of the aged, and social conditions and problems surrounding the aged.

THE POSTPARENTAL PERIOD: THE MIDDLE YEARS

In order to capture the experience of the period after children leave home, a number of phases have been used. Among others are the "stage of the empty nest," the "launching stage," the period of "contracting family size," and the term used here, the "postparental." This period of family life is outlined by Wayne Thompson and Gordon Streib as including 1) the family of late maturity: age 45–54; 2) the family of preretirement: age 56–64; 3) the family of early retirement: age 65–74; and 4) the family of late retirement: age

TABLE 18–1. Marital Status of Men and Women, Age 45–64.
March 1976, Percentage Distribution

	Age of Men		Age of Women	
Marital Status	45–54	55–64	45–54	55–64
Single	5.6	5.6	4.4	4.9
Married	84.5	83.2	77.3	67.4
Separated	3.2	2.7	4.0	3.2
Widowed	1.5	3.7	7.2	19.1
Divorced	5.2	4.8	7.1	5.4
Total	100.0	100.0	100.0	100.0

Source: U.S. Bureau of the Census, *Current Population Reports*, Series P-20, no. 306, "Marital Status and Living Arrangements: March, 1976" (Washington, D.C.: U.S. Government Printing Office, 1977), Table 1, p. 9.

75 and after.[1] This section examines the family of late maturity and the family of preretirement, an age period of from approximately 45–65.

Marital Status and Length of the Middle Years

Of those persons in this age period in 1976, about 85 percent of the men and 70 percent of the women were married (see Table 18–1). Compared with other age categories, the percentage married is high with relatively low percentages of single, separated, widowed, or divorced. For women, the percentage who are widowed begins to climb sharply at ten-year intervals after age 54. The figures change from 7 percent (age 45–54) to 19 percent (age 55–64), 42 percent (age 65–74), and 70 percent (age 75 and over).[2]

The period after the children leave home lasts longer than any other stage in the marital life cycle. Interestingly, this factor is unique to the twentieth century. At the turn of the century, men married at age 26, had their last child at age 36, saw their last child marry at age 59, but lost their spouses at age 57. Women married at age 22, had their last child at 32, saw their last child married at 55, and lost their spouses at 53.[3] The result for both sexes was no postparental period, since the typical or average couple survived two

1. Wayne E. Thompson and Gordon F. Streib, "Meaningful Activity in a Family Context," *Social and Psychological Aspects of Aging* (New York: Columbia University Press, 1962), pp. 905–912.
2. The first two figures were taken from Table 18–1. The last two were taken from Table 18–2 presented later in the chapter.
3. Figures taken from Paul C. Glick, "The Life Cycle of the Family," *Marriage and Family Living* 17 (1955), pp. 3–9.

years short of the time their last child (which on the average was their fifth) was expected to marry.

In contrast today, both sexes marry in their early twenties, have their last child in their mid-to-late twenties, see their last child marry in their mid-to-late forties, but do not lose their spouses until close to age seventy. The result is a postparental period of eighteen to twenty years. Since marriage occurs earlier, with children thus born earlier, and since children are fewer in number, parents gain an earlier release from child rearing. These factors, combined with a longer life span for both sexes, give the average couple several decades together prior to retirement or the death of one spouse.

The Significance of the Middle Years

To many couples, the middle years are the "prime of life" with predictable crises.[4] Business and professional men in particular are likely to hold their top positions and earn their maximum income during this period.[5] Robert Havighurst reports that a Paris newspaper held an essay contest with the title "The Best 10 Years of Life." The Frenchman who won the prize said the best ten years were from fifty to sixty. The reasons he gave were:

1. A man's daughters, if he has them, are married off and their dowries paid.
2. A man's business competitors are either too old to be effective, or too young to be experienced.
3. Inherited wealth has come, if there is to be any.
4. A man can really enjoy his leisure-time interests.[6]

The significance of the early postparental years appears to be much more social and psychological than physical although, particularly for women, many writers believe otherwise. As the author stated in an earlier work,

> What a coincidence that menopause or the cessation of menstruation occurs at the time the children are being launched from the home. The pain caused by the loss of "my babies" can find a socially approved means of expression in the hot flushes, or perhaps flashes, headaches, and digestive disturbances. Any increase in irritability or depression can be more readily attributed to the "change of life" than to the loss of family members.[7]

---

4. A fascinating account of the years between 18 and 50 can be seen in Gail Sheehy, *Passages: Predictable Crises of Adult Life* (New York: E. P. Dutton, 1976).

5. In 1974, the median family income for males age 45 to 54 was $13,641 compared to $8,670 (age 65 and over) and $10,661 (age 25–34). Source: U.S. Bureau of the Census, *Current Population Reports*, Series P-60, no. 99, 1974, Table 9, p. 13.

6. Robert J. Havighurst, "Middle Age—The New Prime of Life" in Clark Tibbitts and Wilma Donahue, eds., *Aging in Today's Society* (Englewood Cliffs, N.J.: Prentice-Hall, 1960, p. 140.

7. J. Ross Eshlemann, *Perspectives in Marriage and the Family* (Boston: Allyn and Bacon, 1969), p. 458.

Middle Age: Oh My

—There may be good reason for middle-aged wives to worry about their husbands and younger women, according to a study by a Wayne State University psychologist.

The Study by Carol Nowack reported that middle-aged men are found by young women to be the "most attractive" of any age group.

Her findings were presented at a weekend meeting of the Midwestern Psychological Association.

She arrived at her conclusions by showing slides depicting attractive, unattractive and plain people to a variety of men and women and then asking them their reactions.

All groups agreed that middle-aged men were generally most attractive and, surprisingly, middle-aged women are regarded as the least attractive. Even the middle-aged women viewing the picture reflected that opinion.

Middle-aged women concerned about wrinkles and gray hairs class themselves as unattractive, the psychologist found.

They also confuse un-attractiveness with age and look upon a young but unattractive woman as old.

If a woman considers herself both middle-aged and old, she has a "double whammy," said Ms. Nowack.

Source: *Detroit Free Press*, May 10, 1976, p. 1-B. Reprinted by permission of The Associated Press.

It seems feasible that menopause serves as an explanatory "catchall" covering any feelings or symptoms that arise between forty and fifty years of age. More than thirty years ago Edward Stieglitz concluded that, more frequently than not, the menopause is cause for relief and increasing pleasure for maturing women.[8]

Debate exists over whether the middle years are depressing and strain-filled or whether they are the prime time as mentioned earlier. The one argument suggests that, combined with the physical processes and changes, it is the time when men are pressured to "get ahead." For many, "it's now or never." The prestigious position they were going to attain, the book they were going to write, or the stardom they were going to achieve may become a reality or may become a dream never to be fulfilled. A man's "handsome ladies' man" image of ten to twenty years earlier may turn into a need to convince himself of his virility. The expenses of weddings or college and the departure of the children may produce restless nights. This argument suggests, then, that the middle years are rough—physically, socially, and emotionally.

The opposite argument suggests that this is a period of life when things are brightest. Income is highest, leisure time is the greatest, child-bearing responsibility is past, and opportunities exist as never before. Which view is correct—or is it possible that both are?

Daniel Levinson and other psychologists refer to a "mid-Life transition" for men around age forty that may go relatively smoothly or may

8. Edward J. Stieglitz, *The Second Forty Years* (New York: Lippincott, 1946), p. 197.

involve considerable turmoil. The transition involves a sense of disparity between "what I've reached at this point" and "what it is I really want." It is a matter of the goodness of fit between the life structure and the self. A man may do extremely well in achieving his goals and yet find his success hollow and bittersweet.[9] The issues involved in this mid-life transition include 1) the sense of bodily decline and the more vivid recognition of one's mortality, 2) the sense of aging, which means to be old rather than young, and 3) the polarity of masculine and feminine including changing relationships to women and an integration of the more feminine aspects of the self. The authors believe this mid-life transition reaches its peak sometime in the early forties and in a three- or four-year period comes to an end. Following this, a new life structure begins to take shape and to provide a basis for living in middle adulthood.[10]

Research by sociologists tends to lend support to a hint of a mid-life transition. Corporation managers who were ambivalent about their career reached a low point in work as a central life interest between the ages of thirty-six and forty-five.[11] A structural analysis of happiness over the life cycle showed the lack of a direct correlation of happiness with various area satisfactions at this time of life.[12] Other evidence suggests as well that for men entrance into middle age is associated with stress and often maladaptive patterns of reaction.[13]

What about women? Is the "empty nest" or postparental stage of the family life cycle a traumatic and unhappy period? According to data from six U.S. national surveys, middle-aged women whose children have left home report, as a whole, somewhat greater happiness and enjoyment of life than women of similar age with a child (or children) living at home, and the former report substantially greater marital happiness than the latter.[14] Thus the children's leaving home does not typically lead to an enduring decline in the psychological well-being of middle-aged mothers. Rather, on balance, the effects seem to be moderately positive.

Other data indicating positive aspects of the postparental period come from Deutscher, who conducted in-depth interviews with forty-nine spouses

9. Daniel J. Levinson, et al., "The Psychosocial Development of Men in Early Adulthood and the Mid-Life Transition," in D. F. Ricks, et al., eds, *Life History Research in Psychopathology* (Minneapolis: University of Minnesota Press, vol. 3, 1974), pp. 253–254.

10. Ibid., p. 255.

11. Daniel R. Goldman, "Managerial Mobility Motivations and Central Life Interests," *American Sociological Review* 38 (February 1973), p. 123.

12. Joseph Harry, "Evolving Sources of Happiness for Men over the Life Cycle: A Structural Analysis," *Journal of Marriage and the Family* 38 (May 1976), p. 295.

13. Stanley D. Rosenberg and Michael P. Farrell, "Identity and Crisis in Middle-aged Men," *International Journal of Aging and Human Development* 7 (1976), pp. 153–170.

14. Norval D. Glenn, "Psychological Well-being in the Postparental Stage: Some Evidence from National Surveys," *Journal of Marriage and the Family* 37 (February 1975), pp. 105–110.

in thirty-three postparental households to determine the extent to which they define this period favorably or unfavorably.[15] His sample provided little support for the argument that postparental life is a time of great difficulty. Only three of the forty-nine interviewed provided clearly negative evaluations. Evaluations of the postparental period as being "better" than was life during earlier stages appeared in twenty-two of the forty-nine interviews. An additional twenty-two either evaluated this period as equal to preceding phases or indicated that a value orientation or change was not clear.

The postparental life as the "good" life was based on one general criterion, the freedom it presented—freedom from financial responsibilities, freedom to be mobile (geographically), freedom from housework and other chores, and finally, freedom to be one's self for the first time since the children came along.[16] Irwin Deutscher mentions that even more important than these "freedoms" was the redefinition of self and the marital partnership that appears to have resulted from them. It may be these new forms of interpersonal relationship and self-conception that were the real dividend for these particular families.[17]

Even though they occurred rarely, the difficulties mentioned in the unfavorable evaluations centered around three areas: 1) the advent of menopause and other disabilities associated with the aging process, 2) the final recognition and definition in retrospect of oneself as a "failure" either in terms of the work career or the child-raising process, and 3) the inability to fill the gap—the empty place in the family that results from the departure of children.[18]

The absence of children symbolizes the children's new independence. Since the children are gone, many mothers form new nonfamilial relationships to fill the void. Many women in this age category become more active in civic and religious affairs, and an increasing number of wives and mothers become employed.

THE EMPLOYED
WIFE AND MOTHER

In 1975, 46 percent of all females age sixteen and over (a total of 36.5 million) were employed in the labor force. This was up from 36 percent (or 25.9 million) just ten years earlier.[19] Of these 36.5 million females, 23.2 per-

15. Irwin Deutscher, "The Quality of Postparental Life: Definitions of the Situation," *Journal of Marriage and the Family* 26 (February 1964), pp. 52–59.

16. Ibid., p. 55.

17. Ibid., p. 56.

18. Ibid., p. 56.

19. U.S. Bureau of the Census, *Statistical Abstract of the United States*, 1976, (97th ed.), Washington, D.C., 1976, no. 574, p. 358.

Go On—Ask Me If I Work

Why is it when a man is a chef or chauffeur,
Or designs interior decoration,
Everybody understands he's working.
Ready for some startling information?
So am I.

Why is it when a husband is a teacher,
Or talented at making sick children well,
Everybody understands he's working.
Ready for less show and more tell?
So am I.

Why is it when a man repairs appliances,

Or practices guidance and counseling,
Everybody understands he's working.
Ready for an important announceling?
So am I.

No Social Security, no old-age pension,
No titles, not even honorable mention.
But if you wonder how much I'm earning,
Even though I'm not working for pay,
Figure out what it would cost to replace me
If I didn't show up just one eighteen-hour day.
                                    —Rochelle Distelheim

Source: *McCalls*, December 1976, Copyright © The McCall Publishing Company.

cent were single, 62.2 percent were married, and 14.6 percent were widowed or divorced. The median age of all females in the labor force was 35.5 with more than one-third of these between the ages of 35 to 54. Thus, as can be seen, a major portion of the female work force is married and in the "middle years" of the life cycle, with the number and percentages increasing sharply.

There were more than 21 million married women (with a husband present) in the labor force in 1975. A total of 4.4 million (21 percent) of these married women had children under six years old. The remaining 9.7 million (46 percent) had no children under age eighteen.[20] The largest percentage of these women were employed in clerical work (35 percent) with an additional 17.6 percent in professional and technical work, 16.6 percent as service workers, excluding private households, and 12.5 percent as operatives and kindred workers.[21] Of those employed, the median earnings of females in 1975 was $3,385 compared to $8,853 for males.[22] The sharpest income discrepancy appears in the $10,000 and over income category, where 45 percent of employed men, but only 10 percent of employed females fall. Much, but not all, of the income gap can be explained by differences in type of work and extent of employment. Again, as can be seen, more than half of the employed wives were also mothers with children under age eighteen and more than a third were employed in clerical work with overall, a median income of slightly over one-third that of males.

---

20. Ibid., no. 576, p. 359.
21. Ibid., no. 577, p. 359.
22. Ibid., no. 666, p. 413.

Reasons for Wife-Mother
Employment

Why do wives and mothers work? They work for the same mysterious reasons that husbands and fathers work, although men are much less likely to be asked. Women are asked because of the strong institutionalized bias that has traditionally existed against married women and mothers working for any reason other than economic remuneration. Since the place of a wife—particularly the mother of preschool-age children—is widely believed to be in the home, the traditional bias will lead again to the question, "Why do wives and mothers work?"[23]

Many individualistic reasons could be given, but all personal and seemingly idiosyncratic factors share much in common. The most frequently articulated reason for working is money. It is doubtful that the percentage of women who work outside the home would be very large if it were not for the income provided. The income needed may be immediate: to pay debts, to buy groceries or household goods, and so forth.

But the income may also be tied in with future needs: college expenses, purchase of a new automobile, or home, or retirement. The motives may not be based on actual financial need but become focused and expressed in monetary terms. Clearly many factors other than money influence the decision to seek paid employment, but a strong bias has existed traditionally against married women and mothers working for any reason other than economic remuneration.

Paid employment has been found to provide many rewards not obtainable from being mother and housewife. The feeling of achievement, success, recognition, creativity, usefulness, status, and importance to society that may result from co-workers and friends are feelings that domestic life does not provide. In addition, many women, particularly those in the middle years or those without children in the home, feel bored. As Lois Hoffman notes, "Technological advances have made the housewife role less time consuming and less satisfying . . . a mother may look to outside employment to fill her day.[24]

Interrelated with money, status, and boredom factors are a long list of influences in the choice to work. Again, as stated by Hoffman:

---

23. The reader may be interested in common misconceptions about women's work motivation. See, for example, Judith Long Laws, "Work Aspiration of Women: False Leads and New Starts," *Signs: Journal of Women in Culture and Society* 1 (Spring 1976), pp. 33–49.

24. Lois Wladis Hoffman, "Psychological Factors," in Lois Wladis Hoffman and F. Ivan Nye, *Working Mothers* (San Francisco: Jossey-Bass, 1974), p. 61. The reader may find the following articles on the housewife and housework to be of interest: Myra Marx Ferree, "The Confused American Housewife," *Psychology Today* 10 (September 1976), pp. 76–80; John Kenneth Galbraith, "The Economics of the American Housewife," *Atlantic Monthly* 232 (August 1973), pp. 78–83; Joann Vanek, "Time Spent in Housework," *Scientific American* 231 (November 1974), pp. 116–120.

Personality variables, such as the needs for achievement and power, a sense of competence, and the attitude toward women's roles, were also considered as motivations for employment. At the present time, however, maternal employment is so common that it is not possible to characterize the working woman in terms of personality traits.[25]

Some key factors that influence the wife's work plans include the number and age of her children, her level of education, work experience and work skills, the income level of her husband, and a range of attitudinal variables, including those of her husband.[26] It is easier to work, as in the middle years, when one does not have children. Generally, it is easier to find a job if one has training, skills, and experience. The absence of a husband, a part-time employed husband, or a husband with low income forces women into the work force. Generally, an *inverse* relationship exists between the husband's level of income and the percentage of wives employed.

Interestingly, a direct relationship exists between economic attainment and an unmarried status. Singleness may be less a "marriage reject" for many employed single women than one of "rejecting marriage."[27] In brief, the lower the husband's income, the higher the percentage of wives employed; the higher the women's income, the more likely she is to be or remain single.

Working Women and Children

Few sociocultural differentials have equaled the strength of the inverse relationship between female labor force participation and fertility. Simply, working women have fewer children. Marital female employment before childbearing was found to be associated with lower fertility levels later, longer first-birth intervals, and earlier use of birth control.[28] On the other hand, there has been a dramatic increase in labor force participation among women with school and preschool age children.

It is often assumed that maternal employment has many effects on a child—all bad. However, research in the last several decades has seriously challenged this view. More than twenty-five years ago, Ivan Nye reported that adolescent children of part-time working mothers had better relationships with their parents than children of either full-time working mothers or

---

25. Hoffman, op. cit., p. 62.
26. See for example, Catherine C. Arnott, "Husbands' Attitude and Wives' Commitment to Employment," *Journal of Marriage and the Family* 34 (November 1972), pp. 673–684.
27. Elizabeth M. Havens, "Women, Work and Wedlock: A Note on Female Marital Patterns in the United States," *American Journal of Sociology* 78 (January 1973), p. 980.
28. H. Theodore Groat, Randy L. Workman, and Arthur G. Neal, "Labor Force Participation and Family Formation: A Study of Working Mothers," *Demography* 13 (February 1976), pp. 115–125.

> **Louise:** *If mothers must work, it should be tempered. My married daughter and my daughter-in-law work part-time and I think it works out alright. I see strains on them that I never had though. Sometimes I feel the child comes second to the job. But they are both in professions and I think it's good that they keep up this contact as long as they keep it part-time.*
>
> **Ann:** *It bothers me that I must work full-time when I have young children. Either my mother or his mother kept them until I put them in nursery school. I prefer them home with me and I prefer being home with them. But if it's gotta work out that way, let it be worked out that way. When we have free times on the weekend, we go places together. We do things. Just the boys and I you know. Sometimes the girls come along. We have a great understanding. But I tell you— my husband being out of the home there's no difference to them. They have just as much love for him as they would if he was in the home.*

mothers who did not work at all.[29] Later, the Gluecks reported that maternal employment was not related to delinquency among lower-class boys.[30] Few studies seem to exist that report meaningful differences between the children of working mothers in general and the children of nonworking mothers. When differences do exist, it is often explained less by the mother working than by chance factors: social class, part- or full-time employment, age of the children, mother's attitude toward employment, or other social and psychological factors.

Hoffman reviewed research organized around five general hypotheses related to maternal employment and its effect on children.[31] Hypothesis one suggested that maternal employment affects the child, particularly the daughter, because the role models provided by working and nonworking mothers differ. Considerable support was provided for this hypothesis. In general, daughters of working mothers had less traditional sex role concepts, a higher level of female competence, and compared favorably with daughters of nonworking mothers with respect to independence and achievement-related variables.[32] The effects on sons was much less clear.

Hypothesis two suggested that a child would be affected by the mother's emotional state: morale or satisfactions from employment status,

---

29. F. Ivan Nye, "Adolescent-Parent Adjustment: Age, Sex, Sibling Number, Broken Homes, and Employed Mothers as Variables," *Marriage and Family Living* 14 (November 1952), pp. 327–332.

30. Sheldon Glueck and Eleanor Glueck, "Working Mothers and Delinquency," *Mental Hygiene* 41 (July 1957), pp. 327–352.

31. Lois Wladis Hoffman, "Effects on Child," in Hoffman and Nye, op. cit., pp. 126–166.

32. Ibid., p. 136.

emotional stress because of dual-role demands, and guilt about the child. The data about the mother's emotional state suggest that the working mother who obtains satisfaction from her work, who has adequate arrangements so that her dual role does not involve undue strain, and who does not feel so guilty that she overcompensates is likely to do quite well and, under certain conditions, better than the nonworking mother.[33] Hypothesis three suggested that maternal employment affects the child through its influence on child-rearing practices. In some studies, maternal employment increased the father's participation in child rearing, while in others the active participation of the father had a positive effect on the child. It is uncertain, however, that these are directly linked; that is, that the father's activities that result from maternal employment are those that have a positive effect. Children of working mothers were found to have more household responsibilities and experience a milder form of discipline.[34]

Hypothesis four suggested that the working mother provides less adequate supervision, this resulting in more delinquency. Data suggests that, particularly in the lower classes, children of working mothers may receive less adequate supervision and this less adequate supervision is linked to delinquency. In the middle class, there appears to be some evidence for a higher delinquency rate among children of working mothers although not for reasons of adequate supervision.[35] Hypothesis five suggested that the working mother's child is a victim of maternal deprivation. No solid evidence supports this hypothesis.[36]

In brief, maternal employment per se appears to be too broad a concept to produce major distinctions in effects on children. The numbers and percentages of women and working mothers do, however, focus attention on other areas such as an increasing interest in, and need for, day-care services. These are mentioned briefly in the final chapter. It also focuses attention on the husband-wife relationship and the balance of power between them.

Working Women and Marriage

The effect of female employment on a marriage and the marital relationship could be expected to vary considerably depending on whether the employment is full-time or part-time, on whether there are preschool children, on the age of the couple, on their stage in the life cycle, and on many other factors. For example, one important predictor of happiness in marriage was found to be a woman's freedom to choose among alternative life-styles.

---

33. Ibid., p. 142.
34. Ibid., pp. 142–147.
35. Ibid., pp. 151–152.
36. Ibid., p. 157.

Both partners were lower in marriage happiness if the wife participated in the labor market out of economic necessity than if she participated by choice.[37]

Employment of the wife is certain to bring changes in the husband-wife relationship. Role changes as a companion, housewife, entertainer, lover, and the like are certain to require readjustments on the part of both spouses. These changes may at times create stress and conflict and at times bring role reversals or renewed vitality to the marital relationship. But are these changes any different from changes brought on in marriages where the wife is not employed?

Nye suggests that while research results concerning a wife's employment are not uniform, the support for a difference in the marital relationship

---

Alex: *Back home upper- and middle-class women don't work. It's a shame for a woman to work. But now they're trying to become like the West and you're seeing middle-class women talking almost like teenagers and going out and work. Mostly its the lower classes that go out and work. But still it's considered a shame.*

                Let's put it this way. If a woman goes out to work, let's say from 8:00 to 8:00, she is considered a loose woman, and she might even have problems to get married some day. They will try to check her background, because marriage is always arranged by the family. She might have a problem getting married, because most of the guys will think that she is loose because she goes out and works, even though she doesn't do anything, just works. Women don't work.

---

is stronger than the alternative of no difference. He then states that having tentatively concluded this to be true, it is important to note the differences in the husband-wife relationship are quite small. No more than 4 percent of the variance in marital satisfaction and other measures of the marital relationship can be explained by the employment status of the wife.[38]

The research of almost three decades is summed up by his conclusions:

> The early studies, in general, showed slightly more marital problems among couples in which the mother was employed; but even in those studies, the difference in tensions and satisfactions occurred mostly at the lower-class levels. Recent studies suggest that the small, sometimes nonsignificant differences in middle-class families found in earlier studies no longer exist; if the wife enjoys her work, the marital satisfactions of this subgroup of wives may average higher than for housewives in general. However, in lower-class families, research sup-

---

37. Susan R. Orden and Norman M. Bradburn, "Working Wives and Marriage Happiness," *American Journal of Sociology* 74 (January 1969), pp. 392–407.
38. F. Ivan Nye, "Husband-Wife Relationship," in Hoffman and Nye, op. cit., pp. 203–204.

The Myth and the Reality

The Myth

A woman's place is in the home.

The Reality

Homemaking in itself is no longer a full-time job for most people. Goods and services formerly produced in the home are now commercially available; laborsaving devices have lightened or eliminated much work around the home.

Today more than half of all women between 18 and 64 years of age are in the labor force, where they are making a substantial contribution to the nation's economy. Studies show that 9 out of 10 girls will work outside the home at some time in their lives.

Women aren't seriously attached to the labor force; they work only for extra pocket money.

Of the 34 million women in the labor force in March 1973, nearly half were working because of pressing economic need. They were either single, widowed, divorced, separated or had husbands whose incomes were less than $3,000 a year. Another 4.7 million had husbands with incomes between $3,000 and $7,000.[39]

Women are out ill more than male workers; they cost the company more.

A recent Public Health Service study shows little difference in the absentee rate due to illness or injury: 5.6 days a year for women compared with 5.2 for men.

Women don't work as long or as regularly as their male co-workers; their training is costly —and largely wasted.

A declining number of women leave work for marriage and children, but even among those who do leave, a majority return when their children are in school. Even with a break in employment, the average woman worker has a worklife expectancy of 25 years as compared with 43 years for the average male worker. The single woman averages 45 years in the labor force.

Source: U.S. Department of Labor, Women's Bureau Publication, "The Myth and the Reality," Stock Number 2916-00015 1974, Washington, D.C.: U.S. Government Printing Office, 1974.

39. The Bureau of Labor Statistics estimate for a low standard of living for an urban family of four was $7,386 in autumn 1972. Today, this figure would likely exceed $10,000. This estimate is for a family consisting of an employed husband age 38, a wife not employed outside the home, an eight-year-old girl, and a thirteen-year-old boy.

Studies on labor turnover indicate that net differences for men and women are generally small. In manufacturing industries the 1968 rates of accessions per 100 employees were 4.4 for men and 5.3 for women; the respective separation rates were 4.4 and 5.2.

Married women take jobs away from men; in fact, they ought to quit those jobs they now hold.

There were 19.8 million married women (husband present) in the labor force in March 1973; the number of unemployed men was 2.5 million. If all the married women stayed home and unemployed men were placed in their jobs, there would be 17.3 million unfilled jobs.

Moreover, most unemployed men do not have the education or the skill to qualify for many of the jobs held by women, such as secretaries, teachers, and nurses.

Women should stick to "women's jobs" and shouldn't compete for "men's jobs."

Job requirements, with extremely rare exceptions, are unrelated to sex. Tradition rather than job content has led to labeling certain jobs as women's and others as men's. In measuring 22 inherent aptitudes and knowledge areas, a research laboratory found that there is no sex difference in 14, women excel in 6, and men excel in 2.

Women don't want responsibility on the job; they don't want promotions or job changes which add to their load.

Relatively few women have been offered positions of responsibility. But when given these opportunities, women, like men, do cope with job responsibilities in addition to personal or family responsibilities. In 1973, 4.7 million women held professional and technical jobs, another 1.6 million worked as nonfarm managers, officials, and proprietors. Many others held supervisory jobs at all levels in offices and factories.

The employment of mothers leads to juvenile delinquency.

Studies show that many factors must be considered when seeking the causes of juvenile delinquency. Whether or not a mother is employed does not appear to be a determining factor.

These studies indicate that it is the quality of a mother's care rather than the time consumed in such care that is of major significance.

Men don't like to work for women supervisors.	*Most men who complain about women supervisors have never worked for a woman.*
	In one study where at least three-fourths of both the male and female respondents (all executives) had worked with women managers, their evaluation of women in management was favorable. On the other hand, the study showed a traditional/cultural bias among those who reacted unfavorably to women as managers.
	In another survey in which 41 percent of the reporting firm indicated that they hired women executives, none rated their performance as unsatisfactory; 50 percent rated them adequate; 42 percent rated them the same as their predecessors; and 8 percent rated them better than their predecessors.

ports the conclusion of continuing differences, favoring couples in which the wife is not employed.

For those wishing to employ these research findings as a basis for making personal decisions concerning their own employment or that of their wives, a caution is in order. Although the average marital adjustment of populations of employed and not-employed wives does not differ substantially, employment of the mother may have a major effect or effects, positive or negative, on any one husband-wife relationship. The consequences are a little more likely to be positive if the number of children at home is small, the job she takes is one she enjoys, the husband's attitude is positive, and the husband and wife have advanced education.[40]

Considerable shifts in power in the husband-wife relationship seem to occur when the wife is employed. In general, the wife's power tends to increase. In an earlier chapter, a resource theory was used to explain shifts in power. Thus, as the wife becomes employed, she gains income, independence, and new contacts (resources) that increase her contribution to the marriage. This increase in power among employed wives appears not only in the United States but cross-culturally as well.

In reviewing the research in this area, Steven Bahr suggests that the increase in power among employed wives tends to be primarily in "external" decisions (for example, finances or the provider role) with less power in "internal" household areas. The effect of employment on power within the child care, socialization, housekeeper, and recreation roles appears to be relatively

---

40. Nye, op. cit., p. 206.

small.[41] The effects of employment may be more pronounced in the lower class, in small families, and in families without preschool children. Among these groups employed women have more power.

Employment of mothers affects far more than their children and their marriage. It affects them as well. It was reported that employed mothers appeared to be in better physical health than housewives, were more likely to enjoy their activities and relationships with children, revealed more positive and fewer negative feelings about themselves, projected an image of ability and confidence, and evaluated their communities as a satisfactory place to live.[42]

In the middle years, with the children gone from the home, the interests of the employed mother are no longer divided between her children and her job. Some women turn from part-time to full-time employment. Some begin work for the first time or at least the first time since the marriage or birth of children. Employment may take on a new meaning, presenting a perspective on the world and her own values considerably different from that known previously. The employment may bring status lost when the children departed from the home. And last but not necessarily least, the mother in the middle years, whether in paid employment or as a housewife, may become a grandmother and assume still another new status with its accompanying new role expectations.

THE GRANDPARENT ROLE

Turning from the employed wife and mother, attention is now focused on another dimension of importance to the middle years: grandparenting. Grandparenting has become a middle-aged rather than an old-aged phenomenon. With the majority of men and women in American society marrying in their late teens or early twenties, and with many of these having children within the first year or two of marriage, parents are becoming grandparents in their early and middle forties. The rocking-chair image and the cane-carrying grandfather image seem grossly inappropriate.

There is a suprisingly small amount of empirical research dealing with the status and roles of grandparents. This may be attributed to the value placed upon the independence of the nuclear family in rearing its own children, as well as the consequent belief that persons other than mother and father contribute little to the socialization of the child. But population

---

41. Steven J. Bahr, "Effects on Power and Division of Labor in the Family," in Hoffman and Nye, op. cit., pp. 180–181.
42. F. Ivan Nye, "Effects on Mother," in Hoffman and Nye, op. cit., pp. 222–225.

> Louise: I have never gotten involved in babysitting with the grandchildren, because I have really strong feelings that mothers should raise their own children. I have a very good relationship with my grandchildren. I love caring for them, but I have no intention of taking over their mother's role. They understand that and whenever they ask me it is a request. And if I can't make it they understand, and there's never any bad feelings.

changes, three- and four-generation families, increases in the employment of women, and redefinitions of marital roles all contribute to a reexamination of the grandparent-grandchildren relationship.

In a worldwide perspective, three or more generation households (which of necessity includes grandparents) are more common than the nuclear family two-generation household. The status they occupy and the roles they are expected to perform would logically appear to be of great significance. Nancy Olsen conducted a study of grandmothers in Taiwan and their role in socialization.[43] She indicated that the grandparent plays two important and interrelated roles in the process of family socialization, as an authority figure and as an alternate caretaker.

In the United States, it would appear that the grandmother would be perceived more as an alternate caretaker than as an authority figure. But in some instances, both these and other roles are performed.[44] To discover the degree of comfort with the role, as expressed by grandparents, the significance of these roles, and the style with which the roles are enacted, Bernice Neugarten and Karol Weinstein conducted interviews with both grandmothers and grandfathers in seventy middle-class families. They discovered that the majority of grandparents expressed comfort, satisfaction, and pleasure in this situation. Approximately one-third did express difficulty in the role, due to the strain associated with thinking of oneself as a grandparent, the conflict with the parents over the rearing of the grandchildren, and the indifference to caretaking or responsibility in reference to the grandchild. For both grandparents the significance of this role related to feeling young again, to emotional self-fulfillment, to being a resource person to the child, and to the vicarious achievement through the child. Slightly less than one-third of the grandparents saw the role as remote, that is, having little effect upon their own lives. Likewise, Joan Robertson found that grandmotherhood is a role

---

43. Nancy J. Olsen, "The Role of Grandmothers in Taiwanese Family Socialization," *Journal of Marriage and the Family* 38 (May 1976), pp. 363–372.
44. Bernice L. Neugarten and Karol K. Weinstein, "The Changing American Grandparent," *Journal of Marriage and the Family* 26 (May 1964), pp. 199–204; Joan F. Robertson, "Grandmotherhood: A Study of Role Conceptions," *Journal of Marriage and the Family* 39 (February 1977), pp. 165–174.

You're as Old as You Feel

The adage has it that you are only as old as you feel. Charles Cavalier's parents must feel pretty young. As does he.

A magazine for retired persons referred to those over 62 as "aged."

So Cavalier wrote a letter to the editor: "I resent, and I'm sure others do, being classi-

fied as 'aged' just because I am over 62. I am 67 years old, run a $2 million business with 30 employees. I work seven days a week and average 10 hours a day.

"If you are not careful, my 92-year-old dad or my 91-year-old mother will kick the hell out of you."

Source: *The Washington Evening Star*, December 18, 1972, p. D-9. Reprinted by permission.

actively enjoyed by 80 percent of the respondents and, for many, it is more enjoyable than parenting because it provides easy joy and pleasure without the socialization responsibilities associated with parenthood.[45]

THE FAMILY OF LATER LIFE

Throughout history, older persons have played significant roles, particularly men who, with increasing age, often receive increasing status, prestige, and deference. In the United States, and apparently in modernized societies in general, old age does not bring with it increased prestige and status but rather brings negative perceptions and definitions.[46] Frequently, old age is defined as a time of dependency and declining productivity and vitality. The socioeconomic status held is generally determined by the achievement of earlier periods of life; if the achievements were limited and provisions for these years were inadequate, opportunities for a full meaningful life are limited.

It is not difficult to remain sensitive to the older person and aging. In tomorrow's community newspaper will be pictures of couples who are celebrating their fiftieth wedding anniversaries, announcements of community and business leaders who are retiring, polls showing attitudinal differences between the old and the young, and of course the obituary notices. All these serve as reminders of the social dimension of aging and of the position of the older person in society.

Social gerontology, the study of older persons and the aging process, as well as the closely related field, the sociology of aging, have both been con-

---

45. Ibid., p. 165.

46. Vern L. Bengtson, James J. Dowd, David H. Smith, and Alex Inkeles, "Modernization, Modernity, and Perceptions of Aging: A Cross-Cultural Study," *Journal of Gerontology* 30 (November 1975), pp. 688–695.

TABLE 18–2. Marital Status of Men and Women, Aged 65 and Over, March, 1976, Percentage Distribution

	MEN		WOMEN	
Marital Status	Aged 65–74	Aged 75 and Over	Aged 65–74	Aged 75 and Over
Single	4.2	4.9	5.9	6.0
Married	81.3	66.7	46.4	21.4
Separated	2.5	2.9	2.2	1.2
Widowed	8.9	23.5	42.0	69.7
Divorced	3.1	2.0	3.5	1.7
Total	100.0	100.0	100.0	100.0

Source: U.S. Bureau of the Census, *Current Population Reports*, Series P-20, no. 306, "Marital Status and Living Arrangements: March 1976," (Washington, D.C.: U.S. Government Printing Office 1977), Table 1, p. 9.

cerned with the social definition of who is thought to be old and how they are old, their interaction patterns and behaviors, the expectations that are imposed upon them, the age, sex, place of residence, and other demographic factors about them, as well as the problems and needs that older members within a society face. Within this framework, the family of later life has come to take on a particular significance in dealing with, and understanding, these other factors of concern to the aged.

Marital Status and Length of the Later Years

In 1976, 81 percent of the men and 46 percent of the women aged 65–74 were married. At age 75 and over, 67 percent of the men and 29 percent of the women were married (see Table 18–2). Relatively few men and women in these age categories are divorced, separated, or single. This is a time when the widowed status becomes increasingly frequent. Whereas less than one in ten men age 65–74 and one in four of the men age 75 and over are widowers, more than four in ten women age 65–74 and seven in ten age 75 and over are widows. This factor is discussed later in this chapter.

Married couples in this over-sixty-five group comprise a high proportion who have been married a long time. Most of them previously celebrated silver wedding anniversaries, and many have or will celebrate their golden anniversaries. Over the years they have shared many joys and weathered many crises. Although it exists, rarely does one read about divorce or incompatibility among these couples. Even when unhappy in their marriage, the experiences of their years, the lives and activities of their children, and perhaps the lack of realistic alternatives to the marriage keep the couple together.

A review of literature concerning older persons' perceptions of their marriage relationships and their present period of life suggests the following:

1. There is evidence that many older persons consider their marriage relationships to be as satisfactory as, if not more than, in previous years.
2. Evidence also exists from other studies that marriage satisfaction declines during the later years, particularly among lower socioeconomic-class couples and among marriages in which a small amount of shared companionship and satisfaction existed in the earlier years.
3. Marriages perceived as satisfactory in the later years have usually been satisfactory from the beginning, while those perceived as unsatisfactory have generally been regarded as such from the beginning.
4. *Love* is the area of greatest marital need satisfaction for both older husbands and wives, while *respect* is the area of least satisfaction for husbands and *communication* is the area of least satisfaction for wives.
5. Housing arrangements, mental health, lack of social participation, physical health, and reduced income are reported to be common problems of the older person.
6. Marriage appears to contribute to morale and continued activity during the later years, and a high degree of marital need satisfaction is positively related to a high degree of morale.[47]

Nick Stinnett et al., in a study of 408 older husbands and wives in Oklahoma, found results that closely parallel the marital-satisfaction data presented in Chapter 15. That is, the respondents tended to perceive their marriage relationships as improving and increasing in satisfaction with the later stages of married life. The older husbands and wives expressed very favorable perceptions of their marriage relationships and present period of life. A summary of their findings is worthy of presentation.

1. The greatest proportion of the respondents rated their marriages as *very happy* (45.4 percent) or *happy* (49.5 percent).
2. The majority of older husbands and wives reported that their marriage had become *better* over time (53.3 percent).
3. The *present* time was reported to be the happiest period of marriage by most respondents (54.9 percent).
4. Approximately 50 percent of the sample felt that most marriages become *better* over time.
5. The two most rewarding aspects of the present marriage relationship were most often reported by older husbands and wives as companionship (18.4 percent) and being *able to express true feelings to each other* (17.8 percent).

47. Nick Stinnett, Linda M. Carter, and James E. Montgomery, "Older Persons' Perceptions of their Marriages," *Journal of Marriage and the Family* 34 (November 1972), pp. 665–666. Reprinted by permission.

TABLE 18–3. Life Table. Expectation of Life at Years of Age: United States, 1974.

Age Interval	TOTAL		
	Both Sexes	Male	Female
0– 1	71.9	68.2	75.9
1– 5	72.2	68.5	76.0
5–10	68.4	64.7	72.2
10–15	63.5	59.8	67.3
15–20	58.6	55.0	62.4
20–25	53.9	50.4	57.5
25–30	49.3	45.9	52.7
30–35	44.6	41.3	47.9
35–40	39.9	36.7	43.2
40–45	35.3	32.2	38.5
45–50	30.9	27.9	33.9
50–55	26.7	23.8	29.5
55–60	22.7	19.9	25.3
60–65	19.0	16.5	21.3
65–70	15.6	13.4	17.5
70–75	12.5	10.7	13.9
75–80	9.8	8.4	10.8
80–85	7.6	6.6	8.2
85 and over	5.7	5.0	6.1

Source: *Monthly Vital Statistics Report*, vol. 24, no. 11, (Washington, D.C.: U.S. Department of Health, Education, and Welfare, National Center for Health Statistics, February 3, 1976), Table 2, p. 5.

6. The two aspects of the present marriage relationship which were most often reported as being troublesome were *having different values and philosophies of life* (13.8 percent) and *lack of mutual interests* (12.5 percent).

7. The two most important characteristics of a successful marriage were most often reported by the respondents as *respect* (38.2 percent) and *sharing common interests* (26.5 percent).

8. The most important factor in achieving marital success was most often reported as *being in love* (48.6 percent).

9. The three most frequently mentioned major problems of the present period of life were *housing* (27.5 percent), *poor health* (21.2 percent), and *money* (20 percent).

10. The *present time* was reported to be the happiest period of life by the greatest proportion of respondents (50.3 percent).[48]

Since the turn of the century, one of the more significant changes in the marital relationship has been that of length. Both sexes marry earlier, stay

48. Ibid., pp. 666, 668. Reprinted by permission.

married longer, and live longer, making possible longer marriages. In 1974, the infant at birth could expect to live 71.9 years. For males this figure was 68.2 years and for females 75.9 years (see Table 18–3). Among the aged, those who reach 65 to 70 can expect to live 15.6 more years (13.4 for men and 17.5 for women).

These figures indicate that there has been little increase in the life expectation of older persons when compared with the 11.9 figure at the turn of the century. That is, in 1900, the person who reached age 65 could expect to live until age 76.9. In 1974, the person who reached age 65 could expect to live until age 80.6 or an average of less than four years longer than his counterpart nearly 75 years earlier. More people are living longer, however. In 1974, 66.6 percent of the men and 81.1 percent of the women reached age 65. In 1900, only 39.2 percent of the men and 43.8 percent of the women reached age 65.[49] Thus, although a much higher percentage of people are living longer, there has been a relatively small increase in the life expectation of older persons.

Living Arrangements of Persons in the Later Years

In 1975 there were an estimated 9 million men and 13 million women in the United States who were 65 years old and over. In 1975 nearly 80 percent of the men and 56 percent of the women in this age group were members of families (see Table 18–4). Nearly 76 percent of all the men were living in families as the head, and 35 percent of the women were living in families as the wives of family heads. As can be seen in the table, these proportions were about the same in 1965, although the overall proportion of men and women living in families has decreased somewhat, particularly for women.

This decrease in older men and women living in families seems to be principally reflected in the decrease observed in the category "other relative," those persons who resided in families but are neither heads nor wives of heads. About 9 percent of all men 65 years old and over were "other relatives" in families in 1965; by 1975 this figure had dropped to 3.7 percent. Among women, these figures were an estimated 19 percent in 1965, a proportion which decreased to 12.7 percent by 1975.

In our society, the norm is for the newly married couple to establish a home of their own (neolocal residence). Nevertheless, through economic necessity, shortage of housing, or sense of responsibility, as shown, a number of persons are living with their children, married or single. A situation of this nature may be a matter of choice or of necessity. Where both parents and children elect to live together, the arrangements frequently work out to the

---

49. *Life Tables,* "Vital Statistics of the United States, 1969," vol. 2, section 5, (Washington, D.C.: U.S. Department of Health, Education, and Welfare, National Center for Health Statistics), Table 5-B, p. 4; and *Monthly Vital Statistics Report* vol. 24, no. 11, Table 2, p. 5.

TABLE 18–4. Family Status of the Population 65 Years Old and Over,
by Sex: 1975 and 1965

	1975		1965	
Family Status	Male	Female	Male	Female
Total, 65 years and over, thousands	9,106	13,105		
Percent	100.0	100.0	100.0	100.0
In families	79.8	56.1	80.3	62.9
Head	76.1	8.5	71.3	10.7
Wife	(X)	35.0	(X)	33.3
Other relative	3.7	12.7	9.0	18.9
Primary individual	14.8	37.3	13.9	30.6
Secondary individual	1.2	1.2	2.3	2.2
Inmate of institution	4.2	5.3	3.5	4.3

X-not applicable.

Source: U.S. Bureau of the Census, *Current Population Reports*, Series P-23, no. 59, "Demographic Aspects of Aging and the Older Population in the United States," (Washington, D.C.: U.S. Government Printing Office, 1976), Table 6–3, p. 48.

satisfaction of both the older member and the children. If a wife is employed, the mother or mother-in-law is likely to assume much of the major responsibility of the household. Babysitting, lawn care, cooking, and fulfilling the daily needs of the home are often functions that older persons can satisfactorily perform. If, however, the arrangement is not one of choice but of necessity, the probability of difficulty is likely to increase. Frequently the relationship is unsatisfactory both for the aging parents and for the children, and in some instances the grandchildren.

Another living arrangement that is frequently satisfactory is for the aging parents and the married children to have separate but geographically close residences where they can maintain close relationships. Many parents like to be independent and want their children to allow them to remain so. This permits both generations to give favors or suggestions with fewer threat feelings. In addition, it permits both to share interests and life-styles without the constant physical presence of one another. Unfortunately, census data are not available on the number or percentage of persons in the later years who maintain residences separate from their children but live close to them.

The proportion of men and women 65 years old and over who maintain their own households in an "unfamily" situation, that is, live apart from any relatives, has increased since the mid-1960s. In 1975, these individuals represented about 15 percent of the men 65 years of age and about 37 percent of the women. This is an increase from 14 and 30 percent respectively in 1965.

The percentage of persons 65 years of age and over who live in institutions has increased since the mid-1960s, but the percentage is still a small proportion of the total. Again referring to Table 18–4, it can be noted that in

1975, 4.2 percent of the men and 5.3 percent of the women were inmates of institutions. This compares with 3.5 percent for men and 4.3 percent for women in 1965.

One study explained that "homes" for the aged originated as a last refuge for the homeless and economically deprived who lacked family ties. For many institutionalized persons, the family as a major resource to draw upon or rely upon was in some way deficient. The applicants to one home for the aged indicated that 45 percent sought entrance because of their own mental or physical impairment; 25 percent sought entrance because of death or impairment of their spouse; 7 percent sought entrance because of poor neighborhoods, loneliness, or relationship problems; and 23.5 percent sought entrance because of death or severe illness of their adult child or their child's spouse.[50]

One alternative to the total institutionalization of the aged family member would be a partial institutionalization plan in which the member could participate in group recreational or work activities during the day and sleep home at night or a night institutional plan where persons would sleep at the institution but be free to participate in community programs and activities during the day. Another alternative would place older persons in "foster homes" in which they would be given the opportunity to actively participate in the activities of the host family.[51] Thereby, a person could maintain healthy social interactions, gain a feeling of usefulness, and have his physical needs provided for as well. The host family would be paid for the services they provide, either by the person himself or by the state (as is frequently done with young children).

Social Conditions and
Problems Facing the Aged

Today there are more than twenty-two million Americans age sixty-five and over. This number makes up more than one-tenth of the United States population, and the rates have been expanding far more rapidly than the nation's population as a whole. Whereas the number of Americans has increased by 60 percent since 1940, the number of people age sixty-five and over has increased by 244 percent (nine million to twenty-two million) and those seventy-five and over are three times (327 percent increase) as numerous as they were just thirty-five years ago. The increase in these figures is due not so much to the fact that individuals are living longer but rather to the larger number of people living. With birth rates declining and with expectations that they will continue to do so, the aged will likely constitute an even larger

---

50. E. M. Brody and G. M. Spark, "Institutionalization of the Aged: A Family Crisis," *Family Process* 78 (March 1966), pp. 76–77.

51. This idea closely parallels the "affiliated family" idea discussed in Chapter 5 as a variant family life-style.

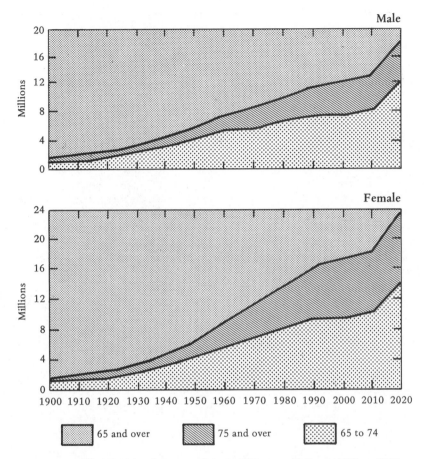

FIGURE 18–1. Growth of the Population 65 Years and Over: 1900 to 2020
Source: U.S. Bureau of the Census, *Current Population Reports*, Series
P-23, no. 43, "Some Demographic Aspects of Aging in the United States,"
U.S. Government Printing Office, 1973, cover page.

proportion of the population for decades to come.

The growth of land-development companies and retirement villages
and the appeal of sunny Florida and Arizona have contributed to the idea
that families upon retirement and later are a highly mobile group. It is true
that in recent decades there have been sizable migrations of these people to
southern and western states. However, as a whole, the aged have proved to
be the least mobile group in an intensely mobile society. The young desert an
area and the aged are left behind.

As suggested in several places, the problems facing the aged are many.
It is a time of life when a disproportionate number of them are isolated, disabled, sick, or poor. For example, ill health almost invariably accompanies
old age. Simone De Beauvoir states that, although they make up only one-
tenth of the population, the elderly accounted for nearly one-quarter of the

Why the Elderly Are Depressed

Old people, as their relatives and their doctors know all too well, are often sad people. The explanation that many students of geriatrics give is that old people are isolated from society. They no longer meet people at work. Their children are grown up and out of the house. Old friends have died and new friends are difficult to make. But, clearly, there is something missing from this explanation, because these things are true for almost all old people—yet not all of them are depressed. Marjorie Fiske Lowenthal and Clayton Haven of the Langley Porter Institute at the University of California, who have done a great deal of work with old people, believe that the missing factor is the presence of absence of an intimate companion that an elderly person can talk to. They believe that a companion can be a buffer against the social losses of old age (American Sociological Review, February 1968).

To substantiate this hunch, the investigators interviewed 280 elderly people three times at approximately yearly intervals. All lived in San Francisco. These elderly people were asked about the number of social roles they performed (whether they were parents, spouses, workers, and so on); and they were asked about their general feelings of being satisfied or depressed. Three psychiatrists rated a subsample of 112 on their level of mental and emotional impairment.

The study showed, first, that social isolation does have a good deal to do with depression in the elderly. The psychiatrists rated as unimpaired some 73 percent of the old people who had a good deal of social interaction—and only 42 percent of those with very little social interaction. Among the respondents rated low, 85 percent reported that they felt depressed.

The study also showed, however, that a confidant can help prevent depression. The investigators found that for those who had a confidant, the level of their satisfaction remained the same (55 percent satisfied, 45 percent depressed) whether or not social interactions and role status had increased or decreased from one interview to the next. Those who did not have a confidant were overwhelmingly depressed, whether their social life had increased (70 percent depressed) or decreased (87 percent depressed).

What about the impact of the blows that befall many of the elderly—retirement, the loss of a spouse, and serious illness? The first two can be greatly softened by the presence of an intimate. Among those respondents who had retired within the past seven years, and had a confidant, half were satisfied and half were depressed. But among those who had retired without a confidant, 64 percent reported that they were depressed. For those who lost a spouse in the last seven years, 45 percent of those who had a confidant were depressed. Of those without a confidant, 73 percent were depressed.

The one burden of age that even a confidant cannot lighten is physical illness. Almost all of the respondents who had suffered a serious illness within the last two years were depressed, whether they had a confidant (84 percent) or not (87 percent).

Source: "Roundup of Current Research," *Trans-Action* 5 (June 1968), p. 4. Reprinted by permission.

fifteen billion dollars spent in 1970 on health care in the United States and for one-quarter of hospital usage.[52] When older people enter hospitals, it has been computed, they are likely to stay for a longer time: an average of fifteen days

---

52. Simone De Beauvoir, "Old Age—End Product of a Faulty System," *Saturday Review* (April 8, 1972), p. 41.

per visit compared to only six days for the strongest and healthiest adults, persons aged twenty-five to thirty-four.

In economic terms, the aged are one of the most sizable segments of the nation's poor. As of 1975, the median total family income was $13,719.[53] However, for families sixty-five and over, the median family income was $7,298. The median income for persons sixty-five and over who were unrelated individuals, that is, not living in or with families, was $2,956.[54]

Using low-income statistics based on the definition developed by a federal interagency committee, a Census Bureau report indicated that in 1974 there were about 24.3 million persons below the low-income level, comprising 11.6 percent of the United States population. Children and the aged represent the largest proportion of persons below the low-income level: children under fourteen years comprised about one-third and persons sixty-five and over approximately one-seventh of the low-income population. There was a seven percent increase in the number of poor persons under sixty-five years of age between 1973 and 1974 while the number of low-income persons sixty-five years of age and over did not change significantly. Substantial increases in Social Security benefits were about equal to the Consumer Price Index during 1974.[55]

Of course, age is simply one factor of significance in the low-income family. The figures would rise tremendously if one were to consider families headed by women (poverty rate of 33 percent compared to 6 percent for families headed by men), race (one of three blacks[56] compared to one of ten whites), geographical distribution (southern poverty rate higher than northern and western), occupation (poverty rate for farm families larger than for nonfarm families), family size (23 percent of all poor families have seven or more persons as compared to 8 percent poor families with three persons), educational attainment (two-thirds of the low-income family heads age twenty-five and over did not complete high school), employment status (38 percent of male heads below the low-income level are unemployed or not in the labor force compared to 5 percent of employed heads), and occupation (poor are heavily concentrated in occupational groups that are low skilled and low paying: service workers, farm workers, and nonfarm laborers).[57]

Extreme caution must be taken in the categorization of the aged as a

53. *Statistical Abstract: 1976*, op. cit., no. 674, p. 416.

54. U.S Bureau of the Census, *Current Population Reports*, Series P-3, no. 59, "Demographic Aspects of Aging and the Older Population in the United States," U.S. Government Printing Office, 1976, Table 6–6, p. 52.

55. U.S. Bureau of the Census, *Current Population Reports*, Series P-60 no. 99, "Money Income and Poverty Status of Families and Persons in the United States: 1974," U.S. Government Printing Office, 1974, pp. 2 and 20.

56. For two articles of particular interest on the plight of the aged black, see Ira F. Ehrlick, "The Aged Black in America—The Forgotten Person," *The Journal of Negro Education* 44 (Winter 1975), pp. 12–23; and Jacquelyne J. Jackson, "The Plight of Older Black Women in the United States," *The Black Scholar* 7 (April 1976), pp. 47–55.

57. Ibid., pp. 18, 21–23.

homogeneous population. Although dependency, sickness, and isolation are frequent, a sizable proportion of these people have few health problems, carry on active lives with families and friends, and continue to make major economic and social contributions to their community and society.

Socialization of the Aged

The tremendous emphasis given to children and youth in socialization literature largely ignores and overshadows the resocialization needs of the aged. In contrast to the aged, the child receives much of his socialization within the family, from peers, schools, job, or community. But what socializing agents exist to direct the aged from one life stage to another? Where is the training for retirement? Where is the training for widowhood? Where is the training or preparation for illness or death? Where is the training for the narrowing of social relationships?

In many ways American society overlooks the fact that persons over sixty-five are social beings, that their world is maintained and meaning is found through interaction with others. As should have become very clear in the previous chapter, of primary importance to the socialization process and to the defining and redefining of the self is the extent and nature of friendship ties, association with significant others, involvement in groups of reference, and social interaction in general. Why should these factors be less important to persons over age sixty-five than to those under age twenty? It could be argued that these social relationships take on increased importance as persons move outside of their occupational spheres and as they experience the deaths of their age-peers.

In a study of sex differences in intimate friendships of old age, the authors concluded that, contrary to stereotypes, men had more frequent social contacts than women, but a smaller proportion of their interaction was with intimate friends.[58] Males did not retreat to workshops, solitary leisure pursuits, or rocking chairs. They had frequent social contacts, usually with friends, children and their families, and spouses. Women more often turned outside the family for emotional support and more often had an intimate friend. Another study indicated that males and females experience approximately the same rates of social interaction with kin and friends, but aged males, particularly widowers, are less likely to participate in religious organizations.[59]

When compared with younger adults, older persons as a group are re-

---

58. Edward A. Powers and Gordon L. Bultena, "Sex Differences in Intimate Friendships of Old Age, "*Journal of Marriage and the Family*" 38 (November 1976), pp. 739–747.
59. Marc Petrowsky, "Marital Status, Sex and the Social Networks of the Elderly," *Journal of Marriage and the Family* 38 (November 1976), pp. 749–756.

moved from primary social roles. Society has provided few role definitions for older persons that would attach them to or keep them active in the social system. Whereas students, parents, and persons in the business or professional world speak with glee of the day when they will be relieved of social responsibility, older persons often find their new "freedom" carries with it grave consequences. Simply providing a variety of recreational activities does not serve as an adequate functional substitute for the responsibilities of gainful employment. For many, the later years brings with it a feeling of uselessness, not with the past but with the present.

An extension of these ideas are expressed in the disengagement theory of aging provided by Elaine Cumming and William Henry:[60] Their theory suggests that aging is an inevitable mutual withdrawal or disengagement, resulting in decreased interaction between the aging person and others in his social system. This process of being disengaged may be initiated either by the individual or by others in his situation. A withdrawal from certain groups may lead to an increased preoccupation with self. In addition, many institutions within society "assist" in this withdrawal.

The results of the Cumming and Henry study supported the ideas that there is a decrease in the number of persons with whom the individual habitually reacts, there is a decrease in the amount of interaction with them, there are qualitative changes in styles and patterns of interaction, and as a result of this decreased involvement with others, changes in the personality system and increased preoccupation with self occur.

Since the appearance of the disengagement theory, crucial questions have been raised about its validity. It has been argued that this process may describe only a fraction of the aged and not the entire population, that the aging process is not a progressive unilineal change, that disengagement is not necessarily inevitable, and finally, that it is unclear whether age in itself is a crucial or a relatively incidental, factor in disengagement.

It seems likely that disengagement will appear for certain people and not for others. For either type of person, the family stands as an available resource. It's importance stems from the fact that intimacy and familiarity characterize the family system and make it more suitable to fulfill many of the needs, services, and interaction patterns of the individual members. However, it should be noted that family factors do not operate independently of the culture in which families operate. To avoid having the aged become "socially disabled," there needs to be a congruity between the cultural goals and structural opportunities that a society provides. The effectiveness of the family as a resource is largely contingent upon the values and services of the larger society: job opportunities, leisure-time activities, health care, clarity of

---

60. Elaine Cumming and William E. Henry, *Growing Old: The Process of Disengagement* (New York: Basic Books, 1961). See also Elaine Cumming, "Engagement with an Old Theory," *International Journal of Aging and Human Development* 6 (1975), pp. 247–251.

role, perception of the aged as fulfilling valuable functions, and socializing opportunities appropriate to the later stage of the life cycle.

RETIREMENT

The problem of retirement involves the resocialization of men and women to new roles and a new life-style. Since men have assumed the major economic responsibility throughout life, this period is crucial for many men, much as the middle years and postparental period is for many women. But as men increasingly take on household tasks and assume a more expressive role, their shift demands readjustment on the part of the wife as well.

Studies of the effects of retirement on marriage have tended to focus on changes in role differentiation[61] and the sharing of household tasks.[62] The role changes moved from a more instrumental type of behavior on the part of the husband and a more expressive type of behavior on the part of the wife to mutually exclusive behavior. As stated by Troll:

> The husband adjusts from the instrumental role of "good provider" to a more expressive role—"helping in the house"—and his wife also adjusts by moving from a relatively more instrumental "good homemaker" to an even more expressive "loving and understanding." The retired husband ends up sharing in household tasks, but whether or not he feels good about it seems to depend on his value system. If, as is true of many working-class husbands, "woman's work" is considered demeaning, the man sharing it feels devalued. This does not seem to be as true for middle-class men.[63]

Wives in Wisconsin were asked what effect they think retirement will have or has had on their relationships with their husbands.[64] Three distinct groups emerged: pessimists (32 percent of the sample), optimists (39 percent of the sample), and neutralists (29 percent of the sample). The pessimists were concerned that their husbands will find themselves with a surplus amount of time and a fear that their husbands will intrude into their domestic domain.

61. Aaron Lipman, "Marital Roles of the Retired Aged," *Merrill-Palmer Quarterly,* 6 (1960), pp. 192–195; Aaron Lipman, "Role Conceptions and Morale of Couples in Retirement," *Journal of Gerontology* 16 (July 1961), pp. 267–271.

62. John A. Ballweg, "Resolution of Conjugal Role Adjustment after Retirement," *Journal of Marriage and the Family* 29 (May 1967), pp. 277–281; and Alan C. Kerckhoff, "Husband-Wife Expectations and Reactions to Retirement," *Journal of Gerontology* 19 (October 1964), pp. 510–516.

63. Lillian E. Troll, "The Family of Later Life: A Decade Review," *Journal of Marriage and the Family* 33 (May 1971), p. 274.

64. Alfred P. Tengler, "Attitudinal Orientations of Wives toward Their Husbands' Retirement," *International Journal of Aging and Human Development* 6 (1975), pp. 139–152.

The optimists saw retirement as a time for an exciting new life together: for gardening, for sleeping in, for fishing, for companionship, for visiting children and grandchildren, for travel, and for doing things together. The neutralists saw no effect, no difference, or didn't know. This group was comprised of a larger number of working class and less educated wives who felt they had less control in the future and would "take what comes."

In studying the family life of old people in London, Peter Townsend found that the men viewed approaching retirement with uneasiness and ill-concealed fear.[65] Many said they would miss being at work and would have nothing to do. Many men preferred to remain at work even though it was arduous and they had experienced recent spells of disability or sickness. Retirement threatened many of the long-standing associations of their lives. Retirement reminded them of their failing strength and skill and that their period of usefulness to others was coming to an end. Often men preferred to step down into a job of inferior status rather than take the bigger step outside into retirement.

After retirement, most of which occurred involuntarily, some of the men were able to take on additional domestic chores. They puttered about in the home doing odd jobs and repairs. They went for a stroll to meet a few acquaintances in the park or stand with them at a street corner. Reading, walking in the park, visiting their children, listening to the radio, tending a few flowers, occasionally going to a club or the cinema—these seemed to be the common recreations of retired men. They were not given much opportunity for self-expression, and the family activities that were left did not provide ways of justifying their lives. They were forced to recognize that it was not their working life that was over, it was their life.[66] Is the situation so different in the United States? Perhaps not, particularly for the working classes. Tending flowers, assisting in housework, and reading tend to represent drastic shifts in life-style and role performance for lower-middle and lower-class men.

Retirement for women tends to represent a less drastic shift in roles, since domestic roles often supplement work roles. Prior to retirement they fulfilled many tasks that they can continue to fulfill after retirement. Women are more likely to retire by choice, and their earnings are less likely to be their sole source of income. Nevertheless, for both sexes retirement necessitates major role readjustments.[67] Health, income, status, and feelings of self-worth tend to decrease at the time of retirement, and often the problems are compounded with the death of a spouse.

---

65. Peter Townsend, *The Family Life of Old People* (London: Rutledge and Kegan Paul, 1957), pp. 158–160.

66. Ibid., pp. 168–169.

67. See, for example, Fred Darnley, Jr., "Adjustment to Retirement: Integrity or Despair," *The Family Coordinator* 24 (April 1975), pp. 217–226.

THE POSTMARITAL FAMILY

The postmarital family, consisting of the widow or widower, is not unique to the aged family but is disproportionately represented after age sixty-five; more women occupy a widow status than any other marital status. Facing the loss of a spouse and making the shift from a married to a widowed status may present extreme difficulty, particulary among those above the poverty level. It was suggested that widowhood at the lowest income levels is relatively insignificant because spouses are not as likely to have been emotionally close nor as interpersonally dependent when married.[68]

Society compounds the difficulty of adjusting to the widowed status by placing an unstated taboo on the discussion of death between husband and wife or parents and children while they are alive. As a result, the widow or widower is often unprepared for the decisions that need to be made. Even if discussions preceded the death, the likelihood is great that loneliness, social isolation, and a need for major readjustments in living patterns will result. There is probably no other period in one's life when there is a greater effort at self-awareness. Feelings of inadequacy and guilt, which lead to depression, are frequent occurrences after the death of a spouse.

Readjustment processes may be less difficult if widowhood follows a major illness or some type of major role change on the part of the spouse. Widowhood is often surmounted best when a person has already built some autonomy of personality, close continuing friendships, a realistic philosophy of life, economic security, and some meaningful personal interests.

Extended-family relationships may not be as significant in the adjustment to widowhood as is often assumed. While research studies indicate a high degree of contact between older people and younger family members, especially adult children, this contact is not directly associated with higher morale or greater personal satisfaction.[69] In contrast to family members, friendship-neighboring is clearly related to less loneliness and worry and a feeling of "usefulness" and individual respect within the community. Friendship relationships are often based upon common interests, a common life-style and a voluntary relationship, while family ties are often marked by dissimilar concerns, different interests, formal obligations, and a role reversal between the elderly parent and the adult children. Certain intergenerational difficulties may be inevitable and be increased by factors such as ill health and economic dependency.[70]

Life expectancy at birth was shown to be 75.9 for females and 68.2 for

---

68. Ira W. Hutchison, III, "The Significance of Marital Status for Morale and Life Satisfaction among Lower-income Elderly," *Journal of Marriage and the Family* 37 (May 1975), pp. 287–293.

69. Greg Arling, "The Elderly Widow and Her Family, Neighbors and Friends," *Journal of Marriage and the Family* 38 (November 1976), pp. 757–768.

70. Ibid., p. 766.

> Louise: *There really are a lot of problems with being a widow. It's been over two years since my husband died. Definitely the faith that we shared was one of my greatest comforts. Without it I don't know how people move ahead. You know, I really don't. If I cried, oftentimes it was for me. It was very lonely. Sometimes for him—he's missing so much you know. But then, after all, our faith tells us this is only part of life, and the real life is in the life hereafter anyhow.*
>
> *I think I've moved into the position of—I'm the boss now. My daughter went through a period after my husband's death when she was constantly testing me. She took the attitude there's no boss in this house, now I do as I please. Well, you know, I can boss, and— there was a lot of conflict to let her know in no uncertain terms there is a boss in this house. If I had just backed off and sat and cried and said I wish your Dad was here and all that stuff I would have let them down I think. There are plenty of times when I wish he was there and could dump the whole mess on him, and he would have been up to it. But, he wasn't there, so I had to do it. And it was good for me and it was good for the children.*

males. Of those who reach age 65 females will live on the average of 17.5 more years, compared to 13.4 for the male. With women thus outliving men, the sex ratio is very unbalanced in these years.[71] Programs to encourage remarriage among widows and widowers could not be successful, at least in a monogamous fashion.

The problem is further compounded in our society by the norm that suggests that women should marry men of their own age or older. The remarriage problem for widowers is less severe since there is both an excess number of women their own age and a social approval given to marrying women younger than themselves.

For women, the death of a husband means a shift from a division of labor and mutual dependency to the joining of forces with a group of unattached women. If his death occurs before retirement, it means a loss of the social identity that was derived from his occupation. For men, the death of a wife means not merely a loss of a companion, but a major shift in his linkage to kin, family, and the social world in general. Evidence indicates that the aged male suvivor experiences a different impact from loss than his female counterpart and that he encounters severe difficulties in adapting to the single status.[72] In many ways the problems of a surviving husband, although far

---

71. The sex ratio becomes even more unbalanced among cigarette smokers. See Robert D. Retherford, "Cigarette Smoking and Widowhood in the United States," *Population Studies* 27 (July 1973), pp. 193–206.

72. Felix M. Berardo, "Survivorship and Social Isolation: The Case of the Aged Widower, *The Family Coordinator* (January 1970), pp. 11–25.

fewer widowers exist, are more serious than those confronting a surviving wife. Whereas most aged widows can care for themselves, the aged widower is more likely to need assistance in meal preparation and general care.

The seriousness of the difficulties faced can be seen in examining the frequency of suicides. Within a given age group, the suicide rates of the widowed are consistently higher than those of the married and the rate of completed suicides is significantly higher for males than females. A review of these studies indicated that both attempted and successful suicides frequently tend to be preceded by the disruption of significant social interaction and reciprocal role relationships through the loss of a mate.[73] A study of aged persons in Florida reported the following major findings:

> 1) The widowed exhibit higher suicide rates than the married; 2) this differential is partially explained by the greater social isolation of the widowed, particularly the widowers; 3) the widowed can find in other types of relationships meaningful alternatives to marriage which help prevent suicidal behavior; 4) widowers have greater difficulty than widows in making effective substitutions for the loss of spouse; and 5) there appear to be limits to the effective mitigation of these alternatives for the widowed, especially the widower.[74]

These problems do not exist independently of retirement—discussed previously—and may be aggravated by it. The widower is removed from his major sources of self-identity: his job and the relationships he had with his co-workers. The result of losing a spouse in old age, particularly among males, is therefore characterized by unhappiness, low morale, mental disorders, high death rates, and high suicide rates.[75] All these seem to be related to the social isolation the widower faces. Not only has he lost a significant other in his spouse, but he becomes isolated from other persons significant to him: friends, neighbors, kin, and those connected with formal organizations. On the other hand, the widow has a greater opportunity for role continuity: housekeeping, interacting with relatives, going to church, and participating in various other kinds of formal and informal relationships.[76]

Some widows and widowers remarry, but the chances of remarriage are, of course, higher for widowers than for widows. The questions centering around the remarriage of widows and widowers are often different from the questions centering around the remarriage of divorced persons. The persons are generally older and face different circumstances surrounding the ending of the previous marriage. A remarriage after the death of a spouse is likely to

---

73. William Rushing, "Individual Behavior and Suicide," in Jack P. Gibbs, ed., *Suicide* (New York: Harper, 1968), pp. 96–121.

74. E. Wilbur Bock and Irving L. Webber, "Suicide among the Elderly: Isolating Widowhood and Mitigating Alternatives," *Journal of Marriage and the Family* 34 (February 1972), p. 24.

75. Ibid., p. 25.

76. Ibid., p. 29.

lead to a comparision of the new spouse with the memory of the deceased. It has been suggested that the perceived quality of marriage improves after the death of a spouse; the tendency is to recall the pleasant experiences and be keenly aware of the spouse's absence. Perhaps it is not accidental that saints exist primarily among the deceased.

INTERGENERATIONAL RELATIONSHIPS

In some ways, a discussion of intergenerational relationships may appear to be an extension of the previous sections on the middle and later years. And so it is. However, at this point, attention is focused on one particular research report of changes in family patterns of planning and achievement over three generations.[77] This is an empirical study of 312 generationally linked families located in the Minneapolis-St. Paul metropolitan and hinterland area. Following the family-development approach, the basic objectives were to establish longitudinal patterns of earning, saving, spending, buying, and financial planning.

Hill demonstarted that the modified-extended-family network relies on the middle or parent generation to serve as the lineage bridge.[78] The parent generation, whose boundaries are contingent to both the married children and grandparents, is most often involved both in intergenerational contacts and in help exchanges. Who needs such an extended-family network? All three generations do. When trouble strikes they turn predominantly first to immediate kin. But the balance between giving and helping is not identical within the intergenerational network and this factor introduces some strains. The married children are high in both giving and receiving. The grandparents give much less than they receive and find themselves in a *dependent* status. The parents give to both younger and older generations more than they receive from either and are in a *patron*-like status.[79]

> These findings lead us to concede that although intergenerational transactions do appear to be governed in part by the norm of *reciprocity* that two other norms are even more apparent, namely the norms of *filial obligation* and of *noblesse oblige*. These latter norms appear to be sufficient to motivate an optimum level of kin keeping activities designed to maintain viable modified extended family networks.[80]

---

77. Reuben Hill with chapters in collaboration with Nelson Foote, Joan Aldous, Robert Carlson, and Robert MacDonald, *Family Development in Three Generations* (Cambridge, Mass.: Schenkman, 1970.
78. Ibid., p. 78.
79. Ibid., p. 79.
80. Ibid., p. 80.

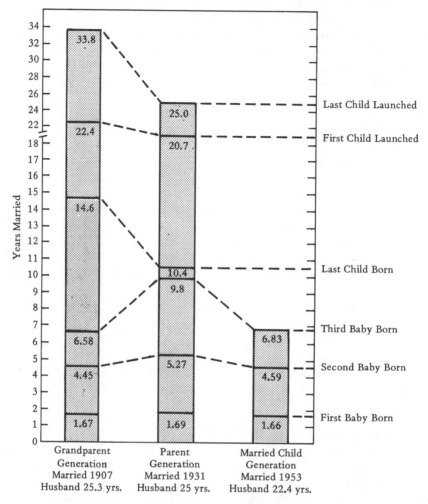

FIGURE 18–2. Profile of the Timing of Family Composition Changes by Generation. Source: Reuben Hill et al., *Family Development in Three Generations* (Cambridge, Mass.: Schenkman, 1970), Chart 4.01, p. 84. Reprinted by permission.

Figure 18–2 demonstrates the similarities and differences between the generations in the timing of family composition changes from age at marriage to launching of the last child. As can be seen, the average grandparent generation married in 1907, the parent generation in 1931, and the married children generation in 1953. All three spent nearly the same time childless, about 1.6 years. Differences of some magnitude appear in the spacing of subsequent births, especially the third and later births. The grandparent generation had its second child 4.45 years and third child 6.58 years after marriage.

They closed their families at 5.2 children, with over one-fourth bearing eight or more children. The last child was born after 14.6 years of marriage, their first child was launched after 22.4 years, and their last child after 33.8 years. The depression-oriented parent generation waited longer than the grandparent generation to have their second and third child, but had their last child much sooner. This generation launched their first and last child at 20.7 and 25 years respectively. The married children generation still has over twenty years of possible childbearing ahead but may not extend its childbearing over as long a period as the previous generations.[81]

In examining the acquisition of the family's divisible goods, it was noted that there is no steadily mounting size of inventory among families as they age. Possession of novel items tended to be higher among children, intermediate among parents, and lowest among grandparents. Durables given as gifts flowed from the oldest to the youngest generation. The speed of acquisition of goods was greater for each successive generation. The child generation does the most forward planning of purchases, and the grandparent generation the least.[82]

These and other findings of the Hill study were examined to construct nine miniature theories and a more general theory that deals with the issue of relations with kin and the synchronization of time, money, and resources. In brief, *family life cycle management* consists of *timing the status changes* of the nuclear family in such a way that each of the family's several careers are mutually supportive of the life-style the family is seeking to achieve.[83] *Resource management*, or *family consumership*, consists of the optimum allocation of energies, information, goods, and expenditures to meet the needs of family members and others within the family's social network. Forward planning on a long-term basis and preplanning of short-term actions are among the components of optimum resource management. Nuclear families in modified-extended-family networks of high solidarity contribute what they can best give and draw on the network for help in solving problems that they cannot solve by themselves. The middle generation serves as the kin-keeping lineage bridge.

Under conditions of rapid change, each generational cohort encounters at marriage a unique set of historical constraints and incentives that influence the timing of its crucial life decisions. This makes for marked generational *dissimilarities* in life cycle career patterns: age at marriage, the number and spacing of children, the changes of jobs by the husband, the wife's entry into the labor force, and the timing of acquisitions.

Intergenerational continuity of *similarities* of three generations occurs with respect to expressive patterns such as religious affiliation, residence loca-

---

81. Ibid., p. 85.
82. These selected findings taken from ibid., pp. 171–172.
83. This brief overview was summarized and selected from ibid., pp. 321–324.

tion, and upgrading of economic and educational competencies. Successive generations not only upgrade but accelerate in performance. It is theorized that this observed acceleration in upgrading from generation to generation reflects increasing responsiveness by successive generations to an interdependence of career achievements. As Hill indicates:

> Among contemporary generational cohorts, for example, the grand-parent generation proved relatively nonresponsive, constrained as it was by lack of competence in controlling family size, by low range of income, limited occupational alternatives and constricted housing possibilities; the middle generation got off to a slow start in the depths of the economic depression, but was more responsive and planful in child spacing, even though erratic in its synchronization of careers, leading in selected careers at the expense of lagging in others. The youngest generation, whose entire marriage span has been spent under conditions of rising affluence of a managed economy making available multiple options has been the most responsive of the three generations, achieving closest fit among its several career achievements, suggesting the best life-cycle planning and management to date.[84]

The study has as its final chapter the application of the research findings for families. The newly married, the family head, the policy maker, or family members at any stage of the life cycle could profit from the suggestions given. Distinctions are made between changes that are possible for families to undertake without professional help, those that are likely to necessitate professional attention, and still others that are likely to require basic changes in economic and social policies through social legislation.[85]

Summary

This chapter included an examination of two major periods of the life cycle: the middle years from approximately age forty to retirement, and the later years from approximately age sixty or sixty-five until the ending of the life span.

The middle years, after the departure of children and prior to retirement, is a period when most men and women are married with small percentages of single, widowed, or divorced. Also, it is one of the longest periods of the marital life cycle, covering a span of approximately twenty years. For men, the middle years are the time when earning power is at its peak. For women, the departure of children and the advent of menopause lead to many shifts in marital and work roles. For many couples, it is a period of "freedom" from certain financial responsibilities, for geographical mobility, and from housework and other chores.

---

84. Ibid., p. 323.
85. Ibid., p. 349.

Many wives accept employment in the labor force during these years. Prior to the middle years, the major concern over employment is the working mother. It is widely believed that maternal employment has many effects on a child, all negative. However, few studies exist that report meaningful differences between the children of working mothers and the children of nonworking mothers. The differences that do exist are explained less by the mother working than by chance factors, social class, part- or full-time employment, age of the children, mothers' attitudes toward the employment, or other social and psychological factors. Maternal employment does create shifts in the balance of power in the marital relationship and changes in marital role expectations and behavior.

It is during the middle years that most parents become grandparents. Thus the rocking-chair image of grandparents becomes glaringly inappropriate.

The family of later life in the United States is often viewed as an undesirable period of life, accented by dependency relationships and declining productivity. This stands in contrast to much of the world where older persons receive increasing status, prestige and deference.

In the United States more than four-fifths of the men and less than one-half of the women age sixty-five to seventy-four are married. After age seventy-five, approximately two-thirds of the man and one-fourth of the women are married. Marriages that do exist are perceived as favorable when compared to preceding periods of the life cycle. Most of the men and women of this age are living in families or living in geographical proximity to their children.

The problems facing the aged population are many, since, for example, they comprise one of the most sizable segments of the nation's poor. Health, loneliness, being needed, lack of status, prestige, and the like all contribute to the social dilemma of the elderly. The state of rolelessness of many persons creates a need for resocialization to a new definition of self in relation to society. Retirement, as well, demands a resocialization to new roles and a new life-style. All of these factors are compounded by the death of a spouse.

The postmarital family, particularly as represented by the widow or widower, while not unique to the aged family is disproportionately represented after age sixty-five; more women occupy a widow status than any other marital status. With the unbalanced sex ratio, remarriage is out of the question for a large number of women. For men, although the availability of a new spouse is less of a problem, his problems may be more severe than those of the surviving wife.

The kin network and intergenerational relationships play a significant role for families of all generations. A three-generational study shows the parent generation, whose boundaries are contingent to both the married children and grandparents, serving as the lineage bridge across the generations. As social conditions change, one consequence is that of marked generational dissimilarities in life cycle career patterns. Yet, despite change, a certain continuity or similarity of generations occurs with respect to expressive patterns such as religious affiliation, residence location, and upgrading of economic and educational competencies.

The family life cycle, while ending for a particular nuclear-family grouping, continues for the multigenerational extended family. Each stage or category of the life cycle has circumstances that are both unique to, and different from, the other stages. This chapter examined selected factors relating to the postparental periods: middle years, retirement, and old age. Conflict, crisis, and marital disorganization, although present at these periods of the life cycle, are not confined to them. The next chapter explores social patterns surrounding crisis and disorganization with particular emphasis on divorce.

Key Terms and Concepts

Discussion Questions

1. What is unique about the middle years or the empty-nest period? How is the period of adjustment different for women and for men?
2. What arguments, if any, exist against the employed wife and/or mother? What social factors are most influential in determining who will work? Explain reasons for the increase in female paid employment.
3. Discuss the consequences of the employed wife and mother on the marriage, on the children, and on the female herself. Are there circumstances in which the negative consequences overweigh the positive?
4. Indicate changes in the grandparent role over the last thirty years. Is this primarily a function of retirement?
5. How true is the argument "you can't teach an old dog new tricks" when applied to the middle-aged or aged couple?
6. A journal article was titled, "Old Age: Product of a Faulty System." In what ways is the United States system faulty in dealing with old age?
7. Discuss changes in husband-wife roles that are likely to accompany illness, retirement, grandparenthood, remarriage, and so forth. How can resocialization be facilitated?

8. *What are the implications of retirement at age sixty, fifty-five, or fifty? Note male-female differences in adjustment patterns after retirement.*

9. *What advantages or disadvantages exist to the widow or widower: if living alone, living with kin, living in a private home with other than kin, living in an institution? What types of conditions make one more favorable than another? Which of these are likely to result in highest/lowest suicide rates?*

10. *Invite several persons over age seventy-five to your class or to a "bull session" (assuming they are not one and the same!) to discuss such topics as their mate-selection processes, wedding practices, views of youth, and marriage practices today.*

11. *Comment on factors that contribute to difficulties in people of different generations living or working together.*

12. *List differences in life-styles, purchasing habits, values, and the like between your generation, your parents' generation, and your grandparents' generation.*

Further Readings

Atchley, Robert C., *The Social Forces in Later Life,* 2d. ed. Belmont, Calif.: Wadsworth, 1977. An introduction to the subject of human aging with particular emphasis on social and sociopsychological aspects.

Dumont, Richard G., and **Dennis C. Foss.** *The American View of Death: Acceptance or Denial?* Cambridge, Mass.: Schenkman Publishing Co., Inc., 1972. A monograph providing the current state of social–science knowledge concerning American death attitudes and an articulation of and suggested resolution to the acceptance—denial controversy.

Hill, Reuben, et al. *Family Development in Three Generations.* Cambridge, Mass.: Schenkman Publishing Co., Inc., 1970. A study of nuclear families in the Minneapolis–St. Paul area linked by three generations: grandparent families, parent families, and young married children families.

Hoffman, Lois Wladis and **F. Ivan Nye.** *Working Mothers.* San Francisco: Jossey-Bass, 1974. *Working Mothers* is an interdisciplinary review of the consequences of employment on the wife, husband, and child.

Jacobs, Ruth H., and **Barbara H. Vinick.** *Re-Engagement in Later Life: Re-employment and Re-marriage.* Stamford, Conn.: Greylock, 1977. A look at senior citizens who experienced losses of a job or spouse but became reemployed or remarried.

Lopata, Helena Znaniecki. *Widowhood in an American City.* Cambridge, Mass.: Schenkman, 1973. The author of *Occupation: Housewife* has provided us with an extensive study and analysis of widowhood. This book is compulsory reading for anyone interested in this area.

Shanas, Ethel, and **Gordon F. Streib, eds.** *Social Structure and the Family: Generational Relations.* Englewood Cliffs, N.J.: Prentice-Hall, 1965. A collection of fifteen articles that coordinates views from the fields of psychiatry, economics, and sociology in an intensive investigation of the three-generation family structure in western society, with special emphasis on generational relationships of the aged.

Sheehy, Gail, *Passages: Predictable Crises of Adult Life.* New York: E. P. Dutton, 1976. A humane and readable revelation of the internal and external forces acting upon adults as they experience changes throughout the life cycle.

Sussman, Marvin B. "The Family Life of Old People," in Robert H. Binstock and Ethel Shanas, eds. *Handbook of Aging and the Social Sciences.* New York: Van Nostrand Reinhold, 1976, pp. 218–243. An examination of a number of themes relating the family life of old people to bureaucratic and organization linkages, kin networks, and variant family forms and intergenerational transfers.

Townsend, Peter. *The Family Life of Old People.* London: Rutledge and Kegan Paul, 1963. A study in two parts describing, first, the family life of 203 people of pensionable age in a working-class borough of East London and, second, a discussion of the chief social problems of old age against the background of family organization and relationships.

Troll, Lillian E. *Early and Middle Adulthood.* Monterey, Calif.: Brooks/Cole, 1975. An attempt to provide a "missing link" in life-span development text between the transition from adolescence and the transition into old age.

Troll, Lillian E. "The Family of Later Life: A Decade Review," *Journal of Marriage and the Family* 33 (May 1971), pp. 263–290. A review of the kinship structure, economic interdependence, family interaction patterns, etc., of families during the second half of life.

Woodruff, Diana S., and **James E. Birren, eds.** *Aging: Scientific Perspectives and Social Issues.* New York: D. Van Nostrand, 1975. A collection of factual, timely, interdisciplinary articles written by colleagues at the Ethel Percy Andrus Gerontology Center.

19

Marital Crisis:
Disorganization and Reorganization

19

Marriages and families have been examined throughout the life cycle. No period in life is without the potential for marital crisis: disorganization and reorganization. You may recall references to parenthood as crisis, low levels of marital satisfaction ten to fifteen years after marriage, a period of disengagement, role conflicts, and the like. Each refers to some event or process that produces or produced stress, conflict, crisis, or disorganization to the marital or family unit.

If eyewitnesses to the American family are to be believed, this institution and the interpersonal relationships within it have been in a state of decline for the past several hundred years. Preachers, teachers, philosophers, political leaders, commentators, and others have recorded their beliefs, irrespective of the generation in which they lived, that parental authority was becoming more lax, sexual taboos were weakening, spouses were rebelling against one another, and so forth. This was usually contrasted to the "old days" when authority was respected, sexual taboos were observed, and spouses were more understanding and tolerant. That each generation makes reference to weakness and decline may indicate dissatisfaction with present events, whatever those events may be, and sentimentality over the past, or it may indicate that actual conditions are never equal to the ideal. In either case, marital and family life is seldom "perfect" either for a given marriage or family as it covers the life cycle or for the marital and family system at any given time within a society. Stressor events produce crisis and disorganization. Let us examine some of these social stresses on the family.

SOCIAL STRESSES ON
THE FAMILY

In a widely quoted article, Reuben Hill speaks of *stressor* or crisis-provoking events.[1] These are situations for which the family has had little or no prior preparation. They are never the same for any given family but vary in striking power by the hardships that accompany them. Hardships are those complications in a crisis-precipitating event that demand competencies from the family that the event itself may have temporarily paralyzed or made unavailable.[2]

Closely related to this idea is Jean Lipman-Blumen's usage of crisis to mean "any situation which the participants of a social system recognize as posing a threat to the status quo, well-being, or survival of the system or any of its parts, whose ordinary coping mechanisms and resources are stressed or inadequate for meeting the threat."[3] Note that both writers extend their definitions beyond events or situations per se. The event or situation need be one in which the family is ill-prepared, demands competencies, is recognized as posing a threat, and stresses the available resources or coping mechanisms.

It is interesting that different families with similar competencies and resources respond very differently to similar events. The key appears to be at the "meaning" dimension. That is, to transform a stressor event into a crisis requires an intervening variable that has been variously termed "meaning of the event" or "definition of the event." This produces a formula as follows: A (the event) $\rightarrow$ interacting with B (the family's crisis-meeting resources) $\rightarrow$ interacting with C (the definition the family makes of the event) $\rightarrow$ produces X (the crisis).[4] Let us examine each of these.

Stressor events (A) may come from a wide variety of sources both within and outside the family. The consequences are likely to differ considerably depending on the source. For example, a general principle in sociology indicates that certain events outside a group such as war, flood, or depression tend to solidify the group. Thus, although stressful, certain external events may tend to unify the family into a more cohesive unit rather than lead or contribute to its breakdown. These same events may not be defined as critically stressful because other persons are in the same situation or worse. For example, it is disappointing to professional researchers to have their writings

1. Reuben Hill, "Social Stresses on the Family," *Social Casework* 39 (February-March 1958), pp. 139–150; see also Donald A. Hansen and Reuben Hill, "Families under Stress," in Harold T. Christensen, ed., *Handbook of Marriage and the Family* (Chicago: Rand McNally, 1964), pp. 782–819.

2. Hill, op. cit., p. 141.

3. Jean Lipman-Blumen, "A Crisis Framework Applied to Macrosociological Family Changes: Marriage, Divorce and Occupational Trends Associated with World War II," *Journal of Marriage and the Family* 37 (November 1975), p. 890.

4. Hill, op. cit., p. 141.

Abused Wives: Why Do They Stay?

Richard Gelles in a series of papers has addressed the issue of violence in the home: physical aggression between husbands and wives, wife abuse, child abuse, pregnancy beatings, and the like. One article attempts to answer the question as to why physically abused wives stay with their husbands.

He found that: 1) the less severe and the less frequent the violence, the more a woman will remain with her spouse and not seek outside aid, 2) the more a wife was struck by her parents, which apparently raises her tolerance for violence, the more inclined she is to stay with her abusive husband, 3) wives who stay with an abusive husband are less likely to have completed high school and are more likely to be unemployed, i.e. they have less power and fewer resources, and 4) the actions

of the wife are influenced by external constraints in the form of police and agency and court lack of understanding about marital violence.

Gelles found some spouses who suffered repeated severe beatings or even stabbings without so much as calling a neighbor. Some spouses reported that it is acceptable for a husband to beat his wife "every once in a while." Divorce appears to be a solution only after a history of conflict and reconciliation, when the wife can no longer believe her husband's promise of no more violence nor forgive past episodes of violence, when the violence is severe and frequent, and when women recognize and have the needed resources for this type of action.

Source: Richard J. Gelles, "Abused Wives: Why Do They Stay?" *Journal of Marriage and the Family* 38 (November 1976), pp. 659–668 and reprinted in J. Ross Eshleman and Juanne N. Clark, *Intimacy, Commitments, and Marriage: Development of Relationships.* Boston: Allyn and Bacon, 1978, pp. 306–318.

rejected by editors of journals. The pain may be less severe if it is recognized that a given publication has a 90 percent rejection rate. To know that many others submitted articles and were rejected, did not get their research funded, lost their homes, had premature births, or were unemployed often makes the event appear less critical. That is, others share similar misfortunes.

Events within the family that are defined as stressful are often more disorganizing because they arise from troubles that reflect poorly on the family's internal adequacy.[5] These events may be nonsupport, mental breakdown, suicide, or alcoholism, among others. The range of events, either within or outside the family, that disturb the family's role patterns are numerous. Not only do they involve losses of persons, jobs, or incomes, but additions as well. The arrival of a child, grandmother, or mother-in-law may be as disruptive as the loss of any of those three. Sudden fame or fortune may be as disruptive as loss of either. Any sudden change in family status or conflict among family members in the conceptions of their roles may further produce family crisis.

The dimensions that characterize any given stressor or crisis-provoking event extend far beyond whether it occurs internally or externally to the family. A crisis-producing event may affect the entire system or only a limited

---

5. Hill, op. cit., p. 142.

part, may occur gradually or suddenly, may be intense or mild, may be a short- or long-term problem, may be expected and predicted or random, may arise from natural conditions or artificial and technological man-made effects, may represent a shortage or overabundance of vital commodities, may be perceived to be solvable or insolvable, and may vary in substantive content.[6] The nature of the crisis event will influence the specific response of an individual or family system.

Hill classifies family crises on the basis of dismemberment, accession, and demoralization.[7] Dismemberment involves the loss of family members (war separation, hospitalization of spouse, death of child, spouse, or parent), accession involves the addition of an unprepared-for member (unwanted pregnancy, deserter returns, step-parent additions, some war reunions, some adoptions, aged grandparents), and demoralization involves the loss of moral and family unity (nonsupport, infidelity, alcoholism, drug addiction, delinquency, and events bringing disgrace). Combinations of these (suicide, divorce, desertion, runaways, institutionalization for mental illness) may be crisis-producing events as well.

Again, what factors make for crisis proneness and freedom from crisis proneness? The explanation lies in B and C in the formula presented earlier. That is, to what extent do families have resources to meet the event (factor B) and to what extent do families define the event as a crisis (factor C)? Crisis-meeting resources (factor B) may include many factors: family adaptability, family roles, family coherence, money income, insurance, friends, religious beliefs, education, good health, and the like. Problem families are often those without adequate resources to meet the stressor events. The extent to which families define the event as a crisis (factor C) reflects the value system of the family and previous experience in meeting crisis. Hill notes that accident proneness is disproportionately high among individuals who lack self-confidence and are characterized by anxiety.[8] Crisis proneness (X) is therefore a function of both a deficiency in family organization resources (factor B) and the tendency to define hardships as crisis producing (factor C). These two factors are combined into one concept of family inadequacy or family adequacy.

TYPES OF FAMILY
DISORGANIZATION

Family disorganization refers to the breakup of a family unit when one or more members are unwilling or unable to perform their role obligations

6. Lipman-Blumen, op. cit., p. 890.
7. Hill, op. cit., p. 142.
8. Hill, op. cit., p. 145.

Childhood Illnesses and Stress

Do children have their first illness at times of great upheaval in their lives—a move to a new neighborhood, a new baby in the family, a parent becoming ill? It seemed so to Arthur Z. Mutter and Maxwell J. Schleifer of the Department of Psychiatry of Boston University School of Medicine as they got to know the patients in the pediatric ward of a city hospital (Psychosomatic Medicine, July/ Aug. 1966). To test their clinical impression against systematic inquiry, they looked into the experiences that 42 of their children patients had had in the six months that preceded their hospitalization. The children were all between the ages of six and twelve; they had been admitted to the hospital with diagnoses that included cat scratch fever, appendicitis, rheumatic fever, meningitis, croup, and pneumonia. Patients with diseases known to have psychosomatic origins—such as ulcerative colitis and bronchial asthma—were deliberately excluded from the study. Mutter and Schleifer interviewed these children and their mothers and compared their stories with those of a group of 45 well children of similar age, race, religion, and family background:

More of the sick children (67 percent) had suffered the loss of someone they cared about than the well children (46 percent).

The families of the sick children were more likely to include someone whose health, mood, or behavior was disturbed—a depressed mother going through her menopause, a rebellious adolescent brother, a moody, hard-drinking father.

The mothers of the sick children functioned less adequately as parents, and their families were less cohesive.

More than half of the sick children had gone through changes that were rated as moderately threatening (a serious illness of a parent, for instance) or seriously threatening (like a parent's death); none of the well children had experienced a severe change and less than 25 percent had gone through even moderate changes.

These results have led the authors to an enlarged concept of disease, where the purely biological factors of injury or infection are only part of a picture that involves psychological and social factors as well. They see disease as the result of a complex interaction between three kinds of stress—biologic, social, and psychological—and the differing abilities of each child to cope with them.

Source: "Roundup of Current Research," *Trans-Action* 4 (November 1966), p. 2. Reprinted by permission.

adequately, as these are viewed by other members.[9] Goode classifies the major forms of family disorganization as follows:

1. *The uncompleted family unit: illegitimacy.* Although the family unit cannot be said to "dissolve" if it never existed, illegitimacy may nevertheless be viewed as one form of family disorganization for two reasons: a) the potential "father-husband" conspicuously fails in his role-obligations as these are defined by the society, the mother, and (later) the child; and b) the parents of both the young mother and the young father fail in their social obliga-

9. William J. Goode, "Family Disorganization," in Robert K. Merton and Robert Nisbet, eds., *Contemporary Social Problems*, 4th ed. (New York: Harcourt Brace Jovanovich, 1976), p. 514.

tion to control the courtship behavior of the two young parents—a major indirect cause of illegitimacy.

2. *Voluntary departure of one or both spouses: annulment, separation, divorce, desertion.*

3. *Changes in role definitions that result from the differential impact of cultural changes.* Social movements such as women's liberation may affect relations between husband and wife, but a major type problem in this category is parent-youth conflict.

4. *The "empty shell" family,* in which individuals live together but have minimal communication and contact with one another, failing especially in the obligation to give emotional support to one another.

5. *The family crisis caused by "external" events,* such as the temporary or permanent *involuntary* absence of one of the spouses because of death or imprisonment, or as a result of such impersonal catastrophes as flood, war, and depression.

6. *Internal catastrophes that cause involuntary major role failures; for example, mental, emotional, or physical pathologies,* such as severe mental retardation of the child, psychosis of the child or spouse, or chronic or incurable physical conditions.[10]

Not all types of family disorganization are viewed by a given society as equally important or worthy of particular sympathy or attention. Even when the disorganization is seen as important, society may only pay attention to one family member. For example, little attention is given to the father of an illegitimate child. Although many types of family disorganization exist, this chapter will not deal with all of them. For example, the first form of family disorganization that Goode listed above—the uncompleted family unit (illegitimacy)—was described in Chapter 16. Changes in role definitions were described in Chapter 17. Empty-shell families are characteristic of many marriages as described in Chapter 15. Family crises caused by internal and external events were included in the discussion at the beginning of this chapter. The remainder of this chapter, then, will be devoted primarily to the voluntary departure of one or both spouses. More specifically, most space will be devoted to divorce, the type of family disorganization in which many marriages end, the type of family disorganization that appears to be at the heart of concern to the general public, and the type that best serves as an index of changes in other aspects of the family.

DIVORCE

Marital systems throughout the world include at least two people, each with their own needs and values, who live together. This factor creates the

---

10. Ibid., p. 515. Copyrighted 1961, 1966, 1971, 1976 by Harcourt Brace Jovanovich, and reprinted by permission.

potential for conflict and voluntary departures. In many societies, including our own, marriage is regarded as a civil contract with the state specifying the conditions under which marriages may be dissolved. Winch classifies the law concerning marital dissolution in the following fashion:

1. In some countries marriage is completely indissoluble except by death. This is in conformity with the Canon Law of the Roman Catholic Church. Countries having this legal feature are heavily Catholic: Spain, Peru, Brazil, Colombia.[11]

2. A divorce is granted if it is shown that one party has been guilty of a grave violation of his marital obligations. Such is the situation in most states of the U.S.A., France, and many other countries.

3. A divorce is granted if it is shown that the marriage is completely broken in fact. In different ways this is the policy in Switzerland, the U.S.S.R., Yugoslavia, Poland, Germany, Rhode Island and Louisiana, and all the Scandinavian countries.

4. Divorce by the mutual agreement of the parties. This is practiced nowhere in Europe. There is provision for it in the civil code of Belgium, but it is so hedged about with formalities that it is equivalent to (3) above. There is also provision for such divorce in Japanese law, but the practice seems to make it the equivalent to "divorce by the husband's unilateral repudiation of his wife."

5. Free power of the husband to terminate his marriage by repudiation of his wife. This is still the official law of Islam and of Judaism. In most Islamic countries and in Israel there are movements to limit the husband's freedom of repudiation and to provide a possibility for the wife to bring dissolution for cause or for factual breakdown, i.e., on the basis of (2) or (3) above.[12]

In the western world, divorce is generally viewed as an unfortunate event for the persons involved and as a clear index of failure of the family system.[13] But in addition to divorce being seen as a personal misfortune or as an index of failure, it may also be viewed as an escape valve, a way out of the tensions of marriage itself. William Goode claims that not only is divorce permitted in nearly all the world's societies, but in most primitive societies the rate of divorce has been higher than in the contemporary United States.[14] In

11. The following eleven countries reported to the United Nations that they have no legal provisions for granting absolute divorces: Argentina, Brazil, Chile, Colombia, Ireland, Italy, Malta, Paraguay, Philippines, Santa Lucia, and Spain.

12. Robert F. Winch *The Modern Family*, 3d ed. (New York: Holt, Rinehart and Winston 1971), pp. 574–575.

13. Feldberg and Kohen trace the failure of family life to its complex dependence on the capitalist corporate order and the particular sex-based division of labor that is a product of that order. Family members are faced with demands from external organizations that prevent them from responding to each other's personal needs. Roslyn Feldberg and Janet Kohen, "Family Life in an Anti-Family Setting: A Critique of Marriage and Divorce," *The Family Coordinator* 25 (April 1976), pp. 151–159.

14. William J. Goode, *The Family* (Englewood Cliffs, N.J.: Prentice-Hall, 1964), pp. 92–93.

addition, a few nations have had higher divorce rates than the United States at different times in the past, such as Japan in the period 1887–1919; Algeria, 1887–1940; Israel, 1935–1944; and Egypt, 1935–1954. At present, the United States has one of the highest divorce rates in the world. The U.S. rate of 4.4 divorces per 1,000 persons in the population in 1973, compared to 2.7 in the U.S.S.R., 2.0 in Sweden, 2.1 in Egypt, 1.7 in Canada, 1.2 in Australia and 0.8 in Israel.[15]

Divorce Rates

Divorce rates are likely to be calculated in one of three ways: by the number of divorces that take place per 1,000 persons in the total population, by the number of divorces per 1,000 married females aged fifteen and over, and by the ratio of divorces granted in a given year to the number of marriages contracted in that same year. Note the difference in rate depending on the figures used.

The number of divorces (including annulments) that took place *per 1,000 persons in the total population* in the United States in 1975 was 4.8.[16] This means that for every 1,000 persons in the population (men, women, children, adults, married, single, etc.), 9.6 persons obtained or 4.8 marriages ended in divorce or annulment. Or said another way, if you come from a city of 100,000 population where 480 divorces were granted in 1975, the divorce rate was 4.8. Since our system is monogamous (two persons per divorce), 960 individuals in the city of 100,000 persons were divorced that year. Note how this divorce rate can be influenced by factors such as the age distribution or the proportion of the married or single population. A country or city with a large family size, a low life expectancy, a late age at marriage, a sizable proportion of the population being children or single teen-agers, and a disproportionate number of the population unmarried, could have a sizable percentage of those married getting divorces and yet have a seemingly "low" divorce rate.

The number of divorces, again including annulments, that took place *per 1,000 married women, age fifteen and over* in the United States in 1975, was probably close to twenty.[17] This means that there were twenty divorces per 1000 married females age fifteen and over. Of the three rates mentioned, this one is probably the most accurate. Unlike the first rate described, men,

---

15. United Nations, *Demographic Yearbook*, 1973, Table 21.
16. U.S. Bureau of the Census, *Statistical Abstract of the United States: 1976*, 97th ed. (Washington, D.C., 1976), no. 97, p. 68.
17. At the time of this writing, the 1975 figures were not available. The 1974 figure was 19.3. Ibid., no. 97, p. 68.

single persons, children, and the like were excluded. It is figured on the basis of the legally married women who constitute the group that is susceptible to divorce. This figure could be used to compare the divorce rate cross-culturally without being influenced by the number, age, or marital status of the total population.

The ratio of *divorces granted in a given year to the number of marriages in that year* was probably close to 40 in 1975.[18] This is the rate used to best illustrate the "breakdown in the American family." See for yourself. Two out of five marriages end in divorce—or do they? Let us assume that your city of 100,000 population issued 1,000 marriage licenses in 1975. The same year, 400 divorces were granted. This would result in a divorce-marriage ratio of 2 in 5 or 40 divorces per 100 marriages. Thus, there were two divorces for every five marriages in your community in the year 1975. Suppose your state passed a no-fault divorce law in 1975 and instead of 400 divorces, 2,000 divorces took place while the number of marriages remained constant at 1,000. Now, according to this rate, we have two divorces for every marriage or a divorce rate of 200. While it may be accurate to speak of twice as many divorces as marriages in a given year, it is not accurate to say that of all marriages two-fifths will end in divorce. The inaccuracy is due to at least three reasons. First, the divorces ended marriages that began over a lengthy time period, not the marriages that began in any specific year. These divorces, the marriages of which began one, eight or thirty years ago, are all compared with the number of marriages in 1975. Second, approximately 20 percent of all marriages that are remarriages are not taken into account. The third reason is based on the fact that the number of marriages is larger than the number of marriage dissolutions. Note an example provided with actual rates:

> Another argument against the use of ratios for forecasting the population to be divorced is based on the fact that the number of marriages is larger than the number of marriage dissolutions. If the ratio of divorces to marriages performed during the same year (0.26 in 1963) were interpreted to mean that 26 per cent of all married couples would eventually divorce, the ratio of deaths of married persons to marriages (0.51) would be interpreted to mean that 51 per cent of all married unions would eventually be dissolved by death. The sum of the two precentages (77) would then be the proportion of unions that would be disrupted either by death or divorce. Thus, the consistent use of ratios in probability statements would not account for 23 percent of all couples.[19]

As of 1975, about 18 percent of the ever-married men and 21 percent of the ever-married women aged forty to forty-four were known to have had a

---

18. Again, at the time of this writing, the 1975 figures were not available.
19. *Divorce Statistics Analysis, United States—1963*, U.S. Department of Health, Education, and Welfare, Vital and Health Statistics, Public Health Service Publication no. 1000, Series 21, no. 13, pp. 2–3.

divorce.[20] While many persons would argue that the rates are "too high," the data do not support, at this time at least, the contention that one-third, two-fifths, or one-half of all marriages end in divorce. It has been estimated, however, that about 34 percent (one-third) of those marriages now in the twenty-five to thirty age group may eventually end in divorce.[21] Glick has estimated that about 40 percent of people born in the 1970s may eventually divorce.[22] He indicated that his estimate may be conservative.

Irrespective of the manner of calculation, readers should be aware that statistics on divorce are not perfect. Even national data reported by the National Vital Statistics Division (NVSD) are based on estimates obtained from states participating in the divorce-registration area (DRA).[23] As of 1976, twenty-nine states and the Virgin Islands participated in the DRA.[24] Thus, actual data from all fifty states are not available. Second, sampling rates vary among the DRA states, depending on the size of their annual divorce totals. All statistics estimated from probability samples have a sampling error. Third, completeness of reporting individual demographic items on divorce records varies considerably among DRA states. For example, some states do not require the reporting of race and others do not require the reporting of the number of this marriage. Fourth, often many items are left blank. This is particularly true of personal characteristics of husband and wife—age, race, and number of this marriage. Although the accuracy of divorce rates and statistics are improving, the divorce data are not perfect. The best available information is presented with the recognition that the figures are based on estimates from selected available data.

Trends in Divorce Rates in the United States

The number of divorces and annulments granted in the United States increased from the pre-World War II figure of 264,000 in 1940, to the post-

20. U.S. Bureau of the Census, *Current Population Reports*, Series P-20, no. 297, "Number, Timing and Duration of Marriages and Divorces in the United States: June 1975," (Washington, D.C.: United States Government Printing Office, 1976), Table G, p. 6.

21. Ibid., Table G, p. 6.

22. Dr. Paul C. Glick, Senior Demographer, Population Division, Bureau of the Census, gave this estimate at a Groves Conference workshop in Kansas City, March 1976.

23. For a history of marriage and divorce statistics programs of the National Vital Statistics Division, with a discussion of research opportunities in divorce statistics and the usefulness of these records, see Carl E. Ortmeyer, "Marriage and Divorce Statistics Programs of the National Vital Statistics Division—Current Developments and Research Potentials," *American Sociological Review* 27 (October 1962), pp. 741–746.

24. *Statistical Abstract of the United States: 1976*, op. cit., p. 49.

TABLE 19–1. Number of Divorces and Divorce Rates: United States, 1945–1975

Year	Number of Decrees	Rate per 1,000 Total Population	Rate per 1,000 Married Women	Year	Number of Decrees	Rate per 1,000 Total Population	Rate per 1,000 Married Women
1975	1,026,000	4.8	—	1959	395,000	2.2	9.3
1974	977,000	4.6	19.3	1958	368,000	2.1	8.9
1973	915,000	4.4	18.2	1957	381,000	2.2	9.2
1972	845,000	4.1	17.0	1956	382,000	2.3	9.4
1971	773,000	3.7	15.8	1955	377,000	2.3	9.3
1970	708,000	3.5	14.9	1954	379,000	2.4	9.5
1969	639,000	3.2	13.4	1953	390,000	2.5	9.9
1968	584,000	2.9	12.4	1952	392,000	2.5	10.1
1967	523,000	2.6	11.2	1951	381,000	2.5	9.9
1966	499,000	2.5	10.9	1950	385,000	2.6	10.3
1965	479,000	2.5	10.6	1949	379,000	2.7	10.6
1964	450,000	2.4	10.0	1948	408,000	2.8	11.2
1963	428,000	2.3	9.6	1947	483,000	3.4	13.6
1962	413,000	2.2	9.4	1946	610,000	4.3	17.9
1961	414,000	2.3	9.6	1945	485,000	3.5	14.4
1960	393,000	2.2	9.2				

Source: *Increases in Divorces: United States, 1967,* U.S. Department of Health, Education and Welfare, Public Health Service Publication No. 1000, Series 21, No. 20, December, 1970, p. 12. Data for 1970 through 1975 obtained from *Statistical Abstract: 1976,* no. 68, p. 51, and no. 97, p. 68.

World War II figure of 377,000 in 1955, to 708,000 in 1970, to 1,026,000 in 1975.[25] The rate per 1,000 population increased from 2 in 1940, to 2.3 in 1955, to 3.5 in 1970, to 4.8 in 1974. The increase was not as steady as it appears from the selected figures given (see Table 19–1 and Figure 19–1).

The number of divorces had a more steady increase. The 1974 figure of 1,026,000 divorce decrees—that is, more than two million divorced persons—was the highest national total ever observed for the United States. During the last few years, the number of divorces has increased more rapidly than the total population and the married population of the United States.

Generally, divorce rates have declined in times of economic depression and risen during times of prosperity (see Figure 19–1). The depression years of 1932–1933 had the lowest rate of divorce per 1,000 married women in the last fifty-five years. Following the depression, the rate of divorce moved upward almost steadily until the first postwar year, 1946. After 1946, the rate

25. Ibid., no. 68, p. 51.

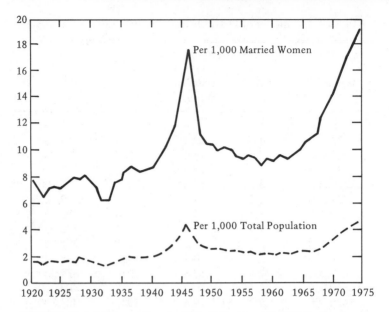

FIGURE 19–1. Divorce Rates: United States, 1920–1975. Source: *Increases in Divorces: United States: 1967*, U.S. Department of Health, Education, and Welfare, Public Health Service Publication No. 1000, Series 21, no. 20, December 1970, p. 1. Data for 1969 to 1975 was filled in by the author on the basis of census material.

dropped sharply until 1950. For about fifteen years, until 1965, the divorce rate showed considerable stability, increasing slightly some years and decreasing during the mini-recession years of 1954 and 1958. Since 1965, the divorce trend has again climbed relatively sharply, reaching the highest rate in the history of the United States during the 1970s.

Variations in Divorce Rates

Divorce rates vary widely by geographic, demographic, and social characteristics. Let us examine several variations and seek explanations for higher or lower rates according to the selected characteristics.

Geographic Distribution

The geographic distribution of divorce rates in the United States indicates a general trend toward an increase as one moves from east to west. This appears to have been true since the nineteenth century. The divorce rate is

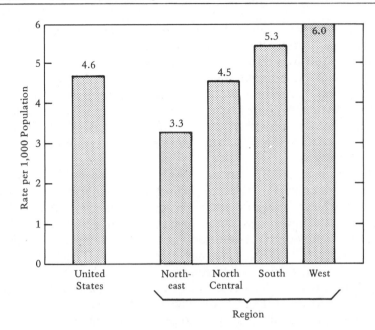

FIGURE 19–2. Divorce Rates per 1,000 Population: United States and Each Region, 1974. Source: Contructed from data provided in U.S. Bureau of the Census, *Statistical Abstract of the United States: 1976,* 97th ed. (Washington, D.C., 1976), no. 103, p. 71.

highest in the western states, followed by the South, the north central states, and the Northeast (see Figure 19–2).

Major variation exists by individual states as well. The divorce rate per 1,000 population in 1974 was lowest in North Dakota (a rate of 2.5) and highest in Nevada (a rate of 17.5). States with a rate of 3 or less per 1,000 population in 1974 included Massachusetts, Rhode Island, New York, New Jersey, Pennsylvania, Wisconsin, North Dakota, and South Dakota. States with rates above 5.5 included Indiana, Florida, Georgia, Tennessee, Alabama, Arkansas, Oklahoma, Texas, Idaho, Wyoming, Colorado, New Mexico, Arizona, Nevada, Washington, Oregon, California, and Alaska.[26] Note how the lowest rates generally occur in the northeast and the highest rates in the south and west.

Even within states, divorce rates vary. For example, rates tend to be higher for standard metropolitan areas (SMAs) than for the remainder of the state.

How can these geographical variations be explained? It is likely that

26. Specific divorce rates by state for 1974 can be seen in the *Statistical Abstract: 1976,* op. cit., no. 103, p. 71.

different factors operate in different areas, but it is believed that divorce rates will be lower in culturally homogeneous rather than heterogamous communities, and in communities with primary face-to-face interactions in contrast to communities with anonymous and/or segmentalized relationships. Primary communities would tend to exert stronger social pressures against "deviant" behaviors (as divorce is often perceived to be) and exert both formal and informal pressure for conformity to community norms. Thus divorce rates might be expected to be lower in rural than urban, or in nonmetropolitan than metropolitan areas.

State and regional differences might be explained by the "liberality" of divorce laws in the newer established sections of the country. The older, more established northeast and mideast areas of the country tend to be more conformist than the newer, less established, fewer multigenerational kin groupings of the West and South. In addition, legal requirements may tend to influence divorce rates.[27] While Nevada may produce a small fraction of the total divorces granted nationally (approximately 2 percent), the divorce rate per 1,000 population within that state can be affected significantly by relatively few in-migratory couples. Except for Nevada and a few other states, it is unlikely that migratory divorce has a major effect on divorce rates within most states. Finally, states with higher proportions of a non-Catholic and young adult population can be expected to have higher divorce rates. Although these factors tend to influence rates, a state-by-state analysis would show many exceptions. Here is one area where current knowledge appears inadequate. At present, precise explanations for state-by-state variation in divorce rates is unknown.

Age of Husband and of Wife

Most typical ages at divorce after the first marriage are twenty-five to twenty-nine for men and twenty to twenty-four for women. In 1975, 27 percent of all divorces among men occurred between the ages of twenty-five to twenty-nine (an additional 22 percent were aged twenty to twenty-four). For women, 44 percent of all divorces occurred between the ages of twenty to twenty-four (an additional 12 percent were aged twenty-five to twenty-nine).[28] Thus, approximately one-half of all divorces occur among persons in their twenties. The median age for divorce after the first marriage is 29.1 for men and 27 for women.

27. Dorothy M. Stetson and Gerald C. Wright, Jr., "The Effects of Laws on Divorce in American States," *Journal of Marriage and the Family* 37 (August 1975), pp. 537–547.
28. *Current Population Reports*, Series P-20, no. 297, op. cit., Table H, p. 7.

The divorce rate is very high among young marriages.[29] The concern over young marriage that was discussed in Chapter 10 included the high incidence of divorce as a factor. Explanations may include emotional immaturity, inability to assume marital responsibilities, greater incidences of early marriage in lower socioeconomic statuses where divorce is more likely, a longer time period in which to get divorced, more premarital pregnancies (also related to higher incidences of divorce), and similar factors. But if factors such as emotional maturity, socioeconomic status, premarital pregnancy, and the like were held constant, it is likely that age would be a less crucial factor in divorce. In other words, it may not be age per se that leads to higher incidences of divorce but a series of factors that intervene between age and divorce that make marriage difficult irrespective of age.

Duration of Marriage

In 1975, the largest number of divorce decrees were granted one to three years after marriage and the number declined relatively consistently with increasing duration. Approximately 5 percent of the divorced were married for less than one year, 8 percent for one year, 9 percent for two years, 16 percent three or four years, 28 percent for five to nine years, and 35 percent for ten years or longer. Thus, about one-third (37 percent) of the divorces were granted to couples who were married for four years or less, another one-third were married for five to ten years and the final one-third were married for more than ten years.[30] These figures represent the time from the legal beginning of the marriage to the legal decree of divorce. Without doubt, the breakup of marriages in all ways except the legal begins well before the actual divorce. Thus, although more divorces occur during the second and third year of marriage (the mode) than at any other time, the first and second year may be the modal ones for marital breakups. Divorces that occur in the seventh or fourteenth year of marriage may simply be a legal break of a marriage broken years earlier.

In 1975, the median interval between the first marriage and divorce was 7.0 years. The median interval between the divorce and a second marriage was 3.2 years, and the median interval between the second marriage and redivorce was 5.3 years.[31] It would appear that the median length of each succeeding marriage that ends in divorce is shorter than the previous one. Perhaps the first experience is the most difficult one. Having been through a divorce, ac-

---

29. See, for example, Robert Schoen, "California Divorce Rates by Age at First Marriage and Duration of First Marriage," *Journal of Marriage and the Family* 37 (August 1975), pp. 548–555.
30. *Current Population Reports*, Series P-20, no. 297, op. cit., Table O, p. 14.
31. Ibid., Table O, p. 14.

cepting the divorce status and later remarrying may tend to make divorce a more acceptable solution to an unsuccessful second, third, or fourth marital relationship.

As indicated in the first sentence in this section, the number of divorces decline relatively consistently with increasing duration. In other words, after the peak years for divorce (years two, three, and four) have been passed, the proportion of divorces by length of marriage gradually diminish. There is no evidence from the 1975 survey (or any other known source) that implies an increase in divorce "after the children have grown up." That phase of the life cycle of the family is reached at quite varied lengths of time after marriage.[32]

Many marriages that never end in divorce are broken in fact except for the legal decree. This leads to a point indicated at various times throughout the book: that length of marriage is not necessarily an index of success or adjustment and that divorce is not necessarily a good index of marital breakdown. Divorce may simply provide an indication of the greater willingness or acceptance to acknowledge a legal ending of a previously ended meaningful marital relationship. Is it possible that higher divorce rates indicate greater success, greater adjustment, and higher levels of satisfaction among existing marriages in the United States?

Race, Religion, and Socioeconomic Status

The success of interracial and interfaith marriages was discussed in Chapter 10. At this point, rather than looking at the success or divorce rate of mixed marriages, the question becomes how rates differ by race, religion, or socioeconomic level in nonmixed or endogamous marriages. Are divorce rates different for blacks or whites, Protestants or Catholics, and lower or higher socioeconomic levels?

Divorce rates by race usually differ within a state as well as for the same racial groupings in different states. For example, for the U.S. as a whole in 1975, white males had a divorce rate per 1,000 persons in the population of 3.6 compared to 4.6 for black males. The rate for white females was 5.0 compared to 7.1 for black females.[33] Yet, in the reporting southern states, divorce rates for blacks were lower than or equal to the rates for whites. In the reporting northern states, the rates for black persons were higher than those for white persons and those for black persons in the southern states. This may be due to the urban and mobile character of large segments of the black population in the north. Or, as mentioned in several chapters, racial differences may be partly explained by social class differences or by differing accessibility to

---

32. Ibid., p. 13.
33. *Statistical Abstract:* 1976, op. cit., no. 97, p. 68.

Divorce and Remarriage Issues Vex the Bishops

Washington—(UPI)—The nation's Roman Catholic bishops went into closed session to discuss one of the touchiest issues facing the church—how to respond to divorce and remarriage among Catholics.

It was understood one reason for the executive session was that the bishops did not want it known how deeply divided they are on the issue and wanted to be able to speak frankly and openly with each other.

No specific action is contemplated on the issue, which has grown in seriousness over the past half decade, spawning organizations of divorced Catholics and their sympathizers seeking changes in the treatment of divorced and remarried members of the faith.

But the bishops are considering a major pastoral letter on moral values which reaffirms the church's traditional principles on marriage.

"Some say even sacramental marriages can deteriorate to such an extent that the marital union is destroyed and the spouses are no longer obliged to keep their promise of lifelong fidelity," the proposed pastoral letter says.

"The church is urged to acknowledge such dissolution and allow the parties to enter new, more promising unions.

"We reject this view."

John Cardinal Dearden of Detroit delivered a ringing defense of the Church's controversial Bicentennial "Call to Action" conference in Detroit.

About 1,340 delegates gathered two weeks ago to tell the bishops of their five-year social action plan to "secure liberty and justice for all."

The conference made recommendations to end automatic excommunication of divorced and remarried Catholics, ease the church's traditional ban on artificial means of birth control, and urge more positive discussion of women priests.

Cardinal Dearden, in his defense of the "Call to Action" conference, said "as a process of consultation and dialogue, the program has been successful."

While there were some "flaws," he urged his fellow prelates to "make clear our continuing commitment to co-responsibility. . . . In framing our response we should affirm the freedom and diversity within the church, which was revealed at Detroit."

Source: *The Detroit News*, November 10, 1976, p. 10-A. Reprinted by permission of UPI.

---

various types of social and economic resources. Generally, the greater accessibility to these resources, the lower the incidence of divorce.

What about religion? What divorce differentials exist by major religious affiliation? Marital survival rates for religious-affiliation types are discussed in Chapter 10. Exogamous and endogamous marriages rank both high and low in survival rates. Is there no consistent pattern? An accurate response to this is difficult to make. For example, lower divorce rates generally exist among groups strongly opposing divorce—as many religious groups do. Yet the total voluntary marital dissolution rate in these groups may be almost as high as that of other groups. Also, no national data on this problem are available. The United States census does not ask about religion, religious studies generally deal with a specific locale or specific religious group, and extreme variations exist in religiosity within specific religious affiliations.

It could be expected that the nonrecognition of divorce by the Roman Catholic Church would result in lower divorce rates among adherents to that faith, and most studies show this to be true. However, it appears that the differences among members of different churches have been declining for some decades. In addition, differences in family behavior between those who attend no church at all and those who attend church regularly are often greater than the differences among people who are affiliated with different churches.[34]

What about socioeconomic level? The increased incidence of divorce has been occurring at all socioeconomic levels; yet, the proportion of persons ever divorced remains clearly the highest for relatively disadvantaged groups.[35] Whether education, occupation, or income is used as an index of socioeconomic level, the divorce rate goes up as socioeconomic level goes down.[36]

Apparently, this was not always the case. Until late in the nineteenth century, the elite administered the divorce law. These elite, who had little interest in the marital problems of the poor, were the only people who could obtain a divorce at all. In many states, it was possible to obtain a divorce only by a special act of the state legislature. Goode notes that whatever the rate of marital instability (desertion, disharmony, separation), the rate of divorce in the United States was higher in the upper classes until some period in the late nineteenth or the early twentieth century.[37] Marriages in the lower classes of course were not necessarily more stable; divorce was simply not an available option to them.

The greater marital instability and higher divorce rates at the lower socioeconomic levels may stem from a number of factors.[38] First, the frustrations involved in the greater difficulty in meeting expenses and the lesser income may affect other areas of marital life. Second, at higher social strata, satisfaction in work and sexual spheres may less necessitate an escape from marriage. Third, the upper strata are more tied in to long-term investment expenditures that are less easily stopped or ended in contrast to the immediate daily need expenditures of the lower strata. Fourth, although the income is insufficient at the lower strata for the type of car, house, or fur coat of the higher strata, the desire for them remains. The purchase of these goods is the responsibility of the husband, and failure to obtain them is the failure of the husband. Fifth, the kin and friend network of the upper strata is larger and

34. See Thomas P. Monahan, "Some Dimensions of Interreligious Marriages in Indiana, 1962–1967," *Social Forces* 52 (December 1973), pp. 195–203.

35. Arthur J. Norton and Paul C. Glick, "Marital Instability: Past, Present and Future," *Journal of Social Issues* 32 (Winter 1976), p. 13.

36. Houseknecht and Spanier found highly educated women (those with five or more years of college) to be an exception. Sharon K. Houseknecht and Graham B. Spanier, "Marital Disruption among Highly Educated Women: An Exception to the Rule," (Unpublished paper sent to the author).

37. Goode, *The Family*, op. cit., p. 88.

38. These factors are discussed more fully in ibid., pp. 88–90, and in Goode in Merton and Nisbet, op. cit., pp. 533–534.

more tightly knit, making divorce more difficult and giving it far greater consequences.[39]

The latter explanation of higher divorce rates among the lower strata was central to Scanzoni in his "reinquiry into marital disorganization."[40] His basic tenet was that the degree of disorganization is inversely related to the integration of the nuclear unit into the kin network. The higher divorce rate among the lower classes in American society is explained by the tendency of lower-class nuclear families to become polarized as a result of each spouse identifying with, and participating in, his or her own blood-kin group. Individual participation in disjunctive and competing kin networks leads to more conflict and higher divorce rates. Many lower-class nuclear units fail to be highly integrated to one dominant set of kin. This lack of integration results in an absence of a common set of values and goals, which gives rise to normative conflict.

In contrast, middle- and upper-class families, who tend to experience fewer divorces, maintain extensive "quasi-kin" networks along with blood-kin relations. Middle-class marital partners are more likely to be mutually involved in external networks with a high rate of social participation. To the extent that the couple is mutually integrated into these external networks, it will share common values and norms and hence resolve conflict by means other than dissolution.

The alert reader may note what appears to be a contradiction in the data. For example, it was shown in Figure 19–1 and mentioned in the text that divorce rates tend to decrease during an economic depression and rise during times of prosperity. Also, it was just mentioned that the incidence of divorce increases as socioeconomic level goes down. How is it possible that divorce rates decrease during depressions when "times are hard," and increases among the lower strata where "times are also hard?"

Several factors are involved. During depressions, divorce rates drop at all class levels. The lower classes during the Great Depression of the 1930s still had the highest divorce rate. Many of the marriages that "survived" the 1930s contributed to the divorce rate of the 1940s, which was the highest in United States history. Also, the ease in getting a divorce varies. If divorce is difficult and expensive to obtain, upper classes have higher divorce rates despite the fact that lower classes have greater marital conflict and disorganization. Finally, the total life-style, the sense of loyalty, the linkages with kin, the occupational and income security, and the group support in general affect rates of divorce. These factors were different for depression families and lower-class

39. For studies on kinship relationships after divorce, see Jerry W. Spicer and Gary D. Hampe, "Kinship Interaction after Divorce," *Journal of Marriage and the Family* 37 (February 1975), pp. 113–119, and Donald F. Anspach, "Kinship and Divorce," *Journal of Marriage and the Family* 38 (May 1976), pp. 323–330.

40. John Scanzoni, "A Reinquiry into Marital Disorganization," *Journal of Marriage and the Family* 27 (November 1965), pp. 483–491.

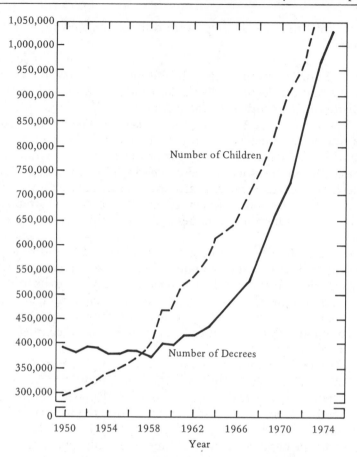

FIGURE 19–3. Number of Divorce and Annulment Decrees
Granted and Number of Children Involved: United States, 1950–
1974. Source: *Children of Divorced Couples: United States
Selected Years*, U.S. Department of Health, Education, and Welfare, Public Health Service Publication No. 1000, Series 21, no. 18,
p. 1. and estimates based on *Statistical Abstracts of the United
States: 1976*, 97th ed. (Washington, D.C., 1976). no. 97. p. 68.

families. Once again we note the powerful influence of the social network in
something perceived to be so "individualistic and personal" as divorce.

Children of Divorced Parents

The number of children involved in divorce has increased more rapidly
than the number of divorces granted (see Figure 19–3). In 1973, an estimated
1,079,000 children were involved in 913,000 divorce and annulment decrees,

an average of 1.17 children per decree. Although the estimated number of children involved in all divorces has been increasing steadily (logically enough, given the overall increase in divorce), the average per decree has been declining in recent years; in 1965, the average reached a peak of 1.36 children per decree.[41] One reason for the decline may be the recent decline in the birth rate. Other reasons include a slight increase in the proportion of childless at divorce (although six of ten divorces in 1973 were among couples who had children) and a decline in the estimated interval between marriage and divorce.[42]

That three of five divorces involve children and that each divorce averages more than one child tends to dispel the myth that "children prevent divorce." However, this can be interpreted in various ways, for the presence of children *is* related to the median duration of marriage at the time of decree. The greater the number of children, the longer the median length of marriage prior to divorce. For example, in 1969, the median length of marriage prior to divorce was 3.8 years for couples with no children under age eighteen. This increased to 5.4 years for those with one child, 9.2 years for those with two children and 13.8 years for those with three or more children.

The trend does seem to be toward a greater willingness to get divorced when children are present, which leads to the question of greater concern: What are the consequences for the children? Should couples, although unhappily married, stay together for the sake of the children? The presumed effect on children is usually negative. That is, the assumption is that divorce is always traumatic for the children, who will suffer psychologically, socially, and economically.

Very few of us would quarrel with the notion that children are better off in happy, stable families than in divorced or unhappy, unstable families. For example, one study indicates that whether black, white, male or female respondents from parental homes that were disrupted by death or divorce during their own childhood had higher rates of divorce or separation in their own first marriages.[43] Research findings such as this confirm the popular notion that divorce is bad for children. This belief is further supported by research results seeming to show that children from broken homes are more likely than others to be low achievers, psychologically disturbed, and delinquent.[44] Recent reviews of many of these studies criticized them on the grounds that they lacked adequate controls and asked the wrong questions. Recent studies, that is in the last fifteen to twenty years, show major disagree-

41. Norton and Glick, op. cit., p. 15.

42. Ibid., p. 15.

43. Hallowell Pope and Charles W. Mueller, "The Intergenerational Transmission of Marital Instability: Comparisons by Race and Sex," *Journal of Social Issues* 32 (Winter 1976), pp. 49–65.

44. For an excellent review of some of this literature, see Karen Wilkinson, "The Broken Family and Juvenile Delinquency: Scientific Explanations or Ideology?" *Social Problems* 21 (June 1974), pp. 726–739.

ment as to the impact of the broken home on children. Rarely do results support the idea that partners in unhappy marriages should avoid divorce or separation for the sake of the children,[45] although the impact may vary considerably according to the age of the children and other factors.[46]

In a Cedar Rapids, Iowa, study of seventh and eleventh graders and more than 1,500 of their parents, Burchinal compared personality and social relationship scores for five groups of adolescents, those from unbroken families, those living with mothers only, and those from three types of reconstituted families: mothers and stepfathers, both parents remarried, and fathers and stepmothers. His two general hypotheses were that 1) there are nonsignificant differences among selected personality characteristics of adolescents from the five family types and 2) there are nonsignificant differences among selected measures of social relationships of adolescents from the five family types.[47] The overall conclusions of his investigation were that data were lacking to reject either null hypothesis. In his words:

> Inimical effects associated with divorce or separation and, for some youth, with the remarriage of their parents with whom they were living, were almost uniformly absent in the populations studied. Acceptance of this conclusion requires the revision of widely held beliefs about the detrimental effects of divorce upon children.[48]

Two earlier studies by Goode[49] and Nye[50] also questioned the assumption that the impact of divorce on children is negative. Goode has produced some of the most significant data available on the process of divorce as it relates to children, custody, and visitation arrangements, and many aspects of the mothers' perceptions of the ways in which divorce (and remarriage) affected their children. In his study of divorced Detroit mothers, he found that most of the mothers (8 percent) were concerned about the possible damage to the child but felt the need to go through with the divorce. Data revealed that only 14 percent of the mothers reported that the children were harder to

45. Mary Jo Bane, "Marital Disruption and the Lives of Children," *Journal of Social Issues* 32 (Winter 1976), pp. 110–111.

46. Three research reports by Judith S. Wallerstein and Joan B. Kelly on the effect of divorce on children at different age categories that may be of interest are: "The Effects of Parental Divorce: Experiences of the Preschool Child," *Journal of Child Psychiatry* 14 (Autumn 1975), pp. 600–616; "The Effects of Parental Divorce: Experiences of the Child in Early Latency," *American Journal of Orthopsychiatry* 46 (January 1976), pp. 20–32; and "The Effects of Parental Divorce: The Adolescent Experience," in J. Anthony and C. Koupernik, ed., *The Child in His Family: Children at Psychiatric Risk* (New York: Wiley, 1974), pp. 479–505.

47. Lee G. Burchinal, "Characteristics of Adolescents from Unbroken, Broken, and Reconstituted Families," *Journal of Marriage and the Family* 26 (February 1964), pp. 46–47.

48. Ibid., p. 50.

49. William J. Goode, *After Divorce* (Glencoe, Ill.: Free Press, 1956), pp. 307–330.

50. F. Ivan Nye, "Child Adjustment in Broken and Unhappy Homes," *Marriage and Family Living* 19 (November 1957), pp. 356–361.

handle after the divorce, and 55 percent saw little impact of the divorce process on the difficulty of handling their children. Of the mothers who had remarried, three-fourths thought their children's life was better than during the previous marriage, 15 percent thought it was about the same, and only 8 percent thought it was worse. Thus 92 percent of the remarried mothers thought that their children's life had either improved or stayed the same.[51]

The Nye study compared selected characteristics of several groups of high-school-aged youth from unhappy but unbroken families, happy and unbroken families, and several types of broken families.[52] No significant differences were found between the adjustments of adolescents in unhappy, unbroken families and those in broken families in the areas of church or school relationships and in delinquency companionship. Adolescents from broken families showed significantly better adjustment than those from unhappy, unbroken families in relation to psychosomatic illnesses, delinquency behavior and parent-child adjustment. In general, children from families broken by divorce did not have poorer adjustment than children from families broken in other ways.

In general, findings comparing the adjustment of children from broken homes with children from unhappy, unbroken homes do not produce results anywhere as detrimental as is commonly believed to occur. The impact of divorce was not psychologically disturbing, major personality differences did not result, and problems with children did not increase.

Grounds for Divorce

Divorce is permitted in every state in the United States. With each state having its own divorce code, with each marriage sharing difficulties of other marriages and having a few unique unto itself, it could be expected that the grounds for divorce would vary widely. An examination of these follows.

Legal Grounds for Divorce

Apart from "no-fault" divorce, the most widely accepted legal grounds for divorce are adultery, cruelty, and desertion. Until 1966, New York had the most stringent divorce law, granting divorce for adultery only. Since that time the grounds have been broadened to include cruelty, desertion, felony conviction, and separation for one year after a formal separation decree.

The legal grounds vary for each state.[53] In at least one state they in-

---

51. Goode, *After Divorce*, op. cit., p. 318.
52. Nye, op. cit., pp. 356–361.
53. These can be seen in *World Almanac and Book of Facts* (New York: Newspaper Enterprise Association, 1977), p. 962.

> **Louise:** *Did I ever consider divorce? Like every day maybe. No, you know I'm being facetious. We never seriously considered it. We had problems but we both knew we would work them through. In spite of problems we never stopped loving each other. We were both definitely commited to the philosophy that marriage is forever, for life. And you worked out your problems, and if they can't be worked out, it really is a serious tragedy. I don't think either one of us could even vision living without the other one.*
>
> **Alex:** *In Turkey, you do not have many divorces. Again, it goes back to religion. Turks are a very religious people and they do not believe in divorces. It is a shame for a woman to be divorced. If she gets married, they fall in love and if it doesn't work out, she will have to put up with it. Man doesn't have to put up with it. He can leave. He wouldn't divorce, just leave.*
>
> **Ann:** *I haven't been able to afford a divorce, and it really doesn't make me a difference. I figure because at the time when I found out that his first wife was also pregnant, I didn't care anymore and I didn't care what I did as far as my relationship with other men was concerned.*
>
> **Mac:** *I'm skeptical about divorce. That's why I'm personally in a trial marriage.*

clude loathsome disease, joining a religious order, disbelieving in cohabitation, refusal to cohabit, impotence, violent temper, epilepsy, gross misbehavior, habitual drunkenness, habitual use of drugs, mental incapacity, idiocy, neglect of marital duties, prostitution by the wife prior to marriage, refusal of the wife to move to a new residence, vagrancy, willful neglect, and the like.

As one might well surmise, the majority of grounds are never used and those that are can be defined or interpreted in a wide variety of ways. For example, cruelty—the most popular legal ground prior to no-fault—may include physical abuse, quarreling, name calling, and the like. One wife might claim cruelty because her husband talks constantly, giving her no peace of mind, while the next wife might claim cruelty because her husband never talks to her. Whereas cruelty once meant physical cruelty or an attack upon the spouse's life, today it may mean little more than "incompatibility," thus covering almost any reason available to the imagination.

It is widely recognized that a tabulation of divorces by legal grounds may bear little resemblance to the "actual" or "real" reasons for the marital conflict. The legal grounds simply reflect the fact that apart from no-fault divorce, the "innocent" spouse must prove that the other spouse is "guilty" in his marital behavior. Most divorces involve an agreement by both spouses before the suit is filed. The legal grounds used are likely to be those within their state that are most effective and socially least accusatory.

Under a "fault" or "guilt" system, the wife brings suit in about seven of ten divorce actions. The social norm favors the wife in terms of cruelty, adultery, drunkenness, physical threat, and the like, which makes the entire process easier to finalize. It is also more socially acceptable for the husband to accept the blame even though common sense alone would attest to the infrequency and unlikelihood of one spouse guilty and the other spouse innocent. Under a "no-fault" system the sex of the filer for divorce shifts drastically. Figures from California and New Jersey following no-fault show a dramatic increase in the percentage of men who filed for divorces.[54]

No-fault Divorce

The adversary divorce system in the United States, in which one party must be innocent and the other guilty, has led numerous states to consider "no-fault divorce." The present "no-fault" trend first reached fruition in California, where traditional fault grounds were abolished January 1, 1970, in favor of dissolution of marriage based on "irreconcilable differences which have caused the irremedial breakdown of the marriage" and incurable insanity. Irreconcilable differences are further defined as "those grounds which are determined by the court to be substantial reasons for not continuing the marriage and which make it appear that the marriage should be dissolved."[55] In California, the term "divorce" was replaced with "dissolution of marriage." Community property was to be "substantially" equally divided. Alimony was to be determined by considering a woman's earning ability and the duration of the marriage. The one-year residency requirement was cut to six months.

California was followed by Iowa, which required "that there has been a breakdown of the marriage relationship to the extent that legitimate objects of matrimony have been destroyed and there remains no reasonable likelihood that the marriage can be preserved."[56] Texas, Florida, Colorado, Michigan, Arizona, Connecticut, Delaware, Georgia, Hawaii, Illinois, Kentucky, Minnesota, Nebraska, Washington, and several other states followed with provisions that dissolution be permissible if it is found that the marriage is "irretrievably broken," following the language of the Uniform Marriage and Divorce Act proposed by the National Conference of Commissioners on Uniform State Laws. This uniform act met strenuous opposition from the American Bar Association.

---

54. Lawrence M. Friedman and Robert V. Percival, "Who Sues for Divorce? From Fault Through Fiction to Freedom," *The Journal of Legal Studies* 5 (January 1976), pp. 61–82.
55. James P. O'Flarity, "Divorce Modern-Style," *Trial* 8 (September-October 1972), p. 15.
56. Ibid., p. 15.

Unmarriage Ceremony: Join Us in Ceremony

Hollywood, Calif.—(UPI)—The same guests who attended Mari and Ed Smith's wedding 15 months ago returned to the couple's apartment last week to celebrate the Smiths' divorce.

Their marriage reception had been a traditional champagne party. The dissolution celebration was casual, with the guests partaking of champagne given as wedding gifts.

"The whole idea is to explain that Ed and I are still buddies," said Mrs. Smith, 24. "Why not? Ed's awfully nice but we just couldn't stand living together."

Smith, 44, a real estate broker, said his wife, who is an insurance account assistant, "just wants to be single, and I want to travel."

At the unmarriage ceremony, Pete Kingsbury, the best man at the Smiths' April 14, 1974, wedding, removed the couple's diamond-studded gold wedding bands and then placed them on the fourth fingers of their right hands.

Their wedding invitations had been engraved. The invitations to the dissolution, which read, "You are cordially invited to join us in celebrating our divorce," were Xeroxed.

They ruled out such activities as throwing rice at their guests, scribbling sexy slogans on the guests' cars and ordering a divorce cake with the small bride and groom split apart.

"I told our friends I could wrap and return their wedding gifts, but nobody accepted my offer," Mrs. Smith said.

Source: *Detroit Free Press*, July 16, 1975, p. 2-C.

The Uniform Marriage and Divorce Act included, among others, provisions to eliminate divorce contests, to eliminate the concept of "fault," to make binding terms dealing with money and possessions, to abolish alimony, to only consider the best interests of the child in determining custody of the children, and to abolish all existing defenses to a divorce action.[57]

Today, more than one-half of all states have a no-fault provision in their divorce laws. As indicated, this means that neither spouse has to prove the other is "guilty." In nearly one-third of the states, it includes the possibility of obtaining a divorce—even if the other spouse is opposed to it—without making a legal claim such as adultery, drunkenness, or mental incapacity.

The extent to which no-fault divorce has altered the legal grounds for decree in Michigan can be seen in Table 19–2. In 1964, 91.3 percent of the divorce cases were legally based on "cruelty." In 1974, 0.3 percent were so legally based. In contrast, 97 percent of all divorces in Michigan in 1974 were legally listed as "no-fault."

Usually, divorce proceedings are relatively routine. Unless some legal requirement, such as the establishment of legal residence or the serving of notice upon the defendant is not fulfilled, divorce proceedings take place quickly and are orderly. Where cases are contested, they can become drawn-out affairs with major bitterness and fighting resulting. The no-fault divorce law at-

57. Ibid., p. 15.

TABLE 19–2. Divorces and Annulments by Legal Grounds for Decree, Michigan Occurrences, 1964 and 1974

Legal Grounds	1964		1974	
	No.	Percent	No.	Percent
Cruelty	17,712	91.3	91	0.3
Desertion	737	3.8	—	—
Nonsupport	362	1.9	1	0.0
Fraud	165	0.9	83	0.3
Bigamy	36	0.2	7	0.0
Conviction of Crime	12	0.1	1	0.0
Adultery	27	0.1	1	0.0
Drunkenness	35	0.2	1	0.0
No Fault	—	—	28,167	97.0
Other	36	0.2	344	1.2
Not Stated	278	1.4	344	1.2
Total	19,400	100.1	29,040	100.0

Source: "Marriage and Divorce: An Overview, 1974," Michigan Health Statistics, Michigan Department of Public Health, 1974, p. 68.

tempts to eliminate the need to establish a defense. Where a marriage is in fact irretrievably broken, even if one party does not want to end the marriage, the courts would recognize that a legal continuation would accomplish little more than the perpetuation of the bitterness and animosity of the parties. It is likely that the use of the available defenses under the fault system has rarely led to the healing of marital rifts.

Social Grounds for Divorce

If the legal grounds for divorce do not reflect the reality of the divorce conflict, what then are the marital difficulties that cause divorce? This answer is far more complex than it may appear at first sight. Are "real" reasons "really real"? That is, if the wife's frigidity is the "real" reason for the husband wanting to end the marriage, could his response to her not have contributed to her frigidity? If the husband drinks too much, and alcoholism is the "real" reason for the wife wanting to end the marriage, could she not have contributed to his drinking in many ways?

These examples are not meant to imply that reasons given are unreal, that all reasons simply serve as rationalizations, or that stated reasons should be ignored. On the contrary, "that which is defined as real is real." However, many factors are involved in arriving at agreements and disagreements, adjustment or maladjustment. In dealing with divorce and family disorganization, it becomes necessary to know more than stated reasons or actual behaviors. It becomes necessary to know the social situation, the class level, the husband-wife interaction patterns, and, in general, the definitions, meanings, standards, and norms by which a specific behavior was judged.

Complaints of husbands and wives tend to differ by variables such as sex and social class. Women were found to be more likely than men to complain about nonsupport, adultery, gambling, drunkenness, and desertion. Men were found to be more likely to complain about unsatisfactory sex relations. Lower-class wives were found to be considerably more likely than middle-class wives to complain about financial problems, physical abuse, and drinking. Middle-class wives were found to be significantly more prone to complain about lack of love, infidelity, and excessive demands.[58] Lower-class wives seem to accept a degree of domination by their husbands that middle-class wives would be less likely to tolerate. Complaints appear to be highly relative to the context in which they occur yet often share threads of commonality that cross sex and class lines.

Levinger says, "When things are going well and the relationship is fruitful, husband and wife tend to obtain very similar satisfaction. After all, their marital satisfaction is derived from one another. . . . When matters are going badly, if positive mutuality breaks down, then husband and wife complaints may still be mainly directed toward their joint relationship, but the verbalized sources of friction are different for the partners."[59]

Disagreements and friction are not by any means usually fatal for the marriage. Nevertheless, the kinds of issues that plague a marriage often reflect its weakest points. Blood and Wolfe asked Detroit wives the main things they and their husbands disagreed about since their marriage.[60] Financial problems came up as the chief disagreement in 24 percent of the marriages. This was followed by recreation as the chief disagreement in 16 percent, and an area of disagreement in 30 percent. Children followed with 16 percent and 24 percent respectively. In fourth place was personality with 14 and 28 percent. Other areas such as inlaws, roles, and religion-politics were chief areas of disagreement by 6 percent of the couples or less. Sex was listed by .5 percent of the wives as the chief area of disagreement, and by only 1 percent as an area of disagreement.

Most disagreements and divorce conflicts extend over a period of years. Although conflict is often depicted as resulting from a single event (adultery, pregnancy, drunkenness), most divorces result from a series of minor malad

---

58. George Levinger, "Sources of Marital Dissatisfaction among Applicants for Divorce," *American Journal of Orthopsychiatry* 5 (October 1966), p. 806.

59. Ibid., p. 806.

60. Robert O. Blood, Jr., and Donald M. Wolfe, *Husbands and Wives* (New York: Free Press, 1960), p. 241.

justments or difficulties, none of which can be singularly listed as the "cause" or "reason." George Levinger[61] claims that people stay in relationships because they are attracted to them and/or they are barred from leaving them and that, consciously or not, people compare their current relationships with alternative ones. If internal attraction and barrier forces become distinctly weaker than those from a viable alternative, the consequence is breakup.

Goode states that it is the reciprocity of the conflict process, the contribution that both husband and wife make to the eventual divorce, that makes the fault theory of divorce so hollow. In every divorce, both parties are offenders, although one party may have offended more than the other, and in practically every divorce both husband and wife agree on the terms of the suit beforehand. Indeed, one might claim that the tragedy of divorce is not so much the breakup of marriage as it is the apparent destruction of two seemingly honest and decent people, to the point where they behave badly toward one another.[62]

Following the divorce, both individuals need to readjust to a new status and life-style. Low levels of stress following the dissolution of a marriage were found to be related to social interaction with friends, involvement in organizations, sexual permissiveness, occupational status, economic independence, an orientation toward change, and low levels of dogmatism. Males experienced less postdivorce stress than females. Among males, those with higher occupational status, those who were older, and those with children experienced less stress than others.[63]

In a longitudinal study of fathers for two years following divorce, all families examined reported distress or exhibited disrupted behavior, particularly during the first year. There was no victimless divorce. Following divorce, stresses were reflected in parent-child relations in life-style, in emotional responses, and attitudes toward the self. The first year for the fathers seemed to be one of exploration and trying out a variety of coping mechanisms. The success of these responses was reflected in the increase in happiness, self-esteem, and feelings of competence in divorced men in the period from one to two years following divorce.[64]

For many individuals who experience a divorce, particularly among those who do not want it, the postdivorce period is likely to be filled with pain, anger, hurt, and loss. For those who sought an end to the marriage, divorce

61. George Levinger, "A Social Psychological Perspective on Marital Dissolution," *Journal of Social Issues* 32 (Winter 1976), p. 43.

62. Goode, in Merton and Nisbet, op. cit., p. 542.

63. Helen June Raschke. *Social and Psychological Factors in Voluntary Postmarital Dissolution Adjustment* (Unpublished Ph.D. dissertation, University of Minnesota, Minneapolis, 1974).

64. E. Mavis Hetherington, Martha Cox, and Roger Cox, "Divorced Fathers," *The Family Coordinator* 25 (October 1976), pp. 417–428.

is more likely to be filled with feelings of relief, liberation, independence, an opportunity for growth and development,[65] and the chance for a new life.[66]

DESERTION

Desertion refers to a separation of the spouses that is against the will of one spouse and is intended by the other spouse to end married life. Compared to divorce, little is known about desertion, and few studies exist on this issue. Unlike divorce, desertion is not institutionalized, no registration takes place with the courts or any other official body, the deserting and nondeserting spouse cannot remarry, and little clarity exists as to exactly what constitutes desertion and what roles are appropriate in legal, economic, or social situations. For example, how many days absence constitutes desertion? When a spouse leaves and returns on multiple occasions, do marital and parental role patterns resemble those of the one- or two-parent family? Is one spouse legally responsible for the expenses and activities of the other? Because of the lack of institutionalized norms and the ambiguity of events surrounding desertion, it is believed that desertion has far more negative effects than divorce.

The Bureau of the Census uses the term "marital separations" in reference to married persons living apart because of marital discord. In addition to desertion, this includes, however, those with legal separations. Sometimes referred to as limited divorce, partial dissolution, divorce from bed and board, or *separtio a mensa et thoro*, a legal separation authorizes husband and wife to live apart. Like desertion, the married couple may not remarry, but unlike desertion, arrangements are formalized as to the support of the wife and children, the couple may not live together unless the court grants permission, and the separation permits a couple to mutually interact in attempts to resolve differences.

It is extremely difficult if not impossible to get accurate statistics on the frequency of desertion.[67] Cases are recorded in certain social agencies, particularly those that work with or provide aid to dependent children. Cases of desertion are noted in courts when a spouse, usually the wife, is seeking support for her children, and cases are recorded as legal grounds for divorce. In Michigan, 3.8 percent of all divorce and annulment cases in 1964 were granted on the legal grounds of desertion. In 1974, no cases were so recorded (See Table

---

65. Laura J. Singer, "Divorce and the Single Life: Divorce as Development," *Journal of Sex and Marital Therapy* 1 (Spring 1975), pp. 254–262.

66. Carol A. Brown, Roslyn Feldberg, Elizabeth M. Fox, and Janet Kohen, "Divorce: Chance of a New Lifetime," *Journal of Social Issues* 32 (Winter 1976), pp. 119–133.

67. For information on desertion in Canada, see Stan Skarsten, "Family Desertion in Canada," *The Family Coordinator* 23 (January 1974), pp. 19–25.

19–2). While it is known that desertion is a major issue, an accurate indication of the frequency of it is unknown.

Effects of Desertion

Divorce was shown at times to involve trauma for the wife and children. But in divorce cases, the legal proceedings are fairly well defined, alimony is frequently awarded, and the wife has the option to remarry. In desertion, a far different picture emerges. The husband may be a chronic deserter, going and coming almost at will. Support by the husband may be very sporadic. The wife may never be quite certain whether she is permanently separated or widowed. In addition, the effect of desertion on the children may be very harmful. Compared to divorce, more children are likely to be involved, remarriage and a new legal and "permanent" parent does not appear on the scene, and psychologically the feeling of being stranded could have traumatic consequences.

In brief, desertion creates uncertainty for all concerned. The husband may be plagued with a loss of self-respect and with the uncertainty of how to act with friends or employers. The wife, uncertain as to when or if the husband will return, is faced with fulfilling the household as well as the wage-earning responsibilities. In addition, she faces the problems of self-esteem and the fulfillment of her emotional, psychological, and social needs. The children face the problem of defining their father, of relating to friends, and of internalizing a stable definition of self. Solutions to problems surrounding desertion may be far more difficult than those surrounding divorce.

ANNULMENT

The word "annul," legally defined, means to reduce to nothing, to obliterate, to make void and of no effect, to abolish, to do away with, to eradicate. To say a marriage has been annulled is to say that a court, acting under the law of the state, found that causes existed *prior* to the marriage which render the marriage contract void. The court is saying that the marriage, when performed, was in fact, no marriage at all, and is annulling it as though it had never existed.[68]

Generally, the distinction between divorce and annulment revolves around the time of the cause or the time in which certain actions occurred. Divorce generally involves an action that occurred *after* the date of marriage

---

68. Morris N. Hartman, "Annulment of Marriage," *The Annals of the American Academy of Political and Social Science* 383 (May 1969), pp. 93–94.

—adultery, incompatability, cruelty, desertion, nonsupport, alcoholism, and the like. Annulment generally involves an action that occurred *before* the date of marriage—being under age, another existing marriage, incurable impotence, incestuous relationship, and the like. While the marriage was a social and psychological reality, legally it never existed. If there are children, the "husband who never existed" may be required by the court to support minor children. Socially, relatives and friends are well aware of the once-existing marriage. Psychologically, both the male and female involved are well aware of once "being married" and the mate selection processes that preceded it.

Void and Voidable Marriages

Sometimes distinctions are made between *void* and *voidable* marriages. Where a marriage is void, no court decree is necessary to terminate it since, by law, the marital status nexer existed. By statute, a well-recognized ground for annulment, available in every state of the United States, is a marriage in existence at the time of a second or other marriage. This second marriage is void. Since bigamy is not legally permissible, the second marriage can never be a valid one. The same is true for marriage to a parent or sibling. Marriages within the kin relationships prohibited by law are void marriages; no status of husband and wife is created at all.

A *voidable* marriage is a valid marriage to start with and remains so until an objection is raised. In certain states, an annulment will be granted where both parties, or either, were at the time of the marriage physically and incurably impotent. This is a voidable, not a void, marriage.[69] For example, the Masters-Johnson research described a sexual problem among certain women known as vaginismus: a psychosomatic illness that affects a woman's ability to respond sexually by virtually closing the vaginal opening to male entry.[70] When vaginismus exists, and medical treatment does not help, legal impotency exists and is sufficient to warrant annulling the marriage.[71]

In most states that provide impotence as a ground for annulment, it is required that the applicant for the annulment must have been ignorant of such incapacity at the time of the marriage. An awareness of the impotency before the marriage, and marriage despite it, eliminates the legal cause for later complaint. In any voidable marriage, the party who has been imposed upon has an option in his or her favor to walk away from the situation when it becomes known and to exercise the option to disaffirm the marriage.[72]

---

69. Hartman, op. cit., p. 97.
70. William H. Masters and Virginia E. Johnson, *Human Sexual Inadequacy* (Boston: Little Brown, 1970).
71. It is of interest to note that the Masters-Johnson research and therapy team claim 100 percent success in the treatment of vaginismus.
72. Hartman, op. cit., p. 97.

Grounds such as insanity or lack of parental consent of an underage marriage, like impotence, are voidable marriages.

There are clear-cut differences between void and voidable marriages. In void marriages (like bigamy) neither the couple not the court has control. On the other hand, the outcome of voidable marriages is dependent upon the wishes of the couple or the ruling of the court. Thus, in marriages that are void the interests of the state and society are at stake. In voidable marriages, the interests of the persons involved are at stake.

REMARRIAGE AND RECONSTITUTED FAMILIES

The United States is recognized as practicing monogamy. Yet it is likely that a greater number, as well as proportion, of people in America experience a multiple number of spouses than in many, if not most, countries recognized as polygamous. This would be especially true for women since polyandry occurs rarely. Whereas the marriage of one man to several women is common, the marriage of one woman to several men is infrequent. In the United States, it can be expected that as and if the divorce and/or annulment rates continue to climb, the number of men and women who have more than one spouse will climb as well. When divorce rates are high, there is likely to be a high rate of remarriage.

Remarriage Rates

An estimated four of every five divorced persons remarry. Remarriage rates are much higher for men than for women, among both the divorced and the widowed in all age groups. Marriage rates of the widowed indicate that men are nearly four times more likely to remarry than women. Marriage rates for the divorced show men remarrying at a rate of a little over one and one-half times the rate for women.[73] The greater likelihood of remarriage for men than for women increases with increasing age.

Remarriages account for a larger proportion of the marriage of white persons than of those for all other groups. About 24 percent of the white brides and 18 percent of all other brides had been married before. Similarly, it was a remarriage for 24 percent of the white grooms and 21 percent for all other grooms.[74]

---

73. *"Marriages: Trends and Characteristics, United States,"* U.S. Department of Health, Education, and Welfare, Public Health Service, Division of Vital Statistics, Series 21, no. 21, September 1971, p. 17.

74. Ibid., pp. 17–18.

The United States Census, taking a cohort of women born from 1920 to 1924, reports that among those whose first marriage ended in divorce, the median age at divorce was 29.6 years. If the divorce occurred at a relatively young age, the chances were correspondingly greater that the woman had remarried. The median age at remarriage of these women whose first marriage ended in divorce was 32.1 years. For those whose first marriage ended in widowhood, the median age at remarriage was about six years older (38.2 years). In 1971, about 14.2 percent of these women born between 1920 and 1924 had been married twice. Of those who married twice, about three-fourths had been divorced after their first marriage and about one-fourth had been widowed before they remarried.[75]

Paul Glick and Arthur Norton show that there has been a consistent forty-year upward movement in the proportion of women who have remarried by a given age, after their first marriage ended in divorce or widowhood.[76] In 1940, less than 1 percent of the women in their early twenties had remarried, but by 1970 the corresponding proportion was 3.5 percent. Among women in their early thirties, the proportion remarried rose from 3.8 percent in 1940 to 11.1 percent in 1970. One major explanation for the continuing rise in remarriage has been the sharply advancing divorce rate, especially among women now in their thirties. These women were born between the disturbed period of the depression and World War II, they had the youngest ages at first marriage ever recorded in the United States, and they have some of the highest birth rates recorded in the United States during the twentieth century.

Marriage among the Remarried

Many of the major studies dealing with remarriage were done in the 1950s.[77] This appears interesting, particularly in light of the increase in the proportion of existing marriages that are remarriages since that time. Nevertheless, some of their findings are of particular interest. One consistent find-

---

75. U.S. Bureau of the Census, *Current Population Reports*, Series P-20, no. 239, "Marriage, Divorce and Remarriage by Year of Birth: June, 1971," U.S. Government Printing Office, 1972, pp. 6–7.

76. Paul C. Glick and Arthur J. Norton, "Perspectives on the Recent Upturn in Divorce and Remarriage," *Demography* 10 (August 1973), pp. 301–313.

77. See for example Jessie Bernard, *Remarriage: A Study of Marriage* (New York: Dryden, 1956); Thomas P. Monahan, "One Hundred Years of Marriages in Massachusetts," *American Journal of Sociology* 56 (May 1951), pp. 534–545; Thomas P. Monahan, "How Stable are Remarriages?" *American Journal of Sociology* 58 (November 1952), pp. 280–288; Thomas P. Monahan, "The Changing Nature and Instability of Remarriages," *Eugenics Quarterly* 5 (June 1958), pp. 73–85; Thomas P. Monahan, "The Duration of Marriage to Divorce: Second Marriages and Migratory Types," *Marriage and Family Living* 21 (May 1959), pp. 134–138; Paul H. Jacobson, *American Marriage and Divorce* (New York: Rinehart, 1959); Paul H. Landis, "Sequential Marriage," *Journal of Home Economics* 42 (October 1950); and William J. Goode, *After Divorce* (Glencoe, Ill.: Free Press, 1956).

ing was that many people who failed in marriages with one mate were quite capable of succeeding in marriage with a different mate. There was nothing intrinsically deficient in their personality that made marital adjustments impossible. Interaction with one mate led only to frustration and defeat, interaction with another, to fulfillment and success.

Granted that the divorced who remarry are somewhat more prone to divorce than those who marry for the first time, the comparison that makes most sense to the remarried persons is between their present (or second) marriage and their own first marriage. Goode found that 87 percent of the remarried divorced mothers stated that their present married life was "much better" than the former, and 8 percent claimed that it was a "little better."[78] Regardless of the exact figures, it is clear that a substantial majority of those who remarry after divorce are and remain relatively happy.

This same finding is supported by more recent data. In a comparison of the reported marital happiness of ever-divorced and never-divorced respondents to three U.S. national surveys, Norval Glenn and Charles Weaver suggest that remarriages of divorced persons are, as a whole, almost as successful as intact first marriages.[79] This suggests that the increased divorced rate in recent years (cited earlier in this chapter) has not been accompanied by any important decline in the marital happiness of remarried divorced persons relative to that of persons who have never been divorced. The prospects for divorced males to enter into satisfactory marriages apparently are somewhat better than for divorced females; however the sex differences are not very great. Remarriage remains a satisfactory "solution" to divorce for a large percentage of divorced persons.

Children among Remarried Parents

It is often assumed that the persons who "pay the price" in divorce and subsequent remarriage are the children. Previous findings were presented on children in one-parent families (Chapter 17) and on children of divorced parents (this chapter). All three factors (one-parent, divorce, and remarriage) as they relate to their effect on children are interrelated, thus it could be expected that findings from studies on each would show results consistent with one another. This appears to be the case.

National data from the 1973 National Opinion Research Center General Social Survey and the 1973 University of Michigan Youth in Transition Survey was used to test the hypothesis that there was no difference between respondents who had experienced stepfather families and respondents who

---

78. Goode, *After Divorce*, op. cit., p. 331.
79. Norval D. Glenn and Charles N. Weaver, "The Marital Happiness of Remarried Divorced Persons," *Journal of Marriage and the Family* 39 (May 1977), pp. 331–337.

had experienced natural-parent families.[80] Used to compare these two groups were social and social-psychological characteristics including demographic, religious, stratification, political, crime, and delinquency, general interpersonal relationships, interpersonal relationships concerning marriage and the family, and personal evaluation. The findings from both data sets were merged to demonstrate that there were *no* substantial differences on these characteristics between individuals of natural or stepfather families. Their findings support the observation of others that a child's experience with a broken home and a subsequent remarriage can be a predominantly positive, predominantly negative, or mixed experience, much as occurs in the "nonbroken" first marriage family. In other words, stepparent families are not found to be inferior to natural-parent families.

The findings just presented should not lead to an assumption that the reconstituted families share no concerns or problems that are absent in first marriage situations.[81] For example, there may now be multiple parents (more than one father, mother, or both), there may be a new sibling relationships apart from newborn; incest may or may not be an item of greater concern; and discipline patterns may vary. But the consequences—products of children from remarriage situations parallels those of first marriage situations.

Summary

Marital crises take place at any stage of the life cycle: after the birth of children, during the school and adolescent years of the children, during the middle years, as well as in old age and retirement. Stressor or crisis provoking events are those situations for which the family has had little or no preparation. The factors that make for crisis proneness or freedom from crisis proneness were said to be in the extent to which families have the resources to meet a particular event and the extent to which the families define the event as a crisis. Adequacy in these dimensions results in no crisis. Family inadequacy in these dimensions leads to crisis.

All societies maintain various mechanisms for keeping interpersonal hostilities within certain limits. All societies permit divorce or the dissolution of a marriage. The laws pertaining to dissolution, the conditions under which the dissolution is granted, and the frequency of these dissolutions vary widely.

In the United States, divorce rates are likely to be calculated by 1) counting the number of divorces that take place per 1,000 persons in the total population, 2) counting the number of divorces per 1,000 married females age

80. Kenneth L. Wilson, Louis A. Zurcher, Diana Claire McAdams, and Russell L. Curtis, "Stepfathers and Stepchildren: An Exploratory Analysis from Two National Surveys," *Journal of Marriage and the Family* 37 (August 1975), pp. 526–536.

81. See, for example, Harris S. Goldstein, "Reconstituted Families: The Second Marriage and Its Children," *The Psychiatric Quarterly* 48 (1974), pp. 433–441.

15 and over, or 3) dividing the number of divorces granted in a given year by the number of marriages contracted in a given year. The long-term trend in each rate is upward, although they vary considerably according to social conditions such as wars, depressions, or periods of prosperity.

Within the United States, divorce rates vary by a wide range of geographic, demographic, and social characteristics. Geographically, the rates increase as one moves from East to West. Rates vary considerably by state as well as by metropolitan areas within the state. Teen-age marriages have higher divorce rates than those married in their twenties. The duration of the marriage is related to the incidence of divorce; persons who are married more than once have a higher likelihood of divorce than those who are married only once. By race, divorce rates are higher for blacks than whites; by religion, divorce rates are higher for Protestants than Jews or Catholics; and by socioeconomic level divorce rates go up as educational level, income, or occupational position go down.

Children are a primary concern to those interested in divorce. About three of five divorces involve children and the trend appears to be toward a greater willingness to get divorced when children are present. The consequence of divorce for the children appears to be less traumatic or negative than the experience of living in an unhappy, unbroken home.

Another means of dissolving or at least drastically altering the marital relationship is via desertion. Desertion is like a legal separation in that the spouses are married and cannot remarry but, unlike a legal separation, desertion includes no formalized arrangement as to visiting patterns, care of the children, financial support, and the like.

A final means of dissolving a marriage is via annulment. Due to causes that existed prior to a marriage, the marriage is eradicated and, in theory at least, never existed. If the causes are in violation of the laws of the state, such as with a previous existing and ongoing marriage, the second marriage is void and, in law, the marriage never existed. If the causes that existed prior to the marriage victimizes one of the spouses, while legal to begin with, the marriage is voidable and annulment is granted.

Most persons who end one marriage enter another. The remarriage rate climbs as the divorce rate climbs. Men are more likely to remarry than women, divorcees are more likely to marry than widows, and younger persons are more likely to remarry than older persons. Although many people failed in their first marriage, the remarriage was generally perceived to be better than the former with an absense of negative effects on the children.

This chapter ends the section on marriage and the family throughout the life cycle. Specifically examined were the marital system, the parental system, parent-child interaction, the postparental system, the later years, and crisis and disorganization throughout these years. As shown previously, the family cycle continues although the family group of a given generation may end. Structures, functions, and relationships change but great persistence exists in the family and marital system and in the family as a social institution. What about the next few decades? What is the family of the future and the future of the family? The next and final chapter explores these questions.

Key Terms and Topics

Discussion Questions

1. *Itemize a list of "stressor events." What ways exist to prepare for events such as these? How is it possible that certain events "strengthen" families whereas others tend to "tear them apart"?*

2. *What factors make for crisis proneness and freedom from crisis proneness? Using the formula given in the chapter, show how "resources" and "meanings" lead to family adequacy or family inadequacy in facing potential crisis situations.*

3. *What features seem to characterize families that are able to respond adequately to stressor events? In what way does the community contribute to these features?*

4. *Make a classification of types of family disorganization. Which types does "society" consider most important? Why?*

5. *How are divorce rates determined? In this chapter, estimated divorce rates for 1975 were 4.8, 20, and 40. How is this possible? What does each mean? What factors influence rates even when the number of divorces remain constant?*

6. *Summarize the trend in divorce rates in the United States. Indicate conditions that are likely to increase or lower the rate of divorce.*

7. *Examine variations in United States rates by geographic distribution. Explain regional, state, and community differences. Find exceptions to the general pattern and explain.*

8. *Why is age at marriage so significant in the likelihood of divorce?*

9. *Divorce rates were found to differ by duration of marriage, marriage order, race, religion, socioeconomic status, and the like. What were the differences and how are these variations explained?*

10. *Discuss the relationship between the presence or absence of children, the number of children, and divorce. What are the consequences of divorce on children? Compare with children from unbroken but unhappy homes.*

11. *Visit a local court which handles divorce cases. Arrange to meet with the judge to discuss the legal process, the legal grounds for the divorce compared to the nonlegal reasons for divorce, his views on marriage and divorce, and changes he would recommend.*

12. *Discuss the implications and consequences of no-fault divorce. What are its pros and cons? What effect it is likely to have on rates, long-term trends, and the like?*

13. *Interview a mother whose husband has deserted her and a divorced mother from similar socioeconomic levels. What similarities and differences exist in the two situations? How are the children affected in each?*

14. *Who gets annulments? Why an annulment rather than a divorce? What happens if children are involved?*

15. *Distinguish between void and voidable marriage. Who cares—that is, what difference does it make if a marriage is void or voidable?*

16. *Discuss the implications of remarriage beyond that presented in this chapter. What about ex-in-law relationships, relationships with step-parents, half-siblings, and other relatives, psychological effects on parents and children, and the like. What is the future trend in regard to remarriage?*

Further Readings

Bohannan, Paul, ed. *Divorce and After.* Garden City, N.Y.: Doubleday, 1970. Nine authorities from sociology, anthropology, psychology, medicine, and the law present chapters on the process and the aftermath of divorce: the reactions of friends, the postmarital social and family relationships, and what divorce means among the Eskimo, Swedish, and Kanuri.

Carter, Hugh, and **Paul C. Glick.** *Marriage and Divorce: A Social and Economic Study.* Rev. ed. Cambridge, Mass.: Harvard University Press, 1976. Using primarily census data, the authors present demographic and socioeconomic data on marriage and divorce in the United States. Chapter 13, "Recent Changes in Marriage and Divorce" is particularly useful.

Duberman, Lucile. *The Reconstituted Family: A Study of Remarried Couples and Their Children.* Chicago: Nelson-Hall, 1975. An attempt to provide professionals, academics, and lay people with a greater understanding of remarriage and the stepfamily and the processes by which it achieves integration and solidarity.

Gelles, Richard J. *The Violent Home: A Study of Physical Aggression between Husbands and Wives.* Beverly Hills: Sage, 1972. A study of violence between marital partners with a concentration on the social meaning of violent acts as felt by the participants.

Glasser, Paul H., and **Lois N. Glasser, eds.** *Families in Crisis.* New York: Harper, 1970.

A book of readings providing multiple views of three problems in the family—poverty, disorganization, and physical and mental illness.

Goode, William J. *After Divorce.* (Also published as *Women in Divorce*). New York: Free Press, 1956. An empirical exploration of 425 divorced urban mothers and their processes of adjustment after divorce.

Goode, William J. "Family Disorganization" Chapter 11 in Robert K. Merton and Robert Nisbet, *Contemporary Social Problems.* 4th ed. New York: Harcourt Brace Jovanovich, 1976. An excellent chapter in a social problems text that covers family-related social concerns such as illegitimacy, divorce, desertion, the "empty-shell" family, parent-youth conflict, women's liberation, and the like.

Harper, Fowler V., and **Jerome H. Skolnick.** *Problems of the Family.* Indianapolis: Bobbs-Merrill, 1962. An extensive project intended to provide the law student with a working knowledge of the findings of other disciplines, as well as principles of law, that could be brought to bear upon problems involving family discord.

Levine, Sol, and **Norman A. Scotch.** *Social Stress.* Chicago: Aldine, 1970. An interdisciplinary discussion of the conceptual and methodological issues of the sources and consequences of social stress. See especially Chapter 2 on the family as a source of stress.

Moles, Oliver C. and **George Levinger, issue eds.** "Divorce and Separation" *Journal of Social Issues* 32 (Winter 1976), pp. 1–213. An issue devoted to the topics of marital instability, marital disruption, marital dissolution, and divorce.

Pavenstedf, Eleanor, and **Viola W. Bernard.** *Crisis of Family Disorganization.* New York: Behavioral Publications, 1971. A series of papers presented at a divisional meeting of the American Psychiatric Association and dealing with programs to soften the impact on children of mentally ill parents or parents under unmanageable stress.

Rheinstein, Max. *Marriage Stability, Divorce, and the Law.* Chicago: University of Chicago Press, 1972. Dr. Rheinstein, a professor of comparative law, provides a view of the history and present status of divorce law and marriage stability in a number of contrasting countries. He argues against making divorce difficult to obtain since it is the marriage breakdown, not the divorce, that has negative effects for societies.

Steinmetz, Suzanne K., and **Murray A. Straus, eds.** *Violence in the Family.* New York: Dodd, Mead, 1974. A major contribution to bringing together a collection of diverse works and viewpoints on violence within the context of the family.

Stuart, Irving R., and **Lawrence E. Abt.** *Children of Separation and Divorce.* New York: Grossman, 1972. A collection of writings that looks at a wide spectrum of the social and emotional issues and problems of divorce and separation. It sets forth conceptions and parental responsibilities toward children, children's perceptions of parents, religious conceptions, children from socially deprived environments, and community resources and assistance available.

Weiss, Robert S. *Marital Separation.* New York: Basic, 1975. Addressed to people contemplating or undergoing separation and to professionals working with them.

Part VI

The Decades Ahead

The Family of the Future   20

20

The Family of the Future

20

What is the family of the future? What is the future of the family? What types of families and societies will exist in the next ten, fifty, or one-hundred years? How do we prepare for them? What type of training do we need to provide for our children and grandchildren (assuming they will be "our" children)? What types of family structures will exist? What functions will the family perform? Will the family be necessary? Will marriage exist? Will women have equal status with men? Will heterosexual partners be necessary for marriage or for children? Will the state regulate family activities? These are a sampling of the questions that can be raised. The answers may depend on who gives them, the basis or theory on which the projection is based, the length of time projected, and perhaps the personal wishes of the projector.

Attempts to predict the future of the family are not new (see the suggested readings at the end of this chapter). Several writers have viewed the family as breaking down and in a state of decay. For example, approximately fifty years ago, Bertrand Russell, who saw the family in an evolutionary perspective, raised the possibility that it may be an obsolete institution or become one before long.

> The decay of the family in quite recent times is undoubtedly to be attributed in the main to the industrial revolution, but it had already begun before that event. . . . The position of the family in modern times has been weakened even in its last stronghold by the action of the State.[1]

Barrington Moore also suggested that the American family may have "obsolete and barbaric features."[2] He suggested that one of the most obviously obsolete features of the family is the obligation to give affection to a particular

---

1. Bertrand Russell, *Marriage and Morals* (New York: Liveright, 1929).
2. Barrington Moore, "Thoughts on the Future of the Family," in Maurice R. Stein, Arthur J. Vidich, and David M. White, eds., *Identity and Anxiety* (Glencoe, Ill.: Free Press, 1960), p. 394.

set of persons on account of the accident of birth. This is a true relic of barbarism. Perhaps no feeling is more excruciating than the feeling that we ought to love a person whom we actually detest.

Comments such as these are highly debatable and open to question. That the family is changing and will continue to change is perhaps, although not necessarily, a definitive statement and one in which we would find widespread agreement. But comments on decay and breakdown or on progress and advancement must be approached cautiously. Prior to speculation on specifics of the family of the future, certain precautions should be mentioned to place projection in perspective.

PROJECTION PRECAUTIONS

In 1970, problems in this country appeared to exceed those of the 1960s. To many, the future looked bleak. College students had been shot at several universities, thousands of youths were on drugs, the stock market was down, inflation and unemployment were up, a war was raging in Vietnam, our natural environment was being destroyed, racial conflict was prevalent, crime rates were climbing with alarming rapidity, much talk existed about a parent-youth generation gap, and divorce, venereal disease, and illegitimacy rates were climbing.

Combined with the publicity given to unmarried couples cohabiting and communal type family groups, many people were convinced that the future of the society and the family looked dark. Some people, including an ex-governor of Michigan, were announcing that these problems were all due to a breakdown in family life. In short, because the family was believed deteriorating and in a state of decay, the United States was therefore overwhelmed with major personal and social problems.

By the mid-1970s the mood of the country had shifted. Crime, divorce, and illegitimacy were still climbing, but an end had come to the Vietnam conflict, a president and most of his circle of advisors had been driven from office, the marijuana and drug scene had been redefined, and an economic depression created a condition of calm if not optimism on college campuses. In just a few short years it appeared, somehow, that the family was less responsible for the nation's ills: oil and energy shortages, environmental problems, unemployment, and the like. Even so, President Carter expressed an urgent need for "strengthening the American family" as the family serves as a major influence in the life experience of virtually every person.

What could be said in response to this shift? Several points have to be stressed. First, changes that take place and will take place in the society or family are not necessarily pleasing or regretful, good or bad, or constructive or destructive per se. Changes are likely to be welcomed or rejected depending largely on one's own frame of reference, the groups with which one identifies,

> Louise: *I feel great, really good, about the future of my family. For society, well it seems to be in trouble. Courses I've taken, like sociology courses, seem to reinforce the idea that families really aren't important, or that you kinda decide for yourself what makes a family and what's gonna work, and I'm not seeing that. I'm seeing that a lot of people do decide for themselves what makes a family, but it isn't working. Me as a taxpayer—pickin' up the tab, you know? I'm paying for kids in foster care, mothers on ADC because husbands ran off, mothers trying to raise kids without fathers. Society can't go that way.*
>
> Ann: *Families will always live. I don't think the family is breaking down. It's just made so public that divorce rates are up. Families that stay together for twenty years don't get publicity.*

and the value orientations to which one adheres. Rising divorce rates can be viewed either as a problem or as a solution to other problems. Homosexuality may be viewed as an illness or as a right to love whomever one chooses. War may be viewed as vital to national defense or as an immoral destruction of life and property. This is not meant to imply that there are not changes that are disruptive to the social order, but it is meant to imply that social matters must be seen in the context in which they occur. It is a rare issue that cannot be interpreted in various manners.

Second, although many people see the family at the core of society and as the most basic of all institutions, it should be made clear that the family cannot be understood as an isolated phenomenon. It must be viewed in relation to the economic, educational, religious, and political institutions. In addition, factors such as population density, mobility patterns, and stratification divisions must be taken into account. It is not by chance that agricultural societies will tend to emphasize extended families, parental involvement in mate selection, and, often, plural marriage. Neither is it by chance that the United States places an emphasis on romantic love, separate households, and monogamous marriages. The central point is that, if accurate family predictions are to be made, it is essential to have an understanding of what is going to take place in other social systems. For example, it has been fairly well established that as educational level increases, the number of children in the family decreases. Generally, divorce rates drop during depressions and increase during periods of inflation and war. In other words, what takes place in the family is highly dependent on, and related to, that which takes place in other aspects of the society. A change in any element of a social system is likely to lead to changes in other elements, including the family.

Third, the family is not a uniform entity. That change will occur is almost without question. But to speak of the changing family or even the American family as if it were a uniform entity can be somewhat misleading.

From the very beginnings of American society, the cultural base of its population was diverse and varied. Then, as today, one could expect to find variations in family patterns by factors such as rural-urban residence, region of the country, religious affiliation, racial and ethnic identity, social class background, or age. And yet, despite the diversity that comprises family life in America, one significant change has been the assimilation of quite different cultural heritages. One must recognize the manifest differences that exist in social class, racial, and religious background and at the same time recognize that within this diversity there are strands of unity that belie heterogeneous origins.

Fourth, any type of social projection into the future is hazardous. Some trends are short-term ones, tied to the economic climate of prosperity that so drastically affects marriage, birth, and divorce rates. Some trends are not necessarily linear or even directional and may be highly or basically unpredictable. Other changes may be internal to the system or external to it, accidental or planned, behavioral or attitudinal, material or nonmaterial, actual or ideal, patterned or nonpatterned, peaceful or violent, continuous or spasmodic, rapid or slow, as well as due to single causes or many causes. This suggests that predictions should be made cautiously—no one can predict the future without error.

PREDICTIONS AND PROJECTIONS

The predictions and projections to be made refer essentially to the United States. It is probably safe to project that the future of the family in this country will be very different from that of much of the world. This is true today and will likely be true for decades.

In the sections that follow, some of the emerging patterns in the organization and functioning of marriage and family life are briefly delineated. The presentation must be regarded as suggestive and tentative rather than exhaustive and final.

Marriage and Family Structures

The organization of the structure of marriage and the family in the near and distant future may take various forms. The diversity of these forms in a pluralistic society should not overshadow the projection that most families will consist of one husband, one wife, and their biological children. However, it is likely that increasing publicity and social recognition will be given to a wide diversity of marriage and family patterns, including each of those mentioned in Chapter 5. A few comments follow on several of those and other patterns.

One-Parent Families

The one-parent family has been given widespread recognition, particularly among lower-class families of all ethnic and racial backgrounds. As indicated earlier, the black family in American society has frequently, although erroneously, been closely identified as a mother-children unit. Accompanying this identification was the connotation of undesirability. This image may be changing. Recently, some social work agencies have permitted the adoption of infants by a single parent. It is highly possible that in the future we will witness more one-parent family units consisting of a single unmarried adult and one or more children. And it could be questioned whether all these unmarried adults will be women. Instances are on record of unmarried men adopting children. Perhaps the day is coming when parenthood will be more fully recognized as a social phenomenon rather than a biological one, and men will be given greater recognition and responsibility in the rearing of children.

Contrary to many of our prejudices, one-parent families need not be a deviant or distorted family form, for in many settings it may be the only viable and appropriate one. Defects in the functioning of one-parent families may stem more from adverse social judgments than from intrinsic failings. Where some sense of stability and continuity is achieved, it can provide a "humane" setting for its members despite certain deficiencies in resources.

Multiadult Households

Marriages with more than one husband or one wife are certainly not new to family scholars either in the United States or around the world. These forms of marriage have existed in experimental forms in the past and present and will in all likelihood occur in the future.

Of the three forms of multiple-partner marriage, polyandry is the least likely to occur in the future. Not only has it been extremely rare in the past, but in the United States, with its excess number of women and an unliklihood that the sex ratio will shift, polyandry will exist infrequently, if at all, as an alternate form of marriage. Certainly many women will have more than one husband; however, these husbands will occur sequentially rather than simultaneously.

Polygyny, again although infrequent, is likely to be the most common form of multiple-spouse marriage. Legally, changes are likely to occur very slowly. If legal changes do take place, however, they may first occur among the older generations—those over sixty (or perhaps today those over thirty). The logic of polygyny for the older population can be well presented by looking at the unbalanced sex ratio at these ages as well as the advantages that this arrangement offers in terms of economic conditions, health care, companionship, joint sharing of household and cooking tasks, sexual partners and psychological factors.

Multiadult households such as communes, family clusters, and affiliated families were discussed in Chapter 5. While these family forms may gradually increase, they are not likely to become predominant forms in the next thirty years.

Extended Families and the Aged

It is likely that extended-family ties will continue to exist much as in the 1950s and 1960s. That is, the majority of family units will not share the same household and in many instances will not even live in the same community but will maintain kin relationships via letters, visiting patterns, financial assistance, and various other means of communication. The general trend may be in the direction of an "isolated nuclear family."[3] However, the "modified-extended" family will exist in a form that does not demand territorial propinquity, occupational involvement, nepotism, or a hierarchical authoritarian pattern.[4] It will, unlike the isolated nuclear family structure, provide significant and continuing aid to the nuclear family.

Margaret Mead says that the nuclear family is a good style of family for change but is hazardous. Whereas the nuclear family of today pushes everyone except cleaning women and babysitters out of the house, the families of tomorrow are going to have a need for more people.

> There is a need to have more people around: more people to hold the baby, more people to pitch in in emergencies, more people to help when the child is sick, when the mother is sick, more children for other children to play with so you don't have to spend a thousand dollars sending them to nursery school, more kinds of adults around for the children to pick models from in case father or mother can't do the things they want to do. The communes aimed to supply these but the bulk of people don't live in communes.[5]

Although it may not happen immediately because it means building new houses and apartments closer together, the time may come when people can live somewhere near youngsters and when places where young married

---

3. Talcott Parsons, "The Kinship System of the Contemporary United States," *American Anthropologist* 45 (January-March, 1943), pp. 22–38.

4. Eugene Litwak, "Geographic Mobility and Extended Family Cohesion," *American Sociological Review* 25 (1960), pp. 385–394; and "Occupational Mobility and Extended Family Cohesion," *American Sociological Review* 25 (February 1960), pp. 9–21.

5. Margaret Mead, "Future Family," *Trans-Action* 8 (September 1971), p. 52.

couples with children will be cherished and cared for and flanked on all sides by people who do not have children at the moment.

Everyone who will be old in the years 2000 to 2040 is now alive. An interesting question to ponder is whether the less traditional forms of marriage or nonmarriage (cohabitation, never married, or communal arrangements) now existing among those in their twenties and thirties will continue when they are in their sixties and seventies?

With more people living longer, it is likely that increasingly, the four- and five-generation family may become the norm. With family size decreasing, the number of children per nuclear family will be less, but the number of children that cover more generations will increase the size of the extended family. It is likely that ties of affection as well as ties of obligation between the generations of families will remain strong. Older persons will probably continue to move away from the roles of economic producer and increasingly become the users of leisure time. With more free time and perhaps more money than previous generations had, they will have more options and opportunities to work out a satisfactory life for themselves.[6]

Permanence of Family Structure and Alternatives to Divorce

Although divorce rates decrease during periods of depression and increase during periods of prosperity, without a doubt, the long-term trend of divorce rates in American society within this century is up, and there seems to be little evidence of a reversal. Any reversal is likely to come in the meaning attached to divorce. It is possible that marriages may be formulated that are clearly not "until death do us part." That is, perhaps we can anticipate an open public acceptance of temporary marriages or of marriages that last only until the children are grown. Today, the expectation of life is over thirty years after the child leaves home. It is Mead's contention that we may move to an ideal of marriage that is vastly different from our present condition.

> At present, they have an ideal of staying together forever, but in fact they get divorced very often. If instead they have as an ideal staying together until the children are grown and not having children until they were ready to do that, not picking out somebody you'd like to spend the weekend with, parenthood will probably become much more solemn, and much more of a commitment. If it doesn't, of course, we're going to have some government putting contraceptives in the drinking water.[7]

---

6. See Bernice L. Neugarten, "The Future and the Young-Old," *The Gerontologist* 15 (February 1975), pp. 4–9; Robert J. Havighurst "The Future Aged: The Use of Time and Money," *The Gerontologist* 15 (February 1975), pp. 10–15; and Erdman Palmore, "The Future Status of the Aged." *The Gerontologist* 16 (August 1976), pp. 297–302.

7. Mead, op. cit., p. 53.

It has been suggested that, unlike fishing, hunting, or automobile licenses, the marriage license is the only one that is not renewed. Thus a failure to renew this license would not necessarily carry the stigma that is attached to divorce and the legal complications that accompany it today. It is also possible that this type of temporary contract may be functional for maintaining the countless number of marriages that break up today.

Mead has suggested that marriage be in two steps.[8] The first may be called an "individual marriage," binding together two individuals only. She suggests it might be called a "student" marriage, as undoubtedly it would occur first and most often among students. But it would also be an appropriate type of marriage for many older men and women who would be committed to each other as individuals for as long as they wished to remain together. This step would not include having children.

The second step is what Mead terms "parental marriage." This type is directed toward the founding of a family. Thus it is not simply a second type but also a second step or stage. It follows an individual marriage and includes its own license, ceremony, and kinds of responsibility. In the individual marriage the central obligation of the man and woman to each other would be an ethical rather than an economic one. The husband would not be ultimately responsible for the support of his wife; if the marriage broke up, there would be no alimony or child support. Parental marriage, on the other hand, would be more permanent. Every parental marriage, no matter at what stage of life, would have to be preceded by an individual marriage. This marriage would be both hard to contract and difficult to break. To contract this marriage the couple would have to demonstrate their economic ability to support a child. Thus every child born would be both wanted and anticipated.

Whether the license idea of Mead's two-step marriage plan will ever become legally and socially sanctioned is uncertain. However, it is likely that the future will witness a continuation of temporary and cohabitation types of living arrangements. As indicated in Chapter 11, many persons are sharing apartments and living as husband and wife without the "benefit" of a marriage license, ceremony, or announcement to parents, friends, or the community. Many of these couples were and are seriously committed to each other and do, after a period of time, obtain a marriage license and make public their legal marital status. Rather than cohabitation as a sign of breakdown or weakness in current courtship and marital patterns, it may simply be an alternative arrangement of preparing for a permanent relationship. Not to be married is not to get a divorce.

Within or outside marriage, the insistence on permanence is already in the process of breaking down. This in no way implies that marriage is on its way out, but rather means that marriage with a particular person is not necessarily in the best interest of the individuals involved or the society at

---

8. Margaret Mead, "Marriage in Two Steps," *Redbook Magazine* (July 1966), pp. 48 ff.

large. Serial monogamy is widely practiced today. One-fifth of all marriages are taking place between persons who have been to the altar previously. As this increases, it is likely that a greater proportion of existing marriages may be more dynamic and vital than marriages at any time in the history of our nation. Marriage will be less likely to exist simply because there is no alternative, but rather, it will exist because it includes a meaningful interpersonal relationship for the persons involved.

The New Birth Technology

M. F. Nimkoff suggests that discoveries in human biology are potentially more significant for the social-psychological aspect of family life than are technological developments.[9] The new birth technology centers around the steroid pill, the contraceptive vaccine, the control of children, the knowledge of how to control the sex of the child, artificial insemination by a husband or a donor, the preservation of human spermatozoa, the collection of ova, the use of hormonal therapy, embryo implants, and a multitude of health, sex-determination, and other scientific discoveries that open up entirely new vistas for change in the family.

Recent developments in biochemistry provide the potential for a major revolution in the near future. The implications of some of these developments are staggering to the imagination. What happens to the "cult of motherhood" if her offspring are literally not her own? How would one maintain a balanced sex ratio since at the present time most societies prefer boys over girls and most parents desire a male child prior to a female child? Who makes the decision of how to "program" the I.Q. or looks of the offspring? What are the implications of being able to produce children at age ninety? What happens to the sexual mores of a society under conditions such as these? Obviously, much of this is speculative at this particular moment. However, many of these developments are already known to science. The cultural lag that exists in the social acceptance of them may lessen considerably in a brief period of time.

Due to the new birth technology, the number of children per marriage is likely to decrease and remain at a reproduction rate approximately zero, that is, a zero population increase. It is Phillip Hauser's contention that this situation must inevitably come about because we live on a finite planet with only fifty million square miles of land.[10] Given that finite planet, any rate of population increase will eventually produce saturation. In the western world,

---

9. M. F. Nimkoff, "Biological Discoveries and the Future of the Family: A Reappraisal," *Social Forces* 41 (December 1962), pp. 121–127.

10. Phillip M. Hauser, "Social Science Predicts and Projects," in Farson et al., *The Future of the Family* (New York: Family Service Association of America, 1969), p. 36.

Beyond the Pill

In the next few years the range of choice in methods of contraception may be vastly expanded. In the July 1971 issue of Family Planning Perspectives, Sheldon J. Segal, vice-president of the Population Council and director of its Bio-Medical Division, reports that at least nine of the 30 promising leads to new birth control methods have moved beyond the stage of animal experimentation in the laboratory to testing with human subjects.

During the past decade, clinical research in contraception was devoted almost entirely to modification of the "pill" and to new forms of IUDs. The success of both these methods, as well as their practical limitations in large-scale family planning programs, and medical anxieties raised over possible long-term effects of hormonal steroids have led to serious efforts to interfere with other critical links in the reproductive chain of events. Mechanical devices and drugs are being used to interfere with contraception at various points: sperm production, maturation and transport in the male, sperm transfer through the female cervical mucus, the muscle activity and openness of the tubes, the preparation of the lining of the uterus for implantation and embryonic development and the functioning of the ovaries.

At some stage of clinical testing with at least limited numbers of human patients are: daily, weekly and monthly pills for use by women; semi-permanent under-skin capsules for men or women; intermittently used vaginal inserts or chronically used intrauterine inserts; pills taken intermittently by women on the basis of coital exposure—before or after; intravenous infusion to terminate an early pregnancy; intrauterine placement of metals to prevent development of the fertilized egg; infusion through the cervix to close the Fallopian tubes; a removable foreign body placed in the vas deferens to impair male fertility— a reversible vasectomy; vaginal tablets to induce menstrual flow whether or not fertilization has occurred or to cause abortion at a later stage.

Several of these new methods involve hormonal interventions which may not eliminate current concerns about their continuous, long-term use; but others under study are mechanical or require only intermittent drug administration, a feature which may relieve some anxieties about the "pill."

Source: "Roundup of Current Research," *Trans-Action* 9 (January 1972), pp. 10, 12. Reprinted by permission.

attaining a zero rate is not a difficult problem; it is accomplished when the American people, on the average, decrease the number of children they have by about one child per couple. The 1970s have already presented evidence of success in reaching a zero rate of growth.

Professional Parents

We are living in an age of specialization. In many large cities today, one does not merely go to a physician; one selects the specialist who is best equipped to handle a particular concern. It would be highly unusual to permit an untrained person to perform heart surgery, teach in a university, or lay bricks. Yet despite the extreme importance we place on the rearing of children, we not only permit but actually require the most untrained persons to perform the task. With few exceptions this is done without regard for psychological, educational, or social qualifications. And from the biased perspective of this writer, were it not so serious, it would be almost humorous the way in which schools resist contraceptive education, education in family life, and preparation for parenthood.

The arguments are well recognized for having parents rear their own children. However, as our society becomes increasingly specialized, as an increasing number of women receive specialized training, as more women enter the world of paid employment, and as children increasingly become a matter of choice rather than chance, part-time parenthood becomes increasingly common. Thus the choice is not an either-or situation in which a mother is totally absent from her children or with them on a twenty-four hour basis. Some combination of the two will become increasingly the norm.

A bulletin published by the U.S. Department of Labor in 1971 noted that at least eleven companies were operating day-care centers for their employees' children. Detailed information was given for nine of them.[11] Only one of these programs was initiated before 1962 and most were started in the later part of the 1960s. The work forces of all the industries were predominately female. These industries provided day-care centers in or adjacent to the plant. Preference in entry was given to children of the employees, but only three of the nine were restricted to employees' children. Each center was open at least eight hours daily with six of the nine open ten or more hours. One company charged no fee whatsoever, and the highest fee amounted to $37.50 a week. Even the latter company paid all but $10 a week for the children of their own employees. Since the day-care centers were established, management of the companies believe that they are reaping rewards in personal recruitment, greater productivity, less labor turnover and absenteeism, and an increase in getting steady and dependable workers.

Most communities today provide day-care nurseries or some other type of educational program for preschool children. At present most are on a private basis, but in the future it is likely that the community and state will increasingly provide this service for employed mothers. One minor step in this direction occurred in 1977, when for the first time child-care was a legitimate deduction on federal tax returns. The frustration experienced by many parents who are forced into a parental role twenty-four hours a day suggests that given the choice, many parents, especially mothers, would welcome the existence of equipped and licensed professional parents. Many biological parents would not only gladly surrender their children for six or eight hours a day but would look upon it as an act of love toward the children, not one of rejection. The time then spent with the children would not be focused on discipline and

---

11. *Day Care Services: Industries' Involvement*, Women's Bureau, U.S. Department of Labor, U.S. Government Printing Office, 1971, Bulletin 296.

National Baby-Sitting: A Shortage of Day-Care Service

Should the federal government get into the day care business? Yes and soon, says Mary Dublin Keyserling, economist and former chief of the Women's Bureau (Windows on Day Care, National Council of Jewish Women, New York, 1972). On the basis of a comprehensive study made in 1970, she concludes that the day care picture is worse than anyone had feared.

Interviewers found that most working mothers are forced to leave their children with babysitters either in their own home or someone else's—and this situation prevails in all groups regardless of socioeconomic position.

The majority of women who work do so from absolute economic necessity. One-third of those surveyed would otherwise be on welfare. In many other cases, the addition of the mother's income was crucial for keeping the family income from falling to a dangerously low amount. Indeed, unless both parents work, the economic problem is as severe for two-parent families as for single-parent

families.

The day care shortage hits all income groups, but hits low income groups the hardest. Unsubsidized quality day care is too expensive for all but a few families.

Fewer than 5 percent of family day care homes are licensed or supervised. Children are frequently ignored and neglected or cared for by incompetent persons in unlicensed home day care situations. Many mothers refuse to work or stop working because of the poor quality, high cost or lack of day care facilities.

Day care services are generally segregated racially, ethnically and by socioeconomic grouping. This is due to de facto segregation of neighborhoods and to the public programs tied to training mothers for jobs to remove them from welfare rolls.

Federal legislation needs to be passed to meet the growing demand for day care and the future needs of a society in which many working women need help in caring for their children.

Source: "Roundup of Current Research," *Society* 10 (November-December 1972), p. 7. Reprinted by permission.

punishment but rather on mutual interchange of affection and enjoyment of one another.

Alvin Toffler and Judith Lorber go a step further than suggesting industrial or private day-care centers.[12] They suggest professional breeders and professional parents where children would be assigned to actual family units and their care would be well-paid for. Such families might be multigenerational by design, offering children an opportunity to observe and learn from a wide variety of adult models, as was the case in the old farm homestead. With the adults paid to be professional breeders or professional parents, they would be freed of the occupational necessity to relocate repeatedly. Such families would take in new children as old ones "graduate" so that age segregation would be minimized. Toffler goes on to suggest that newspapers of the future might well carry advertisements addressed to young married couples:

---

12. Alvin Toffler, *Future Shock* (New York: Bantam, 1970), p. 244; and Judith Lorber, "Beyond Equality of the Sexes: the Question of the Children," *Family Coordinator* 24 (October 1975), pp. 465–472.

Why let parenthood tie you down? Let us raise your infant into a responsible, successful adult. Class A pro-family offers: father age 39, mother 36, grandmother 67. Uncle and aunt, age 30—live in, hold part-time local employment. Four child unit has opening for 1 age 6–8. Regulated diet exceeds government standards. All adults certified in child development and management. Bio-parents permitted frequent visits. Telephone contact allowed. Child may spend summer vacation with bio-parents. Religion, art, music, encouraged by special arrangement. Five-year contract, minimum. Write for further details.[13]

It is doubtful whether Toffler's idea will ever obtain widespread acceptance. However, part-time parents or parent substitutes have and will gain acceptance in most communities and in an increasing number of industries. For several decades one major function of schools has centered around the teacher as a quasi-parent. One does not have to search very hard to find parents who each year look forward to the beginning of school, not merely for the benefit of the children but for the babysitting, child-care function that it provides.

Parent-Child Relationships

Parallel to the previous changes noted, the future family will include numerous changes in the parent-child relationship and methods of child rearing.[14] As noted, it is likely that parenthood will increasingly be defined in a social rather than biological sense, and it is likely that an increasing number of persons will be involved in the child-rearing process. The future is likely to witness an increase in quasi-parents who will contribute to the basic parental function of child rearing: siblings, friends, teachers, grandparents, neighbors, ministers, clerks, babysitters, and others.

Perhaps television should be included as a quasi-parent. Today, American children watch more television than children in any other country in the world. It is estimated that five-year-olds spend an average of two hours per day and twelve-to-fourteen-year-olds spend an average of three hours per day watching television. Obviously this medium will have some effect on what attitudes and values become important to children growing up in the decades ahead.

For teen-agers, there is likely to be a continuation of the peer group as a major source of attitude and value formation. Today, in about the seventh grade, a child turns from his parents to his peers as role models. It is likely that the future will witness an increase in the influence of other individuals in the socialization process.

---

13. Toffler, op. cit., p. 244.
14. Note, for example: Bernice T. Eiduson, Jerome Cohen and Jannette Alexander, "Alternatives in Child Rearing in the 1970's," *American Journal of Orthopsychiatry* 43 (October 1973), pp. 720–731.

The permissiveness or restrictiveness of child-rearing patterns is likely to remain highly related to the social class level of the parents. Working class blue-collar parents are likely to adhere to a set of values that are more closely related to the traditional ones. Children are likely to be taught to conform more closely to externally imposed standards. The stress will be placed on remaining neat, obeying parents, and pleasing adults. On the other hand, middle-class parental values are likely to pay more attention to the internal dynamics of the child. The attempt will be to help the child develop emotionally and socially rather than conform to a rigid routine and adhere to fixed goals. . . . These class distinctions in child rearing are likely to remain highly constant with those found in the occupational and educational world.

Other changes in parent-child relationships are likely to reflect a movement from a formal parent-child relationship, based on differential status position with clearly defined roles, toward the informal, varied, and person-centered relations in the modern family. With this will come a greater participation by children in family decision making, more conscious efforts to help children develop their social and emotional potentialities, the greater use by parents of "psychological" or "symbolic" techniques of discipline, and increasing social support and acceptance being given to family-life educators.

Marital Roles and Division of Tasks

Once again, consistent with the points previously made, various changes will occur in the nature of husband-wife relationships. All marital and family behavior involves a division of labor: the wife does some tasks, the husband does others, children are assigned certain responsibilities, and still other tasks may be performed by either husband, wife, or children interchangeably. Usually these tasks are set to a certain extent by custom. Generally it is regarded as "proper" for the wife to do the cooking, the husband to do the heavy manual labor, and, as the children grow older, for them to assist in household tasks.

The traditional division of labor between men and women seems to have relatively little to do with the biological capabilities and limitations of the two sexes. Except for the bearing and nursing of children, the man is biologically capable of doing anything a woman can do and, conversely, a woman can do anything a man can do including heavy physical labor. For example, on a visit to Bali, in addition to marveling at the beauty of the women, the author was astonished by how they carried heavy loads of rice on their heads. Near the market in Denpasar, women working on a construction project balanced cement on their heads as they climbed a ladder to a third-story rooftop. In Russia, as well as in many other parts of the world, much of the physical manual labor is performed by women.

This is not meant to imply that the American family of the future will have the women doing the heavy physical labor. That, too, would be stereotyping gender roles. The future is more likely to place an emphasis on activities being performed freely by either or both spouses. The division of tasks is more likely to be based on the interpersonal relationships of the couple rather than on traditional and fixed social norms and on role expectations assigned by sex.

The husband-wife relationship will continue to serve as the primary source of affection for adults. The marriage and family of the future will increasingly be visualized as a place of informality and intimacy. If the society increasingly becomes more impersonal, formal, and bureaucratized, the family will serve as an important outlet for openly expressing one's hopes and fears. This function, although performed today, may possibly be one of the most important performed by the family of the future.

Status of Women

The increasing social awareness of discriminatory employment practices and the inferior position given to women could have far-reaching social consequences on family organization. Equal education for men and women, expansion in the frequency and range of employment opportunities, the decline of sexual segregation in work roles, the adoption of masculine dress by women, and a wide range of social contacts before and after marriage are just a few of the signs of the increasingly equal status for men and women. It seems logical to assume that the tremendous changes that are likely to accompany the female roles will have as great an impact and effect on men as they will have on women.

Traditionally, females have been counseled into jobs where they face little competition from men: teaching, nursing, secretarial work, and the like. They have been counseled away from careers in research, business, politics, professional, managerial, and executive positions. If women become trained in mathematics and the physical sciences, Nye contends that several latent consequences of this change are likely to follow. These include:

1. In an increasing number of families the principal or only provider will be the wife, with the husband in some instances becoming the housekeeper in the family in a complete reversal of roles.
2. The divorce rate is likely to increase as the wife's occupation makes more demands on her time, requires her to travel, and leads to her financial independence.
3. Nurseries and day-care centers will increasingly care for children as the number of full-time homemakers decreases.
4. The sexual lives of women are likely to more nearly approximate those of men as women travel more and become less economically dependent on men.

5. The birth rate is likely to continue to decline as interesting and rewarding alternatives to rearing children develop.

6. The age of girls at marriage is likely to increase as the completion of education becomes more obviously useful to them.[15]

To assume that women have made "progress" in achieving equality with men in the areas of occupation, education, and income may be a popular myth. Using United States census data Dean Knudsen reports a gradual but persistent decline in women's occupational, economic, and educational achievements compared to those of men.[16] In general, women's status as defined by such measures appears to have declined. The sources of this lower status are said to include diminished effects by women and institutionalized discrimination. Given the conviction that women should not pursue occupations in competition with men, women and employers together develop a self-fulfilling prophecy.[17] Women, ambivalent about careers, convinced that they will face discrimination, make lesser efforts than men, permitting employers to justify discrimination by appealing to evidence of lower achievement and commitment to employment. The effect is the perpetuation of a belief that sexual equality exists and that only effect is lacking, a belief to which social scientists have offered their support.

And what of the future? Knudsen suggests that given the close correlation of occupation and income with educational achievement, it appears likely that women will remain in an inferior position for the next generation.[18] Perhaps the process of achieving social equality for women is similar to that of minority groups. Women, having achieved some degree of equality in civil rights earlier in this century and political rights in recent years, may ultimately utilize the schools to achieve complete social equality. However, this equality is neither immediately ahead nor easily accomplished.

Sex Norms

Particularly since 1965 significant changes have occurred in the sexual attitudes and behavior of Americans. A "new morality," which judges acts in terms of the degree to which they promote love between people, has been developing. One result for the future is likely to be an increasing permissiveness of sexual norms before, during, outside of, and after marriage. Love and meaningful interpersonal relationships will become the primary goal, which may or may not include sex.

---

15. F. Ivan Nye, "Values, Family and a Changing Soceity," *Journal of Marriage and the Family* 29 (May 1967), p. 247.

16. Dean D. Knudsen, "The Declining Status of Women: Popular Myths and the Failure of Functionalist Thought," *Social Forces* 48 (December 1969), pp. 183–193.

17. Harold M. Hodges, *Social Stratification* (Cambridge, Mass.: Schenkman, 1964.

18. Knudsen, op. cit., p. 192.

It is likely that in the next few years an increasing number of unmarried women will demand sexual equality with men, since it is increasingly possible to separate sex from pregnancy and childbirth. Within marriage, it is likely that an increasing number of couples will place an intrinsic value on sex, that is, valuing it for its own sake. One consequence of this will be an increase in the proportion of married females who experience orgasm and an increase in the proportion of females who take the initiative in sexual behavior.

Marital infidelity will likely increase as marriages place a lower demand on sexual exclusiveness as a prerequisite for marital permanence. In the latter part of the 1960s, reports indicated the presence of mate swapping, group-sex parties, and extramarital affairs involving thousands of marriages. This type of behavior, traditionally viewed as morally deviant and abhorrent to most Americans, today and increasingly in the future will result in couples taking the view that what others do is up to them. This activity is simply a logical extension of the increased sexual permissiveness in American society. The speculation is that in the future the recreational nature and the intrinsic value of sex will continue to increase.

Programs in Marriage and Family Education

As with the other projections into the future, the speed at which changes will occur in family-life education programs is unknown. However, it is likely that increased support will be given to formal programs of education, research, and service dealing with marital and family units as well as with the marriage and family system as a whole within American society.

A large number of these organizations will be continued or established to "strengthen family life," which often means a conservative approach for the perpetuation of traditional values. Even the National Council on Family Relations, established in 1938 and a major interdisciplinary national organization in the marriage and family field, has as its purpose to "advance the cultural values now principally secured through family relations for personality development and the strength of the nation.[19] Only by a large stretch of the imagination could that purpose be interpreted as encouraging or supporting alternative marital and family life-styles or more permissive patterns of behavior.

It is likely that the future will witness a wide variety of programs, both public and private, to ameliorate problems associated with American family life. These programs will not only involve family-life professionals and trained marriage counselors but will center around educational and therapeutic groups of couples. This might involve the development of networks of fami-

---

19. As published on the inside cover of each issue of *Journal of Marriage and the Family*.

> *Ann:*   *Things pertaining to sex were never discussed. I'll never forget when*
> *I started menstruating. I knew nothing about it. When it happened I*
> *tried to stop it. I went home and got in a tub of cold water, I really*
> *did. I told mother because I had to; I couldn't get it to stop. She*
> *says, oh, this is something that happens to all girls; don't worry about*
> *it. And I heard her telling my father that night, you know, "Ann*
> *started," and I thought, oh, God, she told my dad! And I couldn't*
> *look at my father in the face for two weeks.*

lies in the community that can be helpful to one another without the aid or
assistance of trained professionals. As discovered in Head Start programs, in
programs with persons in poverty, and will likely be discovered in family programs, the real benefits to these groups frequently result from the relationships that are developed among group members rather than from the
intervention and direct leadership of a professional. Thus the programs will
probably involve not only doing for others but also providing assistance for
people in groups to help each other. The real task may be to provide the
opportunity, to legitimize the interaction, and to help people be themselves.

The public schools may well serve as the focal point for programs in
marriage and family-life education. As school administrators and community
leaders increasingly become convinced of the need for training in social issues
such as race, crime, population, or social change, so will they recognize the
importance of training in interpersonal relationships that relate to sex, love,
mate selection, and marriage. In addition, although it may be slower in coming, schools will provide training in structural patterns that relate to the family as a social system. Today, it appears that the majority of people want
family-life education in the public schools, but frequently administrative and
community effort is lacking to integrate a program into the existing curricula.

Such is also the case for sex education. In the 1960s sex education in
the public schools attracted national attention. Opponents were certain that
sex education would lead to sexual experimentation and a further breakdown
in the moral fiber of our youth. Proponents for a program argued it would
lead to a decrease in venereal disease and illegitimacy. Both arguments were
likely in error in assuming the impact of a program, grossly overexaggerating
its significance. The exaggeration occurred in large part because 1) many programs were emphasizing venereal disease, menstruation, and the physiology
of pregnancy rather than the social, behavioral, and psychological aspects of
sex, and 2) when these latter areas were handled, it was frequently done by
public school teachers who presented sex on strongly moralistic, propagandis-
tic, and conventional overtones. Chastity, for most, was the correct standard
for the unmarried student.

The future of sex education in the public schools will not eliminate a
stress on physiology nor the moralistic emphasis. But it is likely that these

emphases will be reduced as public school teachers come from college settings where cohabitation, premarital sex, and a new morality is an approved norm. Both the quantity and the quality of sex and family-life education are likely to increase in the high schools as colleges reorient their training programs to serve a changing world. Although this may be more the author's bias and more wishful thinking than fact, it is hoped that these programs will receive increased support, be staffed by increasingly competent and trained persons, and be open and perceptive to the wide variety of family forms that will exist in a pluralistic society.

A PERSONAL NOTE

This author is not as pessimistic about the future of the family as are many other persons with whom he meets or as are various writers who view the rising divorce rates and increased sexual permissiveness as evidence of decay and deterioration. There is little doubt that changes will take place in the American family not discussed in this chapter or throughout the book. It is also inevitable that many of these changes will meet strong resistance and opposition. Furthermore, certain changes will provide additional kindling for certain persons who argue the increased and progressive downfall of the family. However, it seems more realistic to approach these changes as change, to study and understand some of the consequences of new family patterns, and to assist the individuals to cope with the social realities that exist at any given time.

The family will continue to perform various major functions. Most Americans will continue to find marriage and family interaction as a basic source of emotional and psychic stability. Families will continue to be primary sources of socialization, primary sources of security and affection, and primary sources of meaning. Partners within the marriage may change, the expectations of men and women may change, the sexual code and practices may change, and the general family life-styles may be vastly different. These changes are not necessarily to be equated with decay, immorality, or a general deterioration of the American family. If our society is destroyed and the family has a hand in this destruction, it is not likely to be because of change but rather because of an inability to change.

Although to many the future may be quite a shock it may also be one of the most exciting periods in history to be alive. The future does not just come. It is here now and, more than ever before, families in the United States should have the opportunity and social technology for inventing the type of future wanted. Perhaps never in our history has such an opportunity existed to choose the type of marital and family life-style one desires. What will you choose for yourself and support for the society in which you live?

Summary

Attempts to predict the family of the future are not new. For many decades and centuries, writers have been advancing their notions of what is to come in the days and years ahead. Some have forecasted a gloomy picture of the family: moral decay, breaking down, the end of the family. Others maintain optimism and see a bright picture: flexibility, new family forms, freedom for all.

Any speculative activity, positive or negative, needs to be done cautiously. First, changes that take place and will take place are not necessarily decay or progress, good or bad, or constructive or destructive per se. The perspective from which it is viewed may determine what is seen. Second, the family cannot be understood apart from other institutions in society. A change in any element of a social system is likely to lead to changes in other elements, including the family. Third, the family itself is not a uniform entity. This book should have clearly established the widespread diversity in family structures and processes both within the United States and around the world. Fourth, the future cannot be predicted without error. The world in which we live is comprised of many interdependent parts. Change is caused by many factors. Trends clear in one decade are less clear in another. A word of caution as to the hazards of predictions is suggested.

A variety of predictions and projections, primarily for families in the United States, were made. Marriage and family structures are likely to take on many forms, each granted social recognition and approval. Most marriages will remain monogamous, but an increasing number of families may be one-parent families. An increasing number may be multiple-spouse families, if not simultaneously, then consecutively or sequentially. The modified-extended family is likely to play an increasingly important role in providing emotional and economic support to nuclear family units.

Each form of marriage cited may well be more temporary than what has been known. Marriages may be less likely to begin with the idea that they remain until death. Some modification of the "student" and "parental" marriage idea may well become reality and, in fact, may already be happening. Marriage is not likely to disappear, but divorce and remarriage may well occur more frequently.

A new birth technology may well be one of the most significant events in the years ahead. The ability to determine, when, how many, sex, I.Q., color of eyes, and the like of offspring has staggering implications. These infants, no longer tied to the biological parents, if there are two, are likely to be reared increasingly by professional parents in industry, government, or community day-care centers and preschool nurseries. For years to come, school systems are likely to provide child-care functions so that the mother is "free" to pursue her interests, vocationally or aesthetically. Multiple parents will play a role in parent-child relationships.

Husband-wife roles may become more flexible, as appears to be presently happening. That is, what are men's tasks or women's tasks will be less sharply focused. Performance may be based more on ability or interest than on traditional sex typing. Marriage, in whatever form, is likely to continue to serve as one of the most important outlets for primary and psychic stability. Marital infidelity may increase but with less disruption to the marriages.

Programs in family and marriage education are likely to increase, offering a wide variety of programs that advance multiple and alternative marital and family life-styles. Families will continue to fulfill important functions to the individual and to the society.

Perhaps it is fitting that the text ends on a note predicting the family of the future. It will be interesting to examine this chapter with the passing years to reassess the accuracy or inaccuracy of the predictions. While today's crystal ball may be hazy and not 100 percent accurate, tomorrow's crystal ball may be even less clear. That change *will* occur is perhaps our only certainty.

Discussion Questions

1. What methods exist to project into the future? Are they all totally mythical and purely speculative or can we be assured of anything?
2. Describe the family system in America fifty years hence.
3. Can you perceive of a familyless society? Describe the source of affection, the rearing of children, and other aspects.
4. What scientific discoveries are on the horizon today that you believe will have a major impact on the family of the future?
5. What are some of the implications of a new birth technology (predetermining the sex of a child, "programming" its I.Q. and physical features, and others)?
6. What are the pros and cons of communal living, group marriage, or polygamy as compared with monogamy?
7. Discuss the implications of "same-sex" marriages for the persons involved, adopted children, and other persons with whom they interact.
8. As a "family expert," what program recommendations can you make to schools, legislators, and change agents to prepare us as children, youth, and adults for the family of the future?
9. What, in your mind, is the "ideal" marital and family structure of the future?
10. Can man "determine his own future"? Is he simply a product of external forces impinging upon him or do both factors come into play? Discuss.

Further Readings

Bernard, Jessie. *The Future of Marriage.* New York: World, 1972. Dr. Bernard examines where marriage is today and where it is headed. For anyone interested in how marriage is destructive for women or in marriage prophecies, this book is mandatory reading. Marriage has many futures: futures of marital options.

Bernard, Jessie. *The Future of Motherhood.* New York: Penguin, 1974. An examination of the way our society institutionalizes the bearing and rearing of its children and the technological, political, economic, and ethical forces that shape its operation.

Edwards, John N. "The Future of the Family Revisited." *Journal of Marriage and the Family* 29 (August 1967), pp. 505–511. Suggests an increasing interdependence between the economic sphere and the marital union and family sphere.

Farson, Richard E., et al. *The Future of the Family.* New York: Family Service Association of America, 1969. Addresses by a physical scientist, a social scientist, a philosopher, and a behavioral scientist where they attempt to predict and project the future of the family.

Hill, Reuben. "The American Family of the Future." *Journal of Marriage and the Family* 26 (February 1964), pp. 20–28. A presentation of methods to project the family into the future with a summary of properties that family-field professionals seem to want perpetuated in families.

Hunt, Morton. *"The Future of Marriage."* Playboy 18 (August 1971), pp. 116–118; 168–175. A well-illustrated, readable, and stimulating projection into the future of marriage.

Keller, Suzanne. "Does the Family Have a Future?" *Journal of Comparative Family Studies* 2 (Spring 1971), pp. 1–14. A presentation of challenges to the contemporary family with projections of a freer and more flexible future form of family.

Lorber, Judith. "Beyond Equality of the Sexes: The Question of the Children." *Journal of Marriage and the Family* 24 (October 1975), pp. 465–472. A look at alternative arrangements to parenting, with suggestions for their implementation.

Mead, Margaret. "Future Family." *Trans-Action* 8 (September 1971), pp. 50–53. A brief but provocative article that predicts trends infrequently mentioned by other writers.

Otto, Herbert A., ed. *The Family in Search of a Future.* New York: Appleton-Century-Crofts, 1970. Fifteen articles, each dealing with an alternative form of marriage.

Pollak, Otto. "The Outlook for the American Family." *Journal of Marriage and the Family* 29 (February 1967), pp. 193–205. Describes needs created by our bureaucratic way of life and the advances of governmental services in meeting these needs.

Ramey, James. "Multi-adult Household: Living Group of the Future?" *The Futurist* (April 1976), pp. 78–83. A discussion of households that have more than one adult, patterns of diversity in these arrangements, and a projection for the future.

Toffler, Alvin. *Future Shock.* New York: Bantam Books, 1970. A popular best seller which illustrates the transcience and adaptability of American society. Chapter 11 deals with the family of the future.

Winch, Robert F. "Permanence and Change in the History of the American Family and Some Speculations as to its Future," *Journal of Marriage and the Family* 32 (February 1970), pp. 6–15. The 1969 Burgess award lecture to the National Council on Family Relations.

Name Index